IMPERIAL WARRIORS

Tony Gould served in the 7th Gurkha Rifles in Malaya, India and Hong Kong. Invalided out of the army with polio, he read English at Cambridge, and then went on to work as a radio producer for the BBC and as literary editor of the *New Statesman & Society*. His books include *Death in Chile: A Memoir and a Journey, Inside Outsider: the Life and Times of Colin MacInnes* and, most recently, *A Summer Plague: Polio and its Survivors*.

M45
Devou
1.29.04

Imperial Warriors

Britain and the Gurkhas

TONY GOULD

Granta Books
London

Granta Publications, 2/3 Hanover Yard, London N1 8BE

First published in Great Britain by Granta Books 1999
This edition published by Granta Books 2000

A CIP catalogue record for this book is available from
the British Library.

1 3 5 7 9 10 8 6 4 2

ISBN 1 86207 365 1

Typeset by M Rules
Printed and bound in Great Britain by
Mackays of Chatham plc

for TOM

Different generations, different challenges

Contents

The Gorkha Empire at the outbreak of the Anglo-Nepal War, 1814.
The shaded areas represent the extent of Nepal's expansion in comparison with its present-day borders

British India: the North-West frontier

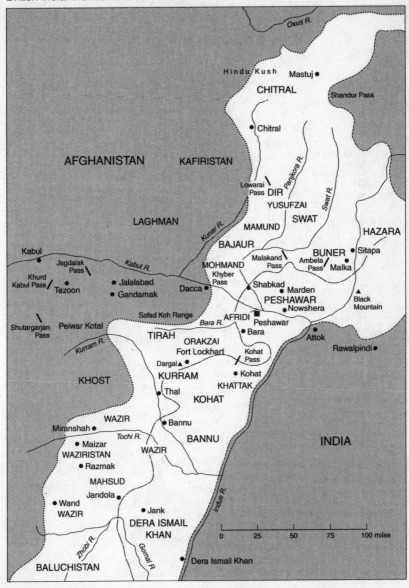

Burma, 1942–5

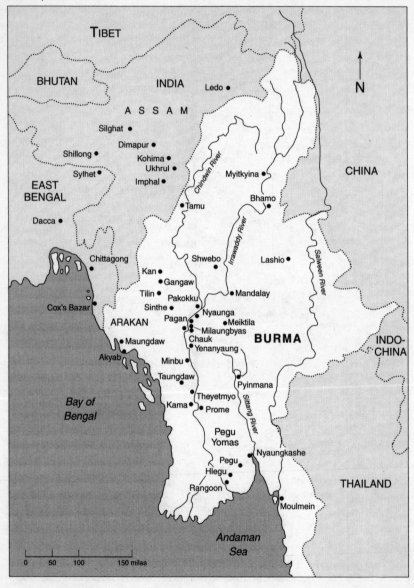

Tribal map of Nepal with shaded areas representing the main *jats* (tribes) recruited as Gurkhas

Tribal areas
- Magar
- Gurung
- Sunwar
- Rai
- Limbu

Acknowledgements

My thanks go to Neil Belton of Granta Books for suggesting that I write this book and then, some years on, justifying his formidable reputation as an editor by reading the finished (as I thought) manuscript with a critical but constructive eye.

I am grateful, not for the first time, to Mark Le Fanu and the Society of Authors for the award of a generous travel grant from the Authors' Foundation which enabled me to spend six weeks in Nepal at the beginning of 1997, and to my old friend Ewan MacLeod for dropping everything and accompanying me there for the first three weeks.

In Nepal, several serving – and retired – officers of the Brigade of Gurkhas helped to smooth my way, in particular Lt-Col. Nigel Mossop, Lt-Col. Nigel Wylie-Carrick and Capt. Gavin Maude, Robin Marston and Kit Spencer of the Summit Hotel and Summit Trekking respectively, Maniprasad Rai (and his wife Mishra, who remembered my taste for tiny dried fishes) and Chandra Pradhan, who gave me a remarkably dispassionate first-hand account of the unfortunate 'Hawaii incident' (in our old battalion) considering that he was a victim of it in more ways than one.

But my largest debt in Nepal is to Lt-Col. John Cross, with whom I was able to pick up where we left off nearly forty years before and resume a friendship and dialogue which has been a continuing delight. John not only gave me the benefit of his long and close relationship with Gurkhas; he also furnished me with introductions to a select group of Kathmandu intellectuals, his old colleagues at Tribhuvan University's Centre for Nepal and Asian Studies (CNAS). My thanks to Ananda Shrestha, Dhruba Kumar, Prayag Raj Sharma, Sridhar Khatri, Nirmalman Tuladhar and Abhi Subedi, all of whom visited me at the Summit Hotel, some more than once, and helped in various ways to broaden my knowledge of Nepal and its politics and history.

At the Queen Elizabeth barracks in Church Crookham, I was helped by Lt-Col. Mike Barrett, Lt. (QGO) Khembahadur Thapa and Sapper Ratnakumar Limbu as I explain at the beginning of the last chapter of this book. At the Gurkha Museum in Winchester, Brigadier Christopher Bullock and his staff and volunteers welcomed me and gave me the run of the archives. Particular thanks to Christopher himself, who kindly read and commented on my manuscript, answered many queries on the phone or face to face, took me out to lunch on more than one occasion and allowed me to interview him at length. I am also grateful to the museum's archivist Gavin Edgerley-Harris and the 'Tuesday group' of volunteers, Maurice Biggs, Mike Broadway, Gavin Jenks and Dulcie Westlake, not forgetting such ever-present stalwarts as Kamal Bahadur Purja and his *buwa*, John Craig, all of whom made my frequent visits to the Gurkha Museum a habit I found hard to break. My thanks, too, to Piers and Maggie Burton-Page for putting their country cottage at my disposal for the period when I was researching there.

The 10th Gurkha Rifles archivist, David Harding, also read and commented meticulously on my manuscript and provided me with several books and documents, while his friend, the ex-CO of the 6th Gurkhas, Lt-Col. Nigel Collett, whom I was fortunate enough to meet in Kathmandu just before I left Nepal, was another extremely valuable source of information.

The staffs at the British Library, Oriental and India Office Collections, at the Public Record Office, at the London Library, at the School of Oriental and African Studies Library and at the National Army Museum (where Clare Wright went to great lengths to help) all contributed in various ways to this book. At the National Army Museum, too, I was lucky enough to meet a visiting Indian, the retired Lt-Gen. S. L. Menezes, author of a recent book on the Indian Army, who enlightened me about many things, particularly Indian attitudes at the time of Partition, and introduced me to another retired Indian Army officer, Colonel Satinder Coomar ('Eno') Singha, with vivid memories of that time.

Chekhov famously remarked that if you want something done, ask a busy man. The Colonel Commandant of the Brigade of Gurkhas, General Sir Sam Cowan, is a very busy man but he still found time to talk and correspond with me about the role of Gurkhas in the modern British Army.

Several other individuals helped and entertained me in my quest for information: Roger Garside, Yubaraj Ghimire, Major Yambahadur Gurung, Colonel David Hayes, Phill Henderson, Lt-Col. Tony Mains, 'Jumbo' Oliphant, Carl and Babs Rogers, Ken, Alison, Jane and Kate Ross, the late Brigadier 'Birdie' Smith and my old company commander, Brigadier 'Lofty' Whitehead.

My debt to my wife Jenny – constant companion and first critic – is immeasurable.

List of Abbreviations

BO	British officer
CGS	Chief of the General Staff
CIGS	Chief of the Imperial General Staff
COS	Chief of Staff
CT	Communist Terrorist
DCM	Distinguished Conduct Medal
GCO	Gurkha Commissioned Officer
GO	Gurkha officer
GOC	General Officer Commanding
GR	Gurkha Rifles
HMG	His/Her Majesty's Government
INA	Indian National Army
IOM	Indian Order of Merit
JIF	Japanese Inspired Fifth-columnists/ Japanese Indian Forces
MCP	Malayan Communist Party
MGBG	Major-General Brigade of Gurkhas
MRLA	Malayan Races Liberation Party
NCO	Non-commissioned officer
QGO	Queen's Gurkha Officer
RAMC	Royal Army Medical Corps
RMA	Royal Military Academy, Sandhurst
RSM	Regimental Sergeant Major
VCO	Viceroy's Commissioned Officer
WO	Warrant officer

Introduction

The Gurkha's legendary prowess with the curved knife which is his trademark weapon is celebrated in a wartime joke. Locked in close combat with a large German, a Gurkha takes a swipe at him with his kukri. The German says, 'Ha, missed!' To which the Gurkha replies, 'Shake your head'.

About Gurkhas, as about Cossacks, myths and legends abound. The kukri is a rich source of mythology: sometimes it is represented as a kind of boomerang; at other times it is said that it cannot be drawn from its scabbard without blood being shed. Neither is true. The kukri is an all-purpose implement which functions more often as a kind of billhook than as a lethal weapon.

At this level, myths are plain falsehoods; but at another level, exemplified in the 'Shake your head' joke, they are more like supertruths, permissible exaggerations of real and defining qualities. They perform a vital function in military lore, establishing the fearsome reputation of – in this case – the Gurkhas for hand-to-hand fighting.

Regimental histories are simultaneously records of fact and repositories of myth, since they are both the regiment's collective memory and its inspiration. Without pride in its particular achievements – its battle honours and its feats of individual heroism – a regiment is nothing; tradition and customs (what the Gurkhas call *kaida*) are what make each regiment, even each battalion, special. To outsiders they may be as alike as two pins, but to themselves they are utterly unique. A spirit of (mostly friendly) competition enhances the performance of a military unit; in attempting to outclass one another, all battalions more nearly approach a peak of perfection.

All this is commonplace; it applies to any regimental system, and quite as much to British as to Gurkha regiments. What is unique to the Gurkhas is that they come from a country which was never part of the British empire, yet they fight for the British monarch rather than the king of Nepal. This has given rise, at least in recent years, and particularly among dedicated nationalists, to adverse comments about mercenaries; it has also led to more myth-making.

A sober and factual historical outline produced by the Brigade of Gurkhas follows a brief description of the Anglo-Nepal war of 1814–16, which provided the British with their first Gurkha soldiers, with these words: 'and from this time stems Britain's friendship with Nepal, a country which has proved a staunch ally ever since and has become our "oldest ally" in Asia'.[1] The suggestion here, and in countless other British accounts of the development of the Brigade of Gurkhas, is that once the war in which Britons and Nepalese formed a mutual admiration society was over, they shook hands and said, 'Now let's be friends' and – lo and behold – they have been friends ever since.

The true story is rather different. For most of the nineteenth century the Nepalese authorities did everything they could to resist the recruitment of Gurkhas by the British. The most bitterly resented clause of the 1816 Treaty of Segauli was the one which imposed a British Resident on the court of Nepal (the Resident was regarded as a harbinger of invasion and loss of autonomy, and it was many, many years before he was allowed even minimal freedom of movement within the valley of Kathmandu). At the time of the first Afghan war (1839–42) the two countries almost came to blows again. Even the much vaunted support provided by Maharajah Jang Bahadur Rana during the Indian Mutiny/Sepoy Revolt of 1857–8 was less the product of amity than of calculation. Jang Bahadur, who had paid a state visit to Britain in 1850, had been sufficiently impressed with its industrial and military muscle to throw his weight behind the side he regarded as the likely winner and reap whatever rewards might then be forthcoming.

If there was any sentiment in the relationship, it was vastly outweighed by self-interest, even after the Shamsher Ranas had conceded recruiting rights to the British in the 1880s in return for recognition following their seizure of power in a family *coup*. And from then until the end of both British rule in India and the Rana autocracy in Nepal the trade in military manpower enriched a succession of maharajahs on whom, in addition, the British showered honours. 'Our "oldest ally" in Asia' was ready to allow Britain to recruit all the Gurkhas it wanted in return for riches and a guaranteed, if circumscribed, independence. That was the reality; the rest is fantasy. The point is underlined by the fact that, on the demise of the Raj, the last maharajah of Nepal, Mohan Shamsher, wooed Nehru in precisely the same way as Jang Bahadur had wooed the British – by offering him Nepalese troops to garrison India while the bulk of the Indian Army was fighting in Kashmir and in Hyderabad – before he, too, was finally ousted.

General Sir Francis Tuker, in a pioneering and influential book on the 'Gurkhas of Nepal', conflates two intertwined but distinct histories by linking the fate of the Gurkhas to that of the Ranas. Gurkha, or Gorkha, in its original meaning (and spelling), derives from the minor mountain kingdom which laid siege to and finally conquered the rich and fertile Kathmandu valley in the eighteenth century. The present-day king of Nepal is a descendant of Prithwi Narayan Shah, who was retrospectively dubbed the father of the nation. The Ranas were usurpers, turning Nepal into a kind of Shogunate for a hundred years or more. Yet the revolution of 1950–1, which put paid to the Rana autocracy and reinstated the king to power, is regarded by Tuker, writing soon after the event, with the deepest foreboding:

> Perhaps the departure of the Maharajah Mohan Shamsher Jang
> Bahadur Rana may mark the end of Gurkha supremacy in Nepal.
> History may allot to it the period from 1768 to 1951. From 1951
> onwards the people of the Valley, the politicians – Brahman, Newars –
> are reasserting themselves against the soldiers, the men of Gorkha.[2]

But who were the men of Gorkha – the Indo-Aryan rulers who claimed Rajput descent or the Tibeto-Burman peasantry of Magars and Gurungs who first acquired a reputation as warriors fighting for them? Generations of Shahs and Ranas did little but exploit and repress these Magars and Gurungs and their equivalent in the eastern hills of Nepal, the Limbus and Rais, who would also enter the ranks of the 'Gurkhas' three-quarters of a century later. To argue, as Tuker does (and most other military writers have followed his lead), that the British 'betrayal' of the Ranas was also a betrayal of the people whom we call Gurkhas is more revealing of his own prejudices than historically accurate.

British officers of Tuker's generation (spanning the two World Wars) had spent many years trying to insulate the Gurkhas from subversive political influence. It is ironic that it was only with the first coming of democracy in Nepal that this policy was reversed and those Gurkhas who were now in the British Army were deliberately encouraged to take an interest in the politics of their country and exercise their newly acquired democratic right to vote. Of course it was in order to achieve the same end: a stable and recruitment-friendly regime in Nepal.

The void at the centre of all histories of the Gurkhas is the voice of Gurkhas themselves. There is a great need (which may soon be met) for an oral history of the Gurkhas. Until that is achieved, Gurkha sources are so rare as to be almost non-existent. Fighting, not writing, is what they are famous for. But British officers who have taken it upon them-selves to tell the Gurkha story have not had it entirely their own way, particularly in recent years when anthropologists working in Nepal have started to question many of their assumptions. The work of Mary Des Chene, who studied both the history of the Gurkhas and the impact of military service in a heavily recruited Gurung district for her Ph.D. thesis, is frequently cited in this book; and another Canadian-born anthropologist, Lionel Caplan, categorizes the writings of British offi-cers as Gurkhas as 'a particular mode of "orientalist" discourse'.[3]

Leaving aside the fact that whenever I hear the word 'discourse' I want to reach for my blue pencil, Caplan is undeniably right when he says that this 'discourse . . . cannot be separated from the issue of power, both in the narrow sense that those in an unambiguously superordinate position (the European officers) produce peremptory knowledge about their military subordinates, and in the wider sense of the unequal eco-nomic, political and social structures within which the depictions occur'.[4] In a book aimed not so much at shooting down British officers as exposing where they are coming from, so to speak, Caplan scores some palpable hits, though his military knowledge is sketchy and his anthropological data on the Gurkhas themselves disappointingly thin, considering the time he spent in Nepal.

My own position is that of an inside outsider. I spent two of the most formative years of my life as a very young officer in a Gurkha regiment; but the vicissitudes of life have since carried me a long way from the scenes of my youth. What I am trying to do here is present the military history of Gurkha units in, first, the Indian and now the British (as well as Indian) Army in the wider context of the diplomatic relations between Britain and Nepal over nearly two centuries, focusing particularly on the chequered history of recruitment in Nepal. That is the macrocosm; the microcosm is the evolving social life and interplay of British officers and Gurkhas within the various regiments during the same period. To achieve this I have sought to combine an insider's understanding of the Gurkha mystique with an outsider's dispassionate assessment of the historical evidence. To what extent I have succeeded must be left to the reader to judge.

NOTE: The word 'Gurkha' has been spelt in many different ways (see the opening of Chapter 1, page 31). The main division, however, is between 'Gurkha' and 'Gorkha'. The former is favoured by the British and the latter, more correct, spelling is used by the Indians. In this book I employ both spellings to indicate the different perspectives and, in modern times, to distinguish between British and Indian regiments.

A Personal Preface: National Service in the 1/7th Gurkha Rifles

In retrospect, my first contact with my future regiment seems entirely characteristic. I was flown out from England on a cold winter's day at the end of 1957. The RAF Comet touched down to refuel at El Adem, Bahrain and Colombo before landing at Singapore just twenty-two hours later. In the UK I had been issued (by our affiliated British regiment, the Cameronians) with three sets of tropical uniform, and I changed into one of these at Colombo. When I stepped out of the plane at Changi airport I felt that at least I looked the part. So I was taken aback when an officer from my regiment, accompanied by two grinning Gurkhas, came up and, instead of shaking hands and introducing himself, grabbed a camera from one of the soldiers and pointed it at me.

'Sorry about this,' he said, clicking away, 'but it's really too good to miss.'

He went on to explain how lucky it was that he had just bought the camera as a present for the rifleman beside him, who was about to finish his stint as his orderly. While he was talking, I compared what the officer and his soldiers were wearing with what I had on and realized why I had become an object of ridicule. I had indeed been issued with tropical kit, but for the wrong theatre of war: my beige shirt and trousers would have been perfect for El Alamein; in the Malayan jungle they would provide no better camouflage than a scarlet tunic.

We walked over to a military Land Rover which was painted the same olive green as my companions' uniforms and I studied my brother officer, who had at last, and rather reluctantly, I thought, introduced himself. Chris Batchelor was short, with broad, hunched shoulders and an attractive bruiser's face. I hoped we might be friends but our conversation during the ninety-mile ride to Kluang, where the 1st battalion, 7th – not yet Duke of Edinburgh's Own – Gurkha Rifles (GR) was stationed, was at best fitful. Chris's answers to my eager and no doubt naive questions were cryptic and after a bit I settled back in silence to take in my new surroundings.

I was uneasily conscious that the soldiers sitting next to me had loaded rifles at the ready. At this late stage of the Emergency, an ambush was highly improbable but I did not know that yet; and my excitement was tinged with fear as I stared out along the rows and rows of rubber trees, drawn up like soldiers on parade, so immaculate were their lines.

Soon it was dark and I turned my attention to the Gurkhas themselves. In addition to the two who had met me off the plane there was the driver of the Land Rover. All three had round, Mongolian faces which, when they smiled, radiated friendliness but were now concentrated and alert to any danger. In their company, as in my absurd uniform, I felt a fraud. I could not speak a word of their language. Indeed, I wondered if I would learn it in time to be of any use to the battalion. I was to discover that this was one reason why the Brigade of Gurkhas was reluctant to take National Service officers: their time was almost up before they could make a contribution; hence their intake was restricted to one or two per year in each battalion.

Eaton Hall, outside Chester, was a magnificent pile owned by the Duke of Westminster and leased by the army for the training of National Service infantry officers. Some intakes were housed in the mansion itself but our company lived in two Nissen huts in the grounds. We all carried canes as a reminder that we were officer cadets, but the use to which these canes were put was not always officer-like. The occupants of the hall, for instance, would hurl theirs at a large painting they passed every day at the bottom of the stairs. The canvas became heavily pitted as a result. It was not until some years later, when I saw it in the chapel of King's College, Cambridge, that I realized that the object of their attentions, now lovingly restored, was Rubens's *Adoration of the Magi*.

Towards the end of our training we were required to state a preference as to which regiment we would like to be commissioned into. I was the only cadet in my intake from the Devons – indeed, there was only one other man from my county regiment in the entire camp and he happened to be my platoon commander. Although he was now in the Devons, Captain Stone had been in the Indian Army during the Second World War. He did not hold it against me that I didn't want to join the battalion in Germany; he merely asked me where I would rather go. When I told him the Far East, because my parents had lived there, he suggested I apply to the Gurkhas.

The Gurkhas? I had very little idea who or what they might be, but they sounded more glamorous than the Devons and were, according to Captain Stone, permanently stationed in the Far East. There were four Gurkha regiments, each with two battalions, and if I succeeded in getting into any one of them I would be bound for either Malaya or Hong Kong. So I applied and, despite losing my footing on the polished floor and involuntarily prostrating myself before the august Major-General R. C. O. Hedley CB, CBE, DSO who interviewed me, I was accepted along with the only other applicant from our intake, an old Etonian called Roger Garside.

All that remained was the ceremonial passing-out parade that marked our transition from cadet to second lieutenant. This was the moment for which the sergeant-majors from the Brigade of Guards – whose names, Lynch, Leech and Blood, give a fair indication of their outlook – had been waiting. Nothing and no one was spared in their efforts to turn us into the best drilled company ever to pass out of Eaton Hall. The ballyhoo was effective and meant that we left Eaton Hall with a higher sense of our calling than might have been expected of mere National Servicemen.

We were officers now and while I relished my newfound status – the pip on each shoulder, the flashes that proclaimed a regiment as exotic as a rare blood group – I secretly awaited the exposure that would, I felt, inevitably follow such undeserved elevation.

The officers' mess of 1/7 GR in Kluang (Malay for 'flying fox', as the big fruit-eating bats which flew over the camp at dusk were called) was on top of a hillock, and the officers' quarters were off to one side. When I had been shown my room and introduced to the Gurkha who was to be my orderly, Chris Batchelor took me to meet the other subalterns who were gathered in one of their rooms. With the curse of the Cameronians still upon me in the shape of my ludicrous sand-coloured uniform, I made the acquaintance of Lieutenants Benthall, Oakden and, my predecessor as a National Serviceman, Ripley. If I looked upon the last-named, who was about to depart, as a potential ally, I was disappointed: he was clearly at one with the other subalterns in regarding this new arrival as an unwelcome intruder. I was, it is true, offered a drink and a cigarette (in those days, we were *issued* with a tin of fifty cigarettes a week on active service) and asked a question or two. But I was not to take this as a sign that I was accepted into their circle; I was, at best, on probation. The first hint of over-familiarity or bumptiousness would result in social ostracization. I had travelled across the world, it seemed, only to be confronted by a simulacrum of the public school I fervently believed I had quitted forever.

Each of the officers – the suave and feline Mike Benthall, the puffed and chunky Henry Oakden, the elegant Richard Ripley and the little toughie, Chris Batchelor himself – was more or less approachable individually, but get them together and they took on a forbidding group personality, at once banal and superior. Years later, when I read the novels of J. G. Farrell and came upon the odious Black and Tan Captain Bolton and his fellow auxiliary officers in *Troubles* and travelled in the company of the delightfully serious young 'griffin' Fleury to Krishnapur (in *The Siege of Krishnapur*), there to meet such self-opinionated nonentities as Burlton, Rayne, Ford and the dashing Lt Cutter – who charges on horseback into Rayne's bungalow, jumps over the sofa and dismounts, only to set about a cushion with his sabre and collapse on the floor in a 'whirlwind of feathers' – I was instantly transported back to the officers' mess at Kluang. But when I was myself a young 'griffin' among the latterday Fords, Raynes, Burltons and Cutters, I wanted nothing so much as to be one of them.

In due course I acquired an olive green uniform and achieved a measure of inconspicuousness. I became familiar with the routines of mess life, the requirements of dress and behaviour. Our adjutant, Iain Elliot, made it plain from the start that the mess made few concessions to

National Servicemen. He explained that, since the overwhelming majority of British officers were regulars and had effectively chosen to live their lives in the Far East, they lived well. He warned me that I would find it difficult to meet my monthly mess bill out of my pay, which was considerably less than a regular's, and with Scots canniness counselled caution in the ordering of drinks. 'Jungle-bashing', as it was called, saved me from embarrassment since it removed me from the mess for weeks at a time.

I suppose I must have primed myself for life in a Gurkha battalion by reading John Masters. Even so I was not fully prepared to enter the world of *Bugles and a Tiger.* I saw myself as a boy among men and I was eager to model myself on my betters. But there were times when I felt that the situation was reversed and I was the only man among boys. Dinner nights, in particular, were an ordeal. These were occasions when everyone dressed up: as a mere National Serviceman I was spared the expense of the full regalia and put on black trousers and a simple white 'monkey jacket' (the sort waiters wear), while regular officers wore rifle-green serge uniforms trimmed with black braid. Such elegance enhanced the scene in the mess when the port was passed along the candle-lit, silver-strewn table and the solitary piper filled the night air with the sound of bagpipes (a reminder that Gurkhas, too, are high-landers); then I felt proud to belong to such a fine regiment. But once the formal dinner was over and the horseplay began, all dignity departed. There were red sweaty faces, straining muscles and the sound of expensive cloth ripping. Everyone behaved as though he were just a little more drunk than he actually was. I did my best to enter into the spirit of the occasion, but was secretly appalled that full-grown men should indulge in such high jinks.

I was made company officer of D Company, which was commanded by Major 'Lofty' Whitehead. Chris Batchelor told me – not without a trace of envy, I thought – how lucky I was. Lofty was indeed a tall man, with a large, thrusting chin. He was generally regarded as an outstanding offi-cer, likely to go a long way (he would retire a quarter of a century later as a brigadier and be appointed colonel of the regiment), and D Company responded to his leadership by winning the title of 'champion company' three times in a row.

My status as company officer was a nebulous one. Though I was theoretically the second most senior officer in the company, being the only other British officer, I was not second-in-command of the company; I was merely the *sano sahib* (the small, i.e. insignificant, sahib); the real second-in-command was Gurkha Captain Tulbahadur Gurung. QGOs – or Queen's Gurkha Officers, to give them their full title – were the post-Indian Army (*British* Indian Army, that is) equivalent to the old VCOs, or Viceroy's Commissioned Officers, who formed a sandwich rank between British officers and Indian, or Gurkha, other ranks. These Gurkha officers – and there were three in each company – had all risen through the ranks. In time, I came to know our three QGOs well but to begin with my lack of the language precluded all but the most rudimentary communication.

The first friend I had among the Gurkhas was the D Company clerk, Corporal Premsing Thapa. All the clerks spoke English, some better than others; most of them came from the Darjeeling area of India rather than the eastern hills of Nepal, where we recruited the majority of our soldiers. These clerks were regarded with deep suspicion by the more hidebound British officers; they were not to be trusted; they were *chalak* – a Gurkhali word meaning 'cunning', 'sly', 'clever-clever' – and could be troublesome. One of our subalterns who was on home leave when I joined the battalion had the reputation of being too friendly with the clerks, and that definitely counted against him in the eyes of his seniors. They preferred the peasant virtues of the ordinary rifleman. Yet the clerks I encountered were docile enough.

Before I went to Malaya, my father had taken me to meet the only officer of the Gurkhas of his acquaintance, Lieutenant-General Sir Francis Tuker KCIE, CB, DSO, OBE, who lived in Cornwall and bought strawberry plants from him. I knew nothing of 'Gertie' Tuker's career except what my father had told me, that he had been a distinguished wartime general whose military career had been cut short by ill-health. By the time I met him, his hands were sadly twisted and crippling arthritis confined him to a chair; but his mind was sharp and he had just published his book, *Gorkha: The Story of the Gurkhas of Nepal*, which I then bought and carried out to Malaya with me. If I'd tried to read it then, I probably would have found it heavy-going and given up – too much obscure Nepali history and not enough about our chaps.

But Tuker must have given me a little lecture about the men I was going out to command. He would have sung the praises of all Gurkhas, but being a 2nd Goorkha (their preferred spelling) himself – indeed, as I would later discover, the ultimate 2nd Goorkha, very much one of 'God's Own' as they were known ironically throughout the Brigade – he would also have managed to insinuate that the *original* Gurkhas, the Magars and Gurungs from west-central Nepal, were somehow superior to the Limbus and Rais from east Nepal, Johnnies-come-lately who had not been seriously recruited until the end of the nineteenth century, fine soldiers though they undoubtedly were.

The four infantry regiments which, along with the Gurkha Signals and Gurkha sappers, at that time made up the British Brigade of Gurkhas were split fifty–fifty between western and eastern Gurkhas: the 2nd and the 6th Gurkhas recruited mainly Magars and Gurungs; the 7th and the 10th predominantly Limbus and Rais (the corps mixed them). This meant that there were a far greater proportion of eastern Gurkhas in the British Army than there had been in the old Indian Army Gurkha Brigade in which just two out of the ten regiments recruited Limbus and Rais. It just happened that (for reasons which will be explained fully in Chapter 8) both these eastern Gurkha regiments were transferred to British service at the time of the Partition of India in 1947, while five of the seven western Gurkha regiments (the 9th Gurkhas were different again, recruiting the higher caste Thakurs and Chhetris) remained in India.

Some officers no doubt exaggerated the differences between easterners and westerners in order to foster regimental rivalry and make each battalion strive to prove itself better than all the others. In terms of actual performance there seemed little to choose between them, and to a newcomer they both looked and sounded much the same. But I had been commissioned into an eastern regiment, so my first loyalty was to the Limbus and Rais who comprised the bulk of our battalion.

Outside formal parades my main contact with the men was through sport. We played basketball, volleyball and football together every day we were in camp. In Kluang, D Company at least seemed to play mainly basketball and, though I was taller than most – if not all – Gurkhas, I often found myself floundering while they weaved intricate patterns of passing all around me. Their speed and sleight of hand left me standing, and they knew how to turn their lack of inches to advantage, bouncing the ball so close to the ground that it was almost impossible to get it away from them, then suddenly leaping in the air to guide the ball into the basket with lethal accuracy. For much of the time, unless someone on my side took pity on the poor sahib and passed him the ball, I was an admiring spectator.

The jungle operations I went on were uniformly uneventful in terms of contacts with the Communist Terrorists – or CTs, as we called them. At that stage of the Malayan Emergency (to call it a war, apparently, would have been bad for trade) the only successful operations came about as a result of propaganda and intelligence work. Auster reconnaissance planes flew over the jungle dropping leaflets aimed at the stubborn remnant of Chin Peng's Malayan Races Liberation Army. These leaflets emphasized the hopelessness of their position and offered attractive incentives to surrender. The tactic worked. Surrendered Enemy Personnel trickled out of the jungle and showed themselves quite ready to betray their comrades in return for the promised amnesty and financial rewards. The challenge was to get them to lead our troops back to their jungle hideouts before the others had time to notice their absence and decamp to another place of refuge. For in the game of hide-and-seek we were playing with the small remaining bands of CTs all they were required to do was to stay put: we could pass within touching distance of them without knowing they were there. The days when they had been on the offensive were long gone. Now they were only interested in survival.

I was eager to make my mark. Secretly, I hankered after a gong; a medal such as the Military Cross, with its elegant purple and white ribbon, would have been such an adornment in years to come when I attended regimental reunion dinners in 'dinner jacket and miniatures'. Mercifully perhaps, I was spared the ordeal by battle, my jungle-bashing being of an unremittingly routine sort: the dawn ride by truck to an unfrequented part of a rubber plantation; the journey on foot, laden with pack, ammunition belt, water bottle and rifle (or, in my case, Sten gun, since it was lighter to carry) into the perpetual twilight of the jungle itself; the frequent halts to work out precisely which map square we had reached when all map squares looked alike; the trudge through swamps infested with leeches that attached themselves to whichever parts of our skin they could get at and had to be burnt off with a cigarette so as not to leave a running sore; the evening halt and – best moment of the day – issue of rum and a handful of tiny dried fishes, the only sort of food I found palatable in the jungle, where I subsisted largely on pint mugs of hot, sweet tea, made with condensed milk, a drink I would normally find disgusting.

According to the late Brigadier 'Birdie' Smith's regimental history of the 7th Gurkha Rifles:

> Both battalions ended their 1958 operational tasks by taking part in a large scale drive against the terrorists still remaining in the Pengarang peninsula of south east Johore. HQ 63 Gurkha Infantry Brigade controlled Operation 'Badak' and had both battalions of the Seventh and 10 GR, as well as The Cheshire Regiment, fully deployed for nearly two months.[1]

I was one of those deployed in this operation; D Company was sent to establish a base at the riverside village of Telok Sengat, where the Gurkha sappers had already built an airstrip for the small Auster planes, which were used both for reconnaissance and as a sort of taxi service – the only alternative approach being by boat across the wide estuary of the Johore river. Our tented camp was on a laterite plateau overlooking the estuary, where, shortly after our arrival, there was a regatta to mark the first anniversary of *Merdeka*, Malayan independence. The fact that this celebration could take place in such an out-of-the-way spot without fear of reprisal is an indication of how one-sided a contest the war had become. Though we took precautions against attack we were essentially engaged in 'mopping-up' – which made it all the more surprising when, on a routine operation, our signaller reported that the company's other platoon, in an ambush position some miles away, had come under fire and one of our men had been wounded.

The next day we emerged briefly from the jungle to be 're-rationed' for a further ten-day stint. Lofty himself came on the lorry bringing our supplies. He took me aside to tell me what had happened. The platoon was due to be rested for the Hindu festival of Dashera (the Gurkha equivalent of our Christmas in terms of celebration) and a Malay police unit was taking over its ambush position. Stealth was essential if the men's whereabouts were to remain unknown to the CTs (assuming there were any in the vicinity). So the police NCOs were shown round in advance of the actual hand-over, which was to take place under cover of darkness. It was during this preliminary manoeuvre that the shot was fired and a Gurkha corporal went down, clutching his thigh. The injury was serious, though it seemed unlikely to be fatal, since the man was immediately evacuated by helicopter. But he died from shock and loss of blood before he reached the military hospital in Singapore.

All attempts to discover an enemy had failed and there was something suspicious about this isolated act of aggression. Then it came out that one of the police NCOs had accidentally let off his rifle but had been too frightened of instant retaliation by the other Gurkhas to say anything at the time. It was only when he was back in the safety of his unit that he confessed.

Lofty urged me to say nothing until we had settled down for the night in the jungle and then to break the news gently to the NCOs. By this time I had sufficient command of the language to play my part. I did not relish the task but was surprised how philosophically the Gurkhas took it. It was not that they did not care; the corporal who had died was universally liked and his promising career – he had been chosen as orderly to the Major-General, Brigade of Gurkhas – had been needlessly ended. But many of these Gurkha NCOs had been in Malaya ten years, and some in Burma before that. They were reconciled to the vicissitudes of war.

Some time before this – and unbeknownst to me – our commanding officer, Lt-Col. Mike Magoris, had written about me to my father:

> The other day he came and asked me whether he could extend his service with us for a further six months. He is keen to go and look round Darjeeling, which we might be able to arrange for him . . . with a view to going into the tea business.[2]

This was an idea I often discussed with Lofty, who had once been stationed in Darjeeling, when we sat outside the mess tent at our company base in the evening, drinking beer and gazing out over the river. But the opportunity to 'go and look round' came sooner than I expected, and when I was posted to Calcutta – to supervise the air-trooping of Gurkhas going on home leave to Nepal – I was sad to leave Telok Sengat, where I had been living an almost ideal existence away from the constraints of the officers' mess with no British officer apart from the avuncular Lofty. There I enjoyed an intimacy with the Gurkhas which would have been impossible with British troops and I was completely under their spell. Hence my search for a non-military career among them.

Before I went to India I returned with D Company to Kluang to celebrate Dashera. During a week of partying, British officers had little to do but keep out of the way, or get drunk with the QGOs when invited to their mess. But their presence was required for the culminating festivities of *Mar*, the day on which animal sacrifices were made to Kali, the goddess of destruction, and the battalion's good fortune for the following year depended on the successful decapitation of an ox with a single stroke of a kukri.

This operation demanded skill as well as strength, though the kukri used was generally twice the size of a normal one, a formidable if rather unwieldy-looking weapon. Should the executioner need more than one clean stroke to sever the ox's head, and thus bring bad luck upon the battalion, he would have to flee from the wrath of the multitude gathered to witness his performance. The lance-corporal entrusted with this task by 1/7 GR in 1958 made no mistake, however, and stood proudly in front of the CO, who honoured him by wrapping a *pagari*, or turban, around his head. And then the dancing began, the *marunis*, young male dancers dressed in women's clothes, swaying sinuously to the rhythms of the drums and tambourines. Their slender figures and beardless faces heightened the illusion of femininity and removed any element of parody that such a drag act would involve in western culture.

My feet had scarcely touched the ground at Calcutta's Dum-Dum airport when I witnessed a row between a British staff officer and an Indian customs official. The official had been amusing himself and a colleague by demanding that one of the Gurkhas from my flight open his trunk for inspection; the joke was that the box was secured with such copious quantities of rope that it would take a long while to unravel. By the time the Gurkha had succeeded in undoing the various strands, the customs man had lost interest and impatiently waved him on. He was unaware that the captain, a heavily-built Yorkshireman, had been watching this.

'You made that man open his box,' the captain said, practically lifting the official off the ground by his lapels. 'Now you bloody well go through it, item by bloody item.'

At first the official seemed disposed to argue the point, but confronted with such a burly, sweaty, red-faced giant he thought better of it and did as he was told.

The captain was consumed with indignation. 'Did you see that?' he said. 'Bloody little *babu*.'

While I sympathized with him, I felt uncomfortable about this encounter, which seemed to epitomize the old colonial relationship, the defunct British Raj.

On my arrival in Darjeeling a month later I witnessed another such altercation, this time involving a European tea-planter and a man who, had he been wearing a uniform, would have been classified as a Gurkha. As they spoke in Hindi I was unable to follow exactly what was being said, but it had something to do with a car which should have been ready for collection and wasn't. The tone, however, was unmistakably hostile.

In Malaya I had seen angry sahibs laying down the law, but this was different. In the army, officers and men trusted and depended on one another; they were bound together by mutual pride and affection. What I sensed in this brief but bitter exchange was something I would not have believed possible between British and Gurkhas – racial tension, if not hatred. It was an inauspicious beginning to my search for a non-military career among the Gurkhas.

When I mentioned this incident to an ex-officer of the 10th Gurkhas who was a tea-planter, he told me that Chinese agents, operating across the border from Tibet and working as shoe-makers in the bazaar, stirred up disaffection among labourers on the estates. I came to the conclusion that tea-planting in Darjeeling was by no means the civilian equivalent of soldiering with the Gurkhas. Despite the loveliness of the place, it was an altogether rougher, tougher life.

Before I left Darjeeling I called at the house of Tensing Sherpa, Edmund Hillary's companion in the first successful assault on the summit of Everest five years earlier; there, my tea-planter friend Mike Cheney had told me, I would be able to hire porters for a trek into east Nepal. This was at least a decade before every self-respecting hippy followed the trail to Kathmandu, and Nepal was still an almost entirely closed country; it was only through the Gurkha connection that I had been able to get a visa, and even then I'd had to specify exactly where I intended to go and how long I planned to stay. My visa, 'Seen at the Royal Nepalese Consulate General at Calcutta', was 'good for a single ["multiple" deleted] journey to ["Kathmandu" deleted] Memeng, Taplejung, Tehrathum, Dhankuta, Dharan and Biratnagar'; it was valid for 'fifteen days only' with effect from 13 December 1958.

Tensing was not at home when I called, but I found two young Sherpas willing to accompany me on what was, for them, no more than a stroll through the foothills of the Himalayas. For me it was a magical journey, through wilder and more magnificent country than I had ever previously traversed, a country without roads or any but the most primitive sort of communications, a country where poverty was endemic except that it was not so much poverty (there being no contrasting riches) as subsistence, a country of high, often cloud-covered hills and deep valleys with cascading rivers and rickety bridges – often a hundred feet or more above the raging torrent – which I sometimes had to close my eyes to cross.

I had become habituated to the dark green, swampy, stagnant, enclosed world of the Malayan jungle; so the openness of the hills, with the occasional tantalizing glimpses of snow-covered peaks rearing out of the high cloud, and the clear and invigorating air afforded me moments of pure pleasure. Perhaps, too, the fact that I was so young and in rude health made this trek through the eastern hills of Nepal, with no companion other than the two Sherpas, Sonagirmi and Nang Pincho, so utterly memorable.

My visit coincided with the first-ever general election in Nepal (and the last for over thirty years). As a gesture towards nascent democracy the British Army had sent small groups of Gurkha signalmen with wireless sets to towns like Taplejung and Dhankuta so that the results of the elections could be transmitted to the capital, Kathmandu. Whenever I came upon these wireless operators, who were instantly recognizable in their western-style mufti (as opposed to the wrap-around tunics and voluminous trousers tapering at the knee favoured by the hill folk), they made me welcome and put me up for the night. Elsewhere we camped in the open or sheltered on the verandahs of the orange-and-white, wattle-and-daub houses of the local peasants, whose hospitality was as generous as their resources were meagre.

As a refugee from the developed world, I was enchanted rather than appalled by the primitiveness of life in the hills which, over centuries, had been carved into thousands of tiny terraced fields where millet and rice were intensively cultivated. The visual effect was as stunning as the labour required to fetch water from rivers and streams to irrigate these narrow plots was back-breaking. Pets, in the western sense, were unknown; humans and animals had an intimate, working relationship and shared the same living space, but humans, particularly women, were the main beasts of burden. Heavy loads were carried up and down the mountains on people's backs in conical baskets called *dokos*, supported by a headband. Men carried kukris tucked in their cummerbunds and used them for chopping firewood. The work was endless, so any break in routine, any excuse for a party, was eagerly grasped.

I attended a Limbu wedding in Khamlalung, where as part of the ritual the bride's father entreated his tearful daughter to stay at home and not to go to the – understandably nervous-looking – bridegroom. I was persuaded to join the wedding dance, or *nach*, and given enough *raksi*, the fiery local spirit, to ensure that I woke up next morning with a throbbing head.

Outside another village we came upon a row of twenty children seated neatly on one side of the track facing two adults on the other; they all had books and this was plainly a school, the first I had seen in the hills. Like the single-tine, ox-drawn plough we had passed earlier in the day, this was an archetypal, almost biblical scene. In the village itself an outdoor meeting comprising every adult male (but no females) was in progress, dominated by the magnificently rotund figure of Subedar-Major and Honorary Captain Gobindsing Limbu OBI, MBE. This was in effect the school's board of governors.

At the time of Partition in India, Gobindsing had been a subedar-major (the equivalent of our Gurkha Major) in the 10th Gurkha Rifles. Lured by the offer of a full commission (and the extra money that went with it), he had opted for the Indian, rather than the British, Army. His influence as subedar-major was such that many others had followed his lead, to the chagrin of his British officers, though they might have been mollified to learn that Gobindsing had lived to regret his decision – or so he told me. The young men of the village, Lance-Corporal Utrabahadur Limbu and Riflemen Padambahadur and Bhaudraj Limbu, who were at home on leave at the time of my visit, were all in British regiments, the 2/7th and 1/10th Gurkhas.

The further south we went, the more signs of civilization we encountered. There were flourishing markets and in Dhankuta, the capital of east Nepal, there was a *maidan*, a piece of common land flat enough to play games on. In Dhankuta, too, the house belonging to the *Bara Hakim*, or local governor, was a three-storey brick building with windows and balconies overlooking a small formal garden. But the detail that caught my eye was a whitewashed hut with a tin roof, which resembled nothing so much as an outside lavatory but was in fact a tiny temple with a bell slung between posts on either side of the door. I came upon a QGO from my own regiment in the streets of Dhankuta, the rather grumpy Gurkha Capt. Keherman Limbu, dressed in such an odd assortment of military and civilian garb – green beret and blazer over the baggy breeches known as *suruwal* – that I insisted on taking his photo.

After Dhankuta the path became almost a highway, it was so well-trodden. One more river, the Tamur Khola, to cross; one more hill to climb; and then, as far as the eye could see, the plain, or Terai, of southern Nepal, stretching down into India. It was like looking out over a vast sea, as impressive in its way as the northern view of the mountains. We finally reached the tented camp of Phusre, which was just above Dharan, where a new British Gurkha recruiting depot was under construction; here I would be sucked back into army life and there would be no place for the Sherpas, Sonagirmi or Nang Pincho, free spirits that they were.

I spent a night at the officers' mess at Phusre, a wooden hut with a verandah surrounded by tents; below it the site of the permanent depot was a wasteland of half-built concrete barracks. My delight in such creature comforts as hot water for bathing and food designed for European palates was tempered with regret at the loss of my Sherpa guides.

After a gruelling twenty-four-hour train journey from Biratnagar, or the Indian railhead Jogbani, to Calcutta, which included crossing the

Ganges in an overloaded ferry at Maniharighat, I arrived back at our transit camp at Barrackpore in the midst of Christmas festivities. It was my twentieth birthday on Boxing Day and that provided an excuse, if one were needed, to continue the celebrations in the mess.

In early January I was appointed second-in-command of a batch of 400 Gurkha recruits about to be shipped to Malaya via Rangoon on SS *Sangola* of the British India line. In command was a captain from the 10th Gurkhas by the name of Mick Cousins. Tall and skinny, Mick was a 'line-boy' (his family connection with, first, the 5th Royal Gurkha Rifles and then the 10th Gurkhas went back to 1915) who as a result spoke impeccable Gurkhali. Our recruits, who had come straight from the hills, had never seen the sea or a ship before, though they were familiar with aeroplanes flying overhead. They gathered on deck and leant on the railings as we steamed out of the Hugli river into the Bay of Bengal. Fortunately the sea was calm, since Gurkhas are notoriously poor sailors.

We disembarked with our recruits at Penang and delivered them to the Depot, Brigade of Gurkhas, at Sungei Patani. Six months earlier I had been at the depot on a language course, along with half-a-dozen other young officers, and we had spent our leisure hours in and out of the swimming pool at the Runnymede Hotel in Penang where, a quarter of a century earlier, my parents had stayed on their wedding night before going on their honeymoon to Sumatra. Now I had to return to my regiment, which had just acquired a new name: no longer plain 7th Gurkha Rifles, we had become the 7th *Duke of Edinburgh's Own* Gurkha Rifles. As the 1/7 GR 'war diary' records for 24 January 1959:

A Tattoo and Regimental Ball was held in Mersing Road Camp [where 2/7 GR were based] in honour of the Royal titles bestowed upon the Regiment by HM The Queen. The Tattoo began at 1930 hours and was performed by the Staff Band Brigade of Gurkhas and the Massed Regimental Pipes and Drums. The guests then went on to 2nd bn. mess for the Regimental Ball. The band was supplied by the 13/18th Royal Hussars (QMO) and buffet supper by the ACC [Army Catering Corps] . . .

2/Lt. Gould arrived in the bn. after duty on the L of C [Lines of Communication] in India and Nepal.[3]

What the battalion war diary does not record was that this was an all-night party with a champagne-and-oyster bar, among other delights, and that cooked breakfast was served in the mess from 0630 hours, or thereabouts. I got back just in time to join in the celebrations.

The Duke of Edinburgh came in person a month later and inspected his new regiment at Blakang Mati barracks in Singapore. He arrived by helicopter and was introduced to the commanding officers of both battalions before being driven round the assembled ranks and garlanded by Gurkha wives and children. Before the parade ended and the Duke departed the way he came, he was presented with a ceremonial kukri by the Gurkha Majors of both battalions.

As a mere National Serviceman, I was excluded from these proceedings, though I was permitted to watch from an upstairs window of the barracks, provided I kept well out of sight.

On the last day of February 1959, I sailed from Singapore to Hong Kong with the advance party of 1/7 GR on board the troopship, HMS *Oxfordshire*; had I not signed on for an extra six months, my National Service would have ended soon after my return to Malaya. As it was, I was one of the team whose task was to take over the camp currently occupied by the 1/6th Gurkhas; they would be moving into our lines at Kluang.

The South China Sea was as rough as the crew of the *Oxfordshire* could ever remember it, and the Gurkha officers and men alike were fearfully seasick. Their genial faces turned green and grim, and the alacrity with which they usually carried out orders was absent. In fact, they became sullen and uncooperative and as near to mutiny as I had ever seen Gurkhas. But the voyage was not long and the weather improved as we approached Hong Kong, so that when we arrived we were able to disembark in some semblance of order. For myself, I was pleased to discover that I was a good sailor, though for days after our arrival the ground seemed to heave like the deck of the ship.

The New Territories, on the mainland of China beyond Kowloon, is an area of intensively cultivated plains and high, grassy hills. The smell of human excrement, used as manure by the Chinese, assailed our nostrils as we drove past smallholdings on our way out to Tam Mei Camp. The camp itself was the usual agglomeration of army huts, nestling in the lee of a hill. But I regarded it with more than usual interest as I had been assigned the task of quartermaster for the duration of the take-over and was responsible, along with a Gurkha officer who knew far more than I did, for checking fixtures and fittings, for spotting missing light-bulbs and cracked washbasins throughout the camp, including the men's married quarters, which were normally out of bounds to British officers.

When the remainder of the battalion joined us in early April, I became more or less redundant. My departure was imminent, so I was assigned not to a company but to the non-job of assistant adjutant. I was in an emotional limbo, too. On one or two evenings during the take-over I had accompanied a group of young and unattached officers from 1/6 GR to a nightclub in Kowloon and watched them make fools of themselves dancing with Chinese 'hostesses' with long, silky black hair, whose encouragement of their buffoonery was strictly professional. While I continued to play basketball and football with the men, I was beginning to withdraw from life in the mess.

I went for a long walk alone, climbing a hill called 'Nameless', and took comfort from the fact that from the top our makeshift military camp looked so small and insignificant, while on the other side the sunlit sea dotted with little islands seemed so invitingly empty. I was thinking that soon I would have to cast off the borrowed plumage of 'Gurkha officer'. Though I had a plan for the future – to join a madcap scheme dreamed up by a 10 GR officer of starting a market garden staffed with Gurkhas on the slopes of Mount Kinabalu in North Borneo – this was no more than a stopgap. What was I doing? Where was I going? Who was I? The one thing I knew with some certainty was that I didn't belong where I was. Yet I had wanted so much to belong, had tried so hard to belong and, if I had failed, had no satisfactory alter-native scenario for myself. Unlike the battalion medical officer, Anthony Hocken, a fellow National Serviceman, I had no civilian activity, no doctoring to return to once my time was up.

The decision was taken out of my hands. We had been practising the drill for the Queen's Birthday Parade in Kowloon and the night before I had dreamed that I was on the parade and didn't know what I was sup-posed to be doing. It was like one of those dreams in which you find yourself on stage and cannot remember your lines. I woke up sweating but, instead of finding relief in the fact that it was only a dream, was so feverish that the dream intensified and turned into delirium, a waking nightmare in which for the most part I really did not know what I was doing.

In the morning they came for me with a stretcher; I protested that I could walk but found it wasn't true, I couldn't even stand. Lying in the ambulance I looked up into the faces of my fellow passengers, uniformed Gurkhas, and found them closed to me, a sahib no longer but a sick man in a sarong. Just how sick I had no means of knowing. When the hospital doctor – a Royal Army Medical Corps colonel with a row of campaign medal ribbons headed by an MC, I noticed – warned me that I might find it increasingly difficult to breathe, 'and you know what that'll mean, don't you?', I had no idea but neither did I care. I trusted him and that was enough. Here was a fatherly man to whom I could hand over responsibility for my life. Let him sort it out.

On 14 May 1959 the adjutant sat down to write his quarterly newsletter:

> ... Before starting this newsletter properly though I must mention the tragic news we have had in the Bn [battalion]. Tony Gould, whom you will know as a national service officer doing an extended tour with us at his own request, is now in BMH Kowloon in an iron lung suffering from polio. He was taken there on 23 April, having been feeling unwell for a few days. The doctors say it will be many months before he can be moved back to UK, and he is at the moment severely paralysed.[4]

While I was incarcerated in the iron lung, paralysed from the neck down – except for my hands, which nevertheless lay useless by my inert body inside the cylindrical tank – I could read a book if somebody turned the pages and replaced it, face down, on a glass shelf above my head. I didn't read much. But one book I recall was an account of the German expedition to Nanga Parbat in the Himalayas in which the climber Hermann Buhl was caught in a blizzard after reaching the summit and had to spend a night in the open at an altitude of something like 27,000 feet before descending to the highest camp. His companions hardly recognized him when he staggered in: he had aged twenty years overnight. He survived only to lose his life on a routine climb in the Alps a few years later.

That much I remember. I don't know that I consciously related this to my own predicament and the fact that downstairs in another ward somebody had died of everyday appendicitis. But what now strikes me as incongruous is reading a book about mountaineering when I could, literally, barely lift a finger. My life as I had known it, an outdoor, active, sporting, military life was over, *khatam*, finished; yet I was apparently unaware of this.

Consciously, that is. For I believe that at another level I knew I had come to the end of something: of what, I could not have said. I had a sense of loss, for sure, but also a measure of relief: it was over – whatever *it* was.

I surrendered to the secret invader and sank into passivity, watching myself from a distance while people came and went, preoccupied with the things they were doing to me or to the machine that was keeping me alive. I wasn't even curious, so that when the doctor finally told me he was taking my name off the danger list and that what I had – in case I didn't know – was polio, I hardly knew how to react. I thought, how strange. Nothing more. Then I was rather impressed; polio sounded so serious. No wonder I'd had three Queen Alexandra's Royal Army Nursing Corps sisters looking after me round the clock. It was something, after all, to have had polio. Already I thought of it in the past. I never for a moment thought that I might not walk again, or that the only mark of distinction I would bring to regimental reunions in London in years to come might be a wheelchair or a pair of crutches.

The fact that I had been in quarantine for two weeks explained the lack of early visitors from the battalion. Then they started to come: Anthony Hocken, who had thought that I was suffering from typhoid when he sent me to hospital, was the first and others followed. John Heelis came; a senior major, he had been in command of the advance party to Hong Kong and, as acting CO in Mike Magoris's absence, had written about me to my father, remarking that: 'In his short time with us he has almost created a record in the number of places he has been able to see and the amount of practical experience he has been able to gain.'[5]

In particular, I remember John Cross's visit; he brought slides of his recent trek in Nepal and embarrassed the sister on duty by asking her what he described as a personal question: 'Are you AC or DC?' John, then a major, was the officer I most admired in the battalion – along with Lofty Whitehead, who had gone on UK leave by this time. John's linguistic brilliance gave him a greater understanding of Gurkhas than any other officer I knew. And Gurkhali was just one of nine Asian languages he spoke fluently. He had attended a party for the local Chinese rubber planters Lofty and I had hosted at the D Company base in Telok Sengat; as soon as the planter sitting next to me heard him speak his language, he looked up in amazement and said, 'how long has he been speaking Chinese?' When I told him John had been learning it for less than three months I could see he didn't believe me. 'Well,' he said, 'he doesn't speak like a European; he speaks like one of us.'

Some officers visited me; others stayed away. The latter may have been afraid of catching polio. My orderly fell ill soon after I had gone into hospital and it was feared that this might be the beginning of an epidemic. But mine remained an isolated case; my orderly recovered from whatever ailed him and life in the battalion went on without me. There was a handwritten PS to the adjutant's newsletter, saying: 'The news of TG is now very much better, and he is out of his iron lung for practically the entire day now, and is expecting to be flown home in a few weeks. He is very cheerful and his father has just been out under the DILFOR scheme. Tony is, in fact, making a remarkable comeback.'[6]

I was, in fact, in a very confused state of mind, troubled by two of the things mentioned so casually in that PS. I was not ready to go home. I had always intended to stay in the Far East and did not see why my illness – a *temporary* form of paralysis, as the doctor had originally described it to me – should alter that. That was one thing. The other was that when I'd heard that one of my parents was being flown out to see me I had assumed it would be my mother, since she was the one who had looked after me during childhood bouts of chicken-pox and whooping cough.

In the end, though, my father's visit made it easier for me to contemplate the inevitable journey home. For single officers at least, regimental life is a simulacrum of home life and I had come to regard the battalion as my second family, with all that that implies of frustration as well as intimacy. Now that the umbilical cord linking me to 1/7 GR had been so abruptly severed, I was adrift in more than a physical sense. I had already rejected the possibility of remaining with the regiment,

but I had set my heart on continuing contact with Gurkhas, as my intention of joining what the adjutant's newsletter described as 'a venture in
Borneo being undertaken by retired officers of the Brigade' illustrates.
I might have felt ambivalent about my fellow officers and military life
in general, but towards the Gurkhas my feelings were strongly romantic and largely unexamined.

This is the hardest thing to recapture after forty years. But at that
time I was totally caught up in the Gurkha mystique; and my removal
from their midst without warning or time for adjustment was a kind of
cold-turkey treatment. In my letter home of 15 May – almost the first I
wrote in my own hand rather than dictated to one of the sisters – I
mentioned in passing 'the pain of leaving my unit' and wrote:

> This morning the Gurkha Major and two other GOs visited me and it
> really was delightful to feel back in the Regt. again for half-an-hour.
> They were very amusing and, apropos of all the [recent] marriages of
> officers in the battalion, suggested that I would get married when I
> recovered – to which I replied that I couldn't afford it. But the old
> Gurkha Major, quite unabashed, said that I should have to look for a
> girl with plenty of money as, after all, that is all that matters![7]

Gurkha Major Bagbir Limbu was wiser than perhaps he knew. My need
for emotional reorientation was quite as urgent as my struggle for health
and strength.

Back in England eight months later I was invalided out of the army, my
military service formally and finally over. The battalion was half a world
away in Hong Kong. For some years I kept in tenuous contact by means
of Christmas cards and would occasionally meet officers on home leave;
but the focus of my life had shifted and I looked at them askance. The
experience of illness had revived my intellectual interests and politi-
cized me. This created a gap between me and my erstwhile colleagues.
I felt out of place at regimental reunions and soon gave up going.

Then the sixties beckoned with their siren songs of freedom – freedom from want, freedom from war (above all, nuclear war), freedom
from the shackles of class and empire. The post-war pall that had hung
over Britain for so long was connected in people's minds with wartime

values, military moustaches and stiff upper lips, uniforms and rank, class distinctions. For the long-haired youth of the sixties, uniforms became fancy dress and Union Jacks decorative motifs for shopping bags. Understatement was out, irreverence in. A defining moment on film was when The Beatles mocked the indignant passenger in the railway carriage who blurted out, 'To think that we fought the war for the likes of you.' There was a sea change in people's perceptions which affected even the army itself, though that would take time to become apparent.

Sartorially, I was once again caught napping. Just as my arrival in Singapore in the wrong tropical uniform had provoked hoots of derision from my brother officer, my too-formal 'civvies' were out of place among the people I now knew. So I jettisoned my rifle-green blazer with its black crossed-kukri buttons, hung up my regimental tie, put on an open-necked shirt and pinned a CND badge to my denim jacket. In the age of Aldermaston I marched – if that's the word – to the music of a different drum.

1

The Gorkha War

In the beginning was the word, and the word – in this case – was Gorkha (or Goorka, Goorkha, Ghoorkha, Goorkah, even Gurkha), a word which has become so encrusted with myth that nowadays some people cannot write it without putting it into inverted commas. Originally it signified a place, as indeed it still does: the hill settlement of Gorkha to the north-west of Kathmandu, home from the mid-sixteenth century to a dynasty of small hill rajahs who, two centuries later, acquired big ambitions. According to tradition, these petty rajahs were the descendants of Rajputs forced by the Muslim invasion of around AD 1300 to flee their homeland and seek refuge in the Himalayan foothills.

These Indo-Aryans gradually imposed their Hindu religion with its classical Varna model of the caste system – Brahman/priests, Kshatriya/warriors, Vaisya/merchants, Sudra/menials (and outcaste Untouchables) – on the Tibeto-Burman inhabitants of the hills, whose own traditions were animist and Buddhist, and communal rather than hierarchical. Converts were made and early intercourse between high-caste Brahmans and mainly Magar women resulted in the elevation of their offspring to Chhetri (*kshatriya*, or warrior) status; these Khas, as they were known, became, like the 'twice-born' Brahmans and Rajputs, wearers of the sacred thread, or *tagadharis*, rather than members of the despised drinking classes, or *matwalis* – those to whom intoxicants are not taboo. But after a while the ranks of the Chhetris closed to the Khas offspring of liaisons between *tagadharis* and hill-women; and with the reinforcement of caste distinctions an insurmountable gap was created between rulers and ruled, which still exists. The first use of the word Gorkha (or Gorkhali, as it was often written), then, referred less to the long-suffering Magar and Gurung foot soldiers it later came to signify than to their Indo-Aryan masters in the House of Gorkha.

In the mid-eighteenth century the rajah of Gorkha, Prithwi Narayan Shah, was in no way distinguishable from the many other hill rajahs in what is now west-central Nepal. Gorkha was both small and poor; according to legend, when Prithwi Narayan set about collecting money to fund the conquest of the rich Kathmandu valley, the amount he could raise from his people barely filled a bison's horn.[1] But the Gorkha rajah was not easily deterred. He knew that the only way to improve the lot of his people and himself was to expand his territory and, since this could only be done at someone else's expense, he needed both military strength and diplomatic powers of persuasion. It took him twenty-five years to achieve his aim of making himself master of Nepal (which in those days meant only the central valley, not the present-day country for the unification of which he is retrospectively honoured). But he never lost sight of his objective.

The secret of his success, according to one modern historian, was 'his disregard of traditional caste rules' in recruiting his army; he did not confine himself to bona fide Chhetris, but spread the net to include (non-Chhetri) Khas, Magars and Gurungs and thereby transformed these peasants into warriors.[2]* Land was the currency in a largely non-

---

*There is a great deal of ambivalence over the exact position of the Magars and Gurungs (and Limbus and Rais) in the caste system. General Sir Francis Tuker argues: 'In caste terms, they should be Kshattriyas or soldiers, no lower; they are, in any case, certainly not Sudras or menials . . . The aspect, the whole mien, of the Sudra in India is of a humble, rather cringing man, but the Gurkha of the Magar and Gurung are proud, self-respecting, genial little men, the equal of any other men on earth, including the [Chhetrified] Khas, and the superior of most.'[3] The historian, John Whelpton, writes:

The Indo-Nepalese had brought the Magars and Gurungs within the caste monetarized economy, and he extended the traditional *jagir* system of land grants, given to military leaders in lieu of pay, to include every soldier in proportion to his rank; in this way he was able both to finance and to motivate his army for an indefinite campaign.[6] But in the process he stimulated the appetite for continuing conquest, which would become the theme of the Gorkha Raj over the next half century until it tangled fatally with the nascent British Raj: 'The circle was really vicious. The need for more land to assign as *jagirs* resulted in further conquests, and new conquests made the expansion of the army necessary ... In 1769 its estimated strength was only 1,200, but by 1775 it had risen to 2,600–3,400.'[7]

Land was central to the historical development of Nepal. Only in the Kathmandu valley, strategically placed between India and Tibet, did trade thrive; elsewhere in the country the economy was a predominantly rural one. It was always hard to scratch a living out of the hills but the long strip of forested plain called the Terai, which separates the hill country from India, provided rich pickings and became known during the nineteenth century as the granary of Nepal. Systems of land tenure favouring the *tagadhari* castes, of which *jagir* was just one, were all part

> framework by granting them a position below the twice-born Khas but above the impure castes, corresponding with the category of *sat* Shudra found in some parts of India. Classed together with these were also castes of Khas origin whose ancestors had not been granted, or who had lost, the right to wear the sacred cord.[4]

Peasants or warriors, *sudra* or *kshatriya*, or somewhere in between, or, alternatively, outside the caste system altogether? The confusion over status reflects the difficulty of slotting the semi-indigenous mountain peoples into a Hindu hierarchy.

Confusion also surrounds the claims of the hill rajahs, including Gorkha's, to fancy Rajput pedigrees. To quote Whelpton again:

> In many cases they were fabrications by court bards to flatter rulers of simple Khas extraction. The specific claim of the rulers of the Shah dynasty, who see themselves as descendants of a fourteenth century prince of Mewar, the premier Rajput state, has been shown to be almost certainly false ...[5]

This gives substance to the frequently heard Magar claim that the king of Nepal is really one of their own kind.

of the long process of Hinduization, accelerated (but not introduced) by the Gorkha conquest. The effect was to subjugate the ethnic communities of Tibeto-Burman origin, some of which – particularly the Limbus in the east – had previously operated a communal form of land ownership. The principles underlying these systems were:

1. All land was understood to be the property of the state.
2. Land, as the principal source of wealth, could not be allowed to remain unproductive.
3. The possession of a freehold right to the land was the sole means to rise to a position of wealth and prestige.[8]

Peasant farmers were traditionally taxed to the extent of half their crops, but the *kut* system, introduced in about 1804, squeezed them further by demanding a 'fixed quantity of their produce and other commodities or else a cash amount'. Since the figure was set in advance, no allowance was made for the failure of a crop:

> The peasant now bore all the costs and risks of marketing. To tide over the difficulties the peasant had to take loans. Rural indebtedness became a common feature and the condition favoured the richer landlords, mostly Brahmans, who now took up on a large scale money lending and other speculative functions.[9]

All that a peasant could offer as surety was his own and his family's labour. From this it was a short step into bondage and slavery and though slavery in Nepal was never as harsh as it could be in other parts of the world the practice survived well into the twentieth century. Here, too, there were caste distinctions: Brahmans and Rajputs were granted immunity to slavery even if they committed adultery, whereas a *matwali* woman could be enslaved for that offence, as Captain William Kirkpatrick, one of the earliest European visitors to Nepal, observed:

> Adultery (termed here, significantly enough, *chak-chukwye*, in allusion to the habits of the bird called by Europeans the Brahminy Goose), is ... fineable in some cases; the injured party, however, is at liberty to put the offenders to death, if he has the power of reaching them

immediately on the commission of the crime. The woman often has her nose slit, or cut off, in which case she becomes a slave, the property in her vesting in the proprietor of the village.[10]

A further burden imposed on the long-suffering peasantry was forced labour. Again, corvée in Nepal did not originate with the Gorkha conquest; but *jhara*, as this economic means of getting repairs and construction work done was called, was extended by the Gorkhalis to include the distribution of official mail and the transportation of arms and ammunition during military campaigns.[11] The nation, for the unification of which Prithwi Narayan Shah is credited, was in fact – and remains to this day – deeply divided, two nations rather than one.

Prithwi Narayan's dream of conquest was aided by the disunity then prevailing in the Kathmandu valley, where the once-powerful Malla dynasty (which also claimed Rajput descent) had in the distant past, Lear-like, divided its empire three or four ways; it was said that there were as many kings as there were *tols*, or wards.[12] Each of the city-states of Kathmandu, Patan and Bhatgaon (now Bhaktapur) had a separate ruler. The Malla kinsmen were too absorbed in internal rivalry to pay much attention to the danger from without. They were also inclined to underestimate the Gorkhali threat – since both Prithwi Narayan's father, Narbhupal Shah, and Prithwi Narayan himself had already been driven out of the valley by Jaya Prakesh Malla, the Kathmandu rajah – or to think they might turn it to their individual advantage in their internecine squabbles. They recognized the seriousness of the challenge only when it was too late, and their failure to combine effectively in their own defence brought about their downfall. Yet they had plenty of warning.

Prithwi Narayan settled on a strategy of gradually encircling the valley, large though it was (roughly sixteen by twenty miles), and cutting off trade, first with Tibet in the north, then from the states to the south. His soldiers policed every mountain pass, rigorously enforcing the blockade, as Father Giuseppe, Prefect of the Roman Mission to Nepal, witnessed at one of the southern passes:

... for every person who was found in the road, with only a little salt or cotton about him, was hung upon a tree; and [Prithwi Narayan] caused all the inhabitants of a neighbouring village to be put to death in a most cruel manner: even the women and children did not escape, for having supplied a little cotton to the inhabitants of Nepal; and, when I arrived in that country at the beginning of 1769, it was a most horrid spectacle to behold so many people hanging on trees in the road.[13]

Worse was to follow when Prithwi Narayan Shah finally succeeded, with the aid of treachery, in entering the outlying town of Kirtipur, whose garrison had valiantly resisted more than one attack. Though he had promised an amnesty, he immediately broke his word and ordered his soldiers to cut off the noses and lips of every inhabitant not considered worthy of being put to death. He contemptuously renamed the town Naskatapur, city of cut-noses.

. . . the order was carried into execution with every mark of horror and cruelty, none escaping but those who could play on wind instruments; although Father Michel Angelo, who, without knowing that such an inhuman scene was then exhibited, had . . . interceded much in favour of the poor inhabitants: many of them put an end to their lives in despair; others came in great bodies to us in search of medicines, and it was most shocking to see so many living people with their teeth and noses resembling the skulls of the deceased.[14]*

---

*Some modern Nepali historians have questioned the objectivity of Father Giuseppe's account, since Prithwi Narayan Shah had later expelled the Capuchin fathers from Nepal. But in 1793 Captain Kirkpatrick recorded his shock at discovering why so many porters he encountered on the way to Kathmandu had no noses;[15] and the *Vamshavali*, or Nepali chronicle, corroborates Father Giuseppe's story, particularly in relation to the savage execution of the nobles of Patan when Prithwi Narayan finally overran the valley. Kumar Pradhan finds Nepali historiography guilty of 'blind prejudice as far as "the father of modern Nepal" and his actions are concerned':

To dismiss the eye witness account on the grounds of its being prejudiced, and another indigenous one, clearly not based on the Capuchin account, on the grounds that it was a later work, can at best be termed as a bias resulting from a false sense of nationalism.[16]

At the same time as he was tightening the noose around the valley of Nepal, Prithwi Narayan Shah had to maintain his base sixty miles away at Gorkha and beat off any attack on it by jealous neighbouring chieftains eager to take advantage of his absence. In 1767, he faced an additional threat from the south when Jaya Prakesh Malla appealed to the East India Company for help in repelling the barbarian invader and reopening the trade route. The English response, described by General Tuker as 'a typical compromise',[17] was to send an ill-equipped and ill-prepared expeditionary force, of less than 2,500 men under a Captain Kinloch, through the Terai during the deadly monsoon season. The fraction of this force which neither succumbed to *aul* fever (a particularly virulent form of malaria) nor deserted was easily put to flight by the Gorkha army. Only a third of his men returned to India with Kinloch.[18] Dr A. Campbell, assistant surgeon at the Residency in Kathmandu during the 1830s, argued that the failure of Kinloch's expedition was the result of 'the little information we possessed regarding the natural obstacles in the early days of our power in India'; and that its 'serious and lasting consequences' could not have been anticipated.

The Gorkha Army consisted only of a few hundred of ill armed, ill accoutred, and undisciplined barbarians, and its chief had not the means of increasing it. The presence of a British force, in the Valley, however small, would have animated the Newars [the indigenous people of the valley] to renewed exertions in defence of their hearths and household Gods, and ours would have been the good fortune to have saved this lovely Valley from the rapacious grasp of a rude, cruel, and war-thirsty race of men, and perpetuated it in the hands of the civilized, lettered, industrious, and commercially disposed people, its aboriginal inhabitants.[19]

The first encounter with a British force on Nepalese soil caused the Gorkhalis to underestimate their future opponents, to view them with suspicion rather than awe; it also, incidentally, yielded them valuable firearms.[20] Dr Francis Buchanan Hamilton, an early British visitor – or perhaps spy, since he spent fourteen months in the vicinity of Kathmandu in 1802–3 and a further two years on the frontier 'collecting information' – wrote:

Prithwi Narayan, besides his personal endowments, was much
indebted for success to the introduction of firelocks, which until his
time were totally unknown among the hills; and, so far as he was able,
he introduced European discipline, the value of which he fully
appreciated. His jealousy of the European character always, however,
prevented him from employing any of them in his service, and he is
said to have strongly recommended to his successors to follow, in this
respect, his example.[21]*

Prithwi Narayan Shah did not long outlive his conquest of the valley.
He died a comparatively young man at the beginning of 1775, five years
after the Mogul emperor in Delhi, still nominally the paramount power
in the Indian subcontinent, had formally endorsed his title of 'Maharaja
Samser Bahadur Jang'.[23] But he did live long enough to set up an
administrative system of military governors in the outposts of the growing Gorkha empire and to deliver words of wisdom which would be
enshrined in a volume called *Dibya Upadesh* ('Divine Exhortation, or
Precepts of Surpassing Excellence').[24]

One of his *obiter dicta* compared Nepal's position with that of 'a tuber
between two boulders', words which became prophetic when, first,
Gorkhali expansion into Tibet brought a mighty Chinese army over the
mountain barrier and down to the very rim of the Kathmandu valley in
1792, and then when border incidents to the south stirred up the wrath
of the Honourable (East India) Company in 1814.[25] Prithwi Narayan's
way of dealing with his mighty neighbours was to keep both at arm's
length; but while the Himalayas provided a natural barrier to the north

---

*Prithwi Narayan's successors evidently failed to follow his example. The historian
of the Gorkha war, John Pemble, records that the Gorkha army learned its drill from
'British deserters who took service with the Gorkha Raja':

In 1814 there were still two of these individuals in Nepal, called Byrnes and
Bell. Byrnes was made schoolmaster and taught the officers English, while
Bell, a gunner, was made colonel of artillery. They even seem to have given
some musical instruction, for in 1816, at Makwanpur, Nepalese fifers
entertained the astonished British troops with their own versions of 'The
Lass of Richmond Hill', 'The Soldier's Wife', and half a dozen other English
marching tunes.[22]

and Peking was anyway remote and reluctant to act, the proximity of the British and their acute interest in the possibility of trade with Tibet made the Company an uncomfortably active southerly neighbour.

Gorkha policy in relation to these two 'boulders' was to invoke the one against the other; so that in 1792, when China, indignant at the invasion of its client state Tibet, sent an army into Nepal, Bahadur Shah – Prithwi Narayan's younger son, who acted as regent during his nephew's (and Prithwi Narayan's grandson, Rana Bahadur's) minority – appealed to the Governor-General for help. The Governor-General, who had already been requested by the Dalai Lama not to help the Gorkhas and was anxious to avoid a confrontation with the Chinese, compromised by sending Captain Kirkpatrick as mediator. But the war was over, and the Gorkhas had agreed to pay tribute in the form of a quinquennial embassy to Peking, before Kirkpatrick arrived; though the captain was allowed to proceed to Kathmandu, it was clear that an extended stay there would not be welcome, so he left in March 1793, the first British official to have set foot in the valley of Nepal.[26]

Likewise, on 8 November 1816, after the conclusion of the Anglo-Gorkha war, the Governor-General and Commander-in-Chief (since 1813), the Marquess of Hastings, recorded in his journal:

> When the Nepaulese found our arms prevailing over them, they sent to the Emperor of China, representing that the British had requested permission to pass across the Nepaulese territories in order to attack China, and that on their refusal of that licence we had waged war on them, and had subjugated part of their country. This appears to have occasioned [a] great sensation at Pekin.[27]

Nepal's attempt to persuade the Chinese to intervene on its side had been as unsuccessful as its earlier effort to involve the British against China. Two days after the previous entry, Hastings noted in his diary:

> There is a strange contrariety in the character of these people. In some things they are tenacious of points of honour to the most punctilious degree, while in a case of this kind they have no shame in acknowledging to us their having been publicly reprobated [by the Chinese] for a profligate lie.[28]

If you are a tuber caught between two boulders, your room for growth is severely limited. Gorkha policy was to avoid being crushed to death by either. Honour did not come into it.

The process which transformed the British in India from traders to rulers was far advanced by the end of the eighteenth century. The survival of the East India Company as the nominal British authority long after substantive power had passed to ministers of the crown was the result of Parliament's reluctance openly to espouse another empire in the wake of the humiliating loss of the American colonies. But the 1773 Regulating Act and Pitt's India Act of 1784 had reduced the Company's role in India to that of agent for the British government, and the 1813 Charter Act effectively completed the process by claiming for the Crown the sovereignty of all the Company's possessions.[29]

To pursue their dream of trading with Tibet (and open the back door, as it were, to China), as well as to look after their interests in general, the British wanted to have a Resident at the court of Kathmandu. But the Gorkhali *bharadars*, or nobles, were bitterly opposed to this idea, seeing it as a Trojan horse tactic which would ultimately undermine their independence; they were well aware that those Indian states which had been obliged to accept the presence of a British Resident had progressively lost their autonomy. In 1793 Captain Kirkpatrick had realized the futility of attempting to impose himself on them in that capacity; but in 1802, after the negotiation of a treaty with the exiled ex-rajah Rana Bahadur living in Benares on sufferance and at the expense of the Company, the British tried again, sending Captain Knox (accompanied by Dr Francis Hamilton) to Kathmandu to be the first British Resident.

Fourteen months later Knox admitted defeat and retired to India, having failed to activate the commercial treaty of 1801. In truth, the court politics of Kathmandu were far too volatile to allow such diplomatic initiatives any hope of success. The nine years of Bahadur Shah's regency, described by one historian as 'the golden age of Nepal's unification', in which time 'Nepal passed definitively from the status of an insignificant state to that of a power in the Indian subcontinent', had ended in 1794.[30] The next half-century witnessed a succession of kings who were either minors or mad or both, of jealous and scheming queen-regents who sought to promote their own offspring at the expense of their rivals' and governed through favourites, and internecine conflict among the nobility, in particular between the Pandes and the Thapas, the two families which more or less alternated in providing chief ministers, according to which royal star happened to be in the ascendant at the time. In the period 1799–1832, there was only one year – 1816 – in which the country was not ruled by a regent.[31] In this Macbethian world, murder was the means to power and the systematic massacre of one's opponents the way to ensure its durability.

In all this mayhem, one man stands out. Bhim Sen Thapa rose to power in the usual bloody way; but he remained chief minister and effective ruler for more than thirty years from 1806 to 1837. In doing so, he provided the model of governance which, a generation on, Jang Bahadur Rana would formalize into a system relegating the king to a religious figurehead and virtual prisoner of the state while elevating the prime minister to maharajah and keeping it in the family by making the post and title heritable.*

From the very beginning of his ascendancy, Bhim Sen was drawn into conflict with the East India Company, whose acquisition of the Nawab-Vizier of Oudh's land in the region of Gorakhpur in 1801 had brought British India into close proximity with the rajah of Palpa, the one remaining more or less independent hill-chieftain within the Gorkha heartland. Intimations of collusion between Palpa and the Company aimed at the destabilization of the Gorkha regime led, first, to the Palpa rajah's imprisonment after he had been lured to Kathmandu on marriage business, then to his assassination in the general massacre of nobles of the Pande faction that accompanied Bhim Sen's assumption of power.

---

*From the days of Prithwi Narayan's grandson, Rana Bahadur – to whom Bhim Sen became adviser when he was a mere captain of the ex-king's bodyguard – scions of the House of Gorkha were from infancy schooled in self-indulgence. What Hamilton writes of Rana Bahadur applies with equal, or greater, force to many of his descendants:

> Rana Bahadur received little or no education from his guardians, but was allowed to indulge in every vice, surrounded by minions and young profligates of the court. These not only assisted him in the pursuit of low vices, but encouraged his natural propensity to cruel diversions.[32]

Following this, Bhim Sen installed his own father, Amar Singh Thapa (not to be confused with his more famous namesake, the Kaji – or chief – of the western army, who, according to some accounts, was Bhim Sen's uncle), as governor of Palpa in order to bring it into line with Kathmandu and nullify British influence. This led to the serious border disputes which culminated in war between the two powers.

The idea of a frontier, in the sense that the British understood and sought to impose it, was entirely foreign to South Asian thinking and practice. Henry Prinsep, writing immediately after the Gorkha war, seems to have grasped this:

> From time immemorial the country within the hills and on the borders has been divided amongst petty Hindoo Rajas, and the forest and Turaee [sic] have naturally been a perpetual bone of contention for them; a chieftain possessing fastnesses in the hills could always enforce contributions, by issuing thence and carrying off booty from those who hesitated to comply. Hence every hill Raja had a sweep of the forest and low country attached to his estate, and this he was continually endeavouring to extend, either by intrigue, or by violence, or by any means that presented . . . The border-war was handed down from father to son, in their respective families.[33]

In other words, there were no fixed boundaries, marked out by stones or frontier-posts, only as it were a fluctuating, wavy line, constantly being redrawn according to the realities of local power politics. Prinsep adds, 'such continued to be the state of this frontier, until the low countries fell under British domination, and the hills were gradually overrun by the Nipâlese, and consolidated by them into one sovereignty'.[34] That was the rub: predatory chieftains were one thing; a united sovereignty with expansionist aims conflicting with Britain's own quite another. It might not have come to war if the Gorkhas had kept their expansion within the hills where they belonged; it was their raids on the plains which threatened British power and its tenuous lines of communication between Calcutta and the north-west. Yet the flatlands of the Terai were 'the prize for which the hill men strove'. As in the case of Palpa, the Gorkhas 'felt that if they brought a raja, no matter how petty or how large, under their rule, they were entitled to the total possessions of that raja, whether they be in the hills or in the plains'.[35]

Small wonder, then, that the Border Commission imposed on Nepal by the Governor-General failed to resolve the problem. Since neither side had any precise idea where the boundary was supposed to be, and oral testimony was both unreliable and contradictory, the British agent tried to browbeat the Gorkhali representatives into accepting his blueprint for it. The latter naturally resented this high-handed approach and the negotiations fizzled out. The raids resumed and at length provided an occasion for the all-out fight for which perhaps both sides had been spoiling. Gorkha domination of 'the mountainous tract stretching between the plains of Hindoostan and the high lands of Tartary and Tibet . . . as far as the river Testa to the east, and westward to the Sutlej' had been achieved, as Prinsep recognized, 'by the systematic prosecution of a policy likened by the Goorkhas themselves, *and not inaptly so*, to that which had gained for us the empire of Hindoostan' [my italics].[36]

Two expanding empires collided and a trial of strength became inevitable. It should have been an absurdly unequal contest and in the end it was. But for several months the outcome was anything but a foregone conclusion; it would be no exaggeration to say that in the winter of 1814–15 the British East India Company's incipient paramountcy in India hung in the balance and might easily have toppled but for one military commander. His name, famous in his own time but largely forgotten by posterity, was David Ochterlony.

At the beginning of the war, Colonel Ochterlony commanded the most westerly of the four columns which the Governor-General and Commander-in-Chief, Lord Moira (not yet Marquess of Hastings, though for consistency it will be simpler to call him Hastings throughout), sent to do battle with the rampant Gorkhas. Immediately to the east of him was another large force commanded by the dashing Major-General Sir Rollo Gillespie. These two columns were pitted against the cream of the Gorkhali army under the command of Kaji Amar Singh Thapa, the warrior who had subdued the many local rajas in the Himalayan regions of Kumaon and Garhwal in Nepal's successful bid to expand its boundaries westwards some years earlier.

To the east, and aimed at the heart of Nepal proper – the mountain

valley of Kathmandu – were two more columns under the command of
Major-Generals Bennet Marley and John Sullivan Wood. Their task
was to cross the Terai and penetrate the enemy's mountain fastness.
(Still further east, on the Sikkim border, was a small token force commanded by Captain Latter with a defensive, rather than offensive, role.)

The four columns were made up mainly of native Indian troops –
though Ochterlony's was the only one without a single British infantry
battalion – and had overwhelming numerical superiority as well as the
inestimable advantage of artillery and arms of all sorts. Against this the
Gorkhali troops had considerable experience of mountain warfare and
limitless confidence in their fighting prowess. For half a century or
more they had been engaged in more or less continual campaigning,
first to subdue the rich and fertile valley of Nepal itself and then to
expand its boundaries in all directions – into Tibet in the north, Sikkim
in the east, Kumaon and Garhwal in the west and, most dangerously for
them, into the British sphere of influence in Oudh in the south.

The East India Company, meanwhile, was consolidating its position
as controller of trade and general power-broker through much of India
from its three bases in Calcutta, Madras and Bombay. There was latent
or open opposition to its expansion in many other parts of the country,
particularly in central India, where the series of Mahratta wars was interrupted by the Anglo-Gorkha war, and in the Punjab, where Ranjit Singh
had his own empire-building aspirations. Should the Company's army
fail against the Gorkhas, the Sikhs and the Mahrattas would not be
slow to take advantage of its discomfiture. So from a British point of
view, much depended on a rapid and successful conclusion to the campaign.

But from the start, this war, in the words of an official historian of the
Bengal Army, contained 'a greater number of disastrous failures and of
ill-arranged and worse-carried-out enterprises, due generally to an entire
want of appreciation of the necessities of hill warfare than had ever
before, or have ever since befallen the arms of the British in India'.[37]
Three of the four columns suffered reverses as a result either of cowardly inactivity or of bold but injudicious activity. In the west, General
Gillespie's frontal assault of 31 October 1814 on the fort at Kalanga
(near Dehra Dun), defended by a mere 600 Gorkha troops, ended in
disaster, with the general himself being killed, along with many of his

officers and men. Hastings, on hearing of the death of Gillespie, noted in his journal: 'That he should have made so rash an attack is astonishing.' He had specifically instructed his generals not to make such attacks on fortresses 'which should be of a quality to require artillery for their reduction'.[38]

Yet despite the 'baneful influence which this reverse must have upon future operations', Hastings thought that trivial when compared with the loss of a brave general whose final 'indiscretion' was far outweighed by his unexampled record of heroic leadership: 'Genius like his would soon have fashioned others to a just conception of the system to be pursued in mountain warfare.'[39] Fortescue echoes this judgement in his *History of the British Army* when he writes that Gillespie was 'not only the bravest man that ever wore a red coat but also extremely capable and resourceful'.[40] Which makes it all the more bizarre that Hastings should have replaced him with a dud like Major-General Gabriel Martindell, imagining that Martindell's previous failure in punitive operations at Rewa in 1813 'would have stimulated him to exert himself in regaining the ground he had lost in the public estimation on that occasion'.[41] Alas, it merely unnerved him.

In the interval before Martindell took over command, the Gorkhas had been bombarded and starved out of Kalanga by Colonel Sebright Mawby; and seventy-odd survivors eventually made their escape in the middle of one night under their leader, Balbahadur Singh. Their stand elicited this tribute from James Fraser, who accompanied his brother William, a political agent with Gillespie's – now Martindell's – army:

> The determined resolution of the small party which held this small
> post for more than a month, against so comparatively large a force,
> must surely wring admiration from every voice, especially when the
> horrors of the latter portion of this time are considered; the dismal
> spectacle of their slaughtered comrades, the sufferings of their women
> and children thus immured with themselves, and the hopelessness of
> relief, which destroyed any other motive for the obstinate defence they
> made, than that resulting from a high sense of duty, supported by
> unsubdued courage. This, and a generous spirit of courtesy towards
> their enemy, certainly marked the character of the garrison at Kalunga,
> during the period of its siege.

Whatever the nature of the Ghoorkhas may have been found in other quarters, there was here no cruelty to wounded or to prisoners; no poisoned arrows were used; no wells or waters were poisoned; no rancorous spirit of revenge seemed to animate them: they fought us in fair conflict, like men; and, in the intervals of actual combat, showed us a liberal courtesy worthy of a more enlightened people.[42]

After taking over from Mawby, Martindell ordered a detachment of 3,000 irregulars under Lieutenant Young to intercept a party of 200 Gorkhas on their way to reinforce the fortress of Jaithak, to which Balbahadur's depleted force had withdrawn. These Gorkhas, recognizing the hopelessness of their situation, resolved to sell their lives dearly and launched themselves on the nearest column of irregulars, who at the sight of these kukri-waving hillmen broke ranks and fled. The panic spread and, despite their fifteen-to-one numerical advantage and Lt Young's efforts to induce them to stand and face the enemy, the entire detachment melted away, leaving the Gorkhas free to continue their march to Jaithak unopposed.*

William Fraser, who had already got himself wounded in the assault on Kalanga which killed Gillespie and had, in the words of a later friend, the French traveller Victor Jacquemont, 'a perfect monomania for fighting',[46] blamed Martindell for this débâcle because the general had

---

*This was the occasion when – as legend has it – the Gorkhas gathered round Young and asked him why he had not run off with his men; to which he supposedly replied that he had not come so far in order to run away, and promptly sat down, thereby eliciting their admiring comment: 'We could serve under men like you.'[43] The source of this almost certainly apocryphal story, reproduced in countless Gurkha histories as though it were gospel, is a biography of Young written by his elderly daughter, Mrs Jenkins, and published more than 100 years after the events it purports to describe. Mrs Jenkins' book begins with an expression of regret at the lack of family records, especially in relation to her father's life: 'While he was with us no one ever thought of putting down notes of all he could have told us' – an admission which scarcely enhances the credibility of what follows. She also writes that her father was taken prisoner (she does not know for how long) and 'treated with every mark of honour as a brave foe'.[44] But as A. P. Coleman points out, there is no contemporary record of Young having been taken prisoner and it is extremely unlikely that he was.[45]

refused to support Young's irregulars with a party of experienced native infantry, although he had been repeatedly requested to do so – 'this old body is worse than none', he commented in a letter.[47] His brother James was no less critical of the column commander; he wrote in his diary on 17 March, 'this old man the General seems gifted with the very soul of procrastination and the marrow of obstinacy', adding two days later, 'the old mule will listen to nothing'.[48] Martindell eventually succeeded in reducing Jaithak to rubble with the aid of his artillery, but then failed to occupy it for fear of counter-attack, despite the vastly superior number of troops at his disposal.

This was bad enough, but the behaviour of the generals in command of the two eastern columns was even more spineless. Marley and Wood both displayed a marked reluctance to engage with the enemy, despite Hastings' persistent prompting. Wood's first encounter with a Gorkha stockade near Butwal promised to be decisive, but he unaccountably ordered a withdrawal at the very moment the enemy had begun to retreat. This gave the outnumbered Gorkhas renewed heart and they harassed their retreating opponents at will. After that, as Fortescue relates, Wood burned a few Gorkha villages but otherwise relapsed into inactivity until he was finally persuaded to advance on Butwal again:

> Arriving before the place on the 17th [April 1815], he drew up his army in battle order, opened fire of artillery and musketry and, after suffering a few casualties, marched back to Gorakhpur, doing a little devastation of Gurkha territory on the way. The manoeuvre before Butwal was of course described as a reconnaissance in force; but, as is not uncommon in such cases, it was really a demonstration in feebleness.[49]

So much for John Sullivan Wood's 'Grand Old Duke of York' style of manoeuvres. Yet Bennet Marley, whose 8,000 strong army was supposed to provide the main striking force on Kathmandu, outdid him in pusillanimity. In failing to support two of his own advance posts at Samanpore and Persa, manned by about 500 men each, Marley practically invited the marauding Gorkhas to wipe them out – which they duly did. Both Wood and Marley excused their inactivity by wildly exaggerating the strength of the enemy, Marley refusing to budge without a battering train. Hastings reported to London that 'the fatal

influence of events on the mind of Major General Marley paralized
[sic] the operations of the British Division and . . . occasioned the total
failure of every object of its formation'.[50]

On 10 February 1815, Marley, according to Prinsep's contemporary
account,

> unable longer to endure the irksomeness of his situation, and feeling
> strongly the impossibility of answering the expectations of his
> commander-in-chief, took the sudden and extraordinary resolution of
> leaving the camp . . . he set off before daylight in the morning, without
> publishing any notification of his intention to the troops, and without
> taking any means of providing for the conduct of the ordinary routine
> of command during his absence.[51]

History may provide instances of armies deserting their generals, but
seldom the other way round: 'Desertion is not a common offence of
generals in the field,' as Fortescue drily remarks.[52]*

Marley was replaced by Major-General George Wood, but for all the
difference this made it might just as well have been his namesake J. S.
Wood. Fortescue sums up the situation with a rather laboured pun,
'Altogether the two Woods showed themselves to be tremulous and
not easy to kindle, aspen rather than oak.'[56] Captain Thomas Smith,
who was assistant political resident in Nepal for five years during the
1840s, puts the blame on 'the defects of the India military system':

> Where length of service alone raises to command, some in situations of
> importance must be naturally beneath mediocrity; while still more are
> incapable from age . . . [57]

---

*Tuker says that Marley was placed on the invalid or non-effective establishment of
the Indian Army, and describes that as 'a merciful end'.[53] But it was by no means the
end of Marley's military career or, indeed, of his advancement. Fortescue records,
'He held lucrative commands for many years, and died, a full general, in 1842'.[54]
This is in marked contrast to the treatment meted out to one of his opponents,
Bhagat Singh, whose failure to attack Marley's fortified post at Baragarhi with a
smaller force resulted in his ritual humiliation: he was obliged to appear in the
Kathmandu *durbar* (court) dressed in women's clothing.[55]

In the words of the historian John Pemble, 'The general stagnation raised the age and depressed the quality even of lieutenant-colonels and majors. When [Sir George] Nugent [C-in-C until he was superseded by Hastings in his dual role as Governor-General and C-in-C] inspected the Bengal army in 1812, he had found two infantry lieutenant-colonels who were demonstrably senile, and had had to remove them to the invalid establishment.'[58] If that was the fate of lieutenant-colonels, what hope was there for doddering major-generals? According to Fortescue, 'the old Indian generals, sapped by the climate and with no traditions but of comfortable and victorious advances in the plains against an enemy which invariably ran away, were helpless in face of a few brave and cunning hill-men'.[59]

The abysmal failure of three of the columns, each bolstered by a British infantry battalion, highlights the achievement of the fourth without one – and Ochterlony was faced with the wiliest Gorkhali military commander and a hard core of very seasoned troops in the most rugged terrain of all. But in his late fifties, David Ochterlony was still in his prime. Though only a colonel when the war started, his career had been impressive, if not yet spectacular.

He was the son of a Scottish seafaring father who had died on a voyage in the West Indies when David was seven, leaving an American wife with a young family of four in straitened circumstances. Mrs Ochterlony crossed the Atlantic to London, and five years later married again. David's stepfather, Isaac Heard, was to become Garter King of Arms and a Knight of Hanover. More to the point, he took a keen and affectionate interest in his eldest stepson for the remainder of his long life (Sir Isaac died at the age of ninety-two in 1822, forty years after his wife and fifteen years after David's only sibling to survive childhood).[60]

When Ochterlony sailed to India in the autumn of 1777, at the age of nineteen, to take up a military cadetship in the East India Company, he left England for good. In those days, conditions of service expressly forbade an officer to return to England, even on furlough, on pain of losing his commission; you stayed in India until you retired – if you were lucky enough to survive that long. 'The service life of British troops in India was rapidly terminated by death, debility or insanity . . . ,' Pemble writes. 'The annual death rate among European troops during the first half of the nineteenth century maintained an average of about one in fourteen, as a result more of alcoholic poisoning, disease and suicide than of battle casualties.'[61] Officers in native infantry regiments were exposed to the same hazards.

Ochterlony survived, though he was wounded in engagements with the French and with Hyder Ali during the governor-generalship of Warren Hastings (1773–85) – not to be confused with his namesake, the Marquess. His superior officers spoke well of him, but he often showed independence, sometimes to the point of recklessness. Despite holding the position of Deputy Judge Advocate General at Dinapore in 1793–4, he participated in what became known as the 'Bengal Mutiny' (though it was more of a threat than an actual mutiny); he was one of many who signed a petition calling for improved conditions in the Company's military service. Some fifty years later Captain Thomas Smith wrote, 'It is now happily forgotten that the Company's military servants were, before that commotion, as much subordinate to those of the royal army, as subadars and jemadars are at present to European officers.'[62]

That was just one of several grievances – that the most senior Company officer was superseded by the most junior King's officer. After 1794 both held commissions from the same source (i.e. the Crown), though Company commissions were only valid east of the Cape of Good Hope.[63] Another arbitrary and unfair rule was that Company officers could not rise above the rank of colonel. All the more senior officers were brought in from the British Army. Then there was the slowness of promotion generally, despite the high casualty rate among officers, which meant that battalions were often commanded by captains, if not mere lieutenants. (After sixteen years' service, Ochterlony himself was still a subaltern.) Harshest of all, in the petitioners' view, was the prohibition against returning to England while in the Company's service.[64]

At this stage there was no Indian Army as such. The three presidencies, Bengal, Bombay and Madras, each had their own separate army, consisting of the Company's European regiments (soon to be phased out) and its native regiments, which were reinforced by King's regiments posted to India for a limited number of years.[65] When the Bengal Army officers threatened mutiny, the Governor-General, Sir John Shore, and his C-in-C, General Sir Robert Abercromby, asked the Governor of Madras to put as many King's troops as he could spare on stand-by. But concessions over promotion and allowances finally satisfied the rebels and these troops were not required.[66] Smith comments: 'Few will now regret the event which, more than justifying and realizing [Ochterlony's] expectations, has placed the Company's on an equality with the Queen's army.'[67]

Ochterlony was made captain in 1796 and major four years later. In 1801 he left Dinapore and returned to regimental duty with the 12th Bengal Native Infantry. His service in the Maratha wars under Lord Lake (who was C-in-C between 1801 and 1807, except for a few months in 1805), earned him the deputy adjutant-generalship of the field army and further promotion to lieutenant-colonel; then he became acting Resident at Delhi, where he supervised the defence of the city against invading Marathas and dealt firmly with the rebels within (two of whose ringleaders, according to Smith, he blew from the end of a gun). As a reward for the 'judgment, firmness, and activity' he displayed in this defence, he was confirmed as Resident at the Court of the Emperor in Delhi at the end of 1804, a lucrative as well as a highly responsible post.[68]

When Sir George Barlow succeeded the Marquess of Wellesley as Governor-General in 1805, Ochterlony received a curt note informing him that he was being replaced as Resident. Lord Lake's protest against such high-handed and undeserved treatment of a loyal officer did not prevent Ochterlony being packed off to command the garrison at Allahabad – the same backwater to which Bennet Marley was later sent in disgrace. Ochterlony continued to resent the fact that he had been, as he put it, 'dismissed ignominiously' from Delhi. But he was restored to favour when he was sent to the frontier of Ranjit Singh's Sikh empire at Ludhiana. There he commanded a military force in support of a young civil servant who was negotiating a treaty with Ranjit, Charles (later Lord) Metcalfe. The two became lifelong friends, writing each other frequent and affectionate letters. When Metcalfe withdrew, Ochterlony stayed on at Ludhiana as political agent. Here he gave evidence of that touchiness which remained a characteristic: a row with the C-in-C (no longer Lord Lake, but Lt-Gen. George Hewett, who succeeded Lake in October 1807) led him to send in his resignation and his career might have ended there and then had not all the authorities, including Hewett himself and the new Governor-General, Lord Minto, agreed to overlook his impetuosity.[69]

At Ludhiana, Ochterlony became acquainted with his future adversaries, Amar Singh Thapa's Gorkhas. His first impression does not seem to have been very favourable; he described them in 1810 as 'a body of ill-armed and undisciplined barbarians who effect a wretched imitation of the dress, accoutrements and constitution of a British native battalion and who might have been successfully resisted in such a country [the valley of Dehra Dun] by less than a third of their numbers'.[70] (It should be noted, however, that he is talking about fighting them on the plains, not in their native hills.)

He encountered Amar Singh Thapa in person on 18 December 1813 and at the Kaji's instigation there was an exchange of presents between Ochterlony's Eurasian son, Roderick Peregrine, who was accompanying his father as his Persian translator, and Amar Singh's second son.[71] To judge by a subsequent letter from Ochterlony to John Adam, political secretary in Calcutta, Amar Singh's gesture was motivated more by self-interest than any warmth of feeling. He left his son in the care of the British doctor, Mr Dickson, for an unspecified medical reason. Four months later, when the doctor pronounced the son fit to return to his father, the latter was insistent that the physician should accompany him. Ochterlony assumed that he wished to recompense the doctor for 'saving the life of the youth' and encouraged Mr Dickson to go. But far from offering him 'any proper compensation for his care and trouble', the Kaji did his utmost to prevent the doctor's return to Ludhiana by denying him transport and assistance with his baggage.[72]

There were other, more serious causes of friction, which may have arisen from the fact that the two countries were now on the brink of war. Ochterlony wrote in exasperation,

It is . . . very difficult to assign motives for the actions of men who seem hardly to possess the faculty of reason, or doubt its existence in those with whom they have a point to carry; and what we have experienced from Ummer Sing [sic] in the late disputes does very little credit to his understanding and carries the fullest conviction of his falsehood and rapacity.[73]

Yet neither Ochterlony nor Amar Singh Thapa were advocates of war, though Ochterlony maintained that 'Goorkha power must be completely overthrown to avoid a constant source of trouble and expense'.[74] As late as 25 August 1814 he was writing privately to Metcalfe, 'To set off with the idea of overthrowing a long-established Government, and for such an unprofitable purpose, appears to me the most Quixotic and the most impolitic measure we have ever attempted – setting aside all the physical difficulties.'[75] For Ochterlony had revised his estimate of his opponents; in a report on the hill districts occupied by the Gorkhas which he sent to John Adam, he wrote: 'Giving the Goorkhas full credit for the reputation they have acquired, an officer must make up his mind to contend with a hardy and brave people, by no means uninformed in the arts and stratagems of mountainous warfare.'[76]

Amar Singh, for his part, combined with the other Gorkhali chiefs in the west to oppose war. When the Kathmandu *durbar* solicited their views, they replied jointly:

The present time . . . is not favourable. The English, seeing their opportunity, have put themselves into an attitude of offence, and the conflict, if war now be undertaken, will be desperate. They will not rest satisfied without establishing their own power and authority, and will unite with the Hill Rajas, whom we have dispossessed. We have hitherto but hunted deer; if we engage in this war, we must prepare to fight tigers.[77]

This cautious and prescient summary of the situation contrasts sharply with the chief minister Bhim Sen's gung-ho response to the Gorkha rajah's question of whether or not to go to war in 1814:

The Chinese once made war upon us, but were reduced to seek peace [in 1792 – an extremely doubtful assertion]. How then will the English be able to penetrate into the hills? Under your auspices, we shall by our own exertions be able to oppose to them a force of fifty-two lakhs of men [an even wilder assertion], with which we will expel them. The small fort at Bhurtpoor [Bharatpur] was the work of man, yet the English, being worsted before it, desisted from the attempt to conquer it; our hills and fastnesses are formed by the hand of God, and are impregnable. I therefore recommend the prosecution of hostilities. We can make peace afterwards on terms as may suit our convenience.[78]

Most of Amar Singh's 'tigers', as we have seen, turned out to be mere paper tigers. But Ochterlony was made of sterner stuff. He was neither reckless nor timid, but canny and cautious; and he tried, wherever possible, to turn the Gorkha positions and build his own stockades so as to encourage the enemy to come out of theirs and attack his, rather than the other way round. It may even have been to his advantage that he did not have a battalion of British infantry at his disposal; he knew that his Bengal sepoys were no match for the Gorkhas in hill combat, so he avoided such encounters as far as he could and placed heavy reliance on his artillery. An eye-witness account of a Gorkha charge likened it to 'a pack of hounds in full cry' in which the fleet-footed mountaineers descended on their prey carrying matchlocks or shields in their left hands and brandishing naked kukris in their right, to the accompaniment of 'several huge trumpets, putting forth a harsh but stirring noise'.[79]

This eye-witness, the anonymous author of *Military Sketches of the Goorka War*, who describes himself as a civilian attached to Ochterlony's column, pays tribute to his leader's tactical skill:

> From those who estimate a general's merit by the numbers whom he has slain or led to destruction, Sir David Ochterlony can claim no praise. No vainglorious assaults, no fatal contempt for the enemy, no conflagrations, no arbitrary executions, marked his route through hostile countries. Disregarding, with the mind of a statesman, the brilliancy of military exploits, and attending exclusively to the efficiency of measures, a battle was his last resort.[80]

The campaign in the western hills was less a series of set-piece battles than a deadly form of chess, with each commander trying to outguess the other. There were occasional brisk and brutal skirmishes in which one or other side gained a temporary advantage, but nothing decisive, though over the months Ochterlony was steadily pushing Amar Singh back higher and higher into his mountain fastness. Eventually, in the middle of April 1815, when Amar Singh occupied his ultimate fortress at Malaun, Ochterlony produced the masterstroke – the checkmate move – complete with feints and diversionary activity, which cut the ridge in two and divided Amar Singh from his most able lieutenant, Bhakti Thapa, and his force. Bhakti tried to rejoin the Kaji by means of an assault also aimed at displacing Ochterlony's force from the position it had gained on the ridge at Dionthal.

This was the decisive battle of the campaign. Amar Singh himself stood within range of the guns, as if his mere presence could command victory. On one side, there was the sheer ferocity of the Gorkha attack on the British stockade; on the other, desperate defence as officers and men struggled to keep the two vital six-pounders manned. The Gorkha sharp-shooters, or 'snipers' (a word which first came into common use in this campaign, according to Fortescue[81]), focused on the artillery and almost succeeded in knocking it out; but Ochterlony's men held their ground and eventually, when Bhakti switched the direction of his assault, made a sortie of their own with fixed bayonets. For a couple of hours, in fading light, the two sides slugged it out without significant advantage going either way. Then for no obvious reason the Gorkhas suddenly seemed to lose heart and gave ground; and a rout turned into a massacre. The campaign was effectively over, though Amar Singh was not yet prepared to concede defeat.[82]

It transpired that the reason the fight had gone out of the Gorkha troops was because their finest and best-loved officer, Bhakti Thapa, had been killed. In a war in which – as James Fraser observed – chivalry and barbarism were oddly intermingled, Ochterlony ordered that his body be swathed in a shawl and returned to Malaun. The day before, when a British officer, Captain Charles Showers, had lost his life after killing a Gorkha officer in single-handed combat, his body had been similarly honoured by the enemy. But on other occasions the Gorkhas had not merely killed their opponents but mutilated their bodies as well.

Amar Singh held on grimly. After the fall of Kalanga on 2 December 1814, when the Kathmandu *durbar* had considered suing for peace, he had written indignantly,

The present . . . is not a time for treaty and conciliation. These expedients should have been tried before the murder of the revenue officer (at Gourukpoor) [the border incident which triggered the war], or must be postponed till victory shall crown our efforts . . . I must gain two or three victories before I can accomplish the object I have in view, of attaching Runjeet Singh to our cause.[83]

By 16 April 1815, the day of Bhakti's death, all hope of bringing Ranjit Singh's Sikhs into the war had vanished. But as Ochterlony besieged Malaun and built a road for bringing up his heavy artillery to deliver the *coup de grâce*, and as the Kaji's troops began to melt away, deserting in numbers to the other side, Amar Singh staked his survival on two eventualities – the expected arrival of Gorkha reinforcements from the east, and the coming of the monsoon. The latter did not come soon enough; and the former never came at all.

Frustrated by Martindell's inactivity and with no troops of his own to spare, Lord Hastings had commissioned two freelance officers to raise levies of irregulars and enter Kumaon with the aim of cutting the Gorkha lines of communication; they could rely on the co-operation of the hill tribes – for whose descendants the words 'Gorkha Raj' were synonymous with oppression. Captain Hyder Hearsey, who was soon captured by the enemy, and Lieutenant-Colonel William Gardner (the founder of 'Gardner's Horse'), who penetrated almost as far as Almora before risking serious engagement with the Gorkhas, had both fought for the Marathas before transferring to British service (Gardner was British and Hearsey Eurasian; both married wealthy Muslims). Gardner was eventually reinforced – and superseded – by Colonel Jasper Nicolls (a future C-in-C in India), who brought with him over 2,000 regular sepoys and several large guns. Together they besieged Almora, whose garrison capitulated on 26 April. Kumaon was now in British hands, and a highly relieved Governor-General praised Nicolls to the skies.

Of the three Gorkhali chiefs in the western hills whom the Kathmandu *durbar* had originally consulted on the wisdom of going to war with the British, one – Hastidal – had been killed in the fighting around Almora, another – Brahma Shah – had been obliged to surrender the entire province of Kumaon, and the third – Amar Singh Thapa – was completely cut off and heavily invested at Malaun. Finally recognizing the hopelessness of his situation, the Kaji grudgingly conceded defeat.

Ochterlony's terms were magnanimous: in recognition of their heroic defence of their respective fortresses at Malaun and Jaithak, he allowed Amar Singh and his son Ranjur to march back to Nepal with all their arms and accoutrements as well as their entourage of 450 crack troops. Promoted to major-general during the campaign, Ochterlony had replaced the ineffectual Martindell as the overall divisional commander.

But his hour of triumph was marred by a personal tragedy. Just days before the surrender, his young ADC, Lieutenant Peter Lawtie, a field engineer whose personal contribution to the campaign was second only to the general's own, had died of typhoid. Ochterlony, who had treated Lawtie like a son, was distraught and adjured his officers to wear mourning for a whole month – and he sent his friend Charles Metcalfe 'a very particular request':

> It is that you will get a slab of marble, and on it cut an inscription of
> your own composition for the tomb of our lamented Lawtie, at
> Ruttinghur. Few will read it; but I do not wish an European visitor to
> pass without knowing that the spot contains the remains of one so
> deservedly valued and lamented.[84]

Clause five of the Convention which Amar Singh was obliged to accept at Malaun in May 1815 provided for the recruitment of volunteers from the Gorkhali western army into the Bengal Army.[85] In those pre-nationalistic days people often changed sides during a war, or from war to war. As James Fraser noted:

> It is well known that in the East no obloquy attaches to a man who
> changes his side, and fights against the cause he once contended for,
> especially if the train of original service has once been broken; and
> although the point of honour seems to be tenaciously kept by the
> Ghoorkhas, and their attachment to their country is perhaps greater
> than among other eastern people, it does not appear to be considered a
> dishonourable act, if, when forced by an enemy to surrender . . . an
> officer of theirs should enter the service of that enemy.[86]

If the likes of Captain Hyder Hearsey and Colonel William Gardner could do it, why not other officers and, even more, ordinary soldiers who had often been dragooned into service in the first place? Many of Amar Singh's troops, for instance, were not 'real Gorkahs' – as they would increasingly come to be known – but conscripts from the conquered hill territories of Kumaon and Garhwal.

Major Frederick Young, looking back to his experiences as a lieutenant during the Gorkha war, described how slave boys conscripted into the Gorkhali army served as camp followers, carrying their particular officer's or soldier's arms and baggage, performing menial tasks for them and helping them build stockades, in return for their keep. They were treated well, being 'frequently adopted by the Goorkahs, and generally furnished with Wives'. According to Young, 'It never was the custom of the Chiefs of the Goorkah Army on the North West frontier to entertain raw recruits from the conquered states.' These boys had to be trained and to prove themselves as hardy and amenable to discipline on active service as their masters were before they could even be considered as soldiers – and it was to this rugged apprenticeship system that Young attributed 'the superiority of the Goorkah army over any other with which the British power has come into contact'.[87]

At the outbreak of the war in 1814, Hyder Hearsey had written a report in which he characterized the Gorkha commanders dismissively as 'ignorant, subtile, treacherous, faithless and avaricious to an extreme, after conquest and victory . . . bloodthirsty and relentless, after defeat mean and abject'. But about the ill-paid and poorly armed soldiery – with their 'infamous' muskets and gunpowder, rather than the fearsome 'crooked instrument called a *kookuree*' (which, he noted, was an all-purpose implement used for cutting branches as well as carving up enemies) – his tone was far more respectful:

> They are hardy, endure privations and are very obedient, have not much distinction of caste, and are a neutral kind of Hindoos eating in mess almost everything they meet with except beef.
>   Under our Government and officers they would make excellent soldiers, and numbers would on the event of a rupture join our standard, for the sake of 6 Rupees per month, and form a proper Corps of Hill Rangers, but who would not serve down in the plains; the change of climate being so very different.[88]

David Ochterlony and the political agent William Fraser were also quick to recognize the potential of Gorkha soldiers in British service.

From the early months of the war, the British were keen to take advantage of defections from the Gorkhali army and employ as irregulars those men from the conquered hill tribes who might naturally wish to avenge themselves on their recent oppressors. About 'real Gorkahs' they were less sure; as John Adam wrote to Edward Gardner, political agent for Kumaon (and a cousin of Colonel William Gardner), 'By your present instructions you are precluded from offering service to such of the enemy's troops as are real Gorkahs', going on to say that the Governor-General now felt 'advantages [might] eventually be lost by a strict adherence to this rule' and His Excellency left it to Gardner's discretion to break it if he thought that 'the separation from the cause of their own Government of the troops or commanders of the enemy [would] be serviceable to our interests'.[89]

Ochterlony was already employing those enemy captives who preferred activity to idleness in various tasks, which he found they performed with alacrity. His confidence in their loyalty was so great that in early April 1815 he proposed forming them into a battalion under Lieutenant Ross to be called the 'Nusseeree Pulteen' (Nasiri *paltan*, regiment or unit).*

Hastings gave the proposal his blessing and what eventually became the 1st King George's Own Gurkha Rifles first saw action on the Malaun ridge in April 1815 under the direction of the lamented Lieutenant Lawtie. Lawtie reported to Ochterlony that he 'had the greatest reason to be satisfied with their exertions': at night they had moved swiftly and silently without losing their shape; the following day they had set about building a stockade with a will, though one man was killed and two more wounded; and after that they were eager for action whenever an opportunity presented itself. Lawtie described their performance in detail so Ochterlony might be 'the better able to judge of the value of a new and so peculiarly formed a Corps', of which he concluded: 'everything they did was done with cheerfulness, good humour and an acknowledgement of gratitude for the kindness of their present

---

*The name Nasiri has puzzled historians. Seema Alavi says it is derived 'from the Nassiri hills from where most of its recruits came'.[90] Pemble, following the regimental historian of 1 GR, claims it is based on a Hindi word meaning 'friendly'.[91] Coleman argues that Ochterlony's personal commitment to the 'Corps in which I feel a great and peculiar interest' – 'I consider myself their Commandant and Patron' – suggests the term Nasiri means more than just friendly and reflects 'the title Nasir-ud-Daula (Helper or victory Giver of the State)' awarded him by the Mogul emperor, Shah Alam, after his successful defence of Delhi against the Mahrattas in 1804, making the regiment effectively 'Ochterlony's Own'. This is the most plausible, as well as agreeable, explanation.[92]

employers'.[93] If these were almost the last words Lawtie wrote, his sentiments have echoed down the years.

When news of Ochterlony's successful use of Gorkha troops at Malaun reached Martindell's column, William Fraser pressed the general to let him enlist prisoners and deserters from Jaithak to stiffen the mixed bunch of irregulars under the command of Lieutenant Young. But Martindell, despite holding the opinion that 'a Goorkah for fighting is worth at least double of any of our irregulars', refused permission, saying that he was not authorized to give arms to 'defectors from the Nepalese army'. So Fraser simply went above his head and obtained the Governor-General's approval through the political secretary, John Adam, who wrote of the Gorkhas, with Ochterlony's experience in mind, 'Of their value in all the essential qualities of soldiers there can be no doubt'.[94] The Sirmoor battalion (later 2nd King Edward VII's Own Goorkha Rifles), Young wrote, 'was originally raised from the remains of the Goorkah Army which so nobly defended itself against the British Force opposed to it at the Seige [sic] of Kalunga and Jaitack'.[95]

What were they like, these men of the hills? After fifteen years' service with them, this was how Young characterized them:

> They are generally short, light bodied, well limbed men, well calculated to bear fatigue, particularly in a Hill Country, they are fiery in dispute, fond to a fault of Gambling, full of energy, and sanguine in all their undertakings. They are naturally dirty and slovenly in their dress, but I consider them smart, intelligent and brave soldiers, attached to their Officers, and embraced [imbued?] with an almost instinctive sense of the necessity for discipline.
>
> In disposition they are loyally attached to the British Service to which they look up for protection. They are at the same time proud of the name of Goorkahs, which carries with it recollections of Martial deeds. They look down on the regular Native Sepoys, to whom they consider themselves superior, but they have the highest opinion of the Europeans as Soldiers, and respect their courage, and discipline, and whenever they have been associated with European Troops a Mutual good understanding and the best feeling has existed.[96]

This profile of brave, tough little men, sunny by nature but prone to sudden, unpredictable outbursts of rage, addicted to gambling, proudly independent yet amenable to discipline, contemptuous of Indian sepoys but with a natural affinity for European troops, and, above all, attached to their officers, remained the template for descriptions of Gurkhas for at least a century and a half.

Just under 5,000 men came into British service in 1815, half to two-thirds of whom were not 'real Gorkahs' but Kumaonis, Garhwalis and other Himalayan hillmen. Out of these Ochterlony formed two Nasiri battalions, Fraser and Young raised the Sirmoor battalion, and the Kumaon battalion (which eventually became the 3rd Queen Alexandra's Own Gurkha Rifles) was formed, according to its regimental historian, Major-General Nigel Woodyatt, from three bodies of men: the remnant of Bhakti Thapa's defeated force at Dionthal, some Gorkha survivors of the fighting around Almora and 300 men from Oudh and Palpa recruited by a British agent to fight the Nepalese.[97]

When Hastings reported the raising of these regiments to London, he sought simultaneously to justify his actions and mollify the Company:

> Your Honorable Committee will be pleased to observe, that the present extent of this Establishment is only temporary. It would neither have been prudent nor consistent with good faith, to discharge from the Service of the British Government any portion of the troops who came over from the enemy. Severed from their own country, they could not be practised upon to any purpose by their former Commanders, therefore for the moment they are efficient for us. But were they cast adrift, they having not either habits or means of industry, must through necessity repair to their old standards, and range themselves in arms against us, or must betake themselves to predatory associations for subsistence. As they fall off, it is not proposed to supply vacancies, until the Corps shall be reduced to the number which may be deemed fit for the permanent establishment.[98]

On such makeshift foundations was built, over the next hundred years, the magnificent edifice of the Indian Army Gurkha Brigade.

The four original battalions formed the core of the defence of the newly conquered territory in the western hills, thus releasing regular British and native infantry units for service against the Marathas or whomever on the plains. None of them took part in the second campaign of the Gorkha war – which followed the failure of the Kathmandu *durbar* to ratify the peace agreement – though the Sirmoor battalion under Lieutenant Young 'marched to Seetapore and joined General [then Colonel] Nicolls' Detachment, destined to invade Nepal'.[99] Nicolls was full of praise for the way in which the battalion was equipped for hill service, but felt he could not trust the men to fight against their own kind so soon after their defection. Young was confident of their loyalty and had no doubt that they would acquit themselves creditably. But on this occasion they did not get the opportunity.[100]

In contrast to the first campaign, which went on for several months, the second was over in a matter of weeks. Unsurprisingly, Hastings placed Ochterlony in command of the invasion of Nepal. The force at the general's disposal consisted of nearly 20,000 men, but the advantage in numbers would only tell if he could penetrate the mountain barrier to the Kathmandu valley; and the known route, the Churiaghati pass to Makwanpur – the gateway, as it were, to Kathmandu – was heavily fortified, with a stockade at every turn. The only hope was to find another way through the mountains, outflanking the enemy to attain the heights, and take them by surprise.

While Ochterlony's campaign against Amar Singh had been characterized by patience and tenacity, his strategy here bordered on the reckless. It was already well into February (1816) and he was aware that with the monsoon pending, and the Terai likely to become a hotbed of fever, time was not on his side. So he took a calculated risk which threw into jeopardy his newly acquired reputation. Without his former ADC, the field engineer Peter Lawtie, Ochterlony relied on his quartermaster-general and head of intelligence, the 'able, however unamiable' Captain Joshua Pickersgill to find the alternative route. A chance encounter with a party of smugglers, who were happy to trade their topographical knowledge for cash, led to the discovery of a path 'unknown to any servant of the Nepaul state'.[101] That was enough for Ochterlony. To deceive the enemy, he left a large force at the bottom of the pass with instructions to make feints at the nearest fortifications, while he took advantage of a moonlit night to slip away with the brigade he had selected for the hazardous march through the mountains.

The fact that he himself accompanied the brigade on foot is a measure of Ochterlony's anxiety over the success of the mission. The utmost stealth consistent with the progress of 3,000 men with artillery and two elephants over appalling terrain was essential throughout, and the last part of the journey was so precipitous that the smallest troop lying in ambush (a tactic much favoured by the Gorkhas) 'might have destroyed the whole brigade, without exposing themselves to much danger', as the author of *Military Sketches of the Goorka War* recorded, adding sternly, 'Such perilous expeditions are justifiable only when undertaken as the means of averting disaster.'[102]

But the ruse worked and the first the Gorkhas knew of it was when, to their amazement, they discovered the British force at the top of the pass: 'They said we were not men, but devils, and that we must have descended from the skies.'[103] Lieutenant Shipp of the 87th (the Royal Irish Fusiliers) pays tribute to 'our gallant general [who] walked every yard of this critical march, encouraging his men', a remarkable achievement for 'an officer seventy years of age' – as indeed it would have been, except that Ochterlony was barely fifty-eight at the time.[104] Ochterlony himself ascribed the success of the march to 'great good fortune, as well as to the most persevering labour, the greatest exertion and most persevering fortitude'.[105]

The remainder of the campaign is best seen through the eyes of Lieutenant Shipp, the only participant-observer to give an account of it (the anonymous author of the *Sketches* not being a soldier). As a writer, he may be a little given to hyperbole, as in this passage comparing the landscape and people of Nepal:

> ... in this paradise of beauty dwelt a cruel and barbarous people, proverbial for their bloody deeds, whose hearts were more callous than the flinty rocks that reared their majestic heads above their woody mountains. They are more savage in their nature than the hungry tiger that prowls through their dreary glens; cruel as the vulture; cold-hearted as their snowy mountains; subtle and cunning as the fiend of night; powerful as the rocks on which they live; and active as the goat upon the mountain's brow.[106]

But when he gets down to particulars, as in the following description of the treatment meted out to a spy caught by the Gorkhas, Shipp can be genuinely shocking:

> This poor creature was seized, and literally cut to pieces; and it was supposed, by the medical people, that he must have died a death of extreme agony, for the ground under him was dug up with his struggling under the torture which had been inflicted on him. His arms had been cut off, about halfway up from the elbow to the shoulder; after which it appeared that two deep incisions had been cut in his body just above the hips, into which the two arms had been thrust. His features were distorted in a most frightful manner . . . [107]

Shipp himself played a notable part in the fighting, once engaging in single-handed combat with a Gorkha chief in front of both armies. 'He was a capital swordsman,' Prinsep writes, 'but his weapon broke early in the conflict, whereupon he threw it away, and trusting to his activity, closed with the Goorkha, and wrenching his sword from him, laid him lifeless with a back-handed stroke.' Prinsep feels bound to add, 'Feats of this kind are not the proper duty of officers, but when they occur are very encouraging to the troops; for the union of personal prowess with gallantry and success will always command admiration.'[108] Quite so. The Gorkhas would certainly not have thought the less of him for momentarily forgetting his duty as an officer.

As the superiority of the British force and its artillery began to make itself felt, Shipp's attitude towards the Gorkhas underwent a change. He was won over by their indomitability:

> The enemy maintained their ground, and fought manfully. I hate a runaway foe; you have no credit for beating them. Those we were now dealing with were no flinchers; but, on the contrary, I never saw more steadiness or more bravery exhibited by any set of men in my life. Run they would not; and of death they seemed to have no fear, though their comrades were falling thick around them, for we were so near that every shot told.[109]

Again and again, Shipp marvels at their steadfastness, 'The havoc was dreadful, for they still scorned to fly' as the six-pounders 'now began to play with grape on the poor and brave fellows'.[110] The unequalness of the contest offended his sense of fair play, and victory in the decisive battle for Makwanpur in February 1816 gave no cause for celebration:

> As long as it was light, we could plainly see the last struggles of the dying. Some poor fellows could be seen raising their knees up to their chins, and then flinging them down again with all their might. Some attempted to rise, but failed in the attempt. One poor fellow I saw get on his legs, put his hand to his bleeding head, then fall, and roll down the hill, to rise no more. This was the scene that the evening now closed upon. Reader, believe me when I assure you that these results of war were no sights of exultation or triumph to the soldiers who witnessed them. Willingly, would we one and all have extended the hand of aid to them, and dressed their gaping wounds. No brave man will ever exult over a bleeding and wounded enemy.[111]

Shipp is prepared to forgive such an enemy even the cruelties he had earlier recoiled from: 'They are taught from their infancy the art of war; they fight under the banner of gloomy superstition; cruelty is their creed; and murder of their foes the zenith of their glory.' For these 'untaught babes of idolatry' pity and commiseration are more in order than condemnation, and in the grim task of burying the 1,100 corpses left in the field, British soldiers and sepoys alike shed tears of compassion.[112]

Among the wounded treated in the British field hospital was one young man whose leg had to be amputated. He submitted to the surgery almost passively, then asked the friend lying next to him when he thought they would remove his other leg; for he would do away with himself if he had to wait too long. An attendant who overheard this remark explained 'that the act was one of kindness, not of cruelty, and done to save his life'. But it was not until he saw the same operation being performed on one of the Company's sepoys that the man accepted 'that we were not such barbarians as he had been taught to suppose'.[113] This story contrasts with an account of a Gorkha who had part of his jaw shot away at the siege of Kalanga during the first campaign and sought medical aid from the British; after he had been patched up, he begged – and obtained – leave to return to his own side to continue the fight.[114]

'I was on the rear-guard the morning we left the valley of Muckwanpore,' Shipp writes. 'The enemy (or, perhaps, I should say our friends) flocked in great numbers, to bid us farewell, or see us depart.' As they moved off, a young stranger came up to Shipp and grasped his hand, saying, 'I love a brave soldier; and the white men are all brave.' It transpired that this man was adjutant of the corps whose commander, Krishna Rana, 'fell under my fortunate sabre', as Shipp tactfully puts it.[115]

The anonymous author of *Military Sketches* asserts that the Gorkhas in the second campaign were 'much inferior, in active valour, to the veterans of Hindur [in the west]' – which hardly seems consistent with John Shipp's experience – though he adds the significant rider, 'when impelled by the energy of Amer Singh'.[116]

Amar Singh might well have made a better fist of defending Makwanpur against his old adversary Ochterlony than the 'nameless Commander' operating under the control of the Nepalese chief minister Bhim Sen Thapa, but the Kaji was out of the reckoning: 'This man, soldier from his infancy, did not seek nor obtain the command of any army when his country was invaded; but retiring to a temple which he had founded in his youth, he died shortly after the termination of the war.' In command of the neighbouring fort at Hariharpur was Amar Singh's son Ranjur, the defender of Jaithak. But he 'forfeited all his renown by an early flight, leaving those companions of his brighter fortune, whom he had distinguished by crescents on their turbans, and called the *Band of the Moon*'.[117] Of the other two outstanding commanders in the western sector during the first campaign, the popular Bhakti Thapa was dead and Balbahadur Singh (the defender of Kalanga) had gone to Lahore to serve under Ranjit Singh and could not return home because, under Nepalese law, his life had 'become forfeited to the vengeance of a countryman, whose wife he had seduced'.[118]*

---

*The common Nepali word for soldier, *lahore*, or one who goes to Lahore, derives from the recruitment of Gorkhas as mercenaries by Ranjit Singh even before the British got in on the act. Coleman quotes a letter from William Fraser to John Adam, dated 27 April 1815, in which Fraser reports that 'the Rajah of Lahore who obtained, at the period that Umr Sing [sic] besieged Kangarh [1806–09], a considerable number [of Gorkhas], found them to be excellent'. After the first phase of the Gorkha war, Ranjit tried to seduce the Gorkhas who had joined the Bengal Army

Defeat at Makwanpur and Hariharpur, and Ranjur Singh's abandon-
ment of his post, left Kathmandu with no alternative but to sue for peace,
and the Treaty of Segauli was signed on 4 March 1816. It suited Ochterlony,
too, to bring the campaign to a speedy conclusion, not simply because of
the approach of the dreaded *aul*-fever season in the Terai but also because
of the number of his European troops suffering from dysentery.

For his great achievement, Ochterlony received the thanks of both Houses
of Parliament and became the first officer in the East India Company's
service to be awarded the GCB. 'You have obliterated a distinction painful
for officers of the Honorable Company,' the Governor-General told him
when he conferred the decoration upon him, 'and you have opened the
door for your brother officers in arms to a reward which their recent display
of exalted spirit and invincible intrepidity proves could not be more
deservedly extended to the officers of any army on earth.'[120] Hastings
demonstrated his gratitude to, and respect for, Ochterlony by eventually
reinstating him as Resident at Delhi, where he lived in the style appropriate to someone who was, 'after the Governor General himself, the most
prominent figure in the service of the East India Company'.[121] But when
Hastings left India and was succeeded as Governor-General by Lord
Amherst in 1823, Ochterlony fell out of favour again.

Early in 1825, the Rajah of Bharatpur died and the six-year-old heir to
the throne, whom Ochterlony had undertaken to recognize, was usurped
by a cousin, Durjan Sal. Sir David demanded Durjan Sal's submission
and, when this demand was ignored, prepared to march on Bharatpur
(whose successful defiance of Lord Lake's armies in 1805 had encouraged Bhim Sen to challenge the Company). The new Governor-General
countermanded his orders, provoking Ochterlony's resignation – as
Amherst had anticipated. To add insult to injury, Amherst replaced
Ochterlony with his old friend Sir Charles Metcalfe (who accepted the

away from British service, but without much success; though he paid his sepoys at
a higher rate, seven to eight and a half rather than six rupees a month, his payments
were irregular and could not be relied upon.
   Balbahadur commanded Ranjit Singh's Gorkha battalion and was killed in the
Sikh–Afghan wars in 1823 when his entire force was mown down by Afghan
artillery. The 'Lion of the Punjab' paid them a fitting tribute. 'Among all my trained
soldiers,' he said, 'only the Gorkhas stood their own against Muslim attack.'[119]

residency only after he had been assured that if he did not, it would be offered to someone else rather than left in Ochterlony's hands). The ailing general took this final reverse badly and died shortly after, on 14 July 1825. Had he lived just a little longer, he would have had the satisfaction of being vindicated yet again when Amherst was finally obliged – and at great expense – to lay siege to Bharatpur.[122]

His memorial, the 165-foot-high Ochterlony monument in Calcutta, might also be seen as a symbol of the passing of an age, the age of ostentatious wealth, princely pomp, harems and huge entourages, great generosity but also corruption (while Sir David himself may have been blameless, his retinue attracted accusations of extortion) – the age, in fact, of the 'nabobs'. But Ochterlony's greatest legacy – and living memorial – is the continuing recruitment of Gurkhas into both the British and Indian armies.*

---

*One of the stipulations of the Treaty of Segauli was that Nepal should accept a British Resident in Kathmandu. William Fraser thought that the appointment would be his. But his brother Alexander wrote to their father from Delhi: 'We hear on good authority that [Edward] Gardner, our second assistant, who is at present Commissioner for the conquered provinces of Cumaoon, goes to Khatmandoo as Resident. See the result of [Hastings'] fine promises. William superseded by his Junior Assistant! Patience!'[123] Perhaps Fraser, like Ochterlony, was regarded by those in authority on the cusp of the new age as not quite sound. There was a touch of the nabob about him too, as Victor Jacquemont recognized:

> He is an original who really ought to be exhibited for a fee, but a very good fellow, whom I love as I do none of his other fellow-countrymen . . . He has six or seven legitimate wives, but they all live together some fifty leagues from Delhi and do as they like. He must have as many children as the King of Persia, but they are all Moslems or Hindus, according to the religion and caste of their mamas, and are shepherds, peasants, mountaineers, etc. according to the occupation of their mother's family. My friend Fraser was a devil of a fellow in his day, but he is verging on the fifties, or rather the fifties have taken possession of him. He is mild as a lamb now. If I were to describe all his eccentricities I should never come to the end of them, but he is a profound thinker withal.[124]

It is a piquant thought that, were all the stories about them true (Edward Thompson relays gossip of 'Ochterlony's thirteen wives on thirteen elephants, every evening taking the air in Delhi'[125]), then the two prime movers of what was to become the Gurkha Brigade had no less than twenty wives between them.

2

Residents, Rajahs,
Ranis – and Ranas

The most influential British Resident in Nepal during the nineteenth century was Brian Houghton Hodgson. Born in 1800 and educated at Haileybury, the school for Indian civil servants, he almost saw the century out, living to the grand old age of ninety-four. Yet he was confined to hill districts (first in Kumaon, then in Nepal from 1821 to 1843) throughout his service in India because of his delicate health, which gave way under the rigours of the climate in the plains.

Hodgson belongs to that select band of imperialist polymaths who made significant contributions to the knowledge of out-of-the-way places and peoples: he was a naturalist, ethnographer and linguist as well as politician and diplomat. His scholarly papers and despatches helped to put Nepal on the map. Insofar as Gurkhas are concerned, he was the staunchest advocate of their recruitment into British service after Ochterlony. But it must have been agony for a man with such an inquiring mind and restless spirit to find himself as physically constrained as he was in Kathmandu. For Bhim Sen Thapa's way of neutralizing British influence was to isolate and imprison the Resident and his entourage in much the same way as he had isolated and imprisoned his own young maharajah.

When Hodgson was first posted to Nepal as Edward Gardner's

assistant in 1821, Bhim Sen had been in power for fifteen years. The chief minister's biggest headache was what to do with an army which had become an expensive luxury, now that the Gorkhas had been penned into what are more or less Nepal's present-day frontiers. He could neither disband it nor, indeed, reduce it without undermining his own strongest support. His way of maintaining a formidable army and, at the same time, cutting expenditure, was to remove numbers of soldiers from the roll of service for a year at a time on a rotating basis, making them *dhakre*, as it was called. Bhim Sen was ever alert to the threat of a British take-over (however unlikely that might actually be in view of Britain's reluctance to provoke the slumbering giant of China). He had not forgotten the warning Kaji Amar Singh had addressed to the rajah early in 1815 when the *durbar* first considered suing for peace.

> Having lost your dominions, what is to become of your great military establishments? When our power is once reduced, we shall have another Knox's mission, under pretence of concluding a treaty of alliance and friendship, and founding commercial establishments. If we decline receiving their mission, they will insist; and if we are unable to oppose force, and desire them to come unaccompanied with troops, they will not comply. They will begin by introducing a company; a battalion will soon after follow, and at length an army will be assembled for the subjection of Nipal.[1]

The first part of this prophecy had already come true – Nepal had been obliged to give house-room to a British Resident, the hateful symbol of its reduction to client status in relation to the British administration in Calcutta. And without a strong army to act as deterrent the rest of it might also be fulfilled. So Bhim Sen's reluctance to reduce the army stemmed from his fear of invasion as much as from fear of losing his power base. As Hodgson's biographer, Sir William Hunter, puts it:

> Bhim Sen was the first Nepalese statesman who grasped the meaning of the system of Protectorates which Lord Wellesley had carried out in India. He saw one native state after another come within the net of British subsidiary alliances, and his policy was steadily directed to save Nepal from a similar fate.[2]

Hodgson, for his part, was satisfied that the *durbar* would not 'court another struggle with us so long as we stand on our present eminence of power, unless' – he went on in his meticulous, not to say long-winded, way – 'driven to arms, in defiance of their deliberate views of policy, by the mere presence of those circumstances of exclusively military habit and excitement into which, without the power of weighing remote consequences, or in the vain hope of events that can never be realised, they have suffered themselves, as easily as unwisely, to slide'.[3]

He thought that the standing army of Nepal was far too large for the country's needs and therefore constituted a danger to British India unless it were substantially reduced. His solution was to press for the introduction into the Company's service of 'Swiss Battalions' of honourable mercenaries. He noted that the Gorkha, like the Swiss, was a true soldier, simple-minded and brave, and with an exceptional love of his native mountains: '. . . the Gorkha soldier, though his vocation be arms, has not, like mercenaries in general, been asked to prostitute his sword in all causes promiscuously and may therefore reasonably be expected to possess, and to manifest in such circumstances, a military chastity, trustworthiness and fidelity to his engagements, which joined to the *reality* of our supremacy and *his consciousness* of it, would constitute, it may perhaps be allowed, a sufficient security to us'.[4] Of the Khas, Magars and Gurungs, who constituted the Gorkha soldiery, he wrote:

> They are in character somewhat choleric, and have a sense of personal dignity and independence not less keen than that of the proudest Rajpoot, or Pat[h]an, yet, unlike those tribes, they are in the highest degree tractable to discipline . . . and [as] steady and peaceable a body of troops as any in the world.

Such a combination of pride and docility was 'an honourable feature in the Gorkha character, which I know not where to seek for a parallel in Asia'.[5]

These Khas, Magars and Gurungs – not to mention the Kiranti, or eastern martial tribes, who he thought would also make excellent soldiers – would be more than happy to serve the British if their government would allow it. Their situation as *dhakres* – 'periodically ejected from the roll of service [and] left without adequate means of subsistence, or occupation' – made them envious of their kinsmen already serving the Company in Kumaon and Garhwal. Hodgson recorded the kind of remarks they were in the habit of making to 'our Seapoys':

> 'Ha Tewaree! you are a lucky fellow, never made *dukhureeuh* [sic], always in receipt of eight siccas [rupees], while we, poor fellows, every other year are left to shift for ourselves to make a mere subsistence by carrying loads like a cooly: for we have no land of our own, we are soldiers – arms are our trade and vocation and gladly would we serve anywhere if we could get regular pay – they say the English is a good service but our Government won't hear of our entering it – nor can we leave the country without permission, obtainable only once in several years under the pretence of pilgrimage – some of our fellows go in this way and visit your stations – and here and there one of us gets service; if not, we pass on, make our *teeruth* [pilgrimage] and come back. Were we to run away our families would answer for the offence, and such being the hazard how can we think of attempting it – especially under such an uncertainty of success?'[6]

Hodgson was at pains to point out that these remarks were not invented, but had been drawn from actual encounters.

As he saw it, enlisting Gorkhas as honourable mercenaries would simultaneously strengthen the Company's Bengal Army and reduce the threat of another war with Nepal by drawing off its surplus soldiery.

Bhim Sen well understood Hodgson's reasoning and was equally determined to prevent the wholesale recruitment of Nepalese soldiers into British service. So these two sparring partners, whose mutual wariness was tempered with respect, set the pattern of diplomatic pressure and pleading on one side and evasion and resistance on the other which prevailed for the next sixty years with regard to Gurkha recruitment. Nepal's most astute ministers might be prepared to come to Britain's aid in times of crisis and offer to send battalions to do battle on its behalf, but neither of the two strong men of nineteenth-century Nepal – Bhim Sen Thapa and Jang Bahadur Rana – was prepared to stand by and watch British agents siphon off the cream of young Magar and Gurung manhood into the Bengal Army.

Nepal had been stripped of the western Terai, as well as its western empire, after the Gorkha war. But Bhim Sen did not merely survive this disaster, he maintained Nepal's precarious independence under the new dispensation and dominated the government for a further twenty years.

In Hodgson, however, Bhim Sen met his match. Unlike his predecessor, Edward Gardner, who followed to the letter British policy of non-interference in the domestic affairs of Nepal, Hodgson was either unsuited by nature or not permitted by events to assume the role of passive spectator. To this day, historians argue about his period in office; no one doubts that his influence was extensive, the only question being whether it was for good or ill. Broadly speaking, British writers credit Hodgson with preventing a second Anglo-Gorkha war, while some Nepali historians accuse him of meddling in affairs he did not fully comprehend and exacerbating, rather then reducing, tensions. Since this was the period in which the foundations of the modern Nepali state were laid and relations with British India – revolving increasingly around Gurkha recruitment – established, it needs to be examined in some detail.

Gardner retired in 1829. Hodgson immediately took over as Acting Resident and then, in 1833, became Resident, a post he held for the next ten tempestuous years. During this time Bhim Sen steadily lost power (particularly after the death in 1832 of the queen-regent, Tripura Sundari, who was said to be his paramour) and the feud between the Pande and the Thapa ruling factions was given free rein by Maharaja Rajendra Bikram Shah, who emerged from his minority a weak and vacillating, but wilful, king. As Bhim Sen's grip on affairs slackened, he could no longer keep the maharajah and the Resident in their separate cages, so the scope for plotting on all sides increased. As one historian has pointed out, the Resident was not just distrusted for his own sake, but also for the use unscrupulous *bharadars*, or nobles, might make of him in their own bids for power; hence Bhim Sen's reluctance to allow Hodgson access to anyone but himself.[7]

However bloody his rise to power may have been, Bhim Sen's fall has a tragic dimension: twice imprisoned on trumped-up charges, the old man was tormented with rumours – such as that his wife was to be paraded naked through the streets of Kathmandu – until he could bear it no longer and sought to end his life with a kukri conveniently placed at his disposal. Unfortunately, he botched his suicide attempt and lingered for nine days before he died on 29 July 1839.

For some years after Bhim Sen's demise there was anarchy in Kathmandu. The war between the Pandes and the Thapas took on a new intensity, and their attitudes to the British reversed themselves: before the rise of Bhim Sen, the Pandes had been considered pro-British; now they were the 'war party' and the Thapas, who had initiated the war with Britain in 1814, were seen as supportive of British power in India. But the Residency Diary for the years immediately following Bhim Sen's death is largely taken up with the doings of the increasingly dysfunctional royal family, whose excesses were in marked contrast to the 'excellent . . . natural habits of subjects and soldiery in Nipal'.[8]

Rajendra's complete lack of sexual interest in women other than his two wives was most unusual among rajahs. But the senior and junior queens conformed to the pattern of Gorkha *ranis* in that they were both much stronger than their pampered menfolk. Samrajya Laxmi, the senior rani, whom Hodgson privately referred to as 'Furiosa', was the power behind the Pande ministry which toppled Bhim Sen Thapa and rekindled the war between the Thapas and the Pandes. Her rival, the junior queen, Rajya Laxmi Devi, therefore supported the Thapa faction. Hodgson had done his best not to get involved in the internal affairs of Nepal through most of the 1830s, but between 1838 and 1840 the aggressively anti-British policy of Ranjang Pande and the senior rani obliged him – in the absence of military back-up, with British forces fully engaged in the ill-judged invasion of Afghanistan – to play a political role and form 'an alliance of convenience' with a third party, that of the *chauntrias*, or royal collaterals, in order to prevent an escalation of hostilities into all-out war.[9]

There was considerable unrest along the border with Company territory, and the Residency itself came under threat in June 1840 when mutineering soldiers were encouraged to believe that a proposed reduction in their numbers and pay had been instigated by the British. The Governor-General, Lord Auckland, took the threats seriously and, as a result of the ultimatums he sent, backed by the deployment of troops euphemistically described as a 'Corps of observation' on the frontier, the maharajah took fright and agreed to the replacement of Ranjang

Pande's administration with what its opponents called 'the British ministry'.[10] But whichever party formed the government, the Pandes or the *chauntrias*, they still had to deal with the king.

> Both distrusted and despised the Maharaja, yet he kept the balance
> between them, and probably would continue to do so. He was averse to
> extremes, a deep time-server, and cunning and timid in the highest
> degree. He had one eye on Calcutta and the other on Pekin, and was
> anxious to discover whether it would be more profitable to side with the
> English or Chinese in the great controversy [i.e., the 'opium war'].[11]

The dismissal of the Pandes led to the departure from Kathmandu of a number of secret agents from the Punjab and other native states with whom the senior queen's party had been conspiring to undermine Britain's growing power. Hodgson had succeeded in frustrating Furiosa, and on 8 August he gloated: 'The Ministers and the Resident together were too much for palace intriguants'.[12] But a month and a half later, there was bad news from Afghanistan: 'Kashmir traders just in from Lhassa reported that the English at Kabul had all been taken and slain, excepting the Envoy, who was kept as a curiosity in a cage. This statement met with ready belief.'[13]

Meanwhile, Samrajya Laxmi had failed in her attempts, first, by 'readmitt[ing] the Maharaja to marital rights after a resolute refusal of three years', to coax her husband into making her chief minister, and then to persuade him to abdicate in favour of her elder son, their heir-apparent and crown prince, Surendra Bikram Shah.[14] She died a disappointed woman on 6 October 1841, earning this tribute from her arch-enemy, the Resident: 'She was a spirit born for dominion, possessed of an indomitable will and incapable of fear. Nothing could make her abandon her purpose.'[15]

The death of the senior queen brought about an improvement in relations between Britain and Nepal. At the beginning of 1842 Rajendra offered to send his forces to serve either in Kabul or in Burma and, although Lord Auckland declined the offer, British troops were withdrawn from the frontier to mark the return to more cordial relations. The maharajah was delighted: 'He observed that he would never have believed, had he not seen it, that the Resident would have unconditionally pardoned him and withdrawn the British force.'[16] The king being who he was, there had to be a reaction of course, and in April news of the extent of British reverses in Afghanistan brought the Pandes back into favour once again.[17]

If the maharajah was an inveterate schemer, however, his son and heir-apparent, who was barely in his teens when his mother died, was simply incorrigible. With his father's acquiescence, if not active encouragement, this pubescent princeling pursued a path of dedicated sadism – as this sequence of entries in the Residency Diary testifies:

10 April. The violence of the Heir-apparent had ceased for a while. It was said that he and his father were ashamed, no less than the Chiefs were disgusted with it. Hands had been mutilated, and scalps laid bare to the cranium, by the young gentleman, and as these hands and heads belonged to men of high rank, or to their sons, it was no wonder that people were wrath . . .

24 April. The Heir-apparent was blustering about cutting the Resident to pieces, and imprisoning or expelling him.

27 April. The Heir-apparent was all day exercising his savage tyranny over sundry persons, gentry and menials, to the risk or loss of their limbs or life. Jung Bahadur, son of Kaji Balnar Singh, and a Chief of the highest character and promise, was made to leap down a well . . . Jung Bahadur was not killed as was at first reported, but he was badly hurt.

5 May . . . Another Chief of rank was subjected to well discipline, which was now so frequent, that the phrase went by way of mutual question, – 'Have you drunk of the well today?'

4 June. The Heir-apparent yesterday dragged his own young sister and brother towards one of his 'must' elephants, amidst the groans and cries of all the spectators. No one dared to interfere until the Maharaja came and rescued the children. The Prince was a Nero in petticoats; he was ruined by his father for the sake of some political intrigue.

11–13 November . . . The Heir-apparent continued to beat, kick, maim and wound the gentry and their sons; it was a question of how long they would endure this. The Heir-apparent had ordered women with child to be brought to him, and all the virgins of rank, in order that he might examine their development and choose himself a wife. A great commotion was raised by these doings . . . [18]

Far from reprimanding, or punishing, this 'Nero in petticoats' for his appalling behaviour, his father rewarded him by making him joint-maharajah along with himself, a move of such imbecility that Hodgson remonstrated with him, demanding that he himself abdicate before his heir be recognized. The Resident commented: 'The great deceiver, it was said, had deceived himself.'[19] Confronted by a princeling who caused the death of his nine-year-old consort by making her stand all day in a water-tank and a king who not only condoned such actions but promoted the thirteen-year-old delinquent, it is hard to disagree with the judgement of the French writer Sylvain Lévi on Prithwi Narayan's successors – that they belong to pathology rather than history.[20]

The great privilege and responsibility of the ruler of Nepal was the *pajani*, the annual review of all civil and military office holders. Since any or all could be confirmed in office or dismissed at will, this was a very effective way of ensuring the loyalty of the nobles and demonstrating where true power lay. The appointments made by Crown Prince Surendra in his new role as joint-maharajah in November 1842 included Jang Bahadur as Kaji. On the face of it this was a rather surprising promotion, given that when last heard of Jang had been ordered by the prince to jump down a well, a feat which might easily have ended his career and his life. But Surendra continued to torment the man even after he had made him Kaji.

1 December . . . Both father and son seemed to have lost their wits, and could not act prudently with so stern a monitor as universal insurrection before them. On the previous night they had conspired to have Jung Bahadur Kower [Konwar] beaten by Captain Jaman Singh Kharttri. Jung Bahadur, however, was released by the soldiery. Jaman Singh escaped with difficulty; his house was sacked for aiding and abetting the Heir-apparent.[21]

As this diary entry indicates, the normally quiescent army had been pushed to the brink of mutiny by the boy prince and his indulgent father. The *chauntria* chief minister, Fatteh Jang, turned to the Resident for advice and support. But in the wake of the Afghan débâcle Lord Auckland had been replaced by Lord Ellenborough (on whose appointment to govern the Indians Macaulay commented: 'We have sometimes sent them Governors whom they loved, and sometimes Governors whom they feared, but they never before had a Governor at whom they laughed'[22]) and Hodgson was under strict instructions from the new Governor-General not to meddle: 'The Premier still attempted to draw the Resident into their proceedings, but the Resident stood steadily aloof; though were he authorized to interfere as arbitrator by and bye, he might perhaps prevent violence and bring about speedy and permanent good . . .'[23] Even in a semi-official record of events, Hodgson could not resist sniping at his new master.

Enter the junior queen, aka Rajya Laxmi Devi. With her rival dead, her rival's son a loose cannon and her husband weak and ineffectual, she was the one remaining hope of stability in Nepal.

> *16–18 December* . . . The soldiery called the father a knave, and the son a madman, to the Maharaja's face. They charged him with incessant breach of word, and declared that they must and would have the Rani made *de facto* Regent, as the sole means of realising the recent engagements, and settling the kingdom . . . [24]

Early in January 1843, when the rani was officially made regent, she summoned the leading Thapa, Bhim Sen's nephew and heir-apparent, Mathbar Singh, from exile in India, where he had been living on a British pension after doing his share of plotting with Ranjit Singh in Lahore. Hodgson had been advising Mathbar from a distance, as his successor, Major Lawrence (later Sir Henry, one of the heroes of nineteenth-century British India), reported in February 1844:

> Mathabar Singh is perhaps entitled to some consideration from me in as much as he appears to have returned to Nepal under some sort of pledge from my predecessor, who had frequent and private meetings with him here and who counselled him repeatedly and most impressively through the Collector at Gorakhpur previous to his return to look to the Rani and to beware of the Raja as the 'darkest and wiliest and most dangerous of deluders'. Mr Hodgson added, 'let Sir Marmaduke (Mathabar Singh's nickname) be assured that no mortal man can give himself to that person (the king) and live. This *nation* has lately pronounced *aut Regina aut ruina* and those who support the

Queen will carry with them *the voice and force of the nation*, the only shield for a Nepalese statesman.'[25]

In conversations with Lawrence, however, Hodgson had never mentioned any understanding with Mathbar and said only that the rani 'though a good woman was untried'.[26] Hodgson, in Lawrence's opinion, 'would never have addressed [General] Matabur Singh at Gorukpore, or forwarded his views on arrival, as he appeared to have done, had he not desired to remove from the General's mind, the impression that he (Mr Hodgson) had been heart and hand with the Chountras; in fact that he was one of them and formed one of their Ministry'.[27] The problem with this sort of interference – Lawrence argued – was that so long as the Resident's party remained in power all was well, but once it was ousted, as it was bound to be sooner or later, the Resident was identified as an enemy and marginalized, or worse. Lawrence was critical of Hodgson for further muddying waters already so opaque as to be impenetrable. He wrote: 'I cannot but feel that to his conduct towards all the leading men of Nepal: the *Gurus* [priestly class], the *Chautarias*, Pandeys and Thapas and the Raja himself, most of my present difficulties are to be attributed.'[28]

But Lawrence had strict instructions to reverse his predecessor's policy and remain aloof from domestic affairs in Nepal; and even such an honourable man as he cannot but have known that in reporting what the administration wanted to hear he was doing his own prospects no harm. In Hodgson's defence it should be said that, in the first place, he had been sucked into political involvement against his better judgement and in response to a crisis. Secondly, if he had followed instructions and dealt only with the maharajah (which had been his own inclination back in the days when Bhim Sen had used his power to keep king and Resident apart), he would never have known where he was since Rajendra 'was wholly wanting in decision, sincerity and straightforwardness, and was liable to occasional fits of passion, such as his eldest son so constantly exhibited'.[29] And finally, he was not, like Lawrence, a bird of passage who would spend two years in Kathmandu and then move on to higher things, but a resident in more senses than one, who cared so passionately about the strange country in which he had made his home, with its mixture of cantankerous court and peaceable populace, that he took his removal by Ellenborough at the end of 1843 badly and (like Ochterlony before him) sealed his fate by reacting impetuously, as his biographer relates:

> Hodgson had not the adroitness of headquarters. Twenty-four years of isolation had made his high-strung and somewhat haughty nature still more sensitive. When wounded by what he regarded as injustice and ingratitude, he could not help showing that he felt it . . . In resigning the service he made a somewhat needlessly emphatic protest against a piece of unfairness in high places which a defter official would have taken as a by no means extraordinary incident in even a prosperous career.[30]

Hodgson's departure from Kathmandu produced 'the most spontaneous outpouring of affection that this period of Nepal's history witnessed'.[31] Even the chameleonic Rajendra was moved. 'At Hodgson's final audience with the Darbar the Raja burst into tears and, referring to the exertions by which Hodgson had so often averted a war, called him "the Saviour of Nepal".'[32]

Mathbar's return to Kathmandu in April 1843 was accompanied by the usual ritual bloodshed. 'Several Pandey Chiefs were confined in irons' on 21 April, and 'all the confiscations that took place on the fall of Bhim Sen Thappa were restored to Matabur Singh'; and on 1 May a number of Pandes were beheaded – one of them being 'dragged to the place of execution with a hook through his breast'. Others were flogged and had their noses (and in one case, lips as well) cut off. The joint-maharajahs, meanwhile, carried on with their double act:

> *16–23 July* . . . The father and son had engaged in a serious scuffle in the presence of many Chiefs and of a large body of troops. Folks said that such a state of things could not last; but gentle and simple Chiefs and soldiery, seemed disposed to let father and son fight out their own battle, and then join the winning party . . . [33]

The trouble was, there did not seem to be a winning party.

This was the situation Major Henry Lawrence walked into on 29 October 1843.*

Apart from the three royal contenders, the joint-maharajahs and the queen-regent – whom Lawrence felicitously dubbed 'Mr Nepal, Master Nepal and Mrs Nepal'[35] – there were the four parties vying for the ministry, *gurus* and *chauntrias* as well as Thapas and Pandes, each with its own agenda. Since the death of the senior rani two years earlier, her son the heir-apparent had become the champion of the Pandes; the queen-regent favoured the Thapas and wanted Mathbar Singh as minister; and the king, as ever, vacillated and, ventriloquist-like, worked his will through others, at the same time refusing to let go of power entirely. His fear was that Mathbar might become the *de facto* ruler of the country in the manner of his uncle Bhim Sen. Rajendra would combine with his son to prevent that, especially since Mathbar made no secret of his contempt for the pair of them, openly telling the soldiers that both were fools.

But Mathbar's own position was precarious, despite the queen's backing. He did not control appointments through the *pajani*. His 'favourite nephew Jung Bahadur', who had been made *kaji*, or military leader, by the prince only the year before, was now excluded from the *durbar*'s four kajiships – perhaps out of fear of the Thapas becoming too dominant, bearing in mind their popularity with the army.[36] Mathbar tried to strengthen his position by getting the Resident on his side, but unlike Hodgson Lawrence refused to be drawn – though this did not prevent him from dispensing moral guidance. For instance, when Mathbar told him that 'there were two or three persons [i.e. Pandes] about the Heir-apparent misleading him; and that until he got rid of them nothing would go right', Lawrence replied

that it was wrong and injudicious to talk of getting rid of people; that there would always be tell-tales, and that he had plenty of experience

---

*When Lawrence was appointed Resident, 'there were "many fears and misgivings that he might not be allowed to take his wife to a country where no white-faced woman had ever been seen"; for as in China, so in Nepal, there was a tradition that "the introduction of a foreign woman would be the downfall of their empire"'.[34] In fact Honoria Lawrence was permitted to accompany Henry to Kathmandu. Hodgson, though he kept a Muslim mistress when he was in Kathmandu, did not marry until long after he left Nepal. So the question had not arisen during his tenure.

that once blood was shed, there was no end to it. The Resident said that on his arrival he had counselled oblivion of the past, and mutual good will, and that he still advised the same line of conduct.[37]

Yet two months later, in October 1844, when the effect of the leniency he had recommended became apparent, Lawrence recorded it with lofty, and rather chilling, indifference:

> At one time during the past month Matabur Singh seemed to have acquired a complete ascendancy in Durbar; but *having failed in effecting the execution of the Pandeys*, he appeared to have lost ground, and they would now probably escape from being punished.[38] [my italics]

In his pursuit of the 'perfect non-interference, but consistently high tone, [which] was in the Resident's opinion the true policy of the British Government', Lawrence seems to have been blind to the inherent contradiction. But Lawrence represented the new generation of Indian officials, muscular Christians to a man – and woman, if one includes memsahibs like Honoria – who now began to make their presence felt. While Hodgson would never have condoned Mathbar's murderous intentions towards the Pandes, he would not have removed himself to a higher moral plane and preached forbearance in a country where, to adapt von Clausewitz, murder was nothing more than a continuation of politics by other means. Where anything the Resident said was, willynilly, charged with political meaning, Lawrence's 'high tone' was inconsistent with a policy of 'perfect non-interference'.

If Mathbar had ignored Lawrence's preaching and made a clean sweep of his political opponents just as Bhim Sen had done before him and Jang Bahadur would do very soon after, then his chances not merely of survival but of instituting a radical – if, in the manner of the time, autocratic – government reflecting his own virtues (which many, including Lawrence, rated highly) would have been much greater.

In March 1845 he complained to Lawrence that Gagan Singh, the queen's favourite, with whom Mathbar had been in alliance, was attempting to divert the succession from the legitimate heir Surendra to the queen-regent's eldest son and might have to be destroyed. Lawrence's reaction was predictable: 'The Resident always took occasion, when opportunity offered, to speak plainly, and express the disgust felt by the British Government at political and party executions.'[39]

In May he received a message that the maharajah and his son were quarrelling (nothing unusual about that, of course) and that Mathbar was in trouble; the minister had been particularly anxious that the Resident should be informed. Lawrence merely sent his salaams by way of reply 'according to custom'. That night Mathbar was murdered. It may not be too fanciful to suggest that Lawrence's uncharacteristic outburst in the Residency Diary on 18 May was directed as much against himself as against Mathbar's assassins:

> In the Durbar, Matabur Singh was as a lion among a pack of curs; every man humbled [himself] before him; they all barked enough now that he was dead. The Minister was a very dangerous man, but he had very good points, much energy, and considerable ability. It would be difficult to find such another man in Nipal . . . Nipal has lost her right arm.[40]

To begin with at least, it was not clear which of the curs had killed this lion. When the king claimed responsibility, his son was alleged to have turned on him and said, 'You killed Matabur Singh indeed, you would not dare kill a rat'.[41] Later in the year, 'Two placards had been posted in the city warning the Heir-apparent to beware of Generals Guggun Singh and Jung Bahadur, who, at the instigation of the Rani, had assassinated Matabur Singh.'[42] Suspicion might well attach itself to Gagan Singh, who stood to gain most by Mathbar's removal, since he was now the unquestioned leader of the queen's party. Gagan's relatively lowly origins – he had been a *chobdar*, or menial in the queen's service – made him unpopular with the other chiefs; and his rumoured *amour* with Mrs Nepal aroused intense dislike and jealousy in Mr and Master Nepal.[43]

> *12 Oct* . . . [The Heir-apparent] came out on the balcony, which runs all along the front of the Durbar buildings, and called out loudly to all below, that if the slave son of a slave Chobdar (Guggun Singh) attempted to make the enrolment (panjani) of the regiments, he would take the skin off his back. On hearing these threats, Guggun Singh appealed to the Rani, who bade him not to be fearful. He had, however, since absented himself from the Durbar.[44]

Sheltering under the queen's petticoats, Gagan was an unlikely assassin, however, whatever he stood to gain by Mathbar's death. Jang Bahadur was a far more plausible killer – but of an uncle, whose favourite nephew and favoured supporter he was? Lawrence considered it improbable, 'Poor as is my opinion of his moral character, I do believe him guiltless of the act of which he is accused.'[45] The fact that Mathbar's legitimate and illegitimate sons both took refuge with Jang Bahadur immediately after the assassination strengthens the case for Jang's innocence.

But though he denied culpability at the time, Jang later freely confessed that he was indeed the one who had fired the fatal shot, adding only that he had no choice; it was by royal command, and either he or Mathbar had to die. He even displayed the murder weapon to European visitors. In 1847 the king – or ex-king as he had become – wrote to the Governor-General, 'On General Martabar Singh's misbehaving himself, I sent for Jang Bahadur, and ordered him to kill Martabar Singh, threatening him with death if he refused to obey.'[46] Not too much credence should be placed on such an admission, however, since by then Jang Bahadur himself was dictating all royal letters. But it seems unlikely Jang would have taken the blame for a murder which showed him in such a bad light unless he had actually done it. Whether he was threatened with death in the event of his refusal to carry out the royal command is another matter: he may have agreed to be the instrument of his uncle's removal simply as a means to his own advancement.

Henry Lawrence left Kathmandu in January 1846, so he did not witness the event for which Mathbar Singh's murder was merely the curtain-raiser, though Honoria Lawrence, writing to a member of the Council of India in London just after she and her husband had left Nepal, saw it coming:

Jung Bahadoor, Matabur's nephew, is . . . a general, and called commander-in-chief. He takes no very prominent part just now, and seems to spend his energies in devising new uniforms. But he is very active and intelligent, and if (perhaps it would be more correct to say, *when*) there is another slaughter in the Durbar, the struggle will probably be between Jung Bahadoor and Guggur [sic] Sing.[47]

Nine months later, Gagan Singh was murdered, if not by Jang Bahadur himself, then probably by his younger brother, Badri Narsingh, though to this day no one can be certain.[48] But whoever murdered the hapless Gagan Singh, his death triggered the pivotal event in modern Nepalese history, known as the Kot Massacre, in which – whether by accident or design – Jang Bahadur disposed of virtually all his rivals for power at one fell swoop.

With Jang Bahadur Konwar (Rana was a later embellishment), it is almost impossible to disentangle the truth from the myth. For some he is the hero of modern Nepal, the strong man who put an end to court strife in Kathmandu, reformed the legal system of Nepal and befriended the British in their hour of need; to others he is the villainous founder of a dynasty which battened on an oppressed populace for more than a hundred years. What no one doubts is that, hero or villain, Jang Bahadur was all-powerful in mid-nineteenth-century Nepal.

Like Henry V and other great leaders of men, Jang Bahadur had a wild, undisciplined youth, in which gambling and dancing girls played a prominent part. As a junior officer he deserted the army and went to Lahore to seek his fortune, perhaps, in the service of Ranjit Singh. But he soon returned to Nepal, where, instead of being punished for his wilful behaviour, he was welcomed as a returning prodigal. No doubt it helped that his father had married a Thapa and was a district governor in the Bhim Sen era.

His physical prowess became legendary – and he contributed greatly to his own myth with the stories he told to gullible Europeans. But Jang does seem to have had a way with elephants, horses – and people. He features largely in the folklore of the Tharu, the indigenous people of the Terai, once rich in wildlife, where Jang hunted on elephants for recreation.[49]

His daredevilry goaded the young Crown Prince Surendra who maliciously ordered him to perform impossible deeds. Apart from the well-jump (which Jang Bahadur himself seems to have stage-managed either by tinkering with the water level or by lining the well with bales of hay, according to which account of it you read), there was an occasion when Jang was riding across a slippery bridge high above a raging river and Surendra ordered him back, knowing that to turn round would mean almost certain death. Again, accounts vary; was Jang Bahadur's horseman-ship so superb that he was able to negotiate this impossible about-turn and reach the safety of the nearer bank; or did he leap on horseback into the torrent eighty feet below and survive by swimming downstream to an island? It hardly matters, since either way this is the stuff of legend.

Jang Bahadur was a gambler who played for high stakes; inevitably he was attracted to politics, where the stakes were highest of all, a life-and-death struggle for supreme power. Whether or not he was involved in the murder of Gagan Singh, he certainly turned it to his advantage in the Kot, the armoury and assembly hall next to the royal palace, to which during the night of 14/15 September 1846 the queen summoned all the high-ranking officials in order to discover who had done away with her paramour. Once again, there is considerable discrepancy over what happened there, but the authorized version, if it does not exactly whitewash Jang Bahadur and his brothers, has Jang faithfully carrying out the queen-regent's orders, rather than initiating a massacre at the end of which he would be the only contender for supreme civil and mil-itary office still standing upright.

At this critical juncture, Britain had only an officiating Resident in Kathmandu, Captain Ottley. At about 2 a.m. Ottley received a summons from the maharajah to discuss Gagan Singh's murder, but declined to go, pleading the lateness of the hour. The following afternoon he received a visit from Jang Bahadur, who was accompanied by two of his brothers and a cousin. The ostensible purpose of this visit was to announce that the so-called *tinon sarkar* – Lawrence's unholy trinity of Mr Nepal, Master Nepal and Mrs Nepal – had appointed him sole minister and commander-in-chief, and to warn the Resident that it would be unwise for him or his staff to 'venture abroad for the next two or three days'. Ottley formally congratulated Jang Bahadur on his appointment and started to express his regret at 'the unhappy occurrences' he under-stood to have taken place when Jang interrupted him and launched into a narrative describing how the queen had summoned everyone to a meeting and then ordered Gagan Singh's regiment to seize the min-isters she accused of plotting the murder of her favourite:

Great confusion followed, the Ministers themselves mutually recriminating one another; swords were drawn; and a son of Chountra

Futteh Jung Sah, it was stated, was the first to use his weapon in wounding a brother of General Jung Bahadoor. The fight then became general, and twenty-six or twenty-seven, mostly principal, chiefs, fell in the mêlée, including Chountra Futteh Jung Sah, General Abhiman Sing Rana, Kajee Dubbunjin Pandy, all three members of the late Ministry, and several of the Chountra's relations. After this occurrence the Maharajah [who had not been present at the massacre] retired in great grief to Pattun [sic], but subsequently returned to Katmandhoo, which was still occupied by the troops.[50]

Ottley reported that the facts as recounted by Jang Bahadur tallied with what he had already heard from other sources, but added: 'it should be borne in mind, that the speaker was a personal and principal actor in the scenes themselves, and evidently no friend of the Chountras, who, with the other members of the late Ministry, and their families, have been the principal sufferers'.[51]

Six months later, the new Resident, Major Thoresby, sent the Governor-General a full and detailed account of what had occurred on the night of 14 September 1846, which makes it perfectly plain that Jang, with well-armed brothers and three regiments at his beck and call, had come to the Kot prepared for all eventualities. Reading between the lines, it is also clear that Jang, or his men, fired the first shot and from then on controlled events, ensuring that none of his major rivals for power survived the night. Since the account emanated from the new minister, however, its aim was to pin the responsibility for what had taken place on to the queen.[52] This prepared the way for his crucial manoeuvre in the ultimate power struggle – with the triumvirate or *tinon sarkar* itself.

So far Jang had been seen as a queen's man. The course he now followed resembled that of his uncle Mathbar Singh, who had also started as a queen's supporter but had changed tack when the queen, backed by Gagan Singh and Abhiman Singh Rana, had pressed for the succession to go to her own eldest son in place of the heir-apparent or his brother Upendra. The switch to supporting Surendra had cost Mathbar his life, just as too obvious a devotion to the queen had cost Gagan Singh his. Too close an alignment with any one of the *tinon sarkar* exposed a minister to the jealousy and probable revenge of the other two, who were capable of acting in concert only in this situation. Jang Bahadur's appreciation of this governed his subsequent actions.

In the immediate aftermath of the Kot massacre, Jang Bahadur – on the queen's orders – confined the crown prince and his brother to their palace at Basantapur. But instead of putting them to death, as he claimed she repeatedly urged him to do, he guarded them closely and visited them daily. This alerted the queen to his defection and a further plot was hatched – to kill Jang. Only he got wind of it and forestalled it by shooting yet another potential rival, Birdhoj Basnyat, and several of Birdhoj's family and other 'conspirators' before going to Basantapur and giving the crown prince and the king (who happened to be visiting the princes) an ultimatum: either they dismissed him immediately, or they invested him 'with full authority to put to death all the enemies of the Crown Prince'.[53] The duo granted him the powers he demanded, and Jang went straight to the queen – this time invoking the crown prince as his authority – to invite her to remove herself into exile or face the consequences of the crown prince's enmity.

The queen had no option but to go. Her only solace was that she managed to persuade the king to accompany her. They headed along the well-worn route to Benares, where they plotted together to overthrow Jang. On 12 May 1847, two ex-soldiers were arrested, carrying a *lal mohar* (royal decree) from the king, authorizing the assassination of Jang Bahadur, which the intended victim promptly read out to the army, inviting them to obey the royal command. The assembled troops wisely resisted any such temptation, vociferously reaffirming their loyalty to the commander-in-chief. Jang used the occasion to depose the king and promote the prince to his long-desired but now barren eminence. The *tinon sarkar* was smashed, Surendra was maharajah, but in name only; in reality he was Jang Bahadur's puppet and all power was vested in the hands of the minister, including the power to conduct the *pajani*, the annual hiring and firing of all civil and military functionaries – which meant of course that he himself could never be removed from office.

The point was re-emphasized when the ex-king, goaded by the ex-queen, launched an invasion to reclaim his throne; Rajendra's small force was defeated and he himself was captured and taken to Kathmandu, where he spent the remainder of his life 'in comfortable confinement'.[54]

*

So assured was Jang Bahadur's ascendancy that he could plan, before the decade was over, a visit to Britain and Europe which would keep him away from Kathmandu for a whole year. In an age of aircraft and easy travel it requires an effort of imagination to recreate the conditions of 150 years ago when travel was not only hazardous and time-consuming, but for a Hindu at least hedged around with prohibitions. To this day, after crossing the *kala pani* (black water, or ocean), an orthodox Hindu is required to undergo a purification ritual; and in Jang's time even to contemplate such a journey was revolutionary. Very few Indians had done it, and no ruling princes.

Yet, just as his model of government with himself as all-powerful minister and the king as impotent but semi-divine figurehead followed Bhim Sen's pioneering practice, so his desire to go to England echoed an earlier attempt by Mathbar Singh, in the latter days of Bhim Sen's ministry and with Bhim's blessing, to arrange such a visit. At that time Hodgson, who rightly saw it as a ruse to bypass both himself and the Governor-General by going straight to the fount of British power in London, used his influence to have the proposed overseas journey downgraded to a ceremonial visit to the Governor-General in Calcutta – which was one of several reasons why Mathbar Singh remained suspicious of him when Hodgson was, in a political sense, wooing him. This time neither the Resident nor Lord Dalhousie (Governor-General from 1847 to 1856), had any objection to Jang Bahadur's proposed visit, the ostensible purpose of which, apart from conveying the compliments of one monarch to another, was 'to see and bring back intelligence respecting the greatness and prosperity of Britain and its capital, the perfection to which social conditions have been raised and the extent to which Art and Science have been made available to the comforts of life'.[55]

The underlying motive, however, was that which had caused Bhim Sen to promote Mathbar Singh's abortive embassy: a desire to have a higher court of appeal than the Resident, whose presence in Kathmandu was a continual irritant to the Nepalese rulers. There were specific questions, both civil and military, that Jang Bahadur wished to raise in London, but above and beyond these was what we would now call a matter of image, his own and his country's. In brief, he wished to raise both in the eyes of the British, and his own, at least, in the eyes of his fellow countrymen. It was as well, perhaps, that as a Hindu he was precluded from taking food or water from his European hosts, because in supping with the British he would require a very long spoon indeed if he was to avoid the fate to which he had consigned his own maharajah: to be worshipped as a god, but treated as a puppet. But Jang had formulated a policy towards British India from which he never deviated, consisting of 'the greatest distrust of the foreigners inside Nepal and the friendliest attitude towards them outside Nepal'.[56]

Jang took a large entourage with him to England in 1850, including his two youngest brothers. The British sent as his interpreter-cum-minder Captain (later General Sir) Orfeur Cavenagh, whom Jang himself had asked for when he learned that Henry Lawrence could not be spared from his duties in Peshawar. In Calcutta, Jang was taken to visit the arsenal at Fort William, which prompted him to remark

> that it was impossible to oppose the British, as they had now succeeded in making fire and water subservient to their will; whilst, alluding to the Chinese he said, that although, in many respects, equal in power and wisdom to the English, yet they must ever remain inferior to them as, owing to their excessive pride, they despised foreigners to such an extent, that they would disdain to learn from them any of the improvements in the arts and sciences now being almost daily discovered . . . whilst . . . the English gladly acquired knowledge wherever it was procurable.[57]

In London Jang Bahadur was lionized. Everywhere he went, he and his entourage created a sensation and the newspapers avidly reported his every move, embellishing the stories of the barbarism of his country and the spectacular nature of his own rise to power. He was a novelty, this gorgeously attired Nepalese minister who shook the hands of Queen Victoria and the Duke of Wellington and thought the prime minister, Lord John Russell, looked a little shabby for the part. Examples of the wit and wisdom of this Noble Savage were greeted with rapturous applause wherever he went, so that as an exercise in public relations the visit was a great success. Both sides were happy with the impression they made, because the British, for their part, made sure Jang was shown enough of the industrial might and military muscle of the country to come away with a healthy respect for its power. After an excursion to the naval dockyard at Plymouth, for instance, Cavenagh reported:

> This visit certainly had a wonderful effect, for, immediately on his
> return, without my having in any way broached the subject, he
> observed that a cat would fly at an elephant if it were forced into a
> corner, but that it must be a very small corner into which the Nepalese
> would be forced before they would fly at the British, or cease to be
> their faithful allies.[58]

According to what Jang Bahadur himself said more than once, the
British owed his support during the 1857 Mutiny to his visit to England
in 1850, which had convinced him that the foundation of British power
was rock-solid.

But behind the glittering façade, the lavish receptions and visits to
the opera as well as to dockyards and munitions factories, Jang's hopes
of short-circuiting the system of Resident and British Indian bureau-
cracy and corresponding directly with the home government received
no encouragement, just as Cavenagh had predicted:

> This latter point, I said, I felt convinced would never be yielded, upon
> which he stated that in that case it would not be pressed, although he
> thought that it was requisite that some check should be placed upon
> the political officers at Katmandhoo, as they sometimes acted in a very
> arbitrary manner. Possibly the truth is that at times he finds the
> restraint that they are able to place upon his proceedings somewhat
> irksome, as well as galling to his pride.[59]

Jang Bahadur returned to India via France, where he met Louis
Napoleon and was once again an object of considerable curiosity. En
route home to Nepal, he acquired another wife, the pretty daughter of
the rajah of Coorg, who became his favourite and whose musical accom-
plishments he was later proud to show off to the European women of
the Residency.[60] In his newfound intimacy with Europeans, he also
encouraged some British officers he met during his return journey to go
with him to Nepal, among them Laurence Oliphant, who afterwards
wrote an account of his journey to Kathmandu.

Oliphant described Jang as 'the most European Oriental, if I may so speak, that I ever met with, and more thoroughly unaffected and unreserved in his communication with us than is the habit with eastern great men, who always seem afraid of compromising themselves by too much condescension'. His story of how Jang got rid of a visiting Indian rajah with exaggerated expressions of regret that he was unable to return his visit illustrates the minister's capacity to flatter Europeans by mimicking their behaviour:

> Thus saying, he politely rose and led the rajah in the most graceful manner to the front door, which was no sooner closed behind him than he returned, rubbing his hands with great glee, as he knowingly remarked, 'That is the way to get over an interview with one of these natives'.[61]

The phrase 'one of these natives' is misleading; it has been pointed out that the word Jang probably used was *deshi*, which may be translated as native, but was generally used by Nepalis to refer to people of the Indian plains, no doubt with a measure of highland contempt, but without the imperialist sneer.[62] Even so, there are hints here and elsewhere in Oliphant's and other accounts that Jang Bahadur's European visit had turned his head. His 'despotic tone', which Oliphant noted, may have predated his journey, but the 'independent manners' that he affected on his return to Nepal provoked mutterings in the *durbar*:

> 'He has become a Feringhee [foreigner].' – 'He wants to introduce their barbarous customs amongst us.' – 'He brings visitors, and is making friends with the English, in order to betray us to them.' This is said by his enemies at court; and, while they watch his every action, esteem him a traitor, who, if they did not know it, is the best friend of their country.[63]

Another European visitor, the Honourable Captain Egerton of the Royal Navy, who had arrived in Kathmandu before Jang returned, remarked on the number of his enemies 'who don't particularly want him back again'. There was a priest who, despite Jang's having undergone purification rites at Benares, maintained that he was still contaminated by his European journey. Egerton comments: 'I suspect the reverend gentleman had better mind what he is about. Jung is not a man to let anybody get to windward of him very easily.'[64]

During his year's sabbatical Jang had left affairs of state in the hands of his brother Bam Bahadur. Soon after he returned in February 1851, Bam Bahadur tearfully revealed details of a plot to assassinate Jang, in which the prime movers were a cousin, Jai Bahadur Konwar, and Jang's brother Badri Narsingh. The king's younger brother, Upendra, was also involved. The plan was to remove not only Jang Bahadur but Surendra as well: Upendra would become king, Bam Bahadur continue as minister and Badri Narsingh as commander-in-chief. On 28 February, the Residency doctor, Henry Oldfield, wrote to his mother from just across the Indian border at Segauli:

> During the last fortnight, and since I left Nepal, [things] have been a little enlivened by the excitement occasioned by the discovery of an extensive plot to assassinate Jung Bahadoor; in consequence of their jealousy at his supposed partiality for the English, and his alleged violation of caste etc. in England, by drinking wine, eating meat, and flirting extensively with English ladies. Fortunately he discovered it in time . . . They must get up very early in the morning indeed to steal a march on Jung; he is so watchful and energetic. You may imagine what sanguinary villains these fellows are when I tell you that the two principal conspirators were *his own brother* (by the same father and mother) and *his first cousin*. The former was to have cut off Jung's head *with his own hands* and then have presented it to the assembled sirdars [government officials] as that of an outcast and traitor. The reigning king's own brother was another ringleader.[65]

Confronted by such disloyalty within the bosom of his own family, the perpetrator of the Kot massacre might have been expected to react ferociously and cut down the offenders without trial. But, according to Laurence Oliphant,

> the minister has learned mercy in England, and, to the astonishment of every one, Budreenath Sing [sic] and his fellow conspirators are only banished for life. It is said that the minister resisted all the representations of his friends as to the propriety of executing the

conspirators by the argument of 'what would the "Times" say?' –
which must have appeared to the majority of the members of the
Nepaul Durbar to be a very extraordinary reason for leniency.[66]

Badri Narsingh and his fellow conspirators were marched off into
British custody at Allahabad, for a term of thirty years. The sentence
was subsequently reduced to five years and, when the cousin died in
prison after just two and a half years, the others were promptly released.
Was Jang Bahadur really so sensitive to what *The Times* might say, or
were there other factors at work in his handling of this conspiracy – if
such it was? More than one modern commentator has argued that Jang
fabricated the plot in order to rid himself of his younger brother Badri
Narsingh, whose popularity with the army and declared opposition to
any concessions to the British he saw as a threat to his own omnipo-
tence; and if he could implicate the royal family at the same time, so
much the better.[67] By destroying the opposition before it could gather
momentum, Jang made sure it never did; and by 'exercising clemency'
he acquired a reputation for statesmanship with the British.

This is not to say that Jang Bahadur's liberal sentiments were a total
sham. In France he had expressed a desire to study the Code Napoléon
and on his return to Kathmandu he had initiated a comprehensive
review of the country's legal system, or *Muluki Ain*. Captain Cavenagh
was impressed by Jang's 'minute supervision . . . over all the other
departments of the State':

> From every quarter in which I made enquiries, I have received
> favorable accounts of Jung Bahadoor's administration. Formerly the
> people were treated almost like serfs by the oligarchy . . . now, on the
> contrary, the lowest peasant is not debarred from demanding justice,
> whatever may be the rank of the party against whom his complaint is
> urged, and consequently putting aside the feelings of a few of the
> Sirdars whose power he has curbed or whose ambition he has checked,
> the Minister is decidedly a popular Ruler.[68]

Nothing illustrates better the double standard Jang Bahadur adopted as
a policy towards Britain – maximum help outside Nepal and maximum
hindrance within the country – than his attitude to military matters. On

the one hand, he repeatedly offered to send regiments to fight alongside the British, whether against the Sikhs in the 1840s or against the rebels in the Indian Mutiny (or Sepoy Revolt) of 1857. Most of these overtures were politely turned down, partly because the British did not want the idea to get around that they could not fight their wars without outside help, and partly because they suspected Jang Bahadur's motives. Oldfield writes of Jang's offer of eight regiments under his personal command during the second war in the Punjab:

> In making this offer it is impossible to suppose that the Minister was influenced by any sincere or active desire to see the British power increased in the north-west. He probably thought it a good opportunity to bring his name personally before the British Government under favourable circumstances, and that, in making an offer which he must have known would be refused, he should get the credit with the British Government of at least friendly intentions.[69]

But though they might quibble over his motives, the British would have reason to be grateful to Jang Bahadur for his support in their hour of need in 1857.

On the other hand, throughout his thirty-year rule, he did his utmost to obstruct, if not entirely prevent, recruiting within Nepal for British Gurkha units. From Bhim Sen's time on, British officers had complained of the near-impossibility of obtaining genuine Gurkha recruits. When the Honourable W. G. Osborne, who was Military Secretary in Lord Auckland's administration, visited Ranjit Singh in May 1838, he asked the Sikh rajah how he managed to obtain recruits for his Gorkha regiments, 'as we had found the greatest difficulty in keeping our own two [sic] regiments complete, from the jealousy of the Nepaulese'. Ranjit replied that he found it difficult, too, but by paying them over the odds he kept them up to strength. 'The truth I afterwards ascertained to be, that not above one man in twenty is a real Goorkha, but they come principally from Cachemire [Kashmir]; and as they are small and active men, they answer very well for the purpose of hill warfare.'[70]

Even before Jang Bahadur came to power, the British frontier posts at Pithoragarh, Almora and Gorakhpur had the double function of keeping an eye on hostile moves on the part of the Nepalese and of launching recruiting drives into the Magar-Gurung heartlands of the western hills. But the penetration of these hills by British agents was fiercely resisted by the Nepal *durbar*, and the *gallawallas*, as recruiters came to be known, had to resort to ever more clandestine methods in mustering their batches of recruits; they could move them only at night and risked execution if they were caught.[71] So Jang Bahadur was not so much initiating a hostile policy as endorsing the traditional resistance to British incursion in any shape or form, regarding it 'as part of their devious design to denude his country of its fighting population, with a view to weakening it militarily'.[72]

In 1850, when the British Gurkha units were being upgraded from local hill battalions to line regiments, Lord Dalhousie used the occasion of Jang's visit to England to seek his help and co-operation. Jang politely consented to do all in his power to help, but had no intention of doing more than go through the motions. A recruiting party was sent to Kathmandu in November 1850 during his absence, and Bam Bahadur put on a charade for its benefit, producing thousands of potential recruits who were then whittled down, under one pretext or another, to fifty-two, twenty of whom absconded. A month later, more than 600 men turned up at the Residency, saying that they had been instructed to come but did not want to leave Nepal. In the Resident's view, the men 'were recently discharged Gorkha soldiers, who had been detained and tutored to play their part'.[73]

If the British laboured under any misapprehension that the obstructions to their recruiting plans were due to Jang Bahadur's absence, they were soon disillusioned. His return made no difference, and in 1854 he made it clear that he would not allow 'a single Gorkha sipahee [sepoy is a corruption of *sipahi*, meaning soldier] in the British service to enter Nepal until he had first taken discharge unless he might come on duty either to purchase weapons for his corps or on recruiting service'.[74] This amounted to denying British Gurkhas access to their homes, a harsh measure for which Jang gave three reasons: that a number of criminals had entered British service as a way of escaping justice and this was bad for relations between the two countries; that he was not permitted to recruit Europeans under the terms of the Treaty of Segauli, so why should the British be allowed to recruit Gurkhas; and that the attractions of British conditions of service would, if not checked by disincentives, denude the country of its soldiers.

The Resident, Major George Ramsay, had an answer to each of these objections: if there were criminals in British units, they were not exempt from punishment for crimes committed in Nepal, but that should not prevent men of proven good character from returning freely to their homes; Jang Bahadur had never raised the question of recruiting Europeans (in fact, one of his reasons for wanting to go to Europe had been to recruit European civil and military engineers); and the number of recruits required by Britain was not so great as to endanger the supply of Nepal's own forces.

But the underlying reason remained unspoken: that Jang Bahadur was at one with the Nepalese *durbar* in regarding Gorkhas in foreign service as an affront to the dignity of an independent state; he may also have feared that in sufficient numbers they might constitute a threat to his own autocratic regime. The Resident concluded, 'My impression is that we must expect fewer liberal measures from General Jung Bahadur, than from any of his predecessors, despite the intentions he proclaims when he is travelling in our provinces.'[75]

Jang Bahadur did relent to the extent of allowing British Gurkhas back into the country under strict conditions, such as that they did not wear uniform but dressed and behaved as Nepalese subjects in Nepal, that they had a passport from the Resident and that they avoided the main thoroughfare across the border from Segauli, as well as Kathmandu itself and all military encampments. (He strongly suspected that these Gurkhas supplied the British with military information he wished to keep from them.) For the time being Britain had to content itself with this 'not very graceful concession'.[76]

While British military interest at this stage focused exclusively on the Magars and Gurungs of west-central Nepal, in 1847 Jang Bahadur had widened his own army's recruitment to include the Kirats, or Kirantis (Limbus and Rais), of the eastern hills. Captain Cavenagh – 'as a soldier' – wanted to learn all he could about the army of Nepal, not least because it was by no means out of the question that there might be another 'collision' between the forces of the two neighbouring countries, though not (in his view) so long as Jang Bahadur remained in power. His *Rough Notes* include these comments on its organization:

With the exception of the Newar tribe, who are considered deficient in courage [a slur upon a people lacking not in courage but in a military tradition], men of all castes are admitted into the Nepal Army and hitherto associated in the same Regiments without reference to religious prejudices; but General Jung Bahadur, having apparently studied the doctrines laid down by European Politicians on the subject of the balance of power, has recently introduced the system of forming distinct corps of Rajputs, Muggurs, Gurungs and K[i]rats, thus, as any class feeling or jealousy which may exist among these different tribes, although perhaps not fostered, is certainly not discouraged by the Government . . . a greater spirit of emulation and *esprit de corps* is thereby engendered amongst the soldiers.[77]

In 1816, Edward Gardner had estimated the strength of the Nepalese army at 10,000 but by 1854, when Jang Bahadur fought a small war with Tibet (Nepal's solitary act of external aggression after 1814–16), it had risen to 27,114; and because of the number of *dhakres* (trained but currently off-the-roll soldiers) at any one time the total number of available troops might be doubled or trebled.[78] But since the heyday of conquest, culminating in the Anglo-Gorkha war, slackness had set in and the standard of training and leadership was not what it had been in Kaji Amar Singh Thapa's time.[79] Cavenagh reckoned that, in the event of another war, 'instead of carrying on a Guerilla warfare, the system best adapted both to their habits and to the nature of their country, they could attempt to operate in masses, and consequently by becoming out-manoeuvred lose all advantage, which, from their courage and activity, they now have over our Native Troops'.[80]* From a tactical point of view he thought their officers were greatly inferior to those of the Sikh army – unsurprisingly, given that every Rana male child was given commissioned rank, not according to ability or even potential, but simply as a birthright. Some were born generals, others mere colonels, according to where their family stood in the Rana hierarchy.

---

*Some historians have argued that the Gorkhas lost the 1815 campaign precisely because they did not adopt guerrilla tactics. If they had, they might have neutralized the British artillery which could pummel them into submission only so long as they remained fortress-bound.

At the end of July 1856, Jang Bahadur suddenly resigned from the posts of minister and commander-in-chief of the army in favour of his brother Bam Bahadur. His motives were not immediately apparent. But a week later, when the king appointed him (i.e., he appointed himself) maharajah of Kaski and Lamjung with extensive powers not confined to those two provinces, it became clear that Jang was not so much relinquishing power as making a bid for even greater authority. He had already established the principle of succession for the ministership, in parallel with that of the king – or maharajadhiraj, as the king was now known (the more grandiloquent the title the more nugatory his function) – except that it was to go from brother to brother rather than father to son. This was to obviate the danger of a son inheriting at so tender an age that he was vulnerable to usurpation, a situation which had plagued the monarchy since Prithwi Narayan's time. But it also meant that there was a limit to Jang's personal power, which he was trying to offset by assuming the maharajahdom of Kaski and Lamjung (which also happened to be the heartland of the Magar-Gurung elements of the army). He clearly intended this title to be hereditary in the traditional father–son manner. Thus, while Bam Bahadur or another of his brothers might assume the mantle of minister, Jang's eldest son would inherit the title of maharajah. (In practice such a division within the Rana hierarchy proved unworkable, and the title simply went with the premiership.)

Jang's dilemma was that once he had laid aside the office of minister the Resident refused to do business with him. Despite the fact that they regarded Jang as an ally, the British were such sticklers for protocol that they would have dealings only with the maharajadhiraj and his chosen representative; it made no difference that the real power in Nepal remained with Jang Bahadur. So when Bam Bahadur conveniently died in 1857, Jang did not hesitate to reinstate himself as minister, to the relief of both sides.

The other way in which Jang sought to enhance the status of his immediate family and at the same time ensure continuity of power was by a series of arranged marriages between his children and those of the king – a practice which persisted throughout the Rana period. (You have only to look at the portraits of the kings of Nepal in sequence to see how they become increasingly Rana-like in appearance.) On 25 June 1857, for instance, Margaret Oldfield and the other two Residency

wives were invited to attend the celebration of the wedding of the
king's eldest son, aged nine, to Jang's eldest unmarried daughter, aged
six. Margaret wrote to her mother-in-law:

> . . . Jung then took us up one by one to the King and his father and
> presented us to them. The King is completely under Jung's thumb and
> is a weak imbecile-looking man though quite young. The old King
> looked quite *daft*, and was dressed in a long white petticoat which gave
> him very much the appearance of an old nurse. Jung *made* them each
> shake hands with us, which they didn't much like, at all events it is the
> first time in their life they have had to shake hands with English
> ladies![81]

Mrs Oldfield went on to say how much she liked Jang, what a complete
gentleman he was, how natural in his behaviour, no forced politeness
about him. His English might be limited to such phrases as, 'Come
here', 'Shake hands', 'Sit down' and other commands; but then her
Hindustani was confined to 'giving a few orders to the servants'.[82]
Unlike the dippy and doddering royalty who tried to avoid shaking
hands (contact with a foreigner defiled a high-caste Hindu), Jang had
style and presence.

His secret ambition, which he confided to the Governor-General
since 1856, Lord Canning, in the euphoria following the recapture of
Lucknow from the sepoy rebels (when Jang Bahadur had thrown his
weight on the side of the British), was to replace these dim-wits –
whether or not they were reincarnations of Vishnu – with himself on the
throne of Nepal.[83] But however grateful the British were to Jang, they
were not prepared to countenance his usurpation of the throne. Reward
him they must, and so they did: in accordance with the advice of the
former Resident, Brian Hodgson, they returned to Nepal the western
Terai they had appropriated after the 1814–16 war.[84] Soldiers were
handsomely remunerated and he himself was knighted. But that was
not enough to satisfy Jang's soaring ambition, and for ever after he held
a grudge against the British for their refusal to facilitate his apotheosis.

The immediate effect of the outbreak of mutiny across the border in
May 1857 was to stir up excitement in Nepal. The army was eager to go

into action, to raid the plains for plunder and gain. The latent anti-British feelings of many of the nobles and army officers came to the surface; here was their long-awaited opportunity to revenge themselves for the humiliation of 1816. If the Bengal sepoys could rise up to such good effect, how much more effective would the Gorkhas be, with their conviction of their own military superiority. Jang Bahadur was under great pressure, not least from his own brothers, to throw in his lot with the rebels, though more cautious nobles advised neutrality, a wait-and-see-which-way-the-wind-may-blow policy.

Characteristically, Jang Bahadur ignored the hotheads and the sober counsellors alike. To the anti-British party, he said, 'we may enrich ourselves for the time being. We may prosper for two or three years, but our time will infallibly come, and we shall then lose our country.'[85] But he knew it would be equally dangerous to deny the army the action it craved. His solution was to offer his troops to the British.

Major Ramsay's provisional acceptance of this offer landed him in trouble with the Governor-General. Canning distrusted the *durbar* and felt that the arrival in Gorakhpur of hordes of Nepali soldiers, far from frightening the rebels, might make them think the Gorkhas were joining them. Hodgson, from his retirement in the hill station of Darjeeling, urged Lord Canning to accept Jang Bahadur's offer, but Government House remained sceptical. Lady Canning told Mrs Hodgson (Anne Scott, whom Hodgson had married in 1853), 'You praise these Gurkhas like your husband, but I can assure you that they are looked on here as being little better than the rebels.'[86] But as the situation deteriorated and forces loyal to the British became hopelessly stretched, the Governor-General changed his mind and instructed Ramsay to accept Jang's offer. In the first place, 3,000 Nepali troops were sent over the border, where they were joined by British officers and performed very creditably in clearing the Gorakhpur area of rebels. A further 9,000 under Jang Bahadur's personal command followed at the end of 1857.

Before leaving Kathmandu Jang told the Resident:

I have three motives for acting as I am now doing.

First, to show that Gorkhas possess fidelity and will shed their blood in defence of those who treat them with honour and repose confidence in them.

Second, that I know the power of the British Government and were I to take part against it, although I might have temporary success for a time, my country would afterwards be ruined and the Gorkha dynasty annihilated.

Third, that I know that upon the success of British arms and the re-establishment of British power in India, its Government will be stronger than ever, and that I and my brothers and my country will all then benefit from our alliance with you, as your remembrance of our past services will render our present friendship lasting, and will prevent your ever molesting us.[87]

This was fine talk but, as one historian has pointed out, 'the Durbar's objections to the use of the Nepali army in India might well have been more vehement if its operations had not been directed against the pre-dominantly Muslim rebel movement in Oudh'.[88]

In contrast to the three regiments he sent out first, Jang Bahadur's own large force destined for Lucknow fought no major battle and moved with unconscionable slowness.[89] *The Times* correspondent, William Howard Russell, who accompanied General Sir Colin Campbell's force for the relief of Lucknow, recorded in his diary on 23 February 1858 the general's extreme irritation with 'that terrible imped-imentum, Jung Bahadoor', for whom he was obliged to wait before he could join battle with the rebels:

Lord Canning strongly urges on Sir Colin not to move without the Goorkhas. He points out that Jung Bahadoor is dying for military distinction, and that if we were to operate against Lucknow before he came up, we might give him offence and drive him back to his mountains in a huff. Is the power of the man, of his State, or the aid of his troops so great, that we should hold our hands for fear of offending him? I see that Sir Colin, who is accused of dilatoriness, is really annoyed at all these impediments.[90]

When Jang Bahadur eventually arrived on 11 March, he insisted on a royal salute not just for himself but for his brothers as well. This further aggra-vated Sir Colin who, having given up waiting and begun the assault, was now distracted from his task by 'a good deal of bowing and salaaming, as the Maharajah introduced his brothers and great officers to the Chief'.

> . . . the English and the Nepaulese were examining each other. Stout
> Calmuck-faced, high-shouldered, bow-legged men these latter, very
> richly attired in a kind of compromise between European and Asiatic
> uniform. As to Jung himself, he blazed like a peacock's tail in the
> sun . . . But brighter than any gem the Maharajah wore is his eye,
> which shines with a cold light, resembling a ball of phosphorus. What a
> tiger-like, cruel, crafty, subtle eye! How it glanced, and glittered, and
> rolled, piercing the recesses of the tent. 'I believe,' quoth one near me,
> 'he is the d——dest villain hung or unhung.'[91]

Five days later Jang was in action on the left of the British force and
sent word that he had been attacked but had beaten off and followed up
the enemy, capturing ten guns. 'That means,' Russell reported the Chief
as saying, 'that he found ten guns the enemy had left there. But I am
glad he has done so well.'[92] On 23 March, Russell, who had turned down
the opportunity to shake the hand of 'a man who has committed cold-
blooded murder', had to modify his hostility towards Jang somewhat:

> McNeill . . . who commands a brigade of Goorkhas, dined with me to-
> day. He says Jung Bahadoor is really a very clever man, active in mind
> and body, 'bloody, resolute, and cruel,' but as brave as steel. His
> officers, many of whom are related to him, are by no means so
> indifferent to danger or prodigal of blood, and they have no influence
> over their men, who will only follow courageous leaders . . . [93]

The looting of Lucknow which followed the defeat of the rebels was
on a grand scale. Russell was appalled by the wanton destruction and
lust for gold he saw on all sides. The phrase 'drunk with plunder'
acquired a new meaning for him. Soldiers staggered out of houses laden
with 'shawls, rich tapestry, gold and silver brocade, caskets of jewels,
arms, splendid dresses'; and beautiful china, glass and jade were all
'dashed to pieces'.[94] The undisciplined behaviour was by no means
confined to the Nepalese troops, but if they did not do much fighting
they certainly took their share of plunder – and created a resentment
that smoulders to this day.

There can be no doubt [the Resident, George Ramsay, reported] that the presence of the Gorkha army in the British provinces under Maharaja Jung Bahadur's command had a fine moral effect, but their services were in a military point of view not what had been expected of them. The Maharaja, who is very weak and very vain, would not allow the slightest semblance of interference or check over his men, who puffed up with braggadocio and conceit covered themselves with ridicule. But had a better system of discipline been observed, and had their officers set them a better example than they did, they would doubtless have behaved with the gallantry which is proverbially characteristic of their race. The march back to the frontier from Lucknow loaded with plunder was more like a rabble than an armed force, and the British officials who were attached to them were heartily glad when they arrived at Sagauli.[95]

Jang Bahadur was certainly vain, but 'very weak'? In the interregnum when Jang had resigned the premiership in favour of his brother Bam and the Resident had refused to deal with him, Jang had taken against Ramsay and attempted to have him removed from office. He had been unsuccessful (indeed Ramsay had been promoted to colonel), but perhaps his denunciation of the Resident in 'a paper containing a series of frivolous complaints' rankled with Ramsay.[96]

According to Margaret Oldfield, her husband Harry effected a reconciliation between the two of them when both were back in Kathmandu, and Jang, 'instead of "retiring to a lonely mountain" as last summer he said he would if Col. Ramsay returned, is rather glad to have someone of *sense* at the head of affairs just now, for he has (owing to the inefficiency of the officer who has been conducting business here for the last nine months for Col. R) got rather into a mesh [mess?] about the rebels who have taken refuge in his territory, viz – "The Nana", the Begum of Lucknow and a host of followers!'.[97]

In the aftermath of the Mutiny there were two potential flashpoints in Britain's relations with Nepal: one was the maharajah's refusal to yield up the more prominent rebel leaders who had sought sanctuary in the Terai; and the other the continuing tug-of-war over recruitment of British Gurkhas. During the Sepoy Revolt, Jang Bahadur had relaxed his opposition to Gurkha recruitment to some extent and the British had taken advantage of this to increase the number of their Gurkha regiments to five. But his fundamental policy had not changed: friendship with Britain stopped at the frontier and, though it was to the advantage of both sides to have an extradition agreement for law-breakers, British penetration of Nepalese territory, whether in search of rebels or of recruits, was taboo.

As the perpetrator of the Cawnpore massacre of 27 June 1857 in which many British women and children, as well as men, were killed, Nana Sahib, aka Dhandu Pant, was the man most wanted by the British; and his presence in Nepal created a dilemma for Jang Bahadur. To hand him over was to condemn a Brahman to certain death, which offended Jang's Hindu sensibility. But to give him shelter offended the British and made them doubt the sincerity of Nepal's friendship. In the end it seemed simplest to concoct a story of the death of the Nana and his brother Bala Rao; nobody believed it and their fate remained a mystery. But in time the British lost interest in these fugitive rebels and were happy to go along with this fiction, discouraging the Resident from pursuing enquiries. Margaret Oldfield was indignant:

> Can you fancy such an indifferent apathetic Government; they ought to be ashamed of themselves! Col. Ramsay is of course very much disgusted at the instructions he has received, and though in his own mind he has not the slightest doubt that these monsters are alive . . . yet he is powerless . . . [98]

In the end the sheer number of rebels in the Terai and the disruption they caused became such an embarrassment to Jang Bahadur that he co-operated with the British in clearing them out, and honour was satisfied.

Continuing recruitment of Gurkhas for British regiments was another matter. On this Jang Bahadur was not prepared to compromise, and in 1859 he forced the British to abandon illegal recruitment drives. Recruiting agents were liable to arrest, and an order went out that 'no subject of the four classes and thirty-six castes of our country [i.e., no Nepali citizen] shall go to India for recruitment without any prior approval'.[99] The punishment for disobedience of this order was confiscation of house and land, and loss of the automatic right to put to death the lover of an offender's wife; any man who ignored this ruling himself incurred the death penalty.[100]

The squeeze on recruiting in the hills meant that more recruits from the borderlands, of dubious background and quality – outlaws among them – were enlisted. That and the often swaggering behaviour of recruiting agents, who attempted to lure volunteers by contrasting the attractions of British service, the power and wealth of the Indian government, with the paltry pay and opportunities provided by the Nepali *durbar*, exacerbated an already tense situation. In 1864 the British officially abandoned the use of recruiting teams and relied on individual contact to bring in volunteers until some formal agreement could be reached.[101] But that would not be in Jang Bahadur's – or his successor's – lifetime.

It is a measure of the control that Jang exercised over the *durbar* and the country that he was almost the only chief minister in nineteenth-century Nepal whose life did not come to a violent end. He died of cholera while on a hunting trip to the Terai in 1877 and was succeeded by his brother Ranodip Singh. There would be another bloody *coup* shortly after, when the Shamsher branch of the Rana family seized power, but the regime initiated by Jang Bahadur held firm for a hundred years.

An autocrat in an age of autocracies, Jang achieved much for his country, even if country came a poor third after family and self. He systematized the law, fought a successful war against Tibet and recovered a 300-kilometre stretch of the Terai from a grateful British Indian government. At the same time, and perhaps most importantly, he never allowed his friendship with the British to undermine his country's autonomy. As one historian remarks:

> Jang Bahadur cannot be blamed like Bir Shamsher and Chandra
> Shamsher, who practically reduced Nepal to a status of a subordinate
> state of the British. So long as Jang Bahadur lived he not only
> maintained the independence of his country, but also did not allow the
> British to recruit the Gorkhas freely.[102]

The interrelatedness of these two phenomena, Nepal's independence and the recruitment of Gurkhas into the British Indian army, was something Jang Bahadur instinctively understood; it made him refuse the Faustian pact to which his successors, in their greed and obsession with the trappings of power, finally succumbed.

3

A Martial Race

Hodgson had called the Gurkhas 'by far the best soldiers in Asia', and argued that 'if they were made participators of our renown in arms, I conceive that their gallant spirit, emphatic contempt of Madhesias (people of the plains), and unadulterated military habits, might be relied on for fidelity'.[1] They might be Hindus, at least nominally, but they were not concerned with caste restrictions in the way the Company's Brahman and Rajput sepoys were.

> These highland soldiers, who despatch their meal in half an hour, and satisfy the ceremonial law by merely washing their hands and face, and taking off their turbans before cooking, laugh at the pharisaical rigour of our *Sipáhis*, who must bathe from head to foot and make *pújá* [say their prayers], ere they begin to dress their dinner, must eat nearly naked in the coldest weather, and cannot be in marching trim again in less than three hours.[2]

From the start of their British service as irregulars policing the hills of Kumaon and Garhwal conquered from their fellow countrymen, Gurkhas created a favourable impression on all European travellers who came into contact with them. As early as 28 November 1824, Bishop Heber recorded meeting Captain Herbert, a geologist, and Sir Robert Colquhoun, commandant of the 'Kemaoon Battalion' (later 3rd Gurkhas), who 'were just returned from a scientific expedition to the eastern frontier, and gave an interesting account of the Ghorkha troops there, whom they described, *as they have been generally represented*, as among the smartest and most European-like soldiery in India' [my italics].[3]

In 1830, the Frenchman Victor Jacquemont went to Dehra Dun, where 'a certain Major Young reigns . . . under the title of assistant resident of Delhi and commandant of the hill militia' (the Sirmoor battalion), and was provided with an escort of Gurkha soldiers for the next stage of his journey. Several months later, Captain Charles Kennedy provided Jacquemont with another small Gurkha escort from the Nasiri battalion at Sabathu. Jacquemont describes Kennedy as 'the most highly paid artillery captain in the sublunary world, a king of kings even more than Agamemnon was, with no Achilles to resist him among all the little hill rajahs, his vassals'. He liked Kennedy, but the trouble with the English, he complained, was that they had no conversation, 'they sit at table for hours on end after dinner, in company with quantities of bottles which are constantly going the round'. But the Frenchman heartily wished he still had Kennedy's Gurkhas with him when he visited Kashmir the following year:

> . . . these two men, disciplined by European training, drilled my band of porters, sometimes numbering as many as sixty, as if they had been a ship's crew. One of them would have been enough. Why have I not a squad of them with me here! They would do more work and spare me more annoyance than all the rabble on foot or on horseback with which I am saddled . . . [4]

In April 1837 Henry Edward Fane, aide-de-camp to his kinsman the Commander-in-Chief, also visited Sabathu and remarked of the 'Goorcahs' stationed there that they 'are very short, yet strong and active fellows, brave to a proverb, and eminently formed for the work they have to do'.[5] And during a visit to Dehra Dun in March the following year, Emily Eden, whose brother George was the Governor-General Lord Auckland, was taken by Colonel Young 'to see his little Ghoorka regiment manoeuvre'. She wrote:

All the mountaineers are very small creatures, but they make excellent little soldiers; and the Ghoorkas beat our troops at this spot twenty-five years ago, and killed almost all the officers sent against them. Now they are our subjects [sic] they fight equally well for us, and were heard to say at Bhurtpore [Bharatpur] that they really thought some of our soldiers were nearly equal to themselves. They look like little black dolls. They are quite unlike natives.[6]

Men of both the Nasiri and Sirmoor battalions had played a prominent part in Lord Combermere's successful siege of Bharatpur in 1825–6 (after Ochterlony had been superseded as Resident at Delhi by Sir Charles Metcalfe), disproving those who thought their effectiveness was limited to mountain warfare. They had also participated in the Sikh wars of the late 1840s, where they earned the approbation of the Commander-in-Chief, Sir Hugh (later Lord) Gough, who wrote in his despatch after the battle of Sobraon:

I must pause in this narrative especially to notice the determined hardihood and bravery with which our two battalions of Goorkahs, the Sirmoor and the Nusseree, met the Sikhs wherever they were opposed to them. Soldiers of small stature but indomitable spirit, they vied in ardent courage in the charge with the Grenadiers of our own nation, and, armed with the short weapon of their mountains, were a terror to the Sikhs throughout this great combat.[7]

Gough's successor as C-in-C, the Peninsular war veteran Sir Charles Napier, was no less enthusiastic. In February 1850 the Brahmans and Rajputs of the 66th Bengal Native Infantry mutinied over the non-payment of *batta* – understandably, when it is considered that this extra allowance given to units serving outside the Company's territory ceased to be paid as soon as that territory was annexed, so that instead of being rewarded for conquering the Punjab the troops immediately had their pay reduced according to a bureaucratic logic incomprehensible to them. Nevertheless the 66th Bengal Native Infantry was disbanded and Napier had no hesitation in handing over its regimental number and colours to the Nasiri battalion (though he was censured for doing so by the incoming Governor-

General, Lord Dalhousie, who thought he had exceeded his powers).
Napier wrote:

> . . . the Ghoorkas will be faithful, and for low pay we can enlist a large
> body of soldiers whom our best officers consider equal in courage to
> European troops. Even as a matter of economy, this will be good; but the
> great advantage of enlisting these hillmen will be that, with 30,000 or
> 40,000 Ghoorkas added to 30,000 Europeans, the possession of India will
> not 'depend on opinions', but on an army able with ease to overthrow
> any combination among Hindoos or Mohammedans, or both together.[8]*

These two themes – Gurkhas as a cheaper version of Europeans, whose
equal they were in courage and fidelity; and Gurkhas as a third force in
India – would be reiterated time and again throughout the history of the
Gurkha Brigade up to 1947 and (as far as economy is concerned) well
beyond that date.

When the Nasiri battalion was upgraded from local infantry to the
regular line and became the '66th or Goorkha Regiment', a new Nasiri
battalion was raised to replace it at Sabathu; and both units, plus the
Sirmoor battalion, sent squads to the School of Musketry at Ambala at
the beginning of 1857 to be trained in the use of the new, but yet to be
issued Enfield rifles. They were placed under the command of
Lieutenant (later General) Donald Macintyre, who wrote:

> After having been encamped for some time with the Native Infantry
> squads, a request was made by the Goorkhas, through one of their own

---

*The phrase 'depend on opinions' refers to the argument over whether India was
held by opinion – i.e. by a more or less willing acquiescence in British paramountcy – or by force. Charles Metcalfe famously maintained that it had to be a
combination of the two:

> We could not keep the country by opinion if we had not a considerable force
> and no force that we could pay would be sufficient if it were not aided by the
> opinion of our invincibility. Our force does not operate so much by its actual
> strength as by the impression which it produces and that impression is the
> opinion by which we hold India.[9]

officers, to be allowed to pitch their tents with those of the British soldiers. The reason stated was that they did not like being mixed up with the '*kala log*' (black fellows), as they called the Poorbeah sepoys [*Purbiya*, meaning eastern, referred to the Brahmans and Rajputs from Oudh who made up the majority of the Bengal Native Infantry], whom they reported to be showing a very bad feeling in their conversations regarding the use of greased cartridges. At the same time they requested that the cartridges might be at once served out to them, in order to show the Poorbeahs that they had no fellow-feeling whatever with them on the cartridge question.[10]

Cartridges thought to be greased with either pork fat (unclean for Muslims) or beef fat (offensive to Hindus, to whom the cow is sacred) were, of course, the final insult which triggered the mass uprising of sepoys who already felt their religion to be under threat from the new generation of British officers, more than a few of whom were proselytizing Christians. Too late, the authorities tried to put things right by issuing ungreased cartridges to the sepoys.

During one firing practice at Ambala, bundles of ungreased cartridges were given to the Gurkhas by mistake and were at once returned by them, 'with the jocular remark "that they were intended for the *kala log*"'.[11] British officers were delighted with this response, and with the Gurkha preference for European soldiers over Native Infantry (NI). It set them apart and though the 66th were technically 'Native Infantry' they did not regard themselves as such, as young Ensign Gepp, who was to lose his life in the Sepoy Revolt, conveyed in a facetious letter to his parents in 1855:

By the by, speaking of Goorkhas, do you know that Regimentally you have been for the last three or four months most desperately insulting my dignity by two very simple letters, viz., NI affixed to the Regimental designation, and even if I have mentioned this before you must forgive the repetition and indulge my (I may say our) conceit whilst I inflict upon you a panegyric on the excellencies of 'The Goorkhas' in general, and their undoubted superiority to the rest of the Indian Army . . . In religion they are Hindus, but far less bigoted than the ordinary Hindu, as they will eat and drink anything; they get on capitally with Europeans, and associate with, but do not condescend to mix with NI's . . . I fear you will be quite tired of hearing their praises sung, but you must forgive my regimental esprit de corps.[12]

The Gurkhas were different: they were not Indian; with their smooth round faces they did not even look like Indians; like all mountain folk they were brave and, in addition, they were amenable to discipline. This was how the litany went. Why, even Sir Colin Campbell made them his 'pet corps when he commanded at Peshawar, for never did an expedition leave that place without Goorkhas accompanying it; he said he could not do without them'.[13]

Yet at the beginning of the Sepoy Revolt in 1857, by no means all the British commanders were confident of the loyalty of the Gurkhas. Doubts seemed to be confirmed when the new, and short-lived, Nasiri battalion (formed in 1851, it was disbanded ten years later) refused an order to march from Sabathu to Phillaur to escort a siege-train to Ambala. The troops complained that their pay had fallen into arrears and took matters into their own hands when 'a detachment of the same corps at Kasauli plundered the treasury, rendering it necessary to send back 100 men of the 75th Foot to reinforce the depot at that place, where a large number of European soldiers' families were collected'.[14] Europeans in the nearby hill station of Simla, already alarmed at reports of mutiny in Meerut and Delhi, evacuated the town in a panic. But the situation was soon brought under control, the regiment – except for the Kasauli contingent – granted an amnesty and almost all 7,000 rupees of government money taken from the treasury voluntarily handed back. Lord Roberts recorded that 'before the year was out the battalion did us good service'.[15]

The Sirmoor battalion, commanded by Major (later Major-General Sir) Charles Reid, had already distinguished itself by firing the first shots on the rebels and executing the first mutineers, including Brahmans (thereby breaking a Hindu taboo), following the uprising at Meerut in May 1857. But instead of the cheers with which the Gurkhas had been greeted by Brigadier-General Archdale Wilson and the (British) 60th Rifles, the Sirmoor battalion was met with silence and suspicious looks when it joined General Sir Henry Barnard's force for the siege of Delhi, where the rebels were gathered under the standard of the eighty-two-year-old emperor and king of Delhi, Bahadur Shah II, long since pensioned off by the British and now, somewhat reluctantly, thrust into the limelight. The Sirmoor battalion was directed to the extreme end of the line on the famous Delhi Ridge, where the men were surprised to find their camp already pitched for them. The reason 'they had so *kindly* pitched tents for us', Reid subsequently discovered, was to place them under the eye of the Artillery, who were close by 'ready to *pound* us if we misbehaved':

> I was not questioned myself, but several asked my officers whether they thought the Goorkahs were to be trusted; when I was told of this, I said, 'Time will show.' 'Shooting Brahmins,' I said, 'was a pretty good test.'[16]

No sooner had the Sirmoor battalion taken up residence in and around Hindu Rao's House on the right of the ridge at Delhi on 8 June 1857 than the alarm sounded and the rebels attacked in numbers. Reid's force, which included two companies of the 60th Rifles, drove them back into the city:

> This, however, was not accomplished until 5 p.m., so that we were under arms for sixteen hours. Heat fearful; my little fellows behaved splendidly, and were cheered by every European Regiment. It was the only *Native* Regiment with the force, and I may say every eye was upon it. The General was anxious to see what the *Goorkahs* could do, and if we were to be *trusted*! They had (because it was a *Native* Regiment) *doubts* about us, but I think they are satisfied.[17]

For the next three months, the Sirmoor battalion occupied Hindu Rao's House 'under the fire of the enemy's heavy bastions morning, noon and night from first to last'.[18] It was not just General Barnard but the rebels, too, tested the loyalty of the Gurkhas. They called out to them, 'Come on, Goorkahs; we won't fire upon *you* – we expect you to join us'.

> 'Oh yes,' was the reply, 'we are coming.' They closed upon their centre, and when within twenty paces they gave the mutineers a well directed volley, killing some thirty or forty of the scoundrels . . . [19]

As a result of their close proximity on the ridge at Delhi where they often felt more like the besieged than the besiegers, the 60th Rifles and the Sirmoor battalion formed an enduring friendship. (The 60th were at that time the only battalion to be fully equipped with the new Enfield rifle; the Sirmoor battalion were then armed with a short musket known as a fusil.[20]) Reid wrote admiringly, 'The 60th Rifles is truly a fine regiment, so totally different to every other. My men are very fond of them, and they get on famously.'[21] And the nineteen-year-old James Hare of the 60th Rifles wrote to his father on 24 June, saying what first-rate soldiers the Gurkhas (and the Corps of Guides, a rare combination of cavalry and infantry, which had come to reinforce them) were:

> Yesterday, a sepoy had gone into a hut and was shooting out at the door, when two little Ghoorkas set out to catch him. They sneaked up, one on either side of the door, and presently the sepoy put out his head to see if the coast was clear, when one grabbed him by the hair, and the other whacked off his head with his cookery [sic].[22]

War might be a grim business, a matter of kill or be killed (or maimed), but that was no reason to go about it grimly. Gurkhas approached it in a lighthearted manner and would extract what fun they could, no matter how serious the situation. They looked upon it as a kind of sport, or *shikar* (hunt).

By mid-July nearly half the Sirmoor battalion, 206 men, had been killed or wounded, and on 19 July Reid recorded the twenty-first attack on his position by the 'Pandies' (after Mangal Pande, the rebellious sepoy doped up on *bhang* whose violent behaviour and subsequent execution at Barrackpore had lit the fuse of mutiny). Still they kept coming and still the vastly outnumbered brothers-in-arms, the 60th Rifles – 'our Rifles' – and the Sirmoor battalion – 'them Gurkees of ours' – vied with one another in beating them off. To add to their difficulties, an outbreak of cholera had spread from the city into the British camp.

For a night and a day over the Muslim festival of 'Id, it seemed that the entire city of Delhi had turned out to drive the besiegers from Hindu Rao's House under the rheumy eye of the old emperor, Bahadur Shah. As many as 10,000 or even 20,000 mutineers attacked Reid's 910 men in successive waves before they were finally forced to retreat. On his way back to Hindu Rao's House, an exhausted Reid came upon a young Gurkha line-boy (i.e. a soldier's son born in the regimental lines), squatting behind a rock with a rifle in his hand. This boy had disobeyed orders by following his father into the field and helping him load his musket until the man had been shot and killed; then he had helped one of the 60th's riflemen until he too had been wounded and had sent the boy (to whom he gave his rifle) to get a 'doolie' to take him to hospital; after that the boy joined in the action and had himself been struck in the leg by a bullet. He proudly showed Reid his wound, and Reid enlisted him on the spot, commenting afterwards:

> He was one of the Fighting class of Goorkah, and was at the time not more than twelve or thirteen years of age. The *esprit de corps* shown by these Line boys throughout the siege was wonderful. Out of twenty-five men who obtained the Order of Merit for Delhi, twelve were Line boys, and out of the seven who received the order for 'Allewal' and 'Sobraon' [in the Sikh wars], five were Line boys. Only those of Goorkah parentage were enlisted, and I never found they deteriorated in the least, or were in any way inferior to the pure Goorkah from Nepaul. They are naturally loyal to the State as *their regiment is their home*.[23]

Reid's attitude stands in marked contrast to the prejudice against line-boys shown by later generations of British officers, who compared them adversely with the 'pure' or 'wild' Gurkhas from the hills.

On 9 August John Nicholson arrived at Hindu Rao's House. Nicholson was one of the extraordinary and dedicated group of men around Henry Lawrence whose exploits in the pacification of the Punjab following the Sikh wars were already legendary – he was even worshipped by a sect of the Sikhs who called themselves the 'Nikal-Seyni Faquirs'. He had been given the rank of brigadier-general to maximize his influence on events. Reid's initial impression of this giant was unflattering: 'I had never seen him before in my life, and I thought I had never seen a man I disliked so much at first sight. His haughty manner and peculiar sneer I could not stand.'[24]

On closer acquaintance, however, like everyone else Reid was won over and he and Nicholson became 'the best of friends . . . I liked him

exceedingly'. They would sit together at night on the top of the increasingly battered Hindu Rao's House and talk. On one occasion a shell
burst right over their heads and the shrapnel hit Reid's telescope and
caught two of the Gurkhas sitting below him, one in the chest and the
other in the right eye, without touching either Nicholson or Reid. On
another occasion, Nicholson warned Reid that he had too many Sikhs
on the ridge: 'Take my advice, and get the General to relieve some of
them. They are all very well in their way, and fight remarkably well, but
don't place too much confidence in them. No man knows them better
than I do.'[25] Nicholson's influence, along with that of the chief engineer,
Colonel Baird Smith, was critical in turning defence into attack; and
even after he had been fatally wounded in the assault on Delhi, his lingering presence on his deathbed ensured that the elderly
Brigadier-General Archdale Wilson (Barnard having succumbed to
cholera) did not give in to the defeatism to which he was prone. Lord
Roberts, who was then a young artillery officer serving on Nicholson's
staff, called him 'the beau-ideal of a soldier and a gentleman'.[26]

The cost of the siege of Delhi to the Sirmoor battalion was 327 out of
an original 490 men, and eight out of nine officers, killed and wounded.
(Roberts gives slightly different figures from those in the regimental
history: 'The Sirmur battalion began with 450 men, and were joined by
a draft of 90, making a total of 540; their loss in killed and wounded
amounted to 319.'[27]) The only time the battalion so much as faltered
was during the final assault on Delhi when Reid himself was wounded
and it was deprived of his leadership.[28] But its prolonged exposure to
daily bombardment and battle more than any other action established
the reputation of the Gurkhas, not simply as courageous and
indomitable soldiers, but as a kind of honorary British, a race apart, *in*
but not *of* the Indian Army. Confirmation of this came in 1858 when the
soldiers of the Sirmoor battalion were designated as 'riflemen' – after
their equally valiant brothers in the 60th Rifles – rather than mere
'sepoys'.

Though the spotlight inevitably falls on the Sirmoor battalion, all the
existing Gurkha battalions distinguished themselves in action in
1857–8. The Kumaon battalion arrived at Delhi in time to play an
important part in Nicholson's assault of the city; and both the new

Nasiri battalion and the 66th (Goorkha) Regiment proved themselves in
action, Lieutenant Gepp losing his life near Nainital, whence Colonel
McCausland wrote sternly to the young man's father on 17 February
1858:

> You have, my dear Sir, much to be thankful for that your poor son died
> a soldier's death and was not brutally murdered as many of our poor
> countrymen, women and children have been. I have to deplore the loss
> of many near and dear relations, particularly a beloved son and
> daughter, in the horrible massacre at Cawnpore in July last . . .[29]

In addition, a new battalion of Gurkhas was raised at Pithoragarh and
Lahughat on the western border of Nepal on 6 August 1857 and went
into training for active service at Almora. This 'Extra Regiment' would
become the 4th Gurkhas. The 5th Gurkhas, who originated in the Sikh
Gurkha force started by Ranjit Singh, was raised as the 25th Regiment
of Punjab Infantry, or the Hazara Goorkha Battalion, in May 1858 and
added to the Punjab Irregular Force.[30] In October 1858, according to the
regimental history of the 5th Royal Gurkha Rifles, 'the first recruiting
party was sent out, not to Nepal, be it noted, but to Kumaon. The
recruits enlisted were Gurkhas, Garhwalis, and Kumaonis, each class in
approximately equal numbers. Many years were to elapse before the
Regiment confined its efforts to the recruiting of Magars and Gurungs
of Central Nepal.'[31]

There were also Gurkhas serving in the north-east of India in the
local Assam Light Infantry battalions from well before the Sepoy
Revolt. They, too, were a mixture of hill peoples, with as many
Kumaonis and Garhwalis as 'pure' Gurkhas. Though the mutiny was
confined largely to the Bengal Army and local troops in Assam were not
directly affected, some battalions, including the Sylhet Light Infantry –
an early incarnation of the 8th Gurkhas – fought against the rebels.
Indeed, the historian of 8 GR finds it incomprehensible that the Sylhet
Light Infantry was not awarded a battle honour 'for their work in the
Mutiny'.[32]

The suppression of the Sepoy Revolt, and the terrible and often indis-
criminate toll exacted by self-righteously vengeful British forces, put an

end to any lingering doubts as to who really ruled India. Neither the aged emperor, Bahadur Shah, who was put on trial and exiled to Rangoon in 1859, nor the fiction of East India Company rule, survived the uprising. India, though not as yet the jewel in the crown, was nevertheless the centrepiece of an expanding British empire.

From 1 November 1858 Indian Army units came directly under the Crown, though this in itself made little difference to their situation; officers continued to feel like poor relations of their British Army counterparts, who took precedence over officers of equal rank in the Indian service. The army reorganization following the Royal Commission of 1858–9 (known as the Peel Commission after its chairman, Major-General Jonathan Peel, the then secretary of state for war) reflected the official British response to the recent strife.

There were many lessons to be absorbed by the authorities, some of them obvious – such as that promotion by seniority rather than merit resulted in elderly and ineffectual commanders, and that siphoning off the brightest officers into the political service left regiments bereft of talent. There were also a number of broader questions to be considered. For example, was the existence of three separate presidency armies justified in an increasingly unified country? Or, what constituted the ideal native regiment: a 'plum-pudding' mixture of class and caste, or an ethnically homogeneous unit? Or again, and crucially, to what extent could a sepoy army ever be trusted?

To take the last question first: Sir Bartle Frere, a member of Lord Canning's executive council and a future Governor of Bombay, argued in the Metcalfe tradition that British rule in India depended on a measure of consent. An army of occupation was out of the question, both politically and economically; therefore Indian troops had to be trusted: 'They could not be *half*-trusted'.[33] Though this argument was logically irrefutable, it was emotionally unacceptable to the majority of British authorities, who did indeed *half*-trust the sepoys. They insisted on abolishing all Indian artillery, except for mountain batteries, and retaining control of the guns in British hands. They were reluctant to put even the new Enfield rifle in the hands of the sepoy, preferring that he should continue to carry a musket and remain at a disadvantage in relation to the British soldier. The Commission, perhaps inevitably, was backward-looking, focusing on tightening internal security rather than planning for external wars, on holding the empire against the enemy within rather than extending its boundaries, still less on preparing for the possibility of having to fight a European army.

Due to the fact that the Madras and Bombay armies had been almost untouched by sedition – and were therefore able to be called upon to help put down the Bengal Army mutineers – the principle of separate armies was upheld. It would not be long before this version of 'divide and rule' would be superseded by another more in tune with contemporary reality, but for the moment this cumbersome and anachronistic division of forces was retained.

Likewise, the idea of mixed regiments on the Madras and Bombay model triumphed in the short term. The southern armies had never pandered to caste prejudices in the way that the homogeneous, high-caste Brahman and Rajput Bengal Native Infantry units had, but had subordinated them to military discipline; and this had acted as a counterweight to the religious feeling which – it was argued – had got out of hand in the Bengal Army. The brightest and best among the pre-Mutiny British officers, such as Henry Lawrence, had disapproved of the clannish nature of the Bengal Army and had recommended recruiting all sorts and conditions of men, including 'the now despised Eurasians' long before this uprising. Lawrence had written, 'Courage goes much by opinion; and many a man behaves as a hero or a coward, according as he considers he is expected to behave. Once two Roman Legions held Britain; now as many Britons might hold Italy.'[34]

But Henry Lawrence was unusual in seeing British rule in India as a kind of stewardship – 'We cannot hold India for ever' – and encouraging what many who came after him, including such luminaries as Lord Roberts, were at pains to prevent: the development of a nationally representative army, officered by Indians as well as British. This might be an acceptable model for civil government, but military thinking after the Sepoy Revolt was deeply reactionary. It is hard to imagine any army officer in 1864 endorsing what Lawrence had proposed in 1844:

> . . . something more is wanted for the sepoy than that at the age of sixty he should, by possibility, have reached the rank of Subadar-Major . . . [F]or the man of better education, the superior character, the bold and daring spirit that disdains to live for ever in subordinate

place . . . for such we firmly believe that is absolutely required some
new grade where, without our risking the supremacy of European
authority, he may obtain command and exert in our behalf those
energies and talents which under the present system are too liable to
be brought into the scale against us . . . [35]

Few British officers shared Lawrence's breadth of vision and sympathy. It was merely because mixed regiments had by and large remained
loyal during the Sepoy Revolt that they were seen as a good thing.
They were politically, rather than militarily, desirable. There was a
growing feeling among officers that the newly conquered and warlike
peoples of the north and north-west, who had proved themselves both
loyal and valiant in the recent conflict, Sikhs from the Punjab and
Gurkhas from Nepal in particular, would make ideal replacements for
the discredited Brahmans and Rajputs of the north-east. This process
became known as the 'Punjabization' of the Bengal army. Sikhs and
Gurkhas might serve in the same units, as they did in some of the
Assamese local battalions, but neither they nor their officers welcomed
too close a proximity. A compromise between the conflicting ideals of
mixed and ethnically homogeneous units was to have mixed regiments
composed of class companies.

In 1865, for example, the 42nd Assam Light Infantry was transformed
into such a regiment, its eight companies comprising Sikhs (two companies), Gurkhas (four companies, a quarter of each composed of Jarwahs,
a local hill people) and Hindustanis (two companies, one Hindu and
one Muslim). But six years later there was sharp disagreement among
the regimental officers over the composition of the 42nd Assam Light
Infantry; all but two senior officers wanted to eliminate the Sikhs.
Colonel Rattray (who, as commanding officer when he was still a major,
had been instrumental in turning the regiment into a class-company
one) and Lieutenant-Colonel Sherriff were in favour of replacing
Gurkhas with Sikhs. The regimental history (of the 6th Gurkhas) comments: 'Captain Brydon and Lieutenant Abbott, both of whom appear to
have been able to exert their influence, saved the regiment from this
fate.'[36] The Gurkhophiles won; fifteen years on, the regiment became
the 42nd Gurkha Light Infantry, a title which reflected the fact that it
was now a class regiment consisting entirely of Gurkhas.[37]

The main architect of the new Indian army from 1879 – the year of the Army Commission under the presidency of Sir Ashley Eden, Governor of Bengal – was General (later Field Marshal Lord) Roberts, the celebrated and popular 'Bobs Bahadur' upon whose words and deeds, including the famous Kabul to Kandahar march of 1880 during the second Afghan war, posterity has cast a cold and doubting eye. His popularity in the Indian Army reflected the fact that he embodied the prejudices of its officer cadre; it would hardly be an exaggeration to say that he institutionalized the warm but patronizing relationship of its officers to their men.

One of his predecessors as C-in-C in India, Lord Napier of Magdala, had argued that if a nation was capable of producing fine civil administrators it could also produce military leaders, but Roberts vetoed the idea of commissions for Indians (other than the junior viceroy's commission), asserting that 'history and experience teach us that eastern races (fortunately for us), however brave and accustomed to war, do not possess the qualities that go to make leaders of men, and that Native officers in this respect can never take the place of British officers'.[38] While another of his predecessors, General Sir Frederick Haines, had warned that 'it would be a mistake to suppose that good military elements could only be found in turbulent races',[39] Roberts was an enthusiastic advocate of the martial races theory, or dogma – the belief that certain races were innately more warlike than others. He wrote:

In the British Army the superiority of one regiment over another is mainly a matter of training; the same courage and military instinct are inherent in English, Scotch, and Irish alike, but no comparison can be made between the martial value of a regiment recruited amongst the Gurkhas of Nepal or the warlike races of northern India, and of one recruited of the effeminate peoples of the south.[40]

Roberts' defenders argue that he was a realist rather than a racist, his sole concern being the perfection of the 'fighting machine' for which he held overall responsibility for seven and a half years between 1885 and 1893. It is true that the martial races theory was relative rather than absolute, allowing that if a once martial people softened and 'degenerated' over years of easy living when not exposed to war, then the process might be reversed too. But while one British historian of the Indian Army may be right in arguing that 'the object of recruiting from fewer "martial classes" [was] . . . simply to obtain the best soldiers', he is completely wrong to suggest that the principle of 'Divide and Rule' was 'never formulated or authoritatively expressed'.[41]

Far from never having been formulated, it was clearly laid out in a government report on the army system in India, published in 1884, which was a blueprint for the future Indian Army:

> Our desire is to maintain the great national divisions of the army, but to systematise and re-adjust them on an intelligent principle, and we, therefore, have determined to recommend that, instead of the three Presidential armies of Bengal, Madras, and Bombay, the armies of India should be divided into four completely separate and distinct bodies, to be called army corps, so distributed that they shall be deprived, as far as possible, of community of national sentiment and interest, and so organised, recruited, and constituted, as to act in time of excitement and disturbance, as checks each upon the other . . .
>
> In working out the details of our proposed division of the army, our main object has been to define the territorial formation of the army of India with due regard to the great principle of *divide et impera* . . . [42]

The replacement of the three presidential armies with four army corps, the so-called 'Punjabization' of the Indian Army – since the Punjab provided the fourth component of this new model army – would not be completed until 1895. The ostensible object of Roberts and other army reformers might be maximum efficiency with minimum expenditure, but despite the second Afghan war (1878–80) and the looming threat of Russia, the focus still had not shifted entirely from internal security, as the continuing argument over the ideal composition of regiments attests. Officers in the Madras and Bombay armies favoured their tried and tested system of mixed regiments 'with no special recruiting ground'; those of the 'Bengal and Punjab' armies preferred class regiments to mixed, or even class-company regiments:

> They argue that the men are more content and happy serving with their own tribesmen; that under such a system there will always be

strong rivalry, not to say antagonism, between regiments, which, *though useful to the State as between regiments*, might be hurtful to discipline as between companies of the same regiment [my italics].[43]

Nevertheless, the report recommended that the northern armies, though they should be allowed to maintain a limited number of Gurkha, Sikh and Hindustani class regiments, should consist mainly of 'class-company regiments, each of which should have its principal recruiting ground, and its fixed depot, in a specified tract of country'.[44]

The Bengali writer, Nirad Chaudhuri (author of such classics as *The Autobiography of an Unknown Indian* and *A Passage to England*), divides the history of British power in India, in terms of military recruitment, into three periods. During the first period, in the eighteenth century, any adventurer who cared to serve was enlisted. This was followed, at the end of that century and in that early nineteenth century, by a spate of campaigns against the indigenous military powers, in which period the Bengal Army was almost exclusively the preserve of Rajputs and Brahmans from the Ganges basin. The third period marked the domination of India following the Sepoy Revolt, 'when the broken up elements of the once hostile military powers are alone enlisted'.[45] As a foreign power, Britain could hardly have been expected to invoke the spirit of nationalism in India, so it had to find an alternative. In the early days of empire it had made use of the Hindu notion of a martial or warrior caste to prevent the army 'from turning into a dangerous mob of mercenaries'; when that backfired, it replaced caste with race, flattering 'the vanity of the Gurkha at the expense of the Sikh, and that of the Sikh at the expense of the Gurkha' – so that the new military order involved 'a constant pampering of . . . parochial vanity'.[46]

But the policy of 'divide and rule' was not simply a matter of fostering the mutual dislike of Sikhs and Hindustanis, or of hillmen and plainsmen, so that no one 'martial race' within the army would acquire the dangerous predominance that the Rajput and Brahman sepoys from Oudh and Bihar had enjoyed before the Sepoy Revolt; it also involved a deliberate separation of the military from civilians, a policy of maintaining the army, in Chaudhuri's words, 'as an insulated body of manhood in the midst of a thoroughly disarmed and emasculated population'.[47]

By categorizing the majority of people of the subcontinent as non-martial, 'effeminate', cowardly even, the British authorities set up an opposition between their pampered favourites and the rest, many of whom took exception, not so much to the idea of martial races as to their involuntary exclusion from them. The rural bias of recruitment in the north made for yet another opposition, between the supposedly slow-witted and unpolitical countrymen who composed the class and class-company regiments and the more educated and politically aware townsfolk who were ruled out of contention. This reinforced both British and Indian prejudices: aspiring Indians came to regard the army as the preserve of the bone-headed and unthinking; and Roberts and his ilk considered Indians unworthy of commissions. In 1885, when the military member of the Governor-General's council, General Sir George Chesney, argued in favour of introducing Indians into higher military commands, 'Roberts at once joined issue with him, grounding his objections on the strong feeling inveterate to all ranks of the British Army that "natives were neither physically nor morally their equals"'.[48]

Finally, there was the opposition between north and south, between the Bengal Army and the other two. Roberts favoured the 'warlike races of northern India' over the 'effeminate peoples of the south', the Tamils and Telegus of Madras and the 'so-called Mahrattas of Bombay'. But since all armies tend to lose their edge in a 'weak piping time of peace', it would have been surprising if the southern armies, which had not been called into action with the same frequency as the Bengal Army since the beginning of the century, had not gone off the boil. It was up to their officers to galvanize them, but for officers, too, the Madras and Bombay armies had less appeal than the Bengal Army; the more motivated among them chose to serve in the north, where the action was, leaving the southern armies in the hands of their less ambitious brethren.

Chaudhuri writes, 'the whole attitude of the British authorities in India in favour of the men of the North was due to a historical circumstance ... that by 1880, due to the growth of the Russian menace, the North West Frontier had become the principal theatre of operations for the Indian Army'.[49]

At the beginning of the 1930s, when Nirad Chaudhuri was exposing the martial races theory as a deliberately divisive means of instilling pride in the Indian Army without recourse to a dangerous nationalism, Lord Roberts' disciple, Lieutenant-General Sir George MacMunn, was using it as a vehicle to promote Aryan views which would have found favour with the new Chancellor of Germany, Adolf Hitler:

> The martial races . . . are largely the product of the original white races. The white invaders [of India] in the days of their early supremacy started the caste system, as a protection, it is believed, against the devastating effect on morals and ethics of miscegenation with Dravidian and aboriginal peoples.[50]

These unsuspecting Aryans, according to MacMunn, by and large succumbed to 'the effect of prolonged years of varying religions on their adherents, of early marriage, of premature brides, and juvenile eroticism, of a thousand years of malaria and hook-worm, and other ills of neglected sanitation in a hot climate, and the deteriorating effect of aeons of tropical sun on races that were once white and lived in uplands and on cool steppes'. This was why 'the mass of the people have neither martial aptitude nor physical courage'.[51] Fortunately, there were exceptions to the rule.

In sum, the tall and fair-skinned people of the north-west were martial; the short and dark South Indians were not. But where did that leave the Gurkhas, who were neither tall nor particularly fair?

Gurkhas were covered by an aspect of the martial races theory mentioned by MacMunn – the philosophy of climatic difference, the supposed superiority of temperate-zone man over tropical man, the idea (old as Herodotus) that 'hard countries breed hard men'.[52] General Sir O'Moore Creagh, C-in-C of the Indian Army in the years leading up to the First World War, puts it more prosaically than MacMunn:

> In the hot, flat regions, of which by far the greater part of India consists . . . are found races, timid both by religion and habit, servile to their superiors, but tyrannical to their inferiors, and quite unwarlike. In other parts . . . where the winter is cold, and the warlike minority is to be found . . . peoples vary greatly in military virtue. Nowhere, however, are they equal in that respect to Europeans or Japanese.[53]

Or Gurkhas? Roberts would certainly have put Gurkhas up there, along with Europeans and Japanese. When the Indian Army invaded Afghanistan in 1878, and the people of the north-west frontier 'saw the little Gurkhas for the first time', they expressed their contempt: 'Is it possible that these beardless boys think they can fight Afghan warriors?' Lord Roberts comments, 'They little suspected that the brave spirits which animated those small forms made them more than a match for the most stalwart Afghan.'[54]

As mountain people the Gurkhas were as renowned for their endurance as for their courage and Roberts had first-hand experience of both qualities during the Afghan campaign, in which the 5th Gurkhas formed as close a link with the 72nd Highlanders (later 1st battalion, the Seaforths) as the 2nd Goorkhas (or Sirmoor battalion) had with the 60th Rifles at the siege of Delhi in 1857: 'The 72nd and the 5th Gurkhas had been much associated from the commencement of the campaign, and a spirit of *camaraderie* had sprung up between them, resulting in the Highlanders now coming forward and insisting on making over their greatcoats to the little Gurkhas for the night – a very strong proof of their friendship, for at Kabul in October the nights are bitterly cold.'[55] In a letter to the Duke of Cambridge, Roberts voiced his hope that 'when the time comes for us to meet a Russian army in the field, our own force will consist mainly of Europeans, Goorkhas, and the best kind of Sikhs and Dogras'.[56]

The Gurkha's highland credentials, along with his evident military ability, then, gave him his ticket of entry to the exclusive martial races club. But at the same time his small stature and beardlessness made him a target of that late Victorian propensity to see all human – or at least all male – relationships in public school terms. The Gurkha was 'a child of nature'; his outlook was 'that of a healthy boy'; 'relations between officers and men are as close as between boys and masters on a jaunt together out of school, and the Gurkha no more thinks of taking advantage of this when he returns to the regiment than the English schoolboy does when he returns to school'; the British officer had to serve a probationary period, as it were, but

once accepted, he is served with a fidelity and devotion that are human and dog-like at the same time. I do not emphasize the exclusive attachment of the Gurkha to his own Sahib as an exemplary virtue; it is a fault, though it is the defect of a virtue. And it is a peculiarly boyish fault. It is the old story of magnifying the house to the neglect of the school.[57]

This sort of well-intentioned but embarrassingly ethnocentric gush litters the pages of innumerable books by British *aficionados* of the 'big-hearted little Gurkhas' from the late nineteenth century through to the present day. It reveals a great deal about the British officer, and almost nothing about the Gurkha.

The martial races dogma spawned a series of Indian Army 'Handbooks', filled with arcane anthropological information, codifying the preferred types of Gurkha, or Sikh, or Dogra, or whomever. In the last hundred years or so there have been half a dozen handbooks on Gurkhas alone.

The first, by Captain Eden Vansittart of the 5th Gurkhas, who was placed in charge of Gurkha recruitment in 1890 – the year in which the Limbus and Rais of east Nepal began to be systematically sought via a new depot in Darjeeling – grew out of his 'Notes on Gurkhas', written that year, and his 'Notes on Nepal', published in 1895. It draws heavily on the work of earlier writers such as Hamilton, Hodgson, Oldfield and Wright. But Vansittart claims that 'the classification of the various races of Nepal is almost entirely my own'.[58] Of the prized Gurungs and Magars, he lists several hundred clans, adding occasional recondite comments, such as: 'Ales of the Roho clan are said not to eat Roho fish'; or, 'The Siris clans of the Ranas and Thapas are the descendants of children who were brought up from babyhood on the milk of goats, their mothers having died in childbirth. No Rana or Thapa of the Siris clans will eat goat's flesh'; or again, 'Bagale means "many". This clan is said to be derived originally from a large family of brothers.'[59]

This 'atomizing ethnographic enterprise', as a recent historian has described it, might produce 'specimens' rather than individuals.[60] But it was all part of the professionalization of the recruitment process.

After the second Afghan war, when the Russian bogey loomed large in the minds of the British authorities, the Indian high command determined to double the number of its Gurkha troops by raising second battalions to all five of its Gurkha regiments. But to achieve this required the co-operation of the *durbar* in Kathmandu. Nepalese expressions of goodwill were no longer enough to satisfy the British Indian government; they must be backed by positive steps to promote recruitment.

But the more pressure the British Resident brought to bear, the more the Nepalese rulers feared that their country would be next to suffer the fate of Afghanistan – invasion, with the possibility of an eventual takeover. (Throughout their rule the Ranas were obsessed with Afghanistan, readily identifying with another tenuously independent mountainous frontier state.) They were convinced that the recruitment of Gurkhas into the Indian Army was a subtle British ruse designed to emasculate their country before marching in to claim it; they could not accept that Britain was not (or was not any longer) interested in territorial aggrandizement, only in Gurkha manpower. Discussing Nepal's military policy in the early 1880s, Brevet-Major E. R. Elles of the Royal Artillery reported 'the ever present fear of a rupture with the British Government':

> There is a general feeling amongst those responsible for the administration, as Mr Girdlestone [the Resident] has more than once represented, that a collision in which the British Government will take the initiative is inevitable, and that its occurrence is only a question of time. It is not so much that the Durbar credits the British Government with a fixed determination to encroach as that it believes that in the irresistible course of events, perhaps by some inadvertence of its own, an occasion for interference will arise, and that Nepal will be threatened with loss of territory.[61]

Despite both sides' protestations of undying friendship, Nepalese suspicions were so ingrained that 'some years ago when the Gorakhpur municipality introduced cast-iron lamp-posts, the Durbar sent agents to satisfy themselves that these posts were not a new kind of gun'.[62]

Nor were suspicions confined to the Nepalese. Elles, like Cavenagh before him, made a careful study of Nepal's military potential, praising the soldiery and dismissing the Rana officers who led 'dissolute lives in the privacy of the zenana' and acquired rank not by merit but by birth – 'the anomaly of boy colonels and grey-headed lieutenants is nowhere carried to such an extreme as in Nepal'. But he also remarked:

View of the Himalayas and terraced foothills from the Kathmandu Valley.
(E. D. MacLeod)

THIS IS INSCRIBED
AS A TRIBUTE OF RESPECT
FOR OUR GALLANT ADVERSARY
BULBUDDER
COMMANDER OF THE FORT
AND HIS BRAVE GOORKAS
WHO WERE AFTERWARDS
WHILE IN THE SERVICE
OF RUNJEET SING
SHOT DOWN IN THEIR RANKS
TO THE LAST MAN
BY AFGHAN ARTILLERY.

The defender of Kalanga 1814,
Balbahadur ('Bulbudder') Singh, in
action and as commemorated in
Dehra Dun. The second obelisk
honours the British dead.
(Courtesy of Gurkha Museum)

James B. Fraser's painting of 'Ghoorkha Chiefs and Soldiers' 1814–15.
(By permission of the British Library)

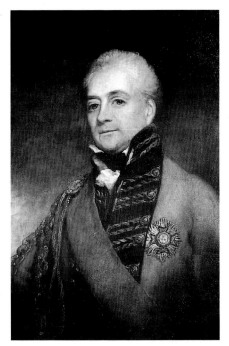

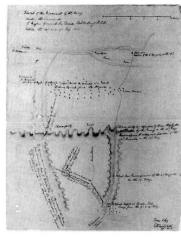

Major-General Sir David Ochterlony
(A. W. Devis © National Galleries of
Scotland); and a sketch map of his
second successful campaign of the
Gorkha War, February 1816.
(Gurkha Museum)

The short-lived new Nasiri Battalion circa 1857 (its predecessor having been upgraded into the regular line as the '66th or Goorkha Regiment', later 1st Gurkha Rifles). (Gurkha Museum)

Men of the Sirmoor Battalion (later 2nd Goorkha Rifles) outside the battered Hindu Rao's House on the ridge at Delhi, 1857. (Gurkha Museum)

Statue of Maharajah Jang Bahadur Rana in Kathmandu.
(E. D. MacLeod)

Jang with one of his many wives (said to number between 17 and 25); and
on a hunting expedition in 1871, accompanied by a brother, a son and two
nephews. (Gurkha Museum)

Mountain warfare: *Illustrated London News* representation of the Afghan fortress of Ali Masjid at the head of the Khyber Pass during the 2nd Afghan war, 1878–80. (Gurkha Museum)

The wounded Piper Findlater of the 92nd (Gordon) Highlanders encourages his comrades and the 2nd Goorkhas at the battle of Dargai Heights during the Tirah campaign on the North-West Frontier, 20 October 1897. (Gurkha Museum)

The 8th Gurkhas in action during Younghusband's Tibetan expedition of 1903–4. (Gurkha Museum)

William Desmond Villiers-Stuart of the 1/5th Gurkha Rifles in 1899, two years after suffering a severe wound during the Tirah campaign of 1897 which left his right leg several inches shorter than his left – hence the stance he adopts here. (Gurkha Museum)

Major A. C. Lovett's paintings of Subedar-Major Santbir Gurung of 2/2 Goorkha Rifles, whose 'vigil' was celebrated in a story by Rudyard Kipling, and of a group of 6th Gurkhas. (Courtesy of the Director, National Army Museum, London)

Men of the 4th Gurkhas 1880s-style. (© D. F. Harding)

> Amongst the NCOs is an important minority who have returned to
> Nepal after a period of service in British regiments . . . This element
> was believed in 1879 by Mr Girdlestone to be on the increase . . . It is a
> serious evil, from a political point of view, thus to give the Nepal
> Government the opportunity of improving its soldiers.[63]

To demand the right to recruit an ever-increasing number of Gurkhas,
while at the same time resenting any incidental increment your alleged
ally might reap from such an arrangement, may seem a little harsh. But
this was an alliance of convenience, not (or not yet) of genuine trust or
friendship. Each country had its own agenda: Nepal was intent on maintaining its fragile independence, and Britain on building up its Gurkha
force. As a visiting English MP remarked about the Nepalese, 'though
externally they are very polite to us, it is a different sort of politeness
from that of the ordinary Native States, and one cannot help seeing that
they have what Shakespeare would have called "a high stomach"'.[64]

At the end of 1883 a crisis in Nepal's relations with Tibet prompted
the Resident, Girdlestone, to suggest that the British government use
the provision of arms and ammunition – access to which it controlled –
as a lever to obtain recruits from Nepal. The crisis passed, but the
policy met with the approval of Jang Bahadur's successor, Ranodip
Singh, and instructions had gone out in his name to provide the British
with the recruits they needed when Ranodip was assassinated in a
palace revolution in November 1885 by the Shamsher branch of the
Rana family. In the 1884–5 recruiting season the British had managed to
recruit only 657 men, which was well short of what they needed to
double their Gurkha force.[65]

The latest *coup*, however, played into their hands. It was a throwback
to the sort of politics at which Jang Bahadur had proved himself so
adept, before transcending them and, as he thought, rendering them
obsolete. Yet by separating the maharajahdom of Lamjung and Kaski
from the ministership – the one to go from father to son, the other from
brother to brother – he was responsible for creating the situation which
brought it about. The impracticability of such an arrangement led
directly to the intra-Rana feuding and blood-letting that brought the
Shamsher Ranas to power.

If the British authorities had chosen to back the direct descendants of

Jang Bahadur, as they were under some pressure to do, Bir Shamsher would have found it difficult to govern. For his *coup* to succeed and in order to establish himself as both minister and maharajah, Bir depended on the recognition and support of the British government. So he wooed the British by doing everything he could to facilitate their recruitment of Gurkhas, short of allowing them to send recruiting teams into the hills. Nepal itself would furnish the recruits Britain required. From Bir's point of view it was as well that Girdlestone, who was a staunch supporter of the Jang party, was away and that the officiating Resident, Colonel J. C. Berkeley, saw the military advantages to be gained from recognizing him. Berkeley wrote:

> Jang Bahadur was steeped in blood and the present minister and his family are as bad as they can be; but they have already rendered us service, and it is conceivable they might be able to do as much for us as Jang Bahadur did . . . Unless we mean to change our whole policy towards Nepal, and to abandon strict neutrality for active interference, it seems to me that it does not matter to us which set of cut-throats has the upper hand.[66]

Britain, though well disposed towards Jang's heirs, followed the officiating Resident's advice and stuck to the policy of non-interference in the internal affairs of Nepal, seeing in it the opportunity to regularize the recruitment of Gurkhas once and for all.

But recruiting through the agency of the Nepalese *durbar* produced disappointing results so far as the regiments were concerned. Reports sent in by officers from the borders of south, east and west Nepal in mid-1886 all tell the same story: far too many physically sub-standard recruits, some actually deformed, many of the wrong castes and sizes and ages, most of them coming from families too poor to pay the 20 rupees which would have bought them immunity from conscription.[67]

British officers were under political pressure not to reject too many of these reluctant recruits for fear of alienating the *durbar*; but they were disgusted with the compulsion employed, which threatened to undermine the popularity of British service. They preferred the old, clandestine, if dangerous, method of recruiting to a system which involved both persuasion and misrepresentation (of rates of pay). A large number of recruits in the newly raised second battalion of the 4th Gurkhas, for instance, 'refused to take their first month's pay, complaining that they had either been forcibly pressed into service, or else cajoled with promises of higher pay'; and no fewer than fifty-one of them deserted.[68]

With the development of the martial races theory officers had also become more choosy over whom they took: they wanted Magars and Gurungs to the exclusion of all other peoples, including Limbus and Rais, of whom Captain Mercer wrote presciently, 'we may yet find that we have as good fighting material among the tribes of eastern Nepal, and should this prove to be the case, we shall have a large additional area upon which to draw for recruits'.[69]

In September 1886 the Adjutant-General reported: 'Second battalions have been raised for the 1st, 2nd and 4th Goorkhas, but . . . there appears to be no prospect of obtaining a sufficient number of *suitable* recruits through the agency of the Nepal Durbar during the coming cold season to complete the formation of *two* additional *Goorkha* battalions', i.e., the 3rd and 5th Gurkhas.[70] So while the raising of a second battalion of the 5th Gurkhas was immediately sanctioned, that of the 3rd Gurkhas was deferred.

The reason the 5th got priority was that earlier in the year there had been an outbreak of mutiny in the 3rd Gurkhas at Almora over reduced allowances. There were two levels of *batta*, or extra money, allowed for food in the Indian Army; *attah* or flour-eaters got a higher rate than rice-eaters. Gurkhas were rice-eaters, and for years various regiments had indulged in a certain amount of jiggery-pokery over food allowances for their men. In 1868, for instance, the agent to the Governor-General on the north-east frontier had witnessed a conversation between a brigadier-general and the commanding officer of an Assam regiment partly made up of Gurkhas:

The General wanted more Nepalese enlisted; wanted, in fact, as I understood him, the Regiment to be Goorkha. The CO objected that the pay was not high enough to be attractive, and was told to calculate his compensation as for *attah*. This was, I suppose, a natural enough course to take. So long as such a source as a compensation fund exists to be drawn upon, a zealous Officer will make the most of it to attract the class of men he believes to be the best.[71]

The commandant of the 3rd Gurkhas was just such a zealous officer; he had been drawing on this 'compensation fund' since 1883, providing his men with a higher *batta* than was strictly allowed under the regulations. It was the sudden and inexplicable reduction of the allowance from 2 rupees 8 annas per man per month to a mere 12 annas when a new and more bureaucratically minded commanding officer took over in 1886 that triggered the mutiny on 12 April. A subsequent investigation uncovered a whole range of complaints and concluded that the battalion was both badly run and poorly disciplined. Four 'ringleaders' were imprisoned for varying lengths of time; and though the previous commandant was held responsible for bringing about the situation in the first place, it was the new CO who was removed from office, since he had 'exhibited such weakness of character in dealing with the conduct of the men as to make it evident that he was quite unfit for the position of Commandant of a regiment'.[72] The mutiny was officially deplored, but it was clearly felt that the mutineers had some cause for complaint.

This mutiny did not prevent the 3rd Gurkhas from objecting that a more recently raised regiment, the 4th Gurkhas, had been granted a second battalion before they had, giving the junior corps opportunities of promotion that they were denied. The following May they too got a second battalion, and the CO of the 3rd Gurkhas used the occasion to get rid of the word 'Kumaon' from the regimental title:

> This regiment was formerly composed of nearly all Kumaonis, and history does not record favourably regarding their services either at Delhi or Bhootan [in the punitive expedition of 1864–6]. The regiment was largely composed of Goorkhas in the late Afghan campaign, and history will record favourably on the performance of the regiment. Courage alone will not make a soldier: many other qualities are required. The Kumaoni failed miserably in Afghanistan in every quality . . . I would not enlist one of them for a soldier . . . but I would the Garhwalis. Good soldiers can be got from Garhwal, but I would not mix them . . . That I could enlist a couple of good regiments from Garhwal I am certain.[73]

The Commander-in-Chief approved the change of name, which was sanctioned in May 1887, and a second battalion was raised consisting of

Garhwalis rather than Gurkhas, despite the name. Major-General Nigel
Woodyatt recalled:

> The selection of Garhwalis was somewhat resented by the officers of
> the old 3rd and especially so by Barry Bishop, our colonel. But the
> Chief [Sir Frederick Roberts, as he then was] was more far-seeing than
> most of us and, having appreciated the great value of the Garhwali on
> his many campaigns, was bent on raising at least one complete unit of
> them, in spite of depressing reports from civil sources regarding their
> disinclination to enlist . . .
> He once asked me, when [I was] at Simla on leave from Almora,
> what I thought of the Garhwali. On my replying that I knew nothing of
> him, he said: 'Well, I'll tell you something. There has always been a
> certain number of them, as well as Kumaonis, in every Gurkha
> battalion, and nearly every so-called Gurkha who has won the Indian
> Order of Merit for gallantry has been a Garhwali or Kumaoni!' Soon
> afterwards I had the curiosity to look this up, and found it was a matter
> of about 90 per cent.[74]

The 2/3rd Gurkhas was eventually reconstructed as the 39th
Garhwalis, and Woodyatt himself was appointed adjutant of the new, all-
Gurkha 2/3rd Gurkhas. But he often thought how pleased Lord Roberts
would have been if he had lived to 'read the glorious record of the
Garhwalis in the Great War'.[75]

The troubles of the 3rd Gurkhas did not cease with the settlement of
the mutiny and the acquisition of a second battalion. Almora had
acquired a reputation as 'a hotbed of venereal disease', and in 1890 the
Adjutant-General wrote:

> The 1st Battalion, 3rd Gurkhas, have suffered terribly for years, and
> probably have at this moment a large body of men radically unsound
> from this cause, whom active service would soon find out. Marriage
> probably is the only antidote in this case, as the battalion is surrounded
> by a hopelessly diseased population. For these reasons His Excellency
> [the C-in-C] would recommend that the men of the 1st Battalion, 3rd
> Gurkhas, be allowed to marry to such an extent as the O[fficer]
> C[ommanding] the battalion may consider desirable.[76]

Another reason for encouraging marriage among Gurkhas and providing facilities for wives and children to settle with their menfolk in India was the difficulties the Nepalese *durbar* put in the way of men going home on furlough. 'The wife makes the home,' so the argument ran, 'therefore, if we are to keep the men, the Gurkha womankind should be encouraged to come freely and settle in India.'[77] Families could be properly looked after, fed and even educated, and line-boys would provide the next generation of soldiers. But that was the rub: 'A race of Gurkhas bred solely from "line boys", "line girls", or settlers in a Gurkha colony, would in time . . . produce a race vastly different to the Gurkha soldier of the present day.'[78] The hardiness of the 'wild', hill-reared Gurkha was valued above the smartness and brightness of the domesticated type.

The particular situation of 1/3rd Gurkhas had demanded immediate action to prevent the further spread of infection, and the good effect on soldiers of bringing their women back to Almora after furlough in Nepal quickly became apparent. In 1892 the CO reported that 'cases of venereal disease are now practically *nil*, in comparison with the numerous admissions into the hospital of former years'.[79] But an extension of this scheme to other Gurkha battalions was vetoed on the grounds that it would be too costly.

For the next few years in Nepal, unofficial and official systems of recruitment co-existed uneasily. When the C-in-C put forward the idea of providing a sweetener to the *durbar* of 20,000 rupees per 1,000 approved recruits, the Resident, C. E. R. Girdlestone, responded derisively:

The members of the Shamshere family now in power are counting their gains, mostly ill gotten, by lacs [a *lakh* is 100,000], not by thousands. So little disposed are they of their own free will to meet the British Government's requirements concerning recruits, that I doubt whether a much larger pecuniary offer would avail.[80]

Girdlestone's counter-suggestion, which was eventually adopted, was that 5,000 rupees given to the recruiting officer at Gorakhpur would be more effective than four times that sum put at the disposal of the

Resident in Kathmandu: 'In the former case the money would reach the persons for whom it was intended, whereas much of that disbursed through the Resident would find its way into the pockets of unscrupulous middle men.'[81] (This will sound familiar to aid-workers in Nepal today.)

As long as the Jang faction found sanctuary in British India, and the anti-Shamsher Girdlestone remained Resident, Nepal's suspicion of British intentions prevented enthusiastic co-operation over recruitment, though Bir Shamsher knew better than to oppose it openly. But after Girdlestone's removal, and the Viceroy Lord Dufferin's sincere attempt to improve relations with Nepal in 1888, Bir responded by means of a proclamation which, for the first time, officially sanctioned Gurkha recruitment into the Indian Army. Relations improved still further when the conciliatory Colonel H. Wylie was appointed Resident in 1891.

It had taken the British over seventy years to formalize the recruiting of Gurkhas into their forces, but their perseverance would pay off a hundredfold over the next seventy years and more.

4

Villiers-Stuart of the Fifth

When the units of the Bengal Native Infantry were renumbered in 1861, the forty-eight regiments of the line included four of the five Gurkha regiments – the 5th was still part of the Punjab Irregular Force. (Local Assam regiments were not then counted as Gurkha regiments, regardless of the number of Gurkhas they contained.) But almost immediately the secretary of state for India instructed that Gurkhas be separated from the main body of Native Infantry; and the units were renumbered 1st to 5th Gurkha Regiments later that same year. It was considered 'highly desirable that these corps should retain in a marked manner, their national and distinctive character'.[1]

(At this stage only the 2nd was a *rifle* regiment, though the 1st as well as the 2nd, when they were the Sirmoor and Nasiri battalions in 1842, had each had one rifle company, and as hill regiments Gurkhas had always worn green jackets, except for the brief period when the 1st Nasiri battalion became the 66th Bengal Native Infantry and its men donned the red coats of the line. The 1st, 3rd, 4th and 5th Gurkhas became rifle regiments in 1891, the denomination 'rifleman' aligning them with the British and distancing them still further from the sepoys.)

In 1864, having regard to 'the different circumstances in which recruits from Nepal entering our service find themselves as compared with other races', the first four regiments were each granted a regimental home in the hills of northern India, where at least some of the men might settle with their families. This was the base to which they always returned from active service on the north-west frontier, or in Afghanistan, or elsewhere. Furthermore, 'It may be distinctly understood that the localities of the existing cantonment lines in which the corps are now located be given over to them in perpetuity as their homes.'[2] The home of the 1st was at Dharmsala, the 2nd at Dehra Dun, the 3rd at Almora and the 4th at Bakloh (the home of the 5th was at Abbottabad, but this was not granted 'in perpetuity').

The four 'chartered' regiments, as they were called, cherished their privileged status and guarded it jealously when it came under threat from no less a personage than Lord Kitchener of Khartoum who, as C-in-C in India at the beginning of the twentieth century, wanted to revoke the charter in order to have greater flexibility in moving the regiments around. But even Kitchener, whose sustained objection to there being a military member on the Governor-General's council not answerable to himself eventually forced Lord Curzon to resign as Viceroy, could not get round that phrase 'in perpetuity' and was obliged to back down.

In addition to acquiring their own homes, these first British Gurkha regiments had developed particular characteristics which helped to distinguish them from one another. Major-General Nigel Woodyatt (of the 3rd) lists them:

The 1st at Dharmsala was renowned for its shooting, marching and band. The 2nd for polo and a wonderful esprit de corps. This, though by no means wanting in others, was so particularly marked at Dehra Dun, that if the men were all dying of scurvy, they would still perform prodigies for the good name of the 'siccon', as the Gurkhas call the regiment. The 3rd was remarkable for its football and, later, its excellent training; the 4th, at Bakloh, for its dress; and the 5th at

Abbottabad, for the good professional knowledge of the officers, their mountaineering prowess and greater experience in hill warfare.[3]*

Regimental pride was – and is – a potent force; and no one in the history of the British or any other army can have been more deeply imbued with it than Brigadier-General William Desmond Villiers-Stuart. His copious memoirs and diaries give a marvellous insight into regimental life at the turn of the century and after. He joined the 1/5th Gurkhas on 29 September 1896 at the age of twenty-four and had to wait another twenty-four years before he achieved his ambition of commanding the battalion in 1920. He was, in many ways, the archetypal regimental officer, whose highly critical attitude towards his fellow officers was offset by a deep paternalistic love of his men. He deserves a chapter to himself.

Like so many army officers, Villiers-Stuart came of an Anglo-Irish family; he was the oldest of three brothers, all of whom went on to serve in the Punjab Frontier Force, or 'Piffers'. William was a keen games player and neglected his studies at boarding school in Newton Abbot, Devon; as a result he failed the army entrance exam the first time he took it. He was commissioned in the Militia (the 4th Durhams) and attended a crammer; when he retook the exam, he passed so well that he obtained one of only three vacancies in the Indian Army.

By this time the Indian service had higher rates of pay and pension for officers than the British Army, and competition to get into it was stiff. The new system, which had just come into force, meant that a young officer, instead of joining a British regiment and eventually applying for transfer to an Indian one, was posted to the 'unattached list' of the

---

*By the time John Masters joined the 4th Gurkhas some fifty years after Nigel Woodyatt had joined the 3rd, there were twice the number of Gurkha regiments, and the comments he records about each – except his own, the 4th, which was of course 'an honourable number' – are flippant and/or dismissive:

> The 1st Gurkhas were earnest, the 2nd idle, the 3rd illiterate, the 5th narrow-minded, the 6th down-trodden, the 7th unshaven, the 8th exhibitionist, the 9th Brahminical (they enlisted high-caste Gurkhas), and the 10th alcoholic.[4]

Indian Army, sent to India and 'attached' to a British regiment for a year, after which he went on probation to an Indian regiment and hoped he would do well enough to be invited to stay. The old system had been open to abuse in the sense that British regiments could offload officers they did not want by encouraging them to transfer to Indian service; so the reforms, particularly the extra incentive of higher pay and pensions, were welcome.

When Villiers-Stuart arrived in Bombay, he warmed to the place but not to the people, too many of whom were 'smelly' and addicted to chewing pan (betel nut). During the train journey to Mian Mir East, the thought of joining a new regiment that wasn't even his, so to speak, filled him with foreboding: 'I seemed to myself to be going to school again, and a new one, or for the first time. And yet I seemed to have been doing this all my life. I was ashamed then of such cowardice. I am ashamed now when I think of it, but so it was.' He could not bear the feeling of being a new boy all over again, and he admits that the sense of 'being different' made the first few days in the 93rd Highlanders (as the 2nd battalion of the Argyll and Sutherlands were still calling themselves, despite their change of name in 1881) difficult. But they were 'extraordinarily kind and good to their "unattached" yet attached people, making them free of everything, helping them all they could, and considering them *of* the regiment', unlike some other regiments, such as the Rifle Brigade and 60th King's Royal Rifle Corps, who treated their 'attached' subalterns 'with nothing short of brutality': 'They allowed them no rights – did not help them at all – made them mess by themselves like outcasts at a separate table always, taught them nothing, took their money, and ridiculed them all the time'.[5]

Yet even with kind treatment it was an anomalous situation; as Villiers-Stuart writes, 'you would have to be a soldier to know what it meant to *belong* to *no* battalion or regiment'. It was particularly hard for someone who came out to India with an 'inferiority complex', someone who, despite his successes at school, in the 4th Durhams, and in passing into the Indian Army so high up 'was still afraid; still felt a fool with strangers, still was shy and desperately self-conscious':

I believe now that though a great deal of this inferiority complex was due to being 'crushed' when young, a great deal was also due to my unconsciously knowing or subconsciously knowing that I did not know, and could not without real miserable embarrassment, any girl alive except my sisters. Anyway that's how it was, a more sad and feeble pessimistic moral coward never left home . . .

He protests too much, perhaps; Villiers-Stuart's background and upbringing were entirely characteristic of upper middle-class males destined to become army officers.

To add to his woes he had to go through the new boy experience twice more, since 'Lord Roberts had made a rule that no one was to go straight off to a Gurkha battalion, and I was told that I must do a year first with a Punjab regiment.' Although this could cause an introverted young officer like Villiers-Stuart agonies, the practice encouraged British officers destined for the Gurkhas to learn Urdu, as they had to, before concentrating on Gurkhali, and to familiarize themselves with Indian life and people.

As Lord Ripon remarked, 'There are probably no conditions of Indian life less favourable for becoming acquainted with the people of the country and seeing them to advantage than service with a British regiment.'[6] After a year with the 93rd Highlanders, Villiers-Stuart regarded the prospect of service with any Indian regiment – even the 20th Punjab Infantry – as 'awful':

I did not like the look of any I had seen, for bearded people of course seemed odd to me after the 4th Durhams, and the 93rd . . . Though I was quite contented to go to the Indian service, at the time from what I'd seen, except a few guards of the 4th Gurkhas, I did not like the style of anything about Indian regiments . . . in fact it seemed to me I was going to an inferior service.

Nevertheless, he gained useful experience with the 20th Punjab Infantry, which was in the process of transformation from an irregular battalion, known after its colonel as 'Brownlow's bounders', to a modern and disciplined regiment of the line. He learned, for instance, that a young officer in an Indian unit could not expect his orders to be carried out as a matter of course, but had to prove his worth first: 'There are two kinds of obedience – automatic to the rank, and personal to the individual. The former was not the practice in the 20th PI. Till I realized this I was worried a great deal.' This lesson applied to Gurkha battalions quite as much as Punjabi battalions.

While he was serving with the 20th Punjab Infantry, Villiers-Stuart was questioned by the colonel as to why he never went to the club, which was the centre of European social life. He pleaded pressure of work and study for (language) exams. The colonel replied: 'Well, I wish you would go. I'm sure of this, unless every subaltern is friends with some nice woman who'll look after him he deteriorates.' Villiers-Stuart comments: 'I'm quite sure he was right that such friendship is good for everyone, but I'm not so sure about the deterioration.' Like many of his kind, he did not approve of 'poodle-faking' (entertaining young women) or ladies' men in general, and writes of one officer he met from the 2nd Punjab Infantry, who later applied to transfer into the 1/5th Gurkhas, 'I put a stop to that. He may have been a good soldier. I don't know – but he certainly was one of those dreadful "ladies' men" – they all adored him – anyone of that sort is best avoided.' Being a ladies' man may not have been this officer's only crime in Villiers-Stuart's eyes; he was a Maltese and Villiers-Stuart 'took a great dislike to him as soon as the first effusiveness had proved that he was not very sincere'.

Racial prejudice of an unthinking kind was endemic among army officers, as Villiers-Stuart's account of the 20th Punjab Infantry's new adjutant, who had transferred from an Assamese Gurkha regiment, illustrates:

> He was a very capable office man, accountant and all that sort of thing. But he didn't look a soldier and certainly appeared to have a strain of dark blood in him and both were hopeless with a smart looking ultra Englishman like P. G. Walker [the colonel], and an Indian battalion so independent as the 20th PI. In fact dark blood is hopeless in any Indian battalion – that is in a so called 'British' officer. I do not think he was a good officer outside the office. He rode badly and was not a good instructor.

So much for the adjutant. But Villiers-Stuart approved of the fact that Ordnance officers in the Indian service had been recruited from 'the best of the Eurasian population as it was then called'. He praised their loyalty and was understanding about their situation, caught between a contemptuous native population and an indifferent government which – at the time he was writing, in the late 1920s – no longer recognized that they had any claim on it. He regretted that in the climate of 'India for the Indians', responsible posts in the railways, telegraph and postal services were no longer reserved for them and 'these excellent people were everywhere pushed out'.

Villiers-Stuart's sporting prowess paid off when it came to getting into a Gurkha battalion, for playing cricket was 'in those days *the* qualification, apart from capacity for work and in work'. He was invited to accept an attachment to the 1/5th Gurkhas 'with a view to permanent appoint-ment in due course'. While he was delighted to get such an opportunity, he dreaded starting all over yet again: 'Once more be the very junior ignoramus of a strange battalion. Once more buy a new kit. I was in despair.' Indeed, his arrival at the 1/5th Gurkhas was the beginning of 'the most miserable time I ever experienced'.

The first officer he met there was the acting adjutant, H. P. Browne, 'who was excessively arrogant and haughty, the sort of person who never can answer a question without losing his position and importance':

> At mess Browne burdened himself with me obviously. I was in a quandary. I did not belong to the battalion, and I had not been made an honorary member. Nor was Browne entertaining me. Should I ask for a drink or what? In the end I did, and beyond the misery of the Abdar or wine butler having a long argument with my khitmatgar [waiter] as to whether I was a 'guest' or not, nothing happened . . . There must have been about fourteen or fifteen people there. After dinner I excused myself as soon as possible and gladly went to bed. Browne had not introduced me to anyone!!

Villiers-Stuart reported to the orderly room at 9.45 a.m. the next day as instructed, only to be kept waiting for nearly two hours before the colonel and another officer, Captain Kemball, deigned to see him; and when they did, they assumed an air of almost terminal boredom. 'But it was all of a piece I found with the tone of the 1/5th Gurkhas, as officers so other ranks. No words can express their arrogance towards and contempt for any new arrival.' Villiers-Stuart was shocked by the bad language (in both senses) of the officers, particularly Kemball, and appalled at the way Gurkha officers, NCOs and men followed their British officers' unworthy example. They too ignored the newcomer, covering their insubordination by pretending not to be able to understand him.

Soon after he arrived Villiers-Stuart took part in a 'field day' exercise:

> Browne with the recruits formed 'the enemy'. When we were
> extending to attack, as the men did it very badly, I had them all back
> and explained how to do it. That is the people I was in charge of.
> Bruce saw this and came flying up and abused me in the most filthy
> language and ordered me to leave them alone. I was quite determined
> to leave the 1/5th Gurkhas after that . . . But I reckoned without Bruce
> who as soon as things were over came up with Browne and howling
> with laughter explained how it really was a great honour to be abused
> like that by him, and he could do much more than that. The beastly
> fellow was so childishly pleased at his disgraceful behaviour that I was
> obliged in spite of myself to laugh too.

The Hon. C. G. Bruce was a legendary figure in his time, a famous mountaineer, a man of enormous physical strength and prodigious appetites. Years after his retirement as a brigadier-general, when a subaltern questioned the subedar-major of the 1/5th Gurkhas about Bruce Sahib, the Gurkha officer asked, 'What do you want to know about him, Sahib?' The young lieutenant said, 'Well, anything,' to which the subedar-major replied, 'I can tell you this, then. He was the only officer who screwed every Gurkha wife in the battalion.'[7] If true, this was certainly unusual: British officers generally kept well away from Gurkha wives; apart from disciplinary considerations they had too much respect for their men to risk provoking their anger. But Bruce seems to have enjoyed breaking the rules.

It was he who started the *khud* or hill race at which Gurkhas excel. Because of their size, they found it impossible to compete on equal terms with Sikhs and Punjabi Muslims in most forms of athletics; so in order to prevent them developing a sporting inferiority complex, Bruce introduced hill running. Though himself an excellent cross-country runner, he had noticed that Gurkhas could easily outstrip him in their own terrain and rightly assumed they would outstrip everyone else. British or Indian troops might compete with them on an uphill stretch, but no one could approach the speed at which they descended a hillside – watching them come down an almost perpendicular slope reminded one officer of 'raindrops falling down a window-pane'.[8]

Given the kind of reception Villiers-Stuart received in 1/5th Gurkha Rifles, it is not surprising that he formed so low opinion of his fellow officers. The CO, Lt-Col. A. R. Martin, was a 'man who broke every rule and made it impossible for subordinates to do their work properly, putting everyone at sea'. Major (later Field Marshal Sir) Arthur Barrett, though he would become a friend in due course, was 'definitely rude to all newcomers, and with no reason'. Kemball (who met his death at Vimy Ridge in 1917, commanding a Canadian battalion with such conspicuous gallantry that the Germans proposed a temporary truce in order that his body might be recovered and themselves brought it into the British lines) was also 'notorious' for rudeness. And of all the many Bs in the battalion:

> Boisragon imagined himself to be the only well bred person in India or anywhere, which resulted in his being an utter snob. Badcock had been a good fellow but was soured by Boisragon getting a VC at Nilt when he did more and 'only' got a DSO . . . Bruce was an insubordinate clever well read man of the world . . . a great sportsman . . . a splendid linguist, and if he had a fault it was perhaps a slight desire to keep in the public eye . . . How did he, only a few years older than me, manage to impress the hidebound 1/5th officers? – because he was 'The Honourable' and because his uncle was Sir William Lockhart, GOC Punjab Command . . . Browne came next. Clever perhaps. Conceited, rude and arrogant. For long I tried to get on with him, but I never did *really*. He could never forget he was senior, I was junior.

But Villiers-Stuart did have one chum; his name was Ketchen, 'a rascal, up to any tricks – but a great sportsman and a pleasant kind friend to me always'. Ketchen's own initiation into mess life in the 1/5th Gurkha Rifles had been painful enough, perhaps, to influence his attitude towards other newcomers. At a guest night soon after his arrival,

Bruce had taken offence at a remark Ketchen had made and, forcing him into a chair, had twisted his neck so hard that it was practically broken by the time the other officers saw the danger, jumped on Bruce and effected Ketchen's release:

> Bruce when really drunk as then was awful. He stopped at nothing and was so powerful no one would do anything with him. It took four or five to quiet him . . . I don't think Ketchen ever forgave Bruce about his neck, and also I'm quite sure Bruce was jealous of him – so there was bound to be trouble.

Since Villiers-Stuart was not writing with an eye to publication, his picture of mess life is unadulterated. But what of the man himself: was he simply subjected to the same treatment as every other new arrival, or was there something about him that made the other officers think he needed 'taking down a peg or two'? Was he 'too full of himself', perhaps? He was certainly ambitious to make a name for himself in a world where ambition was acceptable only if it wasn't obtrusive; he was also highly critical of the lack of discipline in the battalion. He was a martinet in a regiment which rated other activities above square-bashing. And from the beginning he was determined not merely to survive but to transform the battalion into an efficient military machine: 'That in the end I was contented and happy in the 1/5th Gurkhas was merely because by years of labour and unremitting toil I had got them to be very different to what they had been – and I don't care what anyone says, that is known to be true.'

Within six months of joining 1/5th Gurkha Rifles, Villiers-Stuart was in action on the north-west frontier in the 'great tribal outbreak of 1897'.[9] From the time of the Sikh wars right up to the Second World War, the frontier provided British and Indian Army troops with a useful testing ground for the tactics and skills of mountain warfare. Nigel Woodyatt writes:

> There is nothing more fascinating than trans-border warfare. The wild and difficult country, the manly and hardy tribesman, the uncertainty regarding his movements, the element of surprise, the necessity for

ceaseless vigilance, the calls that are made on the stamina of the troops
and on one's own endurance, all tend to bewitch and allure. To try and
compare it with trench warfare on the Western Front is, of course,
ridiculous. One may be aptly termed a *hideous nightmare*, and the other
a very *dangerous sport*.[10]

The Tirah campaign nearly finished Villiers-Stuart's career before it
had properly begun. In this 'dangerous sport' he was so badly wounded
that he ended up with one leg several inches shorter than the other and
could never again participate in less dangerous sports. Another man
might have turned his back on the army, or at least on the infantry, but
Villiers-Stuart was merely strengthened in his determination to succeed in his chosen career.

First, though, he had to spend several months at home recovering
from the wound and trying to build up his strength. On his own evidence, he was not a good patient:

> I could not bear this girl massaging my leg. I put up with it for the
> month ordered and then very gladly saw her depart. She was a pleasant
> looking clean girl, and if it had not been for my inferiority complex and
> anti other sex complex (fear of my parents) I might have got some
> good [out] of her expensive work. I don't know why it was, but I was
> always afraid to speak to one of the opposite sex for fear I'd be thought
> *silly* . . .

He was twenty-five years old, uncertain of his future and moving among
his relatives, particularly the female ones, like a fish out of water:

> [B]ecause Audrey and I had passages of family wit, etc., her mother's
> hawk-eye concluded I was about to propose! Had I not been crippled,
> and quite unaware whether I should ever be able to earn my living *at
> all*, much less continue in the army, also had I had any money with
> which to supplement my very small subaltern's pay, I should have had
> a shot at Norah or Di!! But people in the desperate position I was in
> are not thinking of anything of that sort.

That was that, as far as Villiers-Stuart was concerned; his disability and the fact that he might have to leave the army because of it excused him courting duties; in his memoirs and diaries he never again refers to marriage or the feared opposite sex in relation to himself.

Back in his true home, the regiment in India, he had to work out a way of standing with his right leg slightly bent, or his left leg so stretched that only the toes touched the ground, in order to accommodate the four-inch difference in the length of his legs. One day, after he had fallen off his horse and was feeling particularly weary and sore, Bruce came up and said to him in his sprightly way, 'What a pity you can't stand at ease properly any more! But I expect you'll have to do a lot of "improper" standing at ease – most of your life, in fact, won't you?' and went off, laughing heartily. The incident stuck in Villiers-Stuart's mind: 'I can see the group now and I shall never forget it because I suddenly became aware that unless I could do something about it I should not be allowed to stay long in the regiment.' Since he had yet to be offered a permanent place in the 1/5th he was particularly vulnerable.

Another incident which reinforced his feeling of insecurity was when the new CO, Colonel Barrett, looked him up and down and then turned to Browne and made some remark about polo that afternoon. Villiers-Stuart took this as an indication that he was not wanted, though years later when the two were firm friends and he reminded Sir Arthur of it, Barrett claimed that he had done it 'because he did not wish to be forced "officially" to notice my crippled leg or boots, etc'. Villiers-Stuart was unimpressed.

His sensitivity is understandable, particularly in view of his uncertainty about his future, not to mention the unsympathetic way he had been treated by the officers of the 1/5th from the moment he joined them.

He did everything he could to prove his fitness, including escorting a convoy of arms and ammunition up to the frontier, first in intense heat, then through monsoon downpours when the rains finally came, and finally in the freezing cold of a mountain pass. A few years later he would take part in a forced march which 'became the talk of all India'.[11] He drove others as hard as himself, and the old-style Gurkha officers and other ranks came close to mutiny on occasion. But Villiers-Stuart was hell-bent on disciplining this 'whited sepulchre' of a battalion, as he describes it at this time. He blamed its indiscipline on 'the smug complacency of its senior officers' who made up for their linguistic and other inadequacies by promoting to Gurkha officers those NCOs who could make themselves understood 'irrespective of whether they were good men' (a common enough practice in Gurkha battalions). As a result there were too many commissioned and non-commissioned line-boys who – and here Villiers-Stuart reveals the standard British officer prejudice – 'never are worth enlisting except as signallers, much less promoting'.

Villiers-Stuart's permanent place in the battalion depended on there being a vacancy. At that time the norm in the Indian Army was a minimum of seven British officers per battalion; apart from the commanding officer, there were the second-in-command, the adjutant and four others. Pre-1857, when promotion went even more strictly by seniority, an officer who wished to leave was often helped on his way by his juniors, who might club together to buy him out and move themselves a step up the ladder. This was known as the 'subscription system'.[12] To compensate for his disability and improve his chances of staying on, Villiers-Stuart worked hard to pass the obligatory Parbatiya (Gurkhali) exam. Once he had mastered Parbatiya, he ceased to speak Urdu in the battalion. But as the 5th Gurkhas were part of the Punjab Frontier Force, he also had to pass an exam in Pushtu, the language of Afghanistan and the frontier.

Keen though he was to remain in the 1/5th Gurkhas, he still wondered if it was the right place for him:

> I seemed to be so very much at one with officers of other regiments, but there were so many discordant elements in our mess it was not the same. Boisragon was hopeless, completely antipathetic. Bruce's ways I did not like. Browne could not be friendly. Champain was either condescending or hostile. The rest I got on well with. But it was not happy all through as the 93rd, 4th Durhams, 20th PI had been . . . Anyway, whatever was the case, in the 1/5th one after another of us got more and more wrapped up in the men until, I think now, they became an obsession . . .

Obsession with their men was an abiding characteristic of British officers in Gurkha units. General Sir George MacMunn remarks: 'The rest of the Army . . . is always ready to pull the legs of the officers when they "*gurk*", to use the Army slang, too freely.'[13] Yet this common obsession did not prevent individual units from becoming extremely parochial, and among Gurkha regiments there was a strict pecking order. Villiers-Stuart recalls that when the 42nd Gurkhas came from Assam to Abbottabad, they seemed to the 1/5th 'an astonishing crowd', their men larger and heavier than those of 1/5 GR – 'from lack of hill work'– their officers 'very odd people' and their ideas 'quite out of date'. The CO of the 1/5th, Colonel Barrett, nicknamed his opposite number of the 42nd 'Mozambique' on account of the fact that he had a big nose and 'looked a Jew'. While Villiers-Stuart shared the prejudices of his fellow officers, he was, at the same time, critical of their standoffishness. He writes of the 42nd (who would become the 6th Gurkha Rifles in 1903):

> I should think they had a very easy time in Assam. But there was no excuse for the way all our officers and other ranks laughed at and ridiculed them. The bad feeling started by this infamous behaviour lasted for years, and when I left for good was, among the officers, not dead, though efforts for many years to stop it had got it out of the other ranks. Col. Barrett was responsible for this bad feeling being fostered to a very great extent and as Commanding Officer he ought to have done all he could to prevent it ever forming.

'Piffer' snobbery was at work here: the Punjab Frontier Force regarded itself as an elite, being constantly engaged in sporadic fighting against the tough, merciless but admired Pathan tribesmen; the kudos connected with service on the north-west frontier was absent from service on the less romantic but equally rugged north-east frontier. (The relative neglect of jungle-fighting skills honed on the north-east frontier in favour of the open hill warfare of the north-west frontier would prove costly in the early days of the war against the Japanese in Malaya and Burma in 1942.)

Along with Villiers-Stuart's critical discontent with his battalion went a determination to change it. One of his gripes about his colonel, Arthur Barrett, was that he was 'no organiser, and no regimental officer':

> He could never grasp that 'automatic' was the only word. That is, the officers must wind up the clock, and then it must *go* without anything

more from them than 'seeing the time'. And it could be done, and was done from 1904 onwards [i.e. when his own influence as adjutant took effect].

Villiers-Stuart's vision of the soldier as automaton, the product of intensive discipline and training, was fundamentally at odds with the views of Colonel Barrett and the old irregular habits that the 1/5th had not yet outgrown.

He was at loggerheads with many of his peers and seniors – and with none more than the charismatic C. G. Bruce – over what constituted an efficient fighting unit. These two were polar opposites. Bruce, nick-named '*Bhalu*', the bear, because of his size and strength, was essentially a free spirit, an athlete and mountaineer who had been an active proponent of the idea of forming a special unit of Gurkha scouts, which would take on the hostile frontier tribesmen at their own game – one of mobility, stealth, surprise and superior marksmanship. (It can't have done his cause any harm that his uncle, Sir William Lockhart, was commanding the 1897 Tirah Expeditionary Force in which the Gurkha scouts, made up of contingents from 1/3 GR and both battalions of the 5 GR, distinguished themselves.) John Morris of the 3rd Gurkhas, a mountaineer of the next generation who got to know Bruce well when he went with him on the 1922 Everest expedition after the latter's retirement, describes him as 'the very finest type of paternal Indian Army officer':

He knew the name of every man in his regiment, together with the intimate details of most of their private lives, and it was upon men such as he that the high reputation of the old Indian Army had been built. They were splendid regimental officers, but most of them were temperamentally unfitted for higher command.[14]

Much of this would apply with equal force to Villiers-Stuart who, like Bruce, was fluent in the language and familiar with his men – and also probably temperamentally unfitted for higher command. Both men ended their military careers as brigadier-generals, but neither was really happy except as a regimental soldier. Neither was short of ability: Villiers-Stuart thought Bruce 'had the attributes of a very unusually good C-in-C India in him' and should have gone further than he did; and he might have gone further himself had his ambition been personal rather than regimental. Yet these superficial resemblances mask a deeper dichotomy between the roundhead militarist, professional to his fingertips, and the cavalier soldier-sportsman, who made something of a fetish of amateurism.

One need look no further than to their respective attitudes to leave. After he was 'crippled', Villiers-Stuart writes, '*I dared not ask, either on this occasion or any other* through all the years to come, for any leave off anything *however urgent or necessary*, as if I did, I at once gave a handle to those who *might want to get rid of me*, to make room for themselves.' In blithe contrast, Bruce recalls that 'from the very time I joined [1/5 GR] I did one of those things which has always stood me in great stead – I established a reputation for acquiring leave, and it is perfectly marvellous when such a reputation is established how often leave appears to come round'.[15] No wonder Bruce got under Villiers-Stuart's skin, filling him with envy and contempt. He never missed an opportunity to slight him, as when he wrote, 'the whole battalion was working well, improving daily now we were free of drones and obstructionists like Boisragon and in many ways Bruce . . .' Or again:

> Badcock and I could have got on very well any time. But for Bruce. Badcock was senior to Bruce, and though I did not realise it for a long time, Bruce consistently worked to get Badcock out of his way, so that he, Bruce, might command the 1/5th in due course. Badcock I don't think knew this. So whenever and however Bruce could belittle Badcock he did. Some time later Bruce was responsible for a bad quarrel between Badcock and me, and for having Badcock sent to the 4th Gurkhas.

But even when he is abusing him in his diaries, Villiers-Stuart is obliged to admit, 'No one could help liking Bruce in a way', if only as a prelude to heaping yet more abuse on him: 'but one tired of always being considered a very small person and his requiring one to worship him'. Villiers-Stuart exemplifies the precept that if you really want to put the boot in, begin with a compliment: 'Bruce was a clever man and a genius in many ways, but an insufferable nuisance in all others. The fact remains that when he was present with the battalion things were always difficult, when absent from it everything improved and went smoothly.'

The two men had in common an obsession with their Gurkhas, but Bruce was more liberal and humane than Villiers-Stuart. Under the system of 'half-mounting' then in operation the riflemen had to buy some of their own clothing and feed themselves out of their 'wretched' pay of 7 rupees a month. This meant that 'if they were worked hard during peacetime the very fact that one was making them efficient acted in a way like a fine'.[16] So the lack of training deplored by Villiers-Stuart could be seen in part as an attempt by Bruce and others to avoid unnecessary wear and tear on uniforms and boots for which the men themselves were responsible. Villiers-Stuart would never have allowed such a consideration to stand in the way of greater efficiency.

Yet he had a deep sentimental attachment – to put it no stronger – to individuals, such as the recruit Dhansing Gurung, 'perhaps the greatest friend I ever had in my life'. Bruce had spotted Dhansing's talent as a runner and chosen him for a *khud* race in which the boy came in second. Villiers-Stuart describes what happened after the race:

As I got in the dusk to the end of the bridge by the guard house . . . Dhansing Gurung stepped out from a shadow and in great excitement put his arm through mine and asked eagerly if he might 'come back' to work 'now – with you'. I said of course – and he was ever so delighted. He talked all the way up the hill very fast explaining all he'd had to do and how he'd longed to get away from the training and running all the time and get back to work. It was just like being with a boy at school, only this one was so marvellously put together and so strong he would have shone wherever he went. Spotlessly clean in a white jersey and black shorts only, and the picture of health he seemed a small sized god of strength and energy. And his brain was as good as his body. Bruce of course was furious. He wished to keep Dhansing hanging about him for the future learning nothing and pretending to keep him trained.

But we'd all seen too much of that nonsense to let it go on. The riflemen openly said that if you were chosen 'to run' by Bruce, you lost all promotion and damaged your heart, which was quite true . . .

The roundhead Villiers-Stuart outmanoeuvred the cavalier Bruce on this occasion and, now that he was adjutant – 'miles the best job for anyone till they reached permanent command of a company' – and his place in the battalion was secure, Villiers-Stuart's influence was increasingly felt while Bruce's was on the wane. In any battalion, the adjutant is a key figure, 'the Colonel's Staff Officer'. And as Villiers-Stuart pointed out, 'the majority of Colonels still leave all office work to the adjutant'. The more the colonel left to Villiers-Stuart the better pleased he was.

He was determined that such manoeuvres as pitching and striking camp should be taught properly: 'The work was very hard but we were, or I was, trying for a very big stake. Some understood, others among the officers did not. And one, Bruce, would not.' But Villiers-Stuart felt the tide running his way; the new colonel, Kemball, 'was able to do what no-one else had, i.e. keep Bruce in order. He saw through Bruce completely.' Bruce, however, continued to be a law unto himself; he 'could never work with anyone as he would not realise the necessity for a common system in everything. But as he didn't care what the Colonel said, it didn't matter to him.' Badcock and Bruce had been brought up 'under the old slack and obsolete regime'; neither was 'entirely loyal to the Colonel'. But they were now in the minority, and Villiers-Stuart could afford to be more generous:

> I may as well add here that to the end of their time, like Boisragon, only not so badly, these two were a nuisance to everyone and slowed down all progress. It was not their fault. Circumstances did it. Times changed. They did not see they must change with them.

Villiers-Stuart was an ideal officer in Kitchener's Indian Army, Bruce a hangover from the earlier, wilder days of Bobs Bahadur. Villiers-Stuart's favourites were keen riflemen, like Dhansing Gurung; Bruce's were amiable rogues like his orderly Parbir Thapa, 'a fine hill runner and a good man in camp' who was 'also afflicted by a prodigious sense of fun and the ludicrous, more than any Gurkha I have met ever since, and that's saying a good deal'.[17]

Parbir was the first Gurkha rifleman ever to visit England, when Bruce took him there in 1891 en route to Switzerland, where they were

to take part in an Alpine mountaineering expedition. Despite dire warnings from his fellow officers of what Parbir might get up to in England,
the visit was a great success. Bruce (dressed as an Afghan) and his
orderly staged a mock fight for the benefit of the war artist, Vereker
Hamilton (brother of the future General Sir Ian Hamilton), who was
making studies for his painting, *Taking the Guns at Kandahar*, in which
the men of 2 GR feature largely. Bruce entered into the spirit of the
occasion a little too enthusiastically and nicked Parbir's thigh with his
Afghan knife, drawing blood. As a reward for his pains, Parbir was taken
to London Zoo by the artist, who had not considered that there might
be people who had never heard of, let alone seen, a giraffe; Parbir was
so taken with the absurdity of this creature that, weakened by parox-
ysms of laughter, he collapsed on to the ground and held his head in his
hands in disbelief.

At Sunday evening prayers on the Bruces' estate in south Wales,
Bruce's father looked up from his devotions to discover 'a very solemn
Gurkha in full uniform sitting between the hall boy and the footman
with a particularly pious expression on his face'.[18] But Parbir was more
at home outstripping the leaden-footed gamekeeper in pursuit of
poachers, who roughed him up before he got the hang of things and,
arming himself with a stout stick, cudgelled them into submission and
handed them over in triumph. Despite his lack of English, he made several friends among the Rhondda Valley miners, who welcomed him
into their homes.

But Parbir's greatest adventure – and his nemesis – took place neither
in Britain nor in the Swiss mountains, but back in the regiment while
Bruce was away on detachment. The sport there was seducing the
subedar-major's wife – well, not his actual wife, who was in Nepal, but his
'regimental wife', the 'Cleopatra of Abbottabad' as Bruce dismissively
dubs her.[19] The young 'bloods' of the battalion were so successful in
accomplishing their mission that the enraged subedar-major took to guarding his lady's virtue with men hidden in the bushes around his house. This
merely upped the stakes, and the young men continued to elude him.

Then one day my lad was seen very stealthily creeping into the house.
The place was completely surrounded, but after a strict search lo! and
behold! no Parbir – not a sign. They were just leaving the courtyard

when from underneath the very thinnest bunch of Indian corn stalks
which apparently wouldn't cover a rat, and standing up against the wall
came a violent sneeze! Flung aside and there he was – a corn leaf had
got up his nose – hence the explosion. As they say in Nepali, 'Chor ko
taugo ma Khasingra' – 'On every thief's head there is a little bit of
grass', meaning that something or other is sure to give him away.[20]

This escapade landed Parbir in gaol, where he was sent for a year to
repent at leisure (had it happened in Nepal he would have lost his head
and the erring wife her nose). But Bruce's evident delight in the story
reveals the anarchic streak in his make-up which was anathema to
Villiers-Stuart.

Before he became adjutant, Villiers-Stuart had been the 1/5th's
machine-gun officer, earning this tribute in the regimental history:
'Himself of a mechanical turn of mind, with an eye for detail, and possessed of great administrative capacity, he succeeded in producing a
very high standard of efficiency, and it was not long before the machine
gunners themselves began to take such an immense pride in their work
that there was justification for their claim to be looked upon as a kind of
miniature *corps d'élite*.'[21] As soon as he took over as adjutant Villiers-
Stuart set about transforming the entire battalion in the same way as he
had transformed the machine-gunners. He believed in early indoctri-
nation, and in those days each battalion trained its own recruits:

When . . . recruits joined the ranks the adjutant lost at a blow all these
100 to 150 boys whom he had looked after and cared for for the first
nine months of their life in the army and in a foreign country . . . The
adjutant knew each one of them by name and all about him. He had
watched him grow from an ignorant little animal into a very capable
active strong rifleman; and just as the recruit to the end of his service
would never forget 'my man who taught me' and would render him
enthusiastic obedience at any time, so the adjutant would never forget
in after years the boy who had stolen a place in his heart . . . The
adjutant will begin to teach a new lot of recruits immediately, for the
work never stops; but for a long time he will think of the children he
has lost.

Villiers-Stuart was adjutant for four years in the first decade of the twentieth century. 'And so the new era began, and lasted all through the War with strange officers and all the difficulties for the men of that long time of misery. And I left it in 1924, twenty years later, just the same but a tradition instead of being a new thing.'

Another of the adjutant's responsibilities – and one that was equally close to Villiers-Stuart's heart – was the bugles and band of 1/5 GR. Unlike many Gurkha regiments the 1/5th did not have a pipe band, feeling that it was inappropriate in a regiment which modelled itself upon the Rifle Brigade; the pride of the 1/5th was their bugles. Despite their resistance to the 'vogue for copying Highland Regiments', up to 1905 the regimental march past had been the tune, 'Hieland Laddie'. But this had been adopted by so many British regiments that the 1/5th found themselves having to seek permission to play their own march past, and Villiers-Stuart changed it to the old Irish air, 'Moreen'.[22]

He also gave much thought as to how the bugles should be constituted. In Nepal the low caste *damais* (tailors) doubled as musicians, and traditionally regimental buglers were recruited from *damais* and *lohars* (blacksmiths) as well as from line-boys. From a musical point of view there was little to choose between them, but the line-boys objected to mixing with low caste lads. Villiers-Stuart's solution was to make the bugles the exclusive preserve of line-boys who, unlike *damais* and *lohars*, could be transferred into the ranks if they were good enough; that eliminated caste friction and gave the line-boys hope that they might graduate into riflemen. This policy was later reversed, but Villiers-Stuart reinstated it when he assumed command of the battalion in 1920.

In matters of warfare, Villiers-Stuart disapproved of battalions jealously guarding those secrets which would enable them to beat not just the enemy but other regiments on their own side as well: 'Anything more fatuous could not be conceived but we all grew up in it, and it took the War to break the idea – temporarily – for it is back again I hear as strongly as ever.' Regiments should pool their military expertise to fight a common enemy, not seek glory at each other's expense. But away from battle it was a different story: there inter-regimental competitiveness was a virtue, not a vice. So when Villiers-Stuart heard that while he was on home leave in 1914, the then commanding Lt-Col Boisragon had given all the battalion's band and bugle marches, most of which had been obtained at great trouble and expense from the French army, to 1/6 GR, he was scandalized: 'I never got over it. Our very biggest pride almost was gone!'

It was a cruel irony that the outbreak of war, the time when he most wanted to be with the men he had trained and nurtured, should find him stranded in England on leave – especially given his claim that 'I only once in my whole service had three months or even two months leave.' His efforts to get back to his unit were frustrated; the War Office refused to release Indian Army officers in Britain involved in training the New Army, and Villiers-Stuart found himself second-in-command of a newly raised battalion of the Rifle Brigade. He soon took over command of the 9th Rifle Brigade, which he led with distinction at Ypres on the western front, though sometimes he found it harder to understand the language of the Jews and cockneys and Lancastrians under his command than that of his cherished Gurkhas. His professional dedication, however, was such that even on the western front he took leave only reluctantly.

Despite his readiness to do his duty as a front-line soldier and his commitment to his new battalion – 'It's an odd thing that the 9th RB never did any good after I left it' – Villiers-Stuart yearned to rejoin his own regiment. The opportunity came early in 1916, when he was ordered to Egypt to take temporary command of the 1/5th Gurkhas at El Kubri East.

He was not impressed by the scene which greeted him in the 1/5th mess tent at El Kubri. The officers, including the acting CO, were gambling and there was 'too much whisky about'. He felt their resentment at his arrival and went out among the Gurkhas:

The riflemen seemed very subdued . . . But there were some of the old smiles – and then suddenly my Naré Gurung appeared. He just rushed at me and flung his arms round me and laughed and cried all in one. Then after a minute or two he said, 'My Sahib has come at last – it was very hard to wait . . . oh, what a day! My own Sahib has come' – and much more dear affectionate 1/5th child's talk – for the oldest and best fighters among them were always just affectionate children IF you knew them.

When he had gone on home leave in March 1914, Villiers-Stuart had been so sure that the war was coming that he had left his field service kit with his company. It was there waiting for him when he arrived at El Kubri. While he was checking it over, he drew his kukri to see if it was clean and a piece of paper fell out:

> It was a touching little letter from Rifleman Dhanbir Gurung, my pet batman of A Company. He said in the letter they were off to Gallipoli Peninsula and that he might be killed and never see me again. If that was so – and alas it was – 'when at last you come if you too are not killed, you will get this and remember me, Sahib. If you too are killed, we will be once more together and so happy. Goodbye for now, Sahib'.

After noting Villiers-Stuart's return as acting CO, the regimental history goes on, 'At El Kubri some training was undertaken' – a succinct statement of cause and effect, if ever there was one.[23] But within a month the battalion was ordered back to India, where there was no understanding of the war at all: 'Sometimes it felt as if Army HQ and all under it hated one for having been in the war.'

His first taste of commanding his own battalion was short-lived; he reverted to second-in-command when – 'to my disgust' – one of his seniors, M. R. W. Nightingale, came back: 'He was a very brave man and a very fine leader in war, but he was almost a danger as regards training, reconstructive or office work as he knew nothing of these subjects and never really knew the men.'

Villiers-Stuart had barely got over this disappointment when he learned that he would not be returning with the battalion to the Middle East to take part in the Mesopotamian campaign because an officer of his quality and experience was required to raise the 3rd battalion of the Guides. This was the first of a series of jobs that would keep him away from the 1/5th until he finally assumed command of it at the age of forty-eight.

The least enjoyable of these jobs – Villiers-Stuart called it 'hateful' – was Inspector of Infantry for Northern India. Promotion to brigadier-general may have sweetened the pill, but later he would gladly drop a couple of ranks to take over his battalion. A single story will illustrate why he found the job so distasteful:

At Quetta on my second visit I had a painful thing to do. Scally who was a 4th Gurkha I think, was in command of a newly raised Gurkha battalion there. I heard from the Brigadier that the battalion was very bad, and that Scally complained he could do nothing about it. I knew about Scally. He was one of Arthur Grant's men, when Arthur Grant was the terror of the 4th Gurkhas before the war. So I thought he might have been at some of Arthur Grant's games of brutality. When the inspection began with arms drill, something did not suit Scally, so he walked over and hit a rifleman in the ranks with his cane. I did not do more than make a note of that. A little later, he did it again, more brutally, several times. So I stopped the work which was also far below the usual Gurkha form. We then went to bayonet work and it happened again. So I stopped that and at musketry it happened again. So I told Scally he'd have to be in arrest for striking and he blustered and went on; but I stuck to it and sent him away. I then sent for Collins, also a 4th Gurkha officer, and a good soldier who was second in command. I told him I'd got Scally in arrest and that I'd see that through but I wished to see what the men could do. So I had everything over again, and it was very good. The men were in despair at Scally's bullying ways; when he wasn't there they were willing enough to do their best . . .

. . . [An] enquiry was held and Scally was removed, and the battalion was quite different the next time I saw it . . . He was just like Arthur Grant, he did not know his work so he punished and struck in the hope of getting what he could not teach . . . He should have been cashiered.

It was a great relief to Villiers-Stuart when 'the long hoped for orders' to take command of the 1/5th finally came. Apart from the few unsatisfactory months in 1916, he had been away from the battalion for almost seven years: 'at last I was to get home again'. He found that he was the only pre-war officer left and there were as few as 200 other ranks remaining from that golden age; so he had to set about the task of reinventing, as it were, the highly trained and disciplined force which had gone off to the war.

Not everyone welcomed him back. On his first day as commanding officer he went into the orderly room and, finding a letter carelessly left open, couldn't help but see that it was from one of his officers, who had written, 'Is it really true that this dreadful man is coming to command?' (Four years later, he proudly relates, the same officer travelled an enormous distance to bid him farewell and thank him for all he had taught him.) In the ranks, too, there may have been apprehension at the return of such a strict disciplinarian.

In 1921 the 5th Gurkhas were honoured with the title 'Royal' for services rendered during the war: 'So from now on instead of being the 1/5th GR it would be the 1/5th RG.' This was a further incentive, if any were needed, to make it the finest battalion in India (which is precisely what Lord Rawlinson, the C-in-C in 1920–5, called it). Under Villiers-Stuart, regimental mystique took on a new dimension. In reporting how the Prince of Wales, 'like his father', had fallen in love with the 1/5th Gurkhas – 'Anyone would' – he struggles to give expression to their peculiar magic:

> They were different to everyone – there was that proud 'something' that no other regiment ever had that I saw in my service. 'Something' that puzzled while it haunted everyone with an unbiased mind who ever knew them. Something that made their British officers give up everything to be with them. A strange 'something' never explained. All I can say is, it wasn't there till 1900 and then it came. But whatever it was was beyond price.

Part of the mystique of the 1/5th during Villiers-Stuart's command came from the curious fact that not one of his officers was married (marriage was one of the things they had to give up to be with the 1/5th). Richard Pease, who joined as a subaltern in 1923, recalls that 'we resembled nothing so much as the cast list of *The Barretts of Wimpole Street*, with V-S in the role of "papa"'.[24] The man who had been nicknamed by his contemporaries 'Jane, maid of all work' was now 'known far and wide as a man-eating fish in the Olympic class'.

> No junior officer of any other regiment would come willingly to our mess if there was any danger of encountering him . . . He regarded all other units in the Army as greatly inferior; even our second battalion was looked down upon as definitely sub-human . . . he practised a form of apartheid to ensure that none of us could conceivably be mistaken

for one of [2/5 RGR]. Thus, we wore our shirts outside our shorts while they wore them inside; our leather equipment was brown whilst theirs was black – and so on.[25]

As he was so much older than anyone else, as well as senior in rank, Villiers-Stuart now dominated the mess – and the entire battalion – 'by a mixture of terror and blarney'.

> He subsisted largely on mince, which was available at all meals and which would be placed before him, apparently unsolicited, by Mendez, the head waiter, who seemed to know by intuition that this was what was required, irrespective of what was on the menu. In the evenings he would sit smoking his pipe and drinking whisky and soda with great regularity but to no apparent effect. General conversation was replaced at such times by a monologue of reminiscences relating to past nobilities of the regiment and old customs and procedures now sadly fallen into disuse. This with a 'goonish' humour and turn of phrase which was most entertaining. At times one could not escape the suspicion that the 'old customs' were being invented to further some reform currently being introduced.[26]

Villiers-Stuart's reputation alone was enough to ensure discipline in the battalion; he never had to enforce it in the manner of the Scallys and Arthur Grants of this world. For twenty years he had instilled the need for discipline into generation after generation of recruits and riflemen so that it had become second nature by now. He was delighted when a company commander reported to him that he had overheard a rifleman saying to some of his comrades, 'Eh, don't do that, the Colonel would be sad.' The best discipline was self-discipline; to put someone on a charge and march him in front of the CO in the orderly room was an admission of failure. When someone asked the brigade commander if the 1/5th was concealing crime since they never seemed to have any, the brigadier replied, 'No! V-S sees to that!' Villiers-Stuart thought that was as high a compliment as had ever been paid to him.

Outside the battalion – as for instance, when he was made acting brigade commander – he was quite capable of introducing draconian measures. An outbreak of spitting defeated all attempts by the Military

Police to stop it until Villiers-Stuart ordered that anyone seen spitting in camp was to be made to 'kneel down and lick it up again'. There was only one more case after that.

Villiers-Stuart clung to the job he loved, to the extent of refusing command of a brigade if it meant forsaking his battalion. He had the front-line soldier's loathing for 'successful drawing room staff officers'. It was a them-and-us situation – 'The Bully Beef Eaters and Chlorinated Water Drinkers against the Paté and Caviar Eaters and Champagne Imbibers'. Even as sympathetic a senior officer as Brigadier-General Nigel Woodyatt was tainted by his years on the staff: 'I will say at once that he was a charming man, a kind friend, a tremendous "driver", in the way of getting work out of everyone, an indefatigable worker himself, a perfect soldier to look at, but he had no war service at all, and was one of those people who produce no results whatever, nothing but friction and a feeling that he was forever knocking his troops about.' But Woodyatt was a paragon in comparison with the aptly named Sir Bunkum Hudson:

Sir Bunkum Hudson, a good fellow as a captain, became a Lt-General through being for years at GHQ and promoting himself almost. When the committee to decide on the future composition of the Indian Army was sitting just after the war, Hudson, then Adjutant-General, came in and said, 'Gentlemen, I have only one thing to say – anything black can be made to fight'. Such a remark showed what a cad he had become.

As Villiers-Stuart saw it, in the post-war GHQ 'only the time servers were left at the top'. For a regimental officer there was nowhere to go. In 1923–4, as his time of command ticked away, he became increasingly preoccupied with his incipient departure: 'I had but six months more command and then my life so to speak was over' . . . 'I had been twenty-nine years in the 1/5th RG [more like twenty-seven in fact] and so it was bound to be a sad time for me when I had to go. And I felt that I could do so much more for the battalion still.'

It did not help that the man who was to take over from him was a womanizer and 'a first class swine', who had 'unluckily' injured his left hand with a Verey pistol while serving with the 10th Gurkhas at

Gallipoli and spent the rest of the war on the staff in India – 'I need not say that the Verey light incident was considered by most people to be a "self-inflicted wound".' Now this scrimshanker was to be rewarded with brevet rank and a coveted command. Worse still, he would be the first CO ever to be brought into the 1/5th from outside the regiment, *and* he was married!

The familial nature of the regiment was part of its strength:

> In the 1/5th RG companies were almost always recruited from certain villages in Nepal. We never interfered with that. It meant much greater content and happiness as a rule than the indiscriminate enlistment plan adopted by most regiments. Fathers and sons, cousins, uncles, nephews, friends from childhood and sometimes even for a year or two grandchildren served together. Other regiments objected to this method as being certain to cause favouritism, but I knew no case of it, rather the reverse, in thirty years.

To leave the battalion, for Villiers-Stuart, was the equivalent of leaving his family. His heart ached; he felt as 'Moses must have felt and countless others on giving up their life's work'; he had moulded the battalion in his own image: 'I *belonged* to the 1/5th RG and they to me. And though perhaps it sounds conceited to say so, no-one had ever belonged to them so much before nor had they belonged to anyone so entirely. I had an immense treasure – it was, if anyone ever can understand, "Don't do that, it will make the Colonel Sahib *mad* [sic]" – and so it was not done.'

It is in the nature of things that COs come and go, and the departure of each is generally an emotional time. But Villiers-Stuart had taken his role as paterfamilias to such lengths that when he wound up his valedictory speech with the words, 'Goodbye children – don't forget the regiment is the most wonderful in the world', and stumbled blindly away, this was no empty formulation but a genuine *cri de coeur*.

Partings with individuals were equally painful. As he held out his hand to Naré Gurung, his old favourite 'put it aside and flung himself into my arms and cried and cried and hid his poor boy's head and over and over again said, 'You can't go Sahib, you can't go my own Sahib'". It was, as Villiers-Stuart recalls, 'all very watery'.

That this sort of behaviour was far from typical of Gurkhas was demonstrated the next morning when he set off early on a round of the battalion's frontier outposts and the men did not come out specially to see him go but stood around waiting for a last look: 'It shows the character of the Gurkha – their hatred of any display . . . The better they thought of you the less they would show it.' Yet there was a kind of grand finale at Hangu:

> As the car started the men gave a wild cheer and more and more came running and holding out their hands – and then I looked back waving and they waved – and it was all over – finished – done with for ever. Thirty years I had worked there from youth to 'too old' and I could no more believe it than fly. But it was so.

Brigadier-General W. D. Villiers-Stuart, CBE, DSO, four times Mentioned in Despatches, Order of the Star of Nepal 2nd Class, lived in retirement for nearly thirty-five more years, eight years longer than the entire period of his service in the 1/5th Royal Gurkha Rifles. Yet to all intents and purposes his life ended on 10 April 1924, when he finally left the regiment the day before his fifty-second birthday. After that, all he could do was relive it by writing it, not with an eye to publication, but to keep the memory of it evergreen and minimize the pain of separation.

Richard Pease, the subaltern who had joined the battalion just a year earlier, thought he would visit the old man during his first furlough in England. He planned to call in at Camberley where Villiers-Stuart had retired, still unmarried, and was living with his elderly mother.

> Nevertheless my early training enjoined caution. I therefore halted my car some distance from the house and reconnoitred on foot. Looking over the hedge I saw him on the lawn with what appeared to be a gardener and gardener's boy drawn up in front of him. The scene was too familiar. I stole away and resumed my journey – and I never saw him again.[27]

5

The Gurkha Brigade
Goes to War

Around the turn of the century, the build-up of Gurkhas in the Indian Army gathered momentum. The combination of a newly cooperative attitude towards recruitment on the part of the Nepal *durbar* and the expansion of the British notion of martial classes to include the Limbus and Rais of east Nepal and the higher caste Chhetris and Thakurs who would constitute the 9th Gurkhas meant that in less than two decades the number of battalions in the Gurkha line doubled. By 1908 – the year in which Maharajah Chandra Shamsher (1863–1929) followed in his uncle Jang Bahadur's footsteps and paid an official visit to Britain – there were ten rifle regiments, each with two battalions; what became known as the Gurkha Brigade had a permanent peacetime establishment of around 20,000 men.

The provenance of individual regiments was often tortuous, some having a long history as Assam battalions before being brought into the Gurkha line, others replacing Madras or Bengal Native Infantry regiments deemed unsatisfactory for one reason or another, and yet others being formed out of battalions of existing Gurkha regiments. This gave rise to endless arguments over precedence. Since survival might depend upon seniority, these disputes were not necessarily trivial. The numbering of the units from 1 to 10 might be thought to have resolved the question of seniority – with the 1st as the oldest and the 10th the youngest. But no, if you consider that the original 7th became the second battalion of the 8th and the new 7th was formed out of the 2/10th (the 7th and 10th being the only Limbu-Rai regiments) which then had to be re-raised, you can see it is not so simple. Add to that the pre-Gurkha history of some Gurkha regiments, enshrined in the mess silver and traditions they inherited, and you get an even more complicated picture. Officers of the 8th, 9th and 10th in particular, bringing up the rear numerically, have been known to push the claims of their regiments to venerability to extreme lengths, even claiming honour for the deeds of *their* regiment when it contained not a single Gurkha. If the renumbering had 'been based on the dates on which the regiments were raised', the historian of 8th Gurkha Rifles asserts, 'the order of regiments in the Gurkha Brigade would have been 1st, 2nd, 3rd, 6th, 9th, 8th, 4th, 5th, 10th and 7th'.[1]

But such niceties were an insignificant by-product of the growth of the Gurkha Brigade as a *corps d'élite* within the Indian Army, a third force occupying a special position, as it were, halfway between British troops and Indian sepoys. For facilitating this development, the British had to thank Maharajah Chandra Shamsher Jang Bahadur Rana, whose influence was felt for at least a decade before he superseded his brother Dev in a bloodless *coup* in 1901. Chandra made a virtue of necessity in supporting the British in their desire to expand the Gurkha corps. By going along with Britain's wishes, he could extract favours in return, gaining access to British-controlled arms and ammunition. His argument was that the Nepalese forces would not be of much use to the British in an emergency unless they had been trained in the use of modern weapons. 'We have 40,000 soldiers ready in Nepal,' he had told Lord Roberts in 1892, 'and there is nothing to fight.'[2] (The policy of arming Nepalese soldiers would pay off a quarter of a century later, when 15,778 of them fought for the British on the north-west frontier and in the third Afghan war of 1919.[3])

Chandra was the fifth of seventeen sons of Dhir Shamsher, the ablest of Jang Bahadur's brothers and his staunchest supporter. So it is ironic that while none of Jang's male progeny tasted power no less than five of Dhir's sons became prime minister of Nepal: the first was the eldest,

Bir, after the bloody *coup* of 1885 (which Dhir himself would never have countenanced, though his death a year earlier helped to bring it about); the next was the fourth brother, Dev; and after him came Chandra. Though Chandra remained in office for nearly thirty years, he was succeeded by two younger brothers: Bhim, who outlived him by less than two years, and Judha, who finally resigned at the end of 1945; and the last of all the Rana prime ministers and maharajahs was Chandra's eldest son, Mohan. In the hundred or so years of Rana rule, Chandra's period in office marks the high point of the regime, a peaceful plateau between its violent origins in the *coups* of Jang Bahadur and the Shamsher Ranas and the monarchist plots and popular agitation which darkened its later years and finally combined to bring it down.

Even in the heyday of Chandra's rule, however, there were hints of what was to come. In 1903, the twenty-eight-year-old king, Prithvi Bir, gathered around him a group of supporters from those noble families who had once enjoyed power but had been excluded from political office under the Ranas. But as soon as Chandra got wind of this he exiled the conspirators to distant parts of the country and surrounded the king with his own people. Prithvi Bir's early death in 1911 removed any further threat from that quarter, since his successor, King Tribhuvan, was only five years old.[4] And in 1912, when the writer Babu Ram Acharya published his book, *Nepali Siksa Darpan*, drawing disparaging parallels between the Rana system of government and the Shogunate of Japan, all available copies were seized and impounded by the prime minister.[5] A strong ruler in his uncle's mould, Chandra would brook no challenge to his authority from above or below; and though he introduced a number of important administrative and legal reforms, the plight of the peasants in the hills, the families who furnished the Gurkha recruits, remained much as it had been for the last 100, even 200 years.

Squeezed between landlords and money-lenders, peasants were dependent on good harvests just to stay afloat. In the early part of the nineteenth century a cycle of bad harvests meant accumulated debt and a downward spiral into bondage or slavery. Slavery might even be the less bad option in that the slave-owner had to provide food, clothing and shelter; a creditor was under no such obligation towards a bondsman who worked for nothing, having bartered his labour for the interest on his debt. In the poorest parts of the west-central hills a slave could be purchased for as little as 20 rupees, the price of 500 kg of rice. Jang Bahadur's legal code, the *Muluki Ain* of 1854, had put an end to enslavement for debt but upheld and even strengthened the institution of slavery as a punishment for certain crimes and offences against caste rules. It had also sought to ameliorate the conditions of bondage and prohibited the bondage of children under sixteen.[6] But these reforms, however admirable in themselves, did nothing to mitigate the underlying harshness and impoverishment of the peasant's life.

The liberation of slaves had been one of many, largely abortive, liberal measures introduced by Dev Shamsher when he succeeded his brother Bir as prime minister and maharajah in 1901. His proclamation, freeing all female slaves in the valley of Kathmandu and in his fiefdoms of Kaski and Lamjung, proved to be little more than an empty gesture since Dev had failed to think it through and prepare the ground.[7] The scheme had to be abandoned and another quarter of a century would elapse before the cautious Chandra grasped this particular nettle. (Slavery was more or less confined to the hills – in the Terai it was too easy for a slave to escape across the border into India – and it was never on a large scale even there; when it was finally abolished in 1924 there were a total of 51,419 slaves out of a population of 5.6 million.[8])

Dev had also wanted to give the people a say in government; he started Nepal's first newspaper; and he had even proposed a scheme of universal primary education – some years earlier the Residency surgeon, Daniel Wright, had written memorably: 'The subject of schools and colleges in Nepal may be treated as briefly as that of snakes in Ireland. There are none.'[9] These reforms, moderate as they may seem, were so alarming to the Rana hierarchy that Chandra had little difficulty in gaining enough support from his brothers and peers to remove Dev from office. Dev's personal vanity, his taste for pomp and ceremony and his dilettantism did not help his cause. He was no match for his austere and methodical brother, who did not even have to resort to violence to displace him. Outmanoeuvred and forced to resign after just 114 days in office, Dev went quietly into exile in India where he lived in comfort for the rest of his life on a pension provided by Chandra.

Soon after Chandra came to power, Britain's 1903–4 invasion of Tibet –

euphemistically promoted as a 'peaceful' mission – put him in an awkward situation. Nepal had a neighbourly agreement with Tibet to come to the other's aid in the event of external aggression. But the prospect of a Russian protectorate in Tibet (however unlikely that was) appealed as little to Chandra as it did to the Viceroy, Lord Curzon, and the two made common cause to prevent such an eventuality. The muscle provided by Colonel Francis Younghusband and his expeditionary force, including two of the newer Gurkha regiments, the 1/8th and transport and Maxim-gun detachments from the 1/9th, was backed by a diplomatic offensive from Chandra which, though it did not endear him to the Tibetans, raised his standing in British eyes.

On the ground, Younghusband's 'peaceful' mission soon found itself resorting to arms. To barge into another country on the flimsiest of pretexts was asking for trouble; the Tibetans did not welcome the incursion and put up a stout resistance with the limited means at their disposal. Their tactics – similar to those of the Russians when Napoleon invaded their country – were to lure the enemy on to its destruction by enticing it too far from its base to be reinforced. This preyed on the nerves of the commander of the British troops, the pusillanimous Brigadier-General J. R. L. MacDonald, and he did more to frustrate Younghusband's progress than the Tibetans themselves. It did not help that Younghusband, though junior in rank, was political leader of the expedition; nor that Younghusband was Curzon's man while Kitchener backed MacDonald. The young George Preston, with the 40th Pathans, wrote to his wife:

> They say that General MacDonald is losing his nerve from illness. He wants to move the camp back to the last place, which would be madness, but Colonel Younghusband has flatly refused . . .
> [MacDonald] is not quite what everyone expects. He has a weak-looking face. Is absolutely run by his staff, who are a poor lot, and smokes cigarettes till he is sick.[10]

Preston was new to this or any other sort of warfare and his response to the experience of an attack on a Tibetan fort was anything but gung-ho (in the privacy of a letter to his wife at least):

> It was a weird sight – the whole place strewn with dead bodies. I hate

it Ciskins. These poor devils are brave men and they haven't the
weapons we have. They fight to the bitter end. It's my first show and I
feel awfully sorry for these poor fellows. They are forced to fight and
deserve a better fate.[11]

The Gurkhas, untroubled by scruples about fair play, showed their pen-
chant for comedy as well as their characteristic daring. One night a
jemadar and twenty of his men crept up to a house, where twelve armed
Tibetans were sheltering at some distance from the bulk of their force,
and found them all asleep. The jemadar's plan was to take them prisoner without disturbing their comrades, and to this end he ordered his
men to tie their pigtails together. Unfortunately, this woke them up and
they made such a hullabaloo that the Gurkhas had to beat a hasty retreat
after firing a volley in the direction of the main body of the enemy. The
jemadar's raid, which was made on his own initiative, deterred the
Tibetans from venturing into that house again.[12]

The crucial action of the campaign took place at Gyantze Dzong, a
fort perched on top of so daunting a precipice that it looked impregnable. Indeed, there was 'an old tradition among the Tibetans that
Gyantse Jong was the key to Tibet; and that if it fell into the hands of
a conqueror further resistance was useless'.[13] But on 7 July 1904, an
assault party consisting of two companies of the 8th Gurkhas – with one
company of the Royal Fusiliers sandwiched between them – scaled the
heights, climbing a path 'just like the side of a house', according to
George Preston.

When they got near the top, the Thibetans began hurling stones down
on them and I saw one Gurkha Havildar hurled down the rock.
However he got up and did not appear to be much hurt. It was a
wonderful performance of the Gurkhas. Capt. Humphreys and Lt.
Grant of the Gurkhas were up first and might receive some special
reward for it. The fort was taken by 5 p.m.[14]

The route was now open to Lhasa and the end of the expedition was
in sight. Lieutenant Grant, who was the first into the breach made by
the artillery, was awarded the VC. Havildar Karbir Pun, despite having
fallen at least twenty feet when hit by a rock, was there beside him and

won the Indian Order of Merit First Class (Indian and Gurkha soldiers did not become eligible for the VC until December 1911, when the King-Emperor George V visited India for the coronation *durbar* in Delhi, marking the emergence of that city as the new capital of British India in place of Calcutta).

The Russian scare turned out to be illusory and this was by no means Britain's finest hour, but the Gurkhas had acquitted themselves with honour and Chandra Shamsher had improved his position *vis-à-vis* the government of India. With the Chinese empire in disarray, and Nepal so clearly aligned with British India – Tibet was now the buffer state with China – the *durbar* could see no point in keeping up even the pretence of a subsidiary relationship with the imperial court, symbolized by the quinquennial missions to Peking, which had been going on since 1792. The last one took place in 1906, the year in which Lord Kitchener visited Kathmandu at Chandra's invitation and conferred on the maharajah the rank of general in the British Army. He also made Chandra honorary colonel of the 4th Gurkhas.[15]

The year 1903 saw the initiation of the King's Indian Orderly Officer scheme, the purpose of which was to honour selected senior viceroy's commissioned officers (VCOs) by appointing them to attend the King-Emperor Edward VII in a ceremonial capacity for a limited period of time. In the first year of the scheme, half-a-dozen Indian officers were brought over to England for six months, but there were not enough duties to keep them occupied. So the following year, the number was reduced to four – two from the cavalry and two from the infantry (except in a year in which Gurkhas were chosen, when all four would be from the infantry) – and the time they stayed limited to just three months, from May to July.[16]

In a story published in 1912, Rudyard Kipling celebrates an incident involving king's orderly officers. 'In the Presence', which is set in the cantonment of a Sikh regiment, juxtaposes two anecdotes dealing with 'honour'. The first is told by the pandit, or 'regimental chaplain' as Kipling calls him, with interjections from the subedar-major; this concerns two brothers who served the regiment with distinction but suffered persecution at home. Their land and crops, which were looked after by two younger brothers, were being systematically despoiled by their mother's kin. At length, honour dictated that they should take the lives of their persecutors, which also meant sacrificing their own. 'And what befell the two younger brethren who were not in the service?' asks the subedar-major's nephew, a havildar-major recently returned from England. 'Doubtless they too are dead,' the pandit replies, 'but since they were not in the Regiment their honour concerns themselves only.'[17]

The havildar-major, very much the junior of the trio, is then invited to match this tale with something from his English experience, and he accepts the challenge. In this affair too, he tells his listeners, there were four men – 'and it was an affair which touched the honour, not of one regiment, nor two, but of all the Army in Hind'.[18] And he proceeds to recount the true story of the guard mounted at the lying-in-state of King Edward VII in 1910 by his four Indian Army orderly officers, Subedar-Major Santbir Gurung of the 2/2nd Goorkhas, Subedar-Major Singbir Ghale of the 2/3rd Gurkhas, Subedar Bude Sing Negi of 2/39th Garhwalis and Jemadar Baij Sing Rawat of 1/39th Garhwalis (though Kipling does not name them individually and calls them all Gurkhas – understandably in view of the fact that the 39th Garhwalis were originally, as we have seen, the 2/3rd Gurkhas). This is not a tale of derring-do or revenge killing, but of astonishing endurance in peculiarly trying conditions.

The Gurkha on duty had to stand with head bowed (and high collar cutting into his neck) for an hour at a stretch and, there being just four of them, return for another hour after a break of only three hours, subsisting on water and uncooked grain – since there was no opportunity to cook, and to have accepted food prepared by Europeans would have meant losing caste. They shared this duty with the Grenadier Guards, of whom there were of course any number; but the Grenadiers only stood for half-an-hour at a time and did not have to go without food, or return again the same day. What made the vigil particularly gruelling was the endless procession of mourners shuffling by, whose feet were all the soldiers could see – 'a river of feet, Sahib, that never – never – never stops', as the senior subedar-major tells a British officer in the story.[19] The final test of stamina came when three of the four Gurkhas delivered a wreath to 'Wanidza' (Windsor), leaving the fourth unrelieved for four hours, at the end of which his eyeballs worked 'like weavers' shuttles' from following the unending river of feet:

'And so it was done – not in hot blood, not for a little while, nor yet with the smell of slaughter and the noise of shouting to sustain, but in silence, for a very long time, rooted to one place before the Presence among the most terrible feet of the multitude.'[20]

Kipling's story, which more or less ends there, is a tribute to the fidelity and discipline, rather than the dash and *élan*, of the Indian Army.

After the funeral was over, George V sent a portrait of his father to Santbir Gurung, inscribed, 'In memory of your vigil'. This became a proud possession of the 2nd Goorkhas, to be set alongside the famous truncheon presented to them by Queen Victoria after the siege of Delhi.

There was an unhappy postscript to this affair. When Santbir Gurung returned to Nepal in 1913 he was accused of having gone to England without the maharajah's permission, and was banished both from his caste and from his country by order of Chandra Shamsher, despite the intervention of George V, whose equerry wrote to the viceroy's private secretary:

The King was astounded to hear this story and could not believe that his old friend Chandra Shamsher [with whom he had gone on a tiger shoot in the Terai when he was Prince of Wales] could be a party to such an act, which is, I am sure you will agree, a direct insult not only to the British Raj but to the King both as Sovereign and as Colonel-in-Chief of the 2nd Gurkhas.[21]

Over the next quarter of a century Santbir Gurung made several applications to be allowed to return, but they were all rejected. Not only that, but in 1926 Gurkha officers in general were excluded from the king's orderly officer scheme. In the early thirties, after Chandra's death, the Gurkha officers (GOs) of the 1/8th Gurkhas sent a petition to his successor, in which they asked that the embargo be lifted so that they might take their turn in attending the king-emperor along with the VCOs of other Indian Army units; and GOs in various Gurkha regiments urged their officers to press for the resumption of this coveted overseas posting. Colonel Macrae of the military department of the government of India enquired of the commanding officers of these regiments why the maharajah had forbidden it in the first place.

They all told me that the present trouble would not have arisen but for the actions of several GO's just after the war. They were all apparently suffering from acute wind-in-the-head after their experiences in England, and on their return to Nepal behaved generally in a very lordly manner. They refused to go through the 'purification' ceremonies and to pay, or square, the priests. They were hardly more accommodating with the secular officials. Priests and officials complained to the Maharaja who got very angry. He said in effect, 'Who are these "janglis" to disobey orders? They may be officers in the British Army or even Orderly Officers to the English King, but here they are my subjects and common ryots [peasants] at that. In future no one shall go overseas.'[22]

The British envoy in Nepal, Lt-Col. C. T. Daukes, advised against reopening the question, saying that 'the present Maharaja is extremely conservative and, if anything, even more particular in such matters than the late Sir Chandra Shumshere'. But when Bhim Shamsher died soon after and his brother Judha took over, Daukes reported that the new maharajah was prepared to reconsider the question.[23]

Yet Judha was in no hurry to relax the rules, especially when British officials insisted on linking the particular case of the outcasted eighty-one-year-old Honorary Captain and Subedar-Major Santbir Gurung, Sardar Bahadur, IOM – whose service stretched back to Lord Roberts' famous march from Kabul to Kandahar – with the general question of allowing GOs to go overseas in peacetime. It was not until May 1936, three years after the issue had been raised, that he agreed 'after much deliberation' that Gurkha officers might be permitted to take their turn as king's orderly officers, so long as they upheld caste regulations while they were overseas.[24] Poor old Santbir had to wait a further year, until he was eighty-three, before he was allowed to undergo the purification ceremony of *pani patya* and be readmitted to caste and country. Even that was made conditional on his case receiving no publicity.[25] But at least the hero of Kipling's story, one of the four men who upheld the honour of the Indian Army at the catafalque of Edward VII, did not die an outcast.

Successive maharajahs bemoaned their powerlessness to interfere in religious affairs, which they claimed were the province of the Brahman *raj gurus*. But in 1935 the political secretary in the India Office noted that Sir Clendon Daukes, Britain's former envoy in Nepal (as he now was), regarded this as 'camouflage': 'The Nepalese Government themselves really work the oracle; and the penalty of outcasting, together with the power to give or withhold *pani patya*, or purification, give them a hold over us, by making it necessary or at any rate advisable for their consent to be obtained before Gurkhas can be sent for service overseas.'[26] Certainly in a time of crisis, such as the outbreak of the First World War, Chandra Shamsher had no difficulty in persuading the *raj gurus* to waive the ban on service overseas and to grant returning warriors ritual purification.[27]

This did not mean that Chandra favoured the idea of Gurkhas going to fight in Europe; indeed, he thought it would be as unpopular in France as he knew it would be in Nepal.[28] He certainly did not subscribe to the Viceroy Lord Hardinge's plan to send Indian and Gurkha troops to the western front as a means of removing the 'stigma and . . . colour bar' implicit in the earlier decision not to involve the Indian Army in the Boer War.[29] It was almost a truism that coloured troops could not be employed to fight white troops; should they prove equal – or even more unthinkably, superior – to Europeans in battle, the rationale of imperialism would be undermined. Hence the resistance to Lord Hardinge's policy in many quarters; the king's secretary, Lord Stamfordham, opposed it on the grounds that it would make it impossible to withhold king's commissions from Indians any longer, though surprisingly George V himself was in favour of it.[30] The authorities were in a curious double-bind which made them fear the consequences of success almost as much as those of failure. But the rapid deterioration in the war situation meant that Hardinge got his way.

Chandra followed his uncle Jang Bahadur's example in putting Nepal's own army at the disposal of the British; and the British authorities aped their predecessors by initially spurning his offer, only to change their minds when faced with a manpower crisis. Kitchener, now secretary of state for war, had been keen to accept the offer from the start. But other generals were sceptical of the military value of the Nepalese army without further training, and the political advisers of the secretary of state for India, Lord Crewe, were opposed to the idea for a number of reasons: '(1) independent character of Nepal state, (2) risk of exciting conceit of Gurkhas to dangerous extent, (3) bad effect in India itself, (4) doubts whether Maharaja's offer was much more than an oriental compliment, and (5) barbarous nature of the troops themselves'.[31] Lord Crewe himself suggested that these troops, with further training, might be a useful back-up on the north-west frontier and could later be transferred to Egypt, if required there.

Hardinge did not agree: 'As regards Nepal troops they are quite unsuitable to send abroad. Nor do I want them to train in India as the political effect would be bad, implying a want of confidence.' Though they might be Gurkhas, 'Nepal troops' were neither part of the Indian Army nor officered by the British, so they could not be relied upon. In Hardinge's view they should be kept as a last resort 'in the event of any internal trouble anywhere in India'.[32] In early 1915, however, he telegraphed, 'In view of present conditions in and out of India and depletion of garrisons we consider it highly advisable to accept offer of the Nepal Darbar immediately to despatch a contingent to India.'[33]

The Nepalese contingent consisted of 6,000 men in six battalions and the idea was to train them and send them to the frontier or wherever else troops might be required. Nine months later an offer of a further four battalions, bringing the strength of the contingent up to 10,000 men, was gratefully accepted.[34] These troops were located at Dehra Dun and Abbottabad, and one of the two British officers charged with their training in August 1916 was Major W. D. Villiers-Stuart of the 1/5th Gurkhas. The employment of the Nepalese contingent on the north-west frontier released more Indian Army troops for service overseas.

During the First World War Gurkhas fought in all the main theatres of war, from the fields of Flanders to the hills of Gallipoli and the deserts of Mesopotamia and Palestine. Once they succeeded in coming to terms with the alien conditions and a type of warfare outside their previous experience, they acquitted themselves with honour and enhanced their already high reputation as stalwart warriors.

In the autumn of 1914, two Indian Army divisions, the Lahore and Meerut Divisions, which included several Gurkha battalions, had been sent to Egypt to replace British troops urgently needed in France; but they themselves were almost immediately sent to Flanders and sucked into the maelstrom of modern war for which they were neither equipped nor prepared. Their pre-war functions – maintenance of internal security, dispersal of hostile tribes on the north-west frontier and the first-line defence against (Russian) invasion – were of a quite different order from what was required in France in 1914. Yet they approached Armageddon with the blithe insouciance that characterized all the armies of 1914.

Lieutenant J. L. I. (Hamish) Reid, a descendant of the defender of Hindu Rao's House during the Siege of Delhi in 1857, transferred from the 1/10th Gurkhas in Burma to his famous forebear's regiment shortly before the outbreak of war and sailed from Bombay with the 2/2nd in September 1914. He was worried that the war might be over before the battalion reached Europe, and wrote to his parents:

> ... I wonder how long it will all last, another month or another six months ...
>
> The men are mad with excitement and very pleased with themselves as such a very large proportion of the Indian Expeditionary Force is Gurkhas.
>
> ... I *do* hope to Heaven we will be in the thick of it. Just one really first class battle for four days, like they've just been having ... I hope, on my own small account, that I'm not knocked over before I've had a chance of seeing anything ... [35]

Reid was rearing to go. Six months previously, he had told his parents, 'any idea that one would be leading Gurkhas against Germans would have sounded awful nonsense but here we are on our way and in another month or less, please God, we will be doing it'.[36] He revelled in the good spirits of the men, their feeling that the time of departure for the front, coinciding with the festival of Dashera, was auspicious and their interest in all the new sights that greeted their eyes:

> They take an extraordinary interest in the various places and peoples they have seen on the way and in the Torpedo Boats and French Battleships we saw in Port Said, but more, I honestly think, in the flying fish and porpoises than all the rest put together!![37]

When the Indian Army troops docked at Marseilles they were welcomed as conquering heroes. The 2/3rd Gurkhas, who disembarked with the 2/2nd on 12 October, were surprised to find themselves fêted by what seemed like every man, woman and child in Marseilles. One of their officers remarked: 'This scene, together with the 101 new wonders of a European town, combined to complete the bewilderment of the Gurkha ranks, whose feelings may well be compared to those of Alice in Wonderland.'[38] When the 1/4th Gurkhas arrived, along with the 1/1st, on 1 December, they caused a sensation 'among the ladies of Marseilles' by wearing their newly issued woollen vests and drawers on top of their khaki uniforms.[39]

But Gurkhas are extraordinarily adaptable, as C. G. Bruce had found when he brought his 5 GR orderly to Britain in 1891. In France they quickly overcame any latent hostility they encountered among the natives. 1/1 GR was billeted at Locon, five miles behind the lines at Neuve Chapelle, where some of the farmers were initially less than welcoming. A little later an officer doing his rounds was surprised to discover a farmer who had been particularly prickly inviting the men to help themselves to straw. The Gurkhas had found a number of eggs in his barn and had taken them to the farmer, who told the officer: 'Your men must be good men; if they had been French *poilus* they would not only have kept my eggs but would be cooking and eating my chickens now.'[40] The historian of the 9th Gurkhas remarks:

> Not even the most experienced and knowledgeable pre-war officer of the Gurkha Brigade could have conceived what was now a sight of common occurrence . . . This was 'Johnny Gurk', clad in serge tunic and balaclava cap, sitting in a French peasant's kitchen with his feet on the stove, smoking a pipe and drinking beer or coffee, and discussing life and the war situation in halting and broken French! The Gurkha was deservedly popular with his temporary hostesses for his cheerful spirits, his good discipline and cleanly habits, and for his rather extravagant ideas which appealed very much to the French madame.[41]

The European and the Asian peasants may have had rather more in common than the average British officer realized.

By the end of October, as the 2/2nd Goorkhas neared the front line, the excitement and impatience young Hamish Reid, for one, had been feeling gave way to awe. He told his parents that he would be in the trenches (just north of Neuve Chapelle) before midnight that night and that there had been 'the HELL (no apology, please) of a battle going on':

> . . . The Mons retreat, so Tommies tell us, who have been in both, is
> nothing to what is going on now round here – cheery, isn't it?! Well,
> well – Kismet. The proportion of killed to wounded is very small
> indeed.[42]

This was the last letter Reid wrote. A note scribbled on the envelope records: 'Killed 2 November'.

In addition to the problem all Gurkha units faced – trenches so deep that men as small as they could not see over the parapet, and so water-logged that there was a very real danger of drowning – the 2/2nd came under lethal fire before they could begin to acclimatize themselves to what the commander of the Indian corps in France, General Sir James Willcocks, called 'the uncanny conditions' of the front.[43] According to the general, the 2/2nd had been 'dumped' on an exposed salient on the night of 29/30 October and the Germans 'knew exactly the weakness of the position', which they proceeded to bombard with their vastly superior armaments:

> Here were these gallant fellows just arrived and exposed to every form
> of terror, and they could reply only with their valour and the rifles and
> two machine-guns per battalion with which they were armed [no
> trench mortars or hand grenades], and yet they did it.[44]

Lieutenant W. G. Bagot-Chester of the 2/3rd Gurkhas noted in his diary, 'The Germans got their range accurately and gave them hell with Black Marias, all their officers killed except the Colonel, Corse-Scott and a subaltern; McCleverty wounded. Many casualties amongst the men too. They have been specially commended for the manner in which they underwent the fire.'[45] They were driven from the salient, but the valiant way in which their one-armed CO, Lt-Col. C. E. Norie (who had left his other arm on the north-west frontier), succeeded with the help of the Royal Scots Fusiliers in recapturing trenches overrun by the Germans earned him a brevet-colonelcy. The British Commander-in-Chief, Field Marshal Sir John French, singled him out for special mention in a despatch, and General Willcocks pays tribute to 'the discipline and tenacity of the Gurkhas of Nepal'. Of Lieutenant Reid, we learn that, 'after hard fighting, [he] fell whilst coolly conducting a relieving party of the Connaught Rangers to the Gurkha trenches'.[46]

Not every officer was quite so complimentary about the 2/2nd Goorkhas' initiation in trench warfare. On 1 November the Poona Horse, a mounted regiment acting as additional infantry in conditions inimical to cavalry, were sent in as reinforcements and their D Squadron commander, Captain 'Roly' Grimshaw, recorded a confused situation in his diary: 'At this juncture there appeared some uncertainty as to whether the trenches we were to succour were in the hands of the Gurkhas or the enemy.'[47] It turned out they were in German hands and the CO and the adjutant of the 2/2nd gave conflicting advice – the adjutant urged immediate attack, the CO recommended waiting until after dark – as well as conflicting accounts of what had happened. In the end the salient was abandoned and the Poona Horse withdrawn:

My own belief about the entire affair is that it was carried out to save the face of the 2nd Gurkhas. There is ample evidence that the latter quitted their trenches. Colonel Norie gave everyone to understand that his battalion had been almost annihilated and that if we could succour the remainder it might save the situation . . . His Adjutant [Corse-Scott] was certainly aware of what had taken place, and several artillery officers round about saw many 2nd Gurkha riflemen sneaking about when they ought to have been in the trenches. If Norie did not know, he ought to have known. His Adjutant told me the next day that his men were all over the place and like myself he was trying to round up stragglers. On this search I found 2nd Gurkha men in all kinds of places, ditches, ruins, and even under the culverts, and I regret to say one or two men of [his own regiment's] C Squadron among them.[48]

The 2/2nd was not the only Gurkha battalion to have faltered under such a baptism of fire. On 30 October the 2/8th had likewise been hit by a German avalanche and lost hundreds of men killed or wounded, and ten of their British officers: what was left of them 'broke and straggled to the rear in confusion'.[49] Conditions were so horrendous that two men of the 2/8th drowned in a communication trench. As the regimental historian puts it: 'Pitch darkness, a trench deep to a Gurkha, a heavily laden soldier who slips and falls, and you have a tragedy.'[50] Even the Gurkha's propensity to laugh at his own and others' physical misfortunes was stifled in such conditions. Grimshaw witnessed the stumbling procession of retreating soldiers of all nationalities:

> The state of the wounded beggars all description. Little Gurkhas slopping through the freezing mud barefooted, Tommies with no caps on and plastered with blood and mud from head to foot, Sikhs with their hair all down and looking more wild and weird than I have ever seen them, Pathans more dirty and untidy than usual, all limping and reeling along like drunken men . . . misery depicted in their faces . . . I stopped some Gurkhas and asked why they walked in bare feet. Those that replied said, 'Sahib, our feet hurt terribly, but in boots they hurt worse'.[51]

The 1/4th Gurkhas at Givenchy attempted to raise the floor level of their trenches by stamping mangolds into the mud, but every so often 'these mangold-wurzels bobbed up through the water and hit one on the back'. But that was nothing compared with the effect on the feet of long immersion in freezing water:

> They swelled, turned a greenish-white colour, and became very painful. To walk was an agony. During the march to Auchel we looked like a battalion of cripples. It took us six hours to cover nine miles.[52]

In the trenches at Festubert, the men of the 1/1st developed such bad trench feet that 'if one of them took off his boots, he could never have got them on again'.[53] Their clothing, too, was pathetically inadequate. Until they were issued with greatcoats and serge uniforms months after their arrival in France, i.e., just as winter was turning to spring, the 1/9th (along with everyone else in the two Indian divisions) 'had been wearing the "British Warm" coats and khaki drill tunics and shorts, issued in India, all through the severe conditions of rain, snow and mud; many men were literally in rags, some having nothing on their thighs except the warm drawers received in Orleans'.[54]

One must turn to fiction to get the full flavour of this alien world. Mulk Raj Anand dedicated his 1940 novel, *Across the Black Waters*, to his father, who had been a subedar in the 2/17th Dogras; and this description of conditions on the western front probably derives its authenticity from first-hand information supplied by Subedar Lall Chand Anand:

> Isolated and apart they sat thus, these ghosts from another, warmer world, transplanted into this creeping wet, cold autumnal underworld of 'Franceville', they who had never suffered heavy shell fire, who had no experience of high explosives, who had never seen steel birds fly in the air, who had never been taught anything but the bayonet charge which had been so useful for generations on the frontier, who had only two machine guns to each regiment, and behind whom, Uncle Kirpu believed, were no big guns, facing, what the experience of their repulsed attack and the enemy's expenditure of ammunition proved, the biggest military machine of the iron age invented by that 'incarnation of the Devil, the Kaiser'.[55]

As if these trials were not enough for soldiers for whom regimental pride had to stand in for the patriotic fervour they could not be expected to feel in a war that had no meaning for them, there was the draconian wartime military discipline. 'A wet morning', Bagot-Chester noted on 31 December 1914. 'Yesterday we had the unpleasant duty of being present at the corporal punishment of a Rifleman with thirty lashes for sleeping on his post when a sentry.'[56] A later diary entry tells an even grimmer story – so bad indeed that it has been partially obliterated, though the gist of it is clear. Bagot-Chester had to shoot some of his own men, who had been court-martialed, no doubt for desertion: 'Never do I want to command a firing-party again. They died bravely and it will take a long time to forget this morning's work.'[57]

Given the inadequacy of their weaponry at the beginning, the horrors of an unfamiliar type of war in which they were at risk not only above ground but under it too, where sappers and miners beavered away, and it is hardly surprising that Gurkhas should have proved no more immune to panic than any other race of people who participated in that inferno. At nine o'clock in the morning of 19 December, the Germans exploded a number of mines under the trenches of the Sirhind Brigade and the 1/4th Gurkhas lost an entire double-company. British units stood firm but various Indian regiments broke, including 1/4 GR who retreated without orders: 'all who reported on the retreat agreed that the lack of British officers who had been killed in the attack was crucial.'[58] As a regimental clerk in Rouen would write to his Gurkha friend far away in northern India in 1916:

> . . . This war is very terrible. There is no safety for a man on the earth, or under the earth, in the air, or on the sea. Strong fortresses are overturned like dust, what chance then has anything else? When the artillery fires continuously, hills are converted into dustheaps, and the same thing happens to ships on the sea. Under the sea, submarines go and fight. On land, poisonous gases and liquid fire are used. Under the earth, mines are dug and exploded 200 or 300 yards away. In the air 'Aeroplane', 'Zeppelin', 'Fokker', 'Aircraft', etc., make war amongst themselves . . . The fighting is not confined to one locality. It is spread all over the world. From all this it would seem that God is displeased with the peoples of the world.[59]

This was not war as Gurkhas had previously understood or experienced it; and the lack of movement was as baffling as the sheer scale of it. In 1915 the 1/9th found themselves back in a sector of the front line near Richebourg where they had been the previous year. A Gurkha subedar asked how far it was to Germany and, when he was told it was 200 miles, he shook his head and said with irrefutable logic, 'This war is going to last a long time; we have been here a year and instead of advancing have retired about 100 yards!'[60]

Another anecdote, quite possibly apocryphal but nonetheless telling for that, concerned a German officer in uniform arrested in broad daylight in Vielle Chapelle:

> He explained that when the British bombardment had opened on 10th March [1915] he had hidden in a dug-out. When the artillery fire lifted he came out of the dug-out just in time to see Indian troops appear on the parapet. He promptly went to ground again. The attack swept on,

and he spent the next few days hiding in the dug-out in terror of being
caught and shot as a spy. At last hunger drove him forth. Boldness
being his best policy he walked down the main road into Vielle
Chapelle. 'Did you not meet any of our troops?' 'Oh yes, lots of them;
but they were all Gurkhas and they saluted me!'[61]

This suggestion that they might mistake a German officer for one of
their own is part of the portrayal of Gurkhas as lovable but none too
bright little men favoured by loving but patronizing British officers. A
variation of this is seen in the true story of Rifleman Gane Gurung of
the 2/3rd Gurkhas, who on the very same day (10 March 1915) burst
into a house in Neuve Chapelle and emerged with eight German captives just as the 2nd Rifle Brigade, the spearhead of the 8th Division's
attack, arrived from another direction:

So striking was the sight of this one small man, proudly marching his
eight bulky prisoners out of the building, that he was welcomed with a
rousing cheer by all ranks of the Rifle Brigade who witnessed the
deed . . . Never before had the contemplation of the deed of a single
individual Gurkha been heartily cheered by a British regiment in
action.[62]

The 2/3rd Gurkhas took 300 prisoners in all in their attack on the village
and front-line trenches of Neuve Chapelle, but despite this local success there was no breakthrough. Even more cruelly for the 2/3rd, no
sooner had they been promised relief after enduring what Bagot-
Chester described as 'absolute hell from enemy shelling' than the order
was rescinded and they were told to remain in the trenches.[63]

On 1 May 1915 Bagot-Chester heard a cuckoo call 'amongst the ruins
of Neuve Chapelle', and the next day he had the satisfaction of learning
that the subedars of both his companies had been awarded IDSMs
(Indian Distinguished Service Medals) for bravery. After their shaky
start, the Gurkha units were getting the measure of the western front.
But individuals of any nationality might crack up under the strain, and
Bagot-Chester records in his diary a visit to the 41st Dogras in the front
line who had just suffered massive losses in a bombardment: 'One of
their British officers in the trench had completely lost his nerve and was

rather a pitiable sight. I tried to comfort him a bit . . .' Among his own people, a rifleman called Buddhiman Limbu suddenly became so violent and abusive that he had to be forcibly restrained and sent to hospital: 'Speaking to him quietly afterwards he told me that everybody sought to kill him and he could not live with the men of his company any longer but he said he would come anywhere with me.'[64] (As an easterner in a western battalion, Buddhiman Limbu may have felt not just outnumbered but isolated, and this would have exacerbated his paranoia.)

On 25 May Bagot-Chester expressed his disgust at the state of the trenches the 2/3rd Gurkhas took over from a battalion of the London Regiment:

> Some say Indian troops are dirty and have dirty habits compared to European soldiers but my experience is the reverse. I would much rather take over a trench which had been occupied by an Indian regiment, Gurkha or native, than one occupied by a British regiment. The filth and smell in my trench when I took over was awful . . . [65]

The night before, Bagot-Chester's orderly, Rifleman Tilbir Thapa, had returned from hospital at Boulogne: 'He amused me with his stories of the fearful shamming sick which goes on amongst the Indians of native regiments there. I am glad to say I have not heard of a single case of a Gurkha scrim-shanking in this way.'[66]

In the first months of the war there had been such a rash of wounds to the left hand among Indians in particular – though neither British nor Gurkha troops were entirely immune – that medical officers became suspicious and the authorities threatened soldiers with courts-martial for self-inflicted wounds. The most flagrant self-mutilators were the Sikhs: up to 14 August 1915, the 47th Sikhs had 479 cases of hand wounds and the 15th Sikhs 236 (not all of which, of course, were necessarily self-inflicted), whereas the Connaught Rangers had 54 and the Manchester Regiment 38, the 1/1st Gurkhas 50 and the 1/4th 40.[67]

A wounded Gurkha at the Kitchener Indian Hospital in Brighton wrote to a friend in the 1/4th Gurkhas at the front:

> . . . this hospital is a very bad place. All the natives of India by practising deception have made the doctors in charge displeased with

them. If they are slightly wounded in the hand, they pretend that they cannot move their hands at all. The Gurkhas are disgusted with the natives of India. Here for every work they seek out Gurkhas. But still this place is a very large prison. I cannot put on my belt, nor can I [bend] double; I am troubled with coughing and sneezing; but I tell the Sahibs here that I am all right. Because I say, that from this hospital I have no chance of going direct to India, perhaps I will go to France.[68]

Indian and Gurkha other ranks did not take kindly to the virtual imprisonment – or apartheid – imposed on them in England and called by the commanding officer of the Kitchener Indian Hospital 'an Imperial necessity'. Though they were considered good enough to die or be wounded in Britain's service, these soldiers were nevertheless strictly segregated from the ordinary inhabitants of our islands. A rifleman at Milford Depot in England, sufficiently recovered to be returned to France, complained to a friend in the 2/3rd Gurkhas:

As for exercise, we get about as much as a little pig does in the yard in which he is kept. We are not allowed to say even a single word to the English people. We are permitted to walk 100 yards to the sea, but neither to the right hand nor the left. If anyone is seen talking to a woman, young or old, he is severely punished. As for the town, we are not allowed even to mention its name.[69]

On the other hand, selected individuals – especially those decorated for gallantry – got the red-carpet treatment, and one soldier wrote wonderingly:

On the 17th June I went to London, where they showed me the city, and the Houses of Parliament, and all the great places. Peers showed us these places, and in London they pay us great honour, and great men of royal families always shake hands with us. They make no distinctions of persons in meeting us, and consider us as their brothers. They say, 'You people are our guests, what can we do to entertain you?' They have no pride in their hearts. They show us places which the inhabitants of the city are unable to see even by paying 50 or 100 rupees.[70]

The few letters Gurkhas wrote from the front expressed a kind of numbed awe at the scale of destruction. It hardly mattered who was attacking whom. A wounded and convalescent rifleman wrote of the battle of Neuve Chapelle in March 1915 that 'the piles of the killed on both sides were like heaps of slaughtered goats'.[71]

In the midst of the horror, though, there were lighter moments, usually when battalions were rested from the front line. The appearance of a hare between two of the 2/3rd Gurkha billets caused such wild excitement that a British gunner rushed out of his billet nearby and hailed a passing and uninvolved Gurkha, 'Hi, Johnny – what's up?' The Gurkha solemnly replied, 'Allemand'. Then, seeing the look of alarm on the gunner's face, he smiled. The gunner, who could hardly believe he was having his leg pulled by an 'Indian', called out to a mate, ''Ere, Bill; this 'ere little black is trying to kid me.'[72] Recognition of a shared sense of the ridiculous was (and is) the great bond between British and Gurkha soldiers.

Acts of selfless devotion to British officers by Gurkha soldiers were not uncommon. At Ypres a wounded and exhausted Captain J. R. Hartwell of 1/4 GR crawled into a ditch not far from where Rifleman Motilal Thapa was lying with a shattered shoulder and his arm almost severed from his body:

> When the second line of attackers reached the ditch Captain Hartwell had Motilal carried into the ditch and his arm bound up. The attack passed on, and Captain Hartwell fell asleep and slept for some hours. When he awoke he found Motilal had propped himself up against the side of the ditch and was holding his field service hat over Captain Hartwell's head so as to keep the sun out of his eyes. Poor Motilal was in great pain, and Captain Hartwell heard him muttering continuously that he must not groan or cry out because he was a Gurkha. The devoted man died as he was being carried to the aid post.[73]

The major problem for Gurkha regiments, and for the Indian Army generally, was the paucity of British officers and – given the high rate of casualties in France – the difficulty of replacing them. The regimental system was rooted in familiarity, both men and officers (like Hamish Reid) serving in the same regiment over generations and establishing a

mutual understanding and rapport. On the western front the entire officer cadre of a battalion could be wiped out in a single attack, and this
exposed the (often elderly) Gurkha officers, who at that time were not
expected to show the sort of initiative that would later be demanded of
them.

The withdrawal of the Indian Corps from France had been mooted
from at least the beginning of 1915. If anyone had his ear to the ground,
so to speak, it was the mail censor, E. H. Howell; and he had argued in
January that if the strain on the troops was not to reach breaking point,
'the "door of hope" must be opened somewhere before long'. He
regarded the prospect of the removal of the entire contingent from
France with mixed feelings. On the one hand, the rank and file and all
their relatives would certainly be relieved; on the other, the officers
would not welcome it, nor would 'a large body of public opinion in
India' intent on proving 'that Indian troops were the equals of any that
Europe could produce':

> For the present, however, the regiments which have been heavily
> engaged in France are probably content to let that matter rest. The
> men have had their experience of a European enemy, and have also
> had some chance of feeling their own helplessness without their
> British officers. Man for man some of them may consider themselves a
> match for the Germans; others do not. Each must judge for himself in
> the light of his own experience and behaviour. And the longer the
> question can remain open the better for us. But the burden of proof
> should now be shifted to fresh shoulders and some measure of relief
> accorded where it is most needed . . . [74]

A number of reasons have been given for the supposed failure of the
Indian Corps in France: the wrong sort of training (or training for the
wrong sort of war), inadequate clothing and weapons (at least to begin
with), the hostile climate, the effect of massive casualty rates on units
built on personal relations, inadequate reserves and, above all, the critical shortage of British officers. These were indeed disadvantages, but
none of them would have been insurmountable. That there was an
underlying factor far more important than any of these is shown by
comparison with the performance of the Indian Army in the Second

World War when burgeoning nationalism – where it did not subvert loyalty to the Raj – and something approaching equality (with a number of commissioned Indians on an equal footing with British officers) bolstered the self-esteem of the troops to the extent that they feared no one.

But by the time the Indian Corps (with the exception of cavalry units) was posted away from the western front towards the end of 1915, the Gurkhas at least had gone a long way towards redeeming their early failures – 2/3 GR at Neuve Chapelle in March, and at Loos in September* alongside the largely reconstituted 2/8 GR, of whom General Sir James Willcocks, who had a special affection for the battalion, which he had known as far back as 1886 when it was still the 43rd Gurkha Light Infantry, wrote:

> And what of the 8th Gurkhas who had begun the War on the bleak
> 30th day of October 1914 before Festubert? The old battalion had
> practically disappeared, but although no longer the corps that had
> suffered so terribly in those early days, it was determined to leave its
> mark deep cut on the soil of Flanders . . . and we may well pronounce
> that the 8th Gurkhas indeed did their duty and found their Valhalla.[76]

Gallipoli was the kind of glorious failure that the British, of all nationalities, seem to take greater delight in than outright victory. It contributed most famously, of course, to the self-image of the Australians and New Zealanders whose mettle was tested to the full on those bare hills rising out of the straits of the Dardanelles. But the Gurkhas, too, proved their staunchness in a kind of warfare better suited

---

*At Loos on 24 September 1915, Lt. Bagot-Chester of 2/3 GR was seriously wounded and eighty-six of his 120 men were either killed or wounded. Rifleman Kulbir Thapa of his double company won a VC in this action: he was the only survivor of a small group who fought their way into a German trench; though wounded, he spent the rest of the day and a night beside a seriously injured man from the 2nd Leicesters; the following day he brought him back through the German wire under the cover of mist in addition to rescuing two wounded Gurkhas under fire. Bagot-Chester himself survived his wounds and went on to fight in Palestine, where he won an MC before losing his life in March 1918.[75]

to their talents than the industrial stalemate on the western front. On 2 August 1915, Major Cecil Allanson of the 1/6th Gurkhas wrote in his diary, 'It is gratifying to see that, whatever may have happened in Europe, everyone here admires and speaks well of the Gurkha.'[77] And it was the 'most cherished conviction' of the commanding general, Sir Ian Hamilton, as his secretary wrote on 19 January 1918 in acknowledging a Christmas card from 1/6 GR who made their name there, 'that if he had been given more Gurkhas at the Dardanelles he would never have been held up by the Turks'.[78] In addition to the 1/6th, the 1/5th and 2/10th Gurkhas distinguished themselves in this bitter and hard-fought campaign. The 1/4th also came to Gallipoli, but they arrived after the main battles were over.

In the early part of the campaign, the 1/6th was commanded by Colonel C. G. Bruce, formerly of the 1/5th, but he was badly wounded in the legs. His successor, Major Allanson, wrote of Bruce after visiting him in hospital on 16 July 1915:

He is a fine optimistic man, with but few complaints; he has been about seven weeks in the Gallipoli Peninsula, and said that from start to finish the whole thing was one long nightmare. Shell, maxim and rifle fire, to say nothing of bombs, without intermission, and that for periods of over a fortnight it had been impossible even to take off one's boots or stockings. He said we suffered from a shortage of machine guns and bombs, the latter being nearly all locally made in the Peninsula, and were fighting a very brave enemy, well equipped and in a magnificently defended position.[79]

Allanson was to lead the 1/6th in what was the climax of the campaign, the assault on Sari Bair, the 'Yellow Ridge' which dominated the peninsula. In his diary, which – though not originally intended for publication – was printed for limited circulation, he wrote of the battle on his particular section of the ridge:

At the top we met the Turks; Le Marchand went down, a bayonet through the heart. I got one through the leg, and then, for about ten minutes, we fought hand to hand, we bit and fisted, and used rifles and pistols as clubs; blood was flying about like spray from a hairwash bottle. And then the Turks turned and fled, and I felt a very proud man; the key of the whole peninsula was ours, and our losses had not been so very great for such a result.[80]

This famous battle, commemorated in a painting by the war artist, Terence Cuneo, might have been the turning-point of the Gallipoli campaign if there had been fresh troops to follow up 1/6 GR and consolidate the position it had gained on top of the ridge. But there were no fresh troops; every unit involved in the assault had fought its own battles and lost a number of men. A company of the Warwicks reduced to less than fifty men finally made it to the ridge but lost their third commander in three days, wounded – a young lieutenant by the name of Slim, who was to become much more closely acquainted with 1/6 GR in the years ahead.

Exactly what happened on top of the ridge is shrouded in mystery. The Gurkhas were dislodged by a combination of heavy shelling and a strong Turkish counter-attack, but who was doing the shelling? Allanson blamed the Royal Navy, saying they had mistaken Gurkhas for Turks, but the Navy have always denied it. Allanson also gave more than one version of the death of Lieutenant Le Marchand, on attachment from the 56th Punjab Rifles (Frontier Force). Whether Le Marchand was bayoneted or shot, attacking or retiring or resisting the order to retire, may not matter much at this remove, except that it calls Allanson's credibility into question.

The passage above, with blood 'flying about like spray from a hairwash bottle' certainly has a touched-up feel about it, as if the writer is striving to produce an heroic set-piece (like Cuneo's painting). It is clear, both from Allanson's reputation – when his nephew, Harry Davies, joined 1/6 GR, a fellow officer leaned towards him across the mess table and sneered, 'Of course, your uncle put himself in for a VC' – and from his diary, that he was obsessed with awards and never got over the fact that the VC he had been led to expect was downgraded to a DSO.[81] Since he himself spent most of his service on the staff (he was with the regiment so little that he barely spoke Gurkhali), one has to question his frequently expressed contempt for the way staff officers got themselves decorations. It is not surprising that Allanson was ambivalent about publishing his diary; it is a revealing document and what it reveals about him makes uncomfortable reading.

But this should not detract from the achievement of 1/6 GR at Sari Bair both under his command and after he had been persuaded to relinquish command in order to have a wound in his leg treated. His successor, Captain Tomes of the 53rd Sikhs, was killed within twenty-four hours and command devolved to Subedar-Major Gambirsing Pun, who organized a disciplined and successful withdrawal, communicating with other units and the authorities with the aid of the battalion medical officer.

It was not just heroism in the line that counted, but endurance out of it. By late November 1915, shortly after Kitchener's fleeting visit which, unbeknownst to the troops, determined the evacuation of the peninsula at the end of the year, conditions in Gallipoli rivalled the worst the western front could offer in terms of wintry foulness: trenches filled with water, 'rest pits' turned into quagmires, then frozen over when rain was followed by blizzards of snow and icy winds. Sodden blankets and coats became stiff as boards, and hats so brittle that the brims snapped off. When the men could be persuaded to take off their boots, there were lumps of ice between their toes. Captain Watson-Smyth, in command of B Company, 1/6 GR, marvelled at their stoicism:

> By the morning of the 30th 'B' Company was reduced to an effective strength of about eighty rifles, and eighty per cent of these had their feet more or less frost bitten. Throughout all this time I never heard a single complaint; the men were cheerful and ready to laugh at a joke. No praise could be too high for them.
>
> To give one instance. My field orderly, Hastabir Pun, had accompanied me everywhere during the three days [of relieving the Northamptonshire Regiment]; always he was at my heels, and never had been anything but cheerful and keen. Yet on the 30th, when I made him show me his feet, to my horror I found them black with gangrene from neglected frost bite. He had never said a word to me, and never would have. His case is not an exceptional one, but merely a typical example of the courage these Gurkhas displayed.[82]

Back in the summer of 1915, on 30 July, the troops in Gallipoli had been paraded to hear a message from Lord Kitchener about 'another great victory in Mesopotamia', which had opened up the road to Baghdad.

Privately Major Allanson had had his doubts, confiding in his diary with remarkable foresight (unless this was a later addition, making it unremarkable hindsight): 'With the force at their disposal I cannot imagine how they can ever hope to get there, and if they do how they hope to be able to hold and keep such a vast city.'[83] He was right to be sceptical: Major-General Charles Townshend's 'great victory' at Amara was a prelude to the greatest disaster to befall the Indian Army since the retreat from Kabul in 1842 (and Britain's most ignominious defeat until the fall of Singapore in 1942).

The original aim in sending troops to Mesopotamia had been to protect Britain's oil installations at Abadan. But an ambitious Indian high command was not content with so passive a role and transformed it into an active expedition up the Tigris against the Turks. To begin with, all went well; Townshend's division overcame all opposition, but instead of consolidating his position he colluded with his army commander, General Sir John Nixon, and kept going, all the time stretching his already tenuous lines of communication. He was finally halted at Ctesiphon, where the Turks were massively reinforced; the battle there, according to the official historian, was 'notable for the number of occasions on which both commanders took important decisions on incorrect intelligence'.[84] An enquiry into India's administration of the war in Mesopotamia would later reveal, in a veritable catalogue of errors and incompetence, 'the deplorable treatment of sick and wounded, especially after the battle of Ctesiphon'.[85]

Townshend was obliged to withdraw. But just as he had allowed his lust for glory (and promotion) to outweigh his military judgement in his reckless advance – for Townshend was no fool – so he compounded the error by taking his stand at Kut el Amara, which was neither easily defensible nor within reinforcable distance of his base. He may have been influenced in this by an earlier experience: as a captain on the north-west frontier, he had withdrawn into a fort at Chitral and sustained his besieged force for forty-six days before he was relieved, becoming a hero in the process. The 2/4th Gurkhas claimed 'rather a special interest in the relief of General Townshend's troops in Kut' because they had been part of the relieving column at Chitral in 1895.[86]

Once in Kut, Townshend sat tight and waited to be rescued, putting unnecessary pressure on the force sent to his relief by exaggerating his shortage of food and refusing to make any sorties against the enemy, which had simply bypassed his position and was now concentrated on preventing the relieving force from reaching him. Eventually Townshend's food supplies, which had lasted 117 days longer than he had initially predicted, did run out and he was obliged to surrender on 29 April 1916, thereby condemning his 13,000 blameless troops to brutality at the hands of the Turks and marauding Arabs, to disease and – in far too many cases – death on their 1,200-mile forced march 'across the arid wastes and freezing heights of Asia Minor', while he himself was 'wined and dined, honoured and entertained as the personal guest of the Turkish commander-in-chief'.[87]

The 2/7th Gurkhas were among those rounded up, separated from their officers and taken into captivity:

> From first to last they were magnificent – a class apart. Their conduct
> was not without reward for it won the respect of the Turks and of the
> Germans; it also won the healthy regard of the Arabs so that the
> treatment they were subjected to, deplorable though it sometimes was,
> never reached the callousness of that meted out to some, particularly
> to the abject and to stragglers. In the 2nd Battalion there was no
> straggling; each man took strength from his comrades, cohesion and
> membership were never lost . . . Three remarkable men . . . were
> Colour-Havildar Fatehbahadur Limbu, the senior NCO who took
> command of the Battalion; Colour-Havildar Bhotri Khattri who
> assumed the duties of Adjutant; and Havildar Hari Singh Khattri the
> Sikh QM clerk.[88]

A re-formed 2/7 GR took part in the later stages of the Mesopotamian campaign in 1917–18. The regimental history describes it as 'a strange situation for the 2nd Battalion; as though in a war-game come to life a lost battalion had been revived to play a role in the relieving force whose moves it had so anxiously followed when it was itself besieged . . . [but] we were preparing not to save a surrounded 6 Division but to retrieve its loss'.[89]

As at Gallipoli and on the western front, conditions on the Tigris in Mesopotamia were appalling. The 2/4th Gurkhas felt the force of the Arab proverb, 'When Allah had made Hell he found it was not bad enough. So he made Iraq . . . and added flies.'[90] To the officers of the 1/8th, the British soldiers' characterization of the country as 'miles and miles of fuck all' was 'apt, if unparliamentary':

> Mesopotamia is a hotbed of disease – plague, smallpox, cholera, malaria, dysentery are all prevalent. To these pleasantries could be added heat-stroke when campaigning in temperatures mounting to 120° F in the shade, and on short water supplies.[91]

The campaign petered out when the thrust of the offensive against the Turks switched to Palestine, where General Allenby had assumed command.

There were Gurkhas in Palestine, too, and a detachment of seventeen men from the 2/3rd under Captain Scott-Higgins of the 3/3rd operated with T. E. Lawrence behind the lines in the final phases of his attack on the Hejaz railway, though *unt ko kam* – camel work – did not come naturally to Gurkhas.

A battalion of 4 GR found its way to the Caucasus in 1919, when Bolshevik revolutionaries came up against imperial Russian troops under General Denikin, whose avowed aim of regaining the Daghestan republic for Russia made him unpopular with the Daghestanis. In the prevailing anarchy the British force had an impossible task 'because we were on the one hand assisting Denikin, and on the other endeavouring to maintain the *status quo* as regards the various republics'.[92] Nevertheless the 4th Gurkhas were treated with the greatest respect by all sides. Lurid tales of the prowess of the Gurkhas had preceded them to the Caucasus:

> It was stated that they could progress uphill on all fours at a greater speed than a horse could run on the level; they carried a large flat knife in their mouths and without faltering could fell the undergrowth, even large trees, and so cut their way through the forest. At times, it was said, they would hang head downwards from the branches of trees and slash off the heads of the enemy with this formidable knife; at other times they would throw the knife with such accuracy as to kill their man immediately, and would then rush forward and regain the knife. As they did these things they would laugh with glee; the scowl of a Cossack was nothing to the smile of a Gurkha.[93]

The Argentines in the Falklands war were not the first to fall victim to their own credulity.

Old habits die hard. The pre-Mutiny Indian Army system of Ration Compensation, under which soldiers received an allowance and bought their provisions from a *baniya*, or storekeeper, attached to each company, was not abolished and replaced by free rations until the beginning of 1917. Similarly, the war was half over before the men received a pay rise and a proper system of accounting was introduced.[94] But the biggest administrative headache was recruiting. Men were fed into the war machine and came out mangled or dead. Those who could not be patched up and returned to the front were sent back to India. The dead, the captured and the invalided all had to be replaced and new battalions, even a new regiment, raised.

The short-lived 11th Gurkhas (XI GR) – revived in the post-independence Indian Army – was formed from detachments drawn from other Gurkha units serving in Mesopotamia on 18 May 1918. Four battalions were raised and they served in the Middle East (the 1st and 2nd battalions returning to Iraq to put down the Arab Rebellion in June 1920) and in Afghanistan before they were finally disbanded in 1921–2, in the post-war rundown of the Gurkha Brigade.[95]

There was no end to the manpower demands, and these fell particularly heavily on the Nepal *durbar*, which 'by its efforts not only maintained its own ten State battalions at full strength, but also met adequately the thirty-four battalions, each at twelve hundred, and the equivalent of another three or four battalions for the Guides, and for various State and Military Police establishments':

> This involved the recruitment of no less than 55,000 men between 1914–1919, a generous response, uninfluenced by motives of patriotism, self-advancement, and protection, which is probably unique in history on the part of a self-governing and independent State.[96]

So writes the historian of the 9th Gurkhas, who prefaces these remarks by saying that in order to meet these demands 'the Durbar introduced conscription in Nepal'.[97] Strictly speaking, this was not the case; military service remained voluntary throughout the war, but more and more inducements, in the shape of money and land, had to be offered by the British and Nepalese governments to recruiters and recruited alike to keep up an adequate flow.

In total contrast to the previous century, when British recruitment had been officially frowned upon in Nepal, when not actively obstructed, now it was officially sanctioned and actively – even over-actively – promoted. Seven recruiting centres, later increased to ten, were opened within Nepal itself, and officials were authorized to use gentle persuasion to encourage volunteers to join up. Inevitably there was a reaction. Rumours abounded that Britain was losing the war, and despite all the incentives, inducements and pressures, families – women in particular – began to resist the near-forcible removal of their menfolk, especially when the death toll and the number of the wounded came to be known. Desertions were rife (which itself calls into question the voluntary nature of recruitment): in 1916 alone as many as 1,132 recruits were acknowledged to have deserted, and the real figure must have been considerably higher.[98]

In the country as a whole, though probably not in the Magar-Gurung and Limbu-Rai heartlands, there was some opposition to the notion of fighting another country's wars – which would become more marked with the growth of nationalism in the subcontinent through the century. In a letter to the maharajah written in May 1916, Ganga Bahadur Basnyat pointed out that 'the people like to be recruited for their own country but not for a foreign power'.[99] Chandra Shamsher supported the British even to the extent of apprehending deserters and punishing them, but he did warn the Resident that such steps as he agreed to take applied only to the special circumstances of the war and were not to be regarded as a precedent, and that in taking them at all he was 'some-times overstepping prudent limits, not always a safe thing to do in this country'.[100]

The return of severely wounded Gurkha soldiers, first to hospitals in India and then home to Nepal, was another disincentive to recruit-ment. More than a tenth (and perhaps as many as a fifth) of the 100,000 Gurkhas mobilized during the war were killed or wounded, or missing in action. Early in 1915, Chandra Shamsher's son, General Baber Shamsher, made a tour of inspection at a military hospital in India and talked to over a hundred wounded Gurkhas. Many had lost fingers or toes through frostbite; some had had their noses or eyeballs shot away; one had suffered such dreadful head injuries that he had been transformed into a kind of monster, with his eyes sticking out from the ruins of his forehead. But even more pathetic was a man who had been buried alive in a trench for five days and now lay moaning incessantly because of the pain of his broken back. Baber Shamsher was appalled by what he saw and in the report he sent to his father, asked rhetorically, 'How could life linger in such desperate souls?'[101]

Baber suggested to the British authorities that the maimed and incapacitated should be kept away from depots like Dehra Dun, where recruits gathered, for fear of creating 'an undesirable impression in the minds of raw men'.[102] And Chandra himself requested that the government of India should stop sending news of wounded Gurkhas to their families since they were not in the habit of corresponding and such notices produced a disproportionate alarm.[103]

Despite the demand for recruits, recruiting officers – at least in the early part of the war – rejected large numbers of potential recruits the *durbar* sent them either on health grounds or because they plainly did not belong to the right (i.e. martial) castes; in a survey of rejected recruits carried out at the end of 1914, for example, it was found that the vast majority of these were Chhetris, whose Indo-Aryan appearance would tell against them.[104] By the end of the war, however, the pressure on manpower had become so great that Newars, Tamangs and other races not normally considered martial were enlisted and Nepal even emptied its gaols to feed the voracious war machine (though these ex-prisoners went into the Army Bearer Corps rather than the infantry).[105] Perceval Landon, writing just after the war, doubted 'if any belligerent power directly involved lost so big a proportion of its fighting men'.[106]

Chandra's contribution to the British war effort was not confined to manpower; he also sent donations of money and provided material such as timber from the Terai for railway sleepers.

The Viceroy, Lord Chelmsford, offered the government of Nepal 'an annual present of ten lakhs of rupees [about £75,000 at that time] as a mark of appreciation of the attitude adopted by Nepal during the war, as a recognition of the sacrifices which have been made and in the hope that the gift will not only further strengthen the ties of friendship, which have existed for so long, but will add to the power and prosperity of Nepal'.[107] This was very much second best so far as Chandra was concerned, although he eventually pocketed the money; he had been angling for a grant of territory, according to the precedent set by the return of a strip of the Terai to Jang Bahadur after the Sepoy Revolt. The government of India ruled that such a grant was 'out of the question under modern conditions'. So Chandra had to be content with the annual present 'to be paid in perpetuity unless and until the friendly relations which so happily subsist between the two countries are broken off'.[108]

In 1922, during the negotiations for the Treaty of Friendship which would replace the hated Treaty of Segauli and provide Nepal with written evidence of independence, Chandra tried to have this present capitalized in order to remove 'the apprehension that later it might be interpreted as, or identified with, a subsidy'. He proposed a one-off payment yielding an annual interest of ten lakhs of rupees. But the government of India regretted its 'inability to accede to HH's proposal'.[109] Long after Chandra's death this 'subsidy' continued to rankle with the Ranas, who never gave up hope of a capitalization of the sum; the matter was raised in 1935, in 1938 and again in 1942, but the British would not budge. As the India Office confidentially informed the Foreign Office, 'we do not intend to abandon this lever which we have with Nepal'.[110] Despite the 1923 Treaty of Friendship and the transformation of the Resident into the less threatening figure of an envoy (and from 1934, when Nepal sent a representative to London, minister), the independence of Nepal was still conditional:

Although the Government of India have fully admitted the independence of Nepal to be as complete as that of Afghanistan, it is an essential part of their policy to maintain and secure their influence in the kingdoms of the Indian glacis – a policy which can best be served by the grant of financial or other aid at recurring intervals. The continuance of Nepal within the Indian political, military, and commercial orbit through the maintenance and, if possible, strengthening of existing ties must therefore be a cardinal feature in India's foreign policy. For this reason alone they now on full consideration recommend that the *status quo* should be preserved.[111]

In the early 1920s, when Perceval Landon asked a 'high authority in Simla' about the policy of the Indian government towards Nepal, he was informed: 'We have no policy. We have only friendship.'[112] But such professions of undying amity masked a totally unsentimental *realpolitik* on the part of the British. Their primary consideration remained the recruitment of Gurkhas, and they were happy to reward the Ranas for making this possible, but not to the extent of letting go of the purse-strings. It suited both the British and the maharajah to form a mutual admiration society and if Chandra's long period in office was the high noon of the Rana autocracy, the point at which, in the words of one historian, it 'came closest to meeting its own ideals' – of keeping 'the country secure and the people minimally but sufficiently contented' while at the same time maximizing revenues and appropriating them 'for its exclusive use' – then it was also the period in which the seeds of its destruction were sown.[113]

In the eyes of most British commentators, Chandra was the greatest of the Rana maharajahs: Landon compares him to Cecil Rhodes for force of personality, W. Brook Northey remembers him as 'a man of quite exceptional dignity and distinction, who at the same time with all his charm of manner, was the possessor of a very strong and de-termined character'; Francis Tuker calls him an autocrat, but 'a benevolent one to whom the poorest among his people could bring their complaints': John Morris thinks he was 'an outstanding person-ality and except for his ancestor, the great Jung Bahadur, the only real statesman to emerge from the Rana family' – though he also labels him 'a complete despot', who, like all the Ranas, did not so much oppress his people as 'ignore their existence' (Morris found Chandra's personal dignity was somewhat impaired by 'a mouthful of staringly white false teeth of which he was in only vague control').[114] All these writers remark on his unusual asceticism, the fact that he was so devoted to his one wife that when she was dying he would not consider remarrying, and only agreed to do so when she personally selected a bride for him from Benares. They draw attention to such important reforms as the abolition in 1920 of *sati* (the self-immolation of a widow on her husband's funeral pyre, never as widespread a practice in Nepal as in India and not part of the culture of the hills) and, four years later, of slavery. (It could be argued that the abolition of slavery created as much hardship as it alleviated in that the economic conditions which gave rise to it remained unchanged.)

For Nepali nationalists like D. R. Regmi, however, Chandra behaved 'like a loyal feudatory Prince' and sacrificed several lakhs of Nepali lives (i.e., hundreds of thousands – a huge exaggeration), not to speak of money and war materials, in order to curry favour with the British in 1914–18. He was guilty of accepting British money – to the tune of 'ten lakhs' of rupees annually (no exaggeration this time) – as well as British military rank and British decorations as 'the price of blood which two lakhs sons of Nepal shed in the battle fields'.[115] Regmi also holds him responsible for introducing the king to debauchery at an early age: 'Chandra Shumsher was the man who thought out this device to sterilise the royal puppet.'[116] The ascetic Chandra may have failed to discontinue this practice but he certainly did not initiate it; the commander of the British Resident's bodyguard in 1919 noted:

> For years the Prime Minister's family had retained all power in their own hands and, lest the King should ever evince a desire to rule, he was deliberately encouraged to indulge in every possible vice. He was provided with some 400 concubines and all the alcohol and wine he could be persuaded to consume. The result, of course, was that no King survived much beyond the age of thirty and was invariably dithering and incompetent.[117]

Regmi concedes that Chandra instigated various reforms, such as building a college, a library and a military hospital; but these, like the earlier electrification of Kathmandu, were merely for show, designed to impress visiting foreigners, while 'inwardly the very opposite of what he professed reigned supreme in his mind'.[118]

These two opposing views of Chandra reflect the developing political consciousness and conflict in Nepal, as elsewhere on the subcontinent, from before the First World War right up to Indian independence in 1947 and – in the case of Nepal – beyond. In return for British co-operation in the containment and suppression of the growing anti-Rana forces among Nepali exiles and expatriots in India the Ranas granted Britain the right to recruit an ever-increasing number of Gurkhas into the Indian Army. The more Chandra insisted on outward

and visible signs of Nepal's independence, the more he tacitly acknowledged the political and economic dependence of the Rana regime on
British India.

Perceval Landon failed to discern 'any popular movement whatever'
and therefore assumed that the Nepalese were content to be governed
'in the absolute manner that [Chandra] has proved to be best for his
people at the present day'. The maharajah had told him that attempts
had been made 'to introduce across the border the dangerous virus of
Indian sedition', but these – 'as may be imagined' – had been summar-
ily dealt with.[119] Chandra himself was not so easily fooled. At the
opening ceremony of Nepal's first higher educational establishment, the
Tribhuvan-Chandra College in Kathmandu, he apparently dubbed it
'the graveyard of the Rana rule'.[120]

Rana rule may have been strengthened in the short term by
Chandra's unstinting support of the British cause in the First World
War. But the next thirty years, during which the loyalty of the Gurkha
Brigade would be tested to the full, would see both the Ranas in Nepal
and the British in India come under ever-increasing pressure from the
forces of nationalism.

6

Twilight of the Raj

There is about British Gurkha memoirs of the period between the wars the illusion of timelessness, or of time standing still, which is only heightened by the fragility of the European peace and the sense of impending change in India. This is exemplified by John Masters of the 4th Gurkhas in his classic *Bugles and a Tiger*:

> It was a golden season, and nearing its end, not only for that year but for ever. This was the last time and the first time that I went marching to the plains in the first snap of the cold weather. We knew we would be going to the Frontier for a year or two, but after that we thought that the familiar pattern would again shape our lives – Bakloh [4 GR's permanent home], marching to the plains, manoeuvres, marching to the hills, Bakloh. But the year was 1935, the season Christmas, and Hitler did not hear our confident bugles.[1]

Most Gurkha battalions followed a pattern of what was known as '2 and 4' – two years on the north-west frontier and four years in their home stations. This fixed routine might be interrupted in an emergency, such as the social unrest in Bengal in the years 1930–2. But neither internal nor external threats seemed to disturb the even tenor of regimental life in the inter-war years.

In that time, according to the historian Philip Mason, there was 'a largely subconscious psychological plan for the Indian Army, summed up in the single word "Insulation' – insulation against the forces of nationalism'.[2] It was strong enough in Indian units, but in Gurkha battalions, where neither officers nor men were serving in their home country, it was even stronger; only the suspect Indian-domiciled Gurkhas – and by no means all of them – regarded India as home. Indeed, a large part of the trust and intimacy which characterized the special relationship between (hill) Gurkhas and their officers was the feeling they shared of being aliens in the country in which they served; and this was intensified by the near-inaccessibility of either's home country to the other.

Nepal was a closed country to all but a very few favoured Europeans, and even they were not free to roam the hills where the Magars, Gurungs, Limbus and Rais came from; and Britain was out of bounds to all Gurkhas, at least until Maharajah Judha Shamsher permitted Gurkha officers to participate in the King's Indian Orderly Officer scheme once again towards the end of the thirties. So each remained a mystery to the other, encouraging the growth of mutually sustaining myths. Officers and men found common cause in their mutual liking for hills, sport and *shikar*, and their mutual distaste for the heat of the plains, the unctuousness and 'effeminacy' of a certain type of Indian and the excesses of nationalism.

The road to self-government in India was a bumpy one, and the ride was made considerably bumpier because the British authorities in the driving seat had one foot on the accelerator and the other on the brake. While the Montagu-Chelmsford report of July 1918 had cautiously pointed the way forward, the Rowlatt Acts of 1919, replacing the anti-sedition Defence of India Act, extended wartime restrictions on civil liberty and increased government powers of internment. Gandhi, who had recently come to the forefront of the independence movement, responded by launching his first nationwide *satyagraha* campaign, aiming to embarrass the government by peaceful mass demonstrations and *hartals*, or strikes. He in turn was embarrassed when, in the Punjab in particular, the agitation proved far from non-violent. But the British over-reaction, in which Gurkhas were implicated willy-nilly, played into his hands.

Brigadier-General Reginald Dyer was summoned to Amritsar, where the arrest of two nationalist leaders had sparked off violent demonstrations and rioting in which isolated Europeans were assaulted and killed, or left for dead. Dyer had a very limited force at his disposal and regarded it as providential when a troop train carrying newly trained recruits of the 1/9th Gurkhas from the depot in Dehra Dun to Peshawar stopped at Amritsar in time to furnish much-needed reinforcements and to protect the railway station.

Second Lieutenant (later Brigadier) McCallum, who was not long out of Sandhurst, had just joined 1/9 GR. On the day before the infamous Amritsar massacre, he was sent out with a column to march through the city and proclaim that any assembly of more than five people was forbidden by law. 'As we went through the narrow streets,' he recalled more than fifty years later, 'angry faces looked down on us from the rooftops.'[3] After lunch on the unlucky 13 April 1919, he was ordered to rest by his superior, Captain Gerry Crampton. He sank into a comfortable leather armchair and soon dropped off to sleep. The next thing he remembered was being shaken awake by the captain and told to go out and count the empty cartridge cases at Jallianwala Bagh (though called a garden, at that time it was no more than a barren enclosure walled in by houses):

I found there were 923 empties. Gerry has *never* spoken to me about the 'incident' either then or since but I gathered . . . from the then Jemadar Jitbahadur (later Subedar-Major) that the General Sahib had been informed that a very large gathering was taking place in Jallianwala Bagh and ordered a column of twenty-five rifles from each [of the] 9th Gurkhas and 59th [Scinde] Rifles to go with him into the city. 'He told us to double through the narrow road leading to an open square and then said Gurkhas right, 59th left fire.'[4]

In all some 1,650 rounds were fired into a crowd whose only escape route was past the troops who were shooting at them. Three hundred and seventy-nine people were killed and about 1,200 injured. 'As soon as the firing began, the crowd rushed for the narrow openings between the houses, trampling over each other in their mad retreat. As many people were killed and injured in the stampede as by rifle fire.'[5]

In the immediate aftermath of the massacre, Dyer was lauded for his decisive action which, it was claimed, had put a stop to insurrection not just in the Punjab but throughout India. He was given a prestigious command on the north-west frontier and most soldiers, at least, believed that his subsequent dismissal from the service by an ungrateful government was a travesty of justice. Nigel Woodyatt writes:

> We feel, that whatever excesses or errors of judgment it may be thought he committed, his actions effected the immediate object in view, i.e. the suppression of the rebellion at its very centre, and were primarily approved by the highest authorities. This being so, no political or other influences should have induced the same authorities, later on, to reverse their judgment and let him down.[6]

Woodyatt concedes that the Hunter Committee found against Dyer, and that Dyer's evidence to the committee was 'self-condemnatory', but he still maintains that the proper procedure would have been 'to clearly and emphatically disavow his acts – or rather his subsequent explanation of them – where necessary, while at the same time refusing to be a party to his professional ruin'. The general military view was that Dyer was punished, in Woodyatt's italicized words, *'not so much for what he had done, but for what he had said'*.[7] But Villiers-Stuart is not so complimentary; when he met him during the war he found Dyer 'an excitable lunatic of a man' who was 'irresponsible most of the time for his actions, and all of the time for his tongue'. Dyer was also a ladies' man, no recommendation in the eyes of the misogynistic Villiers-Stuart:

> His ignorance was amazing – I can't attempt to explain it . . . he used to drive about the mountain roads round Abbottabad with a car full of ladies of the station, his great delight being to frighten them by dangerous driving at which he was an expert. The man was insane.[8]

Sir John Smyth VC, who was brigade major in Lahore at the time, describes the deliberations of the Hunter Committee as 'a shambles':

The judge, speaking no Hindustani, was unable to keep order. General Dyer, baited beyond endurance, made some very silly statements. In this respect he was his own worst enemy.[9]

Dyer's divisional commander, Maj-Gen. Sir William Beynon, had warned the brigadier to say nothing. But Dyer condemned himself out of his own mouth when he admitted that he carried on firing after the crowd had attempted to get away: '[I]t was no longer a question of merely dispersing the crowd, but one of producing a sufficient moral effect, not only on those who were present, but throughout the Punjab.'[10] Dyer had exceeded his military role, which was to disperse the crowd with minimal force; he had neglected to give an official warning before opening fire; he had allowed the soldiers, many of whom were inexperienced in crowd control, to fire at random; and he had made no arrangements to succour the wounded before marching his troops away.

There have been far worse massacres on the Indian subcontinent; Hindus and Muslims have slaughtered each other in infinitely greater numbers and in far more dreadful ways; but Amritsar will still be remembered when more horrific massacres are forgotten because of the message it conveyed to Indians – not that, in the last analysis, power rested with the gun (which was never in doubt), but that the liberalism professed by the authorities was a sham, and self-government was not going to be conceded without a struggle. So the victims of the Amritsar massacre became martyrs in the cause of independence, and Dyer the personification of repressive government.

Lt-Col. Tony Mains, who joined the 9th Gurkhas in the thirties, points out that 'modern Indian writing often attributes the action to British troops', adding, 'I have seen a picture in the Information room of the 11th Gorkha Rifles (1974) showing the firing by British troops.'[11] Even Woodyatt, writing at the time, goes so far as to say, 'I believe no Gurkhas were employed to fire on that 13th April, 1919' – despite the fact that he visited Amritsar before the end of that year along with a company from his old regiment, the 3rd Gurkhas, who were sometimes mistaken for their compatriots from the 9th.

The men told me that on first arrival it had been unpleasant, and almost dangerous, for less than a group of half a dozen or so to walk into the city. If they did so, they were met with scowling looks and an offensive remark about shooting down the speaker's brothers . . . [12]

Woodyatt – in his apparent ignorance of Gurkha involvement in the massacre – claims that this was 'most unfair'. But one of the significances of Amritsar, as a historian points out, is precisely that it did 'draw attention to the Gurkhas, who in the eyes of the nationalists were the ultimate in mercenaries as they were not even Indians'.[13]

After Amritsar, the army in India, and in particular Gurkhas, were called upon ever more frequently for aid to the civil power – as riot control was euphemistically known. For officers and men alike, this was a deeply unpopular duty; in that other staple of inter-war soldiering in India, active service on the north-west frontier, at least there were medals to be won. If frontier warfare was like fighting with one hand tied behind your back (in that the rules of the game precluded making a pre-emptive strike: you could not act, only react), then aid to the civil power meant having both hands tied behind your back – you could not fight at all; and if you did, you invariably got it wrong: too much too soon, or too little too late.

When Gandhi launched his civil disobedience campaign in March 1930, repercussions of it reached even the distant and predominantly Muslim North West Frontier Province, where violence erupted in late April in Peshawar. The 2/18th Royal Garhwal Rifles, who were called upon to restore order in the city, were considered by the British to be on a par with Gurkha regiments for political reliability. They were described by British officers in the same patronizing way, too:

> The Garhwali soldier is naturally very staunch – brave and uncomplaining. Blindly obedient to all orders and easily led. Slow in the uptake and in realizing exactly what is required of him when suddenly faced with an entirely novel situation.[14]

On 23 April, two platoons had been physically and verbally abused by a violent mob; and the next day another two platoons had refused to go into the city for more of the same treatment. This 'mutiny' resulted in the immediate disarmament of the 2/18th Garhwalis, who were replaced at Peshawar by the 2/5th Gurkhas. A court of enquiry, which was held at

Abbottabad in the following week, found no evidence of subversion, but ample evidence of provocation.

To prevent a recurrence of Dyer's impulsive action at Amritsar, the rule was that troops had to have warrants signed by a magistrate before they took offensive action against civilians. Since there was no magistrate available on this occasion, the Garhwalis had been obliged to stand by and watch as their British officer and various comrades suffered serious injuries from flying missiles.

> The men saw Government property, Armoured Cars, with Machine Guns in them, damaged and set on fire, a British soldier lying killed, and his body burning in the centre of the street, their own officer struck several times and bleeding, and yet no order came to them or the Armoured Cars to fire or retaliate.[15]

It was to the credit of the Garhwalis that their discipline held in the face of such taunts from the crowd as, 'When we have our Government, we will make the Garhwalis and Gurkhas into sweepers, giving them brooms, and making them do sweepers' work'.[16] Ironically, one of the NCOs who was wrongly found guilty of inciting his platoon to refuse to go into the city underwent a conversion to nationalism in prison and eventually emerged as a political opponent of the regime he had previously served so faithfully. It wasn't until later that the real culprit was found – a disgruntled subedar who took his revenge for the deferment of a pay increment by fomenting disobedience.[17]

The fact that there had been no mutiny as such did not prevent the spread of a myth to the effect that the Garhwalis had defied their officers rather than open fire on an unarmed crowd. In anti-British propaganda aimed at Gurkha soldiers, this was contrasted with the behaviour of the 9th Gurkha contingent at Amritsar:

> The Gurkhas did not display any bravery in opening machine gun fire upon the audience in a meeting at Amritsar, Punjab, in April 1919. The Gurwhalis did not open fire on a procession in Peshawar in June [sic], 1930. By not thus obeying an unjust order, they exhibited real chivalry. They were sentenced to transportation and to imprisonment but were called religious heroes, and they made a name.

In the Mutiny of 1857, the Gurkhas and the Sikhs deprived the
Indians of the Swaraj [self-rule] they had won and gave it to the
English. Now, the Sikhs have made amends for their error and they are
fighting for the achievement of Swaraj. The Gurkhas too should rectify
their mistake and help India.[18]

Gajendra Malla of the 2/9th Gurkhas was a line-boy, born at Dehra Dun
and educated in the regimental school of the 2/2nd Goorkhas before
going on to the town's high school. Because of his educational qualifi-
cations he was enlisted in 9 GR as a clerk. When he was still very junior,
he found himself typing a letter in which the depot commander had
written, 'The Gurkha [before he joins the army] has never worn a pair
of boots, never seen a train, nor a white man'. Gajendra was so incensed
that he protested to the commandant when he took him the letter to
sign, though he knew this might get him into trouble. The officer, however, was understanding and told him that the remark did not apply to
him as an Indian-domiciled Gurkha but only to hill Gurkhas newly
arrived from Nepal. Gajendra said no more but secretly resolved to do
all he could to promote the education of Gurkha children, so that such
supercilious remarks would become obsolete; and, true to his word, he
later helped to found a school in his unit's lines.[19]

Gajendra was ambitious and by dint of working extremely hard and
combining his clerical duties with regimental soldiering he succeeded
eventually in transferring as a naik (corporal) into a rifle company in 2/9
GR. His salary dropped from 67 to 22 rupees a month, and though he
was immediately promoted to havildar (sergeant) his monthly pay was
still only 25 rupees. But his ability was recognized and he was sent on a
platoon commander's course at Kitchener College in Nowgong in central India. He found the course stimulating, but for some of the less
educated, country-bred NCOs it was tough-going. (He recalls that when
they were invited to comment on the course by the chief instructor, a
Pathan havildar stood up and said, 'Sir, a water jug which has the capacity to hold two seers [roughly two litres] of water would certainly not be
able to take any more. If more water is put into it, the water will naturally overflow. Similarly to an Indian soldier, the subjects taught in this
College, though quite interesting, are too many, so our heads cannot
absorb them and they overflow through our nose and ears . . .')[20]

On his return to the depot of the 9th Gurkhas at Dehra Dun, Gajendra was surprised to find himself immediately placed under arrest – for reasons which at first he was unable to ascertain. The depot commander, who was clearly embarrassed by the whole business, finally told him that the order for his arrest had come from Army Headquarters. The case, it transpired, was political: someone had mentioned his name to the authorities as an associate of one Kharagbahadur Bisht, a political activist regarded by the Intelligence Bureau of the government of India as the chief anti-British propagandist among Gurkhas, who had been arrested at the railway station in Delhi en route to Abbottabad on 14 November 1930. Three trunk-loads of Congress pamphlets, full of Nehru's speeches, and several more subversive documents (including the one about Amritsar quoted above) were discovered in Kharagbahadur's possession. These 'clearly proved that he was deeply involved in organising anti-British propaganda amongst Gurkhas and Gurkha regiments and also in helping the Congress Committee of Dehra Dun, Rohtak and Delhi by supplying Gurkha volunteers for picketing etc.'.[21]

Among these documents was a copy of a typed letter in English from Kharagbahadur to Panditji (Jawaharlal Nehru) which distinguished between the different classes of Gurkhas and claimed 'that the domiciled class to which the writer has the fortune or misfortune to belong is indissolubly bound up with the future of India and they have in their hearts a warm and sympathetic corner for the Satyagraha movement'. The 'other class' were represented by 'the soldiery who on account of their cursed ignorance swore by the Union Jack and flared at the name of the Congress and all that it stood for'. Nehru's father, Motilal, had replied on 2 November, regretting that Kharagbahadur's letter had arrived a day late, Jawaharlal having just been arrested and put in gaol. But Motilal had taken the letter in during a visit, and they had discussed its contents and agreed 'that an authoritative declaration on behalf of the Congress that the Gurkhas were their own brethren forming an integral part of the Indian community be issued'.[22]

Another of the impounded documents was a list of names of Gurkha officers of 9 GR who 'had promised to distribute posters' – according to what the disaffected son of a retired 2/9 GR subedar said Kharagbahadur had told him.[23] Gajendra Malla cannot have been one of these as he was not yet an officer. But he did not deny his connection with Kharagbahadur: their fathers had served in the same unit, and they had been playmates almost from birth as well as classmates at the 2/2 GR regimental school.

When Kharagbahadur's father had retired from the army with the rank of jemadar, he had gone to Bengal to work for the railways, and Kharagbahadur had studied at Calcutta University. Then – as now, alas – there was a lucrative trade in young Nepalese girls from the hills, and a rich Marwari (a member of a caste of money-lenders and merchants) in Calcutta had purchased a Nepali girl called Mayu, who was still a minor. According to Gajendra, Kharagbahadur had become an active social worker and, in his concern for the dignity of Gurkha women, had warned the Marwari millionaire 'to curb his tendency to use Gurkha women for immoral traffic'. When the Marwari ignored the warning, Kharagbahadur took the law into his own hands and struck the man dead with his kukri.[24]

At his trial for the murder of Hira Lal Agrawal, Kharagbahadur had apparently 'gloried in his achievement and rejoiced that he had been chosen by God to protect the honour of Nepali girls'; nevertheless he was sentenced to eight years' imprisonment in 1927.[25] He was released after only two years, but not before he had been recruited by one Pratul Ganguly 'for the work of spreading disaffection amongst Hillmen and Indian soldiers'.[26] In March 1930 he published in the Bombay *Chronicle* an appeal to the Gurkhas to 'atone for the misdeeds of their own kinsmen who have fought against their Indian kinsmen', thus alerting the authorities to his new role; 'it is clear,' wrote a senior Indian civil servant, 'that he is capable of great mischief'.[27]

Kharagbahadur was imprisoned for a second time after his arrest at Delhi railway station, but released six months later. After a brief visit to Dehra Dun, he returned to Calcutta, where he disappeared from public view. In 1935 he was reported to be in Nepal, 'where he has obtained employment in the army under an assumed name'.[28]

Gajendra's detention did not last long. As an Indian-domiciled and educated Gurkha, he would have attracted the suspicions of mistrustful British authorities, who greatly feared the subversion of the military and took all possible steps to prevent it. Under the Indian Army Regulations of 1925, officers and soldiers alike were forbidden to take part in political meetings or demonstrations, or to join any political association or movement. But within his own unit Gajendra was known to be a keen and promising soldier with an unblemished record. After a period of leave, he rejoined his battalion, where his intelligence and outstanding ability gained him rapid promotion. He achieved the rank of jemadar in April 1935. But in the eyes of some Gurkhas and British officers he would never be able to live down the stigma of line-boy, no matter how loyally he served.

Major Freddy Poynder (a 1/9 GR officer posted to 2/9 GR as second-in-command before gaining command of his own battalion), for instance, never lost an opportunity of airing his anti-line-boy prejudice. One evening when he was drinking in the Gurkha Officers' Club in Dehra Dun with the GOs from both battalions of 9 GR, 'he very bluntly told me that Gurkha units did not want educated Gurkha Officers like Jemadar Gajendra Malla of 2/9th Gurkha Rifles'. (In the eyes of Poynder and his ilk the words 'educated' and 'subversive' were more or less interchangeable.) Gajendra knew that Poynder had the backing of many of the GOs present, and that made his attack all the more hurtful. He knew he was being picked on and he responded ironically. 'Sir,' he said, 'the Government of India very wrongly established the Army School of Education at Belgaum, where even the uneducated Gurkha soldiers are given education. Isn't it so, Sir?' But irony was wasted on Poynder, who 'gave me a bouquet of abusive language in Gurkhali'.[29] Such bullying tactics were too often employed on people who were in no position to retaliate. Gajendra writes pertinently:

> On the one hand my education was of considerable help to me,
> whereas on the other hand, the same education and my early career as
> a clerk were of a great disadvantage, which was further added [to] by
> my being born in India and known as a Line Boy, or in other words,
> Indian Domiciled Gurkha.[30]

Being born in India was a disadvantage from the point of view of reaching the pinnacle of most Gurkha soldiers' ambition at that time, which was to become subedar-major of their battalion. A sympathetic commanding officer of 2/9 GR told Gajendra what he already knew,

that he would not be made subedar-major since this was more or less
the preserve of the hill Gurkha.* But at the start of the Second World
War, paradoxically, it enabled him to apply for an emergency king's
commission, for which hill Gurkhas were ineligible because they were
not Indians. Gajendra got his commission, though he had to leave the
battalion and move into intelligence – since Indian (or Gurkha) emergency commissioned officers were not then permitted to serve in
Gurkha regiments. In 1948, Gajendra was promoted to colonel and was
the first Indian officer to be made Recruiting Officer for Gurkhas, or, in
the preferred spelling of the post-independence Indian Army, Gorkhas.
But the period after independence 'was not the happiest in Gajendra's
career', according to his old friend, Tony Mains (who also stayed on in
the new Indian Army):

> While he was regarded by the British officers as mildly nationalistic,
> the new senior Indian officers found him far too wedded to the old
> ways of the British and this, added to his somewhat argumentative
> frame of mind, was construed as anti-Indian. The result was
> demotion . . . and finally a return to the Regimental Centre as a major
> where he served out the remainder of his 37½ years' service.[32]

Although Field Marshal Lord Roberts had died while on a visit to the
western front during the First World War, his often-reiterated belief in
the irreplaceability of British officers in command of Indian troops did
not die with him. The instinctive dislike many British officers felt for
line-boys like Gajendra Malla was rooted in the unease such men
aroused in them; with the simple hill Gurkha their intellectual superiority went unchallenged, but educated Gurkhas were seen as a threat to
this comfortable relationship between officers and men – they were
somehow neither flesh nor fowl. The old colonial attitude of Roberts
and Co. died hardest of all in Gurkha units, which were cushioned from

---

*Tony Mains, who served with Gajendra for many years, disputes this. He told me
that the 'real reason why Gajendra didn't become S-M was because he would not
have been accepted – he didn't have the presence – and because he had been a
clerk. Gajendra was very small, he didn't look the part'.[31]

even such minimal change as happened in the rest of the Indian Army between the wars.

As a sop to burgeoning nationalism in India, the British authorities had promised to look into the question of commissioning Indians at the end of the First World War. In 1918 it was announced that king's commissions would be open to qualified Indians and ten places a year were reserved for them at Sandhurst. This was hardly a radical step, but it was the view of General Lord Rawlinson, who assumed command of the Indian Army in 1920, that it would 'take at least two, and probably three, generations to produce Indian officers of the right kind in sufficient numbers'.[33]

The main stumbling-block to progress was the perceived reluctance of British officers to serve under Indians, and the so-called 'eight units scheme' was dreamed up in 1923 to obviate such an undesirable eventuality. Under this scheme two cavalry regiments and six infantry battalions initially were earmarked for Indianization. This was a form of apartheid, or ghettoization, though it was presented (as such policies generally are) as providing a better opportunity for Indian officers to show what they could do. No one was fooled.

In 1927 the 'Indian Sandhurst' committee recommended that an Indian equivalent of Sandhurst be established – 'India should have a military college of her own and thus be self-sufficient in respect of the most important of national needs' – and that it should be inaugurated by 1933.[34] Despite the opposition of the C-in-C in India, Field Marshal Sir William (later Lord) Birdwood, who favoured the (British) Sandhurst option and would not implement these recommendations during his tenure (he retired in 1930), the Indian Military Academy (IMA) at Dehra Dun was opened ahead of schedule, in the autumn of 1932. It took up to sixty regular Indian Army cadets and a further twenty from the State Forces. But the ICO, or Indian Commissioned Officer, was not equal in all respects to the Sandhurst-commissioned Indian (or British) officer. His commission was valid only in India, and he drew lower rates of pay and allowances than his Sandhurst-trained fellow Indians, of whom one historian writes: 'Collectively, they were the most reliable, politically inert, aristocratic, and conservative group the British could select.'[35] But once the IMA came into being Indians ceased to go to Sandhurst.

Indian parents were reluctant to encourage their sons to pursue a military career so long as they felt 'that the Indianisation of the Army is, *in the minds of the authorities*, still suspect and uncertain'.[36] Some British parents in India were equally reluctant to let *their* sons go into the Indian Army, but for the opposite reason. T. J. Phillips was at Sandhurst in the early 1930s:

> When the time came for choosing a regiment, I put down for the Indian Army . . . although my father [in the Indian Police] warned me against it, pointing out that the days of the British in India were numbered and my career would be interrupted by Indian independence or by increasing Indianisation of the Indian Army officer ranks. He turned out to be right of course but I decided to go ahead.[37]

As in the days of Villiers-Stuart, officers passing out of Sandhurst into the Indian Army were placed on the 'unattached list' and had to serve a year with a British battalion in India before they joined an Indian Army unit. They still had to go through the 'vetting' process, spending a week or more with the unit they wished to join, to ensure their acceptability among their peers. John Masters, who is perhaps the best known of all British Gurkha officers as a result of his highly suc-cessful second career as a popular novelist, had a stroke of good fortune while he was being vetted by 2/4 GR at Bakloh; the battalion had been ordered to go to Lahore to quell a religious riot and he begged to be allowed to accompany it:

> I believe the 4th Gurkhas accepted me only because of this lucky chance, that the Shadiganj riots gave me an opportunity to show some military ability and at the same time cut off the social functions to which I would otherwise have been subjected. A few more days in Bakloh and there would have been trouble. I loved parties, and I was wildly excited at the idea of joining this regiment. I was just getting teed up to shine with an erratic brilliance my years were incapable of controlling. The colonel's final word would have been 'No' – regretfully, perhaps, but definitely.[38]

Masters was right about that: he would have been labelled 'unsound'; for 'erratic brilliance', read 'opinionated'.*

Tony Mains, who was vetted by the 2/9th Gurkhas in 1935 – the year in which Masters underwent his ordeal with 2/4 GR – recalls:

> Most cavalry regiments, all Gurkhas, both Frontier Force regiments, Baluch and some others . . . vetted their prospective candidates. This vetting was not to establish social status or anything like that; in fact the next officer to join after me was from the ranks and a poor family background; he was one of our best officers and his death from a mauling by a tiger was a great loss to the regiment. The object was to find out if the prospective candidate was the type who could 'muck in' and turn his hand to any job . . . The CO would say to his officer, 'Is this a chap you are prepared to live with?' The visit, except for being on one's best behaviour, was very pleasant; a shoot in the Nun Nadi beyond Ghangora, football with the troops, a Guest Night in the Mess and a visit to the Gurkha Officers' Club; the time soon passed . . [39]

'Social status' may not have been the sole criterion, but it was certainly an important one: the 'chaps you are prepared to live with' tend to be chaps very much like yourself, polo-playing – in units with a tradition of that – shooting and fishing types, products of public school and Sandhurst almost to a man. Money was a different matter. It did not matter whether or not you had private means. The Indian Army officer was better paid than his British Army equivalent, and a lack of independent means might influence an officer cadet in his choice of regiment. When T. J. Phillips (who later joined 1/9 GR) put his name down for the Indian Army, he recalls, 'Consideration of money did not enter into it although I would have no private means

---

*The consensus about Jack Masters, as he was always known, in the Brigade of Gurkhas when I joined it a decade after he had left the army (and a year or so after *Bugles and a Tiger* was published) was by no means entirely favourable. To adapt Hilaire Belloc's apophthegm, his books might be read, but his sins – intellectual pride, self-seeking, naked ambition, moral turpitude (running off with another chap's wife) – were certainly scarlet.

and that alone would have restricted my choice of regiment in the British army.'[40]

Another 9th Gurkha, R. C. B. Bristow, who ended his military career as a brigadier, had not given finance much consideration before he went into the army either. But when he joined 2/9 GR, he realized he had not chosen the most lucrative profession: 'On Rs 425 a month, about £28, it was barely possible to pay rent, servants, hire of furniture, mess and club bills, to buy clothes and uniform, and to keep Flint [his polo pony] . . . It seemed that the only place where a subaltern could save for home leave was on the frontier, away from the heavier expenses of a peace station, and with field service concessions such as free rations for self, servant and horse.'[41]

Indian Army officers were hardly overworked. In addition to weekends, every Thursday – for some reason that John Morris of the 3rd Gurkhas, at least, never discovered – was a holiday. An officer might take ten days off every month to go shooting; he had two months' annual leave (three if he were serving on the frontier); and every fourth year he went home for eight months.[42] Colonel A. L. Fell of the 2nd Goorkhas found that he had omitted all mention of work in his account of garrison life in the twenties: 'We did not, in fact, work very hard. Apart from morning parades and two hours in the office, our day's work was completed by lunchtime and the afternoons and evenings were devoted to games.'[43] The phrase, 'half a day's work for half a day's pay', did just about sum up the life of an Indian Army officer between the wars.[44]

The leisurely nature of the life was increased by the number of servants employed. Labour was cheap, so that even 'half a day's pay' sufficed to cover the cost of an individual Bearer, whom Tony Mains describes as 'a cross between a Valet and Major Domo', and a share in the services of a Sweeper, a *bhisti*, or water-carrier, and a *dhobi* (washerman). A *syce*, or groom, was a necessity for a polo-playing officer, who, if he were married, also required a *khitmagar*, or waiter, a cook, a *mali*, or gardener, and probably an *ayah* – lady's maid or nursemaid. You could end up with quite a large staff, as Mains recalls: 'When my wife and I were at the Infantry School, Mhow, after Independence, our staff numbered nine – Bearer, Cook, Khitmagar, Chokra [odd-job boy], Sweeper, two Syces and two Malis – to look after two adults, two horses and four dogs; later after our daughter was born an Ayah was added.' Cooks and waiters were likely to be Muslims, as Hindus were ruled out by their caste restrictions on food preparation and their aversion to beef.[45]

Promotion was slow – nine years to wait for a captaincy, eighteen for a majority and a quarter of a century, if you were lucky, for a lieutenant-colonelcy. A. L. Fell remembers his struggle to survive when he started out as a young subaltern in 3/2 GR at the end of the First World War:

> The fact was that regimental life was too expensive and the standard of living too high. Everyone was obliged to observe a common standard in Mess and in one's private life. Etiquette and customs were laid down by regimental fiat even to the extent of approving the hotels where one stayed on leave. It was necessary to possess full-dress uniform at considerable expense in spite of the fact that it was worn less than a dozen times in twenty years. Even one's friends were vetted and, in those days, one accepted such customs and insults as normal.[46]

Fell's concern over money, a recurring theme in his unpublished memoir, led him to seek a transfer from the regiment in which he was proud to serve, 2 GR, to take up a three-year appointment as adjutant of the 1st Assam Rifles – an irregular battalion consisting of a mixture of Gurkhas and Lushais, serving on the unfashionable north-east frontier – entirely because it was better paid: 'On the one hand it was quite impossible to live in my own regiment as a married officer [he had married in 1926] on a captain's pay and some way of augmenting my income had to be found. On the other hand my regiment frowned on officers who spent three years away and one's future prospects were compromised. After careful consideration I decided to take the extra pay and deal with the future when the time came.'[47]

The 2nd Goorkhas certainly did frown on officers, particularly subalterns, who sought a secondment – as is made clear in this extract from No. 7 of 'The Nine Commandments' to be shown to an officer on his appointment to the regiment:

> To apply for an outside seconded job as a subaltern in order to marry is to lay yourself open to the danger of being told to take the job but not

to come back to the Regiment at the end of it, i.e. to go elsewhere
altogether. If an officer is told to do this, he has no complaint.[48]

Fell was allowed back to the 2nd Goorkhas, perhaps because he was
already a captain when he married. In fact he returned to the regiment
twice, though the second time was in the Second World War after he
had officially retired.

Another 'Commandment', No. 4, deals with money in general:

To be in debt is a great drawback and a constant anxiety. This
Regiment is supposed to be expensive. For what it gives it is not
expensive, and an officer can live on his pay provided he is content to
avoid all expensive amusements. The most expensive and least
remunerative of all amusements are drinking and unnecessary
entertaining. A young officer is not expected to indulge in either, and
to live quietly till one can afford to do the things worth doing such as
big game shooting, fishing, polo or exploring is merely a sign of good
sense. To take one's leave poodlefaking in a hill station is forbidden.
Remember that 70 Rs spent in any month on drink represents the
keep of a horse for polo, the cost of a fishing rod or a week in the
jungle or on the mountains.[49]

Other regiments might be less prescriptive than the 2nd Goorkhas, but
in all of them a young officer's behaviour was carefully monitored. T. J.
Phillips found that in the 1/9th, for instance,

There was no objection to a young officer spending part of his two
months [annual leave] on social pursuits in a hill station, but he was
expected to use the greater part of it for shooting big game in the
Himalayas, or climbing, and anyone who consumed the whole of the
period in chasing girls in the hills, rather than Ibex or Markhor was
seldom regarded with favour by his senior officers. It was done
though . . . [and] might incur a sour note in his annual confidential
report as one who found that his CO had written the single
unembellished remark, 'This officer dances beautifully'.[50]

Or, as Masters of the 2/4th puts it: 'When a subaltern applied for leave some colonels would ask him how he intended to spend it, and if it appeared that he was merely going to poodlefake they refused the leave. The young man must pursue animals, not girls.'[51]

Young officers knew what was expected of them and, while they might get away with a bit of poodle-faking, a serious romance was out of the question. When Phillips went on his first home leave, he met a girl on the boat: 'She was very young and I was in love, but for a young officer of the Indian Army, at twenty-four there could be no permanence in a relationship as marriage at that age was professional suicide. He would have to leave the Regiment and go somewhere else.'[52] The received wisdom, if not exactly the rule, over marriage was: 'Subalterns may not marry, captains may marry, majors should marry, colonels must marry.'[53] There was also a financial disincentive to early marriage: an officer had to be thirty before he could draw a marriage allowance.[54]

Phillips defends the system: 'It was felt, and rightly, that marital and financial anxieties would have an adverse effect on the performance of the young officer's duties and on his knowledge of the men and of his profession.'[55] He goes on to cite the example of Villiers-Stuart's 5th Royal Gurkha Rifles, where not just young officers but all officers were discouraged from marrying:

> As a result there were a lot of middle-aged bachelors in the regiment: Briggs, Cameron, Gibbs, Harrison and others. Another, who was a General after the war, was said to have been engaged to the same girl for seventeen years before he married her. These officers . . . had an outstanding knowledge of the Gurkha, and probably there were more interpreters in the 5th than in any other of the regiments . . . It was a fine regiment always.[56]

But the attitude to marriage in the 5th, as Phillips admits, 'paid little regard to the future happiness of the officers concerned'.[57]

There was a strong misogynistic streak in some officers, which John Masters hints at when he writes that one of his brother officers 'made himself popular by announcing at a Bakloh cocktail party that all the wives of the officers of the 4th Gurkhas were either schoolmarms or barmaids'.[58] Masters concedes that there might be 'an element of oblique truth' in this categorization, but is surprisingly sympathetic –

for someone of his background and attitudes – to the plight of 'the women hanging on to the edges' of this 'one-sexed society' ('married or unmarried, their status was really that of camp followers') and of the maligned memsahib in general:

> . . . seldom in history have women been subjected at one and the same time to so many discomforts, so much monotony, and so many temptations. The proportion of women who became hard, idle, and selfish may have been higher than elsewhere, but I doubt it. These faults were just more obvious, as were our own, since privacy was, for the British in India, an unobtainable luxury.[59]

Was the misogyny characteristic of a certain type of officer a cover for latent or blatant homosexuality? Merely to pose the question would be enough to raise the hackles of the more hidebound officers. When John Morris, who in a second career became controller of the BBC Third Programme, dared to write in his autobiography – in the most restrained fashion – of his seduction by his 3 GR orderly, he and his book were roundly condemned. T. J. Phillips, whose memoir reveals a thoughtful and by no means hidebound officer, simply dismisses the story 'which, if it was true would cast a doubtful light on his fitness to be an officer, but which, and I have talked to a number of experienced British officers in Gurkha regiments about it, must be pure fantasy'.[60] Morris himself would probably not have been surprised at this reaction, for he writes:

> I suppose that in those days I should, if asked, have denied my proclivities, especially since homosexuality was a subject that in the mess was sometimes referred to either with ribaldry or disgust. It was known to be common in India but was genuinely believed not to exist in Nepal; indeed, its absence was felt to be one of the main differences between Gurkhas and other soldiers of the Indian Army. It gave them a manly superiority, like the British themselves, such as no mere Indian could hope to possess. In fact it was as common as in any other predominantly male society; nevertheless the myth persisted.[61]

Prejudice equates homosexuality with effeminacy, as John Masters demonstrates when, noting its prevalence among Pathans, he finds 'something startlingly incongruous about the idea when associated with these men, physically the hardest people on earth' and coarsely relishes the thought of a young Pathan, with roses in his long hair and eyes rimmed with kohl, 'entering a gay cocktail party given by Manhattan fairies'.[62] To which Morris might well have replied that – as he once told an interviewer – one has only to read history to find confirmation that it is a commonplace among martial peoples.[63]

Morris was an untypical officer, as he himself stresses, not so much in his sexual orientation perhaps as in his bookishness and unsoldierly attitudes. For one thing, he loathed the north-west frontier; despite his homosexuality he was out of sympathy with the Muslim macho culture of the Pathans (and the desert Arabs) which had such an appeal for so many Englishmen, preferring the landscapes and peoples of north-east India.

A more representative attitude to the frontier is expressed in the history of the 9th Gurkhas – 1/9 GR took their turn there in 1935:

'It was like life at a large English public school,' wrote one officer. 'Freddy Poynder [the CO and Gajendra Malla's *bête noire*] saw that we worked hard and played hard in the stimulating mountain air. Flag-showing columns went out almost every month; while we were in camp there was polo, football, basketball, swimming, racing and field sports. The hills were so peaceful that we could climb and shoot at will, as long as we were accompanied, more or less as a matter of form, by a few khassadars [supposedly friendly local tribesmen].'[64]

This idyll was disturbed in the spring of 1936, when a Pathan from the tribal lands across the border abducted a young Hindu girl from Bannu and, forcibly converting her to Islam, married her. As she had been abducted in India, her parents were able to obtain a court order for her return, which was speedily executed. But this aroused the indignation of the Pathans, 'who began whispering, then shouting, the magic word *Jehad*!'.[65] T. J. Phillips, who did a tour with the Tochi Scouts on the frontier, writes of this celebrated case:

The girl was known as the Islam bibi – as it might be 'Helen of Bannu'.

'Was this the face that launched a thousand ships, and burnt the topless towers of Ilium?' Well, no, though many a man died and many a transborder tower was burnt on her account, long, long after she had been returned to her parents and had been completely forgotten. The troubles that started then, in 1936, went on without intermission until we finally quitted the Frontier and left it to the Pakistanis in 1947.[66]

The Tochi Scouts came under the civil administration and seconded officers were detached from the army – though they kept their rank – and paid an extra 150 rupees a month, plus language pay and extra allowances amounting to roughly ten shillings a day in outposts on active service. The officers with the Tochi Scouts were constantly changing; none of them was married and, with the exception of the three senior officers, all were under thirty. Phillips was twenty-five when he joined them in 1938, and his attachment lasted till 1941 – 'a fine and happy three years', in which he was twice Mentioned in Despatches: 'I had learnt a lot about Pathans, about Scouts and about mountain warfare and soldiering, although I knew that the last two were a long way from war as it was currently being fought in the Middle East and in Burma. But it was a good foundation.'[67]

Before he joined the Tochi Scouts in 1938, Phillips had been posted for a year to the Gurkha recruiting depot at Kunraghat, in Gorakhpur, as an assistant recruiting officer, a wonderful opportunity for a young officer to learn about the men he was serving with and where they came from. His responsibility was for his own regiment, the 9th Gurkha Rifles, and their Dehra Dun stablemate, the 2nd Goorkhas, the *purano paltan* (old regiment) as well as for the Kashmir State Forces, which also recruited Gurkhas from the west-central districts of Nepal. Two other officers looked after the interests of the remaining western regiments, and of the Burma and Assam Rifles. Between them they paid some 300 recruiters and sent them off into the hills where they themselves were not allowed to go: 'For success a recruiter, or *gallawalla*, should arrive home looking prosperous, with money to jingle in his pockets.' The recruiting effort was concentrated on the festival of Dashera, when the *gallawalla* could cast his eye most easily over 'all the talent available'.[68]

As far as local communities were concerned, the arrival of the *gallawalla* was no cause for celebration. Life in a hill village was hard, then as now, and while the extra money a soldier brought home might be welcome, a boy's labour in the narrow terraced fields that transformed the steep hillsides into giant's staircases was often a more immediate necessity. So there was still a surreptitious element about the proceedings:

> . . . the *lahuri* [soldier] usually arranged a secret rendezvous for his *galla*, somewhere outside the village, for after the Dashera and from there they would set off without saying goodbye to anybody, marching double marches for the first few stages to put off parental pursuit. Sometimes a father would come all the way down to Kunraghat and then if he insisted on the boy going back with him, he would have to go, even though he had by then been accepted, but very often the father would change his mind when he saw his son clothed, and fed and paid, and would go back without him . . . [69]

The attitude of mothers, unsurprisingly, was generally less accommodating: 'When Sherbahadur Thapa's mother came down from the Hills to accept his posthumous Victoria Cross from the Viceroy in Delhi, she said to the Commandant of the Depot, "What, after all, is a medal to me? I would sooner have my son any day".'[70]*

---

*Rifleman Sherbahadur Thapa 'wrote a proud page in the history of 9th Gurkha Rifles' by winning the 1st battalion its first VC at Point 366 on the road to San Marino in Italy during the Second World War. The regimental history records his deeds:

> During the advance on Point 366 this young soldier had distinguished himself; he and his section commander had rushed an enemy strongpoint, killing the machine-gunner and putting the remainder of the defenders to flight. The Germans stormed back and the section commander fell wounded. The dauntless rifleman countercharged with his Bren gun, broke the rush and gained commanding ground above a reverse slope . . . For two hours he remained in this exposed position, under constant fire. His platoon, its last round spent, fell back, while Sherbahadur continued to hold the Germans at bay. Major Costeloe, having supervised the withdrawal, returned and ordered the rifleman to retire. Before complying Sherbahadur dashed forward and returned with a wounded Gurkha across his shoulders. With the operation completed and with safety only a few yards away, officer, rifleman and wounded comrade were riddled by a burst of enemy fire – a sad ending to a feat of arms whose glory will not tarnish with the years.[71]

However, the likely lads themselves, whose only alternative to going for a soldier was a lifetime of back-breaking labour for little or no remuneration, understandably took a different view:

> It was small wonder that boys growing up in the villages, with pensioners and furlough men's stories of the wide world, of ships and aeroplanes, of trains, and cities, were filled with a longing to go too, to seek adventure and fortune, so that when the recruiter, the *gallawalla*, came with his velvet waistcoat with the silver buttons, with money in his pocket and with the eyes of the girls on him, they flocked to him as to a pied piper.[72]

Despite the opprobrium the *gallawalla* attracted for whisking off the cream of the village youth in secrecy and haste, recruiting duty was popular. It provided men with extra home leave at Dashera time, and if they brought in a good haul enabled them to earn an extra 40 or 50 rupees in bonuses.

From the day after Dashera ended, recruiting parties started coming into Kunraghat; from eighty-odd on the first day, the numbers rose to 200 a day and, on 22 October 1937, to a record-breaking 360. The target then was about 1,500 men a year. The young men from the high hills, who had never seen flat land, let alone the unending Indian plain, or wheeled transport, or European faces, arrived 'tired, hungry and dirty'. As soon as they came in, they were fed; they washed themselves at the depot well and with the exception of the Puns (a Magar sub-*jat* or clan), who wore their hair long and were spared a haircut until they had been accepted into a unit, went to the barber to have their heads completely shaved but for the *tupi*, or top-knot, by which they hoped eventually to be lifted into heaven.

> They could neither read nor write, and yet they were perfectly self-possessed, not exhibiting the least surprise at any new wonder, though understandably enough they were impressed by the great steam locomotives of the B and NWR [Bengal and North-Western Railway] and used to gather to sit by the side of the track after supper to see them go by, some of the boys still in their hill clothes and others already in shorts and jerseys.[73]

These recruits were supposed to be seventeen or eighteen years old, and there was a limited intake for boys of fifteen. But age was 'a matter of judgement'. One doctor reckoned he could tell the age of a recruit by the amount of pubic hair the boy had, but when Phillips relayed this information to one of his senior GOs the old man laughed and said, 'But I still haven't got any.'[74]

It was not just the recruit's age which was often in doubt, but the ages and even the names of his nearest relatives (since they were known to him by their position in the family – eldest brother, younger sister and so on – rather than by name). When one recruit gave his father's age as sixty, the recruiting officer was so taken aback by his conviction that he asked him how he knew. The boy replied: 'Well, when the *gallawalla* came to the village my father said to me. "There's only you to help about the place now, and I'm getting on. I'm sixty and I need you. If you go off with the *lahuri*, I'll break your neck."'[75]

Recruiting 'blind', i.e., having no direct access to the soldiers' homes, meant that officers had to gather important information about next-of-kin relationships and recruiting districts painstakingly at second-hand. Partly as a result of this, 'the provenance of a recruit was as important as that of an old master'.[76] Caste was a major concern: if a Sarki, or leather worker, succeeded in getting himself enlisted as a rifleman, as had happened in one regiment, there would be religious complications involving costly and time-consuming purification rituals; and at the other end of the scale, a Brahman or half-Brahman might try to pass himself off as a Chhetri in order to gain acceptance in the 9th Gurkhas.

The most painful aspect of the recruiting officer's job was rejecting recruits, who found the prospect of going back to their village so humiliating that in the past they had taken any work in India – as security guards in Calcutta, or worse, in the coal mines of Bihar – rather than return. But for many years now there had been a rule which required that a rejected recruit be escorted back to his village and delivered to the headman by the *gallawalla*.

The critical moment for the recruits came when they were paraded in front of the colonel in charge of recruiting; they were lined up in two files, each individual having the number of his battalion and either a '1' or a '2' marked on his chest to indicate whether or not he was recommended: 'Branded like remounts', a visiting cavalry general was heard

to mutter.[77] After this inspection, the successful ones had a final medical examination before they were despatched to their battalions for
training.

In 1937, Phillips thought the 2 GR recruits for whom he was responsible were particularly splendid: 'I have a photograph which shows them
as like as peas in a pod with not more than an inch or so difference in
height along the line.'[78] He was not so lucky with his own regiment's
recruits, of whom they had to reject 'a disproportionately high percentage', and he got a nasty letter from 'Jumbo' Morris of his battalion,
describing them as 'coarse, not an ounce of breeding, and they look like
coolies or the sweepings of the Nautanwa bazaar' (Nautanwa, a border
town, was the point of departure for *gallawallas* and soldiers going on
leave to Nepal).[79] Morris later apologized for his outburst, which arose
out of his initial disappointment. But it shows how highly each battalion
rated the value of good-quality recruits.

No sooner had the recruits left Kunraghat, around Christmas time,
than the pensioners began to arrive. Collecting their annual pension –
for a rifleman a mere 60 rupees (90 shillings) after fifteen years' service – was a social event. Pensioners walked huge distances with their
wives, in all their finery and wearing the gold jewellery that was a mark
of their wealth, and sometimes with small children, too. One old man
who still came down to collect his pension in 1938 had gone on retirement in 1874. Other claimants were not themselves pensioners but
next of kin to soldiers who had been killed in battle or died of natural
causes. One of these had special need of the money since his deceased
son had taken advantage of his last home leave to impregnate no less
than three of the village maidens, whose families were all clamouring
for compensation.[80]

For a hundred years or more recruitment had been a hazardous business. There were no maps of the areas where the soldiers came from
and ignorance was compounded by disinformation due to the clandestine nature of recruiting almost throughout the nineteenth century.
Over the years a succession of dedicated recruiting officers had doubled
as amateur geographers and ethnographers in an attempt to unlock the
mysteries of their troops' homelands and kinship patterns and customs;
the knowledge they acquired was set down systematically not just in
handbooks, which were updated every so often, but also in the 'kindred

rolls' which recorded the personal details of every enlisted man. This information facilitated the processing of pension claims when a soldier died. The absence of it in the past had caused considerable distress in the hills:

> In the first war, for instance, when 10,000 Gurkhas died in France, Mesopotamia, Gallipoli and other places, boys left their homes and some of their parents never heard of them again. Gurkha mothers must have looked for years at everybody in the distance coming up to the village, hoping it might be their son; pensions and estates remained unclaimed and although every effort was made to trace the next of kin, even in 1937, after nearly twenty years, there were still 400 unclaimed estates and pensions on the files from the 1914 war.[81]

One recruiting officer, Briggs or 'Briggo' of the 5th Gurkhas, had been so frustrated by the lack of information at his disposal in 1917 that he had made it his task singlehandedly to compile what became known as the 'Zilla, or district, book', a gazetteer that took him seven years to complete. Even then he had to publish the first edition at his own expense, though the government paid for a second edition. 'This was the greatest single contribution ever made to the welfare of the Gurkha soldier,' Phillips writes, 'and Briggo was entirely responsible for the initiation of it.'[82] Apart from anything else, it ensured that the errors of the First World War would not be repeated in the Second World War, when pressure on recruitment would once again be heavy.

By March 1938, most of the pensioners had been and gone and Kunraghat more or less closed down for the hot weather. A skeleton staff remained, but 'the rest of us left for the north, like the cranes, back to our battalions'. The experience of recruiting had deepened Phillips' knowledge and understanding of the Nepalese hillmen and made him impatient with misrepresentations:

> As a recruit the Gurkha was sure of his place in the world, and felt no need to impress himself on anyone . . . He was interested in honour and since he had left his home to make his fortune, in saving money. With people he did not know, he was reserved and it might be a year or more before a young British officer was accepted by the men. The

image of the Gurkha smiling and laughing, the friend of all the world, was a superficial one and as false in depth as the belief that he was such a born soldier that Gurkha battalions ran themselves with little effort on the part of officers.

Another misconception about the Gurkha, more common then perhaps than it is now, is that he was stupid and slow. Nothing could be further from the truth though his thought processes were different from ours and he might reach conclusions by a different route from ours. People who were slow to understand this might blame their lack of comprehension on him rather than on themselves.[83]

In a report on Nepal during the years 1929–34 the British envoy, Colonel Daukes, wrote of Judha Shamsher, 'The new Maharaja has little real force of character or intellect and he is being exploited by the rising generation and, in particular, by Generals Sir Mohan, Babar, Kaiser Shumshere, sons of the late Sir Chandra Shumshere Jang Bahadur Rana . . . and also by his own son General Sir Bahadur Shumshere.'[84] These younger, better educated Shamsher Ranas were still very influential at the end of the decade when Lt-Col. Geoffrey Betham was British minister in Nepal; but the maharajah and the Rana regime were coming under increasing pressure from King Tribhuvan (who was now old enough to be frustrated by his powerlessness), as well as from the increasingly restless people. Colonel Betham informed the government of India:

. . . The King and his sons, or at least the Heir Apparent who is now nineteen years old . . . are reported to have said they themselves, and their subjects, have had enough of Sir Joodha and his family and are not willing to put up with them or the present form of government any longer. As for themselves, they are reported to have said, 'We and only we are the descendents of the Sesodia Rajputs and Nepal belongs to us. We, not the descendents of Jung Bahadur nor of Bhir Shumshere, are the hereditary rulers. Under the present system we are kept practically in captivity and have to look to the Maharaja for our daily bread, necessities of life and even our private money. Each Maharaja, while in office, collects all the revenue, pays all salaries, and amasses all the wealth he can for himself and his immediate family, with the result that there is no progress in Nepal nor prospect of development'.

As regards the intelligentsia and the people they are reported to have said that the former want a hand in the Government of Nepal, and the latter a constitutional right to some form of representative Government.[85]

The Viceroy, Lord Linlithgow, was unimpressed. 'I do not rate Betham's capacity very high,' he wrote, unjustly, in a private letter, 'and I am inclined to think he has probably read more into a series of unconnected incidents than is justified . . .'[86] This is a classic case of blaming the messenger for the unwelcome nature of the message. With another full-scale European war looming, the last thing the British authorities wanted was that the social unrest in India should spread to Nepal. Nepal had proved an invaluable ally during the Great War, and there was no reason to suppose that in the event of another war it would not once again come to Britain's aid – so long as the Ranas remained in power. As the indigenous Indian press never tired of reminding its readers, it was for the sake of 'such useful and cheap soldiers' as the Gurkhas that the British 'hold the Ranas of Nepal in so much regard and remain fondly attached to Nepal'.[87]

The radical press in India was an irritant not just to the British, but to the Ranas as well. In July 1939 Judha's son, Bahadur Shamsher, explained to the British minister that Nepal's continuing dissatisfaction with the annual gift of a million rupees was due to the fact that it gave colour to allegations in newspapers like *Naya Hindustan* that 'the English have purchased Nepal with these ten lakhs of rupees. Nepal is today worse than their purchased salves. Like a puppet she moves at the beck and call of the British Government.'[88] Bahadur complained that such remarks were being 'frequently heard' and that 'the Government of India continues to look upon Nepal as an Indian State of secondary importance as the Minister here is nothing but a Second Class Resident'.[89]

Aside from the tactlessness of demeaning the minister to his face (which Lord Linlithgow did only behind his back), Bahadur's comment reveals the frustration the Nepalese rulers felt at their impotence in relation to British India. The article Bahadur found so objectionable referred to the Ranas as 'the foremost messengers of British imperialism' and the exploiters of their own country:

People die of hunger but the Ranas are collecting money in foreign banks. They find it difficult to spend a single pice on the improvement of the country. Trade and agriculture have gone to rack and ruin. For eighty or ninety lakhs population there exists only one school, and for the sake of keeping up a name there is one hospital at Katmandu. Some twenty-five or thirty out of 140 or 150 graduates are without employment. It is only the foolish flatterers of the Ranas who can secure high posts. The word of the Ranas is the law of the land there.

... Gambling, wine, viciousness, debauchery are rampant in the houses of the Ranas. The Ranas are given the ranks of Generals and Colonels even when they are in their mothers' wombs. The reins of government are in the hands of a worthless lot . . . [90]

Betham's own view, though more temperately expressed, was not entirely at odds with this. As he wrote in a secret letter to the secretary to the government of India, 'All the revenue of the country goes into the PM's private treasury which in effect means that the whole administration of the country is paid for out of the PM's private purse. It follows, therefore, that the progress of the country depends on the whims of the PM, governed mainly by the amount of money he has been able to keep.'[91]

Since successive prime ministers (maharajahs) left their wealth to their offspring, rather than in the country's exchequer, every time the country had a new one it started again with an empty treasury. When Chandra Shamsher died in 1929, for instance, he left his sons millions of pounds. 'Until this state of affairs is remedied', an Indian Office official noted, 'there is little prospect of any serious progress in the kingdom as a whole.'[92] Betham recognized that the younger generation of better educated and more widely travelled Nepalis (many of them 'C class' Ranas excluded from the line of succession) was becoming increasingly politically conscious and wanted a say in how public money should be spent. But from a British point of view this was a mixed blessing, as Betham pointed out:

I feel that with one person to deal with who is anxious, for his own advantage, to keep on good terms with the Government of India, the active assistance which we have received in the past is more likely to be forthcoming than with a more constitutional form of Government, especially one on the lines of the Congress Ministries that are now in power in certain of the Provinces of India.[93]

And so, of course, it proved. On the outbreak of war Judha Shamsher did not merely make the now-customary offer of a contingent of the Nepalese army (which the British authorities, following the usual courtship ritual, dithered about accepting); he also emulated his predecessor, Chandra Shamsher, in using his power to facilitate increased wartime recruitment. In the dark days of 1940, according to the highly coloured account provided by Francis Tuker, the British minister requested an interview with the maharajah to obtain permission to raise a further ten Gurkha battalions. Betham found Judha surrounded by his inner core of advisers among whom, he knew, there was dissent. They discussed the critical state of the war and raised the question of whether Britain might not be invaded and conquered. Betham did not deny the gravity of the situation, but maintained that Britain would overcome this 'serious set-back'. When Judha acceded at once to his request to expand the Gurkha Brigade, therefore, Betham was agreeably surprised – and said as much. Tuker goes on:

> Judha retorted that Betham could never have read the Treaty of Segouli of 1816 or the revised Treaty of 1923, for if he had he would have remembered that in them were the words, 'of perpetual friendship'. Betham affirmed that he had of course read both Treaties.
> 'Do you', demanded Judha, 'let your friend down in a time of need?'
> 'No, Sir, but there is often a difference between countries and individuals.'
> 'There should not be. If you win, we will win with you. If you lose, we will lose with you.'
> The Maharajah rose with a smile and conducted the British Minister to his car.[94]

In September 1940, Judha followed this up with another gesture. Hearing of the bombing of London, he sent a donation of 25,000 rupees to the Lord Mayor of the city for the relief of the worst hit areas. (While the Lord Mayor of London was naturally grateful for this gift, the impoverished people of Nepal might have felt differently about it; but they were neither consulted nor considered.)

What Tuker omits to mention is that there was a *quid pro quo*. Like all his predecessors, Judha provided the British with military manpower in return for recognition both of the independence of Nepal and of the hegemony of the Rana regime (which benefited financially from the trade); extra help in wartime called for additional recognition in terms of land or money. These were the ground rules, laid down in 1858 when Jang Bahadur won back a chunk of the Terai as a reward for his part in subduing the Sepoy Revolt.

Despite their awareness of the unrepresentativeness and increasing unpopularity of the Rana regime, the British continued to prop it up. The recruitment of Gurkhas into the Indian Army took precedence over fostering democracy in a client state – especially in time of war.

7

The Second World War

The beginning of the Second World War found the Indian Army as ill-prepared for the titanic struggle ahead as the earlier war had done, only on this occasion the troops were not immediately thrown into the European fray. Initially, indeed, doubts were expressed that – after the experience of the western front during the First World War – they would be used in Europe at all, though ultimately they fought in Italy and Greece as well as in the Middle East, North Africa, Burma, Malaya, Singapore and Java.

John Masters recalls that between the regular officers and the ECOs (Emergency Commissioned Officers) 'there was very little of that friction which had added so greatly to the unpleasantness of the first war'.[1] Regulars refrained from labelling their wartime colleagues 'temporary gentlemen' and the ECOs recognized that not all regulars were Blimps. Perhaps ICOs (Indian Commissioned Officers) were the new 'temporary gentlemen' as far as the regulars were concerned. The Bengali Major-General D. K. 'Monty' Palit recalls that when he joined the army 'they didn't like us, [we were] at best called WOGs (Westernised Oriental Gentlemen) or niggers'; before the war, the rule was, 'No contact, same army, fought the same enemy and carried the same arms, but we never mixed'. The war changed that, with the coming of 'thousands of young Englishmen . . . ECOs, [who] would eat with their fingers, listen to our music . . .'.[2] At the beginning of the war there were fewer than 500 ICOs and nearly 3,000 British officers; by the end of it both figures had risen dramatically: according to recent estimates there were approximately 14,000 Indian and 32,750 British officers.[3] In Gurkha battalions, of course, there were no Indian officers – only British.

The Indian Army in general, and Gurkhas in particular, distinguished themselves in all theatres of war but nowhere more than in Burma, where they were instrumental in transforming – in the words of their great commander, Bill Slim – defeat into victory. But in Burma, too, they found themselves opposed not just by the Japanese, but by their own kind as well, men of the so-called Indian National Army. This division of loyalties affected Gurkhas far less than Indians for the obvious reason that their country was not part of the British Raj; but this did not mean they were untouched by the subcontinental yearning for freedom and democracy.

Among Indians, there was considerable resentment that the Viceroy, Lord Linlithgow, had declared the country to be at war without consulting with their leading politicians; though he was within his constitutional rights, his action was regarded as high-handed by Congress leaders, who promptly resigned from the provincial legislatures in which they held office. Gandhi and Nehru did not go so far as their sometime colleague, the maverick Bengali Subhas Chandra Bose, and align themselves with their enemy's enemy, calling, first, Germany and later Japan their friend; but nor did they give the British authorities their unconditional support, as, for his own anti-Congress reasons, did the leader of the Muslim League, M. A. Jinnah.

Throughout the war, the British endeavour to defeat the external enemy was hampered by internal unrest in India as the nationalist politicians sabotaged the war effort and generally jockeyed for position, maintaining the struggle for independence which the authorities would have preferred to postpone. This unrest had a knock-on effect in neighbouring Nepal as well.

The external role of the Indian Army during the 'phoney war' was limited to providing a few brigades of reinforcements in Egypt and Malaya. But after the fall of France in the summer of 1940, it expanded rapidly and by September the 4th and 5th Indian Divisions under General Sir Archibald (later Field Marshal Viscount) Wavell were preparing to meet – and triumph over – the Italians in Egypt and Abyssinia; and a month later two new brigades were on their way to Malaya to shore up the forces facing the fatally underrated Japanese threat.

Underequipped, trained largely for the wrong sort of war, individual Indian Army battalions laboured under a further disadvantage in the early stages of the war when they were 'milked' of many of their leaders and potential leaders to create new, wartime battalions. The Gurkha Brigade more than doubled its strength during the war, but in order to do so its cadre of trained and experienced VCOs and NCOs, not to mention British officers, had to be spread dangerously thin.

T. J. Phillips returned to the 1/9th Gurkha Rifles in the Middle East in October 1941, after nearly three years on the north-west frontier with the Tochi Scouts, to find an unhappy battalion in which '*nothing* is done without orders, nothing . . . If one leaves them to themselves they become filthy dirty in their persons and in their quarters, they do the very minimum of work, their sentries go to sleep because the NCOs don't go round unless they are afraid they will be punished if their guard is slack, no sanitary arrangements are made and no man is ever checked by an NCO unless there is a BO [British officer] watching him all the time.'[4] Nor was the experience of the 1/9th unique for, as Phillips recorded in his diary:

. . . at about this time the 1/1st were asked to provide a party to board a ship at Basra where the Chinese crew had mutinied. The two BOs took eight or ten men down into the hold where [the British officers] were attacked by the mutineers and beaten up, without any interference from the Gurkhas. When the Naik was asked for an explanation of his behaviour he said, '*Kehi hukum payenna*' ['I didn't have any orders'].[5]

By the time these battalions went to war in earnest they had put their troubles behind them and gave a good account of themselves. But it was fortunate that they had time to sort themselves out before they were put to the test. Several senior officers had doubted the wisdom of dismantling existing battalions and creating new units so quickly: 'Hoghunting with a blunt spear, some called it, but, unfortunately, it was only too clear that the hogs would have to be hunted somehow before 1941 was out.'[6]

Until the end of 1942 the experience of most Gurkha battalions (which had taken no part in Wavell's early victories over the Italians) was restricted to defeat and surrender. In the Far East, the Japanese, having surprised the Americans at Pearl Harbor in December 1941, surprised the British in Malaya and Burma both by the speed of their advance and by their technical and tactical sophistication. In jungle warfare they were light years ahead of the British, whose preference for the barren and rocky north-west frontier over the forested north-east frontier for battle training meant that even among Gurkhas (apart from those in the Assam and Burma Rifles) there was a dearth of troops with jungle-fighting skills and experience.

In Malaya and Burma, British and Indian Army battalions regarded the jungle as more or less impenetrable and stayed close to the roads because of their dependence on lorried transport, whereas the Japanese treated it as friendly cover, moving through it with consummate ease and confusing their enemy by eschewing frontal attacks on defended positions. Their favourite tactic was the so-called scorpion manoeuvre, by which they gripped the enemy in lobster-like claws and then flung out a long tail to encircle it and sting it to death from behind. This worked every time until the allies got wise to it and achieved the air superiority which would enable them to counter such tactics effectively. But that was some years ahead. In the beginning the allies made the fatal mistake of underestimating a ferocious, skilful and well-trained enemy:

> This people who had evolved ju-jitsu as their system of wrestling had applied its principle to war – the principle of using an adversary's strength to his disadvantage. They made the material in which we placed our trust a burden to us, and in this were helped by our lack of training and lack of practice in its use and also by our weakness in the air.[7]

In Malaya and Singapore there was no escape. Defeat brought mass imprisonment and whole battalions were marched into captivity, the

The Second

prisoners were taken, but the escape route
frontier enabled the initial defeat to be turn...
orderly retreat, masterminded by the new army and
Generals Alexander and Slim, with occasional effe...
actions against the enemy.

The nadir of the first Burma campaign was the battle for th... ...g
River bridge. Once the Japanese crossed the Sittang, the ro...d to
Rangoon was open to them, so the bridge, which could not be defended
without heavier weapons than 17th Division had at their disposal, had
to be blown up. The trouble was that most of the division, which had
been outflanked in characteristic fashion by the Japanese, was still on
the wrong side of it. Five Gurkha battalions were caught up in this section, 1/3 GR, 1/4 GR and 2/5 RGR from 48th Gurkha Brigade, and 1/7
and 3/7 GR from 16 and 46 Brigades. The only one of them fortunate
enough to extricate itself and withdraw over the bridge before it was
blown up was the 1/4th Gurkhas, under the command of Lt-Col. (later
Maj-Gen.) W. D. A. 'Joe' Lentaigne – and all because he had opted for
an early breakfast on 21 February 1942.

Brigadier N. Hugh-Jones, commanding 48th Gurkha Brigade, gave
his three Gurkha battalion COs their orders at 9 a.m. The 1/4th had the
least arduous journey to its position, the 1/3rd the longest by several
miles; the COs of the 1/3rd and 2/5th pointed out that their men were
exhausted and they had not yet eaten. As a result Lentaigne was told to
switch positions with 1/3 GR. This meant that his battalion – after finding itself targeted by RAF bombers in the general chaos – was the one
ordered back at midnight to protect the west bank of the Sittang against
an expected landing of Japanese paratroopers the following morning
(which never materialized). So Lentaigne and his men found themselves on the right side of the bridge when it was blown up at dawn on
23 February, while the 1/3rd and the 2/5th – as well as the 1/7th and
3/7th – were left to fend for themselves on the wrong side.[8]

The ultimate responsibility for the decision to blow up the Sittang
River bridge rested with the divisional commander, Maj-Gen. John
Smyth VC, and though it remains controversial on balance it was prob-
ably the right decision. The 17th Division was decimated, but the
Japanese advance was held up sufficiently to allow 7th Armoured

...me to disembark in Rangoon and provide the force which
...rned a potential rout into an organized retreat from Burma. But the
individual battalions caught on the east side of the Sittang suffered terribly. Those troops who escaped death or captivity and made it to the
banks of the river found that there were no boats to help them across
(most Gurkhas at that time were unable to swim and feared the water):

> Many were drowned, but acts of devotion were innumerable, some
> men swimming the swirling river two or three times to bring in the
> wounded. Our guns on the west bank were able to keep down the
> Japanese machine-gun fire, but there were many enemies on that west
> bank also – Burmese snipers and, worse, ghoulish priests in saffron
> with murderous dahs to cut the throats of exhausted swimmers.[9]

Of the four Gurkha battalions left on the east bank of the Sittang, the
remnants of the 1/3rd and the 2/5th combined to form a makeshift (but
still under-strength) battalion; and the survivors of the 1st and 3rd battalions of the 7th also merged. The historian of 7 GR writes that 'it has
never been possible to distinguish which of the Regiment's 900 fatal
war casualties [731 is the official figure for 7 GR deaths in the Second
World War] occurred in or as a direct result of the Sittang disaster, but an
estimate of 350 would not be far short of the mark'.[10] It is remarkable
that just two months after such a setback this composite battalion
should distinguish itself at Kyaukse:

> The honours of the battle go to the 7th Gurkhas who bore the brunt of
> the attack. They broke up and handled very severely three separate
> attacks launched against them during the night of 28th–29th [April].
> Then, not content with that, they planned and carried out a counter-
> attack on the 29th that was quite brilliant and dealt great execution to
> the enemy.[11]

The Gurkhas were gradually discovering that, man for man, they
were quite the equal of the Japanese as fighters. With the right sort of
leadership they would prove more than a match for an enemy who,
physically at least, greatly resembled them. Had they but known it,
there was an exceptional leader already in place as corps commander

during the retreat, a general officer with experience of both the British and Indian armies, whose regimental service had been mostly with the 1/6th Gurkhas, though the battalion he commanded was the 2/7th, a man as remarkable for his modesty as for his courage, intelligence and honesty. Typical of General Sir William (later Field Marshal Viscount) Slim is a story from this time which he tells against himself. In another battle soon after Kyaukse, he found himself exposed to severe shelling in an area manned by 7 GR; he thought it would create a bad impression if he ran for cover, so he kept on walking until Subedar-Major Saharman Rai, an old friend, got up from behind a bush, grinning from ear to ear: 'I asked him coldly what he was laughing at and he replied that it was funny to see the General Sahib wandering along there by himself not knowing what to do.'[12]

It would not take the General Sahib long before he knew precisely what to do.

Slim was very much a soldier's general, rough-hewn, not without a sense of the dramatic, a great communicator who inspired his troops with his bulldog-like resolution and his (uncommon) common sense. His plain-man persona was not an act; if it had been his troops would have seen through it. It was, rather, an expression of his essential honesty. His soldiers of all nationalities identified with him; his extraordinariness was just that, extra-ordinariness; if ever a general had the common touch it was he. His Gurkha service was important to him, a matter of pride but hardly a defining attribute. In this, as in other characteristics, there could hardly be a greater contrast with another fine general who, but for misfortune, might also have reached the very pinnacle of his profession.

'I consider him to be a very promising young officer,' the CO of the 1/2nd Goorkhas wrote in his confidential report on 2nd Lieutenant F. I. S. Tuker in 1914–15; 'he is keen on his work and with a little more experience will be a very good officer. (Temporarily medically unfit.)'.[13] An accurate, if not particularly enlightening, summary, but those last three bracketed words strike an ominous note. Like Slim, 'Gertie' Tuker fought in Mesopotamia in the First World War, and he regarded his first battle there as 'the most arduous, costly and futile of any in his whole career'.[14] He was wounded in the leg and evacuated to India. In

1918 he was attached to the 4th Assam Rifles and took part in a punitive expedition against the Nagas on the north-east frontier before rejoining his battalion (after a period of sick leave) in late 1919 in northern Persia, where he fought against the Bolsheviks.

Colonel A. L. Fell describes Tuker at the time when he was made adjutant of 1/2 GR as 'an unbending martinet . . . [who] expected young officers to spend their money on polo ponies and to spend their spare time training them for polo'.[15] Tuker approached polo as he approached his work, systematically; he even wrote a pamphlet for the regiment on the training of polo ponies. Fell recalls that those 'who frequented the Club, went to dances or to hill stations were frowned upon' by the adjutant and when Tuker married a horsewoman, the sister of one of his fellow officers, 'it was jokingly said that Gertie was marrying her to train his polo ponies – as no one thought of him as a ladies' man'.[16] The marriage, though it endured and produced three daughters, hardly interfered with regimental life, and Tuker noted cryptically:

I lived as a bachelor for all except two and a half years of my married life in India because of my wife's health and dislike of Indian life.[17]

He also wrote (and the italics are his): 'I was very keen on games but never allowed them to come before my profession. *Nor did I allow the female sex to interfere with it.*'[18]

At the beginning of the thirties Tuker became Brigade Major in Delhi and so impressed his seniors that in 1933 he was made a brevet lieutenant-colonel – 'the youngest one in either the British or Indian armies'.[19] This was surprising in view of the fact that he had passed out of Staff College in 1926 with only a 'D' grade, though the reason for that, as his contemporary General Frank Messervy points out, was that he had 'a very critical outlook on the opinions of those above him and a not very tactful way of expressing his disapproval'.[20] One of the Staff College instructors at the time was a certain Bernard Montgomery, who did not take kindly to any sort of criticism.

But Tuker's ability was so evident that even his unwillingness to compromise was condoned; only his health gave continuing cause for concern. When he was posted as a staff officer to Rawalpindi District, he underwent a painful and unsuccessful operation to clear his sinuses, and for a time it looked as though he would be invalided out of the service. His career was saved by the arrival of a new ear, nose and throat specialist, Major (later General Sir) Alexander Drummond, who corrected the condition, which he diagnosed as ethmoiditis, with a minor operation under a local anaesthetic.

When Tuker took over command of his battalion, there was some anxiety among those officers and men who remembered his term as adjutant. But Fell recalls the surprise in 1/2 GR 'that an officer so unpopular in his youth should mature and mellow and, without in any way sacrificing his drive and energy, should eventually become probably the most popular CO the regiment has had'.[21] Tuker was the epitome of the 1/2nd Goorkhas, a highly regarded battalion with a high regard for itself. He was an innovative trainer, concentrating on field exercises designed to raise the tactical awareness of all ranks. When the battalion was posted to the north-west frontier in 1937, it had its chance to test its newly acquired skills, and Tuker to develop his idea about this sort of warfare. He emphasized the importance of mobility and the effectiveness of night operations against snipers. One 2 GR officer remembers that these were 'not very popular with the powers-that-be, who thought that you shouldn't go out after dark – against all tradition'.[22] The tactics Tuker tried out against the Pathans in 1937 would be employed to great effect against the Germans six years later.

With the coming of the war, Tuker's already rapid rise accelerated and at the end of 1941 he assumed command of the famous 4th Indian Division in North Africa. Tuker was not a soldiers' general in the sense that Slim and, in his very different way, Montgomery was; he was too withdrawn, intellectual and artistic. But if he lacked the common touch, he made up for it with an almost motherly concern for his troops. He acquired a reputation for being niggardly with the lives of those he commanded; he might not mix with them easily, but he expressed a lively appreciation of their qualities in his writings:

> One of the most valuable contributions that the Gurkhas made and the Indian units made to the British element was to set a standard of frugality so that everyone learnt to expect hard times and to make the best of them. . . No British, Gurkha or Indian soldier ever passed through the lines of the others without being offered a place and a mug

in the circle round the flickering half-petrol-tin where Tommy-Urdu and Johnny-English made do for banter, for talk of home and for recollections of battles they had fought together. This fellowship was the most inspiring of all worlds to live in – the world of service that each man rendered to his brother.[23]

In the battles of the North African desert as in those of the Burmese jungle, the first round went to the enemy – in this case Rommel's largely German arms and armour. Here the focus of defeat, the equivalent of the Sittang River bridge disaster, was the surrender of Tobruk, when that vital port was overrun by the German Afrika Korps on 21 June 1942.

Two battalions, the Cameron Highlanders and the 2/7th Gurkhas, fought on for some hours after the official surrender, since no word of it had reached their positions, though in the end they too had to give themselves up. This was the second time the 2/7th had been captured in its entirety through no fault of its own; but just as in 1916, after the fall of Kut, the lost battalion was re-raised and went on to fight in the Italian campaign of 1944. (The remnant of the battalion was to have been distributed among other Gurkha units, but this was resisted by three 7 GR subalterns, who – through illness or injury – had missed Tobruk, and a GO; together they put the case for re-raising the battalion so forcefully to a 10 GR major, 'Guinea' Graham, at GHQ Cairo that it was taken up at a higher level and a few days later the original order was rescinded.[24])

It was at this low point that the C-in-C in the Middle East, General Sir Claude Auchinleck – 'at long last', in Tuker's words[25] – took over personal command of the Eighth Army from General Sir Neil Ritchie and laid the foundations on which Montgomery would build his ultimate victory. But it was too late for Auchinleck; Churchill replaced him with Alexander and the arrival of Montgomery as Eighth Army commander meant that the 4th Indian Division was initially sidelined and had only a small part to play in the battle of El Alamein and its immediate aftermath. Monty's failure to pass out of Sandhurst high enough to get into the Indian Army had prejudiced him against it for life. Tuker argued for a more active role, pointing out that his were among the Eighth Army's most seasoned troops, and kept his division training hard while he impatiently awaited his opportunity. Eventually it came: at Wadi Akarit in April 1943.

'Just as Montgomery was a master of the planned battle,' Sir John Smyth (Tuker's biographer and the divisional commander who had had to make the fateful decision to blow up the Sittang River bridge) writes, 'so Tuker was a master of the moving battle in a more tactical setting.'[26] Tuker was highly critical of Montgomery's plan of attack at Wadi Akarit, which was concentrated on the corridor of land between the sea on one side and fortified positions in the mountains on the other. Tuker argued that, rather than expose his division to heavy shelling from above, an assault should be made on the high ground itself; in other words, strike at the most inaccessible position, thereby taking the enemy by surprise: 'Our view was that what appeared to be the strongest part of the position was in reality very difficult to hold unless it was filled full with infantry. It was indeed the weakest part.'[27]

He was, of course, drawing on his experience of the north-west frontier, and what he was suggesting was a night attack spearheaded by Gurkhas on the massif of Fatnassa, described by one writer as 'a fantastic pile, like a fairy-tale mountain, split by chimneys and fissures, layered by escarpments and crowned by rock pinnacles'.[28] If the attack succeeded, the enemy position would be untenable. The 30 Corps commander, General Oliver Leese, put this alternative plan to Montgomery, who most uncharacteristically accepted it: 'it has been said that this was the only time when Monty had changed his plan of battle at the request of a subordinate commander when the orders had actually been issued'.[29] According to one of General Montgomery's staff officers, 'After General Tuker's protest and alternative proposal the Eighth Army commander said, "I don't like people who disagree with me. Nevertheless we will accept Tuker's plan. If he is right we will have a victory. If he is wrong, I shall know what to do with him".'[30]

Tuker himself was under no illusions about the magnitude of the task. But one of his maxims was, 'If the approach to battle is good, then the battle will be easy.'[31] As ever, Tuker was anxious to avoid exposing his troops to unnecessary bloodshed:

The battles worth study and worthy of battle honours are not the bloody ones: they are the ones that yield victory with few casualties. It

is the approach that determines the outcome and we believed that our
approach, our designs and our training, the skill of our individual
platoon and section commanders in this most telling and skilled form
of fighting, this infiltration battle, would suffice for the difficult and
unusual task that confronted us.[32]

The troops to whom he entrusted the critical assault on the heights of
Fatnassa were those of his old battalion, 1/2 GR, whom he knew he
could rely on for this kind of work. Even then he worried that he might
be asking too much of them, sending them up almost unscaleable
heights against a heavily armed and entrenched enemy in a seemingly
impregnable position. But the outcome of the action was now out of his
hands; he might have won the tactical battle with the generals of his
own side but it was up to his troops to turn it into victory on the ground.
'Many a battle,' he writes, 'has been won by a single junior leader. All
that generals can ever do is to give him the chance to win it.'[33] In this
instance the single junior leader was Subedar Lalbahadur Thapa, who
led the two sections under his command up a steep and narrow pathway
studded with anti-tank gun and machine-gun nests.

Subedar Lalbahadur Thapa reached the first enemy sangar without
challenge. His section cut down its garrison with the kukri.
Immediately every post along the twisty pathway opened fire. Without
pause the intrepid Subedar, with no room to manoeuvre, dashed
forward at the head of his men through a sleet of machine-gun fire,
grenades and mortar bombs. He leapt inside a machine-gun nest and
killed four gunners single-handed, two with knife and two with pistol.
Man after man of his sections were [sic] stricken until only two were
left. Rushing on, he clambered up the last few yards of the defile
through which the pathway snaked over the crest of the escarpment.
He flung himself single-handed on the garrison of the last sangar
covering the pathway, striking two enemies dead with his kukri. This
terrible foe was too much; the remainder of the detachment fled with
wild screams for safety. The chimney between the escarpments was
open and with it the corridor through which 5 Brigade might pass. It is
scarcely too much to say that the battle of Wadi Akarit had been won
single-handed several hours before the formal attack began.[34]

The CO of 1/2 GR recommended Lalbahadur for an immediate MC; it was no less a personage than the army commander, Montgomery himself, who upgraded it to a VC.[35] Lalbahadur and his little troop, ably supported by the remainder of 1/2 GR, struck the first blow, and other battalions of 5 Brigade, including 1/9 GR, followed through according to plan. The speed and comprehensiveness of this breakthrough surprised not only the enemy, but also, alas, the commander of the Eighth Army.

When Tuker reported at 8.45 a.m. on 6 April that they had broken through and the way was now clear for an immediate offensive to finish off the campaign in North Africa – 'Now was the time to get the whips out and spare neither men nor machines'[36] – nothing happened. There was a fatal twenty-four-hour delay, during which the Germans had time to fall back and regroup, leaving only pockets of disconsolate Italians to put up a token resistance along the way. With victory presented to him by the 'master of the moving battle in a tactical setting', the 'master of the planned battle' was either too rigid or too cautious to take advantage of it. This did not prevent Monty from taking all the credit for the breakthrough in the signal he sent to Churchill that day. As Tuker's biographer remarks, 'it was ungracious by any standards for Montgomery to make no mention whatever of Tuker's vitally important part in the battle – both in its planning and its execution'. He adds, 'Gertie was perhaps now paying the price for his antagonism to Monty at Camberley Staff College'.[37]

For Tuker, the success of the battle plan was an occasion for pride, certainly, but also for reflection. As soon as he could, he accompanied his chief medical officer on a visit to the wounded in the field ambulances and was deeply touched by the way the two of them were greeted with smiles 'from even the most grievously hurt':

> Always, to meet the bravest of the brave makes one feel as if one's heart will burst from one's chest. I have never known why soldiers are so valiant, and so light-hearted in their greatness. Is there any other profession in which men give so much and ask so little?[38]

Beneath his reserved exterior, Tuker was a highly emotional man. Despite his shyness and lack of flamboyance, he earned the respect of all the nationalities who fought under him. 'Here was a general who had no gift for chatting up the soldiery at all', Sir Arthur Noble, the CO of the only territorial battalion in 4th Indian Division, the 1/4th Essex Regiment, told Sir John Smyth. 'When he came up to see us he was often at a loss for words. And yet my amateur soldiers of the Essex Regiment loved him.'[39]

In the follow-up operation, it was the turn of 1/9 GR to carry out a night attack on the Garci heights and Jemadar Dewan Sing Basnet, like Subedar Lalbahadur Thapa of 1/2 GR before him, engaged in single-handed combat with the enemy. This is his own account of what happened:

I was challenged in a foreign language. I felt it was not the British language or I would have recognised it. To make quite sure I crept up and found myself looking into the face of a German. I recognised him by his helmet. He was fumbling with his weapon, so I cut off his head with my kukri. Another appeared from a slit trench and I cut him down also. I was able to do the same to two others, but one made a great deal of noise, which raised the alarm. I had a cut at a fifth, but I am afraid I only wounded him. Yet perhaps the wound was severe, for I struck him between the neck and the shoulder.

I was now involved in a struggle with a number of Germans, and eventually, after my hands had become cut and slippery with blood, they managed to wrest my kukri from me. One German beat me over the head with it, inflicting a number of wounds. He was not very skilful, however, sometimes striking me with the sharp edge, but oftener with the blunt.

They managed to beat me to the ground, where I lay pretending to be dead. The Germans got back into their trenches and after a while I looked up. I could not see anything, for my eyes were full of blood. I wiped the blood out of my eyes and quite near I saw a German machine-gun. I thought, 'If only I can reach that gun I shall be able to kill the lot'. But now it was getting light and, as I lay thinking of a plan to reach the gun, my platoon advanced and started to hurl grenades among the enemy. But they were also falling very near me, so I thought that if I did not move I really would be dead. I managed to get to my feet and ran towards my platoon. Not recognising me, I heard one of my men call, 'Here comes the enemy! Shoot him!' I bade them not to do so. They recognised my voice and let me come in.

> My hands being cut about and bloody, and having lost my kukri, I
> had to ask one of my platoon to take my pistol out of my holster and
> put it in my hand. I then took command of my platoon again.
>
> I met my company commander, who bade me go to the Regimental
> Aid Post. I said, 'Sahib, there is fighting to be done, and I know the
> enemy's dispositions. I must stay and keep command of my platoon'.
> But he firmly ordered me and I had to go . . . [40]

Dewan Sing earned an immediate IOM (Indian Order of Merit), but he
never recovered sufficiently from his head wounds to return to active
duty.

Under Tuker's intelligent and resourceful command, 4th Indian
Division had been at the forefront of the battles which ended the war in
North Africa and it was therefore appropriate that he should receive the
surrender of General von Armin, whose emissary came to him impec-
cably dressed. Tuker – perhaps with the aftermath of Agincourt in
mind – noted, 'The comparison between the winner and the loser
struck me as quaint.'[41] Tuker had no love for Germans, and when one of
von Armin's generals sought to establish a rapport with his captor by
emphasizing their racial identity he was swiftly and coldly rebuffed:

> Cramer waved his hand out of the window towards the Royal Sussex
> men and said that 'these men are like German men. British and
> German men both white men'. I replied that I could not agree, that
> they were not like the British and our British, Indian and Gurkha
> soldiers were all the same – all white.[42]

Despite the sense of unity among the allied troops which Tuker valued
so highly, when the Eighth Army invaded Sicily it was without the 4th
Indian Division. This time it was not Monty's anti-Indian Army prejudice which kept them out of action but the hesitations of higher
authorities over whether or not Indian troops should be asked to fight
on European soil. Necessity overruled such misplaced scruples and
Tuker was soon in Italy with his division, pondering the problems of
Monte Cassino and its famous monastery.

He was amazed that no one on the Allied side could tell him anything
useful about the construction of the monastery, so he instigated his own

enquiries, combing the bookshops and libraries of Naples for information. What he discovered was that the walls were about fifteen feet
high and ten feet thick at the base and that the monastery had been
converted into a fortress during the nineteenth century.[43] This confirmed his suspicion that to subject such a well-fortified building to yet
another direct attack would be sheer folly as well as costly in lives. He
favoured a flanking movement (in the Japanese mode) which would get
behind the fortress and cut the lines of communication. But before he
had the chance to put his plan into operation, he fell seriously ill:

> After visiting the two French regiments on the front I returned to my
> own Headquarters, still feeling almost totally congealed with a pain
> developing in the back of my neck and a stiffness in the upper part of
> my shoulder blades. Within twenty-four hours it was apparent to
> myself that I was quite unfit to continue in command of anything
> whatsoever.[44]

This was not the beginning of the rheumatoid arthritis which would
slowly cripple and eventually kill Tuker, but a recurrence of the ethmoiditis which might easily have been treated had there been an ear,
nose and throat specialist to hand. In the event, the illness was both
misdiagnosed and mistreated. This was a great blow, not just for Tuker
himself – about whom a report made at this time recommended him for
a Lieutenant-General's appointment, *but not in a fighting formation* – but
also for his division, which 'lost 4,000 men on Cassino and gained nothing'. As an Indian Army historian writes, 'Tuker, on his way back to
hospital in India, must have thought, "I told you so". This was just the
sort of operation he abhorred.'[45] The 9th Gurkhas won renown clinging
to the aptly named Hangman's Hill on the slopes of Monte Cassino
under withering fire, but the price was too high and Tuker would never
have considered paying it. He called it 'the battle which should
never have been fought'.[46]

Conditions at Cassino, as a then junior officer in the 2/7th Gurkhas
recalls, 'were closely akin to those which existed in France during the
First World War'.[47] And as in the earlier war, there were moments of
panic among those Gurkhas who, like the re-raised 2/7th, were coming
under fire for the first time. An exposed position held by one platoon

came under very heavy German fire and the platoon commander, a jemadar whose career up to that point had been one of outstanding promise and rapid promotion, abandoned it, claiming that it had been overrun by the enemy. The jemadar's panic was catching and his (British) company commander ordered a withdrawal in the face of this phantom attack. No serious damage was done, since the Germans were unaware of the effect of their bombardment and did not follow it up; but the company commander was court-martialed and reduced to the ranks (he went on to serve with some distinction as an NCO in a Scottish regiment) and the jemadar dismissed from the service and sent back to Nepal – but at least he was not shot as he would have been in the First World War.[48]

Like the sick general we must now leave Italy, where several Gurkha battalions – particularly those which constituted the misleadingly named 43rd Gurkha Infantry Lorried Brigade (since lorries had little part to play in this sort of warfare) – continued to give a good account of themselves, though the 'tightly-packed, lavishly-armed battlefront and sea flanks did not', as Tuker has it, 'offer the same scope for small enterprises as did the Desert and Burma. The fighting was not so picturesque.'[49]

While 4th Indian Division was battling for Wadi Akarit in the North African desert, Orde Wingate's first Chindit expedition, an experiment in long-range penetration behind enemy lines – dismissed by Tuker as a 'somewhat futile' operation – was under way in Burma. The new Gurkha battalion which was 'unlucky enough' to accompany Wingate on his first operation in February 1943 was the 3rd battalion of Tuker's precious 2nd Goorkhas, and therefore not to be trifled with:

> Regardless of language differences, the unit was broken up, its
> organisation jettisoned, its sub-units mingled with British soldiers,
> complex tactical methods planted upon it and many of the men
> employed as mule drivers – an animal to which the young wartime
> Gurkha was little accustomed and, in any case, a noisy and vulnerable
> means of transport such as no experienced commander would ever
> have borne with for one minute in such operations in such country.
> The Gurkhas lost a lot of men and the whole clumsy expedition

proved nothing that was not known before and achieved little, while
the lessons, if any, that it taught were mainly what never again to do.[50]

What Tuker found unforgivable was that the expedition should be so
profligate with lives and lose as many as a third of its men: 'To some it
may seem strange that life is held so cheaply by commanders.'[51]

Wingate provoked extreme reactions – of adoration as well as abhor-
rence. Nobody was indifferent to this maverick brigadier who seemed
more like a biblical prophet than a professional soldier and who had the
ear not only of Wavell, now C-in-C in India, but also of Churchill. Only
Slim, among senior commanders who had dealings with him, seems to
have kept a sense of proportion about Wingate – another instance of the
extraordinary combination of modesty and authority which characterized 'Uncle Bill'.

According to the regimental history of the 2nd Goorkhas, Wingate's
jungle-fighting technique echoed many of the ideas Tuker had developed in relation to mountain warfare when he commanded the 1/2nd on
the north-west frontier, 'but with the added audacity that [Wingate]
proposed to operate behind the enemy's front and without lines of communication':

> His crisp, sizzling language accentuated the stark boldness of his
> theories. 'Whoever walks in the jungle gets killed. Make the other
> fellow walk into you . . . No lines of communication – bring in the
> goods, like Father Christmas, down the chimney [i.e., by air drops,
> then a novel idea] . . . [52]

The 2 GR historian gives Wingate credit for his revolutionary ideas, but
criticizes him for a training syllabus which, 'although eminently suitable
for his requirements, took no account of Gurkha psychology'; it was
'over the heads of the Gurkhas':

> For the most part they were very young soldiers. Unlike their British
> comrades, they were not stimulated to added efforts by the extraordinary
> nature of their enterprise. The mixing of units likewise reduced their
> efficiency. The Gurkha rifleman is peculiarly the creature of his
> regiment and is apt to feel lost when serving in other formations.[53]

To add to the difficulties, some of the British officers were recent arrivals who were still getting to know Gurkhas and their language.

One recent arrival was Lieutenant Denis Gudgeon, who wrote home: 'My new Brigadier is very good and energetic. He distinguished himself this morning by falling off his horse slap into the river! He has most extraordinary as well as good ideas. He is mad on sand tables [three-dimensional models of battles] and we have them every evening. Yesterday in the middle of it he let off his pistol to see if everyone was alert.'[54] Four months later, Gudgeon was assuring his parents that 'we are certainly going flat out in training to fight the Japs on the right lines, especially with our dynamic Brigadier. Although he is half mad he is just the kind of brass hat you need up top in this war. He has the right ideas . . .'[55]

'Nick' Neill was another young subaltern thrown in at the deep end, but he got off to a bad start with his charismatic commander:

He was wearing his soon-to-be-famous *sola topi*. Whilst inspecting 8 Column's mules, he suddenly turned to me and, pointing to an individual mule, said, 'Neill, what's that mule's number?' I replied, 'Sir, the mules were only branded yesterday and I haven't memorised their numbers yet'. His immediate retort was, 'Well, you should have known them by now, boy'. As far as my Gurkhas were concerned, Wingate showed no interest whatsoever – he certainly didn't ask what anyone's number was. This was typical of the man . . . his interest in man-management – particularly, the care of the wounded – was shallower than that expected and required of an operational field commander.[56]

Neill could not forgive Wingate his indifference to the fate of the wounded: when he received the order that any wounded 'were to be left in the nearest village', Neill refused to pass it on to his Gurkhas, resolving that 'my wounded, if we took casualties, would never be left behind; or if they were, they would be left over my dead body'. To him it was simply incredible 'that any commander should contemplate issuing such a morale-damaging order just as his force was on the point of being launched into the territory of an enemy as brutal and callous as the Japanese'.[57]

Operation Longcloth, as it was known, turned into one long night-mare: 'As in real nightmares, our waking one was of the fear of being chased and caught by a fearsome demon; one would try, as in such a dream, to run away and escape, but one's legs would seem too weak to carry the body forward; and later, during the retreat, this was just how it was to be for us.'[58] The heroes, 'if there were any heroes of Wingate's First Expedition', were (*pace* Tuker) the mules. Neill came to respect and even love these long-suffering beasts, and he sympathized with their minders:

> . . . underneath a sal tree I came across one of my muleteers, 107394
> Prembahadur Rai, sitting cross-legged beneath the heads of his two
> mules, playing to them on the bamboo flute I'd seen him making some
> days previously. I smiled at him and said: '*Bansuli kina bajaeko?*' ['Why
> were you playing the flute?'] He looked up at me and laughed,
> replying: '*Khachcharlai rahar lagchha, hajur!*' ['The mules like it, Sir'].[59]

Prembahadur was one of 300 men in 3/2 GR seconded from the 10th Gurkhas, sixty of whom died; he survived the first Chindit expedition only to fall at Meiktila on 13 March 1945.[60]

The expedition marched deep into enemy-held country, 8 Column getting three-quarters of the way across Upper Burma without, in Neill's estimation, 'achieving anything of significance in the way of either tactical or strategic success'. When the rumour of their impending return to India reached the column, Neill thought to himself as he fell asleep that night 'that we'd marched a very long way for nothing'.[61] Worse was to follow when Wingate, 'still wearing his *sola topi*, but now with a beard like the rest of us' and looking more than ever like a biblical prophet, came hurrying by:

> As though it was only yesterday, I can remember how he looked and
> what he called out to me and the others of my column who were
> standing nearby. As he passed me, he was almost trotting, so fast was
> his step and his speed was causing his pack to bump up and down on
> his back. His eyes were wide and very staring; he cried out as he
> passed, 'Disperse, disperse, get back to India!' I recall thinking to
> myself at the time, 'My God, the man's gone mad. Here we are, a force
> of some 700 men, we have a platoon already across the Irrawaddy, and

he's not prepared to carry on with our crossing. This is too improbable to be true. There must be some other explanation for his behaviour'.[62]

In Neill's view (shared by many others), Wingate went 'one river too far' on this expedition. If he had stopped short of the Irrawaddy, he might have succeeded in extricating his force with fewer casualties. As it was, by breaking it up into 'penny-packets' bereft of communications, he ensured that what followed was less a retreat than a rout – a case of every small group for itself, deprived of administrative or tactical air support. Neill remarked that, though he could not know it at the time, this was to be the greatest challenge of his soldiering life: 'This was it, then, our escape to freedom was to begin – but so was the waking nightmare, which was to torment me from that day on and which was to become more and more frightening as the days, weeks and months rolled by in very slow time.'[63]

Many of the dispersal groups were too small to resist the predations of the Japanese search parties, which were generally about platoon strength. In addition to threading their way through hostile country, the groups had to battle with hunger and thirst. Soon after separating from 8 Column, Neill had his first experience of command in combat when his group ran into a Japanese ambush and lost more than half their number. He suffered agonies of guilt and remorse that he had not known how to protect his Gurkhas by immediately mounting a counter-attack and had failed to rally his men after giving the order to withdraw. But he never repeated these mistakes: 'In later years during the war and in two subsequent campaigns [Malaya and Borneo] afterwards, my Gurkhas and I were able to kill a very great number of enemy as a direct result of lessons learnt the hard way on 14 April 1943.'[64]

Neill had a second encounter with the enemy when a truck-load of Japanese spotted his group and opened fire on them. Rather than risk his men getting hit, he ordered them to run: 'I didn't have time to be ashamed – that would come to me later . . .'[65] Not that there was any occasion for shame, since by this time he and his few remaining men were practically dying of starvation and Wingate's orders had been to avoid enemy contact whenever possible. When they finally reached the Chindwin River at a place called Sahpa, they were literally at their last gasp.

In war, men's fate so often hangs on a very thin and fragile thread. In our case, the thread could not have been thinner. Had we had to delay at Sahpa in order to construct rafts, we would have been caught [by a Japanese patrol which had been tracking them and arrived half an hour later]. Had I not been standing on the Chindwin's edge in that particular clearing and had the Gurkha levy of V Force [a quasi-military formation recruited from the Assam frontier hill tribes] not been passing at that very moment, or had he failed to see me, I would not have been accosted and asked for my identity. Had this encounter not taken place when it did, we would never have been sent the single boat which was to prove to be our salvation . . . The method and timing of our escape was nothing short of a miracle.[66]

Another miracle was that they had beaten the dreaded monsoon by just two days. Defeated, exhausted, starving . . . but alive and still sufficiently disciplined to have kept hold of their arms and ammunition – unlike some other groups which had abandoned their weapons before they crossed the Chindwin.

Denis Gudgeon was not so lucky. He, too, got as far as the banks of the Chindwin, but there he was betrayed to the Japanese by Burmese civilians. He was captured on 20 April 1943 and for the next two years and eight days he lived on one bowl of rice three times a day. On 30 April 1945, he wrote home: 'Never make me a rice pudding again, Mummy.' Three days later he added: 'I am a Chindit so I have discovered.'[67] (The name is a corruption of *Chinthi*, the mythical creature – half-lion, half-griffin – guarding Buddhist temples in Burma.)

By June 1943, two-thirds of the first Chindit expedition had got back to the safety of Assam, having, in the words of the historian of 9 GR, 'lost a thousand men in a series of operations which ranged from conclusive victory to complete fiasco'.[68]

For Neill, the lessons of this 'traumatic' expedition were twofold:

First and foremost, I learnt that Orde Wingate's overall conception of the operation was sound and daring. To dare in war is to win – more often than not. However, unless the training for an operation such as one committed to deep penetration behind a formidable enemy's lines is sound and, equally important, unless its execution is robust and effective, that operation will not totally succeed . . . [69]

(To which Wingate might have replied with the words he uses in his report on the expedition: '. . . training is always insufficient and is bound to remain so. Reports which devote space to lamenting that personnel were "insufficiently trained" in this or that, are stating a truism. No personnel are ever sufficiently trained in any respect.'[70])

Secondly, through exposure to constant fear, Neill had learned something about himself which had a wider application:

> Awful though fear is when it is experienced, when it is conquered it can later become truly beneficial to military men. On being placed in a position where one is able to see fear in others – provided one has known it oneself – a commander can soon know how to detect fear and, with practice, he will learn how far he can push his men, so affected, in battle . . . Very often I have found that a commander, brave and dashing in himself, who cannot appreciate genuine fear in his men, is apt to push his soldiers too hard at the wrong moment, when catastrophe could well result . . . If . . . a commander can bring himself to lead from the front at the same time conquering his own dreads, there is probably nothing that he cannot achieve in war.[71]

The intensity with which Neill recalls his introduction to war many years and several campaigns later shows just how formative an experience it was. His deepest debt, as he acknowledges, is to Havildar Buddhiman Limbu (seconded from 2/10 GR) and the small band of young soldiers who followed him cheerfully and unquestioningly 'through hell and high water' – in this case, almost literally.[72] By succeeding in bringing out his tiny force in some semblance of order, Neill had come of age as an officer and a man; just as important, he had come to be accepted by the Gurkhas.

Orde Wingate is sometimes cited as a rare example of a British officer who served with Gurkhas and was not won over by them. But the critical comments in his report on the expedition are mild enough and he is careful to distinguish between seasoned troops and raw recruits, remarking that 'only Gurkha soldiers of some years standing, with a high proportion of experienced and Gurkhali-speaking British Officers, are fit to take part in operations of this exacting character'.[73] It is true that he refers to the 'slow wits of the Gurkha' (though this is linked to 'the ignorance of Gurkhali even on the part of those GR Officers who had given the subject some study during the short time available') and that he illustrates an argument with a slighting reference to them:

> I regard my maxims of 'When in doubt don't fire' and 'The answer to noise is silence' as having proved invaluable to all Columns . . . It is necessary of course to apply these maxims with the minimum of common sense and not do as one group of Gurkhas was found doing: calmly watch the enemy fire at you while as a matter of principle you clean your rifle . . . [74]

But Wingate was hardly unique in drawing attention to Gurkha intellectual limitations. Another Chindit officer, after paying tribute to the Gurkha's soldierly qualities, writes: 'His weakness lies in his mental capacity. His reactions are slower than the European's and he is apt to rely on his immediate superior to give him all his orders.'[75] And British Gurkha officers themselves are fond of anecdotes illustrating the literal-mindedness of their soldiers. Wingate's offence was more a matter of tone than substance; there was no trace of affection to leaven his criticism and remove the sting from it.

Wavell's verdict on the first Chindit expedition was that

> the enterprise had no strategic value and about one-third of the force which entered Burma was lost, but the experience gained . . . was invaluable. The enemy was obviously surprised and at a loss, and found no effective means to counter the harassment of our columns . . . In general, Brigadier Wingate's theories and leadership were fully vindicated.[76]

Wingate was promoted to major-general and in August 1943 attended the Quebec Conference, where he was able to put his plans directly to Churchill, Roosevelt and their senior military commanders. He could also, to some extent, pick and choose his troops for the next offensive and, though the 13th West African Brigade was included, there were no Indian Army troops other than Gurkhas – of which there were no less than four units, 3/4, 3/6, 3/9 and 4/9 GR. The selection of so many Gurkha battalions probably owed less to Wingate than to his most successful column leaders, Mike Calvert and Bernard Fergusson, who had formed a higher opinion of Gurkha qualities than their commander had.[77]

Wingate's Special Force consisted of six brigades, supported by three wings of the US Army Air Force – such was his influence with the powers-that-be. On the grounds of size alone this could no longer be seen as a guerrilla force, which would blow up bridges and railways and move on; this time 'fortress positions' were to be taken and defended against enemy forces. This would enable the sick and wounded to be evacuated by air from secure bases held by Allied troops – though this had formed no part of Wingate's original intentions.[78]

The second Chindit expedition, launched on 5 March 1944, met with varying degrees of success in its operations behind the Japanese lines. But the death in an aircrash of its commander and inspiration less than three weeks later (24 March) led to the downgrading of the whole enterprise. As Richard Rhodes James, who was cipher officer with 111 Brigade, writes: 'With the death of Wingate our great hopes of the future disappeared. The sense of intoxication we had experienced when waiting to fly in was gone, and in its place was a resignation to do some rather ordinary and pointless soldiering.'[79]

Brigadier 'Joe' Lentaigne, whose call for an early breakfast had saved 1/4 GR at the Sittang River bridge in 1942, left 111 Brigade to take over command of the Chindits; but he had neither Wingate's vision nor his influence in high places. The expedition was deployed in support of the ungracious American General 'Vinegar Joe' Stilwell and his Chinese forces – which had always been the intention; only Wingate, with his own dreams of conquest, had subverted it. Then it was broken up, on the grounds that it was too extravagant with manpower and materials, and its battalions were re-integrated into the military formations invading Burma.

The propaganda value of the Chindits may have outweighed their military worth, but their operations were replete with heroics. To speak only of Gurkha units, an officer, Lt (acting Capt.) Michael Allmand (posthumously) and a rifleman, Tulbahadur Pun, of 3/6 GR both won VCs for spectacular acts of individual bravery in an attack on a strongly defended railway bridge at Mogaung; they were part of Calvert's 77 Brigade. An office in 3/9 GR, temporary Major F. G. 'Jim' Blaker MC, was also awarded a posthumous VC for his part in 111 Brigade's successful assault on Hill 2171 after the Brigade Major, Jack Masters, had taken over command from Joe Lentaigne and the entire brigade was so exhausted that, as Masters put it, 'It is hard to believe that anyone else can be as tired as we.'[80]

Masters distinguished between the Chindit war and normal war. In a normal formation he always had the feeling that he could go on for ever; in the Chindits he knew there was a time limit. Apart from the fact that you could never be relieved or rested, there was 'the absence of supply lines, the knowledge that if you are sick or wounded your future is incalculable, looking always in all directions, always undernourished, always extremely vulnerable to certain types of enemy action'.[81] In 111 Brigade they went well over the planned ninety-day time limit and still somehow managed to function, but the strain was enormous and the benefits more than a little dubious.

The soldiers had to carry everything on their backs. The No. 1 of a Bren gun (light machine-gun) team, for instance, 'when carrying the gun, and just after a supply drop had put five days' K rations in his pack, toted a load of 86 pounds. For a Gurkha with a total body weight of about 130 pounds, who was expected to run up and down mountains, this was a lot.'[82]

So it was not so much the extraordinary flashes of medal-winning bravery as the sheer slog and bloody-minded endurance that Masters celebrates:

A *havildar* passed me at the head of his platoon. I recognised him – Mohbat Sing. He had been a young signaller in the 2nd battalion in the Frontier campaigns of 1936–37 when I was a lieutenant and signal officer. More than once I had sworn at him for his unkempt ways and skill at avoiding work. Now his eyes were dull and he exhorted his platoon in a gasped-out monologue of Gurkhali oaths and endearments – 'Come on, you porcupines' pricks. It's all right. Move, move, kids! We're nearly there. O pubic hairs, keep at it. You,

you . . .' – his head turned as he saw me – '*Salaam, sahib!* Of course we can do it! . . . The Gurkhas are coming! Third-Fourth, *Third-Fourth!*' He broke into a shambling run, followed by all his platoon. How they did it, I do not know. They passed from my view up the path. The firing increased suddenly, grew to a mad clatter . . . at first nearly all Japanese; then even; then nearly all ours, the heavy roar of our grenades and the powerful grunting stammer of the Bren guns. Wounded men came down the path, a corpse sprawled in it right at the limit of my vision as I lay behind a tree peering forward . . .

More firing, again Japanese. Advance held up. What else, on a one-man front against a determined enemy? Only about a third of the way up the ridge, and now late afternoon. I passed the 3/9th Gurkhas through the 3/4th. Found Mohbat Sing and promoted him to a *jemadar* on the spot for gallantry in the field . . . [83]

Mohbat Sing went on to become Subedar-Major of the post-independence 3/4th Gorkhas and finally retired in 1960 or thereabouts.

The war in Burma, it has been said, was the Indian Army's war.[84] In the final analysis it was won, not by the Chindits, however admirable their contribution, but by Slim's British, Indian and Gurkha legions who first repelled the final, desperate, but nonetheless totally focused Japanese onslaught on Imphal and Kohima, the gateway to India, from March to June 1944, then steadily pushed the enemy south-east to the Irrawaddy and beyond. After Imphal and Kohima, Slim outwitted as well as out-fought his opponents, but he had almost been caught out at Imphal when he failed – as he was the first to admit – to get his troops back there fast enough. Imphal was the fulcrum of the entire campaign; a little extra weight on the other side and the outcome might have been very different, though by this time Allied air superiority was beginning to tell. The fact that four of the seven VCs awarded to men of 17th Indian Division in the Burma war (and two out of the three that went to the 2/5th Royal Gurkha Rifles alone) were won in the month of June 1944 is an indication of the severity of the fighting around Imphal.

The 1/7th Gurkhas were fighting alongside 2/5 RGR. B Company's anti-tank gunner, Rifleman Ganju Lama, had already distinguished himself by knocking out two of the five light tanks his company had suddenly come up against – for which he was awarded a Military Medal – when, less than a month later, he singlehandedly took on three enemy medium tanks.

> Three times he was wounded in the arms and legs, his left wrist being broken, but in spite of his handicap he courageously struggled forward and with the utmost coolness destroyed first one and then a second tank, killing the crews. Not content with this he returned for more bombs and dealt with the crew of the third tank which had been knocked out by an anti-tank gun.[85]

Ganju Lama's action not only broke the enemy resistance and enabled 1/7 GR to relieve the hard-pressed 2/5 RGR, but also earned him a VC to pin on his chest in front of his MM.

The words on the memorial for the Allied dead at Kohima – 'When you go home/ Tell them of us and say/ For your tomorrow/ We gave our today' – have the same epic equality as (and were no doubt penned in imitation of) Simonides's famous epitaph on the Spartans killed at Thermopylae, which reads (in Mackail's translation): 'Go, tell the Spartans, thou who passest by,/ That here obedient to their laws we lie'. And the Burma campaign as a whole 'had the shape and pattern of epic drama', as John Masters recognized when, as the senior staff officer in Major-General 'Pete' Rees's 19th Division, he finally reached the Sittang River:

> The first scene of the first act had shown the defeat of Slim and the 17th Indian Infantry Division at this very place, on the banks of the Sittang, early in 1942 [in fact Slim took over command of 1 Burma Corps *after* the Sittang River bridge disaster]; the second scene, their long, disastrous retreat to India, 800 miles away. The second act had covered a year and a half of close, grim fighting in the jungle-covered mountains along the Burma–India border. The third act – the Chindits, Imphal, Meiktila, and the rushing advance back south over those same 800 miles. And now, almost as an *envoi*, this calm, efficient slaughter in the paddy fields, Slim still leading, the 17th Indian Infantry Division still in its place, in contact.[86]

Slim and his once 'Forgotten Army' are now remembered – with advantages. Like any army, it was made up of dozens of small units, pieces of the jigsaw, each privy to some, but not all, of the strategic picture. Let us home in on just one of these units, a wartime battalion, the 4/8th Gurkha Rifles, commanded by Lieutenant-Colonel (later General Sir) Walter Walker, a regular of regulars, three of whose ECOs – one an American – have left accounts of their initiation in jungle warfare under this steely disciplinarian.

'Walter Walker was a martinet; there is no doubt of that,' writes Denis Sheil-Small. 'He was also a perfectionist. If your foxholes or bunkers were not properly dug, you dug them again . . . Officers were far from immune. If your field orders were faulty or imprecise you were rocketed later with withering scorn. Even the latrines did not escape his eagle eye. They must not be less than six feet deep, properly sited and well looked after.'[87]

To the 'very junior, rather diffident, inexperienced' Pat Davis, Walker was 'a beneficial dragon':

He was strict. He insisted on high standards. He was not afraid to punish. He was not afraid to winnow: a few left, other ranks and officers, but not many. Occasionally we thought him unjust, but only occasionally. For myself, I was in awe of him, but committed to his way of running things.[88]

For the American Scott Gilmore, Walker's 'studied nonchalance' was 'part of an act of *savoir faire*, right down to the imperious wave of his cigarette holder':

The American officer taught to rough it with his soldiers might consider such style supercilious . . . To the contrary, Walker's panache was highly admired. Our Gurkhas expected their commander to behave like a commander. Had Colonel Walker's performance been all theater and no substance, they would soon have caught on. But he was first-class at his job, demanding yet efficient, cool and precise. He never showed fear or worry. He was able both to intimate genuine interest in the welfare of the men and to remain sufficiently aloof to keep respect. With his junior officers he seldom unbent.[89]

When Sheil-Small, Gilmore and another young officer arrived a few minutes late for a morning conference, having made tricky journeys through dense jungle from their respective company areas, Walker was not prepared to accept their muttered apologies. He waited until the end of the meeting, then told them coldly that he proposed to set them 'an exercise in punctuality'. This involved doing the rounds of the companies and battalion headquarters three times a night for three successive nights, signing a book at each venue: 'All sentries will be warned so that none of you will get shot during your tours.' After three nights of stumbling through the jungle at regular intervals, grateful at least that this was a training area and there were no Japanese in the vicinity, Sheil-Small sank into the finest night's sleep he could ever remember.[90]

Walker himself, Davis noticed, did not seem to need sleep as other people did; he 'took less sleep than any of us, could never relax, was for all of every day and much of most nights thinking, planning, encouraging, prodding, looking ahead both in time and space, whether on the move or chained to his command post, never inactive'.[91] He had even made himself go without sleep for a night as part of his preparation for the rigours ahead. He compiled 'creeds' for riflemen and junior leaders, made up of aphorisms printed at the head of the battalion orders which were read out to the men daily. 'Shoot to kill – kill to live' was one; 'He who sees first, shoots first' was another. Others included, 'Dead ground, live men', 'If not cover from fire, then cover by fire' and 'In any situation the one unforgivable crime is INACTION'.[92] The idea, of course, was to inculcate good military habits and, by repetition, to make them second nature. 'The only good Jap is a dead one' was not so much a moral sentiment as a practical precept.

In retrospect, Davis finds these maxims – and some of them were fairly bloodthirsty – embarrassing. But the Gurkhas, he remarks, 'did not share our civilized scruples and did not need a pseudo-moral commitment':

> They were paid to be soldiers, not to believe in a cause. They believed in loyalty to the Regiment and to friends, and in courage, and in giving the best of themselves, but not much in King and Empire, and not at all in Western civilisation, freedom, democracy.[93]

This statement is perhaps a little too sweeping; the hill Gurkha might not believe in freedom and democracy as concepts, but independent-mindedness and a strong sense of justice make natural democrats, as the American Scott Gilmore recognizes: 'Every Gurkha is his own man. If he chooses to become a soldier and obey the orders of superiors, this in no way diminishes his individuality.'[94]

On 20 December 1944 the battalion received orders 'to proceed on active operations against the Japanese'. It had been lucky to get five months' rest and training behind the lines at Kohima while other units had 'nagged and pushed at the retreating enemy until we were ready, refreshed, to close on the Irrawaddy and central Burma, territory which had been in enemy hands for more than two years'. There was, Davis recalls, 'the scent of victory about'.[95]

At the time he hardly realized how fortunate he had been to have had time to get to know and grow close to the men he would soon be leading into battle. The experience bolstered his confidence both in himself and in them. In his book he tries to be dispassionate, drawing up a balance sheet of Gurkha virtues and defects.

On the credit side, first and foremost, of course, is the Gurkha sense of humour, not a subtle instrument but 'banana-skin humour' and a 'quick sense of the ridiculous that spared no one, neither the Colonel, themselves, nor me'. Then there is their honesty, which 'permeated all their actions and reactions, a natural integrity, an inborn frankness'. Courage comes only third 'because it seems to me not so uncommon, though I acknowledge that a people without courage are nothing'. Neither is it inexhaustible: 'Courage, said our General Slim, is like having money in the bank. It is an expendable quality.' Finally there is the tenacity for which Gurkhas are famous: 'They led a tough life in their homes which well fitted them for the hardships of active service.'

On the debit side, a propensity for gambling, womanizing and strong drink, limited intelligence – though 'whether Gurkhas were truly less intelligent, or had differently developed intelligence, is difficult to prove. Some of them, bless their ugly flat faces, were certainly very thick-headed' – and a certain insularity. But he would not have wanted to go to war in any other company:

Identification with them was complete, unclouded by the smallest doubt that I might be happier elsewhere. It was always a pleasure, and often a joy, to be among them.[96]

Sheil-Small and Gilmore felt the same way. 'Sometimes,' the latter writes of the aftermath of a battle, 'I looked about at my companions, these uncomplicated moonfaced young stoics, calm, smiling now, smoking their *bidis*, slapping down grimy playing cards with a curse and a chuckle, and thought how privileged I had been to be introduced to battle in their company.'[97] Sheil-Small had felt 'sick' when one of his platoons was badly shot up and 'guilty' that he had not been with them 'at their greatest time of need'. He writes:

It is difficult to explain the bond that united us all in a Gurkha infantry battalion. To describe us as a family would offend the sceptic of today, but like a family we were in our relationship with each other and with the men. We were truly 'brother' officers and we regarded the men with affection and admiration as we would our children.[98]

Pat Davis is careful to avoid such paternalistic comments. He is not blind to the fact that what propelled young men into the army was the economic conditions in the hills of Nepal: 'the Gurkhas had not joined up to worship Lieutenant Smith, but to earn a living':

This [economic] argument . . . would have been anathema to those British officers of the Gurkha Brigade who by training and by nature believed that only they could successfully command Gurkhas. These officers had come to feel such a depth of affection and loyalty for their men that they assumed that it must be unique to them. Up to a point that feeling did exist; had British and Gurkha not respected each other's qualities, and mixed well together, the Gurkha might not have come, or would have come in smaller numbers. But it was a feeling that did not go so deep as many of us like to think.[99]

A Canadian-born anthropologist, in a recent study of Gurung *lahores* in their home setting, argues that what the British officers have identified as 'loyalty' has 'none of the qualities of dog-like devotion often implied in their accounts':

The many British tales of faithful Gurkhas shadowing their officers across battlefields or seeing that they have hot meals or rest are read differently by *lahores*. When I recounted these stories men explained that because the British are likely to be killed due to their incompetencies they must watch out for them. These remarks are not meant to be insulting. Gurungs do not expect wealthy, white, urban people to have such abilities, as they are not the ones they acquire through their lifestyle. This distribution of the abilities required in the army was important to *lahores* in retaining a sense of their equality with their officers.[100]

According to this anthropologist, the attitudes of Gurungs at least precluded a slavish devotion to their officers, 'who were more often found puzzling than seen as father-figures'.[101] In keeping with their sensitivity to 'being treated as inferiors', *lahores* 'uniformly and adamantly insist that the work of an orderly was considered the most demeaning of all army labor. That so many British memoirs describe orderlies as proud of their duties and devoted to their masters is a tribute to *lahores*' forbearance in the face of hardship and humiliation.'[102]

To return to Walter Walker's 4/8th Gurkhas, Pat Davis records an unfortunate incident which shows that even in the best-run battalions bitter hatred could flare up and exact a terrible toll. The duty officer doing his rounds at the evening's 'stand-to' had discovered a naik (corporal) smoking in his trench and roundly abused him in front of several riflemen before putting him on a charge. The next morning the naik was marched in front of his company commander. The duty officer, a subaltern, gave his evidence and then, as he turned away, the naik shot him and, before anyone could do anything, reversed his rifle and shot himself. Davis comments, 'The trouble came perhaps through the conjunction of a Gurkha and an officer both with unstable temperaments. Jimmy had used strong words. The naik felt himself to have been impossibly shamed in front of his juniors, a trust broken.'[103] It was one of the ironies of war that the first dead bodies Davis had ever seen had nothing to do with enemy action.

There would be many more deaths. The 4/8th were soon in the thick of the action. In an exposed position on the west bank of the Irrawaddy at Taungdaw, with Japanese patrols 'sniffing around us', Davis 'felt like the cow that was tied up as bait in tiger shoots: the tiger killed the cow and the hunters killed the tiger'.[104] But he survived while his friend Mike Tidswell – 'gentle, kind and nice; a civilian, not really a warrior' – died a soldier's death, having been mortally wounded leading an attack on an entrenched Japanese position. Many were the feats of bravery on the night of 12–13 May 1945 at Taungdaw but the most celebrated, and the one that brought 4/8 GR a VC, cost Rifleman Lachhiman Gurung an arm and an eye. Under attack from the Japanese, Lachhiman's trench was peppered with grenades; twice he picked up these time-bombs and hurled them back at the enemy, but the third time he was not so lucky; the grenade exploded in his hand and shattered his arm, also wounding his face, body and right leg. The citation reads:

> The enemy, screaming and shouting, now formed up shoulder to shoulder and attempted to rush the position by sheer weight of numbers. Rifleman Lachhiman Gurung, regardless of his wounds, loaded and fired his rifle with his left hand, maintaining a continuous steady rate of fire. Wave after wave of fanatical attacks were thrown in by the enemy, but all were repulsed with heavy casualties. For four hours after being severely wounded, Rifleman Lachhiman Gurung remained alone at his post, waiting with perfect calm for each attack, which he met with fire at point blank range from his rifle, determined not to give one inch of ground.[105]

When the enemy dead were counted, of the eighty-seven found in front of the company's position thirty-one were in the vicinity of Lachhiman's trench. When Pat Davis read the citation for Lachhiman's VC, he found it difficult to relate it to his own confused experience in a trench in the valley below the ridge.

> The words of the citation, by their confident clarity, seemed to me to fictionalize the battle. But I kept this feeling to myself. Only Lachhiman knew what had happened to him. I believed that he had certainly shown exemplary courage; I guessed that the confusions and uncertainties of war could not be reproduced in citations.[106]

The battle of Taungdaw was, nonetheless, a triumph: 'The Colonel had put us into a major battle and brought us out again with remarkably little damage . . . his nerve held (as did the Brigadier's); it was the Japanese who broke.'[107] Walter Walker's wartime battalion had acquitted itself with honour as well as winning the first VC to go to the 8th Gurkhas since 1904, when Lt Grant had won this supreme honour on Younghusband's Tibetan expedition. Walker himself moved on; the battalion took part in further actions, but the war was effectively won; it was only a matter of time – and the atom bomb – before the Japanese surrendered.

In their advance into Burma, the 4/8th Gurkhas, like many other units, had been surprised to find themselves sometimes opposed, not by Japanese, but by Indian troops, who were mostly happy to give themselves up after only a token struggle. On the night of 1–2 May 1945 a 10 GR platoon ambushed a large number of what the British called 'Jiffs' (JIF – Japanese Inspired Fifth-columnists or, more neutrally, Japanese Indian Forces) and beat off a counter-attack by what turned out to be a battalion of about 400 men. The regimental historian's contemptuous comment is that 'probably never in the whole course of the campaign in Burma were so many so utterly routed and put to disorderly flight by so few'.[108]

The origins of the Indian National Army (INA) lay in the crushing defeat of the British forces in Malaya and Singapore, and then Burma, in early 1942. Surrendered Indian and Gurkha troops were separated from their British officers and encouraged to switch their allegiance to the Japanese and help establish the high-sounding 'South-East Asia Co-Prosperity Sphere'. They were subjected to, first, propaganda and then, if that did not move them, to stronger forms of persuasion – near-starvation, solitary confinement, beatings and torture – to induce them to take arms against their employers, all in the name of freedom.

Among INA volunteers there were some who were persuaded on ideological grounds, but many more took the line of least resistance; a third category, several Gurkhas among them, seized the opportunity in order to escape their captors at a suitable moment. The overwhelming majority of Gurkhas remained staunch in their loyalty; the few notable exceptions being mainly from 2/1 GR, a battalion with a high percentage of Dharmsala line-boys, whose Indian origins made them more amenable to nationalist propaganda than native-born Nepalis. One defector, Jemadar Puran Singh of 2/1 GR, however, was later to become Inspector General of Police in Nepal.[109]

Loyal Gurkha officers, NCOs and men were brutally treated by their INA guards, the more nationalistically minded of whom may have felt they had historical scores to settle:

> Subedar (later Subedar-Major) Dilbahadur Gurung and Subedar
> Jitbahadur Gurung seem to have been picked out for special
> persecution. They were both repeatedly knocked senseless, brought
> round, and knocked out again. Dilbahadur had his left wrist broken
> while shielding Jitbahadur from what was likely to have been a final
> and fatal assault. But at last the INA guards desisted and allowed
> medical treatment to be given . . . the GOs had won.[110]

These two 2/1st Gurkha officers were later taken to Penang, along with others from the 2/2nd and 2/9th; there they were comfortably housed in a bungalow with Indian 'servants' and fêted by the Japanese. The object was not to pressurize them by other means into joining the INA, of which the Japanese were openly scornful, but to get them to persuade the three Gurkha battalions to join the Japanese army *en masse*: 'Much propaganda was handed out about the Japanese and Gurkhas being of one kindred race, with common forefathers and similar appearances.' The Gurkha officers unanimously rejected these overtures and 'after a two-and-a-half-month holiday' were sent back to their battalions in prison camp.[111]

Because of the INA recruiting campaign, Indians and Gurkhas were not impressed into labour gangs and set to work on the 'Death Railway' along with the British, Australian and Dutch prisoners. But the Japanese delight in humiliating Europeans and in taking photographs of them performing degrading activities and undergoing torture and execution backfired in at least one case, that of a Sikh havildar who had joined the INA: 'On being shown these abominable pictures he said bluntly, "It is easy to discern which are the men and which the apes". Although put to the torture he continued to revile the Japs until he died.'[112]

In the absence of British officers who, though only a few miles away, risked their lives if they attempted to communicate with their men –

and vice versa – the Gurkhas found a magnificent substitute in Captain (later Major-General) Hari Chand Badhwar of the 3rd Cavalry, whose resistance to Japanese efforts to undermine the loyalty of Indian soldiers cost him dear. In the headquarters of the Japanese equivalent of the Gestapo in Bangkok he and a brother officer from the 3rd Cavalry, Captain (later Lieutenant-General) Dhargalkar, were locked in underground cages, five feet by five feet, sometimes sharing this minimal space with four or five other prisoners, for eighty-eight days on end.[113] Yet when he was transferred to Singapore, he gave such heart to the men of the 2/2nd Goorkhas that at the end of the war they petitioned that he should be elected a life member of the 2 GR mess – 'the first Indian officer ever to be honoured in this fashion'.[114] Their own subedar-major, Hari Sing Bohra, resisted with equal heroism, writing a letter of protest to the Japanese commander, in which he pointed out that since Gurkhas were not Indian citizens they were not interested in serving in the INA, and that as prisoners of war they were entitled to proper treatment according to the laws of war.

> Such undaunted behaviour drew on Subedar-Major Hari Sing Bohra the utmost malice of his captors. Under his orders the men presented a resolute front in the face of every intimidation and every humiliation. The Gurkha officers were locked up separately. They were beaten and starved; they were forced to coolie labours under the orders of coolies. In May 1944, Subedar-Major Hari Sing Bohra, blind from ill-treatment, died of internal haemorrhages caused by beatings – a martyr to his fidelity to the Regimental tradition.[115]

Rifleman Dhanbahadur Rana and twenty-six of his 2/2 GR comrades followed the other route, deciding that to join the INA was 'the shortest way home'. Once on the Burmese front, Dhanbahadur and two others took advantage of the first opportunity to desert into the jungle and made their way over to the British side, carrying with them a detailed map of Japanese dispositions in the area. Dhanbahadur described some aspects of the training he and his comrades had been obliged to undergo:

> We were taught to act as if we were dumb. We were taught to dress

like a gentleman with a tie and collar and stick. We were taught how to pretend that we were mad. We were shown how to tie a loaded pistol above the knee so that it could be drawn at a moment's notice. We were taught to tell all Gurkhas that Subhas Chandra Bose was now ruler of India and that there was no purpose in continuing to serve the English.[116]

The Bengali Subhas Chandra Bose was a late arrival on the scene. He had made his way to Germany early in 1940 to try and persuade the Axis powers to commit themselves to the achievement of a free India. The Germans gave him limited support, seeing his value mainly as an instrument of propaganda and allowing him access to Indian prisoners of war in Europe, but treating with scepticism his dream of raising a revolutionary army. His failure to convert more than a small percentage of POWs to militant nationalism induced Hitler to connive with him only to the extent of shipping him off to the Far East, where Bose hoped to find a more fertile field of action.

The INA predated Bose's arrival and its first leader had no connection with him. Captain Mohan Singh of the 1/14th Punjab Regiment acted simply out of a growing conviction of the justice of the nationalist cause. Because of his evident sincerity, he was successful in attracting Indian volunteers in numbers. But before long he fell out with the Japanese. What he envisioned as a 'liberating army' they saw merely as extra guards for those Indian and Gurkha prisoners who refused to volunteer. So in December 1942 he dissolved the INA.

By this time, however, Bose was on his way to provide a more dynamic political leadership, and the INA survived Mohan Singh's attempt to disband it. Bose addressed its officers and men on 5 July 1943 in a style reminiscent of the imperialist enemy No. 1: 'For the present, I can offer you nothing except hunger, thirst, privation, forced marches and death. But if you follow me in life and in death . . . I shall lead you to victory and freedom.' Nehru's comment was that, if Bose reached India with the assistance of an Axis power, he would personally oppose him 'with open sword in hand'.[117] The question became academic when Subhas Chandra Bose – like that other charismatic leader, Orde Wingate, before him – was killed in an aircrash. But this did not happen until 18 August 1945, by which time Bose had witnessed the disintegration of the INA in Burma. Treachery, he discovered, worked both ways; those who had flouted regimental loyalty and willingly joined the INA were unlikely to prove staunch in battle; and those who had joined it merely in order to escape the rigours of imprisonment deserted at the first opportunity.

Yet there were honourable men among the dross of the INA, as the British officers who took their surrender discovered. The commander of the 2nd INA Regiment, P. K. Sahgal, formerly a captain in the 2/10th Baluch Regiment, impressed Major Purves of the 4/2nd Goorkha Rifles: 'Obviously tired, and limping, he retained some degree of dignity – none of which was obvious in his men, who presented a sorry spectacle.'[118] He also impressed the CO of 4/2 GR, Lt-Col. John Kitson, who interviewed him and recorded his opinions in the battalion war diary:

> I asked him if he disliked the English and he said that amongst
> Englishmen he had some very good friends but that he disliked the
> system of British Imperialism in India.
>
> I don't really know what he thought would happen to him but I
> certainly thought he would be shot or strung up, and so I avoided the
> subject which he did not mention either . . .
>
> Frankly, I couldn't help liking the man; he never cringed like so
> many before or after him have done, and he never spun the yarn about
> being forced to join the INA; furthermore, in spite of his dislike for the
> Japs, he had the guts to stand up for his ideals, even in defeat.[119]

Major Purves separated the forty-five or so officers from the men of the 500-strong 2nd INA Regiment and saw to their disarmament:

> Assisting me was Subedar Makar Singh Gurung and at one point he
> stiffened like a Pointer. The object of his scrutiny was a very nervous
> Sikh, their armourer Lieutenant who turned out to be the 2/2 GR's ex-
> Armourer Havildar who did not relish renewing regimental
> acquaintances! . . . In their ranks were some two dozen Gurkhas. With
> the exception of one ex-3/2 and another ex-1/10 GR, they were all of
> Burma domiciled stock and had been impressed locally.[120]

Not surprisingly, the Indian Army proper saw the INA simply as traitors and had to be restrained from taking justice into their own hands. As Slim put it, 'Our Indian and Gurkha troops were at times not too ready to let them surrender and orders had to be issued to give them a kinder welcome.'[121] Military and political views of how they should be treated were sharply at odds and while the war continued the matter was shelved; they were returned to India as prisoners of war and their existence, insofar as possible, kept secret from the public.

The military view was that anything short of the most condign punishment would be an insult, not just to those Indian and Gurkha prisoners of war who had remained true to their salt despite the sufferings they had been forced to undergo, often at the hands of these same INA volunteers, but to the overwhelming majority of the Indian Army whose loyalty had never been in question and whose task had been complicated by the presence of a fifth column in the enemy ranks.

The political view was, inevitably, more expedient. Philip Mason, the Indian civil servant on whose plate this particular hot potato landed, expresses the dilemma:

> All were guilty of an offence legally punishable with death but, of course, there could be no question of executing 25,000 men. It would have been cruel, impolitic and unjust. On the other hand, the offences of mutiny and desertion could not be condoned – and this in the interest not so much of abstract justice as in the future of the Indian Army. To the new India, that Army would be a valuable possession if it preserved its discipline; without it, a serious danger.[122]

So what was to be done? The first step was to grade offenders according to the seriousness of their crimes. Those who had joined the INA with the intention of deserting were classified 'white' and reinstated in the service. Those who had been misled by Japanese propaganda into believing that the British were defeated and joined simply in order to get home again were classified 'grey' and dismissed. The 'greys' constituted the vast majority – 70 to 80 per cent – of the prisoners. The third category 'black', was reserved for those who had actively supported the Japanese war aims and they should be brought to trial:

> . . . . they were those who had been well aware of what they were

doing and among them the Blackest were those . . . who had tortured, flogged or killed their comrades, either to make them join the INA or, after they joined, to punish them for attempted desertion. For a few of the Blackest, the law should take its course; for the other Blacks, the death penalty would be commuted to imprisonment of varying lengths, in most cases short . . . [123]

Mason maintains that the policy was right, but 'the public handling – as it turned out – was seriously wrong'.[124] A wave of post-war nationalistic feeling led to the INA being acclaimed as heroes, fighting for the freedom of India, rather than turncoats saving their own skins at the cost of their comrades'. Had Bose still been alive, perhaps Nehru and the other Congress leaders would have had to stand up against this feeling (which they secretly abhorred), but for political reasons they publicly aligned themselves with those who had 'fought for the motherland'. Gandhi attempted, in one historian's words, 'to capitalize upon the INA's popularity without associating Congress with its actions' by maintaining that 'whilst it is right and proper for the Congress to defend the members of that body, now undergoing trial, and also to aid its sufferers, the Congressmen must not forget that this support and sympathy do not mean that the Congress has in any way deviated from its policy of attaining independence by peaceful and legitimate means'.[125]

As a result of public pressure, and with independence looming, the punishment for waging war against the king-emperor was downgraded to dismissal, and 'only those who had committed acts of brutality would be liable on conviction to death or imprisonment'.[126] Officers of the Indian Army were both outraged and alienated by this decision. Francis Tuker, promoted to Lieutenant-General and now GOC-in-C, Eastern Command, accuses GHQ in Delhi of offering 'homiletics and suppliant posteriors seductive to the foot of insolence'.[127] But Auchinleck, with the ultimate responsibility as Commander-in-Chief of the Indian Army, was unmoved by the howls of outrage from his senior subordinates. He wrote:

I do not think any senior British officer today knows what is the real feeling among the Indian ranks regarding the INA. I myself believe, from my own instinct largely, but also from the information I have had

from various sources, that there is a growing feeling of sympathy for
the INA and an increasing tendency to disregard the brutalities
committed by some of its members as well as the forswearing by all of
them of their original allegiance. It is impossible to apply our standards
of ethics to this problem or to shape our policy as we would had the
INA been men of our own race.[128]

Auchinleck emerges as the hero of this particular fracas, rising above
factionalism and accusations of weakness and defeatism to reveal statesmanlike qualities of the highest order. But he did make a tactical error
in choosing as the venue for the INA trials the former seat of the Mogul
emperors, the Red Fort in Delhi, a place of enormous and negative
symbolic significance. Luck, too, was not with him in that the first
defendant, an officer who had behaved with great brutality, hanging up
two deserters by their arms and having them flogged so hard that one
died, had his case postponed on a technicality, while the next three – by
chance a Muslim, a Sikh and a Hindu, thus representing the three main
religious communities of the subcontinent – were committed individuals whose actions followed naturally from their initial change of
allegiance. P. K. Sahgal, whom the British Gurkha officers involved in
his arrest had found so congenial, was one of them.

The trials unleashed such powerful emotions that, after reducing the
sentences of Sahgal and his fellow officers from transportation for life to
dismissal from the service in February 1946, Auchinleck put a stop to all
further proceedings in April. Nehru welcomed his decision and on 4
May wrote him a brief letter of thanks, prompting Auchinleck's biographer to put the question, 'who was the greater man in statesmanship or
moral integrity – the writer of this letter or its recipient?'[129] The truth is
that, however much they might differ in other respects, Auchinleck
and Nehru were at one in their desire to guide the Indian Army through
this difficult period of transition with the minimum of disruption. The
Indian Army ethos prevailed over that of the INA, though this might
not have happened so easily had Subhas Chandra Bose still been alive.

Throughout the war the spirit of revolt was alive in India and, though it
did not greatly affect Indian Army Gurkhas (except for the handful
who joined the INA for the 'wrong' reasons and were subsequently

dishonourably discharged), a battalion of the Nepalese Contingent stationed in the North West Frontier Province at Kohat mutinied when its increased ration allowance was used to purchase milk rather than handed over as cash. General Bahadur Shamsher wrote to his father, the maharajah, on 6 January 1941, describing the outbreak as 'unprecedented in our military history'.[130] He was worried about returning these troops to Nepal in case they should spread disaffection there, but since there was no alternative the whole battalion was disarmed and sent home, where twenty-two men were tried. One was hanged and the remainder sentenced to varying lengths of imprisonment ranging from six years to life. Tuker comments: 'Much of the trouble had been due to the incompetence and ineffectiveness of the illegitimate Ranas, their officers.'[131]

But the cliché about there being no bad troops, only bad officers, may have been less applicable than usual in this case. Nepal could hardly remain untouched by the groundswell of revolution abroad in India and indeed the anti-Rana movement had been gaining strength in Kathmandu. An organization founded in the second half of the thirties, the *Nepal Praja Parishad* (Nepal People's Congress), distributed leaflets denouncing the Ranas and accusing the prime minister of misappropriating land and public funds for the benefit of his huge and ever-increasing – legitimate and illegitimate – family. In October 1940 Nepal had its own version of the Gunpowder Plot aimed at the assassination of the leading Ranas. This was as unsuccessful as the original one had been and led to the arrest of forty or fifty members of the Nepal People's Congress who, if they were not themselves responsible, were allied to a group known as *Raktapat Mandal* (the Bloodshed Group) which was behind it.[132]

The fact that King Tribhuvan himself was deeply implicated in the plot added to the alarm of the Ranas, who knew of his frustration but hardly expected him to resort to assassination to get rid of them – especially in view of the generations of intermarriage between Shahs and Ranas, which had effectively bound them into a single family. Judha Shamsher now faced a dilemma: if he publicized the king's involvement and punished him with exile, he risked increasing his own unpopularity to a dangerous extent while providing a focal point for discontent; but to do nothing was tantamount to proclaiming his own vulnerability.

He would have liked to have deposed the king in favour of the crown prince, Mahendra, but the prince would not countenance that. So he had no alternative but to exonerate the king publicly, while in private he tried to woo him away from dangerous alliances and back into the Rana sphere of influence. At the same time he vented his fury on the smaller fry, the imprisoned members of the Nepal People's Congress, who were mostly Newars.

The British minister, Lt-Col. Geoffrey Betham, sought to dissuade the maharajah from inflicting the death penalty on these prisoners (capital punishment for all crimes except treason and certain military offences had been abolished by Judha's predecessor) and from subjecting those he could not put to death – i.e. Brahmans – to 'degradation of a bestial nature'. He wrote, 'I told him that the world of the Twentieth Century simply would not stand for it'.[133] (A quaint notion given that, as an official commented in the margin of Betham's report, 'It is standing for German atrocities!') But the maharajah was unmoved, as Betham, who was in Calcutta at the time, learned from one of his embassy officials in Kathmandu:

On Sunday evening I received a letter from Mr Arnold telling me that one corpse was dangling from a tree near the Customs shed and another on the road to Pashupati; with placards round their necks. Two more of these wretches are being hanged this week . . . The two Brahmins . . . are, according to Arnold's story, to be treated in the most abominable way. They are to be paraded through the streets of Katmandu, Patan and Bhatgaon on donkeys with sucking pigs tied round their necks. At selected places sweepers are to force some foul sort of food into their mouths, thereby depriving them of caste. Of course it is quite obvious that men who are to be treated like this and have then to face imprisonment for the rest of their lives will not eat and will bring their lives to an end as soon as possible.[134]

The maharajah would have done better to have heeded Betham's warnings. In behaving in such a brutal and autocratic fashion he merely intensified popular opposition and gave the anti-Rana movement its first martyrs. Three days later a poster appeared on the tree where the first man had been hanged, promising revenge, and on the following night four men drove up to a statue of the maharajah and draped a sari over it, smearing it with blood in what Betham delicately described as 'a certain place'. These two incidents, according to the British minister, 'have infuriated His Highness but also appear to a certain extent to have broken his heart as it were for he has said that if the people do not realise he is doing his best for them he might as well leave the valley'.[135]

The chastened maharajah now tried to win popular sympathy with a crudely theatrical gesture. A condemned man was taken to a tree on the parade ground, the Tundi Khel; his hands were tied behind his back and preparations made to hang him. At the critical moment, Judha appeared in his car as if by chance and, hearing the condemned man's cries for mercy, magnanimously pardoned him – but to little avail:

> The ruse has been seen through by all in the Nepal Valley and has caused amusement tempered with contempt. Puranman, the condemned man, has also forfeited the respect of the people whereas those who have been executed are considered martyrs.
> On a tree the body of a goat has been hanged with a placard on it similar to those placed on the bodies of the men who were hanged except that it reads as follows:–
> 'This is the punishment for grazing on other people's crops'.
> His Highness . . . has doubled the guard round his residence.[136]

A goat was symbolically apt, since Judha had a reputation as 'a naughty old man' with a hundred or more illegitimate children scattered all over the country. 'It has been and still is, as far as I am aware,' the British minister reported, 'his practice to pick up any damsel that takes his wayward fancy and then to return her, with a few rupees clutched in her hand, to her parents or her husband. Naturally, this kind of behaviour does not earn him the respect or affection of the masses in Nepal.'[137]

Even a commentator as sympathetic to the Ranas as General Sir Francis Tuker calls Judha 'a despot . . . quick-tempered and liable to say and do unwise things in a fit of rage'. Tuker sees him as the last Rana prime minister to exert absolute power, 'living as he did in the past and but vaguely perceiving the future'. 'He insisted that there were rulers and ruled, and that the division between the two was clearly cut.'[138]

Britain's anxiety was, as ever, focused on the possible effects of the

anti-Rana movement on serving Gurkha soldiers. As a secret government minute noted:

> A disturbing feature of the recent unrest is the plan to spread
> disaffection among the Gurkhas in the Indian Army and among the
> Nepalese contingent in India. It will be remembered that serious
> indiscipline occurred recently in one of the Battalions of the Nepalese
> Contingent.[139]*

On the crucial issue of recruitment, however, the British minister
was reassuring. He telegraphed to Whitehall:

> Movement was primarily Newar movement and confined practically
> entirely to the valley. Areas from which Gurkha recruits are drawn
> unaffected and uninterested in the movement.
>   Recruitment of Gurkhas dies automatically in hot summer months. I
> anticipate no, repeat no, dearth of [recruits] between October and
> March.[142]

In an interview with the maharajah on 24 March 1941, Betham discovered how proud Judha was that he had been able to supply 20,000
recruits in just six months without, as he put it, 'any unpleasant incident
occurring during the process of recruitment'. Both the maharajah and

---

*By the end of July 1941, Betham was reporting to the government of India that a
'second phase' of the anti-Rana movement was under way, involving not just
Newars, who had very little money, but rich illegitimate Ranas, who were out of the
running for power, and wealthy Thakurs and Chauntrias whose alignment was with
the royal family, which was once again the pivot of revolt.[140] The government of
India began to play a more active role in its suppression and in 1943 it sent a couple
of Criminal Investigation Department (CID) officers with extensive knowledge of
contacts between Nepalese conspirators and co-conspirators and sympathizers in
India to liaise with Nepalese high officials:

> The great thing about this visit was that confidence was established and it
> looks, by the end of the year, that much has been ascertained and done to
> sift out several skeins of evidence and of contacts in this conspiracy which is
> aimed at the Maharaja and against the constituted Government of Nepal.[141]

the British minister refrained from mentioning the anti-Rana plot and the disaffection of the 2nd Rifles of the Nepalese Contingent, though these things were clearly uppermost in their minds.[143] The level of recruitment, as Betham had predicted in his telegram, was maintained the following year and the target for 1942–3 was 26,000. As the Secretary of State for India, Leopold Amery, was informed:

> The Maharaja has again agreed to co-operate fully and has passed on orders to the Governors of his Provinces and the heads of his Districts to co-operate with the Extra Assistant Recruiting Officers who have been sent into the Districts for Gurkha recruits by the Recruiting Officer for Gurkhas at Gorakhpur. The only stipulation which His Highness has made is that demands should not be made, as far as possible, on 'only' sons, nor should anyone be forced into recruitment against his will.[144]

Just as in the First World War, the political pressure brought to bear on the hill peasantry of Nepal to provide fodder for the voracious war machine prompts the question, when is a volunteer not a volunteer? The anthropologist studying *lahores* in the Kota district (its Gurung, not its Nepali name) – which provided so many 6th Gurkha recruits that 1/6 GR was known locally as 'our battalion' – describes the effect of this pressure at ground level:

> The apparatus of the state, usually fairly remote to Kota residents, came into play in very local ways during the world wars. The *mukhyas* (headmen) of the nine hamlets that comprise Kota were instructed to produce a certain number of men in each recruiting season. This placed them in a difficult position, for most people did not want their sons to become *lahores*. It was thus those who were in debt, or in a position of dependency on the *mukhyas* who were called upon to give up their sons.[145]

It had been easier in the First World War in one respect: slavery had not been abolished then and all the *mukhyas* had slaves they could order to go. During the Second World War the British employed retired soldiers – the Extra Assistant Recruiting Officers referred to above – to gather recruits, and that brought still more pressure to bear: 'Only one Kota man, as far as I know, accepted this service. He was a *Sorajat* Gurung [as opposed to the supposedly superior *Charjat* Gurungs] who had settled in India after his retirement, and returned to recruit during the war. He was not well received, even by his own lineage, and was soon compelled to leave, taking with him only a few recruits.'[146]

The oldest Kota residents recalled both world wars as 'times of great hardship and heartache', when teenage boys would 'disappear in the night, some never to be seen again'. The Ranas, rather than the British, were blamed for the heavy wartime recruitment: 'As one old woman – a World War II widow – said, "Before they took our food, but during that war they grabbed our people too. The government became very greedy."'[147] Second World War veterans themselves recalled that all their mothers, without exception, had tried to prevent their enlistment, hiding them from the recruiters and pleading with them not to go.[148] But the combined force of the British and the Ranas proved irresistible and more than 114,000 Gurkhas were recruited during the war years.[149] These were not all from the recognized martial classes (for whom the official recruiting figure is 104,951[150]): in one eastern regiment, for example, in addition to Limbus, Rais, Sunwars and eastern Magars and Gurungs, 'Tamangs, Sherpas, Bhutias, Lepchas, Newars and Bhujels were also welcomed and proved excellent soldiers'.[151]

At the end of the war there was an exchange of letters between the maharajah, Judha Shamsher, and the Commander-in-Chief of the Indian Army, General Sir Claude Auchinleck, in which Judha – after expressing his pride and pleasure in the fact that nearly half the VCs awarded to the Indian Army in the war had gone to Gurkhas – wrote:

> The information that during the 1945–46 recruiting season Your
> Excellency would not require more than 5,000 recruits to maintain the
> Gurkha units has been noted. Every effort will of course be made to
> make that number available when the time for that comes. Heavily
> recruited as the country has been during the last five years I am afraid
> the quality of the recruits that would then be available would be rather
> poorer. In our army too we are feeling the pinch and recourse has had
> to be taken to fill up vacancies with recruits of lower standard and that
> too with much difficulty.[152]

Auchinleck replied that he was able to reduce his demand to 2,000 recruits and still maintain the Gurkha Rifle regiments at full strength:

> In your letter of 11th March 1945 you stated that your country's wealth lies mainly in her manpower, and it is therefore a matter of very considerable satisfaction to me that I am able to do something towards conserving the vital resources of a staunch and noble ally who has given so unstintingly in the past.[153]

Judha Shamsher, who for some years had wanted to hand over power but had been prevented, first, by the wishes of his family and then by the demands of the war, was now set on retirement. He wrote to Auchinleck asking him to expedite the release of the Nepalese Contingent, as he wished to see his troops back at home before he relinquished office. He also distributed largesse to Gurkha (Rs 50,000), Indian (Rs 25,000) and British (Rs 50,000) prisoners of war through Auchinleck and the Viceroy, Lord Wavell, who wrote: 'I have asked my External Affairs Department to consider what should be done to mark the Maharaja's retirement. Possibly an autograph letter from the King would be suitable. The Maharaja is a strong character who has helped us greatly during the war and I am sorry that he is going . . . His successor is rather an unknown quantity at present.'[154] This was the same maharajah whom, ten years before, the then British envoy had described as having 'little real force of character or intellect'.[155] Judha retired in November 1945 and was succeeded by his nephew, Padma Shamsher, Bhim Shamsher's son, a relatively poor and well-intentioned liberal who was overshadowed by his cousins, the wealthy sons of Bhim's illustrious elder brother, Chandra Shamsher.

But the days of the Ranas, as of their ally the Raj, were numbered. Even the Gurkhas, who had been loyal to both for a hundred years, were growing restless. The end of the Second World War, a chronicler of the Rana dynasty writes, 'brought neither political stability nor tangible rewards to Nepal. Rather, the *darbar* was faced with the problem of reintegrating some 200,000 war veterans [66,206 up to 1 June 1947, in fact] whom the British had demobilised quickly and with minimal financial assistance, many of whom had been exposed to the insidious subversive influences of the Indian nationalist movement.'[156] (The

actual figure the British paid out to released wartime soldiers was over
£3 million, at an average of just under £48 a head.[157]) The maharajah,
however, reaped the benefit of the regime's constant support of Britain
through two world wars when, in 1947, the British government of India
finally capitalized the annuity it had agreed to pay the government of
Nepal 'in perpetuity' with a gift of £1,750,000.[158]

So Padma, when he followed his uncle Judha into retirement a year
later, left office a considerably richer man than he had entered it –
thanks to the exertions of those hillmen whose welfare had been so con-
spicuously neglected by the dynasty he represented.

8

Partition

By 1947, Gurkhas had served as irregular or regular soldiers in the British Indian Army for 132 years. The original four battalions, recruited from deserters and prisoners taken during the Anglo-Nepal war in 1815, with many Garhwalis and Kumaonis among them, had expanded fivefold in peacetime and more than tenfold in the recent war. The Gurkha Brigade was a *corps d'élite* within the Indian Army, with a fighting record second to none: Gurkhas had won no less than ten of the twenty-six Victoria Crosses awarded to other ranks of the Indian Army during the Second World War, though Gurkha battalions comprised only about a fifth of the total number of Indian Army infantry units.[1] Their fame had spread so far that Lt-Gen. Sir Geoffry Scoones, an ex-2nd Goorkha officer, currently Principal Staff Officer at the India Office in London, could report to the Commander-in-Chief in India, Field Marshal Sir Claude Auchinleck, that 'I have heard them . . . mentioned on the London stage and people, like the porter at my flat, have asked me what is to become of them.'[2]

In the context of the huge drama of Indian independence, however, the fate of the Gurkha Brigade is very much a 'play within the play'. The division of ten regiments between the British and Indian armies scarcely merits comparison with the partition of the subcontinent between India and Pakistan – with its subsequent saga of migration, murder and mayhem in the Punjab and elsewhere. The year 1947 witnessed so many upheavals in India that the travails of the Gurkha Brigade attract little more than a footnote, if that, in most accounts of that time; but they marked the nadir of British–Gurkha relations, with both sides put under an intolerable strain. The mutual trust built up over generations, which most officers regarded as the bedrock of this unique relationship, was undermined to the extent that in two of the battalions destined for the British Army there was something akin to a mutiny. For many of the British officers and Gurkha soldiers involved, it was such a traumatic experience that more than thirty-five years later an officer of that era could write to one of his successors, who was enquiring into the origin of the British Brigade of Gurkhas, that the subject was *obviously* (his word) still a touchy one and must be treated as such; he wouldn't want to 're-open old wounds'.[3]

As early as April 1945, Auchinleck had produced a paper for the viceroy, Lord Wavell, in which he enthusiastically endorsed the idea of Britain employing Gurkhas for its Far Eastern garrisons.[4] Five months later, he wrote to the Chief of the Imperial General Staff, Alan Brooke, that since Gurkhas might not be required in the post-war Indian Army and, even if they were, the number of battalions would have to be 'drastically reduced', the British government should 'include as many as possible of the pre-war Gurkha rifle battalions in its strategic reserve' – all twenty perhaps, if they could be used in the Middle East as well as the Far East. He stressed how urgent a matter the reorganization of the Indian armed forces had become.[5] In a follow-up letter to the Vice-Chief of the Imperial General Staff, Lt-Gen. Sir Archibald Nye, Auchinleck added that any offer to take over the Gurkhas must not be regarded as a temporary arrangement, but 'a reasonably permanent commitment'.[6]

As C-in-C of the Indian Army at a time of transition, Auchinleck was obliged to serve two masters, Britain and a future government of India, with very different agendas. He is generally regarded by British and Indians alike as an honourable and incorruptible man, and his record at this critical juncture – his devoted attempt to hold the Indian Army together when the country was falling apart and his statesmanlike restraint in the treatment of INA prisoners – speaks for itself. His impartiality is vouched for by the fact that both Hindus and Muslims accused him of favouring the other side during Partition. Yet his concern for the Gurkhas (as a young subaltern in the Indian Army he almost joined the 1/5th Royal Gurkha Rifles) and for Britain's staunchest wartime ally, Nepal, as well as his strategic thinking about Britain's post-war commitments, may have led him momentarily to overlook India's vital interests. At least, this seems to have been the view of Gen. Sir Mosley Mayne at the India Office in Whitehall, who wrote to Sir Archibald Nye on Boxing Day 1945:

> I feel that before HMG attempts to snap up all the available Gurkha troops, the Indian Government 'of tomorrow' should be given an opportunity of lodging a demand for, at any rate, some of them. From the political aspect – friendly co-operation and interdependence between India and Nepal – and from the point of view of the fighting efficiency of the Indian Defence Services, I feel that it would be a pity if Gurkhas were entirely excluded from the Indian Army; and until very recently Auchinleck thought so too.[7]

Auchinleck may have been influenced by some of his senior generals, the most intransigent of whom was Lt-Gen. Sir Francis Tuker, the GOC-in-C, Eastern Command. While Tuker accepted that the Indian Army, 'to as great an extent as was feasible', had to be 'Indianised', he had no doubt whatever that Britain should take all twenty regular battalions of the Gurkha Brigade – 'for its whole outlook was British and it was at that time bound to the British Crown rather than to any Indian Government of the past, present or future'.[8] This bald assertion ignores the fact that the entire Indian Army, not just the Gurkha Brigade, was at that time 'bound to the British Crown'; that would not prevent it being 'Indianised'.

If the War Office agreed to take some, but not all, of the Gurkha battalions, Tuker's idea was that the rest should be either disbanded or included in 'some form of impartial central army' designed to keep the peace between the armies of the nascent dominions of India and Pakistan. With his Gurkha background, Tuker was less disturbed at the prospect of the break-up of the old Indian Army than Auchinleck, whose own old regiment, the 1st Punjabis, was half Muslim, a quarter

Sikh and a quarter Rajput; and he was an early advocate of splitting it
along communal lines to reflect the evolving and, as he clearly saw,
inevitable political outcome.

Tuker was more far-sighted than his chief over this. The murderous
communal riots of February 1946 in Calcutta, which he had the responsibility of suppressing, convinced him – if he needed convincing – not
just that the subcontinent would be partitioned, but that 'the two States
of India would be at each other's throats before many moons had gone'.[9]
Communalism was the reality, as he saw it; everything else, including
the urge for self-government, was 'froth on the waves'. Even in a united
India, he argued, 'if the Army were to survive then it would only survive
if it were regrouped into its communal classes'.[10] The irony is that
Tuker's scheme was eventually adopted by Auchinleck; but by then it
was far too late, the genie of communal hatred was well and truly out of
the bottle and stalked the land, wreaking havoc beyond the power of
any army to prevent.

Both Auchinleck and Tuker went to Kathmandu before India was
granted its independence, Auchinleck at the invitation of the Nepalese
durbar towards the end of 1945 and Tuker on a private visit a year and
a half later. Auchinleck reported to Wavell that Judha (in his last days as
maharajah) was willing to allow the continued recruitment of Gurkhas
into the Indian Army, should the future government wish to retain
Gurkha units, and that he was even prepared to accept that they be officered by Indians, though 'he obviously did not relish the prospect'.
When Auchinleck raised the possibility of Gurkhas being employed
directly by the British government as part of an imperial strategic
reserve in the Far East and elsewhere, both the maharajah and his son,
Gen. Bahadur Shamsher, who was acting as his interpreter, brightened
visibly:

> Of the two alternatives . . . there is no doubt whatever that they would
> prefer the latter, and they impressed this on me several times before
> the conclusion of the interview.[11]

By the time Tuker reached Kathmandu at the end of April 1947, it
was no longer a question of alternatives: Judha's successor, Padma
Shamsher, accepted that Gurkhas would be serving in the future Indian

Army, and probably in the British Army too; a negotiating team, consisting of an official War Office mission and Indian government representatives, was about to arrive in Nepal to settle the issue.

In discussing the possibility of employing Gurkhas in the British Army with the Chief of the Imperial General Staff, Lord Alanbrooke (as Brooke had become), Auchinleck referred to their potential as 'a sort of Foreign Legion under HMG'. From the beginning, their appeal was twofold: they could be substituted for British troops, who were in short supply, in overseas garrisons; and they were less costly. In a war-bankrupted Britain which had by no means renounced all imperial aspirations, these were vital considerations and Alanbrooke, though he could not commit himself, 'was clearly attracted by the possibilities', as Auchinleck reported to Wavell.[12]

The War Office drew up a plan to create a British Gurkha division, which would entail 'converting a number of Gurkha infantry battalions into Artillery and Engineer units and units of those other arms and services normally included in a division'.[13] This idea did not meet with universal approval; Slim, for example, wrote to his wartime chief, Auchinleck:

> . . . the Gurkha is an almost ideal infantryman and has shown himself
> to be so. While no doubt he could be trained in time to be a useful
> member of any arm of the Service, he will never be as good a gunner,
> signaller, tank man etc., as he is infantryman. It seems to me therefore
> to be unwise to destroy an outstanding infantryman in order to make a
> moderate gunner or what have you.[14]

By the end of May 1946, the Treasury had sanctioned the permanent employment of eight battalions of Gurkhas and the War Office was contemplating the possibility of asking for several more, perhaps all of the pre-war battalions – though it was reluctant to enter into a long-term engagement: 'Unless it is absolutely essential in the negotiations with Nepal we would prefer not to put a definite term of years to our bid.'[15]

But as soon as the War Office had confirmed its bid for eight battalions the India Office put everything on hold. The difficulty, as Wavell and Auchinleck agreed, was that negotiations with Nepal could not go ahead without reference to the interim government of India, and that had not yet been formed. So Wavell requested at least a month's grace.[16] And once the principle that the future government of India should be an equal partner in negotiations was conceded, the possibility of a speedy resolution of the fate of the Gurkha battalions – so urgent from the point of view of the troops and their officers – vanished.

Yet the War Office and India Office were going ahead with plans for a British Gurkha division as though agreement had already been reached. The focus was now on which regiments or battalions should go to which army. This was a highly emotive subject. Although they had an overall loyalty to the Gurkha Brigade, officers identified passionately with their own regiments and each one of the ten was considered non-pareil by its devotees. It was now filtering through to them that the Gurkha Brigade would be split up and some of the regiments handed over to India – a prospect which did not appeal to them or, initially at least, to the men.

Senior officers with experience of Gurkhas were anxious, as Lt-Gen. Sir Geoffry Scoones put it in a letter to Auchinleck, 'to avoid any accusation of picking and choosing individual regiments'.[17] Among various schemes for allocating the Gurkha regiments to Britain and India, Scoones suggested that either the first five went to Britain and the second five to India (or the other way round), or odd numbers to Britain and even numbers to India (or vice versa). He personally favoured the second option, with the even numbers going to Britain; that way, both countries would have a Limbu-Rai regiment and India would get the 9th, whose 'caste customs . . . make them more difficult to deal with overseas'.[18] His impartiality would have been more evident, however, if his own regimental service had not been with 2 GR, one of the units destined for British service according to this scheme.

Other possible scenarios included one in which the 1st battalion of each regiment should go to Britain and the 2nd battalion to India; though this might seem the most equitable, it would have created more problems than it solved – in particular with regard to regimental centres: to whom would they belong? Then there was the argument that, far from excluding 9 GR on account of possible caste prejudices, the higher level of intelligence to be found in that regiment would make it an obvious candidate for conversion from infantry into another arm, as required by a British Gurkha division.

At the beginning of 1947 the War Office was in favour of asking for six regiments (each of two battalions), which should include either the 7th or 10th, and possibly the 2nd – in view of its application for affiliation with the 60th Rifles, the King's Royal Rifle Corps, which it had fought alongside during the famous siege of Delhi in 1857 – and 9 GR, for its potential for conversion to artillery or engineers. The fact that the Treasury had so far authorized the retention or transfer to British service of no more than four regiments seems to have been overlooked.

All this speculation threatened to become academic when the new secretary of state for war, F. J. Bellenger, wrote to Pethick-Lawrence at the India Office saying that the army vote was hardly enough to provide for the British troops needed for defence and internal security, let alone Gurkhas, and – an argument which would be heard with ever-increasing frequency over the years ahead – 'the cost of Gurkhas could not be justified at the expense of cutting down the number of British units below what is considered essential'.[19] The whole question of 'whether it is desirable to include a Gurkha element within the Post War Army' was being raised again; apart from budgetary considerations, this may have had something to do with the fact that the anti-Indian Army Montgomery had recently taken over from Alanbrooke as Chief of the Imperial General Staff.

Despite this setback, discussions went ahead; a War Office delegation, headed by Maj-Gen. L. O. Lyne, was to arrive in Delhi on 24 March.[20] Negotiations would be conducted by Sir Terence Shone, Britain's first High Commissioner in India, with the aim of transferring four Gurkha regiments to the British Army, but for a limited period of five years only. The choice of particular regiments was 'relatively unimportant', but it was 'essential . . . to allow HMG full use of all the available recruiting potential of Nepal' – in other words, 9 GR and either 7 or 10 GR should be included along with two of the other seven regiments, of which 'it would be desirable' that 2 GR be one.[21]

The uncertain future offered to any regiment taken over by the British Army would make the negotiators' task a difficult one. But a week before the War Office delegation was due to arrive in Delhi, the fate of the Gurkhas was discussed at a meeting of the Defence

Committee at the Cabinet Office in London, at which both the prime minister, Clement Attlee, and the Viceroy designate, Lord Louis Mountbatten, were present. Attlee expressed his surprise that the matter had not been raised at an earlier meeting, since it had 'considerable manpower implications'. In view of the shortage of manpower in the UK, he felt that 'there was a strong case for the inclusion of a substantial number of Gurkhas in the Armed Forces'. He was supported by the minister of defence, A. V. Alexander, who mentioned the figure 25,000 as the optimum number of Gurkhas to be employed in the British Army. The secretary of state for war found himself on the defensive. He objected that 'unless they could be used in any part of the world, their employment would not be economical'.[22]

Was Bellenger stating his own view here, or parroting Montgomery's? Gurkhas would certainly be economical: a draft paper prepared for the executive committee of the Army Council at about this time gives the annual maintenance cost of a Gurkha battalion as £150,000, compared with £240,000 for a British infantry battalion in Malaya, a huge difference even allowing for a likely increase in Gurkha pay and allowances and the overheads involved in the construction of depots and training establishments for Gurkhas in Malaya and India/Nepal.[23] And why should Gurkhas not be used in any part of the world, when they had been fighting in Europe, North Africa, the Middle East and all over the Far East in the recent war?

Neither Attlee nor Mountbatten – who, as Commander-in-Chief in Burma, had seen them in action – had any doubts. The Defence Committee resolved that 'the representatives of HMG should make every effort to secure agreement to the employment of up to 25,000 Gurkhas in the regular British Army' and – this was added in ink, as though it were an afterthought – 'that there should be no suggestion of a time limit to their employment' (an instruction immediately relayed to the War Office delegation in Delhi).[24]

If Attlee's intervention cleared the way for the War Office delegation to take a more positive line in negotiations, its experiences in Delhi were having the same effect. 'You will remember that in our preliminary meetings at the War Office we all had grave doubts as to whether a British/Gurkha Division was on for various reasons,' Maj-Gen. Lyne wrote to his deputy, Brig. G. M. Tuck. 'I am quite sure from talks I have had out here that the formation of such a division is both possible and desirable.' He was less certain about the future of the Indian government and armed forces, because of 'the cloud of emotional unreality in which all Indian politicians seem completely enveloped'. Amid the general indecisiveness the one sure thing, however, was that 'what Nehru says goes'.[25]

What Nehru said at an early meeting of the interim government with the British negotiators was that Malaya – where British Gurkha troops would be stationed – with its mixed population of Malays, Indians and Chinese (the last-named being in the majority), was becoming 'a touchy and difficult problem'; in other words, if Gurkhas were used to control civil or communal unrest and suppress freedom movements it would put him in an embarrassing situation. He also said that he understood Nepal was considering applying for membership of the United Nations and, while he was not opposed to that, he could not help wondering if its position 'as a provider of mercenaries' would not damage its international status. When Liaquat Ali Khan, the future prime minister of Pakistan, asked pointedly whether Britain's object in employing Gurkhas was to help Nepal or to fulfil its own obligations, and the War Office delegation replied that it was both, Nehru made it clear where he thought the emphasis lay – and it wasn't on altruism.[26]

Nehru asked a question which sent Gen. Lyne scurrying off to seek telegraphic advice from the War Office as soon as the meeting was over. He wanted to know whether the British Army intended to give Gurkhas commissions – not viceroy's commissions or their equivalent, which they already had, but king's commissions such as British officers held. This became a critical issue in the tripartite discussions between Britain, India and Nepal, and caused dissension in the ranks of those Gurkha units destined for the British Army.

When India announced that it was giving full commissions to Gurkhas in regiments retained in the Indian Army, British officers dismissed this as a trick, a ploy on India's part to curry favour with the Gurkhas. But that was not the whole story, if indeed it was any part of it. Since Gurkhas had been officered exclusively by the British, and Indians had been given no opportunity to get to know them or learn their language, how could they hope to retain control once all the British officers had left and they were in charge? The solution was to promote outstanding VCOs, giving them full commissions, so that they would maintain order and discipline while the Indian officers appointed to each regiment learned the language and the *kaida* (regimental customs, methods, traditions) and generally prepared themselves to assume command.

The War Office brass hats responded unenthusiastically to the idea of commissioning Gurkhas. They referred to the 'colour-bar problem' which had come up in discussions about commissions for Africans and let it be known that they would prefer things to remain as they were, with British officers commanding Gurkha troops; but they recognized that 'ultimately we may be forced to give commissions'. At a Cabinet meeting on 3 June 1947 the secretary of state for war said that 'if non-Europeans were admitted to the ranks of the British Army, they were bound to be eligible in due course for consideration for advancement to commissioned rank. British soldiers would not take kindly to service under coloured officers and discipline would be undermined.'[27] This last sentence was the nub of the argument against granting full commissions to Gurkhas.

For the moment Lyne was advised to 'hedge on this issue'.[28] Other contentious matters included Muslim objections to the employment of Gurkhas in a future *Indian* Army, but these were overruled by a majority vote in Cabinet; and the venue for tripartite talks, since both Nehru and the maharajah of Nepal were determined to 'play only on their home wicket'.[29] The maharajah triumphed here, and the British and Indian negotiating teams traipsed off from Delhi to Kathmandu – at that time a three- or four-day journey into the mountains by air, rail, road and mule-track.

The late Maj-Gen. Rudra, then a brigadier and staff officer at GHQ Delhi, was ordered to accompany the senior civil servant from the Indian Foreign Ministry, Sir Girija Shankar Bajpai, to Kathmandu as the Indian Army observer, but he was expressly forbidden – as he remembered it – to offer any opinion or to exceed his brief as an observer in any way. This made him suspicious, especially as senior Indian officers had not been taken into the confidence of their British colleagues over the future of the Gurkhas, and 'some of us suspected them of trying to take the whole Gurkha force to the British Army'.[30] So he arranged a last-minute interview with Sardar Baldev Singh, the defence member of the interim government, and obtained his authority to participate fully in the negotiations.

In his memoirs, 'Jik' Rudra describes how he and Sir Girija were welcomed in Kathmandu by the British minister, Sir George Falconer, but excluded from consultations with the War Office delegation which had come up with them. He recalls the transparent tactics of the British with amusement:

> For the next two days . . . Lady Faulkner [sic] played her part
> extremely charmingly taking us for endless walks round her flower
> garden, shrubbery and herbarium, feeding us with seemingly endless
> information on her roses, daffodils, tulips, chamomiles and pots of
> basil – whatever.[31]

Every time the two Indians tried to escape from the embassy, some bright spark of an attaché would jump into the car beside them, offering his services as guide. Finally, they hit upon a successful ruse for eluding their chaperons. They announced their intention of worshipping at the Hindu shrine of Pashupatinath, which was closed to the British, and thus were able to make unmediated contact with Nepalese society.

The formal meeting with the maharajah was a success from the Indian point of view. According to Rudra, when the maharajah asked whether the British would accord equal rights to Gurkhas in the matter of commissions, Lyne 'could only prevaricate . . . he was unable (unauthorised, presumably) to allay Nepali suspicions about racial discrimination, especially in regard to promotion to officer status'.[32]

Nevertheless, the maharajah agreed to both armies continuing to employ Gurkhas, provided the troops were willing to serve and were not looked down upon as mercenaries; and provided the terms and conditions 'at the final stage do not prove detrimental to the interest or dignity of the Nepalese Government'.[33] Both the Indians and the British would claim a special understanding with the Nepali authorities, but their relationship with one another was cool. Rudra remarks that although they returned to India on the same day, 'we did not see very much of the two British members during the journey'.[34] Yet this was a man of whom his cousin, Col. 'Eno' Singha says, 'He was more British than Indian, you see, he could speak only in English, more or less, even his Urdu was faulty.'[35]

Gen. Lyne reported that he had had a satisfactory conversation with the maharajah in which the latter had told him how keen he was to maintain the 'intimate relationship with Great Britain' which had existed for 130 years:

> But it was most important for his country to ensure that it was on friendly terms with India . . . HH told Lyne *privately* that he would be prepared to agree to British plan in principle but must know Indian plan in detail. Therefore he could only ask for both plans in detail before approving either.[36]

Before he left Delhi for London on 8 May 1947, Lyne had two interviews with Nehru. Sir Girija Bajpai was present at the first of these, in the course of which Nehru said he hoped that, if the British employed Gurkhas, they would not give them a 'much higher rate of pay' than India could afford. Lyne said that the idea was to base their pay scale on India's, with an additional allowance for overseas service – always provided India did not reduce its pay. Nehru 'laughed and said that the Indian soldier got so little at the moment that it could hardly be reduced lower'.[37]

At their second meeting Lyne found Nehru 'still dubious about use of Gurkhas, at all events by HMG'. The political situation was so difficult, Nehru said, that the Cabinet would not be able to take a decision on the Gurkha question for at least a fortnight.[38] This is hardly surprising in view of the momentous changes that were afoot: by now the emergence of Pakistan was a foregone conclusion and even Auchinleck accepted that the Indian Army had to be broken up and reorganized on communal lines. The splitting of the Gurkha Brigade came a poor third after the division of the country and the army. But that was no comfort to its officers and men.

Throughout May and much of June the project hung fire, waiting for Nehru's go-ahead. Then both Mountbatten and a civil servant in the Ministry of Defence more or less simultaneously had the bright idea of suggesting to Downing Street that the Chief of the Imperial General Staff, who was about to go off on one of his whistle-stop world tours, be the means of settling the Gurkha question when he touched down at

Delhi. The prime minister agreed and arranged that Montgomery, in consultation with the Viceroy, should tackle Nehru.[39] The two men met on 23 June and the fact that Nehru himself made notes of their conversations (there being no other Indian present) is a measure of the importance he attached to these interviews.

Nehru pointed out to Montgomery how the use of Gurkha troops against Indonesians who had been intent on preventing the reestablishment of Dutch rule after the defeat of the Japanese had been deeply resented in that country, and he reiterated India's objections to 'a continuation of the old Imperialist method of holding down colonial territories'. They went around and around the question 'What were the Gurkha troops required for?' without arriving at a mutually satisfying answer. Nehru did not conceal his reluctance to accede to Montgomery's proposals 'because of a large number of implications involved', but felt he could hardly stand in the way of an agreement between Britain and Nepal:

> Therefore, taking everything into consideration, we were prepared to give them the facilities for transit, etc., asked for, subject to further consideration of details and an agreement with the Nepalese Government.[40]

Montgomery professed himself happy with this arrangement and, when Nehru stressed that it was 'beyond my power or authority to commit the future Dominion Government to any course of action', said he would rest content with Nehru's personal assurance.[41]

Because of the 'personal character' of the agreement between Nehru and Montgomery, the British High Commissioner, Sir Terence Shone, recommended that no public announcement be made by the government, and that the War Office mission due to come out and finalize the agreement should 'do its work here as quietly as possible'.[42] So interested parties were still to be kept in the dark in order to spare Nehru embarrassment from his own side.

Once the political obstacles to a British Gurkha force had been overcome, there was renewed urgency about the question of which regiments came over to Britain. Rumours abounded and even before Nehru and Monty had met, Gen. Scoones at the India Office was writing to

Auchinleck that he had had 'some rather violent appeals' about the possible disbandment of the 9th and 10th Gurkhas: 'It is clear that information has leaked out somewhere . . .'[43] Shone, as chief negotiator, certainly assumed that he was to make a bid for the 1st battalions of the first eight Gurkha regiments only.[44]

But General Neil Ritchie, who was in command of South East Asia Land Forces, wondered what would happen to 1/10 GR if Britain intended to take over the 1st battalions of the first eight regiments only. His understanding was that the three Gurkha battalions still in Burma – 1/6, 1/7 and 1/10 GR – 'should (A) be part of the eight battalions to be transferred to British service, (B) come on to Malaya as soon as task in Burma [is] finished estimated Spring 1948'.[45] In India, Auchinleck was also assuming that the three Gurkha battalions in Burma would be selected for the British Army.

The plan to take the 1st battalions of the first eight regiments had now, in fact, been jettisoned in favour of taking over four regiments of two battalions each, and the head of the War Office 'Gurkha Mission', Colonel Duncan Smith, was instructed by Whitehall to bid for 9 GR, either 7 or 10 GR and two other regiments, one of which should, if possible, be 2 GR. The full use of all the available recruiting potential of Nepal remained the 'guiding principle'.[46]

The final choice, however, was left to the mission itself, 'in consultation with GHQ, India'.[47] It was: 2, 6, 7 and 10 GR to Britain; the remainder, including the unique 9 GR and the famous 5 RGR, to India. Despite this, the Chief of General Staff in Delhi, General Sir Arthur Smith, was optimistic about the outcome: 'all here are genuinely satisfied that HMG will not have cause to regret selection'.[48]

As with so many decisions taken in the run-up to independence, administrative convenience triumphed over 'guiding principle': choosing British Gurkha regiments on the basis of which battalions were stationed in Burma (and were due to leave the now independent country) was the easy option. In retrospect, disappointed British officers came up with various conspiracy theories, such as that senior generals influenced the outcome, Tuker and possibly Scoones ensuring the choice of 2 GR, Slim that of 6 and 7 GR. But if these had any influence, it was surely minimal, and Slim, at least, would never have sought to promote some regiments over others merely because he happened to have served in them. Tuker may well have tried to use his influence on behalf of 2 GR, but Scoones had explicitly denied using his when he wrote to Auchinleck in January 1947 about the list of preferred regiments in the brief to the War Office delegation under Maj-Gen. Lyne, 'I would stress that I had nothing whatever to do with the 2nd coming into it!'[49]

Tuker expressed his anger at the effect of such a 'carefree policy' in *While Memory Serves*:

> Thus those who had served Britain longest were discarded and three of
> the newest regiments put in their places. Among the discarded
> regiments were the 1st KGO, raised in 1815; the 3rd QAO raised at the
> same time; the 4th PWO and the 5th Royal with its four VCs in the last
> war. Only one of those which GHQ selected for the War Office bore a
> royal title, the 2nd.[50]

Tuker was careful not to criticize the newer battalions; he emphasized that there was 'little to choose in quality' between any Gurkha battalion, his point being merely that the 'famous regiments allotted to India will one day have their numbers changed, later be deprived of their titles and will have then lost their identity'.[51] History does not bear out this or many other of Tuker's Cassandra-like prophecies. Whereas his beloved 2 GR has ceased to exist, being merged with the remnants of 6 GR, 7 GR and 10 GR into the single Royal Gurkha Rifles, the Indian regiments have proudly maintained both their regimental numbers and their traditions for over half a century.

But this was a time of great bitterness in the Indian Army in general, and Gurkha regiments in particular. Men and officers alike were treated badly by a government and War Office only half-heartedly committed to them. Montgomery's lack of enthusiasm for the 'private army', as he called it, which he had helped to have transferred to British service, was well known, and his attitude was reflected in War Office policy: Gurkhas were not to have their own permanent cadre of officers, but were to be commanded by officers on secondment from British regiments. This flew in the face of traditional wisdom, which asserted that the magnificent performance of Gurkha battalions in war was rooted in the mutual trust and loyalty of officers and men built up over years of service together. The Gurkha, it was said, did not readily give his loyalty; it had to be earned. This would be hard for officers on secondment, though the wartime experience of Emergency Commissioned Officers also showed that both language and customs could be picked up quickly enough by those who put their minds to it.

In August 1947, there were more immediate worries, however. British Gurkha officers were in the same position as other Indian Army officers in that they had been required to decide by 15 July whether to take redundancy terms and leave the army altogether, or to transfer to British service, or to continue serving in one of the new Dominion armies for a limited period, thereby rendering themselves ineligible for future service in the British Army. There was no option for staying on with British Gurkha regiments because at that stage there were no British Gurkha regiments. Even when agreement was reached for the transfer of four regiments, subject to ratification by the Nepalese government, the War Office continued to shilly-shally until finally, on 28 November 1947, the Director of Personnel Administration, Maj-Gen. J. E. C. McCandlish, wrote to all British Gurkha regular officers, giving them the opportunity of opting for 'continued service with Gurkhas . . . whatever their previous election'.[52]

The officers did not relish being – in Tuker's phrase – 'buggered about'.[53] Neither did the troops, who were far from happy with their terms and conditions of service, or the lack of them – since they were not published until 27 December. Gen. Sir Arthur Smith gave the War Office early warning that if the terms were not made sufficiently attractive to the Gurkhas there might well be a shortage of volunteers for British service.[54]

Another, more general warning came from 'an Instructor at Camberley', a certain Lt-Col. J. Masters, who submitted some far-seeing notes on 'The Future of the Gurkhas' in which he argued: 'Paternalism, tradition, isolationism and a fierce regimental pride have in many ways been the source of the Gurkhas' strength. But circumstances in India, the spread of education and the globe trotting which Gurkhas did in the war have altered the situation more than some people realize.' He recommended the formation of a single Gurkha Rifle Corps (GRC), with its own officer cadre, as an alternative to the invidious process of selecting and rejecting individual regiments. This corps would be made up of rifle battalions, a field regiment of artillery, a signals regiment, engineers, rather along the lines of the War Office's proposed British Gurkha division. 'Regimental and battalion pride (and parochialism) must be merged into broader loyalties,' he argued, and in order to achieve a broader base something must be done about the lack of education, which 'the Gurkha is feeling acutely'. Like Gen. Smith, Masters warned that 'the Gurkha will not serve in faraway Malaya unless he is given better pay, better barrack conditions, improved and increased family accommodation – in healthy stations where a Gurkha community can be built up'.[55]

But he went further and insisted that 'the best material' would not come into British service unless better opportunities were provided: 'These opportunities must include the chance of reaching commissioned rank and the chance of learning technical trades useful after Army service.' He wanted a few outstanding Gurkhas to be given king's commissions right away, but he thought their rights and privileges should apply only among Gurkha troops and they should live in the Gurkha officers' mess rather than the British officers' mess: 'It will be years before Gurkha and British officers can live comfortably together on a footing of complete social equality.'[56]

On Wednesday, 13 August 1947, thirty-six hours from independence, the *Statesman* reported that every VCO, NCO and rifleman in all ten Gurkha regiments was to be invited to answer a questionnaire on whether he wished to serve in the Indian Army, or to serve overseas in the British Army, or to leave the army altogether; or again, if he chose to serve in one army, whether he would have any objection to serving in the other.[57] This referendum, or 'opt', as the later version of it came to be known, was in line with the maharajah of Nepal's express desire that the Gurkhas should be consulted about their willingness to serve under the new dispensation.

At the time, probably no one reading India's leading English-language newspaper paid much attention to this brief news item. At midnight on 14/15 August Nehru made his famous 'tryst with destiny' speech and the flag of the 'Indian Union' with its spinning-wheel emblem and three colours representing its different peoples – orange for Hindus, green for Muslims and white for others – was run up flagpoles and eagerly held aloft by milling crowds of people. The celebrations of freedom were short-lived, however, since the birth of not one but two new independent nations was proving a bloody affair. The main flashpoint was in the Punjab, where the border between India and West Pakistan (drawn up by the hapless Radcliffe commission) rendered hundreds of thousands of people on either side of it homeless at a stroke – Hindus and Sikhs in West Pakistan and Muslims in India. The subsequent two-way trek of refugees resulted in a 'frightful holocaust'.[58]

The peace-keeping role had devolved on to the post-war remnant of 4th Indian Division under Maj-Gen. 'Pete' Rees (whose senior staff officer in Burma latterly had been John Masters). It was a thankless task, policing 40,000 square miles of border country in turmoil. As the historian of 4th Indian Division recorded:

> The fanaticism engendered by months of wild talk and rabble-rousing was coming to a head; terror like a pestilence began to walk abroad. In a dark or lonely lane a wayfarer would be accosted and asked his name. If 'of the other community' a knife thrust, a bludgeon stroke or a twisted scarf left a sprawled corpse as the murderers sauntered on. When the stories of such deeds spread, vengeance was sworn above the wails of the women. More and more groups went on the prowl, to slay or be slain.[59]

The Punjab Boundary Force, as Rees's division was called, came into being just weeks before the transfer of power to Nehru's government and from the start it was struggling against hopeless odds to stem the tide of violence. The understandable partiality of Indian troops raised the question of their reliability, so extra responsibility fell on the Gurkha battalions, which had to be supplemented from regimental training centres. On 10 August, for instance, a 7 GR internal security company, commanded by a Captain Wells and made up mostly of recruits, was sent to Dera Baba Nanak to guard a railway bridge over the river Ravi on the line from Amritsar in India to Sialkot in Pakistan, the only border crossing for miles. Capt. Wells recalled:

> We were needed everywhere, and guarding, patrolling, escorting,

investigating went on without stop twenty-four hours a day. There simply were not enough of us to cope with the outbreaks. They were terrible. Villages set on fire, whole families slaughtered in one room – their bodies still burning, women and children with their guts hanging out and slowly dying, heaps of dead feasted on by pi-dogs and vultures. The smell of rotting flesh filled the air.[60]

The 2/4th Gurkhas were posted to Jandiala on the Great North Road near Amritsar, a few miles from the border.

The Battalion's duty was to protect camps and convoys of refugees who were slowly making their way towards the border from Jullundur and the south. A number had bullock-carts, but the majority carried their poor possessions and often their children. The country over which they passed was left desolate as though it had been eaten up by locusts and the stench of death hung over it. Occasionally a train would crawl through, hesitatingly because it was subject to attack, and so packed with people inside and out and on the roof that not a vestige of the carriages was to be seen.[61]

Whole populations on the move, by train, by bullock-cart and on foot, were an easy prey to marauding gangs of Sikhs on one side and Muslims on the other, who materialized, did their worst and vanished at will. The army, hopelessly stretched and, in the case of mixed units, in particular, under 'intolerable strain', could do little to protect the people. At the end of August General Rees had to report to Auchinleck 'that communal tension was rising in some regiments and that he would not be able to answer indefinitely for their performance'. The Auk did not hesitate. From midnight on 1/2 September the Punjab Boundary Force ceased to exist and the armed forces of India and Pakistan took over responsibility for peace-keeping.[62]

Gradually the intensity of communal blood-letting died down and the armies of the two new states gained a measure of control. But the savagery had not entirely burnt itself out as Captain J. P. Cross, who had missed the worst of it because his regiment had been stationed in the comparative safety of the north-west frontier during most of 1947, discovered when 1/1 GR was ordered across the border into Jammu and Kashmir:

Down in Panjab . . . the grim evidence of the unbelievable turmoil, the heartlessness and the senselessness of it all, hit us hard. Myriads of men, women and children, who were of the wrong faith in the wrong country, now with homes broken, impoverished and utterly without hope, made the bewilderingly difficult journey from the Land of Penance to the Land of Promise. Millions never saw the planned end of their journey. Thousands, each morning, would refuse to get up from the side of the road. Death, that merciful releaser, would come soon enough without having the discomfort of looking for it. It was a heart-breaking task for those involved [in peace-keeping]. We passed it by on the sidelines but even so were sickened by it. We saw lorries mow down whole families and the drivers drive recklessly on. With millions dead what were a few more deaths?[63]

When they had crossed the river Ravi, the 1/1st Gurkhas faced another problem. Jammu and Kashmir, an independent princely state with a Hindu ruler and a Muslim majority, had been invaded by hordes of Pathan tribesmen, officially or unofficially backed by the Pakistani army. India swiftly retaliated, creating a situation which the Indian historian of the post-Partition 1st Gorkha Rifles characterized as 'quite extraordinary':

Both India and Pakistan were Dominions in the British Commonwealth. Both had British officers as Commanders-in-Chief of their armies: General Sir Rob Lockhart in India, and Sir Frank Messervy in Pakistan [Auchinleck having been sidelined with the grand but meaningless title of Supreme Commander – of both armies theoretically]. Many senior officers in the two armies were still British as was, indeed, the Indian Governor-General Lord Louis Mountbatten . . . It was Lord Mountbatten who as Chairman of the Defence Committee of the Indian Cabinet had given his assent to the despatch of the Indian troops to Jammu and Kashmir. Sensing that the situation might lead to British officers on two sides fighting openly [with] one another, the British government issued instructions that none of them should be allowed to enter the State. They, however, continued to control the strategic aspects of the war for both India and Pakistan.[64]

John Cross was one of the British officers ordered not to go into Jammu and Kashmir, but since he felt responsible for his company and had as yet no Indian officer to hand it over to, he 'trudged the dusty five miles [in and out of the war zone] . . . morning and evening'. When he gave orders for his troops to dig latrines, this was interpreted on Radio Pakistan as 'Indian troops digging defensive positions at Kathuwa'.[65]

Mutual genocide (by no means confined to the Punjab), followed by war between the two newly independent nations, swiftly snuffed out any joy they might have been expected to feel on achieving self-determination. At the time, most people blamed Mountbatten, the British Labour government and Nehru's Congress Party for failing to anticipate the communal strife and for colluding in bringing forward the date for the transfer of power from June 1948 to August 1947 – thereby transforming what should have been an orderly and dignified British departure into an unseemly scramble for the exit while the inheritors mercilessly butchered one another. Historians have to some extent modified this verdict, since the rundown of British authority may already have been so far advanced that Mountbatten and Co. had little option but to press ahead for fear of creating a power vacuum. 'The only alternative to a divided India was the setting up of a military government', according to General Tuker – and Britain, 'tied to the chariot wheels of democracy', would never have accepted that.[66] Nor could it possibly have sustained it, even if the political will to retain power had been there.

These tumultuous events had an immediate effect on negotiations over the future of the Gurkha Brigade. The Congress Party, in its conversion from opposition to government, no longer regarded Gurkhas as British mercenaries, fit only to be sweepers; it recognized that if it could win their loyalty as the British had done, their value as front-line soldiers in both internal and external wars would be inestimable.

Just one week after the Gurkha referendum was announced it was suspended as a result of a protest from Nehru. He insisted that the government of Nepal must first give its consent to the division of the Gurkha Brigade as agreed by India and Britain; and he argued that the questionnaire should anyway be confined to those Gurkhas serving in regiments allocated to Britain, asking only whether or not they wished to serve His Majesty's Government, since the position of Gurkhas serving in the Indian Army was unchanged.

Auchinleck appealed to Mountbatten. The new Governor-General of India (Jinnah was Governor-General of Pakistan) replied that Nehru 'categorically informed me that it was his policy that every Gurkha soldier should be given the option of volunteering for the Indian Army, volunteering for the British Army or being demobilized'.[67] But moves were being made to ensure that this did not happen. On 5 September 1947 Nehru sent Auchinleck a letter he had received – or elicited – from the maharajah of Nepal stating that in view of the agreed division of the Gurkha Brigade between India and Britain, 'the referendum as a whole is rather redundant'. The fact that the Gurkhas had served all along in the Indian Army made the question of whether they wanted to continue to serve in it superfluous.[68]

The maharajah's letter was Nehru's trump card; he claimed 'personally' to have no objection to a general referendum but did not think it quite tallied with the maharajah's views: 'I suggest, therefore, that this question should be finally settled after the Tripartite Conference.'[69] The British view was that the maharajah of Nepal had been 'got at' and the concession that it was unnecessary for the Indian Gurkha units to hold a referendum forced out of him.[70]

Whatever the rights and wrongs, the British negotiators had to accept that they had been outmanoeuvred by Nehru. No referendum of any sort could be held until after tripartite discussions had taken place in Kathmandu, and this would entail a further lengthy delay. The Commonwealth Relations Office (which had replaced the now redundant India Office) still insisted that all Gurkhas must be allowed to opt – 'to do otherwise would be a breach of faith with Gurkhas both by India and HMG'.[71] But the initiative had passed out of British hands; the newly independent Indians were now calling the shots.

The final act in the political drama went smoothly enough. The tripartite agreement was signed in Kathmandu by all three parties on 9 November 1947, and there were separate bipartite agreements between Britain and India and Britain and Nepal. Three points in the tripartite agreement are still significant:

1. In all matters of promotion, welfare and other facilities the Gurkha

troops should be treated on the same footing as the other units in the parent army so that the stigma of 'mercenary troops' may for all time be wiped out. These troops should be treated as a link between two friendly countries.

2. The Gurkha troops . . . should be eligible to commissioned ranks with no restrictions whatsoever to the highest level to which qualified officers may be promoted.

3. The Gurkha troops should not be used against Hindu or any other unarmed mobs.[72]

The British team noted that the Indian delegation appeared to be badly briefed and that they argued among themselves. The Indians tried to make out that the clauses listed above applied only to British Gurkhas, but the Nepalese C-in-C (and future maharajah), Mohan Shamsher, 'pointed out gently but firmly, that this was not the case and invited particular reference to the point that Gurkha troops should not be used against Hindu or any other unarmed mobs'.[73]

The bipartite agreement between Britain and India laid down that basic rates of pay for Gurkhas should approximate those of the current Indian Pay Code, but that an additional special allowance, 'to compensate for permanent service overseas and high cost of living', would be paid to British Gurkhas.[74] The crucial clause in the bipartite agreement between Britain and Nepal concerned the Hindu cleansing ritual of *pani patya*. It was agreed that the ceremony could be performed – at British expense – in Calcutta or in one of the recruiting depots in India, when Gurkhas came home at the end of their service.

Britain had hoped to get Nepal's agreement to the enlistment of up to 15,000 Gurkhas, but had to be content with the eight battalions allotted to them (or little more than half that number) for the time being, due to the manpower shortage resulting from the heavy recruiting throughout the war. Britain's negotiators did obtain permission to look for suitable sites for recruiting depots within Nepal itself, though they did not put this in writing because the Nepalese feared that they might be asked for similar facilities by India.[75] The long-term objective was to remove all but transit facilities from Indian soil.

At a private meeting with Britain's two senior negotiators, the maharajah stressed the importance of Gurkhas being eligible for king's commissions. He told them this was 'a long-standing grievance'; Gurkhas felt that they had had too little recognition for all they had done in two world wars: 'He knew this was a sore point among Gurkhas since he had received so many letters from them.' He realized that lack of education was a barrier to such promotion but if the Indians were granting commissions, surely one or two Gurkha Officers from each British battalion could be given king's commissions.[76] The British assured him that the matter was being seriously considered at the War Office.

When the idea of a referendum was first mooted, the British were confident of receiving the lion's share of the Gurkha vote. In July 1947, a poll taken in one of the battalions later allotted to India showed 98 per cent of the men in favour of serving the British government; the other 2 per cent opted to take their discharge rather than serve the new Indian government.[77] Even a month later, after the planned division of the Gurkha regiments was announced, the 'figures obtained . . . were generally very favourable to HMG'.[78] But there were warning signs. General Tuker visited a battalion, whose colonel he knew well, and found a very different situation: 'He told me that the men now elected 80 per cent to go altogether, 12 per cent to go to service under HMG and 8 per cent, the domiciled clerks, etc., to serve under the Indian Dominion.' Tuker's conclusion, after talking to the subedar-major and another senior subedar, was that the men were 'hurt and angry' at the splitting up of the Gurkha Brigade and simply did not understand it.[79]

Unofficial soundings like these indicated 'that the Gurkha, despite his loyalty to the British connection, was not going to make his choice blindly'.[80] The War Office mission was aware that Malaya was not as attractive a proposition as India: Gurkhas got home leave every year in India, whereas in Malaya it would be once every three years; in India, Gurkha families lived in well-established Regimental Centres, but they probably would not be able to start going to Malaya for two years and when they did, they would find inferior accommodation and facilities. Then there was the climate, which was regarded as unsuitable for hillmen.[81] In addition to these disincentives, as Tuker wrote: 'By now our men had lost faith in the British'.[82]

British officers were in an impossible position; when their men came to them for advice they could say nothing, because they were under orders not to influence them in any way. John Cross, who experienced to the full the misery of parting with his company of 1/1st Gurkhas, destined for India, writes, 'Those who have never served in as tight-knit a community as a Gurkha battalion can have little idea of the wealth of camaraderie and the warmth of human relationship that exist. But when the soldiers asked us the whys, whens, wheres and hows, we could only give general answers that had no bearing on our limited point of view.'[83]

Despite this, of course, some officers did make their feelings known – to such an extent that the first C-in-C of the new Indian Army, the British General Sir Rob Lockhart, wrote to Scoones, now Military Secretary at the Commonwealth Relations Office, complaining abut their behaviour. He could understand the disappointment of those whose regiments were being handed over to India, but he could not approve of the 'almost defeatist' attitude of some of them, or of their dire predictions of the future of these regiments under Indian officers. He asked Scoones to put pressure on his officers to take a more positive and co-operative line, if only for the sake of the men who had served the Indian Army so well. The Gurkha, after all, 'is a professional soldier and if he is to live he must find employment'.[84]

It was not an easy time even for those whose battalions were destined for British service. The 2/7th, for example, stationed in the industrial city of Ahmedabad in Gujarat, was still adjusting to what was in effect the amalgamation of two separate battalions, one which had been obliged to surrender at Tobruk in 1942 and had spent the rest of the war in prison camp, and the other, its replacement, which had fought in Italy and Greece. Differences of outlook, training and experience, as well as seniority disputes and arguments over who should be demobilized, increased the tension which internal security duties inevitably induced. Add to that an influx of officers from the 1st Gurkhas who could not understand how a battalion lucky enough to have been selected for British service was not united in its commitment to it, and you had a combustible situation.

The relationship between the commanding officer and the subedar-major was the key to the health and harmony of a Gurkha battalion. In the 2/7th both Lt-Col. Bob Houghton and Sub-Maj. Ishorman Rai had been prisoners of war; they were what Gurkhas call *numberis*, i.e. they had joined the battalion at the same time. They had a close familial relationship, so all should have been well. But the wartime experience of the re-raised 2/7 GR had created a different kind of relationship between British officers and Gurkha officers than had existed pre-war, when it had been very much a case of 'Leave it to the GOs'. The exigencies of war had made for a more hands-on approach by British officers.

Houghton was very much in the old style and leaned heavily on Ishorman, his trusted subedar-major. Ishorman had a fine military record; he had been a first-class athlete though now he had grown portly; he had a dominating personality and a fiery temperament. But a wartime incident, in which he had been recaptured after escaping from an Italian POW camp along with two British NCOs who got clean away, may have soured his feelings towards the British. Whatever the reason, disenchantment with the British or personal ambition – the lure of a full commission – Ishorman intended to opt for India and expected everyone else to follow suit.

The adjutant of 2/7 GR, 'Birdie' Smith, discovered this when he was approached by a subedar he knew well and told in confidence that a Gurkha officer and two others who intended to opt for British service had been banned from the GOs' Club. Smith reported this to the colonel, who summoned the subedar-major. Ishorman denied it and Houghton backed him. Smith writes, 'It proved to be a grave error.'[85]

Houghton did not realize his mistake until after the referendum, when Ishorman's influence carried the day. Only forty out of 729 soldiers opted for British service (with 250 still to make their choice): a result which, as Brig. R. C. O. Hedley, the co-ordinator of the British Gurkha force, telegraphed the War Office, 'may cause serious problems full significance of which cannot yet be estimated'.[86] In 2/7 GR itself there was consternation: Houghton was, in Smith's words 'a broken man'; the forty Gurkhas who had dared challenge Ishorman's authority were 'threatened and intimidated'; and although there were no serious incidents, the atmosphere was such that the distraught Houghton seems to have raised the cry of 'mutiny' and a battalion of Bombay Grenadiers was placed on stand-by.[87]

Ishorman's hour of glory was brief. An officer at GHQ in Delhi who was related to him had led him to believe that if the bulk of the battalion opted for India, 2/7 GR would become part of the new Indian Army (which in effect it did: it was redesignated 3/11 GR and first commanded by Major Padam Singh Thapa from the 5th Marathas, who left soon after to take command of 3/5 GR). When Smith, as Adjutant, informed Ishorman that all those who had opted for service with India must leave the battalion, he refused to accept this and demanded to see the relevant order. That was the first shock. The second was that the Indian Army, its senior officers at that time 'nearly all being products of Sandhurst' (rather than the Indian Military Academy which replaced it), instead of welcoming him as a hero took a dim view of his apostasy and that was the end of his career. The irony was that had he opted for Britain, the English-speaking Ishorman Rai, with his better-than-average education, would almost certainly have been one the first GOs to have received a king's commission and would have retired as a major instead of ending up as a local police inspector in Calcutta.[88]

Smith could not forgive Ishorman for 'allowing his personal ambitions to overrule his loyalty to the Battalion he had served for so long', but he recognized that the British were at fault in taking such loyalty for granted and assuming the Gurkhas would opt for them regardless of terms and conditions.[89] The days when they might have followed so blindly were over, if they had ever existed. The British were discovering, at the eleventh hour, that if they wanted the Gurkhas on their side they could no longer pretend to be above the fray – however honourable their motives – but must woo them as they claimed the Indians were doing. Smith took this lesson to heart; as a recruiting officer in Ghoom, near Darjeeling, he knowingly allowed one or two of the brighter 2/7th NCOs to 're-opt' along with many others who claimed to be returning from leave and opting for the first time, and packed them all off to Malaya before the Indian authorities caught up with them. Given what happened at Ahmedabad, and how several of the men had sought out their officers to tell them how they had opted the way they did under duress, he felt no compunction about this.[90]

One month before the tripartite agreement was signed, word reached Gen. Scoones in London that all was not well with the 1st battalion of his old regiment, the 2nd Goorkhas, in Santa Cruz, outside Bombay. He wrote to Maj-Gen. Lyne at the War Office that it was clear to him that, unless they got their Gurkha battalions out of India very quickly, they would be 'got at' just as the maharajah of Nepal had been got at by the Indian government.[91] Exactly a month later, at the very moment when the tripartite discussions were taking place in Kathmandu, Auchinleck sent a telegram to the Chiefs of Staff in London about what he called a 'disturbing and in my opinion probably significant incident' which had occurred on 3 November in 1/2 GR.[92]

Practically the entire battalion, with the exception of the Gurkha officers and some senior NCOs, had refused to parade and had assembled instead outside the quarterguard. When the CO, Lt-Col. G. S. N. Richardson, addressed the men, they told him they did not want to serve the British in Malaya; they did not trust them to look after their interests any longer; the original terms for service in Malaya were not good enough and they were still waiting for new terms; they were finished with their British officers; they would rather serve in India. Richardson had no alternative but to report the situation to the Indian Brig. Brar, commanding the Bombay sub-area. The men repeated their complaints to the brigadier and asked to be allowed to make their opt right away in the presence of Indian officers, since they didn't trust their British officers. This was done, and it seemed likely that almost everyone had opted to serve India.

The 1/2nd Goorkha Rifles was considered a first-class unit; it did not have the internal problems the 2/7th had faced at the end of the war; and Richardson was a highly regarded commanding officer. So what had gone wrong? The trigger seems to have been a warning order of a move to the Punjab (which later turned out to have been issued in error). The men, whose families were to prepare to go to the Regimental Centre at Dehra Dun *en route* to Nepal, took this as a sign that they were being posted to Malaya before they had even opted or seen what new terms were on offer. A recently dismissed educational jemadar was held responsible for stirring up trouble, but Auchinleck and other senior British officers had no doubt that 'a deliberate propaganda campaign' had been going on for some time, the purpose of which was to dissuade Gurkhas from opting British: 'This would accord with my firm belief that India['s] Government is definitely opposed to letting HMG have Gurkha units whatever they may say publicly.'[93]

As with the mass defection of 2/7 GR, 1/2 GR's unanimous refusal to serve Britain – if that was what it amounted to – might entail a 'reconsideration of whole question of allotment of Gurkha regiments unless battalion can be made up by volunteers from other Gurkha regiments'.[94] There was also the question of disciplinary action to be considered. But Auchinleck's next telegram, dated 11 November 1947, discounted the latter because the alleged offence had been condoned by the sub-area commander in allowing the men to record their option on the spot. Anyway, the battalion was 'said to have returned to normal conditions of discipline and behaviour'.[95]

It was this 'disgraceful mutiny' in his old battalion – 'probably the most famous battalion in the Indian Army' – that prompted 'Gertie' Tuker to write an angry, highly critical letter to Gen. Sir James Steele at the War Office. He told his friend Jimmy that he intended to look in on 1/2 GR when he went to Bombay on his way home on retirement later that month. But 'the chances of getting the Gurkhas you want to serve with HMG are becoming smaller and smaller every day'. It took a great deal of provocation to incite Gurkhas into mass disobedience, but 'they have had that provocation all right'. He then listed the causes of the mutiny under six headings:

(a) Splitting the Gurkha Brigade into two parts.
(b) Taking from March 1946 to August 1947 to decide the fate of the GB.
(c) Shilly shallying over terms of service etc.
(d) Stripping the HMG Regiments of all their best officers in whom the men had confidence.
(e) Failure to appoint a Commander for HMG Gurkhas and to concentrate the units.
(f) The action of Indian political parties who use[d] the dirtiest tool they could find to wean these regiments away from their British connection.[96]

Five of these six critical errors might be laid at the door of the British authorities, but the sixth was outside their control. The 'tool' Tuker refers to was the Calcutta-based Nepali National Congress, 'a Communist-Socialist body of revolutionary Indians and low-class Indian-domiciled Gurkhas, led by a shoemaker', and it was the influence of this 'strongly anti-British and strongly anti-the-Nepalese-ruling-family' body on a dozen or so Indian-domiciled eastern Gurkhas transferred into the 1/2 Goorkhas from one of the disbanded wartime battalions that he held responsible for the mutiny. But the 'follies enumerated above have let this party into your regiments'.[97] So the War Office was to blame even for that.

Tuker's valedictory speech to the 1/2nd Goorkhas focused on the famous Truncheon presented to them by Queen Victoria after the 1857 siege of Delhi, the icon on which, as newly joined recruits, they swore their allegiance to the crown. Tuker told the men that if they opted for India *en masse*, the Truncheon would have to be returned to the grandson of Queen Victoria, King George VI.[98] His intervention proved effective and when 1/2 GR re-opted in December, nearly half the battalion chose British service – 340 out of 717. The figures for the Regimental Centre were much the same, and those for 2/2 GR, stationed at Dinapore, better still, with 592 out of 834 opting for Britain.[99]

The opt figures generally were disappointing from a British point of view. Auchinleck had told the Chiefs of Staff that not all Gurkha battalions were affected by the troubles which led to the mutiny in 1/2 GR and that some were willing to serve the British, 'notably 6th Gurkhas now in Delhi who have good reports of Malaya from returning officers'.[100] He was referring to the 2/6th, which provided Mountbatten's bodyguard and for that reason, according to Indian sources, was chosen for British service (but that, if it played any part, was not the main reason, as we have already seen).[101] The Auk's confidence in 2/6 GR turned out to be misplaced.

Maj. 'Eno' Singha had only just arrived at Mathura (on the road from Delhi to Agra) as second-in-command of the 2/1st Gurkhas when the new Indian commandant got a message to say that 2/6 GR were having their opt on Christmas Day and would he please send an officer to take over those Gurkhas opting for India. He sent Singha along with a 15 cwt truck to pick them up and bring them back to 2/1 GR. On arrival at Government House, Singha marched up to the British colonel (Lt-Col. Shaw) and showed him his orders. Shaw said, 'How many Gurkhas do you think have opted for India?' Singha replied, 'Maybe seven, or ten . . . My CO has given me just one vehicle.' 'Guess again,' said the colonel. Singha asked, 'Is it 50?' Col. Shaw snorted, 'No, you'll never guess. It's that damn Congress. 700 have opted for India out of 770 present.'[102] (In fact, it was 692 out of 781.[103])

Brig. Osborne Hedley professed himself baffled by a result which was a reversal of a poll taken two months earlier; that had shown 80 to 90 per cent of 2/6 GR in favour of British service (which explains why Auchinleck was so confident of their loyalty). He listed some of the reasons why the opt might have gone so badly from a British point of view: 'Malaya is a long way from Nepal; difficulties with Brahmins about going overseas; lack of precise information re the grant of King's Commissions to Gurkhas; doubts about married accommodation; and the idea that if the majority of men in any one unit opted for India, then the unit would remain intact and continue to serve the Indian Government.' But the two factors he saw as mainly responsible for Britain's poor performance in the opt were the removal of so many experienced officers from the units (and their replacement by officers the men did not know) and the unconscionable time it took to realize the plan for a British Gurkha force.[104]

In general, the British argued, the nearer to Delhi the more political pressure was brought to bear on the Gurkhas. By far the worst opts from a British point of view were the 2/6th in Delhi and the 2/7th in Ahmedabad; and the 1/2nd near Bombay might have been equally bad had it not been for Tuker's intervention. But even in Burma the opt results disappointed the British, and Lt-Col. Maurice McCready of the 10th recalled how 'propaganda intensified as the date drew nearer' and 'threats of violence to families back to India and reprisals against Indian-domiciled soldiers were received through the post.'[105]

Brig. Hedley reported to the War Office that the attempt to get volunteers from Indian Gurkha regiments to fill vacancies in the British regiments, as had been agreed in November, had been met with various kinds of obstruction from the Indian authorities – 'generally speaking men did not have conditions of service explained to them, nor was it made clear to eligible personnel that they could volunteer. Undoubtedly many names were suppressed.' He claimed that British Gurkha units were often approached by Indian Gurkhas seeking to transfer: 'This unsatisfactory state of affairs cannot fail to have unsettling effect on Indian Gurkha Regiments in which relations between officers and men appear to be deteriorating.'[106]

It is difficult to give a precise final figure for the referendum because even towards the end of January 1948 there were still 1,680 men who had not opted; but about 40 per cent, or less than half the Gurkhas who might have come into British service, chose to do so.[107] In Indian Gorkha regimental histories the figure generally given for those who opted for India is 90 per cent but that, like Gen. Rudra's assertion that 'well over 90 per cent of the men voted not to go with their units to Malaya', is well wide of the mark.[108] Only if it were calculated on the – erroneous – assumption that the entire Gurkha Brigade took part in the referendum, and not just those units destined for British service, could the figure even remotely approach 90 per cent. The only choice given to Gurkhas destined for Indian service was of 'either remaining in the Indian Army and their own unit under Indian officers or leaving the army', which for professional soldiers was no choice at all.[109] Small wonder that 95 per cent opted to remain.

While the troubles in the battalions allotted to Britain were focused on the opt and the divided loyalties it threw up among the Gurkhas, those in the Indian battalions centred on the hand-over to Indian officers and the powerful prejudice this brought out in some British officers. There were ugly incidents in both cases.

Instead of the gradual process of nationalization which by the end of the war had transformed the Indian Army – with the exception of the Gurkha Brigade – the Indian Gurkha units were faced with the sudden departure of one set of officers and their replacement by another. The rapid commissioning of likely Gurkha officers, often on the recommendation of their British officers, eased the transition for the troops. But for the British officers, the wrench of leaving units with which they passionately identified – and men alongside whom they had fought in all sorts of conditions throughout the war – for a very uncertain future brought no comfort; and some of them took it badly. They resented the intrusion of Indian officers on what they regarded very much as their patch and, in some cases, did not trouble to disguise their feelings. In their attitude to India's new masters, traditional military contempt for politicians was magnified when the politicians in question had recently been seen as subversives, whose proper place was in gaol, and were now ordering everybody about and tricking the Gurkhas out of their right to choose whom they served.

The anger of the Indian officers focused on the way the British officers in some of the Gurkha regiments they inherited disposed of their mess silver and funds. And not just Indian officers: several senior British officers, including Brig. Hedley (whose own 5th Royal Gurkha Rifles was one of the offenders) also deplored the fact that in certain regiments mess silver and money had been taken back to the United Kingdom and returned to their donors or had been given to other regiments, rather than handed over to the incoming Indian officers. Some regiments behaved worse than others, as Hedley reported: 'The 4th were alright, 3rd and 8th bad, some battalions have left dud cheques, some fed free or practically free from Mess funds from the middle of August until Indians took over.' But he agreed with the Director of Personnel Services in the War Office that, rather than make an official protest and create a scandal, the best way of handling things would be to approach the colonels of the regiments involved and ask them to arrange for the return of any missing silver and funds.[110]

The most vociferous protester on the Indian side has been Maj-Gen. D. K. 'Monty' Palit who, as a major, took over the 3/9th Gurkhas in 1947; he has told the story, in interviews and in his own writings, several times. As a Bengali, Palit belongs to what the British regarded as the most volatile and least martial of Indian races – 'a low-lying country inhabited by low, lying people' is one typical description of Bengal.[111] So when the brigade commander showed him a letter from the departing adjutant of 3/9 GR saying that the regiment was finished now that a Bengali, 'full of corruption', was coming to take over, Palit understandably felt indignant. The CO Palit was replacing, Lt-Col. David Amoore, asked if he might stay on for a further three weeks in order to qualify for a higher rate of pension; but his continued presence acted as a divisive influence on the GOs, who hardly knew which master they were supposed to be serving. There were tales of a missing machine-gun, of stolen mess property, even cutlery, and whisky bottles smashed by British officers rather than handed over. 'All our mess silver,' Palit writes, 'was either appropriated by individuals or given away to British regiments, though later two British officers got them back from England (our former colonel, General Sir Oliver Twiss and Lt-Col. A. A. Mains)'.[112]

In the 1/5th Royal Gurkha Rifles (Frontier Force) the British officers took legal advice and learned that they might dispose of their mess silver and funds how they wished, since they were their exclusive property, acquired by donation or subscription. At a 1/5 RGR mess meeting, a resolution was passed that there would be free messing for as long as mess funds lasted, and it wasn't until Lt-Col. (later Maj-Gen.) A. S. Pathania arrived to take over 1/5 RGR that this was stopped. On the day that Lt-Col. Pathania arrived, the outgoing CO, Lt-Col. Richard Pease, told him he had better get some other Indian officers in quickly as he had been told by the British officers 'that they would not like to serve under an Indian Commanding Officer'. Pease himself was prepared to stay on for a few days but his second-in-command, Major Nightingale, left that same day.[113]

At the 5 RGR Regimental Centre the mess had been practically stripped of furniture, silver, crockery and cutlery. The paintings had gone; the dining table and chairs and the billiard table had all been given to the Indian Military Academy, whence they were retrieved only 'after some hard persuasion'; the mess silver had been packed away and taken to Britain.[114] Some of the silver was returned to the regiment fairly swiftly, but several items found their way into an officer's attic, where they remained until they were discovered after his death forty-seven years later – when they were returned to India by an embarrassed regimental association.[115]

Legally, British officers may have been within their rights to dispose of mess silver and funds, but morally such action was petty-minded, if not despicable, even allowing for the tensions of that time. The very fact that by no means all Gurkha regiments behaved in this way proves that it was not inevitable. The Indian officers who compiled the most recent volume of the history of 4 GR, for instance, pay tribute to Gen. Sir Arthur Mills, colonel of the regiment at that time:

> He had directed that 'his regiment be handed over intact', indeed a very generous act. His directions were nobly and faithfully carried out by the outgoing British officers. All funds, every item of silver, furniture, carpets, houses, bungalows, invaluable pieces of art, shikar [hunting] trophies collected over years, and the library at Bakloh with thousands of books, some very rare, built over several decades, were all handed over without a hitch, without a complaint, willingly and cheerfully.[116]

The Indians were careful to select only the best officers for their

Gurkha regiments; many of them had previously served in Baluchi, Frontier or Punjabi Mussulman regiments, which were now part of the Pakistan Army. Lt-Col. (later Maj-Gen.) S. K. Korla, who had had a distinguished wartime career with the 7th battalion of the Baluch Regiment in Burma, was chosen to take over the 2/1 GR and he took 'Eno' Singha, who was another Baluchi officer, with him as his second-in-command. When they arrived in Mathura and reported to 2/1 GR at Kosi Kalan, they were coldly received. The outgoing CO, Lt-Col. Dodkins, merely told them that the subedar-major was expecting them and sent an orderly to show them where the GOs' Club was. The two Indians sensed they were being tested, as the GOs plied them with drink and gave them nothing to eat. After two hours, Korla stood up, thanked the subedar-major and said they had to be going. The subedar-major summoned two stretcher bearers and said, 'You don't have to worry, tomorrow is Sunday. We'll send you home.' But the colonel refused, saying, 'I like my drink, but I like to walk home.' The officers made a dignified exit, staggered back to their tents and collapsed into bed without any dinner.

The next morning when they went into the mess, the British officers got up to receive them and said, 'The subedar-major says you're alright, so you're welcome to the regiment.' After that, Singha remembers, the hand-over went smoothly and everyone relaxed:

> Then finally, when they were leaving, we threw a party for them. Colonel Korla had been to Camberley, you see, Staff College, and he knew English cooking. So he got down to the kitchen and cooked for them. My mother having been a pianist, I knew what tunes and when to play, and I arranged the bar and the music and everything. At the end of the party they said, 'If you can do a party like that, we're leaving the Gurkhas in good hands. Congratulations'. We had a very nice time.[117]

But even with such agreeable and understanding officers taking over, the parting of the British and Gurkhas who had been through so much together as comrades in arms was almost unbearably poignant, as 'Fairy' Gopsill, who transferred as a captain from 2/1 GR to 2/7 GR, recalled: 'The final day was beyond description with the Battalion lined up on both sides. As the officers went to the trucks, garlands were placed over their heads until they covered the whole head. Gurkha and British Officers were in tears. I never want to live through a day like it.'[118]

British and Indian officers offer radically different versions of the Gurkha opt. What for one was a great betrayal, with the soldiers' traditional loyalty undermined by insidious propaganda, was for the other a democratic and reasoned expression of popular feeling. Propaganda? How could there be, when the British kept the Gurkhas to themselves, locked up in cantonments away from contaminating contact with ordinary Indians, let alone politicians? Besides, most Gurkhas did not speak Hindi; they were not taught Hindi and that too kept them isolated. No, the massive refusal of British service had more to do with the reluctance of the Gurkha soldier to be sent overseas again after six years of war service abroad.* The Indian offer of short-service commissions certainly attracted senior Gurkha officers who, in turn, influenced the way their juniors voted; but that was a practical necessity, not a devious Indian plot to undermine Gurkha loyalty to the British.

This was all true, but it was not the whole truth. For understandable reasons, Nehru did not welcome a British Gurkha force; he thought it would be used for imperialist purposes which would embarrass his government – as indeed happened. (In August 1948, at the beginning of the Malayan 'Emergency', Sir George Falconer, Britain's ambassador – as he now was – to Nepal, suggested to the Foreign Office that it would be 'unwise' for the BBC and press agencies to draw too much attention to the use of Gurkha troops in anti-communist operations in Malaya: 'This publicity is likely to embarrass Nepal and also India'.[120]) Publicly, though, Nehru did nothing to prevent Britain acquiring Gurkhas

---

*The Gurung Second World War veterans to whom the anthropologist, Mary Des Chene, spoke about the opt claimed that the refusal of British service on the part of so many *lahores* stemmed from their experience of the Hindu-Muslim massacres in India in 1947: 'The animus against going with the British was against going to a Muslim country – Malaya – where presumably such a thing might recur, and they themselves, mistaken for Hindus, might be the target of attacks.'[119] But this rather reinforces the British view that they were 'got at', since this is precisely the sort of scare story a skilful propagandist would put about.

because he did not feel he had the right to interfere with relations between Britain and Nepal. But it would be surprising if his lack of enthusiasm did not communicate itself to those who might be less scrupulous in the way they went about influencing the course of events.

The Gurkhas' lack of Hindi would be no barrier to political infiltration by the Gurkha League (GL) or the Nepali National Congress (NNC), two organizations of Indian-domiciled Gurkhas and Nepali exiles now merged into one, with close links to the All India Congress. The GL/NNC had ready access to friends and relatives serving in various units, and it was known to be active in all four regiments destined for Malaya through September, October and November 1947. The British had always taken comfort in the thought that 'the average Gurkha from the hills normally despises the type he finds belonging to the League'. But the war had brought many changes and Gurkhas were 'now much more susceptible to propaganda put over by the educated Gurkha, i.e., by line boys, clerks and those domiciled in India'.[121]

This raises the question, when does propaganda cease to be propaganda and become something else? Gurkhas were admired by the British for their sturdy independence, along with their other stalwart qualities. What if, their eyes opened by their wartime experiences, they started to question their own position in the larger scheme of things, the role they might be asked to play and their relationship with both a decaying British Raj and its endangered ally, the autocratic ruling dynasty of their own country? Were they succumbing to propaganda, or merely exercising independent political judgement?

As troops who, as their maharajah recognized, might be stigmatized as mercenaries, the Gurkhas inevitably had divided loyalties. Slim, for instance, had written to Auchinleck, 'The ultimate loyalty of the Gurkha is not to India or England, but to his own country.'[122] But it was not that simple either, since the Gurkhas' attitude to the rulers of their own country, in which they were – and are – an ethnic minority, was ambivalent. A 9 GR wartime British officer wrote to the secretary of state for India, Lord Listowel, in August 1947, arguing that endorsement of the hand-over of Gurkha regiments to the 'Congress Raj' by the government of Nepal would not be enough to justify it in the eyes of the Gurkhas themselves:

Just before I left Dehra Dun, I went down to the Gurkha Officers'
Club and when conversation turned to Nepal I was surprised at the
vehemence with which the GOs expressed their opinions on their own
tin sarkar – the Maharaja. The substance of their complaint was: 'He
does everything for himself and nothing for us'. The important point
to him is not what his people want but that they should go on serving
outside the country. So long as they do, the country – and he is the
recipient of its revenues – continues to benefit . . . [123]

In these circumstances it would not be surprising if a substantial body
of Gurkha opinion identified with the nationalist and anti-Rana movement in and outside Nepal, and found nothing objectionable in serving
its ally, the Indian Congress Party, which had already wrested power
from the British in India. In addition, the more far-seeing of the
Gurkhas were well aware of Britain's decline as a world power: 'They
state that we are leaving Palestine, Egypt, India, and have already left
Burma, and that therefore we shall soon be giving up Malaya. Why volunteer, they ask, to serve a country which is in such a decline, when
service in India, which is so much nearer home, is still open?'[124]

Yet despite all the arguments and pressures against serving imperialist Britain, and despite the traumas of the referendum, a large enough
number of Gurkhas rallied to the British cause to enable the British
Gurkha Regiment – as it was initially called – to overcome its inauspicious beginnings. In February 1948, Brig. Osborne Hedley, who never
allowed the massive setbacks he encountered to deflect him from his
aim of getting the project off the ground, estimated that by 1 April the
corps would consist of 7,400 men, made up of 3,900 optees, 2,400
recruits, 300 volunteers from Indian Gurkha regiments and 800 of the
remaining 1,400 men still on leave who had not yet opted.[125] He ended
his analysis of the results of the referendum on a justifiably upbeat note:

Since 1 Jan 1948, the day of transfer to HMG, there has, I am
convinced, been a change of spirit and outlook amongst British Gurkha
units towards the whole scheme. There is now marked enthusiasm.

The child has not been born without labour, and if the weaning is
done patiently and thoroughly, there is no reason why it should not
prosper.[126]

9

Fighting on Two Fronts

In 1948, Britain's corps of Gurkhas, or 'Gurkha Regiment' as it had first been known, officially became the Brigade of Gurkhas with a senior officer designated Major-General Brigade of Gurkhas (MGBG) to look after its interests. The first MGBG was Maj-Gen. Sir Charles Boucher, whose regimental service had been with the 3rd Gurkhas (now part of the Indian Army). Soon the training of recruits and keeping of records were centralized at the Depot Brigade of Gurkhas at Sungei Patani in north Malaya rather than left to individual regiments. This was not merely an administrative convenience; it was felt it would help to foster a corporate identity. The infant Brigade was still reeling from the divisive opt and the loss of so many experienced soldiers – not to mention the traumas of the war and for some, like most of the 2/2nd Goorkhas, years in a prison camp. What it needed most, but did not get, was time to consolidate.

For the first two decades of their service in the British Army, from 1948 to 1966, the Gurkha infantry battalions were almost continually engaged in a war, first in Malaya, where it was known as the 'Emergency', and then in Borneo, where it was called 'Confrontation'. But a war by any other name is still a war; people kill and get killed. In both these conflicts Gurkhas provided the backbone of the military operations; British battalions came for a limited period, then went away again; the Gurkhas remained, each battalion taking an occasional break in Hong Kong but otherwise seldom far from the action in the dense jungles of south-east Asia.

During the first half of this period the British authorities put as much pressure as they dared on the Nepalese to raise the Gurkha manpower ceiling to 15,000 and beyond. But then the emphasis changed, Britain reviewed its overseas commitments in the light of its shrunken role in the post-war, post-imperial world and reductions in the armed forces began to be mooted. Gurkhas, however prized by the military for their soldierly qualities and by the Treasury for their inexpensiveness, were not British; strictly speaking they were not mercenaries either, since they were an intrinsic part of the British Army and the Geneva convention of 1949 specifically excludes from the category of mercenary anyone who is 'a member of the Armed Forces of a party to the conflict'. But in the end they had to be more expendable than the true Brits. The long fight for survival was underway.

To begin with, conditions in Malaya were far from ideal. After their arrival from Bombay on the SS *Strathnaver* on 2 April 1948, the bulk of the five battalions of British Gurkhas from India, including the families which accompanied the men, had to make do with tented accommodation. But first impressions of Malaya were favourable. The relief of getting away from a chaotic India and joining the other three battalions from Burma, as well as the prospect of a fresh start in another country, outweighed the lack of creature comforts. The women, it was reported, 'have not yet abandoned their heavy Nepali dress for something lighter and more suitable for the climate, but it is expected that a New Look will be evolved before much longer'.[1]

Initially the force was both under-strength and bottom-heavy since so many Gurkha officers had left, attracted by the full commissions offered by the Indian Army. This meant many promotions, some of which might well have been considered premature: 'This reward for their staunchness and loyalty is, however, well deserved and a temporarily lower standard is a small price to pay for it.'[2] British officers, too, were in short supply, though the permanent cadre of fifty-six would soon be increased to the establishment strength of 100 with the addition of short-service commissioned officers and volunteers on secondment from British regiments.

The move from the Indian to the British Army involved adjustments of ranks, or at least of their designations. Out went subedar-major, subedar, jemadar, havildar, naik, and in came Gurkha major, Gurkha captain, Gurkha lieutenant, sergeant, corporal; only rifleman remained the same. The old viceroy's commission was retained, though under another name (as in the new Indian Army). VCOs became KGOs, or King's Gurkha officers – and after 1953 QGOs, Queen's Gurkha officers (in the Indian Army they are JCOs, junior commissioned officers).

From the start it was proposed to commission outstanding Gurkha officers as pukka lieutenants, captains and even majors:

> They will rank in all respects as BOs and will take up vacancies in the permanent cadre. They will thus often be commanding young British officers and they will dress as BOs. The ultimate aim is to educate the Gurkha boy from about the age of twelve so that he can take the RMA [Royal Military Academy] Sandhurst exam at seventeen and a half. This proposal is being examined and will be implemented in due course. In this case, of course, there is definitely an FM's baton in his satchel.[3]

The interim measure of introducing 'King's Gurkha Commissioned Officers' (KGCOs or, more commonly, GCOs) was sanctioned by the War Office under a ruling delivered by the judge advocate-general, Sir Felix Cassel, in 1917 that 'aliens', once enlisted, were 'deemed to have all the rights of a British subject, including eligibility for a King's Commission'.[4]

Recruits soon began to arrive from India, though 'some of the first recruits reached their training centres in Malaya dressed in nothing but a towel and a blanket'.[5]

It was not only the army that was clamouring for recruits: the Singapore government wanted a Gurkha contingent in its police force to replace the Sikhs 'whose conduct during the Japanese occupation was such that it was found necessary to disband them on the liberation of Malaya and repatriate them to India'.[6] The difficulty was that the Indian government had banned recruitment of Indians for overseas police forces and without Indian co-operation it would be impossible for Gurkhas to get to Singapore. The solution was to recruit the 144 Gurkhas needed to set up the force from those due to be discharged from the army in Malaya who were willing to stay on. But ever since 1948, the Gurkha contingent of the Singapore police has recruited in Nepal through the agency of the British Army.

Other imminent changes included the conversion of 7 GR to gunners and the creation of divisional sappers from old soldiers and recruits not yet allocated to infantry battalions. The experiment with 7 GR as Gurkha Artillery turned out to be short-lived, however, not because the infantrymen proved inept as gunners but because the endeavour was overtaken by events. In the middle of June 1948 a European rubber planter called Arthur Walker was killed by three young Chinese – the first of many to be murdered on their estates – and the war that was not a war but an 'Emergency' had begun. It would last, at varying levels of intensity, for twelve years, twice as long as the Second World War. Artillery had no part in this guerrilla war and 7 GR soon reverted to infantry as decreed by the man who succeeded Monty, as Chief of the Imperial General Staff, Field Marshal Sir William Slim.

During the Second World War a group of British officers had been infiltrated into the Malayan jungle to orchestrate the resistance to the Japanese of the overwhelmingly Chinese Malayan Communist Party (MCP). The Chinese communist partisans fed and looked after these officers in return for the arms and ammunition they provided. But each was using the other for their own purposes; the ultimate aims of these wartime allies were utterly opposed.

At the end of the war, the officers of Force 136, as it was called, attempted to disarm and disband the guerrillas, offering each of them a campaign medal and 300 Malay dollars in return for their services.[7] (Chin Peng, the leader of the MCP and soon to prove himself a doughty opponent of the security forces, was awarded the OBE for his part in the resistance.) But with the restoration of peace the Malayan People's Anti-Japanese Army instantly transformed itself into the Malayan People's Anti-British Army – later the Malayan Races Liberation Army (MRLA) – dedicated to the removal of another alien power from a land ripe for a Chinese-style communist take-over. Some 4,000 partisans

remained hidden in the jungle and used the arms and ammunition provided by the British against their erstwhile allies.

The Federation of Malaya, bringing together the nine Malay states
and two British settlements (Malacca and Penang) under a central colonial administration in Kuala Lumpur, had come into being on 1
February 1948. Singapore, with its predominantly Chinese population,
remained a separate colony. Of Malaya's five million population, just
under half were Malay, 1.9 million Chinese, 0.6 million Indian and 0.1
million European.[8] Had Singapore been incorporated into the
Federation, Chinese would have outnumbered Malays in the peninsula
as a whole. By keeping them apart the British authorities could count on
the support of the Malays in the war against the overwhelmingly
Chinese Communist Terrorists (CTs).

In the early years of the campaign, the so-called CTs held the initiative, wrongfooting the security forces and ambushing troops and
civilians on the roads almost at will before vanishing into the jungle.
The guerrillas in the jungle relied on the support of the Min Yuen, or
People's Movement, both to keep them informed and to supply them
with food and other necessities. The majority of these people were
recruited from Chinese squatters scratching a living on the fringes of the
jungle. If co-operation was withheld, the CTs did not hesitate to intimidate and even kill people to gain their ends.

On the British side there was an absence of direction at the top and
a lack of savvy on the ground. John Cross, who had transferred as a
captain from 1/1 GR to 1/7 GR, recalls 'thrashing around' in the jungle
in the early days:

> I remember how ill-equipped we were: we carried our water in
> bamboo containers; we were ordered to shoot rubber-estate dogs to
> prevent them from barking a warning of our presence; we had neither
> canvas jungle boots nor waterproof capes, so we slept on and under
> leaves; our 'wireless sets' were so heavy we had to carry them on
> stretchers; and on one occasion the police ordered me out on a job to
> contact guerrillas, then wanted me arraigned for murder when we
> killed one.[9]

The difficulties Cross and other officers of the 7th Gurkhas faced were compounded by their acquisition of gunner officers unfamiliar with either the regiment or infantry tactics. T. J. Phillips was only briefly with the 2/7th, but during that time he was a reluctant witness of an action more characteristic of the later Vietnam war than of the Malayan Emergency. On an operation in which there was 'a great disporportion of Chiefs to Indians' the accidental discharge of a rifle by one of the security forces was mistaken for enemy aggression and the (gunner) CO ordered a punitive burning of a nearby village in which there were only women and children. The villagers lost all their meagre posses-sions, and domestic animals were also consumed in the flames. When Phillips remonstrated, the CO said 'it was a good thing that we had acted as we had, as when troops went into an area they should leave their mark'. After the operation the officers were billeted at a hotel in Ipoh:

> . . . and he came into my room and said that he intended to make a report to the police that we had been fired on and had burnt the village in reprisal. I was still angry and said that I would have no part in it and he replied that that would be all right, provided that I did not tell the police a different story.[10]

Despite this fracas with his CO (who departed when 7 GR officially reverted to infantry in 1949), Phillips looked back on his four months with the 2/7th as 'among the happiest I had in Malaya':

> I had never met the Limbu Rai before, but they were splendid, even with the disorganisation that was bound to follow the sudden outbreak of the emergency, which came so soon after the trauma of their transfer to the British Army . . .
> . . . they were calm, took everything in their stride and were always aggressive on operations, with determination to close with the enemy whenever they could.[11]

But even among the best troops, some were braver than others. Soon after his return to the 2/7th from recruiting duties in India, 'Birdie' Smith found himself in a scout car hurrying towards the spot where a convoy from his battalion had been ambushed. As he approached it, he

ran into two very agitated young Gurkha lance-corporals: 'Incoherent at
first, one of the L/Cpls explained that the driver of their landrover had
been killed by the first burst of enemy fire; then as the vehicle slammed
into the ditch, Chinese "bandits" had rushed out from the jungle edge
to seize their weapons.' What this lance-corporal could not explain was
why there was still firing if, as he said, all the Gurkhas were dead or seriously wounded. Smith urged his driver round the corner, where they
came upon the wrecked Land Rover and two 15 cwt trucks pulled into
the side of the road; he fired the scout car's machine-gun into the jungle
to drive off any lurking terrorists.

> A minute or two later, two grinning, bedraggled young Gurkha soldiers
> emerged from cover behind the rear vehicle. The senior of the pair
> called the other to attention, before reporting to me that they were
> down to their last few rounds, that the *dushman* (enemy) had killed one
> and wounded two, and the two other L/Cpls had disappeared, possibly
> being captives of the terrorists.[12]

The riflemen's bravery had prevented the guerrillas from removing the
weapons of the dead and wounded Gurkhas and Smith recommended
them both for decorations – but only the senior of the two was
Mentioned in Despatches, 'an award that was totally inadequate'. The
two L/Cpls whose instinct had been to run, by contrast, chose to go on
voluntary discharge rather than take postings outside the battalion:
'They knew that their inglorious exit from the scene of the ambush
would never be forgotten – or forgiven – in the Battalion.'[13]

A curious incident occurred in October 1949 when a patrol from 1/10
GR came upon a shack in deep jungle and surrounded it, thinking it
was a CT resort. There was just one man inside and the Gurkha patrol
was amazed to discover that he spoke their language. It transpired that
his name was Nakam Gurung, and he had been a naik in C Company of
the 2/1st Gurkhas when the Japanese overran Malaya. His battalion
had been forced to leave him behind after he had succumbed to malaria;
the subedar-major had given him three months' rations and told him to
hang on until the war ended, when he should rejoin the battalion.

He recovered and built himself a shelter. He cultivated a patch of
land, set traps for wild pig, went fishing and searched for edible plants.

From time to time he came across local Chinese, who informed him of any Japanese in the area and urged him to remain in hiding. He had taken this advice to heart and had stayed there for over seven years. If the patrolmen had any doubts about his identity, these disappeared when he named Major Wylie as one of his regimental officers; by coincidence Charles Wylie was now serving in their own battalion. Four and a half years after the war had ended Naik Nakam Gurung learned for the first time that it was over.

The story has a happy ending. Nakam rejoined the 1st Gorkhas in India and was sent on home leave to Nepal before being discharged with full retrospective pay and allowances and a pension.[14]

On 1 March 1950, a small leave party, also from 1/10 GR, was returning to the battalion in Pahang after visiting their family lines in Johore Bahru when their train was derailed and ambushed by a large body of guerrillas positioned on either side of the cutting. The carriage occupied by the Gurkhas was in the middle of the ambush; it bore the brunt of the attack and four of the men were hit. Under cover of fire one of the guerrillas approached the carriage, calling on the troops to surrender. But the uninjured L/Cpl Sherbahadur Rai shot and wounded him, forcing him back. Another guerrilla came out and Sherbahadur killed him outright, taking advantage of the ensuing lull to leap from the train and charge the enemy. His CO, Lt-Col. C. C. ('Guinea') Graham, relates the story:

> His action inspired the four wounded men to follow him. One was so badly wounded in the chest that Lance Corporal Sherbahadur was compelled to place him under suitable cover from fire. With the remaining three, however, he charged round the flank of the cutting straight at the enemy who immediately withdrew. L/Cpl Sherbahadur Rai and the three wounded men followed the terrorists for one and threequarter miles firing as they went. Eventually, on account of the wounded men, L/Cpl Sherbahadur Rai was compelled to call off the pursuit. On the way back, he picked up the dead body of the terrorist he had shot and returning to the railway line handed the body over to the police. He also dressed and bandaged the wounded GORs. This highly courageous, bold action and inspiring leadership on the part of this young lance corporal undoubtedly prevented a serious incident from becoming a major disaster.[15]

Sherbahadur won the first DCM to be awarded to 1/10 GR in the Malayan war.

The 1/10th, like all the other British Gurkha battalions, had been under-strength and unprepared when the Emergency began; but Guinea Graham, a resourceful commander, soon worked out effective tactics for jungle warfare, based on four principles: secrecy and silence of movement; the need to get between the guerrillas and their jungle bases and sources of supply; the advantage of sending small reconaissance patrols out from platoon jungle bases to search for guerrilla bases and routes; and the use of Gurkhas' natural tracking ability to follow up after encounters.[16] These were soon universally adopted by Gurkha battalions operating in the Malayan jungle.

But the effectiveness of these methods was initially hampered by three strategic deficiencies. Until Lt-Gen. Sir Harold Briggs was brought out of retirement and appointed Director of Operations in 1950 there was no overall plan to deny the guerrillas food by isolating them from the squatter community, or vice versa; there was precious little information coming from police Special Branch; and, crucially, co-ordination between the civil authority, the police and the military was seriously lacking.[17] But then Templer burst upon the scene, doing away with all such distinctions and combining in his person civil and military authority.

General Sir Gerald Templer took over as supremo in 1952 and, in order to isolate the MRLA in the jungle, rigorously enforced the 'Briggs plan' of resettling squatters in fenced-in 'new villages'. Some likened these villages to concentration camps and Templer's draconian measures came in for criticism. But his was a system of rewards as well as punishments and his ultimate aim was to win the 'hearts and minds' of the Malayan people, without whose wholehearted support mere military triumphs would be incomplete. Simple – even simple-minded – though his methods might be, they were strikingly effective. He came, he transformed the situation militarily and politically and by the time he departed two and a half years later ultimate victory was assured.

As a result of his influence, later operations were marked by close co-operation between military and Special Branch, particularly when individual guerrillas let it be known that they were interested in making a surrender deal, as two 'hard-core CTs' did in September 1956. Major

Vivian of 2/2 GR then escorted the European and Chinese Special Branch officers to meet the guerrillas and ensure that this was not a trap. Once their *bona fides* were established, the two CTs enthusiastically entered into Special Branch plans to drug a woman MCP Branch Secretary and her two companions who were due to arrive in a day or two – so that they could be captured alive – and, once that operation was successfully completed, to waylay a VIP, the State Treasurer of the MCP, in another 'Mickey Finn'-type action.

The latter did not go quite as planned and the VIP got away; but three days later news came that he had been killed, 'still in vest and pants', in an ambush nearly fifty miles away. The security forces involved had been guided by a courier who had been captured in Vivian's earlier operation, so 2/2 GR could take some of the credit.[18] By then, of course, the initiative had passed to the security forces, who were constantly tightening the noose around the ever-diminishing bands of guerrillas still in the jungle.

At the height of the Emergency the British authorities tried to gain the Nepalese government's assent to the expansion of the Brigade of Gurkhas – or, in officialese, 'to invoke the enabling clause of the Tripartite Agreement which provided for an increase in Gurkha ceiling from 10,400 to 15,000'.[19] The problem was that the maharajah had made this contingent on the disbandment of seven wartime battalions still operating in India, over which the British, of course, no longer had any control. In November 1950 the Foreign Office in London advised the War Office that 'the crisis which has developed in Nepal . . . makes it impossible for us to continue our efforts to secure Nepalese agreement to an increased ceiling until the situation has again stabilised'. The FO assured the WO that its policy was informed by 'the need for stability in Nepal so that our sources of Gurkha recruitment should not be endangered'. But the immediate outlook was unpromising:

> I am afraid that recent events are likely to make the Nepalese less
> ready to agree to an increase in our recruitment of Gurkhas. Both the
> Chinese occupation of Tibet and the activities of the Nepalese
> Congress Party are likely to make the Nepalese feel that they must
> retain more of their fighting manpower at home.[20]

The crisis was precipitated by an abortive Nepali Congress *coup* against the Rana regime in September in which the king of Nepal was implicated. King Tribhuvan, whose position was becoming increasingly untenable, engineered his escape from the Ranas by tricking them into believing that he and his family were going on an innocent country outing when in reality they were planning to seek asylum in the Indian embassy. The ruse worked and the king was flown to Delhi, ostensibly for medical treatment, five days later, on 11 November, the very day on which the Nepali Congress launched a series of attacks on border towns in the Terai.

In this volatile situation there were basically four different interest groups involved: the ruling Ranas, the king (and his family), the political parties, of which the Nepali Congress was the dominant one, and last but by no means least the Indian government.

Nehru had a difficult course to steer with regard to Nepal. On the one hand, the Nepali Congress was the natural ally of the Indian Congress Party and he believed there would be serious trouble in Nepal if political reforms were not forthcoming. On the other, he was indebted to Maharajah Mohan Shamsher, who had assisted the 'Congress Raj' in the same way that his predecessors had assisted the British: ten battalions of the Royal Nepalese Army were 'loaned' to India in mid-1948, when the new Indian government was under threat both in Kashmir and in Hyderabad, where Hindus were being persecuted in what was still a princely state ruled by the Muslim Nizam – at least until September when the Indian Army moved in and established a military government.

Mohan was canny enough to appease Nehru to the extent of consulting Indian advisers about constitutional changes to Nepal's system of government. But after the Chinese invasion of Tibet in 1950, he turned the threat of incursion across the Himalayas to advantage by negotiating treaties with India over mutual defence and peace and friendship in which the demand for political reform that India had previously insisted on was quietly dropped. These treaties were signed at the end of July 1950. Now, as a condition of allowing Tribhuvan to leave the country, Mohan Shamsher extracted from Nehru an undertaking that the king would not be permitted to indulge in political intrigue in India.

Ex-king, so far as Mohan was concerned. Tribhuvan's defection was regarded as tantamount to abdication, and his son and heir Mahendra's departure with him meant that a four-year-old grandson, Gyanendra, was promptly crowned king in Kathmandu. But on this occasion the old Rana ploy of replacing a recalcitrant monarch with a complaisant minor did not work because Britain and the United States, as well as India, withheld recognition of the new king. (This was the 'betrayal' of Britain's old ally that so enraged General Tuker, among others.) The maharajah was forced to bow to pressure from India and reinstate Tribhuvan, form an interim government with 'popular (i.e. Nepali Congress) representation' and draft a new constitution. Mohan Shamsher stayed on for a few months as prime minister, but on 18 February 1951, three days after the king's triumphant return to Kathmandu, Tribhuvan formally revoked 'all the hereditary powers and privileges that his great-grandfather had bestowed on the Rana family in 1847'; and the 'regime that had lasted 104 years had collapsed in 104 days'.[21]

In a secret telegram to the Foreign Office, Britain's outgoing ambassador, Sir George Falconer, expressed his concern over the future of Gurkha recruitment under the new dispensation: 'Both sections of Nepalese Congress have till now declared their opposition to employment of Gurkhas in the British (though not the Indian) Army.' Perhaps they would change their tune after the manner of the Indian Congress Party, which had once declared that it would never employ 'foreign mercenaries'; but it would be a mistake to count on it: 'Without wishing to appear unduly pessimistic I think it would be wise for the War Office to be prepared to meet the *possibility* of the tripartite agreement being revoked in about three years time by a Congress-dominated assembly.'[22]

Sir George suggested that a way of ensuring the continuation of Gurkha employment in the British Army might be to get the men themselves, 'and through them their relatives in Nepal . . . to take an active interest in political affairs of their country'. He saw that as the best hope for the future, 'assuming of course that India ceases to meddle in Nepal's internal affairs'. But in saying that 'as a class the hill men hold the majority of the popular vote in the country' he revealed his demographic ignorance – pardonable as it was in someone confined to the Kathmandu valley.[23]

His words struck a responsive chord in the War Office and less than two months later General Headquarters, Far East Land Forces, came back with suggestions for 'awakening the political consciousness of Gurkha personnel in the British Army'. These included the appointment of a liaison officer to Nepal – who would be responsible for procuring news and political information for the men, and looking after their interests in Nepal – as well as the dissemination of news and opinion through Radio Malaya, by means of the Gurkhali newspaper, *Parbate*, and in talks and discussions.[24] Given the lengths to which the old British Indian Army had gone to insulate Gurkhas from political influence, there is something mildly comical in this sudden volte-face.*

By April 1952, the new British ambassador in Kathmandu was able to report a 'somewhat improved' situation in Nepal. The ex-maharajah, 'an old and helpful friend', was now ex-prime minister as well. (He had left Nepal for his granddaughter's wedding in Bombay in December 1951 and never came back, settling in Bangalore in southern India, where he died in 1965 at the age of eighty.[27]) His successor was M. P. Koirala, one of two Brahman brothers who were political and personal rivals and boxed and coxed as prime minister and leader of the Nepali Congress over the next few years.

Despite his opposition to Gurkhas serving in the British Army,

---

*It had to be the right sort of political consciousness, of course. When John Cross was appointed Chief Instructor to the new Army School of Education (Gurkhas) in Malaya in 1949 – because of his exceptional linguistic ability – he flushed out a communist agent, C/Sgt. Deoprakash Rai, 'late of the Darjeeling branch of the Gorkha League':

> The idea was that the communists should set up a cell within the school and pick likely material for their cause from among the students. These men would be indoctrinated before going back to their units where, it was hoped, they could influence other Gurkhas to be anti-British and cause as much trouble as they could.[25]

Deoprakash and a handful of others were quietly discharged from the army. Deoprakash went on to become a member, first, of the Bengal state government, and then of the Indian parliament: 'Well known for his communist views, he died of drink in the early '80s, a folk hero among many Indian-influenced Nepali students.'[26]

Koirala – the ambassador wrote – 'told an American last month that it would be ridiculous to reduce our recruitment unless labour conditions inside Nepal improved'. The previous year's 300 per cent rise in the amount of money sent or brought home from Malaya by British Gurkhas increased the economic pressure in Nepal to maintain the British connection, but the ambassador still counselled caution: 'The general political and economic situation here remains unstable and any suggestion of an increase in our ceiling would be loudly criticised by communists both here and in India . . . I am far from confident about how a request to build up our total to 15,000 or so would be received.'[28]

A more immediate worry for the British military authorities was over the continuing use of recruiting depots on the Indian side of the Nepalese border. In 1951, under pressure from India, the 'Act of Enlistment', the ceremony in which Gurkha recruits took an oath of loyalty to the British crown, was removed from Indian to Nepalese soil. Nehru's view was that British recruiting depots in India were an anachronism and the sooner they, too, were removed to Nepal the better. The British shared his view but feared that this might be the thin end of the wedge and that the next thing would be the suspension of transit rights through India.

The end of the first five-year agreement with Nepal in 1953 'provided the opportunity to arrange to remove the recruiting organisation of the "Brigade of Gurkhas" from India to Nepal . . . [and] it was felt that this move would place HMG in a better position in the future to negotiate an extension of the Agreement'.[29] Yet several years of financial wrangling passed before the foundations of the new depot at Dharan in east Nepal were laid at the beginning of 1957. 'Whether the Government should gamble to the extent of £1½ m. (probably an underestimate) on building in one of the most inaccessible parts of the earth to maintain the supply of Gurkha recruits is clearly a matter for high level consideration,' wrote one civil servant.[30] When Treasury officials grumbled about the extra expense involved in setting up and maintaining the Gurkha lines of communication, the War Office reminded them that not only did the Gurkha division form a major part of British land forces in the Far East but it cost approximately £4 million a year less to maintain than an equivalent British force.[31]

In addition to that, by employing Gurkhas Britain was contributing

How the rich live: interior of a Rana palace in Kathmandu with an
imposing portrait of Maharajah Chandra Shamsher at the head of the
staircase. (E. D. MacLeod)

How the poor live: a *chautara*, or resting place, in the hills of East Nepal, for porters carrying loads in their cone-shaped baskets (*dokos*).
(E. D. MacLeod)

On duty: an inspection of the 2/3rd Gurkha Rifles behind the Western Front early in 1915. (Gurkha Museum)

Off duty: men of the 1/9th Gurkha Rifles relaxing on the frontier in the 1930s in what T. J. Phillips describes as 'the best photo of the Gurkhas that I have ever seen'. (Ray Selby/Gurkha Museum)

2/2nd Goorkha recruits at Kunraghat, Gorakhpur, 1937 – 'as like as peas in a pod' according to the assistant recruiting officer, T. J. Phillips. (Gurkha Museum)

Eastern Gurkha hopefuls lined up at the recruiting depot of Ghoom, Darjeeling, in the early 1950s; one of them demonstrates his impressive chest expansion. (Private collection)

Gurkhas in action during the Second World War in the mountains of
North Africa and in house-to-house fighting in Italy.
(Gurkha Museum)

The Burma campaign against the Japanese during the Second World War:
(i) In the trenches, a rifleman with his kukri in the Chin Hills.
(Gurkha Museum)

(ii) Away from the action, a Bren-gunner carrying his weapon.
(Gurkha Museum)

(iii) Out of the line, two 1/10 GR riflemen resting at Ranchi in India, 1944.
(Private collection)

Emergency in Malaya and
confrontation in Borneo:
A 7th GR rifleman in the Malayan
jungle. (Gurkha Museum)

A 2/2 Goorkha machine-gunner in
Borneo. (Private collection)

War artist Terence Cuneo's reconstruction of the action which earned
Lieutenant-Corporal Rambahadur Limbu of the 2/10 Gurkha Rifles his
VC. (© 10 GR Regimental Trust)

Propaganda and psychological operations:
Men of the 1/7 Gurkha Rifles sharpening their kukris in preparation for
the Falklands War of 1982, the sort of photo which struck terror in the
hearts of Argentinian conscripts. (*SOLDIER* Magazine © reserved)

And all smiles in Bosnia as an RGR rifleman hands out a news-sheet in
Banja Luka market. (Gurkha Museum)

aid to Nepal to the tune of some £500,000 annually, or about a sixth of its revenue: 'This figure compared not unfavourably with aid being given by India, China and the United States.'[32] The problem was that this aid was focused on the hills rather than the politically minded Kathmandu valley. Maj-Gen. Pugh suggested that 'if we were to make a gesture, such as providing a hospital, we would obtain advantages out of all proportion to the cost'.[33] (The military hospital built at Dharan would outlive the recruiting depot and be handed over to the Nepalese civil authorities when the camp was finally closed some thirty years after it was built.)

In March 1955 King Tribhuvan died and was succeeded by his son Mahendra, who took a more active part in politics than his father had done. A year later, the British under-secretary of state for war, Antony Head, visited Kathmandu and expressed his concern that not enough attention was being paid to Nepal:

> The trouble, I think, is that we are inclined to regard Nepal as a kind of remote Liechtenstein or Luxemburg, whereas in fact it is in a key position in the cold war . . . We may be sure that if we do not take advantage of the present fluid situation there, the Chinese will.[34]

The foreign secretary, Selwyn Lloyd, agreed: 'We too have been exercised about Nepal for some time.' In time-honoured fashion, Lloyd saw the main purpose of helping the Nepalese as being to 'make them favourably disposed towards the renewal of our agreement on Gurkha recruitment when the time comes in July 1958'. To that end he was pleased that the Treasury had agreed to 'a joint request of our two Departments to waive the tuition and maintenance charges for four Nepalese cadets a year, for three years, at Sandhurst'.[35] (An annex to the tripartite agreement allowed for the provision of officer training for Royal Nepalese Army cadets at Sandhurst, but previously the Nepalese government had had to pay tuition and costs.)

At the same time the first Gurkha boys to be specially prepared for the RMA Sandhurst entry in Malaya were now beginning to filter through the system – with mixed fortunes, as a War Office minute testifies:

We confirm that up to date only three candidates have been sent here for RMAS training, one failed RCB [Regular Commissions Board] after completing training at Eaton Hall OCS [Officer Cadet School], one failed after one term at RMAS, and one is now at RMAS due to pass out in December 1957. A further candidate is due to enter Eaton Hall OCS in August 1957 for subsequent entry to RMAS in January 1958.[36]

In the matter of commissioning Gurkhas, the British were always looking over their shoulders to see what the Indians were up to. In 1953, when Maj-Gen. Perowne was MGBG, he asked the British military attaché in Delhi to find out how many Gurkhas in the Indian Army had been promoted to lieutenant-colonel. The short answer was that the 'Indian Gurkha Officer who gets ahead is invariably Indian bred and educated'. Every one of the eight Gurkha officers to reach the rank of lieutenant-colonel and above (there was one brigadier) was Indian-domiciled and none of them had any connection with Nepal. They had all been granted Indian Army commissions before independence and had only transferred to Gorkha regiments after partition.[37] No serious competition in that quarter, then.

But what sort of pay should a Sandhurst-commissioned Gurkha receive: should it correspond to British or Indian Army rates? The War Office ruled that 'candidates should be informed that on being commissioned they will be paid as second lieutenants at a monthly rate of Rs. 302 (this corresponds to the Indian Army rate for a second lieutenant, less the food element of Rs. 48 per month). In addition, whilst actually serving in Malaya or Hong Kong they will be eligible for a Malaya/HK Addition of Rs. 200 per month'.[38] This pittance would put them on a par with existing GCOs; yet the anomalous position of GCOs was officially recognized, if not rectified:

Though they are more than anxious to play their part as officers they are very conscious of their inability to do so, and cannot join local clubs, have a car, take local leave, or return hospitality.

As a result, except when on duty, they tend to live a life quite apart from the other officers and families, and take no part in the normal life of the community.

This, quite naturally, has the effect of making them retiring and shy, and tends to make them regard themselves as 'poor brethren', who are not considered to be the equal of other officers.[39]

The Brigade of Gurkhas Liaison Officer at the War Office, Lt-Col. C. W. Yeates, argued that since commissioned Gurkhas in the Indian Army were in fact Indians, and were treated as such, 'we should . . . do the same, and pay our Gurkhas as British officers' – though he stopped short of suggesting equal pensions: 'I appreciate that the [pension] scales are governed largely by the country of domicile. The logic of this cannot be disputed . . .'[40]

The argument over the pay and pensions of both GCOs and Sandhurst-commissioned Gurkhas rumbled on; at the end of 1957 the War Office informed the Treasury: 'The problem has some urgency because the first young GCO is to be commissioned from RMA Sandhurst on 14 Dec 1957. The present GCO rates are inadequate for his needs.' Given the differences in the cost of living in Britain and Nepal, the War Office was not seeking parity with British officers, but 90 per cent relativity.[41] Even this was refused, on the grounds that British officers' rates of pay had just gone up; but a compromise was agreed.[42]

A year and a half later, the MGBG, Maj-Gen. J. A. R. Robertson, who had already 'requested that the designation GCO should not be applied to Gurkha officers who are commissioned from RMA Sandhurst, but only to those promoted from QGO or below', wrote indignantly to the War Office:

I consider it quite unacceptable that an officer who has . . . passed into RMAS, lived and trained with his British contemporaries and finally passed out and been commissioned with them into a unit of the British Army as a Regular British Officer should have to be told that because his skin is a different colour he cannot receive the same rates of pay.[43]

But the point was still not conceded, and after another year of wrangling the War Office settled instead for an increase of pay for Sandhurst-trained Gurkha officers. The objection to parity – expressed within the War Office itself as much as in the Treasury – was that it would racially discriminate against *British* officers. The Adjutant-General seems to have had the final word; he noted in a memo to the secretary of state for war: 'I agree with [my staff's] findings that to produce equity you must have different rates of favour of the British officer because his UK financial liabilities are greater than those of the Gurkha officer ex-RMAS. This is particularly so on marriage.'[44]

A novel by Mani Dixit, published in Kathmandu in 1980, compares the relative poverty of a group of Gurkhas at Sandhurst not with their British, but with their Nepali contemporaries there. The two Nepalese Army cadets have money to spend on weekends in London, which are way beyond the means of the five 'Hong Kong' Gurkhas. And that is not the only difference between them:

> . . . It was Madan KC who was always carping to the five lads from Hong Kong about offering their services to fight for a foreign army. 'Quite frankly, I don't see what you boys joined up for. After all, I'm sure that when you are in the British Army and have to fight, it's not and cannot ever be for your homeland,' said Madan.
>
> 'So what. It's a job like any other. If doctors and engineers can go to foreign lands and earn money, they are also working as mercenaries. When such town-based educated elite decide to settle elsewhere, they are deserting their motherland. Why should people like you pick on us poor blighters from the hills and point your fingers at us? After all, there are not enough jobs to go all around, and by joining the British or the Indian Army, some Nepalese lads are at least bettering themselves and perhaps ensuring that they will be able to provide a better future for their families,' replied Top Bahadur.
>
> The Kathmandu boys, in their turn, had also realised that so far as the army life was concerned, the boys from the hills who had come to Sandhurst via Hong Kong had a more healthy attitude and certainly were more professional.[45]

In December 1958, just before the first general election ever to take place in Nepal, the British ambassador reported the arrival in Kathmandu of his opposite number, the Russian ambassador to India and Nepal, bearing such lavish gifts for the king as an Ilyushin-14 aircraft, a car, six motorcycles and twelve bicycles, all made in Russia. 'I find it difficult to believe that this generosity springs from pure benevolence,' Mr Scopes wrote. 'Praise for Nepal's policy of international neutrality was much to the fore in speeches during the King's recent visit to Russia, the contradiction between the proclaimed neutrality of Nepal and continuing Gurkha recruitment is obvious and frequently stressed here and the termination of Gurkha recruitment is point number one in the Nepalese Communist Party's electoral programme.' The ambassador urged the government to compete with Moscow in terms of offering technical training, supplying aircraft and inviting Mahendra on a royal visit to London. Only then would the Nepalese government begin to look favourably on the reiterated request for more Gurkha recruits.[46]

The Nepalese election resulted in a landslide victory for the Nepali Congress and B. P. Koirala became the first prime minister of an elected government. The state visit of Mahendra to London which Scopes, the British ambassador, had been angling for was arranged for 1960. It came at a turning-point in modern Nepalese history, the moment when the country was being transformed from one of the world's most closed societies into one of the more accessible Third World states. Travellers began to penetrate a land previously innocent of tourism, eventually turning Kathmandu into the Mecca of the hippy trail; foreign embassies mushroomed, led by the United States, the Soviet Union and China, and the more Gurkha-minded of British politicians worried about the burgeoning communist interest in the region.

But despite British fears, the Nepalese government did nothing to prevent a gradual increase in recruitment. As Britain's Chief of the Imperial General Staff, Field Marshal Festing, noted in October 1960, 'Both India and the UK have in fact already recruited well over their ceilings . . . whilst the Nepalese are aware of this position they have been content to accept it.' The British figure had crept up to 14,400 and the plan was to increase it to 15,500 in 1963, with the possibility of raising it later to 17,500, though 'it may be wise to avoid any new legal ceiling'. The rationale for such an increase was the difference in the annual cost of British and Gurkha other ranks in the Far East; while a British soldier cost £1,100 a year, a Gurkha cost only £345.[47] So long as both parties to the agreement gained from the trade in military manpower neither was likely to end it, whatever the Communist Party might say.

The democratic experiment in Nepal was anyway short-lived; soon after his return from London, Mahendra, with the support of the army, dismissed the Cabinet, arrested and gaoled its ministers and dissolved Parliament. He reinstated himself as *de facto* prime minister and, though a period of unrest followed, it ceased abruptly when the border war between India and China broke out in late 1962. Mahendra had been on the point of making major political concessions, but the war dramatically changed the picture. India, intent on strengthening the security of its northern frontier, suddenly needed Nepal and was ready to provide 'what amounted to an implicit guarantee of the royal regime against India-based opposition forces'. This enabled Mahendra to introduce a new constitution, replacing parliamentary democracy with what he saw as a more truly national political system based on indigenous village councils, or *panchayats*, that would build democracy 'from the grass-roots'.[48] (The partyless *panchayat* system outlived Mahendra, who died in 1972, and was not finally abolished until 1990, when a series of riots obliged his son and heir Birendra to legalize political parties once again.)

These developments, of course, coincided with British interests. The suppression of political parties in Nepal removed the major obstacle to recruitment and there was nothing now to prevent the implementation of the plan of Gurkha expansion outlined by the CIGS in 1960 – except that the Malayan Emergency was over. Britain's imperial decline, precipitated by Indian independence in 1947, was now gathering pace, blown along by the 'winds of change'; and the Gurkhas' perceived role as imperial troops was therefore shrinking. In 1957, a year after the Suez crisis, the minister of defence had visited the Far East. While on tour, he 'was given a figure of some 4,600 all ranks as the rundown between now and 1 April 1963 of military manpower of all types (UK, Commonwealth, Gurkha, Malayan, etc.)'[49] This was the first ominous sign of what was to become a recurring theme, the reduction of British forces overseas. From the beginning of the 1960s the Brigade of Gurkhas was fighting, not just for the crown in far-flung outposts of empire, but for its own survival. A key figure in both these battles was General Sir Walter Walker, the wartime CO of the 4/8th Gurkha Rifles in Burma.

In 1958, Walker was a brigadier commanding 99 Brigade in the Seremban district of Malaya. Operation 'Tiger' was conceived in 1957, the year in which Malaya achieved its independence (in the absence of a suitable Malay word the Arabic *Merdeka* was used) without benefit of the Malayan Communist Party. The aim of the operation was to eliminate the ninety-six guerrillas believed to be still at large in the jungles of south Johore, the state adjacent to Singapore. Walker planned it meticulously, briefing not just the commanding officers of the four Gurkha battalions involved, the supporting arms, the artillery and the RAF in particular, but also Special Branch and the Psychological Warfare Department. Phase one began on New Year's Day 1958; phase two on 15 April. There was bombing and shelling, aimed at winkling out the largest known remaining CT unit; there was intensive patrolling and, most effective and demanding, there were ambushes.

After the men of 2/2 GR had been sitting in a swamp for twenty-seven days without sight or sound of the enemy, their CO begged Walker to lift the ambush as the conditions were fast becoming unendurable. But the brigadier was unmoved; he was acting on Special Branch information and ordered that the men remain where they were. The very next day three terrorists walked into the trap. Two were killed outright, and the third surrendered after his rifle had been shot from his hands. Only then was Walker satisfied. John Cross comments:

> That one incident encapsulates all that the British have come to expect of the Gurkha on operations: unbelievable stamina, excellent marksmanship and superb fieldcraft. Remembering the standards of ten years before, trust in the Gurkhas, especially at regimental level, had been totally vindicated.[50]

Before the end of the year the whole of Johore was declared 'white' – that is, free of CTs. It was only a matter of time now before the end of the Emergency was announced. Officially, it ended on 1 August 1960 and the Gurkha battalions, whose only post-war peacetime soldiering had been one two-year stint – or at most two – in Hong Kong, where they guarded the border with China, looked forward to a period of well-earned rest and retraining. Not that rest was ever a serious option where Walter Walker, who had been promoted to GOC, 17th Gurkha Infantry Division, and appointed Major-General Brigade of Gurkhas, was concerned.

General Sir Richard Hull, Commander-in-Chief, Far East Land

Forces, was due to leave Singapore towards the end of 1961 to become Chief of the Imperial General Staff. Before he went, he summoned Walker to his official residence to inform him, in the strictest confidence, of what he, as CIGS-designate, and the Army Council were thinking with regard to the future of the Brigade of Gurkhas. Under pressure to economize, the British Army would have to make stringent cuts, he said – the only question was where the axe would fall. If it came to a straight choice between British and Gurkha infantry, the government, the Army Council and he himself all agreed that the cuts should fall on the Gurkhas: 'In the long term it would be the British infantry that would be most important to Britain.'[51]

Although the drift of the conversation had been anticipated by Walker – a mole in the Ministry of Defence had warned him of what was afoot: '. . . you will be presented with a *fait accompli*. For God's sake, fight, fight to the bitter end'[52] – he was aghast to hear that the plan Whitehall was considering would reduce the Gurkhas to the strength of a single infantry brigade group, i.e. 4,000 men. Hull's early service was in the 17/21st Lancers, a cavalry regiment, and his subsequent career had been at the very heart of the British military establishment. There was no personal animosity between him and Walker, but the traditional mutual mistrust between the British Army and the old Indian Army was epitomized by these two generals with their contrasting backgrounds. Where Hull was a War Office man, a 'Whitehall warrior' at home in the corridors of power, Walker was an outsider, an inspiring commander at all levels in the field and a military man to his fingertips, but out of his depth in the world of intrigue and compromise in which politicians moved.

Now he found himself in an impossible position: as MGBG, he was responsible for the Brigade of Gurkhas; but Hull had insisted on confidentiality, and he was honour-bound to keep what he knew to himself. He could not openly oppose a plan he was not supposed even to know about. So he bided his time, bearing in mind that about a year hence he would make his annual report as MGBG in person to the king of Nepal.

At that meeting with the king, Walker read out his official report, which contained nothing in the least objectionable to Whitehall or to the British ambassador who had accompanied him into the royal presence. He informed Mahendra of the arrival in May that year of the 1/6th Gurkha Rifles at Tidworth on Salisbury Plain, the first Gurkha battalion ever to be stationed in the UK, where they would form part of the Strategic Reserve; he mentioned a training scheme in the UK for Gurkha nurses and reported on the fall in the incidence of tuberculosis, to which Gurkhas were peculiarly prone; and he gave an account of mopping-up operations in the jungles of northern Malaya.

His formal presentation over, Walker was invited by Mahendra to speak freely, which – to the ambassador's mounting consternation – he proceeded to do. He asked the king straight out if the government of Nepal had been consulted about the proposed reductions in the number of Gurkhas serving in the British Army. Mahendra confessed his ignorance of any such move and encouraged Walker to tell him more. Walker explained how the governmental consultation process was likely to have gone, with the foreign secretary reminding the prime minister of the extent of Nepalese economic dependence on the British Army, and the Chiefs of Staff, oblivious of the wider implications, insisting that since all the services faced cuts the Gurkhas must accept their share and should certainly not expect to receive more consideration than (if as much as) the British element of the British Army.

Nepal, Walker warned Mahendra, would be presented with a *fait accompli* unless the king made his voice heard in London. Walker's biographer writes:

> Clearly disturbed, the King thanked Walker and said he would
> consider what action to take. Then Walker and an apparently
> discomforted ambassador took their leave.[53]

Walker made things even worse from a British point of view by forging an alliance with the United States ambassador, Henry E. Stebbins, who regarded Britain's employment of Gurkhas as a stabilizing factor in Nepalese affairs and undertook to make his view known in Washington. Secure in the knowledge that 'he had done what he saw as his duty', Walker relaxed and set out in early December to enjoy the trek he had planned in the hills.[54] He was blithely unaware of two storms that were brewing, one of his own making in Whitehall and the other in Brunei, so totally unexpected that when it broke most of the top brass in Far Eastern command (himself included) were absent from Malaya and Singapore. The first would almost undo him but the second, which soon escalated into a full-scale – if still undeclared – border war, would confirm his reputation as a brilliant commander in the field.

In October 1962 *The Times* reported that, as minister of defence, 'Mr Thorneycroft is understood to have approved a plan to reduce the number of infantry battalions in the Gurkha brigade from eight to four, leaving a force of between 8,500 and 9,000 available to the Army.' The idea was either to amalgamate the two battalions of each regiment or, alternatively, to disband one of each. 'Before a final decision is announced,' the defence correspondent of *The Times* went on, 'the Government are to consult the Government of Nepal, where Gurkhas are recruited, and that of India, whose armed forces also include a brigade of Gurkhas.'[55] The wording of the report bears out General Walker's contention that the Nepalese government would be presented with a *fait accompli*: it did not say, 'Before a final decision is *reached*', but before it is *announced*, which suggested little room for manoeuvre.

It might seem perverse to disband Gurkha battalions just at the time when National Service was coming to an end and many British infantry battalions were below strength. But 'the War Office are understood to hold the view that, although the Gurkhas have no difficulty in finding recruits for eight battalions of infantry, it would be wrong to keep them permanently at their present strength while the United Kingdom Army is being reduced in size'. This sounds suspiciously like what the third leader of *The Times* described as 'the view held in some of the darker corners of Whitehall that in the matter of cutting down the armed forces the principle must be equal misery for all'.[56] But the Gurkhas might also be seen as victims of their own success; theirs was the biggest single contribution to victory in Malaya and with the planned incorporation of Singapore and Malaya into a Federation of Greater Malaysia internal security would become a local responsibility and 'not only will the overall task of the British Army be reduced but the four battalions of Gurkhas stationed there will no longer be needed'. The retired and crippled – but by no means inactive – General Sir Francis Tuker took up this point in a letter to *The Times*:

The present hardly seems opportune for proposing the disbandment of half our Gurkha infantry. Has Nepal been consulted? She may well be resentful that we used her men just as long as it suited our purpose to destroy the communist guerrillas in Malaya and to set that country on its feet, and then cast many of them aside.[57]

In March 1963 Walker was summoned to London. Fortunately for the major-general, the Vice-Chief of the Imperial General Staff was ex-Indian Army and an old friend. He warned Walker that he had been recalled from Borneo to answer for what he had done: 'Hull regarded this as gross disloyalty. Profumo [the secretary of state for war] was outraged at his alliance with the American ambassador.'[58] The only thing for him to do was to apologize; he had made his point, now he must eat humble pie, or his career was over; then where would his Gurkhas be?

This was not an easy option for as proud a man as Walker, but even he could see the logic of it. Nothing else could save him, not even the rumours which now reached his ears of John Profumo's involvement with a young woman who was also the mistress of the Russian naval attaché.

The interview with the CIGS was predictably tense. First, Hull kept him waiting for forty minutes. Then he greeted him coldly, without a smile or a handshake. He demanded an explanation of his behaviour which Walker, bearing in mind the VCIGS's warning, made no attempt to defend, offering an apology instead. 'Had you not apologised,' Hull told him, 'I would have had to sack you.' As it was, though he would remain MCBG in name, Walker would no longer advise the Army Council on Gurkha affairs; Maj-Gen. J. A. R. Robertson was being called out of retirement to take on the role of Gurkha liaison officer at the War Office. Walker, who might easily have been court-martialed, had got away with the equivalent of a sharp rap over the knuckles. His biographer attempts to exonerate him by contrasting Hull's old-fashioned, terribly British concern with acceptable social conduct with Walker's thoroughly modern, thrusting, US-style approach: he 'had behaved as senior American officers customarily behaved: rallying a powerful lobby to produce results which conventional methods could not'.[59]*

---

*Perhaps this was what inspired Walker, on his retirement in the seventies, to launch the campaign for vigilantes which briefly turned the media spotlight on him and earned him, once again, the disapprobation of his seniors. When a retired major-general told Templer that he was working for Walter Walker's 'Civil Assistance', Sir Gerald dismissed him curtly, saying, 'You must be mad.'[60]

As a result of Walker's undiplomatic intervention, Field Marshal Viscount Slim was hauled out of a very busy retirement (though field marshals never officially retire) and sent on a top secret mission to Kathmandu to square the king of Nepal over War Office policy. As his biographer writes:

> Slim's cover for this mission was perhaps the most implausible disguise attempted by a famous figure since Churchill, faced with the need to change transport at Gibraltar during one of his wartime journeys, suggested to Alanbrooke that he should hide behind a grey beard. The late commander of the 14th Army flew to India as 'Mr Phipps', ostensibly on a business visit for ICI. But as Churchill himself once observed to Lord Moran about Slim, 'Oh yes, he has a hell of a face'. It was hardly likely that he would pass from India to Nepal unrecognized, and inevitably one of his pilots, who had flown under him in Burma, gave a rapturous greeting to Uncle Bill. However, though the deception plan was less subtle than that for the Meiktila victory, the result of Slim's foray was satisfactory.[61]

In contrast to Walker, Slim's professionalism was unimpeachable. He explained the British government's difficulties to Mahendra and readily obtained the king's consent to reductions on the understanding that the War Office would do everything possible to minimize their impact. It helped that the four most senior officers in the Royal Nepalese Army had all served under Slim during the war. Profumo expressed his gratitude to Slim in a fulsome letter, but the old field marshal was under no illusions as to the advisability of the policy. He wrote privately to Field Marshal Lord Harding (ex-colonel of the 6th Gurkhas) on 1 April 1963, 'I again told the Secretary of State for War that I thought anyone who reduced the Gurkhas in the present world situation was "crackers".'[62]

Events would quickly prove him right and put a stay of execution on the reduction of the Gurkhas. A minor revolt in Brunei escalated into a major confrontation along a thousand miles of border between Sarawak, Brunei and North Borneo (Sabah) on one side, and Indonesian Borneo, or Kalimantan, on the other. Maj-Gen. Walter Walker would describe 1963 as 'a year which began with the end of a revolution and ended with the beginning of an undeclared war'.[63]

Borneo, if it meant anything at all to most Britishers, meant the country known as Sarawak, which up to the Second World War had been ruled by the 'White Rajahs', the Brooke family, as a kind of personal fiefdom. A few might have heard of the wartime exploits of Tom Harrisson, who had organized the resistance of the Borneo tribes against the Japanese (and was once again called into action against the Indonesians); others might know that much of the land was mountainous and covered with tropical forest even denser in places than the Malayan jungle, and that inland villagers lived communally in 'longhouses'. But that would be about the extent of most people's knowledge.

In the political events of the early 1960s there were three key players. Tunku Abdul Rahman, the prime minister of the Federation of Malaya, who had been something of a playboy prince until General Templer had groomed him for office, first floated the idea of *Malaysia*, an economic and political union of Malaya, Singapore, North Borneo, Brunei and Sarawak, in May 1961. This seemed an admirable scheme to the decolonizing British government but was anathema to the second player, President Sukarno of Indonesia, who had long dreamed of a pan-Indonesian empire stretching from the Indian Ocean to the Pacific and incorporating the whole of Borneo and Malaya. The third player in this power game was the Sultan of the small but oil-rich Brunei, whose aim or 'problem', as the regimental historians of 2 GR nicely put it, 'was to preserve an old feudalistic order while giving it the outward appearance of a parliamentary democracy'.[64]

In September 1962 the People's Party won an overwhelming victory in the Brunei elections but was still outnumbered by the Sultan's nominees in the legislative assembly. The trouble which flared up in early December was fomented by the secret and militant wing of the People's Party, which had strong Indonesian links and backing.

Not only were all the Far Eastern service chiefs 'in the wrong place', as Walter Walker put it when he heard the news of the Brunei revolt on a transistor radio in the mountains of east Nepal, but the British battalion on stand-by in case of trouble, the Queen's Own Highlanders, was seriously depleted at the time, with five platoons out on anti-piracy patrols off the coast of Borneo.[65] So the 1/2nd Goorkhas had to break off their annual inspection and be ready to move at once – provided planes could be found to fly them. By late afternoon on 8 December 1962 two rifle companies and a small HQ under the command of the battalion second-in-command were on their way to Brunei, with the remainder of the battalion due to follow the next day.[66]

The second-in-command of 1/2 GR was greeted at Brunei airport with a gloomy prognosis. Armed rebels had made attacks in several different places, including the Shell oilfield at Seria, some seventy miles away. The situation was chaotic and the two rifle companies, without maps of the town and expecting to be engaged in riot control rather than armed insurrection, had to adjust quickly to the new reality. The troops fought through the night; the remainder of the battalion joined them the next day; and 1/2 GR was soon reinforced by the Queen's Own Highlanders and two other British battalions, as well as a Royal Marines company from 42 Commando (under the command of Jeremy Moore, who became a household name in the Falklands war), which landed under fire at Limbang on the border with Sarawak. They divided the country between them and went after the rebels in the jungle: 'The [2nd Goorkha] Battalion's bag exceeded 800 prisoners. That the rebellion was both short-lived and ineffective was due in no small measure to the determination and speed shown by the two companies that landed on the evening of 8 December.'[67]

On 19 December, Maj-Gen. Walter Walker, who was now in the right place, was appointed Director of Borneo Operations with the object of clearing the rebels out of Brunei before Malaysia was established in August 1963, a task he achieved with some months to spare. But the proposed unification did not quite go according to plan. The three Borneo countries were due to merge with Malaya and Singapore on 31 August, but Indonesian and, to a lesser extent, Philippine opposition to the scheme prompted a United Nations fact-finding tour of the area designed to discover what people really wanted. This visit, according to John Cross, whose linguistic skills and proven empathy with tribespeople led to his being summoned from UK leave by Walter Walker to take over command of the Border Scouts, was stage-managed by the pro-Malaysia (and anti-Chinese) lobby to such a degree that it was a farce: 'I had never been so close to international decisions before but my opinion of that august body, the United Nations, which I bitterly described as a High Level Platform for Low Level Propaganda, has never been the same since.'[68] As it was, Malaysia did not come into being until 16 September, and by then Brunei had opted out, preferring independence under British protection. (Two years later the predominantly Chinese Singapore also pulled out.)

By this time cross-border raids all along the Indonesian border with the former British colonies confirmed General Walker's fear that the Brunei revolt was not a one-off event but the prelude to a larger and far more serious conflagration.

The 2/6th Gurkhas lost a British officer in one of these early Indonesian raids into Sarawak and though they exacted a measure of revenge, inflicting a dozen or so casualties on the enemy, they were moved to another area before the battle was completed, to be replaced by 1/2 GR.[69] Another raid led to a furious battle between a small detachment of seven 1/2nd Goorkhas, supported by twenty-one Border Scouts – until it got too hot for all but one of them. Only three of the Gurkhas survived unscathed after two hours of mortar bombing, machine-gun and small arms fire, yet with the help of the one remaining Border Scout they dragged their two badly wounded comrades out of the immediate danger area, and made them as comfortable as they could before heading for the nearest village, which was many miles away: 'Living off roots, they had a long and hazardous journey as it was four days before they reached the outpost at Belaga, weak and exhausted but with weapons spotlessly clean and able to give a first-hand account of the battle.'[70]

The 1/2nd Goorkhas then moved into the area in force, set up ambushes and shot up two boats carrying some thirty men, causing them to collide and then capsize in the fast-flowing river. The two wounded Gurkhas were eventually rescued and evacuated. The enemy force, which had consisted of around a hundred soldiers and almost as many porters, was commanded by a Major Muljono. The career of this dedicated guerrilla had begun during the Japanese occupation, continued with the return of the Dutch and now brought him up against the British, whose Jungle Warfare School in Malaya was one of several he had attended.[71]

Cross-border raids, commanded by such men, presented the British security forces with a problem; as long as they were confined to their own side of the border they were forced on to the defensive and could only react to enemy initiatives, rather than take offensive action of their own. From the start, Walter Walker pressed for permission to make retaliatory raids across the border. But, in his own words, 'As usual the politicians were afraid of their own shadows and dragged their feet.'[72] It would take another year and an escalation of the conflict through an alarming, if abortive Indonesian sea and air raid on the mainland of Malaya itself before the British government allowed limited penetration into Indonesian territory; and even then the strictest secrecy was imposed both at the time and for several years afterwards. Unlike later conflicts in the Falklands and in the Gulf, the Confrontation in Borneo was a largely unreported war.

From the beginning, Walker concentrated on getting early information of enemy movements and winning the battle for the 'hearts and minds' of the people, the importance of which Templer had demonstrated in Malaya. The Border Scouts had a crucial role to play in both these objectives; unlike the SAS patrols which were operating in small numbers in enemy territory, even before permission to cross the border had been granted, the Border Scouts were intelligence-gatherers rather than warriors, the 'eyes and ears' of the regular forces who would relay information back to battalion and brigade commanders. Their other important function was to strengthen the spirit of resistance along the border, to demonstrate by their presence the government's commitment to the defence of the border peoples. They could make the difference between defeat and victory, General Walker told John Cross when he briefed him on 28 July 1963. 'I was told that it was up to me to make the organisation work,' Cross recalled. 'It was an enormous responsibility.'[73]

But the Indonesians played into Walker's hands by their campaign of terror: 'Their cold-blooded murders, coupled with the looting of the villages, resulted in the news of their brutality being passed from longhouse to longhouse. This meant that I had won the hearts and minds of the border villages – in fact of all the people of Borneo.'[74] The war itself was not so easily won. Walker leaned heavily on the SAS and all eight Gurkha infantry battalions, each of which served a series of four-month tours in Borneo, because these were the troops with experience of jungle warfare. But so long as the Indonesians could operate from safe bases just over the border in Kalimantan, they called the shots and Walker could only gnash his teeth in frustration. After the ill-conceived

invasion of Malaya by the Indonesians in 1964, however, he was given
the go-ahead to make secret and limited cross-border raids. These operations, code-named 'Claret', took the fight to the enemy and
transformed the fortunes of the war.

Both sides relied on ambushes to achieve their ends. These could be
very uncomfortable experiences – and not just as a result of enemy
action. Captain C. J. D. Bullock, commander of 2/2 GR's Support
Company, set up an ambush on what was supposed to be a riverbank
but had been turned into a swamp by heavy rain. For nearly three days
he and his men (who had to be regularly relieved because the water was
so icy) stood up to their shoulders in this swamp before their vigil was
rewarded with the sight of an enemy boat. They opened fire and killed
all four of the boat's occupants. But another, bigger boat coming up
behind the first fired on them in retaliation and Bullock had to beat a
hasty retreat:

> As we trudged through the swamp I had plenty of time to think about
> the ambush. Although it had been a limited success we would have
> done better to let the first boat go by and engage the second one which
> probably contained far more men. Nevertheless not being an entirely
> dedicated soldier I could not help but be secretly glad that only four
> Indonesian women would be without their sons, husbands or lovers as
> a result of our activity.[75]

Less than a month later, the same tough but humane officer set up
another ambush beside a river, well inside Indonesian territory. This
time the enemy approached by land, a considerable force of more than
a hundred men opposing Support Company's forty-strong ambush.
Rifleman Ramparsad Pun waited until the leading scout was practically on top of him before firing his Bren gun. He killed four men with
his opening burst and several more were wounded. But the Indonesians
now attacked in force and a fierce battle ensued:

> A young L/Cpl called Birbahadur was an absolute tower of strength
> rushing from threatened sector to sector directing fire and shouting
> encouragement. The real Section Commander, a man of great promise
> in peace, was nowhere to be seen having taken cover behind a tree. He

was subsequently branded a coward and his career ended, yet how natural an impulse is self-preservation?[76]

Bullock had lost contact with his gunner officer, a Captain Masters from New Zealand, and wandering off in search of him in the jungle gloom mistook a couple of Indonesians for him and another man. These were just taking aim when one of them let out a yell and both went down. Looking round, Bullock was surprised to see Rifleman Hariprasad Thapa who had taken it upon himself to shadow his company commander and, seeing the danger he was in, opened fire. His action, Bullock felt, was 'a fine example of that special Gurkha fidelity and courage, and there is little doubt that he saved my life'.[77]

But the danger was far from over. In the face of another Indonesian assault, Bullock ordered his men to withdraw. Still without his gunner officer, he could not bring down artillery fire on the enemy, and his company's escape from the ambush position was as eventful as the ambush itself, involving acts of outstanding bravery from several individuals, including the lost Captain Masters, who carried and dragged a wounded Gurkha company sergeant major through 6,000 yards of thick jungle and swamp before being obliged to leave him with all the food and water he had and set off alone the next day to get help.

Masters got back to the company base late in the afternoon and immediately returned with Bullock and a doctor, and twenty men, to rescue the wounded CSM. It took all night and most of the next day to locate him, by which time his condition had become critical and the doctor recommended immediate evacuation. The rule was that helicopters were not to be flown across the border except in the direst emergency, and this might have given pause to a less redoubtable commanding officer than Lieutenant-Colonel Neill, the man who as a young officer with the Chindits had been so disgusted with Wingate for his cavalier attitude towards the wounded. Neill did not hesitate. A helicopter went in, darkness and heavy rain notwithstanding, and the wounded man was winched out on a stretcher. The CSM, who would otherwise have lost his leg, underwent a successful operation and was soon walking again without so much as a limp.

This cross-border action produced a number of gallantry awards: both Masters and Bullock – as well as an SAS company sergeant major – got

MCs (though Bullock's award was not for this action alone); L/Cpl Birbahadur Pun won a DCM and Rfn. Ramprasad Pun an MM. But the ultimate *bahaduri*, the one VC of the campaign, went to L/Cpl Rambahadur Limbu of 2/10 GR (battalion recently under threat of disbandment) for actions described in the official citation as reaching 'a zenith of determination and premeditated valour which must count among the most notable on record'.[78] The lance-corporal had been in action only once before when he found himself leading his support group along a very narrow ridge against a strongly entrenched enemy. When he and his two companions came under machine-gun fire Rambahadur rushed forward, killed the machine-gunner with a hand grenade and took the first trench. His group now became the focus of fire from two other machine-guns which he knew would have to be knocked out; but in going forward his two comrades were both hit and wounded. Rambahadur, though the target of close-range and accurate fire, succeeded in rescuing them both and carrying them to safety. It took him twenty minutes to bring them in and both, alas, had already died of their wounds. But Rambahadur, miraculously unscathed, made a third foray into the maelstrom of battle, this time to recover an abandoned Bren gun which he then used to good effect, finally leading a charge through the jungle, firing from the hip and personally accounting for at least four Indonesians. After an hour of intense fighting the hill-crest was taken; and it was successfully held against a series of counter-attacks.

'In scale and achievement this engagement stands out as of the first importance', the citation reads, 'and there is no doubt that, but for the inspired conduct and example set by Lance Corporal Rambahadur at the most vital stage of the battle, much less would have been achieved and greater casualties caused.'[79] The action is misleadingly described as having taken place 'in the Bau District of Sarawak'; the citation could not reveal the true location for fear of compromising the secret Claret operations. Therefore it was unable – in the words of the 10 GR regimental historian – to 'do justice to the unique psychological pressure created by operating 4,000 yards inside enemy territory in a garrison complex sited for mutual support and covered by artillery and mortars; pressures which were magnified two fold at a stroke as soon as casualties were suffered at the very outset of the action'.[80]

Konfrontasi did not formally end until 11 August 1966, but by the time Walter Walker handed over command to Major-General George Lea in 1965 the outcome was no longer in much doubt. Borneo could easily have turned into another Vietnam but for the quality of the military leadership and the jungle skills of the troops. The Gurkhas did more than their share of the fighting: 'there was not a day throughout Confrontation when at least one Gurkha battalion was not involved'. The historians of the post-war 2nd Goorkhas (and of the Confrontation) attribute Indonesia's defeat to the fact that 'the Security Forces had the advantage of a major military base in the right place – Singapore; had complete command of sea and air; and had a good intelligence service'.[81] The long-drawn-out war also ruined Indonesia economically and the downfall of Sukarno, and his replacement by Suharto, ushered in an era of peaceful co-existence with Malaysia.

In the eighteen years of more or less continuous, mostly low-level warfare in Malaya and Borneo between 1948 and 1965 the Brigade of Gurkhas had lost thirteen British officers and nearly 200 Gurkhas killed in action and ten British officers and 382 Gurkhas wounded.[82] In that same period it had proved its military value over and over again. Yet the ceasefire in Borneo had barely been ratified before reductions and redundancies were back on the War Office agenda. Was this base ingratitude, or the inevitable outcome of political and military withdrawal east of Suez? The heart dictates one answer, the head another. Christopher Bullock of 2/2 GR, one of the heroes of *Konfrontasi*, expresses the regimental officer's point of view:

Many of our splendid soldiers had soon to leave as the Brigade of Gurkhas was cut by over half once Confrontation had ended. When I returned as Adjutant to the Battalion after leave it was my distasteful duty to send many fine men away on enforced redundancy after all we had been through together. However much I explained, they never really understood why I, of all people, should do this to them. Sometimes after long exhausting sessions with them I returned to my room in the Mess totally disillusioned with the system which, in its unseemly haste to dispense with those that had helped win Confrontation, affronted human dignity to such an extent.[83]

10

Rundown

Once Malaysia was established and British troops were no longer required there, Hong Kong became the home of the Brigade of Gurkhas. And so it remained for the next thirty years. Though there were no wars to fight – with the exception of the Falklands war in 1982, in which just one Gurkha battalion was involved – there were disturbances in Hong Kong itself following the cultural revolution in China and again in the post-Mao era, with the massive influx of illegal immigrants from the mainland. As in the last days of the Raj in India, so in the last days of the empire in Hong Kong, the Gurkhas had a vital internal security role.

At the same time, and not entirely coincidentally, they faced not just one, but two separate rundowns, in which units were broken up and large numbers of soldiers made redundant; and in the interval between them there was in one battalion a serious and widely publicized disciplinary lapse that became known as the Hawaii incident.

It was a period of profound change for the Gurkhas – as Hong Kong braced itself for the hand-over to China; as Nepal renewed the struggle for democracy; and as they themselves adapted to their changing circumstances. They were no longer the simple children of nature so memorably portrayed, for example, in George MacDonald Fraser's memoir of the Burma war, *Quartered Safe Out Here*, but Hong Kong sophisticates just as much, if not more at home in the modern world than in their native hills. And the final twist in this 184-year saga has seen them, or what remains of them, gathered into the bosom of the British Army and trained – and stationed – in the United Kingdom itself.

Walter Walker's successor as Major-General Brigade of Gurkhas was Maj-Gen. A. G. ('Pat') Patterson, originally of the 6th Gurkhas, whose colonel he was shortly to become. Unlike his immediate predecessor, Patterson did not attempt to fight his senior officers and the politicians who dictated the rundown of the Gurkhas, questioning the 'why' of it, but concentrated on how it was to be done and on getting the best possible terms for those made redundant.

He insisted on certain basic principles, designed to ease the painful process and at the same time to keep all units in a state of operational readiness. These included: a ceiling of 2,200 redundancies a year so as not to put undue pressure on the depots in Nepal, which were offering short resettlement courses in agriculture, building and carpentry; an equal rate of rundown for all units and a minimum of six months' notice for every man made redundant; and a continuation of recruitment of not less than 300 men per year in order to maintain the structural balance of age and rank in the Brigade. The plan was to reduce the number of Gurkhas from 14,500 to 10,000 over three years, the process to be completed by the end of 1969. The two battalions of the 10th Gurkhas would be the first to amalgamate, in 1968, and the following year it would be the turn of 6 GR. But the first phase had hardly begun when the government's decision to withdraw from east of Suez precipitated yet another round of cuts, so that in four and a half years the overall strength would have been reduced to a mere 6,000 if the plan had not been revised. By the end of 1971 what remained of the Gurkha units would all be stationed in Hong Kong, Britain having pulled out of Malaysia, Singapore and Brunei.[1]

In practice, however, it did not work out quite like that. Britain's considerable oil interests in Brunei and the Sultan's continuing need of troops – and willingness to pay for them – postponed the planned amalgamation of the two battalions of the 2nd Goorkhas in 1971; and in addition to Hong Kong and now Brunei, in that same year 7 GR became the first Gurkha battalion to be posted to Church Crookham barracks in the United Kingdom for a regular tour of duty. The Ministry of Defence in the new Conservative administration announced that the Brigade of Gurkhas would not be run down below an overall strength of 6,700. This partial reprieve was a result of the worsening situation in Northern Ireland, which meant that an increasing number of British troops were being sent there, leaving gaps elsewhere.[2]

The biggest battle, inevitably, was with the Treasury over compensation terms. Those that were being negotiated when the 1962 reduction programme had been suspended were found to be 'little short of appalling'.[3] Now Patterson and his team, which included the future Field Marshal Sir John Chapple, succeeded in getting better terms for those who would be made redundant. Men would become eligible for a pension after ten, rather than fifteen, years and gratuities of up to £360 would be paid to those who missed out on a pension; so 'there was no shortage of volunteers [for redundancy] from men with eight or nine years service, for they looked upon a £300 or more gratuity as a never-to-be-repeated chance to acquire capital swiftly'.[4] It was just unfortunate that, as John Cross points out, 'the oil crisis and inflation would hit everybody soon afterwards, thus making the amounts seem, in retrospect, a pittance'.[5]

Gurkha regiments had always been family affairs. In 1963, when *Soldier* magazine carried an item recording the fact that the first battalion of the Royal Scots had nineteen sets of brothers currently serving, Major J. A. Lloyd-Williams of 1/2 GR wrote from Singapore to say that his battalion had forty-five Gurkha brothers – 'Perhaps this is a British Army record?' – consisting of eighteen sets of two and three sets of three.

Probably the oldest family in the Regiment is that of Maj (QGO) Hirasing Gurung and his young brother, L/Cpl Sherjang Gurung, whose connection goes back in an unbroken line, father to son, to 1815, when their ancestor was one of the first to be enlisted when the Regiment was raised.[6]

Nineteen years later, when the *Soldier* returned to the subject, Lt-Col.

Paul Pettigrew, CO of the now amalgamated 6 GR, recalled that on the previous occasion the magazine had featured claims from various units and the number of brothers they had serving, he, as adjutant of his battalion, had started counting, but 'I gave up when I reached 100'.[7] The close kinship which characterized Gurkha units meant that the severe cuts affecting them all, with the equivalent of a platoon of men leaving every six weeks for a period of four years, carried strong overtones of family bereavement. Taking into account the normal arrivals and departures, in addition to redundancies, John Cross worked out that: 'By the end of 1971, when the rundown had finished, units had lost over 70 per cent of those who were serving when the process started.'[8] This was a massive turnover and the biggest upheaval in the Brigade since the miserable days of 1947.

Lt-Col. Alastair Langlands of 2 GR describes the scene at Paklihawa, the British Gurkha Centre in west Nepal at that time, when the families of a party of redundant men who had completed their resettlement courses were leaving for the last time in hired lorries and taxis: 'The children, clutching dolls bought in Singapore, mothers armed with feeding bottles and colourful paper flowers, fathers with radios and umbrellas, all dressed in their best, packed into the transport. As the vehicles moved away towards the hills, the Gurkhas cheered.' These were not quite the circumstances in which they might have envisaged returning home from the wars, but their discipline and good humour were so remarkable that Langlands felt doubly distressed over their likely fate:

For the first few months their children could get dysentery, some dying even before they reached their homes. Their small pension or gratuity would not be sufficient to feed them, so they would have to fight to win their food from the soil, and overcome hail, landslides, floods and fire. A few would invest their gratuity in a share of a taxi or a little shop. There were some who had no land to return to and their future was grim. Many would apply for work as civilians in Paklihawa, or in one of the British projects in Nepal. Failing this, their search might take them far afield, ending as watchmen in Bombay, Delhi or Calcutta. Even those with land could soon find themselves unable to make ends meet and have to search for work.[9]

A similar recognition of the hard times that lay ahead for many of the redundant men led Maj-Gen. Patterson to give a high priority to welfare, reporting to the king of Nepal in December 1967 that he was doing all he could 'to increase the efficiency of our Ex-Servicemen's Welfare Organisation and the funds available for charitable grants and pensions to those in need'.[10] His initiative led to the establishment, in 1969, of the Gurkha Welfare Trust, a charitable body supported by the Ministry of Defence which, by 1 August 1970, had already raised £620,500 in the United Kingdom, Brunei, Singapore and Malaysia.[11] Since then it has greatly expanded, but so, too, has the need for it – with the discovery of destitution not merely among those who were made redundant at the end of the sixties but also among non-pensioned survivors of the Second World War and their families.

Maj-Gen. James Lunt was Defence Adviser to the British High Commissioner in New Delhi at the time of the cuts, and the Ministry of Defence, fearing that the Indian Army might disapprove of their unilateral action, directed him to break the news personally to the Indian Chief of Army Staff, General J. N. ('Muchu') Chaudhuri:

> Chaudhuri's reaction was hardly as anticipated. After listening politely
> to the message from the CGS [Chief of the – no longer Imperial –
> General Staff], he commented that it was a matter of indifference
> where the Government of India was concerned. In fact he rather
> welcomed such a reduction since it meant all the more Gurkhas for the
> Indian Army to recruit! He then changed the conversation to polo.[12]

If India was unconcerned about the reduction of Britain's Brigade of Gurkhas, Britain was not disposed to question the fact that the Indian Army's recruitment of Gurkhas was far in excess of the number allowed by the tripartite agreement. Britain's world role had been so dramatically reduced in the twenty years following Indian independence that the two armies were in no danger of having to compete with one another for recruits. With one expanding while the other contracted there were more than enough volunteers to satisfy both.

The sharp decrease in British Gurkha numbers greatly increased the desirability of service in the British Army. The anthropologist Mary Des Chene, studying the effects of Gurkha military service on Gurung village life, sees the difference between 'Malaya *lahores*' and 'Hong Kong *lahores*' as one 'between the many and the privileged few':

> For the many Malaya *lahores* who returned with smaller pensions than they expected, or with none at all, searching out additional sources of cash income looked like necessity not opportunity. Many of them have carved out lives of what I will call 'permanent transience', with complex consequences for their sense of identity, place and belonging.[13]

The increased allowances paid to the 'Hong Kong' generation of Gurkhas, particularly while they were stationed in Brunei or in Britain – to bring them into line with the British troops whom they served alongside – means that, in retrospect, 1971 can be seen as a watershed in their fortunes:

> Gurkhas were no longer engaged in constant war, and there was suddenly an opportunity to amass significant wealth. At the same time places in the Brigade of Gurkhas became a particularly scarce resource . . . land [and other resources] . . . were also becoming increasingly scarce. Satellite communities in Pokhara and the Terai, created by migrating Malaya *lahores*, gave people connections and a sense that there existed not entirely alien places to which they could move. The opportunities for education for their children and an easier lifestyle made the idea of leaving the village increasingly attractive. Taken together, these transformations, both in the army and at home, combined to turn service in the British Gurkhas into a sought after opportunity.[14]

Military writers might argue that, with the exception of the two world wars, during which the element of compulsion undermined the traditional, voluntary nature of recruitment, service in the British Gurkhas had always been 'a sought after opportunity'. But there can be no doubt that, with fewer places and considerably more money on offer, British service grew more attractive. Paradoxically, though, as the Gurkhas became ever more integrated into the British Army, improvements in pay and conditions served only to highlight residual inequalities. In April 1970 the defence attaché in Kathmandu reported a conversation he had had with a high official of the Nepalese Foreign Ministry, in which 'the apparent discrimination between British and Gurkha troops in the recent Armed Forces Pay Revision' was questioned. The attaché asked for guidance, remarking, 'Any indication that a pay rise for Gurkhas is being or is likely to be considered would of course be well received here though we would still need to be able to explain why the Gurkhas lag behind.'[15]

In the British Army, as in Orwell's *Animal Farm*, it would seem, some are more equal than others. The continuing difficulty for the pro-Gurkha lobby in the army and government was that, insofar as the Treasury was concerned, the main reason for employing Gurkhas was that they were a cheap army; if they were to achieve parity with British troops they would become not just as expensive but considerably *more* expensive, given the additional cost of maintaining the lines of communication in Nepal. So perhaps it is not surprising that there is no record of a reply to the defence attaché's request for guidance on file in the Public Record Office.

In the days of the Rana autocracy, the British appeased the maharajahs by loading them with honours. Now, in 1971, they made the ailing King Mahendra honorary Colonel-in-Chief of the new slimline Brigade of Gurkhas. *Plus ça change . . .*

An indication of how right General Patterson had been to insist on all units remaining operational throughout the period of rundown was demonstrated when 'Confrontation' in Borneo was succeeded by 'Disturbances' in Hong King. The cultural revolution in China inevitably spilled over into Hong Kong and there were a number of incidents – riots, arson, a poster campaign, strikes – in Kowloon and on the island itself in the long hot summer of 1967.

The police quelled the riots and generally kept things under control; the government's policy of minimum force meant that the military stayed in the background, a visible presence rather than an active participant, though the communist press drew a fantastic poster-like picture of the 'masses facing the Beast soldiers and Wolf policemen . . . without fear'.[16] But when trouble erupted in the New Territories frontier village of Sha Tau Kok on 8 July, the 1/10th and the 1/7th Gurkhas were soon drawn into the action, with the 1/6th in reserve. By the time the 2/7th, brought over from Malaya to reinforce these battalions, joined in, there were incidents at every border crossing.

Just as in India during the civil disturbances of the twenties and thirties, the Gurkha soldiers – and Pakistani riot police – were subjected to pamphlet and broadcast propaganda, on the one hand, taunting them as 'mercenary officers and soldiers' of the 'British Imperialists', and on the other, calling on them to change sides: 'We are your friends. Lay down your arms. Come over here and we will welcome you. If you do not take this chance, you will be totally defeated. It is a matter of life and death.'[17] In this situation the troops were hampered by not being permitted to meet force with force, or to retaliate when made the target of bottles and stones. The rioters were protected, if not actively encouraged, by the Chinese Army, dug in on the other side of the border overlooking the trouble spots.

One flashpoint was at Man Kam To bridge, where the peasants who traded across the border fiercely objected to a barrier having been erected by the security forces. After hours of fruitless parleying between the villagers and a group comprising the British District Office, the CO of the 1/10th and a senior police officer, the Chinese seized the three officers and held them hostage while the debate continued into the night. The brigade commander ordered that 'the situation be resolved by dawn'. Two platoons of 1/10 GR took up positions on either flank and Major Bruce Niven prepared a Saladin armoured car and a third platoon to make an assault. The situation became even more tense when Niven heard that some of the battalion's weapons had been removed to the bridge by the Chinese.

> I decided to wait one minute longer or until they began to move the
> CO and DO and [Superintendent Bill] Paton towards the Bridge, when
> I would have ordered the Saladin and Lieutenant Nima forward.
> Fortunately, only photographs – a propaganda victory – were required
> by the other side and our weapons [were] then moved back from the
> centre of the bridge to our side again. They were then returned to the
> (by now) somewhat confused men of 'C' Company . . . [18]

After the photo call the hostages were released, but it had been 'a damned close thing'.[19]

To prevent further incidents of that kind the government closed all the gates in the frontier fence. But this only aggravated the local farmers, who could no longer come over to work their fields on the Hong Kong side. At Ta Ku Ling they took the law into their own hands and, punching a hole through the fence, attacked a platoon of 1/6 GR with sticks and stones, forcing them to shelter in a police station since they were under orders not to shoot unless their lives were threatened. Reinforcements were sent in but, rather than provoke the Chinese further, the Hong Kong authorities ordered that the gate be re-opened.

This task fell to Major Bob Duncan; as a token of his peaceful intentions he took only his Gurkha orderly and a small police escort. But as soon as he opened the gate he was grabbed by an angry mob from the other side and forced to sign a statement of apology and promise of future good behaviour. A considerable force of Gurkhas sent to rescue him had to fight their way in bare-handed, while the police detachment rather rashly fired rubber bullets, which in the heat of the moment could well have been mistaken for the real thing. The watching Chinese soldiers responded with a warning burst of automatic fire over the heads of the troops and police before order was restored. For a moment, the CO of the 1/6th remarked, it 'seemed to bring World War III appreciably closer'.[20]

But the moment passed and by the end of 1967 there were 'fairly clear indications that Peking had told the local hot-heads to stop unseemly violence, probably since the use of force failed to intimidate the British, alienated the vast majority of Hong Kong citizens and reflected adversely on China's image in the rest of Asia'.[21] Though there were some further incidents in 1968, the sting had largely gone out of the Red Guard movement.

The next crisis on the Hong Kong border was the less dramatic but longer running influx of illegal immigrants when the regional Communist power structure broke down, following the demise of Chairman Mao, and people voted with their feet. This climaxed a decade later, and in the year 1979 the number arrested almost reached 90,000. At one time there were five battalions deployed along the frontier. In June 1979 the daily rate of captures was over 400 and 7 GR alone apprehended nearly 17,000 Chinese that year, not a score they were particularly proud of, but a measure of the desperation of the mainland Chinese people under a 'people's government'.[22]

At the beginning of the seventies the last British troops left Malaysia and Singapore, following the government's policy of withdrawal east of Suez (the Depot, Brigade of Gurkhas, after nearly two decades in northern Malaya, had already been transferred to Hong Kong); and in 1973 the closure of the British Gurkha transit camp at Barrackpore removed the final British Army toe-hold in India. Troops now flew directly in and out of Nepal. But the major shift of the seventies was the introduction of Gurkha battalions to Britain, on a rotating basis, for regular tours of duty, which opened up other geographical areas to them. Not Northern Ireland, of course, since even the most Gurkhaholic of soldiers agreed that it would be political dynamite to send Nepalese nationals to try and keep warring Catholic and Protestant British subjects apart. But Cyprus, where the 10th Gurkhas helped restore the peace between Turks and Greeks in 1974–5, and Belize, where 6 GR were the first of several Gurkha units to be sent as a deterrent to Guatemalan aggression in 1978–9, provided fresh fields of operation.

Before either posting could be confirmed, Foreign Office 'reservations' about the use of Gurkhas in explosive situations outside south-east Asia had to be surmounted. So there was some satisfaction when, at the end of the 10th Gurkhas' six-month tour of duty in Cyprus, the British High Commissioner wrote to the Foreign Office in praise of 'their efficiency, determination, good behaviour and personal charm' which, he said, had won the respect of the Turks and the Greeks alike. He concluded that the choice of a Gurkha battalion 'was not only justified – it was most successful. They were able to adapt lessons learned on the China border to the different needs of the SBA [Sovereign Base Area].'[23]

This did not prevent the Foreign Office expressing doubts all over again when the question of sending a Gurkha battalion to the Falklands arose in 1982. By this time the illegal immigrant crisis in Hong Kong and the need to man the Chinese border more extensively had brought about a small expansion in the Brigade of Gurkhas and 2/7 GR was re-raised for the third time in the 7th Gurkhas' relatively brief history. But it was the 1/7th, not the 2/7th, which was a part of the newly formed

5 Airborne Brigade in England when the Argentinians invaded the Falklands.

This brigade was just beginning to function as a unit when it was broken up; the two British parachute battalions were detached and sent to the south Atlantic with 3 Marine Commando Brigade, while the 7th Gurkhas faced 'a distinct possibility that they would be left behind in the UK'.[24] The Foreign Office did not want the Gurkhas to go for fear of giving offence to Third World countries. The army replied that Gurkhas would be ideal for the cold and miserable conditions and argued that their removal from their assigned brigade would undermine its budding *esprit de corps*.[25] The Chief of Defence Staff, Field Marshal Sir Edwin (now Lord) Bramall, who was also colonel of 2 GR, and the secretary of defence, John Nott (who had served with the 2nd Goorkhas in Malaya in the fifties), helped to overrule Foreign Office objections; and the defence attaché in Kathmandu, Keith Robinson of 7 GR, worked to ensure that the Nepalese government would not oppose the use of Gurkhas in this conflict.

So 1/7 GR set sail for the Falklands on board the chartered liner *QE2* on 12 May 1982. Before the battalion left, press and television reporters descended on the Queen Elizabeth barracks at Church Crookham to interview the men and take pictures of them with their kukris unsheathed – a distraction which, according to their commanding officer, Lt-Col. David Morgan, they could have done without.[26] Yet these photos found their way to Port Stanley and Goose Green, where they struck terror into the hearts of young Argentine conscripts.

For tyro Rifleman Baliprasad Rai, forming up at 6 a.m. on 12 May 1982 in full battle order was the start of a big adventure: 'It was a wet and windy morning and I thought it was a fitting day to go off to a place where I was told it would be wet and windy all the time.' When he got to Southampton he was amazed at the sheer size of the *QE2*.

Why, it was even larger than any building I had seen back home! Soon we were ushered into her labyrinth[ine] depths to the accompaniment of our regimental march on the pipes, and shown to our allocated quarters. And what luxurious quarters! Never had I slept in such beautiful surroundings or in such a big, soft bed, or perhaps I ever will! If I was to go to war, then there was no better way to go.[27]

The battalion soon settled into a routine of training and keeping fit on the long voyage south: 'Life on the *Queen Elizabeth 2* was much the same as in Queen Elizabeth Barracks'. Lulled into a sense of security by the luxurious liner, the good food, the videos of Hindi and English films provided for the troops' entertainment, the lectures on the history and geography of the Falklands, the continuous sunshine – 'sometimes it was hotter than in Dharan during summer' – the men had a rude awakening when they transferred from the *QE2* to the ferry ship *Norland* at South Georgia and, in (ant)arctic clothes and weather, 'swayed, shook and rolled towards . . . the East Falklands'. Never the best of sailors, the Gurkhas succumbed to sea-sickness and the 800-mile journey seemed more like 80,000 miles of stomach-churning agony:

> All around me I could see the same scenes, people huddled against the cold and the wind, straining to gain some semblance of balance as we were bounced and buffeted like rag dolls. I would have willingly sat through hours of Argentine torture [rather] than go through another minute of this ordeal![28]

Land, any land, even east Falkland seemed preferable to tossing about in a ship on the heaving sea. But scarcely had 1/7 GR disembarked and dug their holes in the ground before 'the first wave of Argentine jets swooped in very low over the hills – streaks of green and silver coming from the south, with all their cannons firing'. The Gurkhas put on their helmets, jumped into their freshly dug trenches and watched the fire-work display as the fighters attacked the ships in the Falkland sound, running the gauntlet of British guns and rockets: 'on the third run . . . one of the aircraft was hit by a Rapier or small arms fire, I don't know what, but it veered off towards the nearby hills trailing flames before exploding in the sky before our very eyes . . . The full and harsh reality of war was upon us.'[29]

While D Company marched the fifteen or so miles to Goose Green and Darwin, which had already been captured by 2 Para, the remainder of the battalion was airlifted in by helicopter. The weather was grim; rain, mist and low cloud reduced visibility to ten yards and icy, antarctic winds penetrated no matter how many layers of protective clothing: 'It was colder and wetter than ten English winters combined.'

Baliprasad saw his first Argentine soldiers, all prisoners of war: 'They looked uncomfortable, ill-ke[m]pt and ill-disciplined, like Mexican bandits in the cowboy films I had seen on video. Some of them looked even younger than me!'

At the end of a week at Goose Green, Baliprasad's company was transported by helicopter (after the lethal Argentine air attack on the landing ships *Sir Galahad* and *Sir Tristram* had rendered a sea journey too hazardous) to Bluff Cove near Port Stanley, where they came under mortar and shell fire for the first time. They spent most of the night digging in and faced more heavy artillery fire the next morning.

> 105mm shells whistled and whined above our heads and crashed around with a deafening noise, showering everyone with dirt. My ears ached from the terrible din but I could faintly hear the OC, Capt Holley saheb screaming for everyone to keep their heads down. I don't know if anyone else heard him. The shells seemed to come even closer and I would not be telling the truth if I said I was not at all frightened. I was thoroughly but I was also angry. This was no way to fight I thought, and a No. 1 gunner was no use in this situation, no matter how good. A shell landed perilously near, about twenty feet away, and I heard my trench-mate, 21160801 L/Cpl Gyanendra Rai, cry out. He had been hit by flying shrapnel on his shoulder. I told him, 'There is blood pouring down your back'. He looked at me and replied, 'You are also hit. There is blood all over the back of your head'. Yes, a piece of shrapnel had penetrated my tin-hat and lodged itself in the back of my head. Only then did I feel the pain.[30]

That was the end of the Falklands war for Rifleman Baliprasad Rai. He had 'the dubious distinction of being the first Gurkha casualty' to be treated at the field hospital, a converted sheep-shearing station near San Carlos, before he was evacuated in stages back to Britain.

The remainder of the battalion supported the Scots Guards in the assault on Tumbledown where, in the confusion, there was an 'accidental firefight' with the Scots Guards in which the Forward Observation Officer with D Company was hit in the chest, though the bullet fortunately missed his heart.[31] Despite this mishap, 'as soon as D Company crossed its start line, the Argentinians decided that they had endured enough: streams of their soldiers were seen heading towards the Scots Guards to give themselves up, or even back to Stanley'. The Gurkhas felt cheated of the battle for which they had keyed themselves up, but that was it, 'the war was effectively over, and the battalion had simply "punched at air"'. Their one fatality happened after the war was over, when they were clearing the battlefield and a lance-corporal was blown up by an unexploded grenade he struck with a spade. The commandant did his best to assuage his battalion's disappointment, writing later: 'If we can win wars by our reputation, who wants to kill people?'[32]

But as professional soldiers, the Gurkhas could not but feel that their great opportunity to show the world what they were capable of had passed them by. As an American journalist reported, they 'arrived two weeks before the war ended, fired few shots, took three prisoners [ten, in fact], suffered only a handful of casualties and never reached the Falklands capital, Port Stanley'.[33] Yet if Argentinian accounts, given a wider currency through the journalistic writings of the Columbian novelist Gabriel García Márquez (who coincidentally was awarded the Nobel Prize for Literature in 1982) are to be believed, then the Gurkhas played a far more vivid role in winning the war.

In an article which appeared in the Bogotá daily, *El Espectador*, Márquez wrote that 'the most terrible memory kept by the Argentine survivors is of the savagery of the Gurkha battalion, those fierce and legendary decapitators who preceded the English troops in the battle of Puerto Argentina [Port Stanley]':

'They advanced, shouting and beheading', wrote one witness to the merciless butchery. 'The rate at which they cut off the heads of our poor boys with their assassins' scimitars was one every seven seconds. In their strange custom, they held the severed head by the hair and cut off the ears'. The Gurkhas confronted the enemy with such blind determination that of 700 who disembarked only 70 survived. 'These beasts were so ferocious that once the battle for Puerto Argentina was finished, they continued killing the English themselves until the English had to shackle them to subdue them'.[34]

In another article, Márquez was a little more circumspect, conceding that the British government denied the 'accusations of cruelty and savage acts committed by its Gurkha soldiers' and insisted that these were 'pure fairy tales inspired by black propaganda'. But he was unconvinced, preferring to believe an Argentinian account in which a soldier returned from the war was reported as saying:

> The Gurkhas seemed completely drugged. They even killed one
> another. They advanced screaming without even protecting
> themselves. It was not difficult to kill them but there were too many.
> Sometimes you killed one or two but the next one would then kill you.
> They were like robots: one Gurkha trod on a mine and went flying
> through the air, but the one following him didn't show the slightest
> concern – he ran over the same area without changing course and also
> went flying almost as if not at all expecting it. They seemed to have no
> survival instinct . . . Nothing interested them, not even their own lives.
> The British who came behind the Gurkhas had it very easy: they
> found the path practically cleared.[35]

Though a sceptical friend suggested that this account might have been 'magnified by the narrator out of fear', Márquez remained unshaken, recalling that 'a Gurkha battalion [sic] under the command of Brigadier-General Reginald Dyer opened fire indiscriminately and under safety on a peaceful civilian demonstration with complete certainty of hitting the participants, killing 379 people'. The Amritsar massacre, Márquez added, was 'reconstructed with chilling accuracy in the film *Gandhi* . . . by a British knight of the realm, Sir Richard Attenborough'. So it must be true.

The fact that Gurkhas were 'paid warriors in the service of a foreign army . . . most certainly defines their status as *mercenaries*', according to Márquez, and the modern mercenary is, almost by definition, an unscrupulous rogue. In Hong Kong, they were 'trained like animals in the job of killing'. Márquez reiterated the myth about Gurkhas that 'once they have unsheathed their famous knife it cannot be put back without blood'; and his clinching argument was that since they constituted 'a real, anachronistic and shameful colonial force which Britain keeps as an unworthy fragment of its times of glory, so there is nothing strange in its criminal behaviour in the Falklands [or Malvinas, as he must have written in the original], nor is there any reason to believe that the testimonies of so many Argentine survivors are raving nonsense'.[36] QED.

Rifleman Baliprasad Rai would have been even more amazed by the scale of the Argentine fictions peddled by the Nobel prize-winning novelist than he was by the size of the *QE2*.

The battle of words – so much more dramatic than the actual fighting in which the Gurkhas were involved – was not confined to the pages of the world's newspapers. There was some sparring in the General Assembly of the United Nations where Argentina, backed by Cuba, accused Nepal of allowing its citizens to be used as mercenaries by a colonial power, namely Britain. The Nepalese government refuted the accusation, referring to the UN definition of mercenaries, which specifically excluded foreign troops who were an intrinsic part of a native army – as Gurkhas were in both the Indian and the British armies – and did not neglect to point out that Argentina had missed five earlier opportunities to protest, these being the occasions on which India had employed Nepalese subjects in battle against either Pakistan or China.[37]

In this instance, the Chief of Defence Staff and an ex-Gurkha defence minister triumphed over Foreign Office opposition to the use of Gurkha troops in a politically sensitive situation; and a Nepalese government presided over by a king who had been educated at Eton stood by its ally on the world stage, choosing to see the war as a dispute over self-determination rather than de-colonization. But there would not always necessarily be such favourable circumstances, and the propaganda focusing on the mercenary status of the Gurkhas, though it backfired on the Argentines in the short run, would resonate in Nepal for years to come and, in the volatile atmosphere of the re-established democracy, could still influence the fate of the British Gurkhas. At the very least, it showed that Foreign Office objections were not without some foundation, despite the ire they aroused in military breasts.

The 1/7th Gurkhas were a little embarrassed to be welcomed as conquering heroes on their return to Southampton. In the Falklands, the hungry soldiers had killed more geese than enemy – so many, indeed, that Gurkha-Major Lalbahadur Rai suggested that Goose Green be renamed simply 'Green'.[38] Yet though they had not had a chance to prove themselves in battle they had done all that was asked of them in the disciplined manner characteristic of Gurkhas. Four years later, when 1/7 GR hit the headlines again, it was, alas, a very different story.

There was a mutinous outbreak in May 1986 among the men of Support Company who had been sent to Hawaii on a training exercise under the command of an officer on secondment from a British regiment. The men had a number of complaints: about the quantity and quality of the rice they were given, the level of overseas allowances and the fact that all available vehicles were monopolized by the 'white officers' so that they had to walk to and from the camp, with the result that, as L/Cpl Prakash Sunuwar told a *Sunday Times* reporter, 'When we would come back late, the mess would be closed and there would be no food'.[39]

In addition to these gripes, they had taken offence at remarks Major Corin Pearce (who had been with 1/7 GR for little over two years and was due to rejoin the Royal Anglian Regiment later that year) had apparently made at a screening of a BBC documentary film on Nepal for the benefit of the Americans on the exercise about the ignorance and poverty of the hillmen recruited into the army. 'He humiliated us', Prakash Sunuwar was quoted as saying. 'He said the Gurkhas come from the hills, they don't have homes, they are not educated, they don't get adequate food, they cannot afford to wear shoes. They work for us because of their poverty. "Now, look how we have trained them up".'[40]

As a seconded officer with less than fluent Nepali, Major Pearce's intentions may have been misunderstood; his wife later spoke of his fondness for the Gurkhas. But the company commander had clearly failed to gain the trust of the men. Among his Gurkha officers, he leaned heavily on Capt. (QGO) Chandra Kumar Pradhan, because Chandra spoke excellent English. This further complicated matters since Chandra, being a Newar rather than a Limbu or Rai, was himself something of an outsider, despite the fact that his father had served in 7 GR in Burma during the war.[41]

Things came to a head at a party to celebrate the conclusion of the joint exercise with units of the US 25th Infantry Division. The company commander made a heavy-handed attempt to stop the men drinking; but since they had contributed towards the cost of the party, they resented his interference and returned to the camp in a dangerously disgruntled mood. Pearce's second-in-command, Capt. (QGO) Amiraj Rai, who was serving out his last days, seems to have left it to Chandra Pradhan to try and calm the men. But it was too late. As Chandra stood in a pool of light shed by the solitary lamp, trying to restore order, he was aware of the men jostling and pushing one another in the dark fringe between the tents. Then they surged forward and knocked him unconscious.[42]

When he regained consciousness, he was alone. The men had vanished. He picked himself up and found an American military policeman who told him that Major Pearce had also been attacked and was now having his head stitched up in the medical centre. The company commander had been kicked and badly beaten about the head, which required some fifteen stitches. Chandra went to see him and afterwards mustered the company sergeants; he ordered a parade for the following morning, at which he announced that the incident was closed, as it might well have been had it not been for the official reaction – or overreaction – in Hong Kong.

An attack on a British officer was a serious matter, but in Chandra's view the correct procedure would have been for the commandant immediately to have sent to Hawaii a trusted senior British officer, along with the Gurkha major, to conduct an enquiry and sort things out on the spot – there were still two or three days left before the company was due to fly back to Hong Kong. Instead of which, on arrival in Hong Kong, the entire company was herded into wire cages on the backs of trucks and generally treated as criminals, being kept apart from their families – Chandra included – for two days while attempts were made to discover the ringleaders.[43] Faced with this sort of witchhunt, the Gurkhas closed ranks and withheld co-operation, precipitating their dismissal *en masse*; in the end, 120 men were sent back to Nepal.[44]

Media interest in the 'Hawaii incident' was intensified by the coincident drug-smuggling trial of six men from 2/2 GR stationed in the UK, five of whom were found guilty and imprisoned. The *Daily Telegraph* editorial comment was headed 'End of Empire' and argued that the Gurkhas were 'no longer the simple mountain boys that they once were' and that the dismissal of over a hundred men from 1/7 GR 'must be seen against the background of this loss of innocence':

There has always been great mystification among the Gurkhas about the lifestyle of the officer caste. But that mystery has been dissipated now. The much sought-after two-year tours of duty in Britain have shown just how unmysterious and unworthy of respect the once-hallowed lifestyle really is. The men, whose loyalty to their officers was hitherto unquestioned, now regard their superiors with increasing scepticism . . .[45]

Several papers stressed the outdated paternalism of the British–Gurkha relationship and the *Guardian* opined that:

Their regimental tradition, essentially 19th-century colonial and based on strict paternalism, would surely be impossible to maintain in Europe, where they would have to learn mechanised and high-technology warfare. No doubt they could adapt: the question is whether they should be required to. They would surely feel more at home with their fellow-countrymen in today's Indian Army, which has much more obvious uses for natural light infantrymen with jungle and tropical experience. It is possible to detect in the various present troubles of the Gurkhas a sudden overexposure to the late 20th century. They can hardly be blamed if this upsets them. Britain should be preparing a handsome golden handshake for the Gurkhas on leaving Hong Kong in 1997. It would be unforgivable to spring it on them when it is so obvious now that the parting of the ways is coming.[46]

Passing over the newspaper's own (perhaps unconsciously) patronizing tone, was the Hawaii incident symptomatic of the kind of malaise described in both the *Guardian* and the *Telegraph* editorials? On the face of it, and in the opinion of most British officers, no: this was an entirely local, not to say parochial affair, and it would have been better for everyone if it had been hushed up in the way that such – or worse – events generally are. There have been rumours of 'incidents', to say nothing of mutinies, in Indian Gorkha battalions and even in the Nepalese forces, but these have not been subjected to media scrutiny.

Most officers would have agreed with the *Sunday Telegraph* writer who suggested that 'if any other body of troops had been involved, it would not have been regarded so seriously. Suppose the Paras had indulged in a punch-up (not that they ever would) after a night out in the Aldershot saloons and they refused to talk. I doubt very much if they would be kicked out of the Army.' But the article continued: 'With the Gurkhas it is different. The breakdown of trust between them and their officers strikes at the very heart of the paternalistic system'; and this writer, too, links events in Hawaii with the smuggling of heroin and cannabis into Britain by men of 2/2 GR, asserting that 'modern times are catching up with the Gurkhas and their "mafia"'.[47]

Several factors may have contributed to the creation of a state of unrest in Support Company, 1/7 GR, which consisted – as the *Daily Telegraph* defence correspondent, John Keegan, pointed out – not of recent recruits but of soldiers with at least seven years' service.[48] For these men the Falklands war, despite the fuss made over it, had been more frustrating than fulfilling and, that apart, Gurkhas had not fought a war for twenty years. Garrison duties in Hong Kong were no substitute, and by the early nineties one 2 GR officer was looking forward to the Brigade's recovery from what he called 'the apathy of soldiering in Hong Kong'.[49]

Then there were the psychological stresses of successive rundowns, punctuated by mini build-ups (a Gurkha Reinforcement Battalion, known unromantically as GRUB until it became the fourth incarnation of 2/7 GR, was, as we have seen, raised in 1981 to help police the Sino–Hong Kong border in the anarchic situation following the death of Mao, but then disbanded again in November 1986); and there was a distinct possibility of total disbandment in 1997 when Hong Kong reverted to Chinese rule.

In Nepal, political agitation against the *panchayat* form of monarchical government and the corruption associated with it had yet to come to a head, but there were other changes affecting Gurkhas more closely, such as their migration in numbers from the hills to the towns and the Terai in search of an easier life and an education for their children.

Finally, the Gurkhas themselves were changing. They were now, in the words of the 2 GR officer quoted above, 'rootless cosmopolitans posted around the world . . . amongst the jet-setting *nouveaux riches* of [their] nation'.[50]

The question of the future of the Gurkhas in the British Army after the return of Hong Kong to China was recognized by officers of the Brigade as an increasingly urgent one. The Major-General Brigade of Gurkhas warned, 'We would . . . be deluding ourselves if we thought that we will have the Brigade as it is today after 1997, and that we will still enjoy the same terms and conditions of service. Everyone is being realistic and is prepared for some future reductions and reorganisations.'[51]

In July 1988 there were reports in the press of a study – the 'so-called Gurkha Paper being circulated among the General Staff' – recommending cut-backs in the 8,000 strong Brigade of Gurkhas. The extent of these reductions could be anything from one battalion to complete disbandment, though the latter option was considered improbable. The consensus was that there had to be a military role for Gurkhas after the hand-over of Hong Kong, the only question being: for how many of them? The defence secretary, George Younger, was expected to make an announcement in the House of Commons later in the year.

This announcement did not come until 22 May 1989, but it was, according to the Brigade's own journal, *The Kukri*, 'arguably the most significant decision to be made about Gurkhas by the British Government since 1947'. Younger stated that while it was 'not possible to be definitive at this stage about the future for the Gurkhas after 1997', due to other impending changes – 'particularly in the size of the British Army as a whole' – he planned a future for the Gurkhas 'based on a viable Brigade structure':

> At present we see this force being a balance of four Gurkha Infantry battalions, squadrons of the Queen's Gurkha Engineers, the Queen's Gurkha Signals and the Gurkha Transport Regiment, together with the necessary infrastructure. It would comprise about 4,000 personnel. I would expect the future Gurkha force to have roles that lie within the main stream of the Army's Defence commitments, including, as now, a substantial Gurkha presence in the UK.[52]

The Brigade of Gurkhas was once again to be reduced almost by half, but its survival into the twenty-first century now seemed to be assured. Maj-Gen. Garry Johnson, colonel of 10 GR, suggested that the way to look at it was as 'a cup half full, not as a cup half empty'.[53] Two years later, when the defence secretary Tom King made *his* announcement on the future size and shape of British forces under the misleading rubric 'Options for Change', the Brigade was to be reduced still further to 2,500 by mid-1997[54] – a cup two-thirds empty, or perhaps one-third full.

In between times there had been considerable infighting in the army and Ministry of Defence. The fact that the army as a whole, not just the Gurkhas, faced massive cut-backs brought latent hostilities and envies to the surface. British regiments, which had been proud to be affiliated with Gurkha regiments, forgot their chums, or knifed them in the back, when their own survival was at stake. Their point of view is well expressed in a study of the British Army published at the time of these upheavals:

> Gurkhas may arouse strong, protective emotions in some British
> military breasts . . . but all this rather exasperates officers in other
> regiments who talk of the 'infatuation for little Johnny Gurkha' as a
> romantic nostalgia for imperial days, pillbox hats and all. The Gurkhas
> may be superb, they say, in their specialist role of jungle warfare (some
> dispute even this), but put them in Osnabrück for five or six years, and
> they are liable to go to pieces.[55]

There was a strong feeling, represented by the Director of Infantry, Maj-Gen. R. J. Hodges, and the colonels of British regiments he assembled, that all Gurkhas should go before a single British regiment was touched.[56] It was, in a sense, a last re-run of the old British Army/Indian Army rivalry and mutual mistrust, except that Gurkhas were now part and parcel of the British Army and a senior officer like Lt-Gen. Sir Garry Johnson (as he had become), as both Colonel Commandant Light Division *and* colonel of the 10th Gurkha Rifles, inevitably had divided loyalties and might have been seriously embarrassed if it had come to a showdown.

Once survival, albeit in a skeletal state, had been secured, the priorities were to obtain the best possible terms for those made redundant and to apply the lessons learned from the previous round of redundancies in managing the painful process of severance from the regiments. The MGBG, Maj-Gen. Peter Duffell, and the Brigadier Brigade of Gurkhas, Christopher Bullock, had both been adjutants of their respective battalions of the 2nd Goorkhas at the end of the sixties, so they were determined to avoid the mistakes made at that time. Bullock still remembers the strain of having to break the unwelcome news of their redundancy to soldiers he had commanded in action in Borneo:

> Operational ties are incredibly close and to see some of these guys who were first-class people going, well, it was grim – especially when they turned round and said, 'Look, Saheb, you've got the power to stop me going, why don't you?' You know, 'We're chums, now's the time to come out on my side. Just give me one more year, let me get a pension.' Grim, it was really grim, it knocked you out a bit.[57]

In 1990, the redundancy terms – achieved after a long and arduous struggle with the Treasury – were a great improvement on those of the sixties, even allowing for inflation. The fact that British troops were also being made redundant and were getting reasonable terms helped. Pensions after just four years' service, as part of the redundancy package, compensation payments of several thousand pounds and the setting up of a re-employment organization with offices in Nepal, Hong Kong and the UK – which was Peter Duffell's personal initiative – all contributed to sustaining morale and preventing a breakdown of discipline through the period of what was euphemistically called 'drawdown'. Lt-Col. Nigel Collett, who had been Brigade Major, Brigade of Gurkhas, and had helped to frame the policy he then had to implement in his own battalion as CO of the 6th Gurkhas, sums it up by saying, 'No doubt many were disadvantaged, and bitterness was frequent, but many men whose careers were almost over were happy to take the money and go.'[58]

Negotiations over the terms of service of the Gurkhas remaining in the British Army were less satisfactory and dragged on until 1996. According to Collett,

> This was mostly not the Brigade's fault, as the arguments over length of service, quarters and accompanied service, pensions, leave flights, baggage entitlements, medical facilities and education were complex, and not only involved money but political problems such as the nationality of Gurkha babies born in the UK. The arguments tended to

get bogged down in the Foreign and Commonwealth Office (which didn't want to change anything, and would not countenance renegotiating the Tripartite Agreement) and the Home Office, which was paranoid about special cases creating immigration precedents.[59]

While these kinds of argument were probably inevitable, the officers involved in negotiating the survival of the Brigade of Gurkhas found some of the interventions of their own Council of Colonels – the colonels of the four rifle regiments and three corps units – less than helpful. As guardians of their own regimental traditions, the colonels of the infantry regiments, at least, were inclined to take what Nigel Collett describes as 'a sort of buttons and bows approach to military service', busying themselves – and creating work for the staff – on such 'priorities' as uniforms and mess property rather than focusing on the future size and shape of the Brigade as a whole.[60]

Essentially it came down to an internecine struggle between the 2nd Goorkhas and the rest, with 2 GR – whose colonel was no less a personage than the Chief of the General Staff, General Sir John Chapple – intent on preserving its historical pre-eminence and the other three regiments united in determination to avoid a 2 GR take-over. Discord focused on the fate of the Queen's Truncheon and the incorporation in the new regimental uniform of the red piping which distinguished the 2nd Goorkhas from the other rifle regiments.*

Where the colonels' influence was decisive was in the designation of the organization to emerge from the drastic cut-backs. There were two options: the amalgamation of the existing pairs of regiments into two one-battalion regiments, or the formation of one large new regiment. Among the Brigade staff, Christopher Bullock favoured retaining the historic numbering of the regiments, even if it meant amalgamating

---

*Although the majority view prevailed at the time, 2 GR may be said to have had the last word, since both the Queen's Truncheon and red piping are back as essential features of the Royal Gurkha Rifles, with the approval of all ranks. But it could be argued that, just as it was right and proper to give all four regiments equal status in the formation of a new regiment, so it is appropriate that that regiment should now bear the historical honours which marked the emergence of *all* Gurkhas from the ruck of sepoys into the elite of riflemen.

them along the lines of, say, the 14th/20th Lancers; so that you would have the 2nd/6th Gurkhas, made up of westerners, and the 7th/10th Gurkhas, comprising easterners. But against all expectations the colonels unanimously resolved to create a new regiment, the Royal Gurkha Rifles, with initially three, but ultimately two mixed battalions – though these are now once again being streamed, with the first battalion consisting largely of westerners and the second of easterners, an arrangement the Gurkhas themselves by and large prefer.

The British infantry itself was divided into those who had followed the order to create large regiments and those who had refused, fighting for the retention of old regiments even if they had only a single battalion, which complicated the process of either cutting or expanding them. Field Marshal Lord Bramall, who sat in on the deliberations of the Council of Colonels as a very senior elder statesman and ex-colonel of 2 GR, favoured the large regiment option and this probably swayed the council.

To General Sir Sam Cowan, who was colonel of the Queen's Gurkha Signals before becoming the first Colonel Commandant of the Brigade of Gurkhas (equivalent of the old MGBG), the decision to go for a large regiment was 'very wise'. It enabled the Royal Gurkha Rifles – immediately after the disbandment of its third battalion – to move into the breach created by under-recruiting in the army and provide 'reinforcement companies' for three British infantry battalions without internal haggling over which regiment was to provide how many soldiers.[61]

The Gurkhas may have survived as a token force in the British Army, but the Gurkha world, created out of an intense interaction between officers and men in an environment where both were far from home and looked to each other for more than military camaraderie, came to an end with the return of Hong Kong to Chinese rule. Nigel Collett, who took voluntary redundancy in 1994 and started up a Gurkha re-employment agency in Hong Kong – 'to build something of my own and maybe help re-weave together some of those strands I had spent so many years unravelling' – observed from the sidelines the close-down of the Gurkha garrison there:

I was present at the closure of Tam Mei Lines at Cassino, Borneo

Lines (28 Army Education Centre) and Malaya Lines (by then 1
RGR), where in 1996 the last of the old-style beating of retreats took
place. For the last time dusk and the backdrop of the mountain of Tai
Mo Shan silhouetted the white tunics, gleaming teeth and
accoutrements of the Pipes and Drums of the Brigade. The Governor,
Chris Patten, made a fine speech, thanking the Brigade for keeping
the peace in Hong Kong for the last thirty years, and so contributing to
what the British were proud to leave behind. It was an emotional
night – to those who had seen Hong Kong's Gurkha Garrison at its
height more so than the formal Colony handover some months later. It
was on that night that the real Garrison ceased to exist; what was left
was only in passage or the remnants of staff who had always been just
temporary residents. The Garrison had been Gurkha for so long, and
for so long to be a Gurkha had meant that Hong Kong was your home.
It was on that day that it all felt at an end.[62]

Once they left Hong Kong, Gurkhas were serving in a totally alien
military environment, as Christopher Bullock points out: 'Hong Kong
was Gurkha homeland; the English troops were the aliens; Gurkha
world obtained. There is no Gurkha world now, no place in which he is
safe in a Gurkha military environment. It's gone, there are not enough
Gurkhas left to create a Gurkha military environment.' And environment, as Bullock recognizes, 'is the key thing':

I mean, before you were with soldiers because there was nowhere else.
Subalterns weren't paid much. You worked hard in the day and played
games with soldiers in the evenings. What else were you going to do?
You could go down to the bazaar, but that was costly and anyway you
only did that once a week. The rest of the time there were no
distractions; like it or not you were there; so it wasn't all that difficult
to accept that way of life. It doesn't happen now. The British officer
has his girlfriend or his wife and his problems and his interests and his
car and his everything . . . When I was in a British regiment in 1960,
you wouldn't dream of suggesting to your soldiers – unless it was a
company football match – that you should be with them in their own
time after their tea. It was considered enough of an imposition to be
with them *up to* their tea. They didn't really want to see an officer

while off-duty under any circumstances. To join a Gurkha battalion, where they couldn't have enough of you, where you were with them all the time, was a complete contrast. Now I suspect the Gurkha battalion is becoming more and more like a British battalion.[63]

In view of all this – the loss of the Gurkha world with everything that made it special, the disbandment of all the regiments brought over from the Indian Army in 1947–8, the endless, heart-breaking redundancies – was this not perhaps the moment to draw a line under 182 years of history and end a unique relationship which might otherwise peter out in boredom and indifference, if not conflict and bitterness? Not according to Bullock:

People used to say to me, it should have ended. They've said that for the last twenty years, we should have finished then. Why? So that you can feel better in your old age? If you turn to the people for whom you suggest it should have ended, their answer will resoundingly be: 'No, it's our career, our life, our future, our hopes – how can you let us down by saying complacently it should have ended just because we've stopped wearing blazers and grey flannel trousers when we go out? You can't say that.' Who are we to say it should have ended? We are only in the Brigade of Gurkhas to try and ensure its survival for as long as possible under any circumstances until Gurkhas themselves can no longer fit into the environment either through the inability of the soldier or through the inability of the political system in Nepal to accommodate the arrangement.[64]

For the moment neither proviso applies: the political situation in Nepal since the restoration of the democratic process in 1990 is unsettled but not – as yet – actively opposed to British recruitment of Gurkhas, which brings precious wealth to a poor country; and Gurkha soldiers continue to impress with their adaptability, keenness to learn new skills and propensity for making friends wherever they go.

In Brunei, they are preferred to British troops for cultural reasons and since the Sultan pays the piper (or Ministry of Defence) he can call the tune, which means Gurkhas for garrison duty there. His largesse has ensured a continuing British presence in south-east Asia after 1997 and has helped to maintain Gurkha strength – along with the formation and deployment of Gurkha reinforcement companies in the Princess of Wales' Royal Regiment, and 2nd Battalion, the Parachute Regiment, and the Royal Scots, which took place in December 1996 in the wake of the disbandment of the 3rd battalion RGR in November. This has kept numbers in excess of the projected 'around 2,500 by 1998'.[65]

In Christopher Bullock's estimation, 'the Brigade of Gurkhas has risen phoenix-like out of the ashes and is in a very strong position at the moment because, contrary to all senior and informed opinion at the time, the British Army has not been able to recruit. I think it's interesting that the Scottish Division, the division of infantry that was keenest – or at any rate very keen – to see the end of Gurkhas, is now saying how delighted they are to have a Gurkha reinforcement company in the Royal Scots.'[66]

Nigel Collett agrees that 'to some degree the new Brigade is leaner, fitter and better (it kept the best of the good, so the standard has to be high), and is proving itself again wherever it goes'. But he remembers the period of 'drawdown' as 'a foul time, over-long to live through'. As CO of the 6th Gurkhas, he had the unpleasant task of interviewing all those selected to go 'on the basis of a strict merit points system':

> Each marched in individually, and I read out the redundancy paper, listing entitlements. I then asked them if they had anything to say. One never knew what the men were going to say; some reeled out in shock, many were content or even pleased, some made complaints and blamed partiality, *gaunli*-ism [favouring people from one's own village], unfairness, tribalism or whatever. One tried always to be as decent in riposte as one could be, and not shoot them down for insolence or stupidity. They all had their say if they wanted it. No-one was abusive or aggressive, no-one threatened anyone. A few burst into tears.

He characterizes this distressing time succinctly: 'One was always saying goodbye.'[67]

The Gurkha world may have gone, but it would be wrong to strike too elegiac a note. The Brigade of Gurkhas soldiers on, now consisting of two battalions of Royal Gurkha Rifles, one squadron each of Gurkha

Engineers, Gurkha Signals and the Gurkha Transport Regiment, plus three Gurkha Reinforcement Companies and two Gurkha Demonstration Companies in the UK, not to mention the recruiting organization and infrastructure in Nepal. Terms and conditions of service, so long a bone of contention, have been amended and updated to take account of the new, post-colonial position of Gurkhas in the British Army and to provide parity of take-home pay with British soldiers.

Pay was not the only issue considered in the terms and conditions settlement; leave was another. British soldiers get four weeks' leave a year; so do Gurkhas. But Gurkhas also get long leave to Nepal every three years. With the ease and speed of modern transport, the six-month period specified in the tripartite agreement might have been substantially reduced and most soldiers would have settled for two months. But General Cowan felt that the tripartite agreement had to be honoured and, taking into account improved transportation methods, concluded that the optimum period of long leave should be five months. In reaching this decision he was also influenced by some other considerations:

> It is a very good thing to get people back to Nepal to remind them that they are Nepalese citizens, that this is their country, that this is where their roots are; and the younger element can get properly married according to arrangements made by their parents. It also reminds people of what their basic pay is, because when they go on home leave there is no 'universal addition' [the allowances that put them on a par with British troops]. It just reminds them that this is the level of pay appropriate to the land where they are now living, the basic pay that Indian Gurkha soldiers risking their lives in all the various insurgencies are also getting.[68]

Cowan, who had recently visited the training centres of the 11th Gorkhas, recruited in east Nepal and based in Lucknow, and of the 1st and the 4th Gorkhas at Sabathu, was impressed both by the toughness of the training programme – the chances of young recruits swiftly going into action in one or other of the internal security operations going on in India are high – and by the pride that all Indian Gorkha regiments take in their traditions. He was amused to discover that in India, too, the senior officers who become colonels of Gorkha regiments form 'quite a Gorkha "mafia"'.[69]

Both the Indian and the British Army have retained the sandwich ranks that the Indians call JCOs (Junior Commissioned Officers) and the British QGOs. To abolish these ranks in the Indian Army would merely aggravate the shortage of officers there.[70] That consideration does not apply in the British Army where, for some years, there was a lively debate in Gurkha circles on whether or not to dispense with the QGO ranks. A study conducted by the then colonel of the Gurkha Transport Regiment, Maj-Gen. (now Rev.) Morgan Llewellyn, which served as a kind of blueprint for the Gurkha aspects of 'Options for Change' in its earlier, and more optimistic, phase, when the target figure for reductions was nearer 6,000 than 2,000, specifically recommended that the QGO ranks should eventually be replaced by short service commissions on the model of the British Army's short service quarter-master commissions.

But the Llewellyn study was overtaken by events, and in its struggle for survival the Brigade of Gurkhas was forced to undergo changes enough without the additional burden of introducing such a major structural alteration. The move was aborted, partly on the advice of the QGOs themselves, many of whom – particularly those in the infantry – thought they might be disadvantaged on educational grounds. The new terms and conditions of service determined that the QGO ranks would continue. In General Cowan's view, 'there is still a key role for the Queen's Gurkha Officer, for someone who knows the men, who stands in that intermediate position and can exercise more flexibility than the British officer' – particularly, perhaps, in the new and largely unfamiliar circumstances in which the Gurkha now finds himself soldiering.[71]

It is impossible to predict how long the present arrangement will continue into the twenty-first century. At the time of writing, the feeling within the Brigade of Gurkhas is bullish. The speed with which Gurkhas have adapted to the latest demands made upon them and the success of the reinforcement companies in British infantry battalions have been a cheering antidote to the dismal round of cuts and the wounding rejection by British infantry divisions which immediately preceded them. But the Gurkhas' success is predicated on the failure of the British Army to meet its recruiting targets. Should that change for any reason, or should the pressure from the Gurkha Army Ex-Servicemen's Organization (GAESO) in Nepal for parity with the British soldier in pensions as well as pay escalate, then the future of the Gurkhas could once again be cast into doubt.

In an article in the Nepalese magazine *Himal*, the ubiquitous Mary Des Chene (here billed as an editor of the journal *Studies in Nepali History and Society*) offers uncritical support for GAESO's case. 'Whether successful or not', she maintains, 'GAESO has already challenged the nation to think about why Nepali and British governments have quietly allowed Gurkhas to be treated as second to their British counterparts, even while their British officers proclaimed them to be second to none.' Of the 182-year-long British–Gurkha connection she writes:

> From one political perspective, this history is read as a record of glorious military service and unparalleled loyalty. From another position, it is read as a history of mercenaries, fighting fascism and independence movements with equal enthusiasm, and as a blot on the record of Nepali sovereignty.[72]

In the ideological dispute between professionalism and nationalism, there is no doubt which side Des Chene is on. She rehearses the mercenary argument – 'As the legitimate right to muster armed forces became increasingly reserved to nation-states, and military service became tied to citizenship and patriotism, the term "mercenary" had, by the 20th century, taken on increasingly ugly connotations' – and concludes that since Gurkhas 'swear loyalty to foreign powers . . . some will probably continue to call them mercenaries, no matter how the Geneva Conventions define the term'. The implications of this for Nepali sovereignty 'help to explain why passions often run high when questions about Gurkha service are raised'.

GAESO challenges the validity of the tripartite agreement, or rather the bilateral agreement between Britain and India over basic rates of pay which the Ranas allowed to stand despite their insistence elsewhere that 'Gurkhas be treated on an equal footing with other soldiers of the armies they served'. The rationale for this bilateral agreement was the necessity for more or less equal terms when the British and

Indian armies were competing for recruits during the immediate post-war manpower crisis. This situation no longer obtains, if indeed it ever really did. Des Chene notes that

> the Indian government has thus far declined to make the obvious statement that a few thousand Nepalis serving in the British army poses no challenge to India's ability to recruit Nepalis for its own army – and thus that there is absolutely no need today to tie the British Gurkhas' remuneration to the Indian army pay code. Indeed, despite the fact that Britain says its hands are tied by the bi-partite treaty with India, the Indian Embassy in Kathmandu tells GAESO that this is a matter for the British and Nepali governments to decide.

For Des Chene, it all comes down to a 'simple question' for the 'British military': 'Having proclaimed far and wide, for over a hundred years, that Gurkhas are among the best infantry soldiers in the world, how can it be just that they received less rather than more than other British soldiers for their service?'[73]

The short answer, of course, is that justice does not come into it: had they not been cheaper than British soldiers to employ, Gurkhas would not have been taken into the British Army in the first place. And if Gurkhas are still the victims of what Des Chene calls 'colonialist arithmetic' (in relation to pensions), then they are willing accomplices in their victimhood, as the associate editor of *Himal*, Deepak Thapa, acknowledges in an accompanying article in the same issue of the magazine.

Deepak outlines the British case, that British soldiers are required to serve twenty-two years – as opposed to the fifteen years that most Gurkhas serve – before receiving a pension and that those with shorter service must wait until they are sixty before they get their pension (calculated according to the number of years they have served). If GAESO's demands for equality were met, he argues, the long-term gain of pensions twenty times larger would be seriously offset by the immediate withdrawal of monthly payments to a considerable number of Gurkha pensioners, who would be told to apply again when they reached the age of sixty; and even 'taking into consideration that the average life expectancy of Gurkha pensioners is slightly higher than the national average of fifty-four, there is the question as to how many would be around to collect the amount'.[74]

Then it has to be remembered that Gurkhas are volunteers; whatever pressures might have been put upon them during the two world wars, nobody can deny that nowadays they enlist of their own free will and regard themselves as extremely fortunate if they succeed in getting into the British Army. The immediate rewards – not to mention longer-term opportunities, such as the Gurkha Reinforcement Unit (a preserve of ex-soldiers) in Brunei and other second careers specifically designed for ex-Gurkhas – are such that equal pay and pensions are the last thing on their minds when they sign up: 'While not every ex-Gurkha is successful in building a second career, it is certainly true that the British army connection has helped many former Gurkhas to live comfortable lives in relation to other servicemen.'[75]

Gurkhas made redundant through no fault of their own but as a result of reductions in the size of the army 'were given a raw deal'. Veterans of the Second World War who did not qualify for a pension 'felt cheated when they were sent packing with nothing more than their last salary, and a service medal'. Veterans of the Malay campaign in the late sixties, whose service was not long enough to be pensionable, were, like their British counterparts, given eighteen months' salary; but 'given the huge disparity in the [basic] pay scales of Britishers and Gurkhas, the latter got a pittance in comparison'. Deepak Thapa agrees with GAESO's demand for pensions for these people, but points out that it is inconsistent with 'its "equal-treatment" demands'. What neither he nor Des Chene mentions is that the Gurkha Welfare Trust is paying welfare pensions to both categories of veteran.

But GAESO has two further demands. One is that the British government assist in creating educational and training institutions for the children of Gurkhas. Though there are no such facilities for the children of British soldiers, GAESO maintains that since most Gurkhas are separated from their families for twelve out of fifteen years' service, their children are deprived of a father figure and, as a result of this and of the inevitable disruption of their education through travel to and from the United Kingdom and elsewhere, tend to be 'wayward'. The other is that Gurkhas – since they have 'given the best years of their lives to serving the British' – be given work permits to enable them to have jobs in the

UK after their retirement from the army. Deepak sees the logic of these demands but quotes a 'former British officer' as saying: 'The Gurkhas want to have their cake and eat it too. They want to be treated equally, but then again they want preferential treatment.'

He wonders, too, if GAESO is not putting the very existence of the Brigade of Gurkhas at risk with its legal challenge to the British government:

> The possibility that the British Gurkhas may be disbanded as a result of its activities does not seem to bother GAESO. Why should 3,000 matter when a hundred thousand stand to gain? . . . GAESO fails to consider the fact that 3,000 is not an absolute figure. It means many times that number of soldiers over the years.[76]

Serving Gurkhas have been 'subtly warned by their officers "not to rock the boat" since their very future may be at stake', but their attitude seems to be one of 'conditional support for GAESO'. A young Gurkha sergeant on leave in Kathmandu was thrilled that his earnings would be on a par with British soldiers' when the new pay code came into force (on 1 July 1997), but this did not prevent him 'silently' supporting GAESO's pension demands, which 'would secure him a lavish future'. If GAESO won, so much the better; if it failed, they were still doing pretty well.

GAESO is undoubtedly a thorn in the side of the British authorities. But Des Chene's contention that 'if the Gurkha connection is ended it will most likely be because of assessments of military needs in an ever-dwindling British Empire' stretches credibility.[77] It is not the ever-dwindling empire (now surely at vanishing point, anyway) that dictates the continuing recruitment of Gurkhas, but – as we have seen – the failure of the army to attract British recruits in sufficient numbers, combined with the adaptability and high professional standards of the Gurkha soldier.

If the Gurkha connection were indeed to come to an end, it is more likely to be through the inability of the political system in Nepal to accommodate the arrangement than through anything the British authorities might do. The two main political parties are both involved in the pensions dispute, with the United Marxist-Leninists supporting

GAESO and the Nepali Congress supporting the more moderate Nepal Ex-Servicemen's Association (whose demands for increased pensions the British government has already gone some way towards meeting).

Deepak Thapa comes from a family in which nine generations enlisted in the army before his father broke the mould by becoming a civil servant instead. Deepak himself was a teacher, first in Pokhara and then near Hile in the eastern hills, before he joined *Himal*. He believes the diplomatic fracas over Gurkha involvement in the Falklands/Malvinas war brought the fact that Nepalis were fighting in foreign armies to the forefront of national consciousness. The widely reported Hawaii incident, coming on top of that, made people wonder what the real causes of Gurkha discontent might be. There was some resentment among British Gurkha ex-servicemen against the *goras* (Europeans, whites). Ex-soldiers were often critical of the behaviour of their British officers, though residual loyalty and pride in their military tradition prevented them speaking out openly; in that sense they had developed schizoid personalities. But it is probably true there would be less resentment had it not been for the recent reductions.[78]

The editor of the Nepali-language version of *Himal*, Basanta Thapa – like Deepak, a Magar (though he hails from Dhankuta in the east) – denies that there is any resentment, or at least considers it to be very much a minority attitude; most old soldiers, he says, enjoy telling stories of army life and talk about their 'sahibs' with obvious affection. Basanta does not come from a military family, though his sister is married to a *lahore* who is now serving the Sultan of Brunei in the GRU (Gurkha Reinforcement Unit).

Basanta himself was once an extreme nationalist, opposed to all foreign recruitment, but over the years he has changed his mind and now he supports recruitment on the grounds that it provides much-needed employment; indeed he would welcome more of it, in the Middle East or elsewhere. He is critical of the 'long-nosed [i.e. Bahun (Brahman)/Chhetri] government' for limiting opportunities, not so much for enlistment as for legitimate labour migration. As things stand, people are forced to migrate illegally to the Gulf States, South Korea, Malaysia, or Japan in search of work and the government simply washes its hands of all responsibility for them.[79]

Among Nepali intellectuals, there are some who cherish Nepal's links with Britain as a counterweight to India's influence. Prayag Raj Sharma, who specializes in the pre-Rana period of history, approves of British recruitment of Gurkhas, but he summarizes others' objections to it under three headings: the stigma associated with the word 'mercenary'; the effect on the dignity of the nation; and inequities in terms and conditions of service. He emphasizes that these objections are not so much anti-British as anti-foreign, but there are constraints in speaking against India that do not apply to Britain, which is no longer a power in the region.[80]

Another academic and writer, Ananda Shrestha, identifies two schools of thought in Nepal. One is vehemently opposed to recruitment, seeing the provision of mercenaries for foreign armies as an affront to national dignity. The other is less nationalistic and more pragmatic, taking the line that if recruitment is the means to a better life, who can deny people the choice? Any curtailment of opportunities abroad should at least have as a concomitant the development of alternative employment within Nepal. Ananda himself is of the latter persuasion, though he too is critical of the British over pensions and the denial of the right to live in the United Kingdom to those who might wish to retire there, and of both the British and Indian armies for their apparent reluctance to promote Gurkhas above the rank of major.

Nepal and India are indissolubly linked by common interests, in defence particularly, but deeply distrust one another and the weaker country, Nepal, struggles to maintain a separate identity. If it were simply a question of economics, Ananda Shrestha reckons, Nepal would be better off if it were a part of India. 'They don't allow us to live, and they don't allow us to die' is how he puts it. Since the 1950 peace treaty with India, which Nepal has been trying unsuccessfully to renegotiate, there has been an open border between the two countries. In the last days of the *panchayat* regime, the king incurred India's displeasure by resisting the Indian penetration of Nepal. In order to reduce the influx of Indians, who were swamping the Nepali population, the *panchayat* government introduced identity cards and work permits. India responded by closing the border, which sent prices rocketing and contributed to popular discontent. This, in turn, provided fertile ground for the pro-democracy movement, supported by an Indian government not always so keen to promote democracy in Nepal, whatever it may profess.

Ananda Shrestha once had hopes that the United Marxist-Leninists (UML) would prove less susceptible to Indian influence than the Nepali Congress Party has been, but the UML has close links with the Marxist government in West Bengal and he has been disappointed by its performance in government. In his view it has been 'a power game all along'.

The 'politics of vendetta' have held sway throughout Nepalese history: first it was the war between the Pandes and the Thapas; then, after the Thapas had triumphed in the person of Jang Bahadur, between Jang's offspring and the Shamsher Ranas; and later between the Ranas and the Shahs. In more democratic times, it was between B. P. and M. P. Koirala, representing two factions of the Nepali Congress, and now the UML is split into opposing factions. These vendettas have played into the hands of the Maoist guerrillas who are particularly active in the western hills, since democracy is manifestly failing when parties are interested only in power, not performance. The extent of political disillusionment is such that there are many, even among the Kathmandu elite, who sympathize with the Maoists' cause, though they deplore their terrorist methods.[81]

The situation in Nepal following the restoration of democracy in 1990, then, remains highly volatile and it would be rash to attempt to predict what might happen there in the next few months, let alone years.

Ananda Shrestha is from Palpa in the west; he grew up in Magar country and, though more of a journalist than a writer of fiction, he was moved by a real incident to write a short story. It is about a young man from a military family going back three or four generations, whose self-image as one of the chosen few is so shattered when he is turned down by the British Army on medical grounds that he contemplates suicide. The story hinges on his dilemma – to jump or not to jump, as it were – and Ananda admits that he had a hard time deciding on a suitable resolution. In the end the boy does not jump; an only son, he feels responsible for his widowed mother. But the point of the story is the intensity of his dream and his commensurate disappointment:

The crushing defeat was hard for him to accept. He knew he could never go back to his village, a reject, and a disgrace to the family. How could he, the son of Bir Bahadur Pun, the grandson of Khagda Bahadur Pun and the great grandson of Samar Bahadur Pun return and be accused of breaking the fine family tradition where soldiering was the only profession and bravery an inheritance. 'No,' thought Nar Bahadur, 'there is no way I can go back.'[82]

Ananda has no difficulty in identifying with his protagonist; other contemporary Nepalese writers take a more distant, even disapproving stance in relation to *lahores*. Michael Hutt, a lecturer in Nepali at London's School of Oriental and African Studies, calls the attitude of these 'inherently nationalistic' writers 'somewhat censorious'.

In general, nationalism and left-wing ideology probably grow more readily in a climate of literacy and relative prosperity. In rural areas, where life is an unremitting struggle, patriotic feeling may be outweighed by economic imperatives. It seems unlikely that the Gurungs and Magars of the central hills, or the Rais and Limbus of the east, perceive any conflict between their Nepali patriotism and the tradition of service in foreign armies which has become an unquestioned way of life in many of their mountain villages.[83]

There may be a gulf of mutual incomprehension between the inward-looking urban intellectual and the outgoing rural *lahore*, but in 1938 Bisheshwar Prasad Koirala, the man who went on to become Nepal's first elected prime minister, attempted to bridge it in a short story about a chance encounter between a student and a soldier.

The student (Koirala himself perhaps) is walking in the eastern hills towards Ilam, when he is overtaken by a soldier on leave from Quetta. At first anxious to be rid of this alien and rather frightening creature – 'I had heard a lot about the brutality of soldiers' – the student gradually warms to a man who can speak so openly and cheerfully about his life and loves, can greet all strangers as friends and flirt outrageously with any girl he meets.

The soldier, who prides himself on recognizing people by the clothes they wear and the way they talk, guesses at once that his companion is a student but is otherwise incurious about him. While they are together, he will look after this thin and pale young man chance has sent his way, deciding when to make a halt and where to stay for the night, but that is the limit of his involvement.

The student, on the other hand, wants to know all about life in the army and is shocked to discover that the soldier enjoys fighting and looks forward to the war that is rumoured to be imminent (and for which he is gathering recruits), holding that death in battle is the quickest and surest route to heaven. The student has some difficulty in reconciling his companion's matter-of-fact joviality with the gruesome nature of his trade; yet when the soldier shakes him awake in the early hours of the following morning to say goodbye, he feels bereft:

> I had begun to grow fond of him, but he cared for no-one. He strode off down the path, and I stood there watching him go. Many times I have seen stone memorials to soldiers killed in battle. But this was the only chance I had to meet a soldier in the flesh.[84]

B. P. Koirala's surprisingly sympathetic story portrays the soldier as a romantic figure, living a life of enviable freedom – though the passing mention of the forthcoming Second World War and the reference to war memorials in the last lines hint at a darker reality. The fact that it was written at all suggests that the Gurkha may not be entirely without honour in his own country. But the Tibeto-Burman peoples who over nearly two centuries have made the name of Nepal famous throughout the world are treated with scant respect at home; in a society dominated by Indo-Aryans they are still regarded at best as simple peasants, at worst as rank outsiders.

With the economic and social emancipation of the few thousand Magars, Gurungs, Limbus and Rais who have survived successive rundowns and migrated to the lowlands and towns in search of educational opportunities for their sons and daughters, this may be about to change. Should that happen, then the long march of 'Johnny Gurkha' will not have been in vain.

11

Return to Nepal: A Personal Postscript

Between 1959 and 1996, when I began my research for this book, I had almost no contact with Gurkhas. In the beginning it would have been too painful, too sharp a reminder of a life of action and physical expression from which I had been forever excluded. If I continued to make no effort to see them, even after they came in numbers to the United Kingdom, it was because I felt I no longer belonged, the vital connection had been broken, their language forgotten; and perhaps I was also afraid I might be disillusioned and come to wonder how I had managed to invest so much of my youthful self in them. Would this ethnic romance turn out to be like a first love affair, fatal to revisit, the object of one's longing having thickened and coarsened and grown garrulous in middle age?

For these reasons, when I broached the subject of this book with the Brigade of Gurkhas, I proceeded – as the police would say – with caution. My first foray took me to the Queen Elizabeth barracks at Church Crookham, near Aldershot. At the gate, when my car was stopped by a khaki-clad sentry wearing a 'hat, felt, Gurkha' at the prescribed jaunty angle and carrying a rifle at the ready, I was instantly transported back thirty-nine years to my arrival in Malaya, tongue-tied and clad in the wrong uniform.

My sense of being in a time-warp increased when I made myself known to Lt-Col. Mike Barrett, a retired officer of the Gurkha Signals, as it turned out he had also been stationed at Kluang in 1958. He outlined the current situation in the Brigade of Gurkhas for me and then took me to the unit library, where he left me to browse through publications he thought I might find useful.

Among these was a 1991 issue of the English-language 'alternative bi-monthly' journal *Himal*, emanating from Kathmandu, an issue devoted to 'Nepalis in Foreign Uniform'. Published a year after the re-establishment of the democratic process in Nepal, when people were suddenly free to speak their minds, this series of articles gave a distinctly Nepalese perspective on the Gurkha phenomenon.

Two things were immediately apparent: one was the politicization of 'the Gurkha issue' in Nepal; the other that, in the words of a Nepalese sociologist, 'Gurkha recruitment offers the only lucrative and prestigious employment to Nepali hillmen, who would otherwise have to seek menial labour in Nepal, India and elsewhere.'[1] The two largely cancelled one another out. As long as remittances from Nepalis serving in the Indian and British armies constituted the fourth largest source of the country's foreign currency earnings and provided 'the biggest infusion of cash into the economy of the hinterland', no political party was likely to grasp this particular nettle, however fiery its rhetoric.[2] Much of the argument, particularly in the highly charged discussion on the subject of 'To Fight or Not to Fight' organized by *Himal*, focused on such weighty matters as nationalism versus colonialism. But as a retired Royal Nepal Army officer reminded the academics who formed the majority of those involved in the discussion:

> Questions relating to recruitment must be asked not in Kathmandu gatherings but amongst communities that send soldiers into the Gurkhas. I can vow that you would not dare discuss these issues under a pipal tree in those communities.[3]

While I sat there reading these words, I became aware of a Gurkha wrestling with the intricacies of a computer not far away from me. People drifted in and out of the little library, but for much of the time we were alone and before long we started to talk. We soon established a link: Ratnakumar Limbu was a grandson of the formidable Bagbir Limbu, who had been Gurkha Major of the 1/7th Gurkhas throughout my service with the battalion. Ratna himself was a Gurkha sapper, whose military career had stalled when he had been medically downgraded as a result of a heart condition. His openness and warmth were so infectious that within minutes and with no effort on my part, it seemed, I had been re-admitted into the charmed circle of the Gurkha family. Later, when he was posted to the Gurkha Museum in Winchester, where I spent several months researching, I would see Ratna almost daily and we would, as it were, formalize our relationship in familial terms with me becoming his 'uncle' – *thulo babu* (literally, big father) – and he my *chhora*, or son. But the unaffectedness of his initial welcome dispelled at a stroke all my doubts about the wisdom of re-entering the world of my youth. I was delighted to discover how potent the Gurkha magic still was.

From the beginning I was determined to revisit Nepal. Hong Kong or Brunei might have been more productive from a purely military point of view, but I thought I would get a broader picture from a spell in the homeland of the Gurkhas. I had to prepare myself for that trip by relearning the language, or enough of it to establish my credentials. Latterday Gurkhas like Ratna might be fluent in English, but in Nepal I would feel no better than a tourist if I could not conduct at least a simple conversation in Nepali, as I was learning to call it – not Gurkhali. I had discussed with Mike Barrett the possibility of getting on to a beginners' course and he had put me in touch with Lieutenant (QGO) Khembahadur Thapa, the senior Gurkha officer at 28 Army Education Centre in Church Crookham. Khembahadur tested me with a few questions and then delivered his verdict; however much I might have forgotten I still knew too much Nepali to benefit from the beginners' course.

I was disconcerted by the bluntness of his rejection and asked him what I was to do then, since even if I taught myself again from books I needed practice in speaking if I was to acquire any degree of fluency before I went back to Nepal. He could easily have shrugged his shoulders and shown me the door, but instead he thought about what I had said and came up with a plan.

When was I going to Nepal? In January, four or five months away. Khem himself was going to Nepal a couple of months earlier, but we could still get together a few times before then. One evening he would take me to the officers' mess for beer and *bhat* (cooked rice, or curry) and introduce me to other Gurkha officers there; another evening he would arrange for his friend Warrant Officer II Ramesh Limbu to be my host in the warrant officers' and sergeants' mess; and he thought I would also benefit from an evening, which he would organize, with the junior ranks. On each occasion we should eschew English and speak in Nepali. These meetings would familiarize me with the sound of the language again, as well as give me the incentive to pursue my private studies. He waved aside my protests that this would put him to too much trouble and expense on my behalf and made our first appointment.

Over the next two months I had several meetings with Khem, sometimes on his own, often in the company of other Gurkha officers or NCOs; and because I insisted on a measure of reciprocity he allowed me to take him and his friend Ramesh out for a meal in a Nepali restaurant in Fleet. We did converse in Nepali some of the time, and being among Gurkhas certainly stiffened my resolve to relearn the language; but more often we lapsed into English, my desire to quiz him and the others on their thoughts and feelings outweighing the ostensible purpose of our encounters. As with Ratna, we substituted a familial relationship for an inappropriate military one; so Khem became my *bhai* (younger brother) and I his *daju* or *dai* (older brother).

Khem was a line-boy; his father had served in the 1/6th Gurkhas and he had grown up largely in Malaya. With his education and intelligence he was an obvious candidate for one of the corps units and he had enlisted in the Queen's Gurkha Signals. His forthcoming trip to Nepal was in connection with recruitment and he told me that in the debate over what type of recruit was most desirable the old line-boy/'wild man' dichotomy still prevailed, as much in the minds of Gurkha officers and NCOs as among British officers, though the technical and linguistic demands made on modern Gurkha soldiers in the British Army necessitated a higher standard of education than previously. As to why young men should still be queueing up to join the British Army neither Khem nor his QGO colleagues had the slightest doubt that money was the major incentive. If there was also an element of family tradition about it they did not say so. But they did insist that, once they had joined, Gurkhas gave their all; theirs was not the nine-to-five attitude so prevalent among British contemporaries.

According to Khem, the two fundamental virtues of the Gurkhas were trust and loyalty. Both derived from the rawness and nearness to the edge of life in the hills: 'If somebody says to a goatherd that he will bring food on such-and-such a day and fails to do so, it may well mean the goatherd starves to death.'[4] Keeping your word was sacrosanct to a Gurkha, so when he swore his allegiance to the Crown on joining a regiment that was no light matter. But trust needed to be reciprocal and, in Khem's view, the British had recently shown themselves less worthy of it than heretofore. The rot had set in with the heavy reduction of the Brigade of Gurkhas at the end of the sixties and (in September 1996) they were still awaiting the new terms and conditions of service promised two years earlier. He no longer knew how to counsel the young men who came to serve: what would be their future? His own service would soon be coming to an end, but what were the prospects of those whose service was just beginning?

Khem was critical of the way Gurkhas were so often represented in books by British officers as *kukri*-waving little supermen; by extolling their bravery above all other qualities these officers succeeded only in dehumanizing them. Courage, or the lack of it, was an individual, not a racial, trait and if it was indeed more common among Gurkhas than in some other peoples then that was a product of the harsh conditions of their life, not some mysterious, innate force.

What concerned Khem more was the fact that throughout their history Gurkhas had been followers rather than leaders: in the days of Nepal's expansion they had followed the Indo-Aryan others; then they had followed the British; and now they followed the Indians in the Indian Army, too. But in the contemporary Indian Army at least there were equal opportunities of promotion – Gurkhas had risen as high as brigadier – whereas in the British Army Lt-Col. Bijaykumar Rawat of 1 RGR was the first Gurkha to get beyond the rank of major and command a battalion. (I did not know enough then to question whether any high-ranking Gurkha in the Indian Army was a Nepali national rather than Indian-domiciled.)

In Nepalese politics, too, Gurkhas had yet to assert themselves as leaders; if they ever did, they should challenge the corruption which was endemic in the country, regardless of which system operated – *panchayat* or democracy – or which party was in power. There was a party known as 'Maguraile' (a combination of Magar, Gurung, Rai and Limbu) which theoretically represented their interests, but it had too narrow a focus and too oppositional a stance to attract the likes of Khem, who wanted a party which sought to unite *all* the diverse ethnic elements of the country, not just the Gurkha element.

Yet, at a more parochial level, Khem and his fellow western Gurkha officers were of the opinion that a mixed eastern and western Gurkha regiment, such as the Royal Gurkha Rifles, was less harmonious than the old segregated regiments had been – though Khem's own Gurkha Signals was mixed and he counted several easterners among his close friends. Khem attributed this to social differences in the hills of east and west-central Nepal. Whereas westerners clustered together in villages with their fields spread out around them, easterners tended to be homesteaders rather than villagers, each house surrounded by its own land at some distance from the others. The effect of this was to make the individualistic Rais and Limbus more defensive, hostile and suspicious of outsiders than the more clubbable Magars and Gurungs.[5] ('Cats and dogs', said John Cross cryptically, if politically incorrectly, when I later put the question of their difference to him. In his book on Nepal, he elaborates: 'The eastern Gurkha is like a cat: friendship cannot be forced and the chemistry takes some time to work. The westerners are more like dogs: it was productive to make positive advances.'[6])

At Church Crookham, the Gurkha officers did not have a separate mess but shared one with the British officers. The British officers, because they were in their home country, often went out in the evenings and were away at weekends, so that the feeling of regimental closeness which had obtained when both British and Gurkhas were serving in a country other than their own was lacking. There were very few British officers present on either of the two occasions when I went to the mess with Khem, and the atmosphere seemed more hotel-like than mess-like. British and Gurkha officers greeted each other casually and ate in separate groups at some distance from one another on the long tables. Khem and his colleagues admitted to a measure of dissatisfaction with the sharing arrangement; since it did not reflect a true equality of status they felt constrained by it and would have preferred to have had their own mess. The ambience in the WOs' and Sgts' mess was considerably more relaxed, cheery and uninhibited.

At that time I was unaware that the future of the QGO ranks had been the subject of intense debate within the Brigade of Gurkhas, but it would certainly have lightened the atmosphere in the officers' mess if everyone there, British and Gurkha, had had the same sort of commission, if the QGOs could have felt that they were there as a matter of right rather than on sufferance. Khem contrasted the situation at Church Crookham with the close contact between British and Gurkhas of all ranks within the Gurkha Signals squadron, where the similarity of the work they all did made for greater equality.[7]

The one night I stayed as Khem's guest in the QGOs' quarters made me aware of the primitiveness of the facilities in the Queen Elizabeth barracks at Church Crookham. The rooms were poky and uncomfortable; the entrance smelt of drains. Indeed, the whole camp had long since been condemned and the Gurkhas were due to move out eventually; but no British unit would have been expected to put up with conditions that Gurkha battalions had endured uncomplainingly for years.

I flew into Kathmandu on the morning of Sunday, 5 January 1997. I had persuaded an old friend, Ewan MacLeod, who had also done his National Service in the 7th Gurkhas – though he had left the second battalion shortly before I joined the first battalion – to accompany me for the first part of my stay in Nepal. We had shared a house in Cambridge when we were both studying there in the early sixties but had subsequently lost touch until we met again at a regimental reunion, the first I had attended for many years. I had cast Ewan as my minder, whose physical support I might need when we ventured into the mountainous interior which, seen from the air as we came in to land, looked quite as dauntingly magnificent as I remembered it.

I had never been to Kathmandu, but Ewan, an architect, had spent a year there at the beginning of the sixties studying the classical Newar architecture of the valley. My first impression of the city was that it was typical of the Indian subcontinent, noisy, dusty and bursting with life, the streets a free-for-all in which people, cars and animals jockeyed for position.

We did not stay there long. The Deputy Commander, British Gurkhas Nepal, Lt-Col. Nigel Mossop, arranged for us to hire a Gurkha Welfare Land Rover and driver, which would pick us up at the hotel early one morning to take us first to Gorkha, then on to Pokhara. We would be away from Kathmandu for at least two weeks, the plan being to spend two or three days at Pokhara and then descend to the Terai and drive along the east–west Mahendra highway as far east as Dharan, where my 1958 trek had ended.

It was dank and misty when we loaded our luggage and ourselves into the Land Rover and crawled out of town, following a stream of noisy lorries and buses, all emitting noxious exhaust fumes, up into the surrounding mountains. Earlier Nigel Mossop had said, 'Gurkha drivers come in two kinds – fast and slow'. Bombahadur Tamang, or BBT as he was more commonly known, belonged to the second category. He was gentle, quietly spoken and, since he had served in the Indian – rather than the British – Army, spoke little or no English. That suited me. In the long journey ahead I would have ample opportunity to practise my Nepali.

Once we had left the Kathmandu valley and penetrated the rim of mountains surrounding it, the mist began to lift and our spirits with it. After an hour or so we turned north off the Pokhara road and began to climb through cloud towards Gorkha. We were rewarded with our first glimpses of the high Himalayas since our aerial descent into Kathmandu, where persistent smog mostly obscures the Himalayan vista. Gorkha itself was a sizeable village, or small town, strung out on a steep hillside. We were welcomed with garlands of flowers by the newly appointed area welfare officer (AWO), ex-Gurkha Major and Hon. Lt. (GCO) Haribahadur Thapa, and his staff.

In the euphoria of our arrival in Kathmandu I had expressed a desire to see Gorakhnath, the citadel-cum-temple which is the *fons et origo* of the modern Nepali nation as much as of the Gurkhas as a fighting force. Now I could see the enormity of what I had so lightly proposed. The shrine was perched on top of a high ridge in an impregnable position. Pilgrims had to climb some 1,600 steps to reach it. My conveyance was not some kind of palanquin with two men at either end and perhaps another two at the side, as I might have imagined in my sahib-like fantasies, but an ordinary kitchen chair to be hoisted on to one man's back and carried like a *doko*, the large, cone-shaped basket with a headband used to transport everything in the hills. I looked at the chair, with a veritable cat's cradle of ropes attached to it, and I looked at the porter, a slightly built man nicknamed 'Bhote' – Tibetan or Sherpa, or in his case Tamang – and I was appalled. But I could see no way out of this self-inflicted dilemma without serious loss of face. That we got to the top of the hill and down again without mishap was entirely due to Bhote's strength and skill.

The welfare centre, the first of several we would see, was a simple, two-storey building with a cluster of outhouses, surrounded by a high wire fence. Each centre was run by an area welfare officer, who was a retired QGO, and his assistant – another retired QGO or warrant officer – a medical orderly, a runner and, in many of the centres, an agricultural assistant. This one had been opened in 1982. Magnificent poinsettias (bearing little resemblance to the pot-plants sold at Christmas in England) and other shrubs graced the garden, where a hummingbird flitted from flower to flower in search of pollen. For me the welfare centres were oases in the sense that each had one European-style lavatory in addition to the hole-in-the-ground variety, thanks to the late Brigadier Abel Dacre, in whose honour they have been dubbed the 'Dacreloo Line'.

While we were at the Gorkha welfare centre, two old men who had served in the 2/2nd Goorkhas during the war came in to collect their welfare pensions (which had recently gone up several hundred per cent from 90 rupees – about £1 – to 700 rupees a month). One of them told us how he would have been awarded a Military Medal if only his CO had lived long enough to endorse the recommendation. This must have been during the Japanese invasion of Malaya, before 2/2 GR became prisoners of war *en masse*. The ancient warrior would have gone on talking indefinitely if Haribahadur had not gently shepherded him and his companion out of the compound so that we could sit down and eat before continuing our journey to Pokhara.

My main reason for wanting to go to Pokhara was to visit John Cross, whom I had not seen for nearly four decades. We had been corresponding for the previous six months and I had been reading his books, particularly *The Call of Nepal*, in which he tells of his fifty-year fascination with the country and its peoples and how he acquired a surrogate family and earned the right to settle in Nepal. When I was an impressionable young officer John had impressed me more than most; his linguistic flair, amounting almost to genius, had awed me, while his complete absence of military pomposity or any desire to pull rank had endeared him to me; his kindness, too, as when he had brought his slides of Nepal to show me in hospital in Hong Kong. These qualities had endeared him to many Gurkhas as well, though his standing among his peers was more ambivalent. He writes: 'As regards my brother officers and superiors, I was a puzzle. I did not fit the conventional mould so had to prove myself many times over before being taken seriously.'[8]

Perhaps John exaggerates his unconventionality: his views are generally orthodox, though his behaviour might be considered erratic from a military point of view. His tendency to speak his mind, irrespective of his audience, the mimic in him which makes him so brilliant a linguist, a propensity for clowning as a cover for shyness – these could be mistaken for a lack of soundness. In another career he might have achieved more tangible rewards, but in many ways the military life suited him well; if he did not go quite as far as he might have wished in terms of promotion (it was a particularly bitter blow that he had been passed over for command of his battalion), or receive the recognition he deserved in the form of medals, the army was tolerant of his foibles, his eccentricities, and made imaginative use of his linguistic and people skills. He retired as a lieutenant-colonel with an OBE and, though lesser men have climbed higher up the greasy pole, few have had as active or varied a career. Denis Healey could hardly have been more wrong when, on a tour of Borneo as minister of defence during Confrontation, he looked John up and down and said contemptuously, 'I suppose you are one of those office-wallahs who only come out into the open during such a visit as this.'[9]

As we drove slowly up the street where John lived, looking for his house, the man himself materialized in front of us, waving a stick in the air by way of greeting. He looked just as I remembered him, though when I remarked on this he whisked off his little Nepali hat to reveal his baldness. But it scarcely mattered; he had that tough, stringy, outdoor and ageless look that I associate with someone very different, the late Dr F. R. Leavis of Downing College, Cambridge. (Perhaps they have more in common than their appearance; certainly both acquired

the reputation of mavericks among their colleagues.) He was wearing
shorts he claimed to have had since the fifties – and asked me if I recognized them – and socks that he said he had put on for our benefit.
The only uncharacteristic touch was the pair of very dark glasses concealing his eyes, but these were necessary to preserve what sight he had.
For John had gone blind at the end of the seventies while he was still
serving in Pokhara as recruiting officer, and this was not long after he
had 'met up with a penniless and fatherless hill lad from the Gurkha
heartland called Buddhiman Gurung'.

> He had run away from home because there was not enough food for
> them all had he stayed there any longer. He had spent five years
> scraping a living to feed his younger brother and sister who, by 1976,
> were hungry enough to eat more food than there was. I ensured that he
> need never go hungry again and he looked on me as his father.
> Buddhiman guided and guarded me as I progressively lost my sight
> and I looked on him as my son, relying on him as I had never relied on
> anyone before except when I was a small baby . . .
>   By the time my sight was restored we were as one tree, I the roots
> and he, with his wife, the branches.[10]

Buddhiman's version of what happened is that, coming from a village
which provided numerous Gurkha recruits, he had heard of an officer
called J. P. Cross long before he met him. A cousin, who was a soldier,
had described him as a kind of paragon:

> Why, he likes us more than he does his own kind, is envied by his own
> people and should have been made a general by now. He knows all
> about us. He speaks our language just the same as we do. He tries so
> hard at everything. When he was young he loved his cold beer after
> games, inviting everybody to join in before he went to change. Now he
> has given up drinking beer; he never did like *raksi* [spirits] or smoking.
> He asks the men what the 'white stuff' drifting up from the end of
> their cigarettes is and, when they say 'smoke', he shows mock surprise
> and says he thought it was their money they were burning. And the
> songs he sings at *Dashera*. The soldiers always laugh loudly and the
> British sahebs laugh because the Gurkhas laugh.[11]

Buddhiman himself had wanted to enlist but it was his misfortune to be too small to be considered. Nevertheless, he had made his way to the depot at Paklihawa, close to the Indian border, and had thrown himself on the mercy of his uncle, Birkharaj Gurung, who had just been made Gurkha Major there. Buddhiman had been accompanied by another village lad, who was equally poor, and both had been put to work in one of the cookhouses, where at least they would be fed. The arrangement was strictly informal, not to say clandestine, and the boys had had to hide whenever the colonel did his rounds. This had not been difficult since this officer's routine never varied. Then there had been a farewell party for the colonel:

> I was happy; no Colonel saheb, no hiding. I said as much and was told not to be so stupid; there was always a Colonel saheb. The old one was going and a new one was coming.[12]

That afternoon Buddhiman had been accosted by 'an elderly British officer' in sports gear who'd come running in his direction. This officer was smaller and thinner than any Buddhiman had seen before – though he had always observed the species from a safe distance. On this occasion he had had no time to hide. The officer had fired a string of questions at him, what was he doing, where did he live, how old was he, was he married and so on: 'He spoke in fluent Nepali, with a smile, and seemed so happy'. Buddhiman had answered him naturally, though this was the first British officer he had ever spoken to and his heart had 'felt it was about to burst'. He was afraid he had been found out and would have to leave the camp and start worrying all over again where his next meal was coming from: 'In great sadness I went back to the head cook and told him all about my unexpected bad luck.' The cook's reply had surprised Buddhiman:

> He smiled and said, 'Oh, that's the new Colonel saheb. Have no worries about him. He always talks to people like that. He is a good man who never turns away the poor and needy. His name is J. P. Cross.'[13]

At the time John had had weightier matters on his mind than the fate of one poor Gurung boy. He had discovered that the recruiting process was rife with corruption and that the camp at Paklihawa was the venue for a lucrative trade in contraband masterminded by Birkharaj's predecessor as Gurkha Major. On top of which there was no security in the camp, where there was a Hindu temple open to all; the locals came and went as they pleased and petty thieving was rampant. John was learning the truth of what his brilliant language teacher, Colonel G. G. Rogers, had told him when he joined 1 GR in 1944: that 'the Gurkhas were not the same in their own country as they were in uniform, serving under the British'.[14]

Yet he had not forgotten his encounter with Buddhiman, and had raised the question of his presence in camp with Birkharaj, who had told him that there were two such lads, both 'dirt poor' and both from his village. John had 'sighed inwardly': was this another scam; 'was even Birkha Raj going to prove unable to resist such pressures?' He asked what would happen if they were told to go, saying that 'we were not a rest camp for Nepali paupers, however much people might think we were'; and Birkharaj had simply said:

'Saheb, they have nothing. I did not want them to starve or go to India without hope of anything positive.' He spoke with great feeling and my heart warmed to him. 'I was going to tell you about them.'[15]

John ruled that they should join some other young hopefuls who were employed as office runners and so live openly in the camp. A move to Pokhara was imminent and the camp was due to close, much to the annoyance of the local people, among whom many Gurkhas had settled because of the proximity of the camp.

Amid all his professional worries, John had had a personal one: 'for the fourth or fifth time' he had been on the brink of getting married; his *enamorata* had come out to Nepal but – like at least one of her predecessors who had gone out to Malaya to marry John in the fifties – had found that he was already too married, so to speak, to a people and a way of life to leave room for a conventional marriage. So she, too, had left him.[16]

I had never expected that first year would be the unhappiest in my career. More regimental gilt had worn off the ex-serviceman gingerbread than I could have imagined. I had found scandals in every department of my little unit that no decent commander should have countenanced; I had found unhappiness in the military and civilian staff, and I hated the disdain in which the name of the British was held outside the camp – the result of 'the slow defeat of never doing anything properly' ever since Paklihawa started. I had failed yet again to get married.[17]

The only cheering thought was that his two years as Deputy Recruiting Officer (DRO), West, were to be extended to three and a half; so he could remain in Nepal as he wanted to do, despite his distaste for the way things were done there even among Gurkhas (or ex-Gurkhas), until his retirement in 1980. But if he stayed he needed a new batman. Instead of appointing an enlisted man, he had asked Gurkha Major Birkharaj if he thought his kinsman Buddhiman would make a suitable orderly. Birkharaj had assented and John had sent for Buddhiman, whom he had been watching for more than a year with ever-increasing approval. He was intending to pay Buddhiman 300 rupees a month but, rather than create a dependency which would have to be broken on his retirement, he had 'decided to set him up so that he would not go hungry again' with money to buy enough land to support him, a wife – as he would certainly want to marry – and two children:

> That way I could make a clean break when the time came; yet I was being pulled in another direction by the inchoate desire for a son such as he, that I had never had and probably never would.[18]

Buddhiman had been overwhelmed by John's offer and, when John had asked him what he should call him, had answered at once: 'Son. We are now father and son.'[19] Later he confided in John how this offer had affected him at the time: 'when told that I would never allow him to go hungry again and, as he was too small for the army, I would look after him, he thought of his dead father, and . . . "I wept inside"'.[20] Buddhiman's main concern had been that, however hard he worked, he would never be able to repay such kindness. But his chance to prove his devotion would come sooner than either man could have anticipated.

John was still wrestling with the recruiting scandal, his certain knowledge that at least one area recruiting officer and his *gallawallas* had been using their power to promote or obstruct the fortunes of aspirant recruits as a means of enriching themselves. In his first season he had caused something of a sensation by refusing to recruit from the third largest village in the Gurkha heartland, Ghandrung, which had 'provided more recruits and had bred more Gurkha Majors than any other single village in the West'.[21] When he had visited the village, he had had a frosty reception and Buddhiman had feared for his safety. John had let the villagers have their say, then he got up and addressed them:

> I was punishing the village, did they say? Punishment? My writ and jurisdiction lay within the barbed wire of Paklihawa and Pokhara camps, nowhere else in the country. Who had mentioned punishment? Not I. If they had thought they were doing wrong, that was up to them. If there was a taker of favours, there must also be a giver.[22]

He had told the villagers that if they accepted his conditions, he was prepared to resume recruiting there the next season. But if he 'heard so much as a mouse squeak out of place', he would close the area again. Then he had sat down and waited.

His words had struck home; they triggered an orgy of confession: 'I had never heard such openness before and I doubt I'll ever hear it again.'[23]*

---

*John Cross's efforts to clean up recruiting practices may or may not have been entirely successful. When I ran into his successor as Deputy Recruiting Officer, Lt-Col. Bill Smart (who had gone on to become the representative in Nepal of the Kadoorie Agricultural Aid Association, the brainchild of the late Sir Horace Kadoorie, one of the brothers whose firm provided Hong Kong with electricity), he was sceptical, remarking on how endemic corruption was in Nepal. And the anthropologist Mary Des Chene, writing of the mid-eighties, states: 'Most people insist that it now requires either inside influence or upwards of Rs 10,000 [when the going day labour rate is Rs 10–13] to secure a berth in the British Gurkhas . . . Those whose sons have been enlisted deny that any monetary bribes are necessary, but agree that it is helpful to have a high-ranking serving or former officer put in a word for a candidate.' She qualifies this statement in a footnote: 'If bribes and influence affect selection it [sic] seems to do so at this first stage, when Nepali recruiters go into the hills. Once in Pokhara . . . British officers make the final selections, and at this stage no-one suggested that any influence could be exerted' (though in her reluctance to give British officers as a class any credit Des Chene cannot resist adding: 'I do not suggest that British officers are by definition incorruptible, only that they are not part of social networks . . .').[24]

All this time John's personal predicament had been worsening. His sister, with whom he had planned to set up house in retirement now that his final attempt to get married had failed, was killed in a road accident in America; and his sight was troubling him more and more: 'Looking into sunlight was a penance, so was walking where shadows dappled the ground.' Despite his failing sight John walked hundreds of miles in the hills every year and Buddhiman had become ever more indispensable to him, pointing out obstacles in his path and hovering half a pace behind him ready to catch hold of his pack-straps if he stumbled or fell. At his lowest point, when he did not know if his sight could be saved or not, John had contemplated suicide; but Buddhiman's devotion, unaltered by his recent marriage, pulled John through this dark night of the soul:

> If ever anyone repaid a debt of gratitude by personal love, it was Buddhiman's wonderful and unremitting care and concern to and for me during those long months of increasing darkness and difficulty.[25]

In April 1980 John's army service was extended by a further two years, which enabled him to have his eyes operated on while he was still serving. The operation was performed in Hong Kong and his sight was restored, though he was left with the tunnel vision which obliged him to wear very thick dark glasses.

When at last he retired from the army at the age of fifty-seven he did not return to England (except for a period of leave) but stayed on in Nepal where he was employed in Kathmandu at Tribhuvan University's Centre for Nepal and Asian Studies (CNAS or 'see-nas'). His original intention had been to update Professor Sir Ralph Turner's pioneering Nepali dictionary, but since, rather bizarrely in view of his fluency in nine Asiatic languages and membership of the Institute of Linguistics, his contract was as an assistant lecturer in *history*, his research project – which he later turned into the book *In Gurkha Company* – was 'The Nepalese Contribution to the British Army'.[26]

His main preoccupation then was to be allowed to remain indefinitely in Nepal and, after many petitions, he was granted permanent residence and the right to buy property and a house in his own name – a unique honour for a foreigner. From time to time he visited his elderly mother in England (she died just two years short of a personal century in 1998), but he had now made his home in a sizeable house in Pokhara, in the garden of which he introduced Ewan and me to a now prosperous – rather than hungry – looking Buddhiman, whose attractive wife Bhim Kumari brought us tea and biscuits.

John suggested that the fundamental conflict of ideas in Nepal was between, on the one hand, democracy, which sought to eliminate or at least reduce inequality, and on the other, Hinduism, which perpetuated it through caste divisions. He said that the Maoist campaign of terror in the western hills, which was very much in the news just then, and the communist rhetoric of the United Marxist-Leninist party were both symptoms of a frustration with feudalism.

A few months later he wrote to me that the Maoists had caused massive disruptions in local elections in five 'mid far west' districts 'by killing, or otherwise threatening, those Congress or National Democrat hopefuls who had wanted to stand'. He found it 'bitterly ironic that, after all I have done against the Communists and been through physically and mentally during that time, the one haven I thought would be "fireproof" has turned out nonsensically to be the opposite'.[27]

We broke our eastward journey across the Terai at Chitwan and, instead of visiting the national park there, decided to call on a local celebrity, Lachhiman Gurung VC, late of the 4/8th Gurkhas (see p. 268). In 1995, on the fiftieth anniversary of the end of the Second World War, Lacchiman had been among the five, out of seven, surviving Gurkha recipients of the VC to be fêted in Britain. *The Kukri* reported:

> Lacchiman Gurung VC, in his twilight days, was very much in the limelight; in August he was received outside 10 Downing Street by Prime Minister John Major, who presented him with a cheque for £100,505 for the GWT [Gurkha Welfare Trust] which was raised from the British public, mainly by readers of the *Sunday Express* newspaper. It has been a profitable year for the old and the brave; the seven surviving VCs received a substantial increase to their annuity, it is now £1,300 per annum. Lacchiman Gurung VC also acquired a new house through the generosity of the 8 GR Association and the British public through an appeal in the UK following publicity generated by a UK newspaper reporter, Miss Deborah Sherwood.[28]

Lachhiman had, in fact, become a bit of an embarrassment since he had joined forces with – or been co-opted by – the Gurkha Army Ex-Servicemen's Organization. In GAESO's magazine, *Gorkha Sainik Awaj*, he was quoted as saying, in reply to a question on whether he would recommend the army as a career:

> I joined a foreign army; was involved in a war and lost my arm. I could have died but with luck I lived. Many of my friends died in the war, some froze to death, many were blinded when engaged in war in the high Himalaya [a reference, presumably, to the Indian border war with China in 1962, the 8th Gorkhas being now part of the Indian Army]. Anybody who sends an able young person to the army to experience all the *dukha* [trouble, pain, grief] is guilty of *paap* [sin]. I cannot do such *paap*. I cannot recommend anybody to join the army.[29]

As a holder of the VC, Lachhiman lent a certain authority to an organization like GAESO and was proudly wheeled out in the front of its demonstrations for equal pensions.

His new house, built roughly equidistant from the Indian Army pension-paying post and the Chitwan area welfare centre, looked attractive from a distance, but Ewan's professional eye soon discerned that it had been shoddily built. We had asked the area welfare officer what would be a suitable present to take and he had said *raksi*, for Lachhiman was known to be fond of his drink. So we presented him with a bottle and were offered tea in return by one of the two women ministering to his needs. Lachhiman himself, now old and frail, seemed rather lost and confused, the showhouse too big for him, his sudden celebrity after years of obscurity unsought and not particularly welcome except insofar as it brought relief from destitution. We did not linger but, after some polite conversation and group photographs, took our leave. It was an uncomfortable thought that this tiny, distracted old man should have become a pawn in a political game whose ramifications were almost certainly beyond him.

From Chitwan it took twelve hours to reach Dharan. Though flat, the countryside was far from uninteresting. Much of the forest had been cleared, though there were still stretches of it where little groups of monkeys squatted at the roadside, scattering at our approach. Different kinds of kingfishers perched at intervals along the telegraph wires, keeping watch on the streams and ditches below; and a sudden, breathtaking flash of turquoise and navy blue proclaimed the passage of a jay, or Indian roller. But this was Nepal and, though most of the road was paved, at one point we were diverted for several miles on to a dusty track from which we could see above us, running parallel, a smooth and pristine highway where bicycles sped with ease while we lurched from pothole to crevice in ever-mounting frustration.

Dharan was unrecognizable as the place I vaguely recalled from 1958. I had no recollection at all of the town, and the military camp had then been no more than a forest of concrete posts and steel rods pointing skywards. On the face of it, this had not been the ideal place to build a military base. In the late fifties, as John Cross writes, Dharan was 'the centre of the communist movement' in Nepal. The army had looked askance at a site with 'a water problem and no access road'. But in every other place inspected by the British reconnaissance group '"civil unrest" made it move away until the most unsuitable site of all, Dharan, was "offered" a few days before the group would have had to report their mission unsuccessful'. Thus the authorities in Kathmandu had 'neatly turned a potentially embarrassing situation from themselves to one positively so against the British', and if it had not been for the military hospital 'and the dedicated work done by British doctors and nurses to "non-entitled" patients, the presence of the camp might well not have been tolerated'.[30]

If the cantonment had originally been an unwelcome development, by the time it closed thirty years later it had come to play such an important part in the life of the district that it was sorely missed. The hospital treated over 45,000 outpatients a year and in 1988, when an earthquake killed more than 700 people and destroyed innumerable buildings, the military machine slipped into gear and worked round the clock for three days, saving lives and restoring vital water supplies, and by its actions earned both the thanks of the king of Nepal and the 1989 award of the Wilkinson Sword of Peace.[31]

The depot had now been closed for almost a decade, yet the signs of British occupation which had led to its being dubbed 'mini-London', even as far away as in Kathmandu, were still evident in the treed and spacious grounds, with several football pitches, a swimming pool and a golf course. The military hospital and the bulk of the cantonment had been taken over by the Nepalese government and the hospital renamed the B. P. Koirala Hospital. Most redolent of the recent past was the well-kept cemetery, now under threat of being built over as part of the hospital's expansion programme.

The welfare centre at Dharan had opened in 1988 even before the depot had closed; it was the largest of all the area welfare centres since it combined welfare with the recruiting of eastern Gurkhas; it was also the most active on the medical side. Some 200 chronically sick persons came regularly for their medication and in the previous year alone the medical orderly and the visiting doctor had treated well over 5,000 people – 'lots of medicines being given away', as the ex-7 GR area welfare officer, Hon. Capt. Khagendra Bahadur Limbu, put it. This was a legacy of the military hospital, where everything had been free.

During our ten-day stay in Dharan, I ventured into the hills twice and on neither occasion did I reach my destination. We had lost our Land Rover and driver, BBT, as they had been summoned back to Kathmandu. Khagendra offered us his car and driver and our first journey over the mountain roads, which had replaced the footpaths I had walked in 1958, was to Tehrathum, whence Ewan was to go on a five-day trek accompanied by two porters he had hired in Dharan. Beyond Dhankuta, the old capital of east Nepal, as far as a place called Hile the road was graded and sealed, a magnificent feat of British engineering, the equal of any Swiss Alpine road. But after that we were on a much rougher track and it was not long before we and all our belongings were smothered in fine red dust.

The faces and clothes of the peasant farmers and their *doko*-bearing wives and sisters, the thatched wattle-and-daub, orange-and-white houses and the spaciousness of the landscape were all familiar. But this was a country for walking, not driving, and try as I might I could not feel a part of it in the way that I had during my earlier trek through these same hills. All of us – Ewan, his porters Kumar and Bolbahadur, the driver A. B. Rai and I – lapsed into silence as the difficulty of the road, the need to scrutinize its surface for hidden hazards, the ubiquitous dust and the increasing chill of the afternoon as the sun began to sink, got through to us. A simple journey had turned into an expedition. In this awesome landscape our vehicle suddenly seemed like a frail bark in a towering sea. We looked forward to reaching Tehrathum and the relative comfort and familiarity of a welfare centre.

We did not get to Tehrathum. Rounding a bend, we came upon an insurmountable obstacle, a missing bridge over a chasm. This was journey's end, or at least car journey's end. It was getting dark and we had no alternative but to return to the last ridge, almost an hour away, and seek out a hostelry at Lasune – the end of the bus route from Dharan and many, many miles from the Dacreloo Line. There we passed a bitterly cold and uncomfortable night.

The next morning it was still dark when Ewan and his porters set off on foot for Tehrathum and A. B. Rai and I began the long drive back to Dharan. A mile down the road the engine failed and had it not been for the fortuitous arrival of a bus I might have had to spend another night at Lasune.

A few days later, his vehicle repaired, A. B. Rai and I drove into another part of the eastern hills – to meet Ewan and his porters at the end of their trek. This time we were defeated by the weather. Unseasonably heavy rain made the unsurfaced road impassable and forced us to turn back. We called at Damak in the Terai, where the most recently opened area welfare centre was located. Our unheralded arrival there meant that I was spared the usual briefing from the area welfare officer, Hon. Lt Krishnabahadur Limbu, ex-10 GR. Instead, he allowed me to sit in on his interviews with clients, which were far more revealing.

The one that touched me most was with an old man, very deaf and practically blind, who had served in the 1/3rd Gurkhas between 1941 and 1947. He had been on the wrong side of the Sittang River in Burma when the bridge was blown up in 1942. Though he had survived that military disaster, he was now in a confused and obviously destitute state. He had been deserted by his three children, who had disappeared into India years before and – as happened all too often – had never contacted him again. A neighbour, who was also a distant relation, had brought him into the centre.

The area welfare officer could not give him any more money since he had already been given a handout less than three months before and his case was being considered. All he could do was reimburse his bus fare.

I asked Krishna (in English) if I might give the old man something, and he encouraged me to do that. So I tried to work out an appropriate amount, neither too large nor too paltry, and settled for 500 rupees, less than £6 but a substantial sum to the old man. He was pathetically grateful. I think there were tears. Certainly my eyes pricked. And when he got up to go, instead of joining his hands together in the civilian salutation, he stood to attention and – to my great embarrassment – gave me a military salute. I left, hoping that if he no longer possessed his precious discharge certificate there might be someone from his regiment who could vouch for him, so that he would qualify for a regular welfare pension.

A. B. Rai eventually succeeded in reaching Ewan and his porters, who had made their way by bus to the point where the surfaced road began. Their return marked the end of our stay in Dharan; the next day we were back in Kathmandu.

I was saddened by the fact that, though I had met several 7th Gurkhas on this visit to the eastern hills, I had not met a single one from my era. This was largely my own fault. If I had sent a list of names in advance to the welfare centre, I would certainly have had the opportunity to meet some. But after nearly forty years my memory of individuals, with a few exceptions, was hazy. The exceptions tended to be older ones, Gurkha officers, some of whom were already dead. Yet I learned later from John Cross that the QGO I would have liked to have seen most, the Gurkha lieutenant who had shared with me the labour of taking over Tam Mei camp in Hong Kong in 1959, was living within easy reach of the welfare centre in Dharan. This QGO had won a DCM in Malaya and John rated him the finest jungle fighter he had ever met.

I was not surprised to hear that he had fulfilled his promise and become Gurkha Major of the battalion ten years later. But almost immediately on achieving this pinnacle of a Gurkha soldier's ambition he had gone on leave and was caught smuggling 200 watches into Nepal; as a result, he had been dismissed from the service, and retired at once without the customary honorary GCO rank. His sin was venial rather than mortal, but it underlined the schizophrenic existence of the Gurkha, who remains a Nepalese citizen throughout his service in the British Army and is therefore susceptible to double standards. As his old friend and company commander, John Cross, remarked: 'He's no worse than many others but, okay, he fouled his nest, he shat in his *bhat khane thal* [dinner plate], as they say. But I must say this: he was the only Gurkha Major who wasn't invited to the 7th Gurkha disbandment parade with the Duke of Edinburgh, and I said, "But you punished him once; you can't go on punishing him". This was to give a bugger a bad name and the bastard's hanged for life. That is part of the British culture which I think stinks.'[32] John also said that he had become a Christian, changed his name and was now so crippled with arthritis he could barely walk.

Until the re-establishment of democracy in 1990, Christianity had been a proscribed religion in Nepal. Hinduism then lost its protected status and other religions flourished. High up in the hills, on the road to Tehrathum, A. B. Rai had pointed to a little corrugated iron building and said '*Girja*' (church) and I had expressed disbelief, thinking it must really be a *mandir*, or temple. But he insisted it was a church and as we got nearer to it I could see a simple crucifix sticking out of the roof. I asked how many Christians there could possibly be in such a place and A. B. replied that nowadays it was all *chyas-mis* – a kind of pick-and-mix of religions obtained. Christianity has made many converts, particularly among untouchables and the *janajatis* (loosely, ethnic minorities). A Newari intellectual I spoke to later clearly thought this was one freedom too many, arguing that it eroded the culture of the country. Except that, as he said, professing Christians often still performed Hindu rites and untouchables remained untouchable.[33]

Major Maniprasad Rai, now retired, was one of the first Sandhurst-commissioned Gurkhas. His father, the late Hon. Capt. Dalbahadur Rai MBE MC, generally known as 'Smiler', had succeeded Bagbir Limbu as Gurkha Major of 1/7 GR. Mani had joined the regiment soon after I had left, but I was introduced to him and his wife Mishra (who had trained as a nurse in England at the same time as Mani was at Sandhurst) at the house of mutual friends a few years ago.

We met several times in Kathmandu and on Ewan's last day in Nepal, Mani, accompanied by his son Roshan who was on a visit from England, took us to lunch in a restaurant. Roshan brought along a friend, the son of a Gurkha officer who had been head clerk in one of the regiments. Raja was working for an American aid organization in Kathmandu and, having just agreed to an arranged marriage with a Darjeeling girl, was now having second thoughts. Roshan, at twenty-seven, had so far resisted all parental attempts to marry him off, pointing out that Mani and Mishra's own marriage had not been an arranged one. Mishra was a Tamang from Darjeeling, Mani a Rai from the Nepali hills, and their different backgrounds and *jats* meant that both sets of parents had initially opposed their marriage; but they had soon become reconciled to what was obviously a loving and successful partnership. Mani had also encountered regimental opposition in marrying young but had weathered that particular storm, though it meant that the newly-weds had had very little money until he qualified for a marriage allowance.

When I questioned Mani on the differences between eastern and western Gurkhas he said that while the Gurungs were clever and got on well with the sahibs, they could be tricky; the Limbus were the best leaders; the Rais were somewhere in-between – 'a middling sort of people we are' – and the Magars were similar to the Rais.

One of his many projects was to research into the pre-history of Nepal, the misty era when Rais were the Kiranti kings, paramount in the Kathmandu valley. This reminded me of the interest in *jat* – or tribal – pride expressed by another Sandhurst alumnus, Major Yambahadur Gurung, who had stayed one night in Dharan while I was there. Yambahadur, who had served mostly in the 2nd Goorkhas, had said he was planning to leave the army later in the year to look for a job in Nepal. He had spent so much of his life out of his homeland that he now wanted to do something for it. Shortly after he was posted to Kathmandu, he said, he had been invited to a Sunuwar party, where the dances were authentic Sunuwar *nautches*, and he had been so impressed by the efforts of this tiny *jat* to maintain its cultural identity that he felt Gurungs, too, should do more to preserve their language and culture.

There are estimated to be about forty principal minority languages in Nepal today, most of them Tibeto-Burman, and the language issue has become critical. The unification of Nepal two centuries ago by Prithwi Narayan Shah created a state, but not, according to the archaeologist and historian Prayag Raj Sharma, a 'nation-state', which he defines as having 'a common destiny of remaining together, despite differences in language, culture, religion and political ideology'. Prithwi Narayan established feudal authoritarian rule on the basis of 'four key ideas: the unquestioning power and authority of the Hindu King of Gorkha; the supremacy of the Hindu ethos in national life; social integration through the Hindu social system based on caste division; and recognition of Nepali as the language of government, administration and, in more recent times, education'. The way Prithwi Narayan united the kingdom was not by treating other ethnic groups as foreign or alien, but by subsuming them into the caste system; and this process was taken a stage further by Jang Bahadur, whose 1854 *Muluki Ain*, or legal code, took into account the caste of both the offender and the victim in determining appropriate punishments for crimes. King Mahendra's 1963 *Muluki Ain* made it illegal to discriminate on the basis of caste, but 'did not do away with the idea of caste altogether'. The new Nepali Constitution of 1990 finally 'acknowledges the cultural pluralism of Nepal and guarantees the right of every community "to conserve and promote its language, script and culture"'.[34]

As a result, what Mary Des Chene calls 'the triumvirate of the Nepali state under the Panchayat', the Nepali language, Hinduism and the monarchy, is under threat.[35] The ethnic minorities, which now call themselves *janajatis*, were all lumped together within the caste system as the touchable but liquor-drinking *matwali* (as opposed to the non-drinking and sacred-thread-wearing *tagadhari)*:

> Some *janajatis* are now actively representing themselves as outside the Hindu caste hierarchy not as untouchable, but as non-Aryan and non-Hindu. Thus they reject the legitimacy of Hindu-based definitions of their social status and rights.[36]

The Tamu (i.e. Gurung) writers whose work Des Chene is discussing are not calling for revolution so much as for pluralism. '[W]e should not oppose any *jati*, language and religion,' S. P. (Siri Prasad) Gurung writes. 'We should instead oppose that communal thinking and tendency that gives special rights to only one while disregarding others.'[37] Even so, Des Chene concludes that '*janajati* cultural projects challenge the very heart of Nepali nationalism, lovingly fostered by some, cynically utilised as a mechanism of social control by others'.[38]*

The language question – which is, of course, by no means confined to Nepal – is complex, especially when considered in relation to universal education, a recent development in Nepal. As John Cross said, 'If a child is to be allowed to study in Maithili, Magarkura, Newari or whatever, then good, it means that the tribal language is not lost. But then the child has to catch up with Nepali, and Nepali is a very difficult language.' He sees tribal language revival as a 'short-term palliative': 'The cost of getting textbooks and teachers, and the waste and delay in getting the person back to the Nepali medium, is too expensive for this country.'[39]

I was surprised initially that so 'westernized' and cosmopolitan a Gurkha as Major Yambahadur Gurung should espouse the parochial cause of the Gurung language and culture, but then I realized it was a natural reaction to the process of deracination his life to date had exemplified, at one with his desire to leave the army and commit himself to his homeland. His friend Maniprasad Rai showed similar tendencies. Groomed and trained from an early age to become British officers, these two educated Gurkhas occupied the awkward middle ground between the western world, in which they had largely moved during their service careers, and the traditional Gurung or Rai worlds of their fathers, who had been QGOs, and their troops.

Mani had two sons and both had been educated in English private schools. Roshan was the younger and he freelanced in computer graphics; the elder, Milan, had written a book about the American linguistic philosopher, Noam Chomsky. They were therefore now so far removed from their roots that it was probably less of

---

*Des Chene is referring to the historical irony by which the development of the Nepali language and the celebration of the unification of Nepal and pre-Rana culture so 'lovingly fostered' by political opponents of the Rana autocracy in exile in India during the twenties and thirties became the new orthodoxy under the *panchayat* regime and were 'cynically utilised' as a means of suppressing other languages and cultures. Among these other languages, only Newari, with its rich literary history, was to some extent immune – though Newars, too, are demanding greater recognition of their language *vis-à-vis* Nepali.

an issue to them than it was to their parents, who still had a foot in either camp.

Ewan's departure left me with time to reflect. We had both been welcomed back into the Gurkha fold, no questions asked. For three weeks we had travelled around the country as guests – albeit paying guests – of the Brigade of Gurkhas. We had stayed in the officers' mess at Pokhara and at various welfare centres, and we had visited many more. We had sat through innumerable briefings from British and Gurkha officers about recruiting and welfare, pay and pensions. We had even met a few pensioners, young and old. The organization was impressive; the area welfare centres were imbued with the family spirit of the Gurkhas.

For me this was both comforting and a little disconcerting. It was like returning to the bosom of the family after you have grown up and left it; you know in your heart you no longer belong. The magic was still there, but the person I had become in the forty years since I had first encountered it was more questioning and less prone to enchantment. Many parts of the Gurkha myth that I had once swallowed whole I now found indigestible – not least the imperialist assumptions underlying it, which linger to this day.

India largely escaped the kind of criticism routinely levelled at Britain in the Nepali press over its use and treatment of Gurkhas. There was a good and a less good reason for this. The less good – but perfectly understandable – reason was Nepal's dependency on India and reluctance to offend a Big Brother more than capable of retaliation. The better one was that Indian Gorkhas were more fully integrated in the Indian Army than British Gurkhas had ever been in the British Army, since both pay codes were based on Indian – not British – Army rates, which were the same throughout the Indian Army.

However strongly British officers might protest that their Gurkhas were treated fairly – indeed more than fairly in some instances, when levels of allowances pushed their pay up so far as to put it in excess of their British equivalents, even officers – they were not treated identically. They might have achieved parity with the British soldier in terms of take-home pay but they were still a special case because of the tripartite agreement; and even if this could be shown sometimes to work in their favour it remained a mark of difference and could therefore be stigmatized as 'colonialism' or even 'racism' by political opponents, no matter how much better off British Gurkhas were than their Indian counterparts. And whereas Indian Gorkhas were free to settle in India – and many of them did – British Gurkhas did not have the option of settling in the United Kingdom.

And yet, and yet . . . Politics was not the whole story. From my own experience and observation I had no doubt that the spirit and traditions of the Gurkha regiments had touched all who had ever served in them, British and Gurkha, and made them the better for it. Such things were not measurable, but this did not mean that they did not exist. Pride – an impersonal pride that is the opposite of vanity – was still an evident characteristic of Gurkha soldiers and their better officers. This counted for something, however much it might be undervalued in the contemporary world.

Let me conclude these personal reflections, not with the oft-quoted final paragraph of the preface of Sir Ralph Turner's Nepali dictionary, visualizing the 'stubborn and indomitable peasants of Nepal . . . disappear[ing] into the smoke and wrath of battle' (though I know it by heart), but with the observations of a witness not so well disposed towards the Brigade of Gurkhas, the anthropologist Mary Des Chene.

In her thesis, Des Chene tells the story of a rare intervention in village affairs by local *lahores*. Rival gangs of teenagers threatening to fight one another might be nothing out of the ordinary, but when these gangs began to arm themselves with kukris and sticks their elders became alarmed and this was where the *lahores* came in. They summoned the youths to a meeting, where the latter might have expected to be lectured on the evils of fighting and violence; instead they were given 'a lesson in military tactics':

> The young men were told they were hopelessly disorganized, barging around like alarmed elephants. They needed to camouflage themselves, to split up into small parties and perform reconnaissance. They needed a proper plan of battle, and to establish potential lines of retreat. And so on.[40]

Both the anthropologist and the new village policeman, a Chhetri, who had agreed to let the *lahores* hold the meeting to try and sort out the trouble, were taken aback by such an approach.

Other onlookers were thoroughly enjoying the spectacle; only the *lahores*, it seemed, were taking it seriously, inviting the lads to nominate one of their number as leader. But when the ex-Gurkhas went on to offer their own services as officers the youngsters muttered something about thinking it over and slunk away. The old soldiers had made their point and there was no more trouble after that. One of them, questioned by Des Chene, shrugged it off as 'a simple matter of "reverse psychology"'.[41]

Gurkhas have always been granted a sense of humour but, historically, they have also been the butt of 'Irish' jokes, ones that make them out to be none too bright. What I like about this story is that it reveals the wit and wisdom of the Gurung *lahores* in their home environment and shows them using their military experience imaginatively to defuse a potentially explosive social situation. It makes me laugh and, at the same time, it makes me proud ever to have been associated with such people.

A Note for the Non-Military

I have assumed some familiarity with military ranks and formations in this book. But for non-military readers, here is some basic information. First, officers in hierarchical order from the top:

Field Marshal
General
Lieutenant-General
Major-General
Brigadier (once Brigadier-General)
Colonel
Lieutenant-Colonel
Major
Captain
Lieutenant
Second Lieutenant

Next in seniority in the Indian Army/Gurkha regiments are what were formerly known as Viceroy's Commissioned Officers and are now known as Queen's (or King's) Gurkha Officers (and in today's Indian

Army as Junior Commissioned Officers) – a sandwich rank between officers and other ranks:

Subedar-Major/Gurkha Major
Subedar/Gurkha Captain
Jemadar/Gurkha Lieutenant

Other rank Indian infantry and British Army (including Gurkhas) equivalents are as follows:

Havildar-Major/Sergeant-Major (warrant officer)
Havildar/Sergeant
Naik/Corporal
Lance-Naik/Lance-Corporal
Sepoy/Rifleman/Private

Every soldier belongs to a regiment. That is his home, so to speak. A regiment may have just one battalion (theoretically about 800 to 1,000 men, but very often fewer) or as many as five or six – particularly in wartime. A regiment is not itself a fighting formation, but a battalion is. Here, in order of numerical strength, are the key fighting units (the emphasis here is on infantry and no mention is made of supporting units such as artillery, engineers, supply and transport):

Army (made up of 3 corps)
Corps (consisting of 3 divisions)
Division (consisting of 3 brigades)
Brigade (consisting of 3 battalions)
Battalion (consisting of 3 or 4 rifle companies, plus Support
    Company & Battalion HQ)
Company (consisting of 3 platoons)
Platoon (consisting of 3 sections)
Section (usually 8 or 9 men)

This is only a very rough guide, and all these numbers are subject to change according to the exigencies of service.

Generally speaking, armies, corps and divisions are commanded by generals, brigades by brigadiers, battalions by lieutenant-colonels, companies by majors (sometimes captains), platoons by lieutenants or second-lieutenants (in Gurkha regiments by Gurkha lieutenants) and sections by corporals or lance-corporals.

Copyright
Acknowledgements

For permission to make use of unpublished copyright material, the author gratefully acknowledges the following: Colonel D. F. Neill for extracts from his unpublished Chindit memoir, *One More River*; Denis G. F. Gudgeon for quotations from letters from Burma to his parents about Orde Wingate and the Chindits; Mrs H. C. Gay for a quotation from her late husband, Major H. C. Gay's unpublished Burma memoir; and Lt-Colonel A. A. Mains for extracts from Gajendra Malla's memoirs of his service in the 9th Gurkha Rifles.

Every effort has been made to clear copyright of published material, and thanks are due to Cassell plc for permission to quote from the late Philip Mason's Introduction to *The Springing Tiger: A Study of a Revolutionary* by Hugh Toye and from Lt-General Sir Francis Tuker's *While Memory Serves* and *Approach to Battle*. But in too many cases the trail went cold where either publishers or agents had gone out of business (or simply failed to respond to repeated requests for copyright clearance), or individual authors or executors to whom copyright had reverted proved untraceable. Full details of all works quoted are given in the references and bibliography.

References

The following abbreviations are used in the References:

BL–OIOC   British Library, Oriental and India Office Collections (India Office Records)
GM   Gurkha Museum
IWM   Imperial War Museum
NAM   National Army Museum
PRO   Public Record Office

Introduction

1. Brigade of Gurkhas, 'An Outline History of the Brigade of Gurkhas', RHQ/History, 1 May 1996.
2. Francis Tuker: *Gorkha*, p. 265.
3. Lionel Caplan: *Warrior Gentlemen: 'Gurkhas' in the Western Imagination*, p. 1.
4. Ibid., pp. 1–2.

Preface

1. E. D. Smith: *East of Kathmandu*, p. 96.
2. Lt-Col. M. H. F. Magoris to J. R. Gould, dated Kluang, Malaya, 10 July 1958.
3. GM: Diaries G.39, 1/7 GR War Diary 1957–61, 24 January 1959.
4. GM: 1/7 GR Newsletters 1954–70, 14 May 1959.
5. Maj. J. E. Heelis to J. R. Gould, dated Hong Kong, 2 May 1959.
6. GM: 1/7 GR Newsletters, 14 May 1959.
7. Tony Gould to J. R. and H. B. Gould, dated BMH Kowloon, Hong Kong, 15 May 1959.

1 The Gorkha War

1. Kumar Pradhan: *The Gorkha Conquests*, p. 30.
2. B. D. Sanwal: *Nepal and the East India Company*, pp. 44–5.
3. Francis Tuker: *Gorkha*, pp. 26–7.
4. John Whelpton: *Kings, Soldiers and Priests*, p. 7.
5. Ibid., p. 12.
6. Ludwig F. Stiller, 'Modern Nepal' in Kamal P. Malla (ed.): *Nepal*, p. 101.
7. Pradhan, op. cit., p. 112.
8. Ludwig F. Stiller: *The Rise of the House of Gorkha*, p. 15.
9. Pradhan, op. cit., p. 176; Stiller, op. cit. [*The Rise of . . .*], pp. 59–60.
10. Colonel Fitzpatrick: *An Account of the Kingdom of Nepal*, p. 104.
11. Pradhan, op. cit., pp. 176–7.
12. Ibid., p. 15.
13. Father Giuseppe, 'An Account of the Kingdom of Népál', *Asiatick Researches*, Vol. 2, xvii, Calcutta, 1790, p. 317.
14. Ibid., p. 319.
15. Fitzpatrick, op. cit., p. 164.
16. Pradhan, op. cit., pp. 104–5.
17. Tuker, op. cit., p. 52.
18. Stiller, op. cit. [*The Rise of . . .*], pp. 126–7.
19. BL–OIOC: Hodgson MSS 1, 'Sketch of the Relations between the British Government and Nepal from their commencement down to AD 1834 . . . with occasional observations by A. Campbell Assistant Surgeon', 1 April 1837.
20. Pradhan, op. cit., p. 103.
21. Francis Buchanan Hamilton: *An Account of the Kingdom of Nepal*, p. 246.
22. John Pemble: *The Invasion of Nepal*, p. 26.
23. Pradhan, op. cit., p. 105.
24. Stiller, op. cit. [*The Rise of . . .*], pp. 136–7.
25. Pradhan, op. cit., p. 142.
26. Stiller, op. cit. [*The Rise of . . .*], pp. 212–13.
27. The Marchioness of Bute (ed.): *The Private Journals of the Marquess of Hastings*, pp. 144–5.
28. Ibid., p. 147.
29. John Keay: *The Honourable Company*, pp. 362–91.
30. Stiller, op. cit. [*The Rise of . . .*], p. 173.
31. Stiller, op. cit. ['Modern Nepal'] p. 102.
32. Hamilton, op. cit., p. 250.
33. Henry T. Prinsep: *History of the Political and Military Transactions in India during the Administration of the Marquess of Hastings 1813–1823*, Vol. 1, pp. 61–2.
34. Ibid., p. 63.
35. Stiller, op. cit. [*The Rise of . . .*], p. 246.
36. Prinsep, op. cit., p. 55.
37. Lt F. G. Cardew: *A Sketch of the Services of the Bengal Native Army to the Year 1895*, p. 118.

38. Bute, op cit., pp. 222–4.
39. Ibid.
40. Hon. J. W. Fortescue: *A History of the British Army*, Vol. XI, p. 129.
41. Cited in Tuker, op. cit., p. 83.
42. James Baillie Fraser: *Journal of a Tour* . . . , p. 29.
43. Tuker, op. cit., p. 86.
44. L. Hadow Jenkins: *General Frederick Young*, pp. 1, 47–8.
45. Arthur Percy Coleman: *So Peculiarly Formed a Corps* (unpublished Univ. of London M. Phil. thesis), pp. 126–7.
46. Victor Jacquemont: *Letters from India 1829–32*, p. 149.
47. Cited in Coleman, op. cit., p. 126.
48. Ibid., p. 135.
49. Fortescue, op. cit., p. 147.
50. East India Company: *Papers Respecting the Nepaul War*, p. 745.
51. Prinsep, op. cit., p. 129.
52. Fortescue, op. cit., p. 146.
53. Tuker, op. cit., p. 80.
54. Fortescue, op. cit., p. 146.
55. Francis W. Stubbs: *History of the Bengal Artillery*, p. 29.
56. Fortescue, op. cit., p. 147.
57. Captain Thomas Smith: *Narrative of a Five Years' Residence*, Vol. II, p. 175.
58. Pemble, op. cit., p. 111.
59. Fortescue, op. cit., p. 149.
60. Major F. G. Cardew, 'Major-General Sir David Ochterlony, Bart., GCB, 1758–1825', *The Journal of the Society of Army Historical Research*, Vol. X, No. 39, January 1931, pp. 40–63.
61. Pemble, op. cit., p. 92.
62. Smith, op. cit., pp. 161–2.
63. T. A. Heathcote: *The Indian Army*, p. 122.
64. Cardew, op. cit. ['Ochterlony'], p. 44.
65. Pemble, op. cit., pp. 90–3.
66. Sir Penderel Moon: *The British Conquest and Dominion of India*, p. 269.
67. Smith, op. cit., p. 164.
68. Cardew, op. cit., p. 48; Smith, op. cit., p. 167.
69. Cardew, op. cit., pp. 50–2.
70. Coleman, op. cit., p. 87; Pemble, op. cit., p. 40.
71. Coleman, op. cit., p. 99.
72. BL–OIOC: *Records of the Ludhiana Agency*, Ochterlony to Adam, 26 May 1814.
73. Ibid.
74. Cited in Coleman, op. cit., p. 106.
75. Cited in Edward Thompson: *The Making of the Indian Princes*, pp. 188–9.
76. BL–OIOC: *Records* . . . , Ochterlony to Adam, 29 August 1814.
77. Cited in Prinsep, op. cit., p. 460.
78. Ibid., p. 458.
79. Anon.: *Military Sketches of the Goorka War*, pp. 13–14.

80. Ibid., p. 48.
81. Fortescue, op. cit., p. 131.
82. Pemble, op. cit., pp. 281–3.
83. Prinsep, op. cit., pp. 466–7.
84. Edward Thompson: *The Life of Charles Lord Metcalfe*, p. 163.
85. Coleman, op. cit., p. 112.
86. Fraser, op. cit., p. 151.
87. BL–OIOC: *Bengal Military Consultations*, Vol. 57, No. 35, dated Deyrah Dhoon 29 December 1829.
88. Hearsey to Adam, 24 August 1814, cited in Dr Banarsi Prasad Saksena (ed.): *Historical Papers Relating to Kumaon 1809–1842*, pp. 3–4.
89. Adam to Gardner, 7 March 1815, ibid., pp. 63–4.
90. Seema Alavi: *The Sepoys and the Company*, p. 277.
91. Pemble, op. cit., p. 275.
92. Coleman, op. cit., pp. 146–7.
93. BL–OIOC: L/MIL/5/391/Coll. 138, Lawtie to Ochterlony, 18 April 1815.
94. Cited in Coleman, op. cit., pp. 154–5.
95. BL–OIOC: *Bengal Military Consultations*, No. 35, Young to Col. Fagan, Adj-Gen., 29 December 1829.
96. Ibid.
97. Nigel Woodyatt: *The Regimental History of the 3rd QAO Gurkha Rifles*, p. 9.
98. BL–OIOC: L/MIL/5/391/Coll. 138, Hastings to Honorable Committee, EIC, 2 October 1815.
99. BL–OIOC: *Bengal Military Consultations*, No. 36, Young to Fagan, 25 August 1830.
100. Smith, op. cit., pp. 232–3.
101. Ibid., p. 179.
102. Anon., op. cit., p. 40.
103. Lt John Shipp: *Memoirs of the Extraordinary Military Career of John Shipp*, p. 73.
104. Ibid., pp. 62, 69.
105. Cited in Cardew, op. cit., p. 57.
106. Shipp, op. cit., pp. 81–2.
107. Ibid., pp. 89–90.
108. Prinsep, op. cit., pp. 199–200.
109. Shipp, op. cit., p. 102.
110. Ibid., pp. 104–5.
111. Ibid., p. 109.
112. Ibid., pp. 113, 116.
113. Ibid., pp. 117–18.
114. Fraser, op. cit., p. 29.
115. Shipp, op. cit., pp. 139, 141.
116. Anon., op. cit., p. 46.
117. Ibid., pp. 34, 46–7.
118. Stubbs, op. cit., pp. 19–20.

119. Coleman, op. cit., pp. 210–11.
120. Cited in Pemble, op. cit., pp. 339–40.
121. Cardew, op. cit., p. 60.
122. Ibid., pp. 61–2.
123. Cited in Coleman, op. cit., p. 175.
124. Jacquemont, op. cit., p. 354.
125. Thompson, op. cit. [*The Making . . .*], p. 184.

2 Residents, Rajahs, Ranis – and Ranas

1. Henry T. Prinsep: *History of the Political and Military Transactions . . . 1813–23*, pp. 464–5.
2. Cited in B. D. Sanwal: *Nepal and the East India Company*, p. 217.
3. BL–OIOC: Hodgson Papers, Vol. 9, 'Nepal Army 1825'.
4. Ibid. – underlinings in original.
5. BL–OIOC: Hodgson Papers, Vol. 10, 'Memoir on the army of Nepal submitted to the Government when I was Secretary to the Embassy'.
6. Ibid.
7. Ludwig F. Stiller: *The Silent Cry*, p. 231.
8. BL–OIOC: L/P&S/20/D6, 'Diary of Events in Nipal 1841 to 1846', compiled by J. Talboys Wheeler.
9. Ludwig F. Stiller: *Letters from Kathmandu*, p. 122.
10. John Whelpton: *Kings, Soldiers and Priests*, p. 100.
11. BL–OIOC: L/P&S/20/D6, 'Diary . . .', 12 July 1841.
12. Ibid., 8 August 1841.
13. Ibid., 28 September 1841.
14. Whelpton, op. cit., p. 73.
15. BL–OIOC: L/P&S/20/D6, 'Diary . . .', 6 October 1841.
16. Ibid., 16 February 1842.
17. Ibid., 23 April 1842.
18. Ibid.
19. Ibid., 16–22 October 1842.
20. Cited in Whelpton, op. cit., p. 104.
21. BL–OIOC: L/P&S/20/D6, 'Diary . . .'.
22. Cited in Perceval Landon: *Nepal*, Vol. 1, p. 102.
23. BL–OIOC: L/P&S/20/D6, 'Diary . . .', 16–17 November 1842.
24. Ibid., 16–18 December 1842.
25. Lawrence to Government, 6 February 1844, cited in Stiller, op. cit. [*Letters . . .*], p. 231 – italics in original.
26. Ibid.
27. BL–OIOC: L/P&S/20/D6, 'Diary . . .', 15 October 1844.
28. Cited in Stiller, op. cit. [*Letters . . .*], p. 232.
29. BL–OIOC: L/P&S/20/D6, 'Diary . . .', 22–24 May 1843.
30. Sir W. W. Hunter: *Life of Brian Houghton Hodgson*, p. 238.
31. Stiller, op. cit. [*Letters . . .*], p. 190.
32. Hunter, op. cit., p. 234.
33. BL–OIOC: L/P&S/20/D6, 'Diary . . .'.

34. Sir Herbert Edwardes and Herman Merivale: *Life of Sir Henry Lawrence*, Vol. 1, p. 449, citing Mrs Lawrence's *Journal*.
35. Ibid., p. 470.
36. BL–OIOC: L/P&S/20/D6, 'Diary . . .', 31 December 1843.
37. BL–OIOC: L/P&S/20/D6, 'Diary . . .', 20 August 1844.
38. Ibid., 15 October 1844.
39. Ibid., 14 March 1845.
40. Ibid., 18 May 1845.
41. Ibid., 3 July 1845.
42. Ibid., 21 October 1845.
43. See H. A. Oldfield: *Sketches from Nipal*, p. 353.
44. BL–OIOC: L/P&S/20/D6, 'Diary . . .'.
45. Cited in Whelpton, op. cit., p. 137; Stiller, op. cit. [*Letters* . . .], p. 274; and in Oldfield, op. cit., p. 347.
46. Rajendra to Governor-General, 15 August 1847, cited in Oldfield, op. cit., p. 348.
47. Honoria Lawrence to George Clerk, January 1846, cited in Edwardes and Merivale, op. cit., Vol. 2, p. 40.
48. Rishikesh Shah's Introduction to John Whelpton: *Jang Bahadur in Europe*, p. 63.
49. Ibid., p. 8.
50. BL–OIOC: L/P&S/20/G10/3, Geo. R. B. Ottley to Secretary to the Governor-General, 17 September 1846.
51. Ibid.
52. Stiller, op. cit., p. 377.
53. Thoresby to Government, 18 March 1847, cited in Stiller, op. cit., p. 316.
54. Whelpton, op. cit. [*JB in Europe*], p. 86.
55. Ibid., p. 98.
56. Sanwal, op. cit., p. 67.
57. General Sir Orfeur Cavenagh: *Reminiscences of an Indian Official*, pp. 108–9.
58. Ibid., p. 141.
59. Ibid., p. 131.
60. BL–OIOC: MSS.Eur.C.193, Oldfield letters, Margaret Oldfield to her mother-in-law, 8 July 1857.
61. Laurence Oliphant: *A Journey to Kathmandu*, pp. 20–1.
62. Whelpton, op. cit. [*JB in Europe*], p. 124 – Whelpton mistakenly attributes this story to Cavenagh.
63. Oliphant, op. cit., p. 118.
64. Hon. Capt. Francis Egerton RN: *Journal of a Winter's Tour in India*, p. 209.
65. BL–OIOC: MSS.Eur.C.193, Oldfield letters – italics in original.
66. Oliphant, op. cit., p. 90.
67. M. S. Jain: *Emergence of a New Aristocracy in Nepal*, pp. 111–20; Adrian Sever: *Nepal under the Ranas*, pp. 74–9.
68. Capt. Orfeur Cavenagh: *Rough Notes on the State of Nepal* . . . , pp. 54–5.
69. Oldfield, op. cit., pp. 380–1.
70. Hon. W. G. Osborne: *The Court and the Camp of Runjeet Sing*, pp. 107–8.
71. Kanchanmoy Mojumdar, 'Recruitment of the Gurkhas in the Indian

Army, 1814–1877', *United Services Journal*, Vol. 83, No. 391, p. 148; Purushottam Banskota: *The Gurkha Connection*, p. 29.

72. Mojumdar, op. cit., p. 149.
73. Ramakant: *Indo-Nepalese Relations 1816–1877*, pp. 270–1.
74. Ibid., pp. 271–2.
75. Ibid., p. 272, Ramsay to Government, 29 June 1854.
76. Cited in Mojumdar, op. cit., pp. 149–50, 163.
77. Cavenagh, op. cit. [*Rough Notes . . .*], pp. 10–11.
78. Krishna Kant Adhikari: *Nepal under Jang Bahadur*, Vol. 1, pp. 159–65.
79. Ibid., p. 167.
80. Cavenagh, op. cit. [*Rough Notes . . .*], pp. 12–13.
81. BL–OIOC: MSS.Eur.C.193, Oldfield letters, Margaret Oldfield to her mother-in-law, 8 July 1857 – italics in original.
82. Ibid.
83. Leo E. Rose: *Nepal*, p. 131.
84. Mojumdar, op. cit., p. 73.
85. Ibid., p. 71.
86. Hunter, op. cit., pp. 255–6.
87. Oldfield, op. cit., pp. 29–30; Ramakant, op. cit., p. 287.
88. Rose, op. cit., p. 128.
89. Ramakant, op. cit., p. 289.
90. W. H. Russell: *My Diary in India*, pp. 197–209.
91. Ibid., pp. 309–10.
92. Ibid., p. 350.
93. Ibid., p. 359.
94. Ibid., pp. 330–3.
95. 'Events at the Court of Nepal III, 1852–61', by Col. G. Ramsay, in B. J. Hasrat (ed.): *History of Nepal . . .* , pp. 335–6.
96. Ibid.
97. BL–OIOC: MSS.Eur.C.193, Oldfield letters, Margaret Oldfield to her mother-in-law, 28 February 1859.
98. Ibid., 13 December 1860.
99. Rose, op. cit., p. 133.
100. Ibid.
101. Ibid.; Mojumdar, op. cit., p. 165.
102. Ramakant, op. cit., p. 344.

3   A Martial Race

1. B. H. Hodgson, 'Origin and Classification of the Military Tribes of Nepal', paper given to the Bengal Asiatic Society on 9 January 1833, reprinted in *Essays on the Languages, Literature, and Religion of Nepal and Tibet*, p. 41.
2. Ibid., p. 40.
3. Bishop Reginald Heber: *Narrative of a Journey through the Upper Provinces of India*, Vol. 1, p. 273.
4. Victor Jacquemont: *Letters from India 1829–32*, passim.

5. Henry Fane: *Five Years in India*, Vol. 1, p. 194.
6. Emily Eden: *Up the Country*, pp. 112–13.
7. Cited in Loraine Petre: *The 1st KGO Gurkha Rifles*, p. 31.
8. Ibid., p. 34.
9. Cited in Philip Mason: *A Matter of Honour*, p. 192.
10. BL–OIOC: L/MIL/17/2/489, 'Historical Record of the Services of the 2nd Goorkha (the Sirmoor Rifle) Regiment', pp. 6–7.
11. Ibid.
12. Cited in Petre, op. cit., p. 47.
13. Ibid.
14. Lord Roberts: *Forty-One Years in India* (1-vol edition of 1898), p. 54.
15. Ibid.
16. 2 KEO Goorkha Rifles: *1857–1957 Centenary of the Siege of Delhi as recorded by Major Charles Reid Commanding the Sirmoor Battalion*, p. 13 – italics in original.
17. Ibid., p. 14 – italics in original.
18. Ibid., p. 15.
19. Ibid., p. 16.
20. Information from David Harding, archivist of 10th Gurkha Rifles and author of *Smallarms of the East India Company 1600–1856*.
21. 2 KEO GR, op. cit., p. 28.
22. BL–OIOC: MSS.Eur.C.254, James Hare to his father, 24 June 1857.
23. 2 KEO GR, op. cit., p. 40 – italics in original.
24. Ibid., p. 44.
25. Ibid.
26. Roberts, op. cit., p. 33.
27. Ibid., p. 139.
28. Christopher Hibbert: *The Great Mutiny*, p. 308.
29. Cited in Petre, op. cit., p. 67.
30. *History of the 5th Royal Gurkha Rifles (Frontier Force) 1858–1928*, p. 3.
31. Ibid., p. 8.
32. Lt-Col. H. J. Huxford: *History of the 8th Gurkha Rifles 1824–1949*, p. 18.
33. Mason, op. cit., p. 318.
34. Sir Henry M. Lawrence, 'Military Defence of Our Indian Empire' (1844), reprinted in *Essays, Military and Political, Written in India*, pp. 29–30.
35. Ibid., p. 57.
36. *Historical Record of the 6th Gurkha Rifles, Vol. I, 1817–1919*, pp. 27–8.
37. Ibid., p. 33.
38. Roberts, op. cit., p. 533.
39. Cited in K. M. L. Saxena: *The Military System of India (1850–1900)*, p. 264.
40. Roberts, op. cit., p. 532.
41. Charles Chenevix Trench: *The Indian Army and the King's Enemies 1900–1947*, p. 13.
42. BL–OIOC: Government Report: *East India (Army System)*, pp. 30–3.
43. Ibid., p. 92.
44. Ibid., p. 94.
45. Nirad C. Chaudhuri, 'The "Martial Races" of India', *The Modern Review*

(Calcutta), Part IV, February 1931, p. 218.

46. Ibid.
47. Ibid., p. 225.
48. Ibid., Part I, July 1930, pp. 50–1.
49. Ibid., Part II, September 1930, p. 306.
50. Sir George MacMunn: *The Martial Races of India*, pp. 9–10.
51. Ibid., p. 2.
52. T. A. Heathcote: *The Indian Army*, p. 93.
53. Cited in Stephen P. Cohen: *The Indian Army*, pp. 47–8.
54. Roberts, op. cit., p. 356.
55. Ibid., p. 418.
56. Cited in David Omissi: *The Sepoy and the Raj*, p. 13.
57. Edmund Candler: *The Sepoy*, pp. 7–9.
58. Eden Vansittart: *Gurkhas*, p. i.
59. Ibid., pp. 89–91.
60. Omissi, op. cit., p. 31.
61. Major E. R. Elles: *Report on Nepal*, pp. 44–5.
62. Ibid.
63. Ibid., pp. 41–2.
64. Sir Richard Temple MP: *Journals Kept in Hyderabad, Kashmir, Sikkim and Nepal*, p. 260.
65. Purushottam Banskota: *The Gurkha Connection*, pp. 67, 86–7.
66. Cited in Kamal Raj Singh Rathaur: *The Gurkhas*, p. 72, Berkeley to W. J. Cunningham, Secretary to the Government of India, February 1887.
67. GM: Recruitment reports by Capt. C. Chenevix Trench, Lt. E. M. F. Martin, Lt. A. V. Hatch, Capt. C. A. Mercer and Lt. G. H. Loch, July/August 1886.
68. Ranald MacDonell and Marcus Macauley: *A History of the 4th PWO Gurkha Rifles, 1857–1937*, Vol. I, pp. 76–8.
69. GM: Recruitment report by Capt. C. A. Mercer, July/August 1886.
70. BL–OIOC: L/MIL/7/7028, Maj-Gen. Sir T. D. Baker to Secretary, Military Department, Simla, 15 September 1886.
71. BL–OIOC: L/MIL/7/4193, Col. H. Hopkinson to Secretary, Government of Bengal, 13 March 1868.
72. BL–OIOC: L/MIL/7/7267, Military Department to Rt. Hon. the Earl of Kimberley, Secretary of State for India, Simla 30 July 1886.
73. BL–OIOC: L/MIL/7/7031, Col. H. H. Lyster, Commanding 3 GR, to Col. H. Collett, Deputy Adjutant-General, 12 October 1885.
74. Nigel Woodyatt: *Under Ten Viceroys*, pp. 85–6.
75. Ibid.
76. BL–OIOC: L/MIL/7/7051, Maj-Gen. W. Galbraith to Secretary, Military Department, Simla 21 October 1890.
77. Ibid.
78. Ibid.
79. BL–OIOC: L/MIL/7/7051, Lt-Col. E. B. Bishop, CO 1/3 GR, to GOC Rohilkhund District, Almora, 4 August 1892.
80. BL–OIOC: L/MIL/7/7031, C. E. R. Girdlestone to Secretary, Foreign

Department, Camp Motihari, 29 November 1887.

81. BL–OIOC: L/MIL/7/7031, Col. P. Harris to Secretary, Military Department, Fort William, 13 February 1888; and Col. A. C. Toker, Deputy Secretary, Military Department, to Adjutant-General, Simla, 2 April 1888.

4 Villiers-Stuart of the Fifth

1. Military Despatch from India, No. 100 of 8 June 1861, cited in K. M. L. Saxena: *The Military System of India (1850–1900)*, pp. 200–1 (footnote).
2. Military Despatches of 18 March and 29 June 1864, cited in Perceval Landon: *Nepal*, Vol. II, pp. 191–2.
3. Nigel Woodyatt: *Under Ten Viceroys*, pp. 174–5.
4. John Masters: *Bugles and a Tiger*, p. 103.
5. GM: W. D. Villiers-Stuart papers – all the remaining quotations in this chapter come from this source unless otherwise identified.
6. Lord Ripon to Lord Hartington, 29 October 1881, cited in David Omissi: *The Sepoy and the Raj*, p. 105.
7. Charles Chenevix Trench: *The Indian Army and the King's Enemies 1900–1947*, p. 25.
8. Woodyatt, op. cit., p. 172.
9. Sir Penderel Moon: *The British Conquest and Dominion of India*, p. 908.
10. Woodyatt, op. cit., p. 235 – italics in original.
11. Robert Maxwell: *Villiers-Stuart on the Frontier 1894–1914*, p. xii.
12. T. A. Heathcote: *The Indian Army*, p. 132.
13. Sir George MacMunn: *The Martial Races of India*, p. 197.
14. John Morris: *Hired to Kill*, p. 147.
15. C. G. Bruce: *Himalayan Wanderer*, p. 70.
16. Ibid., p. 54.
17. Ibid., p. 72.
18. Ibid., p. 74.
19. Ibid., p. 80.
20. Ibid., pp. 79–80.
21. *History of the 5th Royal Gurkha Rifles (Frontier Force) 1858–1928*, p. 162.
22. Ibid., p. 171.
23. Ibid., p. 274.
24. Robert Maxwell, *Villiers-Stuart Goes to War*, p. 326.
25. Ibid.
26. Ibid.
27. Ibid.

5 The Gurkha Brigade Goes to War

1. H. J. Huxford: *History of the 8th Gurkha Rifles 1824–1949*, p. 51.
2. Perceval Landon: *Nepal*, Vol. II, p. 86.
3. GM: Field Marshal Sir John Chapple, 'Numbers of Gurkhas serving in WW1 and WW2', 30 April 1996.
4. Adrian Sever: *Nepal under the Ranas*, pp. 281–2.

5. Satish Kumar: *Rana Polity in Nepal*, p. 139.
6. Sever, op. cit., pp. 220–2.
7. Ibid., p. 223.
8. Ibid., p. 275.
9. Daniel Wright (ed.): *History of Nepal*, p. 31, cited in Sever, op. cit., p. 224.
10. NAM: Acc. No. 6510–111, G. W. Preston, Letters to His Wife 1904–1919.
11. Ibid.
12. W. J. Ottley: *With Mounted Infantry in Tibet*, pp. 154–5.
13. Ibid., p. 191.
14. Preston, op. cit.
15. Sever, op. cit., p. 241.
16. BL–OIOC: L/MIL/7/5910, Note on King's Orderly Officers for 1904 by Col. H. D. Hutchinson, War Office.
17. Rudyard Kipling: *A Diversity of Creatures*, p. 223.
18. Ibid., p. 225.
19. Ibid., p. 231.
20. Ibid., p. 235.
21. BL–OIOC: L/P&S/12/3053, demi-official letter from Maj. C. Wigram to Sir James DuBoulay, 15 May 1913.
22. Ibid., Note from Col. Macrae, 14 August, 1933.
23. Ibid., confidential letter from Col. Daukes to Maj. W. K. Fraser-Tytler, Foreign Secretary to the Government of India, 30 June 1933.
24. Ibid., letter from PM of Nepal to British Envoy, 11 May 1936.
25. Ibid., cypher telegram from F. M. Bailey, British Minister in Nepal, to Rt. Hon. Anthony Eden, Secretary of State for Foreign Affairs, 27 May 1937.
26. Ibid., comment by J. C. Walton on a Political Department minute paper, 9 July 1935.
27. Sever, op. cit., p. 259.
28. Asad Husain: *British India's Relations with the Kingdom of Nepal 1857–1947*, p. 189.
29. Lord Hardinge to Lord Crewe, Secretary of State for India, cited in Gregory Martin, 'The Influence of Racial Attitudes on British Policy towards India during the First World War', *Journal of Imperial and Commonwealth History*, Vol. 14, No. 2, January 1986, p. 92.
30. Ibid., p. 93.
31. BL–OIOC: L/MIL/7/17321, Employment of Nepalese troops in India – 1914 war, telegram from Secretary of State to Viceroy, 28 August 1914.
32. Ibid., Viceroy to Secretary of State, 30 August 1914.
33. Ibid., 2 February 1915.
34. Ibid., 18 November 1915, sanctioned 6 December.
35. BL–OIOC: MSS.Eur.F206/315–16, Lt. Hamish Reid to Col. and Mrs Reid, 9 September 1914.
36. Ibid., 4 October 1914.
37. Ibid., 11 October 1914.
38. Nigel Woodyatt: *The Regimental History of the 3rd QAO Gurkha Rifles*, p. 103.
39. Ranald MacDonell and Marcus Macauley: *A History of the 4th PWO Gurkha Rifles 1857–1937*, Vol. 1, p. 168.

40. F. Loraine Petre: *The 1st KGO Gurkha Rifles*, p. 128.
41. F. S. Poynder: *The 9th Gurkha Rifles 1817–1936*, p. 81.
42. BL–OIOC: MSS.Eur.F206/315–16, Lt. Hamish Reid to Col. and Mrs Reid, 30 October 1914.
43. Sir James Willcocks: *With the Indians in France*, p. 56.
44. Ibid., pp. 82–7.
45. NAM: Acc. No. 6012–337–1, Capt. W. G. Bagot-Chester, War Diary, 4 November 1914.
46. Willcocks, op. cit., pp. 82–7.
47. Cited in Charles Chenevix Trench: *The Indian Army . . .*, p. 34.
48. Ibid., p. 35.
49. Jeffrey Greenhut, 'The Imperial Reserve: The Indian Corps on the Western Front, 1914–15', *The Journal of Imperial and Commonwealth History*, Vol. xii, No. 1, October 1983, p. 56.
50. Huxford, op. cit., pp. 72–3.
51. Chenevix Trench, op. cit., p. 37.
52. MacDonell and Macauley, op. cit., p. 188.
53. Petre, op. cit., p. 135.
54. Poynder, op. cit., p. 61.
55. Mulk Raj Anand: *Across the Black Waters*, pp. 177–8.
56. NAM : Bagot-Chester War Diary, 31 December 1914.
57. Ibid., 5 February 1915.
58. Greenhut, op. cit., pp. 59–60.
59. BL–OIOC: L/MIL/5/858, Censored letters 1914–18, Arkan Das to L/Naik Chaman Gurung, 31 May 1916.
60. Poynder, op. cit., p. 89.
61. MacDonell and Macauley, op. cit., p. 212.
62. Woodyatt, op. cit., p. 124.
63. Chenevix Trench, op. cit., p. 41.
64. NAM: Bagot-Chester War Diary, 1, 9 and 22 May 1915.
65. Ibid., 25 May 1915.
66. Ibid.
67. Greenhut, op. cit., p. 57.
68. BL–OIOC: L/MIL/5/858, Censored letters, letter dated July 1915.
69. Ibid., letter dated 27 October 1915.
70. Ibid., letter dated 5 July 1915.
71. Ibid., letter dated 31 March 1915.
72. Woodyatt, op. cit., p. 142.
73. MacDonell and Macauley, op. cit., p. 238.
74. BL–OIOC: L/MIL/5/858, Note by the Censor, 25 January 1915.
75. J. W. B. Merewether and Sir Frederick Smith: *The Indian Corps in France*, pp. 414–18
76. Cited in H. J. Huxford and H. S. Gordon: *A Short History of the 2nd Battalion 8th Gurkha Rifles*, pp. 38–9.
77. Harry Davies: *Allanson of the 6th*, p. 37.
78. D. G. J. Ryan et al.: *Historical Record of the 6th Gurkha Rifles: Vol 1, 1817–1919*, p. 144.

79. Davies, op. cit., p. 24.
80. Ibid., p. 51.
81. Ibid., Prologue and passim.
82. Ryan et al., op. cit., p. 136.
83. Davies, op. cit., p. 35.
84. Cited in J. N. Mackay: *History of the 7th DEO Gurkha Rifles*, p. 47.
85. Ibid., p. 81.
86. MacDonell and Macauley, op. cit., p. 288.
87. Norman Dixon: *On the Psychology of Military Incompetence*, p. 105.
88. Mackay, op. cit., p. 56.
89. Ibid., p. 61.
90. MacDonell and Macauley, op. cit., p. 290.
91. Huxford, op. cit., p. 92.
92. MacDonell and Macauley, op. cit., p. 374.
93. Ibid., p. 375.
94. B. R. Mullaly: *Bugle & Kukri: The Story of the 10th PMO Gurkha Rifles*, Vol. 1, pp. 149–50.
95. GM: H. R. K. Gibbs, 'A Brief History of the XI Gurkha Rifles 1918–1921', pp. 30–6.
96. Poynder, op. cit., p. 169.
97. Ibid.
98. Prem R. Uprety: *Nepal*, p. 137, Adjutant-General, India, to Gen. Baber Shamsher, 3 August 1917.
99. Ibid., p. 136 (footnote).
100. Ibid., p. 139, letter dated 23 August 1918.
101. Ibid., p. 106.
102. Ibid., p. 106, Gen. Baber Shamsher to Gen. C. Roe, 14 May 1916.
103. Ibid., pp. 146–7.
104. Ibid., p. 140.
105. Ibid., pp. 148–9.
106. Landon, op. cit., p. 145.
107. BL–OIOC: L/P&S/12/3017, Lord Chelmsford to Maharaja Sir Chandra Shumshere, 27 December 1919.
108. Ibid., 'The annual gift of Rs. 10 lakhs by the Government of India to the Government of Nepal', undated memo.
109. Ibid.
110. Ibid., J. C. Walton, India Officer, to C. W. Orde, Foreign Office, 26 March 1935.
111. Ibid., confidential letter from J. G. Acheson, Foreign Secretary to the Government of India, to J. C. Walton, India Office, 22 August 1935.
112. Landon, op. cit., p. xiii.
113. Sever, op. cit., p. 237.
114. Landon, op. cit., p. 89; W. Brook Northey: *The Land of the Gurkhas*, p. 86; Francis Tuker: *Gorkha*, p. 176; and John Morris: *A Winter in Nepal*, pp. 25–7.
115. D. R. Regmi: *A Century of Family Autocracy in Nepal*, pp. 180–1, 189.
116. Ibid., pp. 175–6.

117. GM: Acc. No. 90/12/05, Col. A L. Fell, unpublished memoir (written 1953–55), p. 24.
118. Regmi, op. cit., p. 181.
119. Landon, op. cit., p. 208.
120. Kumar, op. cit., pp. 138–9; and Sever, op. cit., p. 360.

6   Twilight of the Raj

1. John Masters: *Bugles and a Tiger*, pp. 131–2.
2. Philip Mason: *A Matter of Honour*, p. 466.
3. BL–OIOC: MSS.Eur.D.1114/8, 'Amritsar, April 1919' by Brig. F. McCallum, June 1975.
4. Ibid.
5. GM: Acc. No. 94–10–9, T. L. Hughes: *Man of Iron: A Biography of Maj-Gen. Sir William Beynon KCIE, CB, DSO*, unpublished typescript, p. 136.
6. Nigel Woodyatt: *Under Ten Viceroys*, p. 293.
7. Ibid.
8. GM: W. D. Villiers-Stuart papers.
9. Cited in Hughes, op. cit., p. 137.
10. Cited in David Omissi: *The Sepoy and the Raj*, p. 218.
11. GM: Lt-Col. A. A. Mains, 'Gen. Dyer and Amritsar', p. 15.
12. Woodyatt, op. cit., p. 294.
13. Stephen P. Cohen: *The Indian Army*, pp. 93–4.
14. BL–OIOC: L/MIL/5/861, Proceedings of a Court of Enquiry . . . , 28 April–7 May 1930.
15. Ibid.
16. Ibid.
17. S. L. Menezes: *Fidelity & Honour*, p. 332; Philip Mason, op. cit. p. 452.
18. BL–OIOC: L/P&S/12/3005, Secret No. 5/1. A. /30, A Note on Anti-British Propaganda, Intelligence Bureau, Home Department, Government of India, 19 January 1931, Appendix D 'Om Bande Matraun'.
19. NAM: Acc. No. 9601–71, 'Rifleman to Colonel: The Memoirs of Major Gajendra Malla, 9 GR', compiled by Tony Mains and Elizabeth Talbot-Rice, pp. 1–4.
20. Ibid., p. 6.
21. BL–OIOC: L/P&S/12/3005, Secret No. 5/1. A. /30.
22. Ibid.
23. Ibid.
24. NAM: Gajendra Malla, op. cit., p. 7.
25. BL–OIOC: L/P&S/12/3005, Note on Kharagbahadur Singh, 18 July 1935.
26. Ibid.
27. Ibid., confidential letter from S. N. Roy, ICS, Deputy Secretary to the Government of India, to Chief Secretaries to the Governments of Bengal, UP, Bihar & Orissa, Assam 10 January 1931.
28. Ibid., Note on Kharagbahadur Singh.
29. NAM: Gajendra Malla, op. cit., p. 12.
30. Ibid., p. 13.

31. Author interview with Lt-Col. A. A. Mains, 9 September 1997.
32. NAM: 'Gajendra Malla, an Appreciation', by Lt-Col. A. A. Mains.
33. Mason, op. cit., p. 454.
34. *Report of the Indian Sandhurst Committee*, HMSO 1927, p. 37.
35. Cohen, op. cit., p. 119.
36. *Report of the Indian Sandhurst Committee*, p. 21.
37. GM: Acc. No. 87/2/11, Maj. T. J. Phillips, unpublished memoir, p. 13.
38. Masters, op. cit., p. 76.
39. GM: Lt-Col. A. A. Mains, 'Joining the 9th Gurkhas in the Thirties', pp. 2–3.
40. Phillips, op. cit., p. 13.
41. R. C. B. Bristow: *Memories of the British Raj*, pp. 36–7.
42. BL–OIOC: MSS.Eur.T.49, 'The Raj' interviews, BBC/Charles Allen, John Morris, p. 8.
43. GM: Acc. No. 90/12/05, Col. A. L. Fell, unpublished memoir, p. 30.
44. Cited in Charles Chenevix Trench: *The Indian Army*, p. 118.
45. GM: Lt-Col. A. A. Mains, 'Further Jottings on Service in the Army in India, 1934–39', pp. 83–4.
46. Fell, op. cit., p. 23.
47. Ibid., p. 35.
48. GM: 2 GR/711, 'The Nine Commandments'.
49. Ibid.
50. Phillips, op. cit., pp. 20–1.
51. Masters, op. cit., p. 152.
52. Phillips, op. cit., p. 41.
53. Cited in Masters, op. cit., p. 151.
54. Chenevix Trench, op. cit., p. 118.
55. Phillips, op. cit., p. 43.
56. Ibid.
57. Ibid.
58. Masters, op. cit., p. 158.
59. Ibid., pp. 153, 162.
60. Phillips, op. cit., pp. 157–8.
61. John Morris: *Hired to Kill*, pp. 114–15.
62. Masters, op. cit., p. 213.
63. BL–OIOC: MSS.Eur.T.49, John Morris, p. 4/5.
64. G. R. Stevens: *The 9th Gurkha Rifles (Vol. 2) 1937–1947*, p. 3.
65. Masters, op. cit., p. 202.
66. Phillips, op. cit., p. 37.
67. Ibid., pp. 93, 217.
68. Ibid., pp. 48–9.
69. Ibid., p. 50.
70. Ibid.
71. Stevens, op. cit., pp. 110–11.
72. Phillips, op. cit., p. 49.
73. Ibid., p. 56.
74. Ibid., p. 57.

75. Ibid., p. 61.
76. Ibid., p. 57.
77. Ibid., p. 58.
78. Ibid.
79. Ibid., p. 59.
80. Ibid., p. 63.
81. Ibid., p. 60.
82. Ibid., p. 61.
83. Ibid., pp. 64–7.
84. BL–OIOC: L/P&S/12/3051, Lt-Col. C. Daukes, 'Nepal 1929–34'.
85. BL–OIOC: L/P&S/12/3012, Lt-Col. G. Betham to Secretary to the Government of India, 22 June 1939.
86. Ibid., Lord Linlithgow to Lord Zetland, 17 August 1939.
87. *Naya Hindustan*, 6 May 1939.
88. Ibid.
89. BL–OIOC: L/P&S/12/3012, Aide-memoire of interview between Lt-Col. Betham and Gen. Sir Bahadur Shamsher, 7 July 1939.
90. *Naya Hindustan*, 6 May 1939.
91. BL–OIOC: L/P&S/12/3012, Secret letter from Lt-Col. Betham to Secretary to the Government of India, 22 August 1939.
92. Ibid., India Office Political Department notes on despatch No. 47 from Lt-Col. Betham to Foreign Office, 27 July 1940.
93. Ibid., Betham to Government of India, 22 August 1939.
94. Francis Tuker: *Gorkha*, p. 213.

7   The Second World War

1. John Masters: *The Road Past Mandalay*, p. 22.
2. BL–OIOC: MSS.Eur.R.193 (cassette 9), Maj-Gen. D. K. Palit.
3. S. L. Menezes: *Fidelity & Honour*, p. 367; J. G. Elliot, in *A Roll of Honour*, p. 16, gives the figures as 8,300 Indian and 34,500 British officers.
4. BL–OIOC: MSS.Eur.C.393, T. J. Phillips, diary entry for 26 March 1942.
5. GM: Acc. No. 87/2/11, Maj. T. J. Phillips, memoir/diary, 1 March 1942.
6. E. V. Bellers: *The History of the 1st KGO Gurkha Rifles, Vol. II, 1920–1947*, p. 58.
7. J. N. Mackay: *A History of the 4th PWO Gurkha Rifles, Vol. III, 1938–1948*, p. 75.
8. Compton Mackenzie: *Eastern Epic, Vol. 1. Sept 1939–March 1943*, pp. 436–49.
9. Ibid., p. 448.
10. J. N. Mackay: *History of the 7th DEO Gurkha Rifles*, p. 180; official figure in Col. R. G. Leonard: *Journal of the Gurkha Recruiting Depots and Record Offices, 1939–47*, p. 43.
11. Mackay, op. cit. [*History of 4 GR*], p. 111.
12. William Slim: *Defeat into Victory*, pp. 102–3.
13. BL–OIOC: L/MIL/7/17024, Confidential reports on regiments/officers.
14. GM: Sir John Smyth: *Gurkha Fighter: The Life of a Gurkha General – Lt-Gen.*

Sir Francis Tuker, unpublished typescript, p. 8.
15. Cited in ibid., p. 13.
16. Ibid., p. 14.
17. Ibid., p. 20.
18. Ibid.
19. Ibid., pp. 18–19.
20. Ibid., p. 17.
21. Ibid., p. 13.
22. BL–OIOC: MSS.Eur.R.14, Lt-Col. E. H. M. Parsons.
23. Cited in Smyth, op. cit., p. 26.
24. Mackay, op. cit. [*History of 7 GR*], pp. 240–1.
25. Francis Tuker: *Approach to Battle*, p. 137.
26. Smyth, op. cit., p. 5.
27. Tuker, op. cit., p. 318.
28. Charles Chenevix Trench: *The Indian Army*, p. 225.
29. Smyth, op. cit., p. 65.
30. Cited in G. R. Stevens: *The 9th Gurkha Rifles (Vol. 2) 1937–1947*, p. 29 (footnote).
31. Cited in Smyth, op. cit., p. 98.
32. Tuker, op. cit., pp. 321–2.
33. Ibid., p. 322.
34. From *The Tiger Kills*, cited in Tuker, op. cit., pp. 322–3.
35. Smyth, op. cit., p. 68.
36. Tuker, op. cit., p. 325.
37. Smyth, op. cit., p. 75.
38. Tuker, op. cit., p. 331.
39. Smyth, op. cit., p. 108.
40. Stevens, op. cit., pp. 39–40.
41. Tuker, op. cit., p. 375.
42. Ibid., p. 378.
43. Smyth, op. cit., p. 116.
44. Ibid., p. 117 – from Tuker's private papers.
45. Chenevix Trench, op. cit., p. 246.
46. Francis Tuker: *Gorkha*, p. 227.
47. E. D. Smith: *Even the Brave Falter*, p. 22.
48. Ibid., pp. 22–4.
49. Tuker, op. cit. [*Gorkha*], p. 227.
50. Ibid., pp. 220–1.
51. Ibid.
52. G. R. Stevens: *2nd KEO Goorkha Rifles, Vol. III, 1921–1948*, p. 199.
53. Ibid., p. 200.
54. IWM: Acc. No. 85/8/1, Lt Denis G. F. Gudgeon, 3/2 GR, letter of 28 June 1942.
55. Ibid., 20 October 1942.
56. GM: Ref. No. N1, Col. D. F. Neill: *One More River*, unpublished typescript, p. 5.
57. Ibid., p. 13.

58. Ibid., p. 14.
59. Ibid., p. 19.
60. Information from David Harding, archivist of 10 GR.
61. Neill, op. cit., p. 23.
62. Ibid., pp. 25–6.
63. Ibid., pp. 28–30.
64. Ibid., p. 36.
65. Ibid., p. 52.
66. Ibid., p. 62.
67. IWM: 85/8/1, Lt Gudgeon, letters of 30 April and 3 May 1945.
68. Stevens, op. cit. [*9 GR 1937–1947*], p. 226.
69. Neill, op. cit., pp. 75–6.
70. BL–OIOC: L/MIL/17/5/4270, Brig. O. C. Wingate: *Report on Operations of 77th Indian Infantry Brigade in Burma, Feb–June 1943*, p. 24.
71. Neill, op. cit., pp. 78–9.
72. Ibid., p. 80.
73. Wingate, op. cit., p. 4.
74. Ibid., p. 41.
75. Richard Rhodes James: *Chindit*, p. 100.
76. 'Despatch on Operations in the India Command, 1 Jan to 20 June 1943', cited in H. R. K. Gibbs: *Historical Record of the 6th Gurkha Rifles, Vol. II*, p. 116.
77. Stevens, op. cit. [*9 GR 1937–1947*], p. 227.
78. Ibid., p. 226 (footnote).
79. Rhodes James, op. cit., p. 95.
80. Masters, op. cit., p. 276.
81. Ibid., p. 287.
82. Ibid., p. 166.
83. Ibid., pp. 272–3.
84. Elliot, op. cit., p. 182.
85. Mackay, op. cit. [*History of 7 GR*], p. 223.
86. Masters, op. cit., p. 320.
87. Denis Sheil-Small: *Green Shadows*, p. 32.
88. Patrick Davis: *A Child at Arms*, pp. 68–9.
89. Scott Gilmore (with Patrick Davis): *A Connecticut Yankee in the 8th Gurkha Rifles*, pp. 185–6.
90. Sheil-Small, op. cit., pp. 51–4.
91. Davis, op. cit., p. 219.
92. Ibid., pp. 60–5.
93. Ibid., p. 65.
94. Gilmore, op. cit., p. 93.
95. Davis, op. cit., pp. 97–8.
96. Ibid., pp. 99–103.
97. Gilmore, op. cit., p. 147.
98. Sheil-Small, op. cit., p. 183.
99. Davis, op. cit., p. 106.
100. Mary Des Chene: *Relics of Empire*, unpublished Ph.D. thesis, pp. 317–18

(footnote).
101. Ibid., p. 318.
102. Ibid., p. 319 (footnote).
103. Davis, op. cit., pp. 130–1.
104. Ibid., p. 202.
105. Ibid., p. 236.
106. Ibid., p. 237.
107. Ibid., p. 219.
108. B. R. Mullaly: *Bugle & Kukri: The Story of the 10th PMO Gurkha Rifles*, p. 354.
109. Menezes, op. cit., p. 381.
110. Bellers, op. cit., p. 146.
111. Ibid., p. 148.
112. Stevens, op. cit. [*History of 2 GR*], p. 193.
113. Menezes, op. cit., p. 382.
114. Stevens, op. cit. [*History of 2 GR*], p. 194.
115. Ibid., p. 196.
116. Ibid., p. 195.
117. Cited in Menezes, op. cit., pp. 385–6.
118. IWM: Acc. No. 87/23/1, Maj. D. C. Purves: *Forty Years On*, unpublished typescript.
119. IWM: Acc. No. 88/48/1, cited in 'Extracts from the Memoirs of Maj. H. C. Gay, 4/2 GR', unpublished.
120. IWM: 87/23/1, Maj. Purves.
121. Slim, op. cit., p. 327.
122. Philip Mason, Foreword to Hugh Toye: *The Springing Tiger*, pp. viii–ix.
123. Ibid.
124. Ibid.
125. Stephen P. Cohen: *The Indian Army*, p. 160.
126. Ibid.
127. Francis Tuker: *While Memory Serves*, p. 59.
128. Cited in Smyth, op. cit., p. 140.
129. John Connell: *Auchinleck*, p. 819.
130. Asad Husain: *British India's Relations with the Kingdom of Nepal 1857–1947*, pp. 230–1.
131. Tuker, op. cit. [*Gorkha*], p. 208.
132. Ibid., p. 208; and Adrian Sever: *Nepal under the Ranas*, p. 334.
133. BL–OIOC: L/P&S/12/3012, Secret letter from Betham to Secretary to the Government of India, 28 January 1941.
134. Ibid.
135. Ibid., 7 February 1941.
136. Ibid., 13 February 1941.
137. Cited in Sever, op. cit., p. 334.
138. Tuker, op. cit. [*Gorkha*], pp. 209–10.
139. BL–OIOC: L/P&S/12/3012, Secret Political Department minute on the 'Anti-Rana movement', 21–28 April 1941.
140. BL–OIOC: L/P&S/12/3013A, Betham to Government of India, 28 July

1941.

141. Ibid., Extract from Annual Report on Nepal for 1943.
142. BL–OIOC: L/P&S/12/3012, Secret telegram from Betham to Secretary of State for Foreign Affairs, undated.
143. BL–OIOC: L/P&S/12/3017, Aide-memoire of Betham's interview with HH the Maharajah of Nepal, 24 March 1941.
144. Ibid., Briefing note on Nepal for 1942 interview between Secretary of State for India and the Nepalese Minister (in London).
145. Des Chene, op. cit., p. 274.
146. Ibid., p. 275.
147. Ibid., pp. 247–8.
148. Ibid., p. 255.
149. A. E. C. Bredin: *The Happy Warriors*, p. 292.
150. Leonard, op. cit., p. 4.
151. Mackay: *History of 7 GR*, p. 275.
152. Judha to Auchinleck, 11 March 1945, cited in Husain, op. cit., pp. 252–3.
153. Ibid., Auchinleck to Judha, 30 June 1945.
154. BL–OIOC: L/P&S/12/3013A, Private and secret letter from Lord Wavell to Lord Scarbrough, 9 July 1945.
155. BL–OIOC: L/P&S/12/3051, Secret letter from Lt-Col. C. Daukes to Sir John Simon, 15 January 1935.
156. Sever, op. cit., p. 375; for the figure of 66,000, see Bredin, op. cit., p. 292.
157. Leonard, op. cit., p. 12.
158. Tuker, op. cit. [*Gorkha*], p. 254.

8 Partition

1. Francis Tuker: *While Memory Serves*, p. 629; BL–OIOC: L/WS/1/1023, Wavell to Pethick-Lawrence, 1 January 1946.
2. BL–OIOC: L/WS/1/1027, Scoones to Auchinleck, 22 January 1947.
3. GM: Col. R. C. Jackman to Maj. R. H. Duncan, 16 May 1983.
4. PRO: W032/13252, Auchinleck: Secret paper, forwarded by Lord Wavell to Lord Brooke, CIGS, 13 April 1945.
5. Ibid., Auchinleck to Brooke, 30 September 1945.
6. Ibid., Auchinleck to Nye, 11 December 1945.
7. Ibid., Mayne to Nye, 26 December 1945.
8. Tuker, op. cit., pp. 628–9.
9. Ibid., p. 24.
10. Ibid., p. 22.
11. BL–OIOC: L/WS/1/1023, Auchinleck to Wavell, 6 November 1945.
12. Ibid., 20 November 1945.
13. PRO: W032/13252, J. J. Lawson, Secretary of State for War, to Lord Pethick-Lawrence, Secretary of State for India, 14 March 1946.
14. BL–OIOC: L/WS/1/1027, Slim to Auchinleck, 15 November 1946.
15. BL–OIOC: L/WS/1/1023, Lawson to Henderson, 31 May 1946.
16. PRO: W032/13252, Pethick-Lawrence to Lawson, 12 July 1946.
17. BL–OIOC: L/WS/1/1027, Scoones to Auchinleck, 25 October 1946.

18. Ibid.
19. BL–OIOC: L/WS/1/1023, Bellenger to Pethick-Lawrence, 7 February 1947.
20. BL–OIOC: L/P&S/12/3093, telegram from Cabinet Office to UK High Commissioner, India, 11 March 1947.
21. Ibid., Brief for British Negotiators in Discussion with Government of India as to the Employment of Gurkha Troops under HMG.
22. BL–OIOC: L/WS/1/1023, Extract from DO (47) 8th meeting, Defence Committee, 17 March 1947.
23. PRO: W032/13252, Draft paper for the Executive Committee of the Army Council, undated.
24. BL–OIOC: L/WS/1/1023, Defence Committee, 17 March 1947; and telegram from Cabinet Office to UKHC, India, 20 May 1947.
25. PRO: W032/13252, Lyne to Tuck, 1 April 1947.
26. Ibid., telegram from UKHC, India, to Cabinet Office, 9 April 1947.
27. PRO: CAB 128/10, Cabinet minutes, 3 June 1947.
28. PRO: W032/13252, telegram from Vice Adj-Gen., War Office, to Maj-Gen. Lyne, 12 April 1947.
29. BL–OIOC: L/P&S/12/3093, telegram from Lyne to DCIGS, 21 April 1947.
30. Maj-Gen. D. K. Palit (ed.): *Major General A. A. Rudra*, p. 298.
31. Ibid., p. 301.
32. Ibid., pp. 303–4.
33. PRO: W032/13252, Maharajah's statement, undated.
34. Palit, op. cit., p. 307.
35. Author interview with Col. Satinder Coomar Singha, 20 July 1997.
36. BL–OIOC: L/P&S/12/3093, telegram from UKHC, India, to Cabinet Office, 7 May 1947.
37. Ibid., record of interview with Nehru, Sir Girija Bajpai and Maj-Gen. Lyne, 6 May 1947.
38. Ibid., Lyne to DCIGS, 7 May 1947.
39. PRO: W032/13252, telegram from Viceroy to Secretary of State for India, 13 June 1947; BL–OIOC: L/WS/1/1024, J. M. Addis, 10 Downing St., to R. Wood, Ministry of Defence, 18 June 1947.
40. BL–OIOC: L/P&S/12/3093, Nehru's note of his interview with FM Montgomery, 28 June 1947.
41. Ibid.
42. PRO: WO32/13252, UKHC, India, to Cabinet Office, 29 June 1947.
43. BL–OIOC: L/WS/1/1027, Scoones to Auchinleck, 11 June 1947.
44. BL–OIOC: L/WS/1/1025, telegram from UKHC, India, to Cabinet Office, 15 July 1947.
45. PRO: W032/13252, telegram from Ritchie to VCIGS, 20 July 1947.
46. Ibid., telegram from Ministry of Defence to Col. D. M. W. Smith, 25 July 1947.
47. Ibid., telegram from War Office to C-in-C, India, 31 July 1947.
48. Ibid., telegram from CGS, India, to VCIGS, 7 August 1947.
49. BL–OIOC: L/WS/1/1027, Scoones to Auchinleck, 22 January 1947.

50. Tuker, op. cit., p. 638.
51. Ibid.
52. BL–OIOC: L/WS/1/954, McCandlish to British officers, 28 November 1947.
53. PRO: WO32/13252, Tuker to Steele, 12 November 1947.
54. Ibid., telegram from CGS, India, to VCIGS, 21 August 1947.
55. Ibid., Notes on 'the Future of Gurkhas' by Lt-Col. J. Masters, July 1947.
56. Ibid.
57. The *Statesman*, 13 August 1947.
58. B. R. Mullaly: *Bugle & Kukri: The Story of the 10th PMO Gurkha Rifles*, p. 386.
59. Cited in G. R. Stevens: *The 9th Gurkha Rifles (Vol. 2) 1937–1947*, p. 327.
60. Cited in J. N. Mackay: *History of the 7th DEO Gurkha Rifles*, pp. 286–7.
61. J. N. Mackay: *A History of the 4th PWO Gurkha Rifles, Vol. III 1938–1948*, p. 506.
62. Stevens, op. cit., p. 328.
63. J. P. Cross: *The Call of Nepal*, pp. 44–5.
64. Chandra B. Khanduri: *The History of the 1st Gorkha Rifles, Vol. III, 1946–1990*, p. 71.
65. Cross, op. cit., p. 45.
66. Tuker, op. cit., p. 130.
67. BL–OIOC: L/P&S/12/3093, Mountbatten to Auchinleck, 24 August 1947.
68. Ibid., Padma Shamsher to Nehru, 24 August 1947.
69. Ibid., Nehru to Auchinleck, 8 September 1947.
70. BL–OIOC: L/WS/1/1027, Scoones to Lyne, 9 October 1947.
71. BL–OIOC: L/P&S/12/3093, telegram from E. P. Donaldson, CRO, to A. C. B. Symon, UKHC, India, 29 October 1947.
72. BL–OIOC: L/P&S/12/3093, Annexure III, Tripartite Agreement, 7 November 1947.
73. BL–OIOC: L/P&S/12/3094, Tripartite Agreement, Appendix VIII, Notes of a meeting held at the Maharajah's Palace at Kathmandu, 7 November 1947.
74. BL–OIOC: L/P&S/12/3093, Agreement between the Government of the Dominion of India and HMG in the UK, 7 November 1947.
75. Ibid., telegram from Col. Duncan Smith to War Office, 10 November 1947; Symon to Donaldson, 14 November 1947.
76. BL–OIOC: L/P&S/12/3094, Tripartite Agreement, Appendix VII, Notes of a private meeting between Padma Shamsher, A. C. B. Symon and Col. Duncan Smith, 7 November 1947.
77. Tuker, op. cit., pp. 637–8.
78. PRO: WO32/13252, Analysis of the Reasons for the Results of the Gurkha Referendum by Brig. R. C. O. Hedley, undated.
79. Tuker, op. cit., pp. 638–9.
80. PRO: WO32/17640, R. G. Alexander, Gurkha Mission, to H. W. Fry, 26 August 1947.
81. Ibid.
82. Tuker, op. cit., p. 639.
83. Cross, op. cit., p. 45.

84. BL–OIOC: L/WS/1/1025, Lockhart to Scoones, 18 October 1947.
85. E. D. Smith: *Wars Bring Scars*, p. 21.
86. BL–OIOC: L/WS/1/1026, telegram from Hedley to War Office, 22 December 1947.
87. Smith, op. cit., pp. 21–3 and personal communication to the author; S. L. Menezes: *Fidelity & Honour*, p. 427 and author interview with Lt-Gen. S. L. Menezes, 26 June 1997.
88. Smith, op. cit., p. 22.
89. Ibid.
90. Ibid., p. 24.
91. BL–OIOC: L/WS/1/1027, Scoones to Lyne, 9 October 1947.
92. BL–OIOC: L/WS/1/1025, telegram from Auchinleck to Chiefs of Staff, 7 November 1947.
93. Ibid.
94. Ibid.
95. Ibid., telegram from Auchinleck to COS, 11 November 1947.
96. PRO: WO32/13252, Tuker to Steele, 12 November 1947.
97. Ibid.
98. Cross, op. cit., p. 46.
99. BL–OIOC: L/WS/1/1026, Gurkha Mission, Delhi, to War Office, 9 December 1947.
100. BL–OIOC: L/WS/1/1025, telegram from Auchinleck to COS, 7 November 1947.
101. Menezes, op. cit., p. 427; Palit, op. cit., p. 307.
102. Author interview with Col. Singha.
103. PRO: WO32/13252, telegram from Hedley to War Office, 28 December 1947.
104. PRO: WO32/13252, Hedley to Maj-Gen. C. H. Boucher, 30 December 1947.
105. R. W. L. McAlister: *Bugle & Kukri: The Story of the 10th PMO Gurkha Rifles, Vol. 2*, pp. 14–15.
106. BL–OIOC: L/WS/1/1026, telegram from Hedley to War Office, 12 February 1948.
107. PRO: WO32/13252, telegram from Hedley to War Office, 20 January 1948.
108. Palit, op. cit., p. 309.
109. C. N. Barclay: *The Regimental History of the 3rd QAO Gurkha Rifles, Vol. II (1927–1947)*, p. 95.
110. PRO: WO32/13252, Hedley to Boucher, 24 January 1948.
111. Mullaly, op. cit., p. 45.
112. Maj-Gen. D. K. Palit, 'Indianisation: A Personal Experience', *Indo-British Review*, Vol. XVI, No. 1, March 1989, p. 63.
113. Col. R. D. Palsokar: *History of the 5th Gorkha Rifles (FF) Vol. III: 1858–1991*, pp. 102–4.
114. Ibid.
115. *5th Royal Gurkha Rifles Regimental Newsletter*, 1994.
116. Brig. H. S. Sodhi and Brig. P. K. Gupta: *History of the 4th Gorkha Rifles: Vol.*

IV, 1947–1971, p. 3.
117. Author interview with Col. Singha.
118. Cited in Khanduri, op cit., p. 61.
119. Mary Des Chene: *Relics of Empire*, unpublished Ph.D. thesis, p. 291 (footnote).
120. PRO: WO32/13252, telegram from Falconer to Foreign Office, 10 August 1948.
121. Ibid., Analysis . . . of the Gurkha Referendum by Brig. Hedley.
122. BL–OIOC: L/WS/1/1027, Slim to Auchinleck, 15 November 1946.
123. BL–OIOC: L/WS/1/743, D. H. Jordan to Lord Listowel, 24 August 1947.
124. PRO: WO32/13252, Analysis . . . of the Gurkha Referendum by Brig. Hedley.
125. Ibid., telegram from Hedley to War Office, 11 February 1948.
126. Ibid., Analysis . . . of the Gurkha Referendum by Brig. Hedley.

9 Fighting on Two Fronts

1. BL–OIOC: L/WS/1/956, The Brigade of Gurkhas Liaison Letter No. 1, 6 May 1948.
2. Ibid.
3. Ibid.
4. PRO: WO32/13252, Executive Committee of the Army Council paper, 'Grant of commissions to Gurkhas', 7 October 1947.
5. J. P. Cross: *In Gurkha Company*, p. 212.
6. BL–OIOC: L/P&S/12/3096, D. M. Man, Colonial Office, to A. N. Gilchrist, India Office, 31 May 1947.
7. Harold James and Denis Sheil-Small: *A Pride of Gurkhas: the 2nd KEO Goorkhas 1948–1971*, p. 5.
8. R. W. L. McAlister: *Bugle & Kukri: The Story of the 10th PMO Gurkha Rifles, Vol. 2*, p. 26.
9. J. P. Cross: *'A Face like a Chicken's Backside'*, p. 22.
10. GM: T. J. Phillips, unpublished memoir, pp. 407–9.
11. Ibid., p. 427.
12. E. D. Smith: *Wars Bring Scars, pp.* 44–5.
13. Ibid., pp. 45–6.
14. *Parbate*, No. 47, 25 November 1949; E. D. Smith: *Johnny Gurkha*, pp. 78–9.
15. Cited in McAlister, op. cit., p. 42.
16. 10 GR Archive: Brig. C. C. Graham, draft chapter, 'The Terrorist Emergency – Malaya: Early Years 1948–50', p. 12.
17. Ibid., p. 24.
18. James and Sheil-Small, op. cit., pp. 85–90.
19. PRO: WO32/14623, Loose minute from Maj-Gen. R. A. Hull to CIGS, 24 August 1950.
20. Ibid., R. H. Scott, Foreign Office, to Maj-Gen. R. A. Hull, War Office, 20 November 1950.
21. Adrian Sever: *Nepal under the Ranas*, pp. 392–3.

22. PRO: WO32/14623, Telegram from Falconer to the Foreign Office, 22 January 1951.
23. Ibid.
24. Ibid., C-in-C FARELF to War Office, 12 March 1951.
25. J. P. Cross: *The Call of Nepal*, pp. 64–5.
26. Ibid., pp. 66–7.
27. Sever, op. cit., p. 400–1.
28. PRO: WO32/14623, Secret despatch No. 15, C. H. Summerhayes to Foreign Office, 2 April 1952.
29. PRO: WO32/15599, Secret War Office minute by Brig. Lewis Pugh, 19 March 1954.
30. Ibid., Secret memo by H. W. Smith, War Office, 24 March 1954.
31. Ibid., Secret War Office memo, February 1957.
32. Ibid., Ministry of Defence working party on assistance to Nepal, 14 March 1957.
33. Ibid.
34. PRO: WO32/16718, Antony Head to Secretary of State for War, Fitzroy Maclean, 17 July 1956.
35. Ibid., Selwyn Lloyd to Antony Head, 24 July 1956.
36. PRO: WO32/13381, Loose minute, War Office, 22 May 1957.
37. Ibid., Brig. Sir Andrew Horsbrugh-Porter, Military Attaché, India, to War Office, 10 June 1953.
38. Ibid., War Office to GHQ FARELF, 24 August 1954.
39. Ibid., 'The present position of GCOs', document on pay of Gurkha officers commissioned through the RMA Sandhurst, undated.
40. PRO: WO32/17641, Paper concerning the pay and pensions for Gurkhas commissioned from RMAS, 4 December 1953.
41. PRO: WO32/13381, War Office to Treasury, 3 December 1957.
42. Ibid., Treasury to War Office, 12 March 1958.
43. Ibid., MGBG to War Office, 20 November 1959.
44. Ibid., Adjutant-General to Secretary of State for War, undated.
45. Mani Dixit: *Come, Tomorrow*, p. 131.
46. PRO: WO32/16718, Scopes to Selwyn Lloyd, 10 December 1958.
47. Ibid., Secret memo on Gurkhas from CIGS to Secretary of State for War, 18 October 1960.
48. Leo Rose and John T. Scholz: *Nepal*, pp. 49 and 124–5; and Sever, op. cit., p. 403.
49. PRO: WO32/15525, Maj-Gen. G. S. Thompson, War Office, to R. G. K. Way, Ministry of Defence, October 1957.
50. J. P. Cross: *In Gurkha Company*, p. 82.
51. Tom Pocock: *Fighting General*, p. 118.
52. Ibid., p. 119.
53. Ibid., pp. 124–5.
54. Ibid., p. 126.
55. *The Times*, 22 October 1962.
56. Ibid.
57. Ibid., 1 November 1962.

58. Pocock, op. cit., p. 149.
59. Ibid., p. 151.
60. Walter Walker: *Fighting On*, p. 299.
61. Ronald Lewin: *Slim*, p. 319.
62. Ibid., p. 320.
63. Cited in Smith, op. cit., pp. 94–5.
64. James and Sheil-Small, op. cit., p. 120.
65. Pocock, op. cit., p. 127; E. D. Smith: *Britain's Brigade of Gurkhas*, p. 163; information from Brig. Christopher Bullock.
66. Smith, op. cit. [*Britain's Brigade . . .*], p. 164.
67. Ibid., p. 166.
68. Cross, op. cit. ['*A Face . . .*'], p. 150.
69. Charles Messenger: *The Steadfast Gurkha*, pp. 65–9.
70. Smith, op. cit. [*Britain's Brigade . . .*], p. 169.
71. Ibid., p. 170.
72. Walker, op. cit., p. 162.
73. Cross, op. cit. ['*A Face . . .*'], p. 143.
74. Walker, op. cit., p. 162.
75. Christopher Bullock: *Journeys Hazardous*, p. 55.
76. Ibid., pp. 98–9.
77. James and Sheil-Small, op. cit., p. 202.
78. Cited in Cross, op. cit. [*In Gurkha Company*], p. 119.
79. Ibid.
80. McAlister, op. cit., p. 429.
81. James and Sheil-Small, op. cit., 218.
82. Cross, op. cit. [*In Gurkha Company*], p. 119.
83. Bullock, op. cit., p. 177.

10   Rundown

1. Harold James and Denis Sheil-Small: *A Pride of Gurkhas: The 2nd KEO Goorkhas 1948–1971*, pp. 225–7.
2. E. D. Smith: *Johnny Gurkha*, p. 106; J. P. Cross: *In Gurkha Company*, p. 148; James and Sheil-Small, op. cit., p. 238.
3. James and Sheil-Small, op. cit., p. 222.
4. R. W. L. McAlister: *Bugle & Kukri: The Story of the 10th PMO Gurkha Rifles Vol. 2*, p. 244.
5. Cross, op. cit., p. 147.
6. *Soldier*, October 1963.
7. Ibid., November 1982.
8. Cross, op. cit., p. 148.
9. Cited in James and Sheil-Small, op. cit., pp. 231–2.
10. Cited in *The Kukri*, 1968, p. 6.
11. *The Kukri*, 1970, p. 199.
12. James Lunt: *Jai Sixth!*, pp. 130–1.
13. Mary Des Chene: *Relics of Empire*, unpublished Ph.D. thesis, pp. 249, 251.
14. Ibid., pp. 252–3.

15. PRO: WO32/15599, Telegram from Kathmandu to FCO, MOD (Army), 13 April 1970.
16. E. D. Smith: *East of Kathmandu: The Story of the 7th DEO Gurkha Rifles Vol. II, 1948–1973*, p. 166.
17. Ibid., p. 168.
18. Cited in McAlister, op. cit., p. 255.
19. Ibid.
20. Charles Messenger: *The Steadfast Gurkha: Historical Record of 6th QEO Gurkha Rifles, Vol. 3, 1948–1982*, pp. 92–3.
21. McAlister, op. cit., p. 262.
22. E. D. Smith: *The Autumn Years: Vol. III of the History of the 7th DEO Gurkha Rifles*, p. 57.
23. Cited in McAlister, op. cit., pp. 472–3.
24. D. P. de C. Morgan, 'The Falklands War 1982', in Smith, op. cit. [*The Autumn Years*], p. 63.
25. Lawrence Freedman and Virginia Gamba-Stonehouse: *Signals of War: The Falklands Conflict of 1982*, p. 384.
26. Morgan, op. cit., p. 64.
27. GM: 7GR/606, 21164257 Rfn. Baliprasad Rai, 'From Bagsila to Bluff Cove (A Soldier's Story of the Falklands War)'.
28. Ibid.
29. Ibid.
30. Ibid.
31. E. D. Smith, 'Gurkhas in Command', *The Elite*, Vol. 3, No. 26, p. 515; Morgan, op. cit., pp 71–2.
32. Morgan, op. cit., pp. 72–4.
33. Peter Osnos, 'The Gurkha Myth', *New York Herald Tribune*, 4 May 1983.
34. *El Espectador*, 3 April 1983.
35. Gabriel García Márquez, 'The Queen's Gurkhas', *Clarín*, 25 May 1983.
36. Ibid.
37. Cross, op. cit., pp. 171–2.
38. Morgan, op. cit., p. 73.
39. Amit Roy, 'A question of Gurkha honour', *Sunday Times*, 10 August 1986.
40. Ibid.
41. Author interview with Chandra Kumar Pradhan, 15 February 1997.
42. Ibid.
43. Ibid.
44. E. D. Smith, op. cit. [*The Autumn Years*], p. 82.
45. *Daily Telegraph*, 6 August 1986.
46. *Guardian*, 12 August 1986.
47. Christopher Dobson, 'One scrap too many for Johnny Gurkha', *Sunday Telegraph*, 10 August 1986.
48. John Keegan, 'Senior Gurkhas recommend dismissal of 111 soldiers', *Daily Telegraph*, 12 August 1986.
49. Maj. J. J. Burlison, 'Some Place Else', *The Kukri*, 1994, p. 172.
50. J. J. Burlison, 'Triple Twilight', *The Kukri*, 1995, p. 11.
51. GM: 7GR/759, MGBG's message . . . , 13 November 1986.

52. Statement by the Rt. Hon. George Younger MP, reprinted in *The Kukri*, 1990, p. 18.
53. *The Kukri*, 1990, p. 19.
54. *The Kukri*, 1992, p. 15.
55. Antony Beevor: *Inside the British Army*, pp. 260–1.
56. Author interview with Christopher Bullock, 25 June 1998.
57. Ibid.
58. Lt-Col. Nigel Collett to the author, 18 May 1998.
59. Ibid.
60. Ibid.
61. Author interview with General Sir Sam Cowan, 6 July 1998.
62. Nigel Collett to the author, 18 May 1998.
63. Author interview with Christopher Bullock, 25 June 1998.
64. Ibid.
65. *The Kukri*, 1997, p. 5.
66. Author interview with Christopher Bullock, 25 June 1998.
67. Nigel Collett to the author, 18 May 1998.
68. Author interview with Sir Sam Cowan, 6 July 1998.
69. Ibid.
70. Author interview with Lt-Gen. Stanley Menezes, 26 June 1997.
71. Author interview with Sir Sam Cowan, 6 July 1998.
72. Mary Des Chene, 'Loyalty *versus* Equality', *Himal*, July/August 1997, pp. 15–23.
73. Ibid.
74. Deepak Thapa, 'Mercenary Position', *Himal*, July/August 1997, pp. 24–6.
75. Ibid.
76. Ibid.
77. Des Chene, op. cit.
78. Author interview with Deepak Thapa, 11 February 1997.
79. Author interview with Basanta Thapa, 11 February 1997.
80. Author interview with Prayag Raj Sharma, 10 February 1997.
81. Author interview with Ananda Shrestha, 31 January 1997.
82. Ananda Shrestha, 'The Storm and the Flame', *Kathmandu Post*, 25 December 1994.
83. Michael Hutt, 'A Hero or a Traitor? The Gurkha Soldier in Nepali Literature', *The Kukri*, 1991, pp. 168–75.
84. Ibid; and B. P. Koirala, 'The Soldier (*Sipahi*)', *Himal*, November/December 1994, pp. 45–7.

11   Return to Nepal

1. Anup Pahari, 'Ties that Bind: Gurkhas in History', *Himal*, July/August 1996, p. 12.
2. Ibid.
3. Keshar Bahadur Gadtaula, 'To Fight or Not to Fight', ibid., p. 23.
4. Author interview with Lt (QGO) Khembahadur Thapa, 20 September 1996.
5. Ibid.

6.   J. P. Cross: *The Call of Nepal*, p. 60.
7.   Author interview with Khembahadur Thapa.
8.   Cross, op. cit., p. 4.
9.   J. P. Cross: '*A Face Like a Chicken's Backside*', p. 181.
10.   J. P. Cross: *The Call of Nepal*, pp. 1–2.
11.   Ibid., pp. 155–6.
12.   Ibid., p. 160.
13.   Ibid.
14.   Ibid., p. 38.
15.   Ibid., p. 167.
16.   Ibid., p. 169.
17.   Ibid., p. 180.
18.   Ibid., p. 181.
19.   Ibid.
20.   Ibid., p. 185.
21.   Ibid., p. 179.
22.   Ibid., p. 186.
23.   Ibid.
24.   Mary Des Chene: *Relics of Empire*, unpublished Ph.D. thesis, pp. 277–8.
25.   Cross, op. cit.[*The Call of Nepal*], pp. 191, 201.
26.   Ibid., p. 232.
27.   Lt-Col. J. P. Cross to the author, 24 May 1997.
28.   *The Kukri*, 1996, p. 11.
29.   Cited in Pratyoush Onta, '*Dukha* during the World War', *Himal*, November /December 1994, p. 24.
30.   Cross, op. cit., pp. 162–3.
31.   Brig. D. P. de C. Morgan, 'Dharan – a Few Final Thoughts', *The Kukri* 1991, pp. 139–42.
32.   Author interview with Lt-Col. J. P. Cross, 5 February 1997.
33.   Author interview with Ananda Shrestha, 31 January 1997.
34.   Prayag Raj Sharma, 'How to Tend This Garden?', *Himal*, May/June 1992, pp. 7–9.
35.   Mary Des Chene, 'Ethnography in the *Janajati-yug*', *Studies in Nepali History and Society*, Vol. 1, No. 1, June 1996, pp. 124–5.
36.   Ibid., p. 125.
37.   Ibid., p. 113.
38.   Ibid., p. 147.
39.   Author interview with John Cross.
40.   Mary Des Chene, op. cit.[*Relics of Empire*], p. 358.
41.   Ibid.

Bibliography

The main documentary sources for this book were the Gurkha Museum at Winchester, the National Army Museum in Chelsea, the Public Record Office (PRO) at Kew, the British Library, Oriental and India Office collections (BL–OIOC), then at Blackfriars, and the nearby Imperial War Museum. The public and private papers consulted in these repositories are specified in the references to each chapter. The following is a selection of books and articles consulted, with occasional brief comments.

Adhikari, Krishna Kant: *Nepal under Jang Bahadur 1846–1877*, Vol. 1 (Kathmandu, 1984)

Alavi, Seema: *The Sepoys and the Company: Tradition and Transition in Northern India 1770–1830* (Delhi, 1995)

Anand, Mulk Raj: *Across the Black Waters* (London, 1940). A fine novel dealing with the experiences of an Indian Army unit on the western front in 1914–15.

Anon.: *Military Sketches of the Goorka War in India in the Years 1814, 1815, 1816* (London, 1822). John Pemble (see below) surmises that the author of these *Sketches* was David Ochterlony's Eurasian son, Roderick Peregrine; if this is so it would detract from what he writes about the general as well as providing an interesting gloss on some of his racial remarks.

Anon.: *History of the 5th Royal Gurkha Rifles (Frontier Force) 1858–1928* (Aldershot, n. d.)

Bibliography 459

Anon.: *History of the 5th Royal Gurkha Rifles (Frontier Force) Vol. II: 1929–1947* (Aldershot, 1956)

Banerji, Brajendra Nath, 'The Last Days of Nana Sahib of Bithoor', *Bengal: Past and Present*, XXXIX, April-June 1930

Banskota, Purushottam: *The Gurkha Connection: A History of the Gurkha Recruitment in the British Indian Army* (Jaipur, 1994)

Barclay, Brig. C. N. (ed.): *The Regimental History of the 3rd Queen Alexandra's Own Gurkha Rifles, Vol. II (1927–1947)* (London, 1953)

Beevor, Antony: *Inside the British Army* (London, 1990)

Bellers, Brig. E. V. R.: *The History of the 1st King George V's Own Gurkha Rifles (The Malaun Regiment), Vol. II: 1920–1947* (Aldershot, 1956)

Birdwood, Field Marshal Lord: *Khaki and Gown: An Autobiography* (London, 1941)

Bishop, R. N. W.: *Unknown Nepal* (London, 1952)

Bista, Dor Bahadur: *Fatalism and Development: Nepal's Struggle for Modernization* (Calcutta, 1991)

Blaikie, Piers, Cameron, John and Seddon, David: *Nepal in Crisis: Growth and Stagnation at the Periphery* (Oxford, 1980)

Bolt, David: *Gurkhas* (London, 1967)

Bristow, Brig. R. C. B.: *Memories of the British Raj: A Soldier in India* (London, 1974)

Bruce, Brig-Gen., Hon. C. G. *Himalayan Wanderer* (London, 1934)

Bullock, Christopher: *Journeys Hazardous: Gurkha Clandestine Operations Borneo 1965* (Worcester, 1994)

Bute, the Marchioness of (ed.): *The Private Journals of the Marquess of Hastings* (London, 1858)

Candler, Edmund: *The Sepoy* (London, 1919)

Caplan, Lionel, '"Bravest of the Brave": Representations of "The Gurkha" in British Military Writings', *Modern Asian Studies*, Vol. 25, No. 3, 1991

Caplan, Lionel: *Warrior Gentlemen: 'Gurkhas' in the Western Imagination* (Providence, RI and Oxford, 1995)

Cardew, Lt. F. G.: *A Sketch of the Services of the Bengal Native Army to the Year 1895* (Calcutta, 1903)

Cardew, Maj. F. G., 'Major-General Sir David Ochterlony, Bart., GCB, 1758–1825', *Journal of the Society of Army Historical Research*, Vol. X, No. 39, January 1931.

Carew, Tim: *All This and a Medal Too* (London, 1954)

Cavenagh, Capt. Orfeur: *Rough Notes on the State of Nepal, Its Government, Army, and Resources* (Calcutta, 1851)

Cavenagh, Gen. Sir Orfeur: *Reminiscences of an Indian Official* (London, 1884)

Chant, Christopher: *Gurkha: The Illustrated History of an Elite Fighting Force* (Poole, 1985)

Chaudhuri, Nirad C., 'The "Martial Races" of India', Parts I–IV, *The Modern Review* (Calcutta, July 1930 to February 1931). The centenarian in early, radical vein rather than in his later pro-imperialist mode.

Chenevix Trench, Charles: *The Indian Army and the King's Enemies 1900–1947* (London, 1988)

Cohen, Stephen P.: *The Indian Army: Its Contribution to the Development of a Nation* (Delhi, 1971 and 1990)

Coleman, A. P.: *So Peculiarly Formed a Corps: The beginnings of Gurkha service with the British* (M. Phil. thesis, April 1995 – published in 1999 by the Pentland Press, Bishop Auckland, under the title, *A Special Corps*)

Connell, John: *Auchinleck: A Biography of Field Marshal Sir Claude Auchinleck* (London, 1959)

Cross, Lt-Col. J. P.: *In Gurkha Company: The British Army Gurkhas, 1948 to the Present* (London, 1986)

Cross, J. P.: *Jungle Warfare: Experiences and Encounters* (London, 1989)

Cross, J. P.: *The Call of Nepal* (London, 1996)

Cross, J. P.: *'A Face like a Chicken's Backside': An Unconventional Soldier in South East Asia, 1948–1971*(London, 1996)

Davies, Harry: *Allanson of the 6th: An account of the life of Colonel Cecil John Lyons Allanson CMG, CIE, DSO, 6 GR, compiled from his diaries, letters and personal papers* (Worcester, 1990)

Davis, Patrick: *A Child at Arms* (London, 1970). The best Gurkha memoir by a British officer I have read; Davis was a young Emergency Commissioned Officer with the 4/8th Gurkhas in Burma during the Second World War.

Des Chene, Mary Katherine: *Relics of Empire: A Cultural History of the Gurkhas, 1815–1987* (unpublished Ph.D. thesis, 1991). An historical and anthropological study of enormous interest, well researched and provocative. This was one of two works, from opposite ends of the political spectrum, with which I found myself constantly engaging (for the other, *see* Tuker below).

Des Chene, Mary Katherine, 'Ethnography in the *Janajati-yug*: Lessons from Reading *Rodhi* and other Tamu Writings', *Studies in Nepali History and Society*, Vol. 1, No. 1, June 1996.

Digby, William: *India and Nepal: 1857, A Friend in Need; 1887, Friendship Forgotten* (London, 1890)

Dixit, Mani: *Come, Tomorrow* (Kathmandu, 1980)

Dixon, Norman: *On the Psychology of Military Incompetence* (London, 1976). A unique and fascinating study and an old favourite of mine.

East India Company: *Papers Respecting the Nepaul War* (London, 1824)

Edwardes, Sir Herbert and Merivale, Herman: *Life of Sir Henry Lawrence* (London, 1872)

Egerton, Hon. Capt. Francis, RN: *Journal of a Winter's Tour in India: With a Visit to the Court of Nepaul* (London, 1852, 2 vols)

Elles, Brevet Maj. E. R., RA: *Report on Nepal* (Calcutta, 1884)

Elliott, Maj-Gen. J. G.: *A Roll of Honour: The Story of the Indian Army 1939–1945* (London, 1965)

Fane, Henry Edward: *Five Years in India* (London, 1842, 2 vols)

Farwell, Byron: *The Gurkhas* (New York & London, 1984)

Forbes, Duncan: *Johnny Gurkha* (London, 1964)

Forteath, Lt-Col. G. M.: *Pipes, Kukris and Nips* (Edinburgh, 1991)

Fortescue, Hon. J. W.: *A History of the British Army*, Vol. XI (London, 1923)

Fraser, George Macdonald: *Quartered Safe Out Here* (London, 1992). A very fine 'other rank' memoir of the war in Burma by the author of the Flashman series, with a brief but memorable evocation of the Gurkhas of that era.

Fraser, James Baillie: *Journal of a Tour through Part of the Snowy Range of Himala Mountains and to the Sources of the Rivers Jumna and Ganges* (London, 1820)

Gibbs, Maj. H. R. K.: *The Gurkha Soldier* (Calcutta, 1944)

Gibbs, Lt-Col. H. R. K.: *Historical Record of the 6th Gurkha Rifles: Vol. II* (Aldershot, 1955)

Gilmore, Scott (with Patrick Davis): *A Connecticut Yankee in the 8th Gurkha Rifles: A Burma Memoir* (Washington/London, 1995)

Giuseppe, Father, 'An Account of the Kingdom of Népál', *Asiatick Researches*, Vol. 2, xvii (Calcutta, 1790)

Greenhut, Jeffrey, 'The Imperial Reserve: The Indian Corps on the Western Front, 1914–15' *The Journal of Imperial and Commonwealth History*, Vol. XII, No. 1, October 1983. A seminal article to which all subsequent chroniclers on the Indian divisions on the western front in the First World War are indebted.

Hamid, Maj-Gen. Shahid: *Disastrous Twilight: A Personal Record of the Partition of India* (London, 1986). Gossipy, malicious memoir by the officer who was Auchinleck's military secretary in 1947. Biased but fun.

Hamilton, Francis Buchanan: *An Account of the Kingdom of Nepal and of the Territories Annexed to this Dominion by the House of Gorkha* (London, 1819)

Harding, David (ed.): *10th Gurkha Rifles: One Hundred Years* (1990)

Hasrat, B. J. (ed.): *History of Nepal, As Told by Its Own and Contemporary Chroniclers* (Hoshiapur, Punjab, 1970)

Hayter, Adrian: *The Second Step* (London, 1962)

Heathcote, T. A.: *The Indian Army: The Garrison of British Imperial India, 1822–1922* (Newton Abbot, 1974). Very informative and useful.

Heber, Bishop Reginald: *Narrative of a Journey through the Upper Provinces of India* (London, 1843, 2 vols)

Henneker, Brig. M. C. A.: *Red Shadow over Malaya* (Edinburgh, 1955)

Hibbert, Christopher: *The Great Mutiny: India 1857* (London, 1978)

Hodgson, Brian Houghton: *Essays on the Languages, Literature, and Religion of Nepal and Tibet* (London, 1874)

Hodgson, Brian Houghton: *Miscellaneous Essays Relating to Indian Subjects* (London, 1880)

Hunter, Sir William Wilson: *Life of Brian Houghton Hodgson, British Resident at the Court of Nepal* (London, 1896)

Husain, Asad: *British India's Relations with the Kingdom of Nepal 1857–1947* (London, 1970)

Huxford, Lt-Col. H. J.: *History of the 8th Gurkha Rifles 1824–1949* (Aldershot 1952). For me, the most readable of the regimental histories.

Huxford, Maj. H. J. and Gordon, Capt. H. S.: *A Short History of the 2nd Battalion 8th Gurkha Rifles* (Quetta, 1927)

Jacquemont, Victor (translated by Catherine Anne Phillips): *Letters from India 1829–32* (London, 1936). A very perceptive French view of the rise of the British Raj. Sadly Jacquemont, a naturalist and friend of Stendhal, died young in India.

James, Harold: *Across the Threshold of Battle: Behind Japanese Lines with Wingate's*

Chindits, Burma 1943 (Sussex, 1993)

James, Harold and Sheil-Small, Denis: *A Pride of Gurkhas: The 2nd King Edward VII's Own Goorkhas (The Sirmoor Rifles) 1948–1971* (London, 1975). A lively regimental history.

James, Lawrence: *Mutiny in the British and Commonwealth Forces, 1797–1956* (London, 1987)

Jenkins, L. Hadow: *General Frederick Young: first commandant of the Sirmur battalion (2nd Gurkha Rifles)* (London, 1923). More family piety than factual history (see footnote on page 46).

Kaye, J. W. and Malleson, Col. G. B.: *History of the Indian Mutiny of 1857–8* (Cabinet ed., London, 1889)

Keay, John: *The Honourable Company: A History of the East India Company* (London, 1991)

Khanduri, Brig. Chandra B.: *The History of the 1st Gorkha Rifles (The Malaun Regiment) Vol. III: 1946–1990* (Delhi, 1992)

Kirkpatrick, Col. William: *An Account of the Kingdom of Nepaul, Being the substance of observations made during a Mission to that Country, in the year 1793* (London, 1811)

Kumar, Satish: *Rana Polity in Nepal: Origin and Growth* (Delhi/London, 1967)

Landon, Perceval: *Nepal* (London, 1928, 2 vols)

Langer, V.: *Red Coats to Olive Green: A History of the Indian Army 1600–1974* (Bombay, 1974)

Lawrence, Sir Henry M.: *Essays, Military and Political, Written in India* (London, 1859)

Leathart, Scott: *With the Gurkhas: India, Burma, Singapore, Malaya, Indonesia 1940–1959* (Ely, Cambridgeshire, 1998)

Lewin, Ronald: *Slim, the Standardbearer* (London, 1976). One of the better military biographies, but then Slim was one of the better generals – and, as a writer himself, a gift to a biographer.

Lunt, James (ed.): *From Sepoy to Subedar, being the life and adventures of Subedar Sita Ram, a Native Officer of the Bengal Army written and related by himself* (London, 1970). Translated and first published in 1873 by Lt-Col. Norgate, it may also have been written by him – in other words, it is probably a fake.

Lunt, Maj-Gen. James: *Jai Sixth!: The Story of the 6th Queen Elizabeth's Own Gurkha Rifles 1817–1994* (London, 1994)

McAlister, Maj-Gen. R. W. L.: *Bugle & Kukri: The Story of the 10th Princess Mary's Own Gurkha Rifles*, Vol. 2 (1984)

MacDonell, Ranald and Macauley, Marcus: *A History of the 4th Prince of Wales's Own Gurkha Rifles, 1857–1937*, Vols I & II (Edinburgh, 1940)

Mackay, Col. J. N.: *A History of the 4th Prince of Wales's Own Gurkha Rifles, Vol. III, 1938–1948* (Edinburgh, 1952)

Mackay, Col. J. N.: *History of the 7th Duke of Edinburgh's Own Gurkha Rifles* (Edinburgh, 1962)

MacMunn, Lt-Gen. Sir George: *The Martial Races of India* (London, 1933)

Mains, Lt-Col. A. A., 'Handover to Indian Officers – 9th Gurkha Rifles 1947', *Indo-British Review: A Journal of History*, Vol. XVI, No. 1, March 1989

Malla, Kamal P. (ed.): *Nepal: Perspectives on Continuity and Change* (Kirtipur, 1989)

Marks, J. M.: *Ayo Gurkha!* (London 1971). An enjoyable novel by an ex-officer of the 10th Gurkhas in which a young Limbu joins up and soon finds himself in action during the Malayan Emergency. Fluent and only slightly romanticized. Strong on life in the hills of Nepal.

Martin, Gregory, 'The Influence of Racial Attitudes on British Policy Towards India during the First World War', *The Journal of Imperial and Commonwealth History*, Vol. XIV, No. 2, January 1986

Mason, Philip: *A Matter of Honour: An Account of the Indian Army, Its Officers and Men* (London, 1974). Classic account by the doyen of imperial Indian historians, who died at the beginning of 1999, aged ninety-two.

Masters, John: *Bugles and a Tiger: A Personal Adventure* (London, 1956). The Gurkha officer memoir: responsible for attracting many Brits to Gurkha regiments.

Masters, John: *The Road Past Mandalay: A Personal Narrative* (London, 1961). An exceptionally strong war memoir, gritty and gripping.

Masters, John: *Pilgrim Son: A Personal Odyssey* (London, 1971)

Maxwell, Robert: *Villiers-Stuart on the Frontier 1894–1914* (Edinburgh, 1989)

Maxwell, Robert: *Villiers-Stuart Goes to War* (Edinburgh, 1990). The Villiers-Stuart diaries and papers edited for publication.

Menezes, Lt-Gen. S. L.: *Fidelity & Honour: The Indian Army from the 17th Century to the 21st Century* (New Delhi, 1993)

Merewether, J. W. B. and Smith, Sir Frederick: *The Indian Corps in France* (London, 1918).

Messenger, Charles: *The Steadfast Gurkha: Historical Record of 6th Queen Elizabeth's Own Gurkha Rifles Vol. 3, 1948–1982* (London, 1985)

Mojumdar, Kanchanmoy, 'Recruitment of the Gurkhas in the Indian Army, 1814–1877', *United Services Institute Journal*, Vol. 83, No. 391, 1963

Mojumdar, Kanchanmoy: *Anglo-Nepalese Relations in the 19th Century* (Calcutta, 1973)

Moon, Penderel (ed.): *Wavell: The Viceroy's Journal* (London, 1973)

Moon, Sir Penderel: *The British Conquest and Dominion of India* (London, 1989)

Morris, John: *Hired to Kill: Some Chapters of Autobiography* (London, 1960). An intelligent and literate memoir of service in the 3rd Gurkhas which scandalized British officers by being explicit about a homosexual incident. In a second career Morris became Head of the BBC (Radio) Third Programme.

Morris, John: *A Winter in Nepal* (London, 1964)

Mullaly, Col. B. R.: *Bugle & Kukri: The Story of the 10th Princess Mary's Own Gurkha Rifles* (Edinburgh, 1957)

Northey, Maj. W. Brook: *The Land of the Gurkhas* (Cambridge, 1937)

Northey, Maj. W. Brook and Morris, Capt. C. J.: *The Gurkhas: Their Manners, Customs and Country* (London, 1928)

Oldfield, H. A.: *Sketches from Nipal* (London, 1880)

Oliphant, Laurence: *A Journey to Kathmandu* (London, 1852)

Omissi, David: *The Sepoy and the Raj: The Indian Army, 1860–1940* (London, 1994)

Onta, Pratyoush, '*Dukha* during the World War', *Himal*, Nov/Dec 1994

Onta, Pratyoush, 'Creating a Brave Nepali Nation in British India: The

Rhetoric of *Jati* Improvement, Rediscovery of Bhanubhakta and the Writing of *Bir* History', *Studies in Nepali History and Society*, Vol. 1, No. 1, June 1996

Osborne, Hon. W. G.: *The Court and Camp of Runjeet Sing* (London, 1840)

Ottley, Brevet Maj. W. J.: *With Mounted Infantry in Tibet* (London, 1906)

Pahari, Anup, 'Ties that Bind: Gurkhas in History', *Himal* 'Nepalis in Foreign Uniform' issue, July/August 1991. One of many searching articles to have appeared in this and many other issues of *Himal*.

Palit, Maj-Gen. D. K., 'Indianisation: A Personal Experience' *Indo-British Review: A Journal of History*, Vol. XVI, No. 1, March 1989

Palit, Maj-Gen. D. K.: *War in High Himalaya: The Indian Army in Crisis, 1962* (New Delhi, 1991)

Palit, Maj-Gen. D. K.: *Major General A. A. Rudra* (New Delhi, 1997)

Palsokar, Col. R. D.: *History of the 5th Gorkha Rifles (FF) Vol. III: 1858–1991* (Shillong, 1991)

Pant, Mahesh Raj. 'Nepal's Defeat in the Nepal-Britain War', *Regmi Research Series*, 10 (Kathmandu, 1978)

Pearson, Hesketh: *The Hero of Delhi: A Life of John Nicholson, Saviour of India, and a History of His Wars* (London, 1939)

Pemble, John: *The Invasion of Nepal: John Company at War* (Oxford, 1971). Definitive account of the Anglo-Gorkha war, 1814–16.

Perowne, Maj-Gen. L. E. C. M.: *Gurkha Sapper: The Story of the Gurkha Engineers 1948–1970* (Hong Kong, 1973)

Petre, F. Loraine: *The 1st King George's Own Gurkha Rifles (The Malaun Regiment)* (London, 1925)

Pett, Maj-Gen. R. A., 'India's Infantry in the mid-Nineties', *Army Quarterly and Defence Journal*, Vol. 126, No. 2, April 1996

Pocock, Tom: *Fighting General: The Public and Private Campaigns of General Sir Walter Walker* (London, 1973)

Poynder, Lt-Col. F. S.: *The 9th Gurkha Rifles 1817–1936* (London, 1937)

Pradhan, Kumar: *The Gorkha Conquests* (Calcutta, 1991)

Prawal, Maj. K. C.: *Indian Army after Independence* (New Delhi, 1987)

Prinsep, Henry T.: *History of the Political and Military Transactions in India during the Administration of the Marquess of Hastings 1813–1823*, Vol. 1 (London, 1820, 'enlarged' 1825)

Proudfoot, C. L.: *Flash of the Khukri: History of the 3rd Gorkha Rifles (1947–1980)* (New Delhi, 1984)

Rai, Capt. Maniprasad, 'The Man', *The Kukri*, July 1966

Ramakant: *Indo-Nepalese Relations 1816 to 1877* (New Delhi, 1968)

Rana, Netra Rajya Laxmi: *The Anglo-Gorkha War (1814–1816)* (Nepal, 1970)

Rathaur, Kamal Raj Singh: *The Gurkhas: A History of the Recruitment in the British Indian Army* (Jaipur, 1987 and 1995)

Regmi, D. R.: *A Century of Family Autocracy in Nepal* (Nepali National Congress, 1950). Anti-Rana propaganda. Weak on facts, strong on feeling.

Roberts of Kandahar, Field Marshal Lord: *Forty-One Years in India* (London, 1898, 2 vols). As popular in its day as the man who wrote it, this has not worn well.

Rose, Leo E.: *Nepal: Strategy for Survival* (Berkeley, California, 1971)

Rose, Leo E., and Scholz, John T.: *Nepal: Profile of a Himalayan Kingdom* (Boulder, Colorado, 1980)

Russell, William Howard: *My Diary in India, in the year 1858–9* (London, 1860)

Ryan, Maj. D. G. J., Strahan, Maj. G. C. and James, Capt. J. K.: *Historical Record of the 6th Gurkha Rifles: Vol. 1, 1817–1919* (1925)

Saksena, Dr Banarsi Prasad (ed.): *Historical Papers Relating to Kumaon 1809–1842* (Allahabad, 1956)

Sanwal, B. D.: *Nepal and the East India Company* (London, 1965)

Saxena, K. M. L.: *The Military System of India (1850–1900)* (New Delhi, 1974)

Sever, Adrian: *Nepal under the Ranas* (New Delhi, 1993)

Shakespear, Col. L. W.: *History of the 2nd King Edward's Own Goorkha Rifles (The Sirmoor Rifles)* (Aldershot, 1912)

Shakespear, Col. L. W.: *History of the 2nd King Edward's Own Goorkhas (The Sirmoor Rifle Regiment) Vol. II, 1911–1921* (Aldershot, n. d. but 1924)

Sheil-Small, Denis: *Green Shadows: A Gurkha Story* (London, 1982)

Shipp, Lt. John: *Memoirs of the Extraordinary Military Career of John Shipp, Late a Lieutenant in HM's 87th Regiment* (London, 1829). Swashbuckling and riveting, if not entirely reliable.

Slim, Field Marshal Viscount: *Defeat into Victory* (London, 1956)

Smith, E. D.: *Britain's Brigade of Gurkhas* (London, 1973 & 1982)

Smith, E. D.: *East of Kathmandu: The Story of the 7th Duke of Edinburgh's Own Gurkha Rifles Vol. II 1948–1973* (London, 1976)

Smith, E. D.: *Even the Brave Falter* (London, 1978). A man who proved his own valour by winning a DSO that might easily have been a VC as a young officer in Italy during the war, the late Brig. 'Birdie' Smith writes interestingly about fear and the failure of nerve both in this memoir and in its sequel, *Wars Bring Scars* (see below).

Smith, E. D.: *Johnny Gurkha: 'Friends in the Hills'* (London, 1985)

Smith, E. D.: *Wars Bring Scars* (Aylesford, 1993). The highlight, if that's the word, of this second volume of 'Birdie' Smith's autobiography is his account of the helicopter crash in Borneo in which he had to have his arm amputated without an anaesthetic in order to be released from the wreckage.

Smith, E. D.: *Valour: A History of the Gurkhas* (London, 1997)

Smith, E. D.: *The Autumn Years: Vol. III of the History of the 7th Duke of Edinburgh's Own Gurkha Rifles* (Staplehurst, 1997)

Smith, Capt. Thomas: *Narrative of a Five Years' Residence at Nepaul* (London, 1852, 2 vols)

Snellgrove, David: *Himalayan Pilgrimage* (Oxford, 1961)

Sodhi, Brig. H. S. and Gupta, Brig. P. K.: *History of the 4th Gorkha Rifles (Vol. IV) 1947–1971* (Delhi, 1985)

Spaight, W. M., 'Gurkha Ghosts', *Journal of the Royal Central Asian Society*, XXIX, April 1942.

Stevens, Lt-Col. G. R.: *History of the 2nd King Edward VII's Own Goorkha Rifles (The Sirmoor Rifles) Vol. III, 1921–1948* (Aldershot, 1952)

Stevens, Lt-Col. G. R.: *The 9th Gurkha Rifles (Vol. 2) 1937–1947* (1953)

Stiller, Ludwig F.: *Prithwinarayan Shah in the Light of Dibya Upadesh*

(Kathmandu, 1968 and 1989)

Stiller, Ludwig F.: *The Rise of the House of Gorkha: A Study in the Unification of Nepal 1768–1816* (New Delhi, 1973)

Stiller, Ludwig F.: *The Silent Cry: The People of Nepal 1816–1839* (Kathmandu, 1976)

Stiller, Ludwig F.: *Letters from Kathmandu: The Kot Massacre* (Kathmandu, 1981)

Stubbs, Maj. Francis W.: *History of the Bengal Artillery* (London, 1877)

Temple, Sir Richard, Bart. MP: *Journals Kept in Hyderabad, Kashmir, Sikkim and Nepal*, Vol. II (London, 1887)

Thompson, Edward: *The Life of Charles Lord Metcalfe* (London, 1937)

Thompson, Edward: *The Making of the Indian Princes* (London, 1943)

Thompson, Edward and Garrett, G. T.: *The Rise and Fulfilment of British Rule in India* (Allahabad, 1962)

Toye, Hugh: *The Springing Tiger: A Study of a Revolutionary* (London, 1959)

Tuker, Lt-Gen. Sir Francis: *While Memory Serves* (London, 1950)

Tuker, Lt-Gen. Sir Francis: *Gorkha: The Story of the Gurkhas of Nepal* (London, 1957). This pioneering British account of Nepalese history, strongly weighted in favour of the Rana dynasty, is the other work (*see* Des Chene above) that I found most challenging when it came to writing this book.

Tuker, Lt-Gen. Sir Francis: *Approach to Battle* (London, 1963)

Uprety, Prem R.: *Nepal: A Small Nation in the Vortex of International Conflicts 1900–1950* (Kathmandu, 1984)

Wakeham, Eric: *The Bravest Soldier: Sir Rollo Gillespie 1766–1814* (Edinburgh, 1937)

Walker, Gen. Sir Walter: *Fighting On* (London, 1997)

Whelpton, John: *Jang Bahadur in Europe: The First Nepalese Mission to the West* (Kathmandu, 1983)

Whelpton, John: *Kings, Soldiers and Priests: Nepalese Politics and the Rise of Jang Bahadur Rana, 1830–1857* (New Delhi, 1991)

Willcocks, Gen. Sir James: *With the Indians in France* (London, 1920)

Wingate, Brig. O. C.: *Report on Operations of 77th Indian Infantry Brigade in Burma, Feb–June 1943* (New Delhi, 1943)

Woodyatt, Maj-Gen. Nigel: *Under Ten Viceroys: The Reminiscences of a Gurkha* (London, 1922)

Woodyatt, Maj-Gen. Nigel G.: *The Regimental History of the 3rd Queen Alexandra's Own Gurkha Rifles from April 1815 to December 1927* (London, 1929)

Wright, Daniel (ed.): *History of Nepal* (London, 1887)

Index